Environmental & Natural Resource Economics

10th Edition

Tom Tietenberg
Emeritus, Colby College

Lynne Lewis
Bates College

Routledge
Taylor & Francis Group
LONDON AND NEW YORK

First published 2009 by Pearson Education, Inc.

Published 2016 by Routledge
2 Park Square, Milton Park, Abingdon, Oxon OX14 4RN
711 Third Avenue, New York, NY 10017, USA

Routledge is an imprint of the Taylor & Francis Group, an informa business

---

Library of Congress Cataloging-in-Publication Data
Tietenberg, Thomas H.
Environmental & natural resource economics / Tom Tietenberg, Emeritus, Colby College, Lynne Lewis, Bates College. — 10th Edition.
pages cm
Includes index.
ISBN-13: 978-0-13-347969-0
ISBN-10: 0-13-347969-2
1. Environmental economics. 2. Environmental policy. 3. Natural resources—Government policy. 4. Raw materials—Government policy. I. Lewis, Lynne. II. Title.
HC79.E5T525 2014
333.7—dc23 2013050399

Environmental & Natural Resource Economics

10th Edition

Contents in Brief

Contents

20 The Quest for Sustainable Development 508

21 Visions of the Future Revisited 531

Preface

A glance at any newspaper will confirm that environmental economics is now a major player in environmental policy. Concepts such as cap-and-trade, renewable portfolio standards, block pricing, renewable energy credits, development impact fees, conservation easements, carbon trading, the commons, congestion pricing, corporate average fuel economy standards, pay-as-you-throw, debt-for-nature swaps, extended producer responsibility, sprawl, leapfrogging, pollution havens, strategic petroleum reserves, payments for ecosystem services, and sustainable development have moved from the textbook to the legislative hearing room. As the large number of current examples in *Environmental & Natural Resource Economics* demonstrates, not only are ideas that were once restricted to academic discussions now part of the policy mix, but they are making a significant difference as well.

New to This Edition

New Features

- New chapter on ecosystem services that covers the state of ecosystem services, valuing ecosystem services, and policy mechanisms to protect and maintain ecosystem services (Chapter 13)
- Updated data on water pricing (Chapter 9), energy (Chapter 7), e-waste (Chapter 8), land use (Chapter 10), forests (Chapter 11), fisheries (Chapter 12), ecosystem services (Chapter 13), air quality (Chapter 15), climate change science (Chapter 16), climate change finance (Chapter 16), carsharing (Chapter 17), and oil spills and water quality trading programs (Chapter 18)
- New Self-Test Exercises (Chapters 13 and 16)
- Many new economic studies discussed
- New and updated tables and figures

New or Expanded Topics

- Dealing with asymmetric information problems (Chapter 2)
- Scale and aggregation issues in benefit-cost analysis (Chapter 3)
- Compensating and equivalent variation approaches to valuation (Chapter 4)

- Combining revealed preference and stated preference approaches to valuation (Chapter 4)
- Benefit transfer and meta-analysis (Chapter 4)
- Innovative responses to valuation challenges (Chapter 4)
- The economics of hydraulic fracturing (fracking) on energy supply (Chapter 7)
- The impact of the Fukushima accident on the role of nuclear power (Chapter 7)
- The relative costs of alternative fuels for electricity generation (Chapter 7)
- Impact of fracking on water demand and local air and water quality (Chapter 7)
- Recycling and fairness issues associated with e-waste (Chapter 8)
- Water markets in Australia (Chapter 9)
- Catch shares and territorial use rights fisheries (Chapter 12)
- Special challenges and innovation in ecosystem valuation (Chapter 13)
- Game theory as a window on climate negotiations (Chapter 16)
- The environmental effectiveness and cost effectiveness of existing carbon pricing programs (Chapter 16)
- The special role of natural gas in climate policy (Chapter 16)
- Carbon pricing design issues: offsets, price volatility, and linking regional systems (Chapter 16)
- Pricing public transport (Chapter 17)
- The effectiveness of tax credits for electric vehicles (Chapter 17)

New Examples and Debates

- Estimating the Benefits of Carbon Emissions Reductions: The Social Cost of Carbon
- Using the Travel Cost Method to Estimate Recreational Value: Beaches in Minorca, Spain
- Valuing the Reliability of Water Supplies: Coping Expenditures in Kathmandu Valley, Nepal
- The Green Paradox
- The Relative Cost-Effectiveness of Renewable Energy Policies in the U.S.
- Energy Efficiency in Rental Housing Markets
- Does Packaging Curbside Recycling with Incentives Promote Efficiency?
- Moving Rivers or Desalting the Sea? Costly Remedies for Water Shortages
- ITQs or TURFs? Species, Space, or Both?
- The Value of Coral Reefs in the U.S. Virgin Islands
- Costa Rica's "Pago por Servicios Ambientales" (PSA) Program
- The Agglomeration Bonus
- The Sulfur Allowance Program after 20 Years
- Three Illustrative Carbon Pricing Programs

- External Benefits of Fuel Economy Standards
- Discounting over Long Time Horizons: Should Discount Rates Decline?
- Willingness to Pay versus Willingness to Accept: Why So Different?
- Distance Decay in Willingness to Pay: When and How Much Does Location Matter?
- What Is the Value of a Polar Bear?
- Does the Advent of Fracking Increase Net Benefits?
- Paying for Ecosystem Services or Extortion?: The Case of Yasuni National Park
- Tradable Quotas for Whales?

An Overview of the Book

Environmental & Natural Resource Economics attempts to bring those who are beginning the study of environmental and natural resource economics close to the frontiers of knowledge. Although the book is designed to be accessible to students who have completed a two-semester introductory course in economics or a one-semester introductory microeconomics course, it has been used successfully in several institutions in lower-level and upper-level undergraduate courses as well as lower-level graduate courses.

The structure and topical coverage of this book facilitates its use in a variety of contexts. For a survey course in environmental and natural resource economics, all chapters are appropriate, although many of us find that the book contains somewhat more material than can be adequately covered in a quarter or even a semester. This surplus material provides flexibility for the instructor to choose those topics that best fit his or her course design. A one-term course in natural resource economics could be based on Chapters 1–13 and 20–21. A brief introduction to environmental economics could be added by including Chapter 14. A single-term course in environmental economics could be structured around Chapters 1–4 and 14–21.

In this tenth edition, we examine many of these newly popular market mechanisms within the context of both theory and practice. Environmental and natural resource economics is a rapidly growing and changing field as many environmental issues become global in nature. In this text, we tackle some of the complex issues that face our globe and explore problems and potential solutions.

This edition retains a strong policy orientation. Although a great deal of theory and empirical evidence is discussed, their inclusion is motivated by the desire to increase understanding of intriguing policy problems, and these aspects are discussed in the context of those problems. This explicit integration of research and policy within each chapter avoids a problem frequently encountered in applied economics textbooks—that is, in such texts the theory developed in earlier chapters is often only loosely connected to the rest of the book.

This is an economics book, but it goes beyond economics. Insights from the natural and physical sciences, literature, political science, and other disciplines are scattered liberally throughout the text. In some cases these references raise outstanding issues that economic analysis can help resolve, while in other cases they affect the structure of the economic analysis or provide a contrasting point of view. They play an important role in overcoming the tendency to accept the material uncritically at a superficial level by highlighting those characteristics that make the economics approach unique.

Intertemporal optimization is introduced using graphical two-period models, and all mathematics, other than simple algebra, is relegated to chapter appendixes. Graphs and numerical examples provide an intuitive understanding of the principles suggested by the math and the reasons for their validity. In the tenth edition, we have retained the strengths that are particularly valued by readers, while expanding the number of applications of economic principles, clarifying some of the more difficult arguments, and updating the material to include the very latest global developments.

Reflecting this new role of environmental economics in policy, a number of journals are now devoted either exclusively or mostly to the topics covered in this book. One journal, *Ecological Economics*, is dedicated to bringing economists and ecologists closer together in a common search for appropriate solutions for environmental challenges. Interested readers can also find advanced work in the field in *Land Economics*, *Journal of Environmental Economics and Management*, *Review of Environmental Economics and Policy*, *Environmental and Resource Economics*, *International Review of Environmental and National Resource Economics*, *Environment and Development Economics*, *Resource and Energy Economics*, and *Natural Resources Journal*, among others.

Two discussion lists that involve material covered by this book are ResEcon and EcolEcon. The former is an academically inclined list focusing on problems related to natural resource management; the latter is a wider-ranging discussion list dealing with sustainable development.

A very useful blog that deals with issues in environmental economics and their relationship to policy is located at http://www.env-econ.net/.

Services on the Internet change so rapidly that some of this information may become obsolete. To keep updated on the various Web options, visit the Companion Website of this text at http://www.routledgetextbooks.com/textbooks/9780133479690. The site includes an online reference section with all the references cited in the book. The site also has links to other sites, including the site sponsored by the Association of Environmental and Resource Economists, which has information on graduate programs in the field.

Supplements

For each chapter in the text, the *Online Instructor's Manual*, originally written by Lynne Lewis of Bates College and revised by Nora Underwood of the University of Central Florida, provides an overview, teaching objectives, a chapter outline with key terms, common student difficulties, and suggested classroom exercises. PowerPoint® presentations, prepared by Hui Li of Eastern Illinois University, are available for instructors and include all art and figures from the text as well as lecture notes for each chapter. Professors can download the *Online Instructor's Manual* and the PowerPoint® presentations at the Instructor Resource Center (http://www.routledgetextbooks.com/textbooks/9780133479690).

The book's Companion Website, http://www.routledgetextbooks.com/textbooks/9780133479690, features chapter-by-chapter Web links to additional reading and economic data. The site also contains Excel-based models that can be used to solve common depletable resource problems numerically. These models, developed by Arthur Caplan and John Gilbert of Utah State University, may be presented in lecture to accentuate the intuition pro-vided in the text, or they may underlie specific questions on a homework assignment.

The Companion Website also provides self-study quizzes for each chapter. Written and updated by Elizabeth Wheaton of Southern Methodist University, each of these chapter quizzes contains 10 multiple-choice questions for students to test what they have learned.

Acknowledgments

The most rewarding part of writing this book is that we have met so many thoughtful people. We very much appreciate the faculty and students who pointed out areas of particular strength or areas where coverage could be expanded. Their support has been gratifying and energizing. One can begin to understand the magnitude of our debt to our colleagues by glancing at the several hundred names in the lists of references contained in the Name Index. Because their research contributions make this an exciting field, full of insights worthy of being shared, our task was easier and a lot more fun than it might otherwise have been.

We also owe a large debt of gratitude to the following group who provided detailed, helpful reviews of the text and supplied many useful ideas for this revision:

Jan Crouter, *Whitman College*
Kevin J. Egan, *University of Toledo*
Ana Espinola-Arredondo, *Washington State University*
Rebecca Judge, *St. Olaf College*
Pallab Mozumder, *Florida International University*
Michael L. Nieswiadomy, *University of North Texas*
Christopher Worley, *Colorado School of Mines*

In addition, we received very helpful suggestions as we were writing this edition from the following:

Robert Johnston of Clark University, who helped us to think about how to organize the new chapter on ecosystem services, and Sahan Dissanayake of Colby College, who provided us with several helpful suggestions for refining it.

And, finally, we want to acknowledge the valuable assistance we received during various editions of the writing of this text from the following:

Dan S. Alexio, *US Military Academy at West Point*
Elena Alvarez, *State University of New York, Albany*
Gregory S. Amacher, *Virginia Polytechnic Institute and State University*
Michael Balch, *University of Iowa*
Maurice Ballabon, *Baruch College*

Edward Barbier, *University of Wyoming*
A. Paul Baroutsis, *Slippery Rock University of Pennsylvania*
Dana Bauer, *Boston University*
Kathleen P. Bell, *University of Maine*
Peter Berck, *University of California, Berkeley*
Fikret Berkes, *University of Manitoba*
Sidney M. Blumner, *California State Polytechnic University, Pomona*
Vic Brajer, *California State University, Fullerton*
Stacey Brook, *University of Sioux Falls*
Nancy Brooks, *University of Vermont*
Richard Bryant, *University of Missouri, Rolla*
Linda Bui, *Brandeis University*
David Burgess, *University of Western Ontario*
Mary A. Burke, *Florida State University*
Richard V. Butler, *Trinity University*
Trudy Cameron, *University of Oregon*
Jill Caviglia-Harris, *Salisbury University*
Duane Chapman, *Cornell University*
Gregory B. Christiansen, *California State University, East Bay*
Charles J. Cicchetti, *University of Southern California*
Hal Cochrane, *Colorado State University*
Jon Conrad, *Cornell University*
John Coon, *University of New Hampshire*
William Corcoran, *University of Nebraska, Omaha*
Maureen L. Cropper, *University of Maryland*
John H. Cumberland, *University of Maryland*
Herman E. Daly, *University of Maryland*
Stephan Devadoss, *University of Idaho*
Diane P. Dupont, *Brock University*
Frank Egan, *Trinity College*
Randall K. Filer, *Hunter College/CUNY*
Ann Fisher, *Pennsylvania State University*
Anthony C. Fisher, *University of California, Berkeley*
Marvin Frankel, *University of Illinois, Urbana-Champaign*
A. Myrick Freeman III, *Bowdoin College*
James Gale, *Michigan Technological University*
David E. Gallo, *California State University, Chico*
Jackie Geoghegan, *Clark University*
Haynes Goddard, *University of Cincinnati*
Nikolaus Gotsch, *Institute of Agricultural Economics (Zurich)*
Ben Gramig, *Purdue University*
Doug Greer, *San José State University*
Ronald Griffin, *Texas A&M University*
W. Eric Gustafson, *University of California, Davis*
A. R. Gutowsky, *California State University, Sacramento*
Jon D. Harford, *Cleveland State University*
Gloria E. Helfand, *University of Michigan*
Ann Helwege, *Emmanuel College*
Joseph Herriges, *Iowa State University*
John J. Hovis, *University of Maryland*
Charles W. Howe, *University of Colorado*
Paul Huszar, *Colorado State University*
Craig Infanger, *University of Kentucky*
Allan Jenkins, *University of Nebraska at Kearney*
Donn Johnson, *Quinnipiac College*
James R. Kahn, *Washington and Lee University*
Tim D. Kane, *University of Texas, Tyler*
Jonathan D. Kaplan, *California State University, Sacramento*
Chris Kavalec, *Sacramento State University*
Richard F. Kazmierczak, Jr., *Louisiana State University*
Derek Kellenberg, *Georgia Institute of Technology*
John O. S. Kennedy, *LaTrobe University*
Joe Kerkvliet, *Oregon State University*
Neha Khanna, *Binghamton University*
Thomas C. Kinnaman, *Bucknell University*
Andrew Kleit, *Pennsylvania State University*
Janet Kohlhase, *University of Houston*
Richard F. Kosobud, *University of Illinois, Chicago*
Douglas M. Larson, *University of California, Davis*
Dwight Lee, *University of Georgia*
David Letson, *University of Miami/RSMAS*
Hui Li, *Eastern Illinois University*
Scott Elliot Lowe, *Boise State University*
Joseph N. Lekakis, *University of Crete*
Ingemar Leksell, *Göteborg University*
Randolph M. Lyon, *Executive Office of the President (US)*

Robert S. Main, *Butler University*
Giandomenico Majone, *Harvard University*
David Martin, *Davidson College*
Charles Mason, *University of Wyoming*
Ross McKitrick, *University of Guelph*
Frederic C. Menz, *Clarkson University*
Nicholas Mercuro, *Michigan State University*
David E. Merrifield, *Western Washington University*
James Mjelde, *Texas A&M University*
Michael J. Mueller, *Clarkson University*
Kankana Mukherjee, *Worcester Polytechnic Institute*
Patricia Norris, *Michigan State University*
Thomas C. Noser, *Western Kentucky University*
Lloyd Orr, *Indiana University*
Peter J. Parks, *Rutgers University*
Steven Peterson, *University of Idaho*
Daniel R. Petrolia, *Mississippi State University*
Alexander Pfaff, *Duke University*
Steve Polasky, *University of Minnesota*
Raymond Prince, *University of Colorado, Boulder*
H. David Robison, *La Salle University*
J. Barkley Rosser, Jr., *James Madison University*
James Roumasset, *University of Hawaii*
Jonathan Rubin, *University of Maine*
Milton Russell, *University of Tennessee*
Frederic O. Sargent, *University of Vermont*
Salah El Serafy, *World Bank*
Chad Settle, *University of Tulsa*
Aharon Shapiro, *St. John's University*
W. Douglass Shaw, *Texas A&M University*
James S. Shortle, *Pennsylvania State University*
Leah J. Smith, *Swarthmore College*
V. Kerry Smith, *North Carolina State University*
Rob Stavins, *Harvard University*
Tesa Stegner, *Idaho State University*
Joe B. Stevens, *Oregon State University*
Jeffrey O. Sundberg, *Lake Forest University*
Gert T. Svendsen, *The Aarhus School of Business*
David Terkla, *University of Massachusetts, Boston*
Kenneth N. Townsend, *Hampden-Sydney College*
Robert W. Turner, *Colgate University*
Wallace E. Tyner, *Purdue University*
Nora Underwood, *University of Central Florida*
Roger von Haefen, *North Carolina State University*
Myles Wallace, *Clemson University*
Xiaoxia Wang, *Renmin University of China*
Patrick Welle, *Bemidji State University*
John Whitehead, *Appalachian State University*
Randy Wigle, *Wilfred Laurier University*
Mark Witte, *Northwestern University*
Richard T. Woodward, *Texas A&M University*
Anthony Yezer, *The George Washington University*

Working with Pearson has been a delightful experience. Our Executive Acquisitions Editor Adrienne D'Ambrosio and Editorial Project Manager Sarah Dumouchelle have been continually helpful since the initiation of this edition. We would also like to acknowledge Nancy Freihofer and Heidi Aguiar on the production side, Samantha Graham, who managed permissions; and Lisa Rinaldi, who managed the Companion Website content. Thanks to you all!

Lynne's most helpful research assistant for this edition was BoRa Kim. Working with all of the fine young scholars who have assisted with this text over the years has made it all the more obvious why teaching is the world's most satisfying profession.

Finally, Tom would like to express publicly his deep appreciation to his wife Gretchen, his daughter Heidi, and his son Eric for their love and support. Lynne would like to express her gratitude to Jack for his unwavering support, patience, and generosity. Thank you.

Tom Tietenberg
Lynne Lewis

Visions of the Future

1

From the arch of the bridge to which his guide has carried him, Dante now sees the Diviners . . . coming slowly along the bottom of the fourth Chasm. By help of their incantations and evil agents, they had endeavored to pry into the future which belongs to the almighty alone, and now their faces are painfully twisted the contrary way; and being unable to look before them, they are forced to walk backwards.

—Dante Alighieri, *Divine Comedy: The Inferno*, translated by Carlyle (1867)

Introduction

The Self-Extinction Premise

About the time the American colonies won independence, Edward Gibbon completed his monumental *The History of the Decline and Fall of the Roman Empire*. In a particularly poignant passage that opens the last chapter of his opus, he re-creates a scene in which the learned Poggius, a friend, and two servants ascend the Capitoline Hill after the fall of Rome. They are awed by the contrast between what Rome once was and what Rome has become:

> *In the time of the poet it was crowned with the golden roofs of a temple; the temple is overthrown, the gold has been pillaged, the wheel of fortune has accomplished her revolution, and the sacred ground is again disfigured with thorns and brambles. . . . The forum of the Roman people, where they assembled to enact their laws and elect their magistrates is now enclosed for the cultivation of potherbs, or thrown open for the reception of swine and buffaloes. The public and private edifices that were founded for eternity lie prostrate, naked, and broken, like the limbs of a mighty giant; and the ruin is the more visible, from the stupendous relics that have survived the injuries of time and fortune. (Vol. 6, pp. 650–651)*

What could cause the demise of such a grand and powerful society? Gibbon weaves a complex thesis to answer this question, suggesting ultimately that the seeds for Rome's destruction were sown by the Empire itself. Although Rome finally succumbed to such external forces as fires and invasions, its vulnerability was based upon internal weakness.

The premise that societies can germinate the seeds of their own destruction has long fascinated scholars. In 1798, Thomas Malthus published his classic *An Essay on the Principle of Population*, in which he foresaw a time when the urge to reproduce would cause population growth to exceed the land's potential to supply sufficient food, resulting in starvation and death. In his view, the most likely response to this crisis would involve rising death rates caused by environmental constraints, rather than a recognition of impending scarcity followed either by innovation or self-restraint.

Generally, our society seems remarkably robust, having survived wars and shortages, while dramatically increasing living standards and life expectancy. Yet, actual historical examples suggest that Malthus's self-extinction vision may sometimes have merit. Example 1.1 examines two specific cases: the Mayan civilization and Easter Island.

EXAMPLE 1.1

A Tale of Two Cultures

The Mayan civilization, a vibrant and highly cultured society that occupied parts of Central America, did not survive. One of the major settlements, Copán, has been studied in sufficient detail to learn reasons for its collapse.

After A.D. 400 the population growth began to bump into environmental constraints, specifically the agricultural carrying capacity of the land. The growing population depended heavily on a single, locally grown crop—maize—for food. By early in the sixth century, however, the carrying capacity of the most productive local lands was exceeded, and farmers began to depend upon more fragile parts of the ecosystem. Newly acquired climate data show that a 2-century period with a favorable climate was followed by a general drying trend lasting four centuries that led to a series of major droughts. Food production failed to keep pace with the increasing population.

By the eighth and ninth centuries, the evidence reveals not only high levels of infant and adolescent mortality but also widespread malnutrition. The royal dynasty, an important source of leadership, collapsed rather abruptly sometime about A.D. 820–822.

The second case study, Easter Island, shares some remarkable similarities with both the Mayan case and the Malthusian vision. Easter Island lies some 2000 miles off the coast of Chile. Current visitors note that it is distinguished by two features: (1) its enormous statues carved from volcanic rock and (2) a surprisingly sparse vegetation, given the island's favorable climate and conditions. Both the existence of these imposing statues and the fact that they were erected at a considerable distance from the quarry suggests the presence of an advanced civilization, but current observers see no sign of it. What happened? According to scholars, the short answer is that a rising population, coupled with a heavy reliance on wood for housing, canoe building, and statue transportation, decimated the forest (Brander and Taylor, 1998). The loss of the forest contributed to soil erosion, declining soil productivity, and, ultimately, diminished food production. How did the community react to the impending scarcity? Apparently, the social response was war among the remaining island factions and ultimately, cannibalism.

We would like to believe not only that in the face of impending scarcity, societies would react by changing behavior to adapt to the diminishing resource supplies, but also that this benign response would follow automatically from a recognition of the problem. We even have a cliché to capture this sentiment: "necessity is the mother of invention." These stories do point out, however, that nothing is automatic about a problem-solving response. Sometimes societies not only fail to solve the problem but their reactions can actually intensify it.

Sources: Webster, D., Freter, A., & Golin, N. Copan: The rise and fall of an ancient maya kingdom. (2000). Fort Worth: Harcourt Brace Publishers; Brander, J. A., & Taylor, M. S. (1998). The simple economics of Easter Island: A Ricardo-Malthus model of renewable resource use. *The American Economic Review, 88*(1), 119–138; Turner, B. L., & Sabloff, J. A. (2012). Classic period collapse of the central Maya lowlands: Insights about human–environment relationships for sustainability. *Proceedings of the National Academy of Sciences, 109*(35), 13908–13914; Pringle, Heather. (9 November 2012). Climate change had political, human impact on ancient Maya. *Science*, 730–731.

Future Environmental Challenges

Future societies will also be confronted by resource scarcity as well as with accumulating pollutants. Many specific examples of these broad categories of problems are discussed in detail in the following chapters. This section provides a flavor of what is to come by illustrating the challenges posed by one pollution problem (climate change) and one resource scarcity problem (water accessibility).

Climate Change

Energy from the sun drives the earth's weather and climate. Incoming rays heat the earth's surface, radiating energy back into space. Atmospheric "greenhouse" gases (water vapor, carbon dioxide, and other gases) trap some of the outgoing energy.

Without this natural "greenhouse effect," temperatures on the earth would be much lower than they are now and life as we know it would be impossible. It is possible, however, to have too much of a good thing. Problems arise when the concentration of greenhouse gases increases beyond normal levels, thus retaining excessive heat somewhat like a car with its windows closed in the summer.

Since the Industrial Revolution, greenhouse gas emissions have increased, considerably enhancing the heat-trapping capability of the earth's atmosphere. According to the Intergovernmental Panel on Climate Change National Research Council, 2010, "Warming of the climate system is unequivocal, and since the 1950s, many of the observed changes are unprecedented over decades to millennia." It also noted that based upon multiple lines of evidence "Human influence on the climate system is clear."

As the earth warms, the consequences are expected to affect both humans and ecosystems. Some damage to humans is caused directly by increased heat, as shown by the heat waves that resulted in thousands of deaths in Europe in the summer of 2003. Human health can also be affected by pollutants, such as smog, that are exacerbated by warmer temperatures. Rising sea levels (as warmer water expands and previously frozen glaciers melt), coupled with an increase in storm intensity, are expected to flood coastal communities with greater frequency. Ecosystems will be subjected to unaccustomed temperatures; some will adapt by migrating to new areas, but many others are not expected to be able to adapt in time. While these processes have already begun, they will intensify slowly throughout the century.

Climate change also has an important moral dimension. Due to their more limited adaptation capabilities, many developing countries, which have produced relatively small amounts of greenhouse gases, are expected to be the hardest hit as the climate changes.

Dealing with climate change will require a coordinated international response. That is a significant challenge to a world system where the nation-state reigns supreme and international organizations are relatively weak.

Water Accessibility

Another related class of threats is posed by the interaction of a rising demand for resources in the face of a finite supply. Water provides a particularly interesting example because it is so vital to life.

According to the United Nations, about 40 percent of the world's population lives in areas with moderate-to-high water stress. ("Moderate stress" is defined in the U.N. Assessment of Freshwater Resources as "human consumption of more than 20 percent of all accessible renewable freshwater resources," whereas "severe stress" denotes consumption greater than 40 percent.) By 2025, it is estimated that about two-thirds of the world's population—about 5.5 billion people—will live in areas facing either moderate or severe water stress.

This stress is not uniformly distributed around the globe. For example, in parts of the United States, Mexico, China, and India, groundwater is already being consumed faster than it is being replenished, and aquifer levels are steadily falling. Some rivers, such as the Colorado in the western United States and the Yellow in China, often run dry before they reach the sea. Formerly enormous bodies of water, such as the Aral Sea and Lake Chad, are now a fraction of their once-historic sizes. Glaciers that feed many Asian rivers are shrinking.

According to U.N. data, the continents most burdened by a lack of access to sufficient clean water are Africa and Asia. Up to 50 percent of Africa's urban residents and 75 percent of Asians are estimated to lack adequate access to a safe water supply.

The availability of potable water is further limited by human activities that contaminate the remaining supplies. According to the United Nations, 90 percent of sewage and 70 percent of industrial wastes in developing countries are discharged without treatment. And climate change is expected to intensify both the frequency and duration of droughts, simultaneously increasing the demand for water and reducing its supply.

Some arid areas have compensated for their lack of water by importing it via aqueducts from more richly endowed regions or by building large reservoirs, but this solution can promote conflict when the water transfer or the relocation of people living in the area to be flooded by the reservoir is resisted. Additionally, aqueducts and dams may be geologically vulnerable. For example, in California, many of the aqueducts cross or lie on known earthquake-prone fault lines (Reisner, 2003). The reservoir behind the Three Gorges Dam in China is so vast that the pressure and weight are causing tremors and landslides.

Meeting the Challenges

As the scale of economic activity has proceeded steadily upward, the scope of environmental problems triggered by that activity has transcended geographic and generational boundaries. The nation-state used to be a sufficient form of political organization for resolving environmental problems, but is that still the case? Whereas each generation used to have the luxury of being able to satisfy its own needs without worrying about the needs of generations to come, intergenerational effects are now more prominent. Solving problems such as poverty, climate change, ozone depletion, and the loss of biodiversity requires international cooperation. Because future generations cannot speak for themselves, the current generation must speak for them. Current policies must incorporate our obligation to future generations, however difficult or imperfect that incorporation might prove to be.

International cooperation is by no means a foregone conclusion. Global environmental problems can result in very different effects on countries that will sit around the negotiating table. While low-lying countries could be completely submerged by the sea level rise predicted by some climate change models, arid nations could see their marginal agricultural lands succumb to desertification. Other nations may see agricultural productivity rise as warmer climates in traditionally intemperate regions support longer growing seasons.

Countries that unilaterally set out to improve the global environmental situation run the risk of making their businesses vulnerable to competition from less conscientious nations. Industrialized countries that undertake stringent environmental policies may not suffer much at the national level due to offsetting increases in income and employment in industries that supply renewable, cleaner energy and pollution control equipment. Some specific industries facing stringent environmental regulations, however, may well face higher costs than their competitors, and can be expected to lose market share accordingly. Declining market share and employment resulting from especially stringent regulations and the threat to outsource production are powerful influences. The search for solutions must accommodate these concerns.

The market system is remarkably resilient in how it responds to challenges. As we shall see, prices provide incentives not only for the wise use of current resources, but also for promoting innovations that can broaden the menu of future options.

Yet, as we shall also see, market incentives are not always consistent with promoting sustainable outcomes. Currently, many individuals and institutions have a large stake in maintaining the status quo, even when it poses an existential threat. Fishermen harvesting their catch from an overexploited fishery are loath to reduce harvests, even when the reduction may be necessary to conserve the stock and to return the population to a healthy level. Farmers who depend on fertilizer and pesticide subsidies will give them up reluctantly. Coal companies resist any attempt to reduce carbon emissions from coal-fired power plants.

How Will Societies Respond?

The fundamental question is how societies will respond to these challenges. One way to think systematically about this question involves feedback loops.

Positive feedback loops are those in which secondary effects tend to reinforce the basic trend. The process of capital accumulation illustrates one positive feedback loop. New investment generates greater output, which when sold, generates profits. These profits can be used to fund additional new investments. Notice that with positive feedback loops, the process is self-reinforcing.

Positive feedback loops are also involved in climate change. Scientists believe, for example, that the relationship between emissions of methane and climate change may be described as a positive feedback loop. Because methane is a greenhouse gas, increases in methane emissions contribute to climate change. The rise of the planetary temperature, however, could trigger the release of extremely large quantities of additional methane currently trapped in the permafrost layer of the earth; the resulting larger methane emissions would further increase temperature, resulting in the release of more methane, and so on.

Human behavior can also intensify environmental problems through positive feedback loops. When shortages of a commodity are imminent, for example, consumers typically begin to hoard the commodity. Hoarding intensifies the shortage. Similarly, people faced with shortages of food may be forced to eat the seed that is the key to more plentiful food in the future. Situations giving rise to this kind of downward spiral are particularly troublesome.

In contrast, a negative feedback loop is self-limiting rather than self-reinforcing. Perhaps the best-known planetary-scale example of a negative feedback loop is provided in a theory advanced by the English scientist James Lovelock. Called the *Gaia hypothesis* after the Greek concept for Mother Earth, this view of the world suggests that the earth is a living organism with a complex feedback system that seeks an optimal physical and chemical environment. Deviations from this optimal environment trigger natural, nonhuman response mechanisms that restore the balance. In essence, according to the Gaia hypothesis, the planetary environment is characterized by negative feedback loops and, therefore, is, within limits, a self-limiting process.

As we proceed with our investigation, the degree to which our economic and political institutions serve to intensify or to limit emerging environmental problems will be a key focus of our analysis.

The Role of Economics

How societies respond to challenges will depend largely on the behavior of human beings acting individually or collectively. Economic analysis provides an incredibly useful set of tools for anyone interested in understanding and/or

Ecological Economics versus Environmental Economics

DEBATE 1.1

Over the last decade or so, the community of scholars dealing with the role of the economy and the environment has settled into two camps: ecological economics (http://www.ecoeco.org/) and environmental economics (http://www.aere.org/). Although they share many similarities, ecological economics is consciously more methodologically pluralist, while environmental economics is based solidly on the standard paradigm of neoclassical economics. While neoclassical economics emphasizes maximizing human welfare and using economic incentives to modify destructive human behavior, ecological economics uses a variety of methodologies, including neoclassical economics, depending upon the purpose of the investigation.

While some observers see the two approaches as competitive (presenting an "either-or" choice), others, including the authors of this text, see them as complementary. Complementarity, of course, does not mean full acceptance. Significant differences exist not only between these two fields, but also within them over such topics as the valuation of environmental resources, the impact of trade on the environment, and the appropriate means for evaluating policy strategies for long-duration problems such as climate change. These differences arise not only over methodologies but also over the values that are brought to bear on the analysis.

The senior author of this book has published in both fields and has served on the editorial boards of the leading journals in both fields, so it probably will not be surprising that this book draws from both fields. Although the basic foundation for the analysis is environmental economics, the chapters draw heavily from ecological economics to critique that view when it is controversial and to complement it with useful insights drawn from outside the neoclassical paradigm, when appropriate. Pragmatism is the reigning criterion. If a particular approach or study helps us to understand environmental problems and their resolution, it has been included in the text.

modifying human behavior, particularly in the face of scarcity. In many cases, this analysis points out the sources of the market system's resilience as embodied in negative feedback loops. In others, it provides a basis not only for identifying the circumstances where markets fail, but also for clarifying how and why that specific set of circumstances supports degradation. This understanding can then be used as the basis for designing new incentives that restore a sense of harmony in the relationship between the economy and the environment for those cases where the market fails.

Over the years, two different, but related, disciplinary approaches have arisen to address the challenges the future holds. As shown in Debate 1.1, both ecological economics and environmental economics can contribute to our understanding.

The Use of Models

All of the topics covered in this book will be examined as part of the general focus on satisfying human wants and needs in light of limited environmental and natural resources. Because this subject is complex, it is better understood when broken into manageable portions. Once we master the components in individual chapters, we will be able to coalesce the individual insights into a more complete picture.

In economics, as in most other disciplines, we use models to investigate complex subjects such as relationships between the economy and the environment. Models are simplified characterizations of reality. For example, although a road map by design leaves out much detail, it is nonetheless a useful guide to reality. By showing how various locations relate to each other, a map gives an overall perspective. Although it cannot capture all of the unique details that characterize any particular location, a map highlights those characteristics that are crucial for the purpose at hand.

The models in this text are similar. Through simplification, less detail is considered so that the main concepts and the relationships among them become clear.

Fortunately, models allow us to study rigorously issues that are interrelated and global in scale. Unfortunately, due to their selectivity, models may yield conclusions that are dead wrong. Details that are omitted may turn out, in retrospect, to be crucial in understanding a particular dimension. Therefore, models are useful abstractions, but the conclusions they yield depend on the structure of the model. Change that structure and you are likely to change the conclusions. As a result, models should always be viewed with some skepticism.

Most people's views of the world are based on models, although frequently the assumptions and relationships involved may be implicit, perhaps even subconscious. In economics, the models are explicit; objectives, relationships, and assumptions are clearly specified so that the reader understands exactly how the conclusions are derived.

The validity and reliability of economic models are tested by examining the degree to which they can explain actual behavior in markets or other settings. An empirical field known as econometrics uses statistical techniques, primarily regression analysis, to derive key economic functions. These data-derived functions, such as cost curves or demand functions, can then be used for such diverse purposes as testing hypotheses about the effects of policies or forecasting future oil prices.

Examining human behavior in a non-laboratory setting, however, poses special challenges because it is nearly impossible to control completely for all the various factors that influence an outcome beyond those of primary interest. The search for more control over the circumstances that provide the data we use to understand human behavior has given rise to the use of another complementary analytical approach—*experimental economics*, as discussed in Example 1.2. Together, econometrics and experimental economics can provide different lenses to help us understand human behavior and its impact on the world around us.

EXAMPLE 1.2

Experimental Economics: Studying Human Behavior in a Laboratory

The appeal of experimental economics is based upon its ability to study human behavior in a more controlled setting. During the mid-twentieth century economists began to design controlled laboratory experiments with human subjects. The experimental designs mimic decision situations in a variety of settings. Paid participants are informed of the rules of the experiment and asked to make choices. Perhaps, for example, in an experiment to mimic the current carbon trading market, the participants are told how much it costs to abate carbon emissions and they are asked to place bids to buy carbon allowances. The team running the experiment would then calculate the resulting market price as well as how many allowances each successful participant would acquire, based on all the bids.

To the extent that the results of these experiments have proved to be replicable, they have created a deeper understanding about the effectiveness of markets, policies, and institutions. The large and growing literature on experimental economics has already shed light on such widely divergent topics as the effectiveness of alternative policies for controlling pollution and allocating water, how uncertainty affects choices, and how the nature of cooperative agreements affects the sustainability of shared natural resources.

While experiments have the advantage of being able to control the decision-making environment, the artificiality of the laboratory setting raises questions about the degree to which the results from laboratories can shed light on actual human behavior outside the lab. While the degree of artificiality can be controlled by careful research design, it cannot be completely eliminated. Over the years, however, this approach has provided valuable information that can complement what we have learned from observed behavior using econometrics.

Sources: Cummings, R. G., & Taylor, L. O. (2001/2002). Experimental economics in natural resource and environmental management. *The International Yearbook of Environmental and Natural Resource Economics* (H. Folmer and T. Tietenberg, Eds). Cheltenham, UK: Edward Elgar, 123–149; Smith, V. L. (1998). Experimental methods in economics. *The New Palgrave Dictionary of Economics*, Volume 2, J. Eatwell, M. Murray , & P. Newman, Eds. London, UK: The Macmillan Press Limited, 241–249.

The Road Ahead

Are current societies are on a self-destructive path? In part, the answer depends on whether human behavior is perceived as a positive or a negative feedback loop. If increasing scarcity results in a behavioral response that involves a positive feedback loop (intensifies the pressure on the environment), pessimism is justified. If, on the other hand, human responses serve to reduce those pressures or could be reformed so as to reduce those pressures, optimism may be justified.

Not only does environmental and natural resource economics provide a firm basis for understanding the behavioral sources of environmental problems, but also this understanding provides a firm foundation for crafting specific solutions to them. In subsequent chapters, for example, you will be exposed to how economic analysis can be (and has been) used to forge solutions to such diverse areas as climate change, biodiversity loss and water scarcity. Many of the solutions are quite novel.

Market forces are extremely powerful. Attempts to solve environmental problems that ignore these forces run a high risk of failure. Where these forces are compatible with efficient and sustainable outcomes, those outcomes can be supported and reinforced. Where the forces diverge, they can be channeled into directions that restore compatibility. Environmental and natural resource economics provide a specific set of directions for how this compatibility between goals and outcomes can be achieved.

The Issues

The two opposing visions of the future identified in Debate 1.2 offer not only rather different conceptions of what the future holds but also dissimilar views of what policy options should be chosen. They also suggest that to act as if one vision is correct, when it is not, could prove to be a costly error. Thus, it is important to examine these two views (or some third view) as a basis for forging your own view.

In order to assess the validity of these visions, we must address some basic issues:

- Is the problem correctly conceptualized as exponential growth with fixed, immutable resource limits? Does the earth have a finite carrying capacity? If so, how can the carrying-capacity concept be operationalized? Do current or forecasted levels of economic activity exceed the earth's carrying capacity?
- How does the economic system respond to scarcities? Is the process mainly characterized by positive or negative feedback loops? Do the responses intensify or ameliorate any initial scarcities?
- What is the role of the political system in controlling these problems? In what circumstances is government intervention necessary? What forms of intervention work best? Is government intervention uniformly benign, or can it make the situation worse? What roles are appropriate for the executive, legislative, and judicial branches?
- Many environmental problems involve a considerable degree of uncertainty about the severity of the problem and the effectiveness of possible solutions. Can our economic and political institutions respond to this uncertainty in reasonable ways or does uncertainty become a paralyzing force?
- Can the economic and political systems work together to eradicate poverty and social injustice while respecting our obligations to future generations? Or do our obligations to future generations inevitably conflict with the desire to raise the living standards of those currently in absolute poverty or the desire to treat all people, especially the most vulnerable, with fairness? Can short- and long-term goals be harmonized? Is sustainable development feasible? If so, how can it be achieved? What does the need to preserve the environment imply about the future of economic activity in the industrialized nations? In the less-industrialized nations?

The rest of this book uses economic analysis to suggest answers to these complex questions.

What Does the Future Hold?

DEBATE 1.2

Is the economy on a collision course with the environment? Or has the process of reconciliation begun? One group, led most notably by Bjørn Lomborg, President of the Copenhagen Consensus Center, concludes that societies have resourcefully confronted environmental problems in the past and that environmentalist concerns to the contrary are excessively alarmist. As he states in his book, *The Skeptical Environmentalist*

> *The fact is, as we have seen, that this civilization over the last 400 years has brought us fantastic and continued progress. . . . And we ought to face the facts—that on the whole we have no reason to expect that this progress will not continue.*

On the other end of the spectrum are the researchers at the Worldwatch Institute, who believe that current development paths and the attendant strain they place on the environment are unsustainable. As reported in that institute's *State of the World 2012* report

> *In 1992, governments at the Rio Earth Summit made a historic commitment to sustainable development—an economic system that promotes the health of both people and ecosystems. Twenty years and several summits later, human civilization has never been closer to ecological collapse, one third of humanity lives in poverty, and another 2 billion people are projected to join the human race over the next 40 years.*

These views not only interpret the available historical evidence differently, but also they imply very different strategies for the future.

Sources: Lomborg, B. (2001). *The skeptical environmentalist: Measuring the real state of the world.* Cambridge, UK: Cambridge University Press; The Worldwatch Institute (2012). *The state of the world 2012.* Washington: Island Press.

An Overview of the Book

In the following chapters you will study the rich and rewarding field of environmental and natural resource economics. The menu of topics is broad and varied. Economics provides a powerful analytical framework for examining the relationships between the environment, on one hand, and the economic and political systems, on the other. The study of economics can assist in identifying circumstances that give rise to environmental problems, in discovering causes of these problems, and in searching for solutions. Each chapter introduces a unique topic in environmental and natural resource economics, while the overarching focus on development in a environment characterized by scarcity weaves these topics into a single theme.

We begin by comparing perspectives being brought to bear on these problems by economists and noneconomists. The manner in which scholars in various disciplines view problems and potential solutions depends on how they organize the available facts, how they interpret those facts, and what kinds of values they apply in translating these interpretations into policy. Before going into a detailed look at environmental problems, we shall compare the ideology of conventional economics to other prevailing ideologies in the natural and social sciences. This comparison not only explains why reasonable people may, upon examining the same set of facts, reach different conclusions, but also it conveys some sense of the strengths and weaknesses of economic analysis as it is applied to environmental problems.

Chapters 2 through 6 delve more deeply into the economic approach, highlighting many of the tools used by environmental economists including cost-benefit analysis, discounting, and methods available for monetizing nonmarket goods and services. Specific evaluation criteria are defined, and examples are developed to show how these criteria can be applied to current environmental problems.

In Chapters 7 through 13 we turn to some of the topics traditionally falling within the subfield known as natural resource economics. The topics covered in these chapters include depletable and renewable energy resources, recyclable resources, water, and land, as well as forests, fisheries and other ecosystems.

We then move on to an area of public policy—pollution control—that has come to rely much more heavily on the use of economic incentives to produce the desired response. These chapters reveal the unique aspects of local and regional air pollution, global problems such as climate change and ozone depletion, vehicle air pollution, water pollution, and toxic substances as well as the effectiveness of the various economic approaches used to control these pollutants.

Following this examination of the individual environmental and natural resource problems and the successes and failures of policies that have been used to ameliorate these problems, we return to the big picture by assembling the bits and pieces of evidence accumulated in the preceding chapters and fusing them into an overall integrated response to the questions posed in the chapter. We also cover some of the major unresolved issues in environmental policy that are likely to be among those commanding center stage over the next several years if not decades.

Summary

Are our institutions so myopic that they have chosen a path that can only lead to the destruction of society as we now know it? We have briefly examined two points of view that provide different answers to that question. The Worldwatch Institute finds that the path is destructive, while Lomborg strikes a much more optimistic tone. The pessimistic view is based upon the inevitability of exceeding the carrying capacity of the planet as the population and the level of economic activity grow. The optimistic view sees initial scarcity triggering sufficiently powerful reductions in population growth and increases in technological progress bringing further abundance, not deepening scarcity.

Our examination of these different visions has revealed questions that must be answered if we are to assess what the future holds. Seeking the answers requires that we accumulate a much better understanding about how choices are made in economic and political systems and how those choices affect, and are affected by, the natural environment. We begin that process in Chapter 2, where the economic approach is developed in broad terms and is contrasted with other conventional approaches.

Discussion Questions

1. In his book *The Ultimate Resource*, economist Julian Simon makes the point that calling the resource base "finite" is misleading. To illustrate this point, he uses a yardstick, with its one-inch markings, as an analogy. The distance between two markings is finite—one inch—but an infinite number of points is contained within that finite space. Therefore, in one sense, what lies between the markings is finite, while in another, equally meaningful sense, it is infinite. Is the concept of a finite resource base useful or not? Why or why not?
2. This chapter contains two views of the future. Since the validity of these views cannot be completely tested until the time period covered by the forecast has passed (so that predictions can be matched against actual events), how can we ever hope to establish *in advance* whether one is a better view than the other? What criteria might be proposed for evaluating predictions?
3. Positive and negative feedback loops lie at the core of systematic thinking about the future. As you examine the key forces shaping the future, what examples of positive and negative feedback loops can you uncover?
4. Which point of view in Debate 1.2 do you find most compelling? Why? What logic or evidence do you find most supportive of that position?

Self-Test Exercise

1. Does the normal reaction of the price system to a resource shortage provide an example of a positive or a negative feedback loop? Why?

Further Reading

Batabyal, A. A., & Nijkamp, P. (2001). Introduction to research tools in natural resource and environmental economics. In A. A. Batabyal & P. Nijkamp (Eds.), *Research tools in natural resource and environmental economics*. Hackensack, NJ: World Scientific Publishing. An introduction to the most frequently used theoretical, empirical, experimental, and interdisciplinary research tools in natural resource and environmental economics.

Delbeke, J., Klaassen, G., van Ierland, T., & Zapfel, P. (2009). The role of environmental economics in recent policy making at the European Commission. *Review of Environmental Economics and Policy*, *4*, 24–43. This article examines how environmental economics has been used at the European Commission in climate change, energy, and air pollution policy.

Repetto, R., Ed. (2006). *Punctuated equilibrium and the dynamics of U.S. environmental policy*. New Haven, CT: Yale University Press. A sophisticated discussion of how positive and negative feedback mechanisms can interact to produce environmental policy stalemates or breakthroughs.

Stavins, R., Ed. (2012). *Economics of the environment: Selected readings* (6th ed.). New York: W. W. Norton & Company, Inc. An excellent set of complementary readings that captures both the power of the discipline and the controversy it provokes.

Additional References and Historically Significant References are available on this book's Companion Website: **http://www.routledgetextbooks.com/textbooks/9780133479690**

The Economic Approach: Property Rights, Externalities, and Environmental Problems

2

The charming landscape which I saw this morning, is indubitably made up of some twenty or thirty farms. Miller owns this field, Locke that, and Manning the woodland beyond. But none of them owns the landscape. There is a property in the horizon which no man has but he whose eye can integrate all the parts, that is, the poet. This is the best part of these men's farms, yet to this their land deeds give them no title.

—Ralph Waldo Emerson, *Nature* (1836)

Introduction

Before examining specific environmental problems and the policy responses to them, it is important that we develop and clarify the economic approach, so that we have some sense of the forest before examining each of the trees. By having a feel for the conceptual framework, it becomes easier not only to deal with individual cases but also, perhaps more importantly, to see how they fit into a comprehensive approach.

In this chapter, we develop the general conceptual framework used in economics to approach environmental problems. We begin by examining the relationship between human actions, as manifested through the economic system, and the environmental consequences of those actions. We can then establish criteria for judging the desirability of the outcomes of this relationship. These criteria provide a basis for identifying the nature and severity of environmental problems, and a foundation for designing effective policies to deal with them.

Throughout this chapter, the economic point of view is contrasted with alternative points of view. These contrasts bring the economic approach into sharper focus and stimulate deeper and more critical thinking about all possible approaches.

The Human–Environment Relationship

The Environment as an Asset

In economics, the environment is viewed as a composite asset that provides a variety of services. It is a very special asset, to be sure, because it provides the life-support systems that sustain our very existence, but it is an asset nonetheless. As with other assets, we wish to enhance, or at least prevent undue depreciation of, the value of this asset so that it may continue to provide aesthetic and life-sustaining services.

The environment provides the economy with raw materials, which are transformed into consumer products by the production process, and energy, which fuels this transformation. Ultimately, these raw materials and energy return to the environment as waste products (see Figure 2.1).

FIGURE 2.1 The Economic System and the Environment

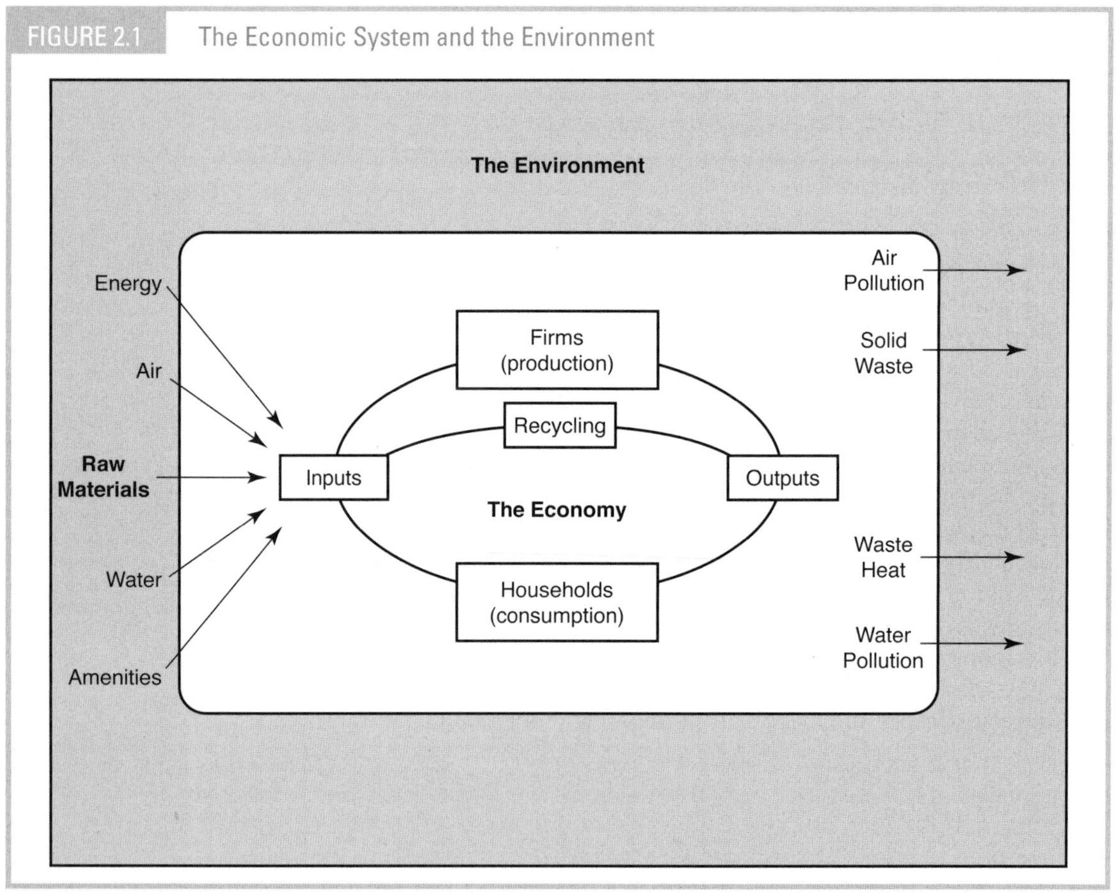

The environment also provides goods and services directly to consumers. The air we breathe, the nourishment we receive from food and drink, and the protection we derive from shelter and clothing are all benefits we receive, either directly or indirectly, from the environment. One significant subclass of these, *ecosystem goods and services*, incorporate the benefits obtained directly from ecosystems, including biodiversity, breathable air, wetlands, water quality, carbon sequestration and recreation. Anyone who has experienced the exhilaration of white-water canoeing, the total serenity of a wilderness trek, or the breathtaking beauty of a sunset will readily recognize that ecosystems provide us with a variety of amenities for which no substitute exists. (Chapter 13 provides a closer look at the role economics plays in maintaining and protecting these very special goods and services.)

If the environment is defined broadly enough, the relationship between the environment and the economic system can be considered a *closed system*. For our purposes, a closed system is one in which no inputs (energy or matter) are received from outside the system and no outputs are transferred outside the system. An *open system*, by contrast, is one in which the system imports or exports matter or energy.

If we restrict our conception of the relationship in Figure 2.1 to our planet and the atmosphere around it, then clearly we do not have a closed system. We derive most of our energy from the sun, either directly or indirectly. We have also sent spaceships well beyond the boundaries of our atmosphere. Nonetheless, historically speaking, for *material* inputs and outputs (not including energy), this system can be treated as a closed system because the amount of exports (such as abandoned space vehicles) and imports (e.g., moon rocks) are negligible. Whether the system remains closed depends on the degree to which space exploration opens up the rest of our solar system as a source of raw materials.

The treatment of our planet and its immediate environs as a closed system has an important implication that is summed up in the *first law of thermodynamics*—energy and matter can neither be created nor destroyed.[1] The law implies that the mass of materials flowing into the economic system from the environment has either to accumulate in the economic system or return to the environment as waste. When accumulation stops, the mass of materials flowing into the economic system is equal in magnitude to the mass of waste flowing into the environment.

Excessive wastes can, of course, depreciate the asset; when they exceed the absorptive capacity of nature, wastes reduce the services that the asset provides. Examples are easy to find: air pollution can cause respiratory problems, polluted drinking water can cause cancer, smog obliterates scenic vistas, climate change can lead to flooding of coastal areas.

The relationship of people to the environment is also conditioned by another physical law, the *second law of thermodynamics*. Known popularly as the *entropy law*, this law states that "entropy increases." *Entropy* is the amount of energy unavailable

[1]We know, however, from Einstein's famous equation ($E = mc^2$) that matter can be transformed into energy. This transformation is the source of energy in nuclear power.

for work. Applied to energy processes, this law implies that no conversion from one form of energy to another is completely efficient and that the consumption of energy is an irreversible process. Some energy is always lost during conversion, and the rest, once used, is no longer available for further work. The second law also implies that in the absence of new energy inputs, any closed system must eventually use up its available energy. Since energy is necessary for life, life ceases when useful energy flows cease.

We should remember that our planet is not even approximately a closed system with respect to energy; we gain energy from the sun. The entropy law does remind us, however, that the flow of solar energy establishes an upper limit on the flow of available energy that can be sustained. Once the stocks of stored energy (such as fossil fuels and nuclear energy) are gone, the amount of energy available for useful work will be determined solely by the solar flow and by the amount that can be stored (through dams, trees, and so on). Thus, in the very long run, the growth process will be limited by the availability of solar energy and our ability to put it to work.

The Economic Approach

Two different types of economic analysis can be applied to increase our understanding of the relationship between the economic system and the environment: *Positive* economics attempts to describe *what is*, *what was*, or *what will be*. *Normative* economics, by contrast, deals with what *ought to be*. Disagreements within positive economics can usually be resolved by an appeal to the facts. Normative disagreements, however, involve value judgments.

Both branches are useful. Suppose, for example, we want to investigate the relationship between trade and the environment. Positive economics could be used to describe the kinds of impacts trade would have on the economy and the environment. It could not, however, provide any guidance on the question of whether trade was desirable. That judgment would have to come from normative economics, a topic we explore in the next section.

The fact that positive analysis does not, by itself, determine the desirability of some policy action does not mean that it is not useful in the policy process. Example 2.1 provides one example of the kinds of economic impact analyses that are used in the policy process.

A rather different context for normative economics can arise when the possibilities are more open-ended. For example, we might ask, how much should we control emissions of greenhouse gases (which contribute to climate change) and how should we achieve that degree of control? Or we might ask, how much forest of various types should be preserved? Answering these questions requires us to consider the entire range of possible outcomes and to select the best or optimal one. Although that is a much more difficult question to answer than one that asks us only to compare two predefined alternatives, the basic normative analysis framework is the same in both cases.

EXAMPLE 2.1

Economic Impacts of Reducing Hazardous Pollutant Emissions from Iron and Steel Foundries

The US Environmental Protection Agency (EPA) was tasked with developing a "maximum achievable control technology standard" to reduce emissions of hazardous air pollutants from iron and steel foundries. As part of the rule-making process, EPA conducted an *ex ante* economic impact analysis to assess the potential economic impacts of the proposed rule.

If implemented, the rule would require some iron and steel foundries to implement pollution control methods that would increase the production costs at affected facilities. The interesting question addressed by the analysis is how large those impacts would be.

The impact analysis estimated annual costs for existing sources to be $21.73 million. These cost increases were projected to result in small increases in output prices. Specifically, prices were projected to increase by only 0.1 percent for iron castings and 0.05 percent for steel castings. The impacts of these price increases were expected to be experienced largely by iron foundries using cupola furnaces as well as consumers of iron foundry products. Unaffected domestic foundries and foreign producers of coke were actually projected to earn slightly higher profits as a result of the rule.

This analysis helped in two ways. First, by showing that the impacts fell under the $100 million threshold that mandates review by the Office of Management and Budget, the analysis eliminated the need for a much more time and resource consuming analysis. Second, by showing how small the expected impacts would be, it served to lower the opposition that might have arisen from unfounded fears of much more severe impacts.

Source: Office of Air Quality Planning and Standards, United States Environmental Protection Agency. (November 2002). *Economic impact analysis of proposed iron and steel foundries.* NESHAP Final Report; National Emissions Standards for Hazardous Air Pollutants for Iron and Steel Foundries, Proposed Rule. (April 17, 2007). *Federal Register, 72*(73), 19150–19164.

Environmental Problems and Economic Efficiency

Static Efficiency

The chief normative economic criterion for choosing among various outcomes occurring at the same point in time is called *static efficiency*, or merely *efficiency*. An allocation of resources is said to satisfy the static efficiency criterion if the economic surplus derived from those resources is maximized by that allocation. Economic surplus, in turn, is the sum of consumer's surplus and producer's surplus.

Consumer surplus is the value that consumers receive from an allocation minus what it costs them to obtain it. Consumer surplus is measured as the area under the demand curve minus the consumer's cost. The cost to the consumer is the area under the price line, bounded from the left by the vertical axis and the right by the quantity of the good. This rectangle, which captures price times quantity, represents consumer expenditure on this quantity of the good.

Why is this area above the price line thought of as a surplus? For each quantity purchased, the corresponding point on the market demand curve represents the amount of money some person would have been willing to pay for the last unit of the good. The *total willingness to pay* for some quantity of this good—say, three units—is the sum of the willingness to pay for each of the three units. Thus, the total willingness to pay for three units would be measured by the sum of the willingness to pay for the first, second, and third units, respectively. It is now a simple extension to note that the total willingness to pay is the area under the continuous market demand curve to the left of the allocation in question. For example, in Figure 2.2 the total willingness to pay for Q_d units of the commodity is the shaded area. Total willingness to pay is the concept we shall use to define the total value a consumer would receive from the amount of the good they take delivery of. Thus, total value the consumer would receive is equal to the area under the market demand curve from the origin to the allocation of interest. Consumer surplus is thus the excess of total willingness to pay over the (lower) actual expenditure.

Meanwhile, sellers face a similar choice (see Figure 2.3). Given price P^*, the seller maximizes his or her own producer surplus by choosing to sell Q_s units. The *producer*

FIGURE 2.2 The Consumer's Choice

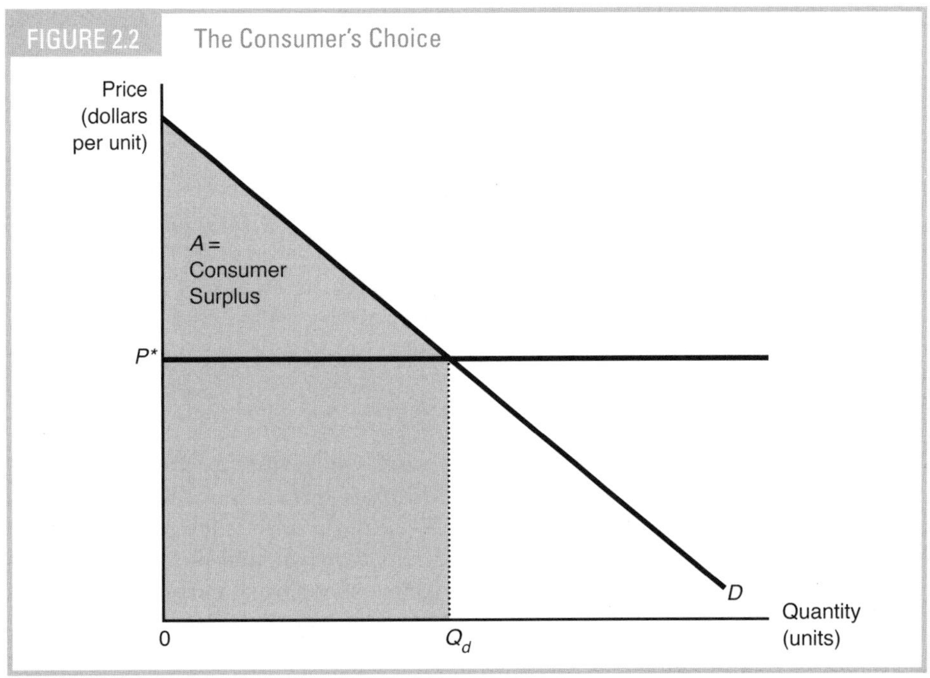

FIGURE 2.3 The Producer's Choice

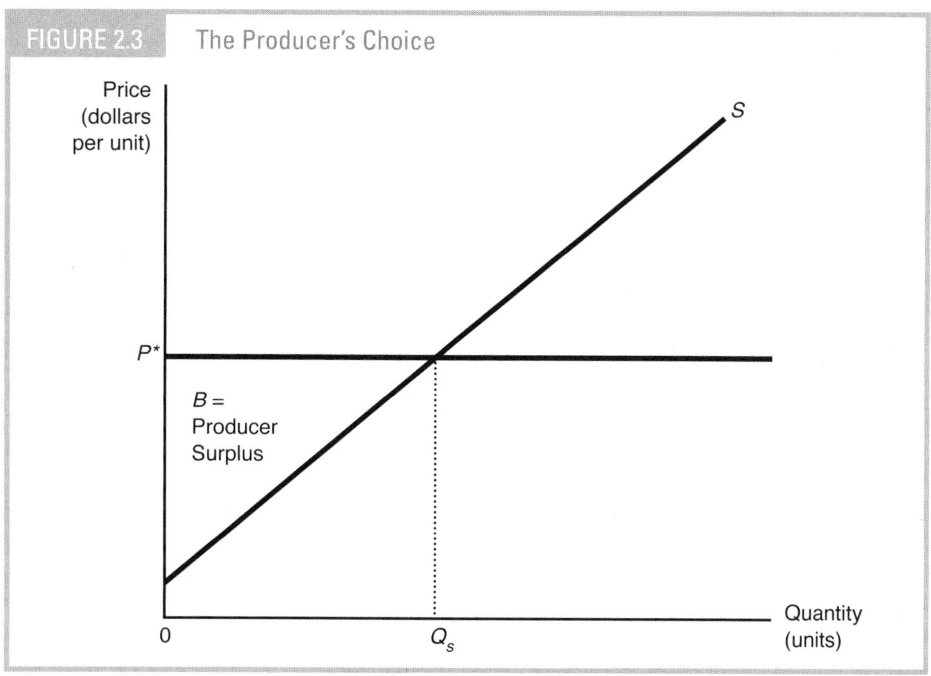

surplus is designated by area *B*, the area under the price line that lies over the marginal cost curve, bounded from the left by the vertical axis and the right by the quantity of the good. To calculate producer or consumer surplus, notice that as long as the functions are linear (as they are in the figures), each area is represented as a right triangle. Remember that the area of a right triangle is calculated as 1/2 × the base of the triangle × the height of the triangle. Using this formula, try calculating these areas in the first self-test exercise at the end of this chapter.

Property Rights

Property Rights and Efficient Market Allocations

The manner in which producers and consumers use environmental resources depends on the property rights governing those resources. In economics, *property right* refers to a bundle of entitlements defining the owner's rights, privileges, and limitations for use of the resource. By examining such entitlements and how they affect human behavior, we will better understand how environmental problems arise from government and market allocations.

These property rights can be vested either with individuals, as in a capitalist economy, or with the state, as in a centrally planned socialist economy. How can we tell when the pursuit of profits is consistent with efficiency and when it is not?

Efficient Property Rights Structures

Let's begin by describing the structure of property rights that could produce efficient allocations in a well-functioning market economy. An efficient structure has three main characteristics:

1. *Exclusivity*—All benefits and costs accrued as a result of owning and using the resources should accrue to the owner, and only to the owner, either directly or indirectly by sale to others.
2. *Transferability*—All property rights should be transferable from one owner to another in a voluntary exchange.
3. *Enforceability*—Property rights should be secure from involuntary seizure or encroachment by others.

An owner of a resource with a well-defined property right (one exhibiting these three characteristics) has a powerful incentive to use that resource efficiently because a decline in the value of that resource represents a personal loss. Farmers who own the land have an incentive to fertilize and irrigate it because the resulting increased production raises income. Similarly, they have an incentive to rotate crops when that raises the productivity of their land.

When well-defined property rights are exchanged, as in a market economy, this exchange facilitates efficiency. We can illustrate this point by examining the incentives consumers and producers face when a well-defined system of property rights is in place. Because the seller has the right to prevent the consumer from consuming the product in the absence of payment, the consumer must pay to receive the product. Given a market price, the consumer decides how much to purchase by choosing the amount that maximizes his or her individual consumer surplus.

Is this allocation efficient? According to our definition of static efficiency, it is clear the answer is yes. The economic surplus is maximized by the market allocation and, as seen in Figure 2.4, it is equal to the sum of consumer and producer surpluses (areas $A + B$). Thus, we have not only established a procedure for measuring efficiency, but also a means of describing how the surplus is distributed between consumers and producers.

This distinction is crucially significant. Efficiency is *not* achieved because consumers and producers are seeking efficiency. They aren't! In a system with well-defined property rights and competitive markets in which to sell those rights, producers try to maximize their surplus and consumers try to maximize their surplus. The price system, then, induces those self-interested parties to make choices that also turn out to be efficient from the point of view of society as a whole. It channels the energy motivated by self-interest into socially productive paths.

Familiarity may have dulled our appreciation, but it is noteworthy that a system designed to produce a harmonious and congenial outcome could function effectively while allowing consumers and producers so much individual freedom in making choices. This is truly a remarkable accomplishment.

FIGURE 2.4 Market Equilibrium

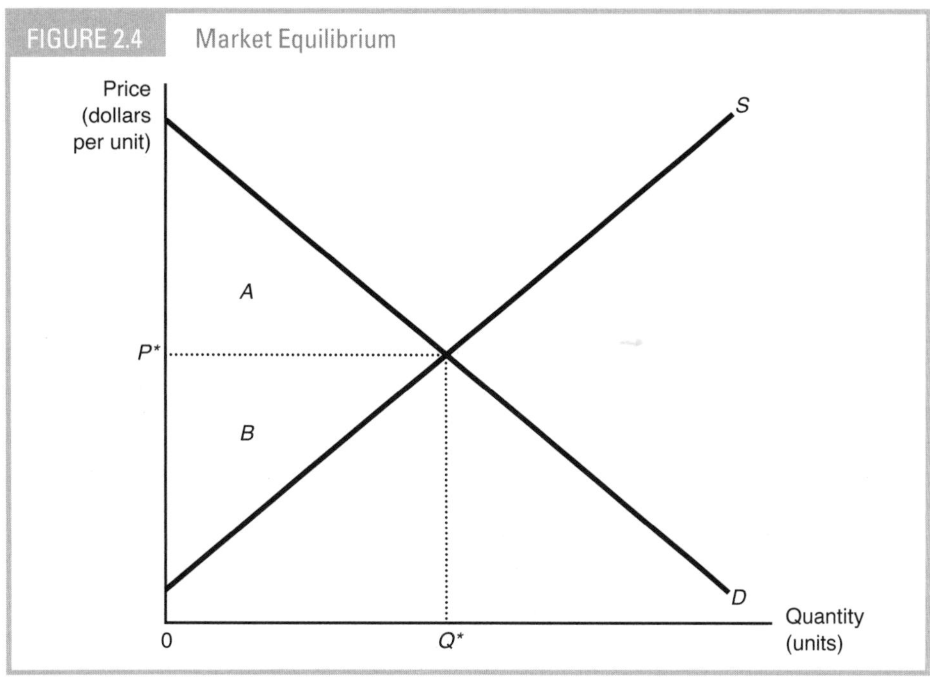

Producer's Surplus, Scarcity Rent, and Long-Run Competitive Equilibrium

Since the area under the price line is total revenue, and the area under the marginal cost curve is total variable cost, producer's surplus is related to profits. In the short run when some costs are fixed, producer's surplus is equal to profits plus fixed cost. In the long run when all costs are variable, producer's surplus is equal to profits plus rent, the return to scarce inputs owned by the producer. As long as new firms can enter into profitable industries without raising the prices of purchased inputs, long-run profits and rent will equal zero.

Scarcity Rent. Most natural resource industries, however, do give rise to rent and, therefore, producer's surplus is not eliminated by competition, even with free entry. This producer's surplus, which persists in long-run competitive equilibrium, is called *scarcity rent.*

David Ricardo was the first economist to recognize the existence of scarcity rent. Ricardo suggested that the price of land was determined by the least fertile marginal unit of land. Since the price had to be sufficiently high to allow the poorer land to be brought into production, other, more fertile land could be farmed at an economic profit. Competition could not erode that profit because the amount of high quality land was limited and lower prices would serve only to reduce the supply of land below demand. The only way to expand production would be to bring additional, less fertile land (more costly to farm) into production; consequently, additional production does not lower price, as it does in a constant-cost industry. As we shall see, other circumstances also give rise to scarcity rent for natural resources.

Externalities as a Source of Market Failure

The Concept Introduced

Exclusivity is one of the chief characteristics of an efficient property rights structure. This characteristic is frequently violated in practice. One broad class of violations occurs when an agent making a decision does not bear all of the consequences of his or her action.

Suppose two firms are located by a river. The first produces steel, while the second, somewhat downstream, operates a resort hotel. Both use the river, although in different ways. The steel firm uses it as a receptacle for its waste, while the hotel uses it to attract customers seeking water recreation. If these two facilities have different owners, an efficient use of the water is not likely to result. Because the steel plant does not bear the cost of reduced business at the resort resulting from waste being dumped into the river, it is not likely to be very sensitive to that cost in its decision making. As a result, it could be expected to dump too much waste into the river, and an efficient allocation of the river would not be attained.

This situation is called an externality. An *externality* exists whenever the welfare of some agent, either a firm or household, depends not only on his or her activities, but also on activities under the control of some other agent. In the example, the increased waste in the river imposed an external cost on the resort, a cost the steel firm could not be counted upon to consider appropriately in deciding the amount of waste to dump.

The effect of this external cost on the steel industry is illustrated in Figure 2.5, which shows the market for steel. Steel production inevitably involves producing pollution as well as steel. The demand for steel is shown by the demand curve D, and the private marginal cost of producing the steel (exclusive of pollution control and damage) is depicted as MC_p. Because society considers both the cost of pollution and the cost of producing the steel, the social marginal cost function (MC_s) includes both of these costs as well.

If the steel industry faced no outside control on its emission levels, it would seek to produce Q_m. That choice, in a competitive setting, would maximize its private producer surplus. But that is clearly not efficient, since the net benefit is maximized at Q^*, not Q_m. Can you see the deadweight loss?

With the help of Figure 2.5, we can draw a number of conclusions about market allocations of commodities causing pollution externalities:

1. The output of the commodity is too large.
2. Too much pollution is produced.
3. The prices of products responsible for pollution are too low.

FIGURE 2.5 The Market for Steel

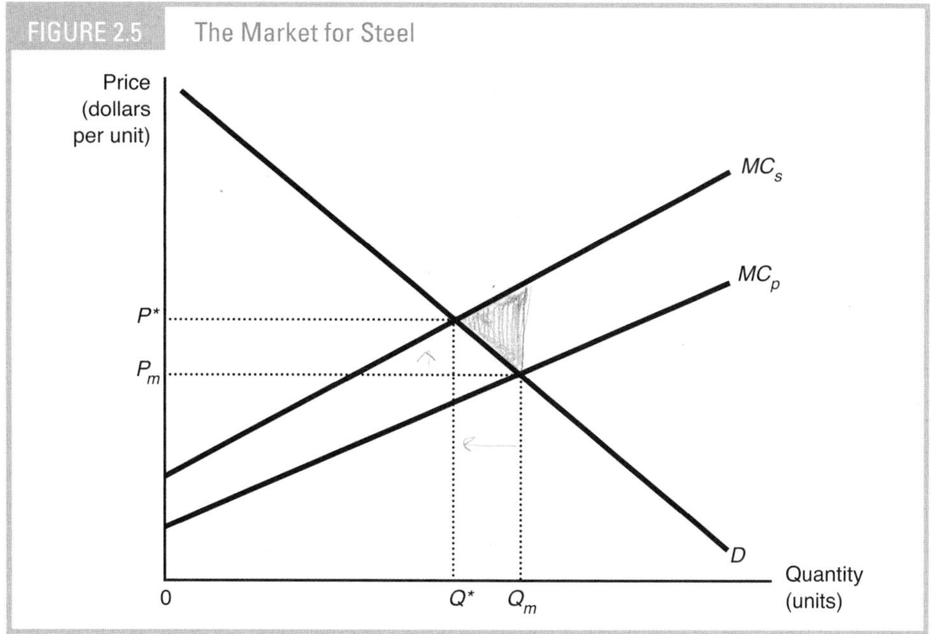

4. As long as the costs are external, no incentives to search for ways to yield less pollution per unit of output are introduced by the market.
5. Recycling and reuse of the polluting substances are discouraged because release into the environment is so inefficiently cheap.

The effects of a market imperfection for one commodity end up affecting the demands for raw materials, labor, and so on. The ultimate effects are felt through the entire economy.

Types of Externalities

External effects, or externalities, can be positive or negative. Historically, the terms *external cost* (*external diseconomy*) and *external benefit* (*external economy*) have been used to refer, respectively, to circumstances in which the affected party is damaged by or benefits from the externality. Clearly, the water pollution example represents an external diseconomy. External benefits are not hard to find, however. As noted in the opening quote to this chapter, private individuals who preserve a particularly scenic area provide an external economy to all who pass. Generally, when external economies are present, the market will undersupply the resources.

One other distinction is important. One class of externalities, known as *pecuniary externalities*, does not present the same kinds of problems as pollution does. Pecuniary externalities arise when the external effect is transmitted through altered prices. Suppose that a new firm moves into an area and drives up the rental price of land. That increase creates a negative effect on all those paying rent and, therefore, is an external diseconomy.

This pecuniary diseconomy, however, does not cause a market failure because the resulting higher rents are reflecting the true scarcity of land. The land market provides a mechanism by which the parties can bid for land; the resulting prices reflect the value of the land in its various uses. Without pecuniary externalities, the price signals would fail to sustain an efficient allocation.

The pollution example is *not* a pecuniary externality because the effect is not transmitted through prices. In this example, prices do not adjust to reflect the increasing waste load. The damage to the water resource is not reflected in the steel firm's costs. An essential feedback mechanism that is present for pecuniary externalities is not present for the pollution case.

The externalities concept is a broad one, covering a multitude of sources of market failure (Example 2.2 illustrates one). The next step is to investigate some specific circumstances that can give rise to externalities.

EXAMPLE 2.2

Shrimp Farming Externalities in Thailand

In the Tha Po village on the coast of Surat Thani Province in Thailand, more than half of the 1100 hectares of mangrove swamps have been cleared for commercial shrimp farms. Although harvesting shrimp is a lucrative undertaking, mangroves also serve as nurseries for fish and as barriers for storms and soil erosion. Following the destruction of the local mangroves, Tha Po villagers experienced a decline in fish catch and suffered storm damage and water pollution. Can market forces be trusted to strike the efficient balance between preservation and development for the remaining mangroves?

Calculations by economists Sathirathai and Barbier (2001) demonstrated that the value of the ecological services that would be lost from further destruction of the mangrove swamps exceeded the value of the shrimp farms that would take their place. Preservation of the remaining mangrove swamps would be the efficient choice.

Would a potential shrimp-farming entrepreneur make the efficient choice? Unfortunately, the answer is no. This study estimated the economic value of mangroves in terms of local use of forest resources, offshore fishery linkages, and coastal protection to be in the range of $27,264–$35,921 per hectare. In contrast, the economic returns to shrimp farming, once they are corrected for input subsidies and for the costs of water pollution, are only $194–$209 per hectare. However, as shrimp farmers are heavily subsidized and do not have to take into account the external costs of pollution, their financial returns are typically $7,706.95–$8,336.47 per hectare. In the absence of some sort of external control imposed by collective action, converting mangroves to shrimp farming would be the normal, if inefficient, result. The externalities associated with the ecological services provided by the mangroves support a biased decision that results in fewer social net benefits, but greater private net benefits.

Source: Sathirathai, S., & Barbier, E.B. (April 2001). Valuing mangrove conservation in southern Thailand. *Contemporary Economic Policy*, *19*(2). 109–122.

Perverse Incentives Arising from Some Property Right Structures

Private property is, of course, not the only possible way of defining entitlements to resource use. Other possibilities include

- state-property regimes (the government owns and controls the property);
- common-property regimes (the property is jointly owned and managed by a specified group of co-owners); and
- *res nullius* or open-access regimes (in which no one owns or exercises control over the resources).

All of these create rather different incentives for resource use.

State-property regimes exist not only in former communist countries, but also to varying degrees in virtually all countries of the world. Parks and forests, for example, are frequently owned and managed by the government in capitalist as well as in socialist nations. Problems with both efficiency and sustainability can arise in state-property regimes when the incentives of bureaucrats, who implement and/or make the rules for resource use, diverge from collective interests.

Common-property resources are those shared resources that are managed in common rather than privately. Entitlements to use common-property resources may be formal, protected by specific legal rules, or they may be informal, protected by tradition or custom. Common-property regimes exhibit varying degrees of efficiency and sustainability, depending on the rules that emerge from collective decision making. While some very successful examples of common-property regimes exist, unsuccessful examples are even more common.

One successful example of a common-property regime involves the system of allocating grazing rights in Switzerland. Although agricultural land is normally treated as private property, in Switzerland, grazing rights on the Alpine meadows have been treated as common property for centuries. Overgrazing is protected by specific rules, enacted by an association of users, which limit the amount of livestock permitted on the meadow. The families included on the membership list of the association have been stable over time as rights and responsibilities have passed from generation to generation. This stability has apparently facilitated reciprocity and trust, thereby providing a foundation for continued compliance with the rules.

Unfortunately, that kind of stability may be the exception rather than the rule, particularly in the face of heavy population pressure. The more common situation can be illustrated by the experience of Mawelle, a small fishing village in Sri Lanka. Initially, a complicated but effective rotating system of fishing rights was devised by villagers to assure equitable access to the best spots and best times while protecting the fish stocks. Over time, population pressure and the infusion of outsiders raised demand and undermined the collective cohesion sufficiently that the traditional rules became unenforceable, producing overexploitation of the resource and lower incomes for all the participants.

Res nullius property resources, the main focus of this section, can be exploited on a first-come, first-served basis because no individual or group has the legal power to restrict access. *Open-access resources*, as we shall henceforth call them, have given rise to what has become known popularly as the "tragedy of the commons."

The problems created by open-access resources can be illustrated by recalling the fate of the American bison. Bison are an example of "common-pool" resources. *Common-pool resources* are shared resources characterized by nonexclusivity and divisibility. *Nonexclusivity* implies that resources can be exploited by anyone, while *divisibility* means that the capture of part of the resource by one group subtracts it from the amount available to the other groups. (Note the contrast between common-pool resources and public goods, the subject of the next section.) In the early history of the United States, bison were plentiful; unrestricted hunting access was not a problem. Frontier people who needed hides or meat could easily get whatever they needed; the aggressiveness of any one hunter did not affect the time and effort expended by other hunters. In the absence of scarcity, efficiency was not threatened by open access.

As the years slipped by, however, the demand for bison increased and scarcity became a factor. As the number of hunters increased, eventually every additional unit of hunting activity increased the amount of time and effort required to produce an additional yield of bison.

Consider graphically how various property rights structures (and the resulting level of harvest) affect the scarcity rent (in this case, equivalent to the economic surplus received by consumers and producers), where the amount of rent is measured as the difference between the revenues received from the harvest minus the costs associated with producing that harvest. Figure 2.6 compares the revenue and costs for various levels of harvest. In the top panel the revenue is calculated by multiplying, for each level of hunting activity, the (assumed constant) price of bison by the amount harvested. The upward sloping total cost curve simply reflects that fact that increases in harvest effort result in higher total costs. (Marginal cost is assumed to be constant for this example.)

In terms of the top panel of Figure 2.6 the total surplus associated with any level of effort is measured as the vertical difference between the total revenue curve and the total cost curve for that level of harvest.

In the bottom panel the marginal revenue curve is downward sloping (despite the constant price) because as the amount of hunting effort increases, the resulting bison population size decreases. Smaller populations support smaller harvests per unit of effort expended.

The efficient level of hunting activity in this model (E_1) maximizes the surplus. This can be seen graphically in two different ways. First, E_1 maximizes the vertical difference between the two curves in the top panel. Second, in the bottom panel E_1 is the level where the marginal revenue, which records the addition to the surplus from an additional unit of effort, crosses the marginal cost curve, which measures the reduction in the surplus due to the additional cost of expending that last unit of effort. These are simply two different (mathematically equivalent) ways to demonstrate the same outcome. (The curves in the bottom panel are derived from the curves in the top panel.)

FIGURE 2.6 Bison Harvesting

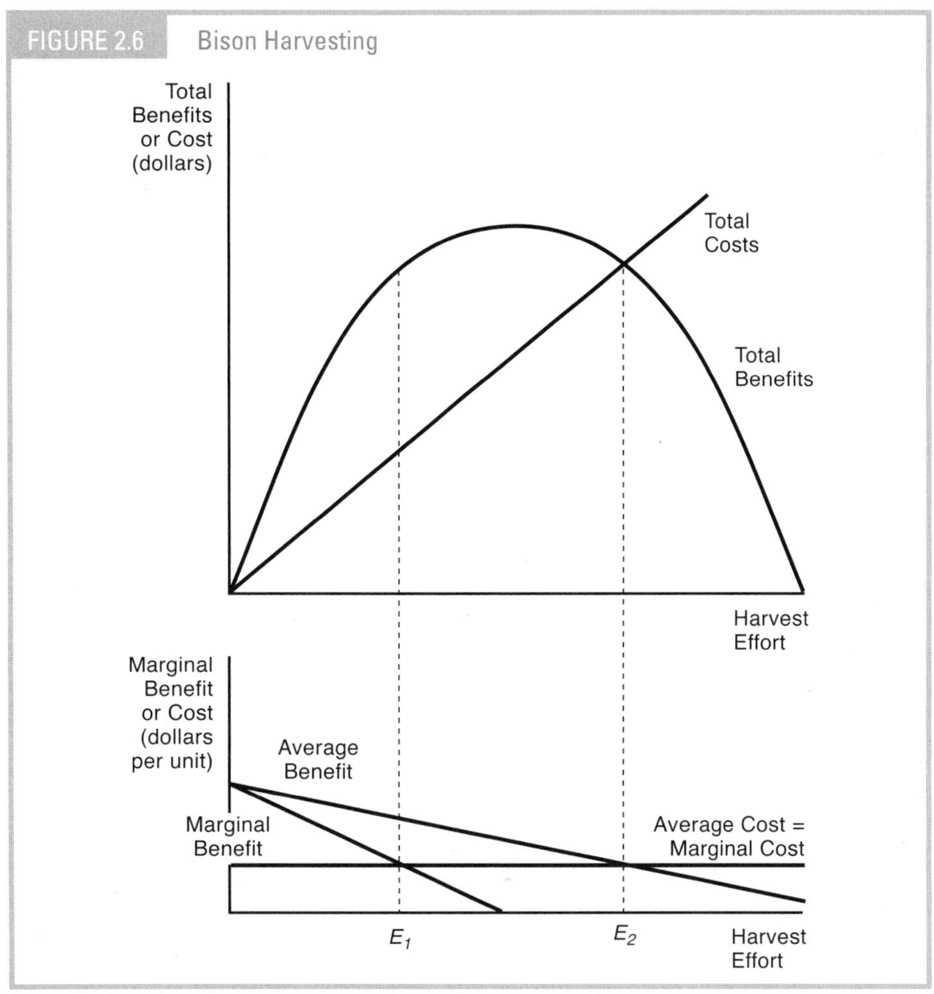

With all hunters having completely unrestricted access to the bison, the resulting allocation would not be efficient. No individual hunter would have an incentive to protect scarcity rent by restricting hunting effort. Individual hunters, without exclusive rights, would exploit the resource until their total benefit equaled total cost, implying a level of effort equal to (E_2). Excessive exploitation of the herd occurs because individual hunters cannot appropriate the scarcity rent; therefore, they ignore it. One of the losses from further exploitation that could be avoided by exclusive owners—the loss of scarcity rent due to overexploitation—is not part of the decision-making process of open-access hunters.

Two characteristics of this formulation of the open-access allocation are worth noting: (1) In the presence of sufficient demand, unrestricted access will cause resources to be overexploited; (2) the scarcity rent is dissipated; no one is able to appropriate the rent, so it is lost.

Why does this happen? Unlimited access destroys the incentive to conserve. A hunter who can preclude others from hunting his stock has an incentive to keep the herd at an efficient level. This restraint results in lower costs in the form of less time and effort expended to produce a given yield of bison. On the other hand, a hunter exploiting an open-access resource would not have an incentive to conserve because the potential additional economic surplus derived from self-restraint would, to some extent, be captured by other hunters who simply kept harvesting. Thus, unrestricted access to scarce resources promotes an inefficient allocation. As a result of excessive harvest and the loss of habitat as land was converted to farm and pasture, the Great Plains bison herds nearly became extinct (Lueck, 2002). Another example of open-access, fisheries, is the principal topic of Chapter 12.

Public Goods

Public goods, defined as those that exhibit both consumption indivisibilities and nonexcludability, present a particularly complex category of environmental resources. *Nonexcludability* refers to a circumstance where, once the resource is provided, even those who fail to pay for it cannot be excluded from enjoying the benefits it confers. Consumption is said to be *indivisible* when one person's consumption of a good does not diminish the amount available for others. Several common environmental resources are public goods, including not only the "charming landscape" referred to by Emerson, but also clean air, clean water, and biological diversity.[2]

Biological diversity includes two related concepts: (1) the amount of genetic variability among individuals within a single species, and (2) the number of species within a community of organisms. *Genetic diversity*, critical to species survival in the natural world, has also proved to be important in the development of new crops and livestock. It enhances the opportunities for crossbreeding and, thus, the development of superior strains. The availability of different strains was the key, for example, in developing new, disease-resistant barley.

Because of the interdependence of species within ecological communities, any particular species may have a value to the community far beyond its intrinsic value. Certain species contribute balance and stability to their ecological communities by providing food sources or holding the population of the species in check.

The richness of diversity within and among species has provided new sources of food, energy, industrial chemicals, raw materials, and medicines. Yet, considerable evidence suggests that biological diversity is decreasing. Biodiversity is a valuable ecosystem service. Ecosystem services will be covered in detail in Chapter 13.

Can we rely solely on the private sector to produce the efficient amount of public goods, such as biological diversity? Unfortunately, the answer is no! Suppose that in response to diminishing ecological diversity we decide to take up a collection to provide some means of preserving endangered species. Would the collection yield sufficient revenue to pay for an efficient level of ecological diversity? The general answer is no. Let's see why.

---

[2]Notice that public "bads," such as dirty air and dirty water, are also possible.

In Figure 2.7, individual demand curves for preserving biodiversity have been presented for two consumers A and B. The market demand curve is represented by the vertical summation of the two individual demand curves. A vertical summation is necessary because everyone can simultaneously consume the same amount of biological diversity. We are, therefore, able to determine the market demand by

FIGURE 2.7 Efficient Provision of Public Goods

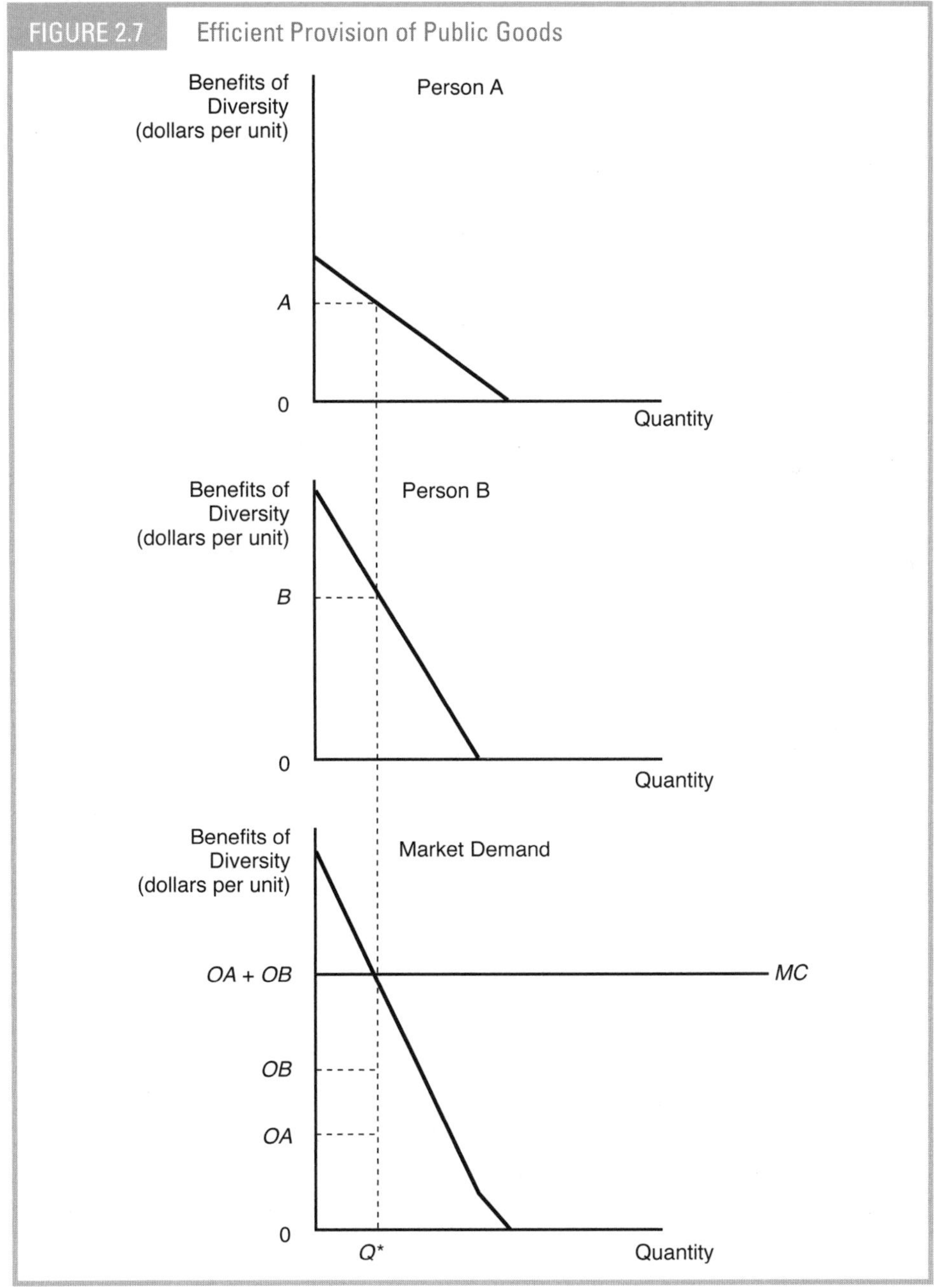

finding the sum of the amounts of money they would be willing to pay for that level of diversity.

What is the efficient level of diversity? It can be determined by a direct application of our definition of efficiency. The efficient allocation maximizes economic surplus, which is represented geometrically by the portion of the area under the market demand curve that lies above the constant marginal cost curve. The allocation that maximizes economic surplus is Q^*, the allocation where the demand curve crosses the marginal cost curve.

Why would a competitive market not be expected to supply the efficient level of this good? Since the two consumers have very different marginal willingness to pay from the efficient allocation of this good (*OA* versus *OB*), the efficient pricing system would require charging a different price to each consumer. Person *A* would pay *OA* and person *B* would pay *OB*. (Remember consumers tend to choose the level of the good that equates their marginal willingness to pay to the price they face.) Yet the producer would have no basis for figuring out how to differentiate the prices. In the absence of excludability, consumers are not likely to choose to reveal the strength of their preference for this commodity. All consumers have an incentive to understate the strength of their preferences to try to shift more of the cost burden to the other consumers.

Therefore, inefficiency results because each person is able to become a free rider on the other's contribution. A *free rider* is someone who derives the value from a commodity without paying an efficient amount for its supply. Because of the consumption indivisibility and nonexcludability properties of the public good, consumers receive the value of any diversity purchased by other people. When this happens it tends to diminish incentives to contribute, and the contributions are not sufficiently large to finance the efficient amount of the public good; it would be undersupplied. (In Chapter 16 we shall use the lens provided by game theory to show how the free rider effect helps to shape climate policy.)

The privately supplied amount may not be zero, however. Some diversity would be privately supplied. Indeed, as suggested by Example 2.3, the privately supplied amount may be considerable.

Imperfect Market Structures

Environmental problems also occur when one of the participants in an exchange of property rights is able to exercise an inordinate amount of power over the outcome. This can occur, for example, when a product is sold by a single seller, or *monopoly*.

It is easy to show that monopolies violate our definition of *efficiency* in the goods market (see Figure 2.8). According to our definition of *static efficiency*, the efficient allocation would result when *OB* is supplied. This would yield consumer surplus represented by triangle *IGC and* producer surplus denoted by triangle *GCH*. The monopoly, however, would produce and sell *OA*, where marginal revenue equals marginal cost, and would charge price *OF*. At this point, although the producer's surplus (*HFED*) is maximized, the sum of consumer and producer surplus is clearly

EXAMPLE 2.3

Public Goods Privately Provided: The Nature Conservancy

Can the demand for a public good such as biological diversity be observed in practice? Would the market respond to that demand? Apparently so, according to the existence of an organization called The Nature Conservancy.

The Nature Conservancy was born of an older organization called the Ecologist Union on September 11, 1950, for the purpose of establishing natural area reserves to aid in the preservation of areas, objects, and fauna and flora that have scientific, educational, or aesthetic significance. This organization purchases, or accepts as donations, land that has some unique ecological or aesthetic significance, to keep it from being used for other purposes. In so doing they preserve many species by preserving the habitat.

From humble beginnings, The Nature Conservancy has, as of 2012, been responsible for the preservation of 119 million acres of forests, marshes, prairies, mounds, and islands around the world. Additionally, The Nature Conservancy has protected 5000 miles of rivers and operates over 100 marine conservation projects. These areas serve as home to rare and endangered species of wildlife and plants. The Conservancy owns and manages the largest privately owned nature preserve system in the world.

This approach has considerable merit. A private organization can move more rapidly than the public sector. Because it has a limited budget, The Nature Conservancy sets priorities and concentrates on acquiring the most ecologically unique areas. Yet the theory of public goods reminds us that if this were to be the sole approach to the preservation of biological diversity, it would preserve a smaller-than-efficient amount.

Source: The Nature Conservancy, http://nature.org/aboutus/

not, because this choice causes society to lose economic surplus equal to triangle *EDC*.[3] Monopolies supply an inefficiently small amount of the good.

Imperfect markets clearly play some role in environmental problems. For example, the major oil-exporting countries have formed a cartel, resulting in higher-than-normal prices and lower-than-normal production. A *cartel* is a collusive agreement among producers to restrict production and raise prices. This collusive agreement allows the group to act as a monopolist. The inefficiency in the goods market would normally be offset to some degree by the reduction in social costs caused by the lower levels of pollution resulting from the reduction in the combustion of oil.

---

[3]Producers would lose area *JDC* compared to the efficient allocation, but they would gain area *FEJG*, which is much larger. Meanwhile, consumers would be worse off, because they lose area *FECJG*. Of these, *FEJG* is merely a transfer to the monopoly, whereas *EJC* is a pure loss to society. The total pure loss (*EDC*) is called a *deadweight loss*.

FIGURE 2.8 Monopoly and Inefficiency

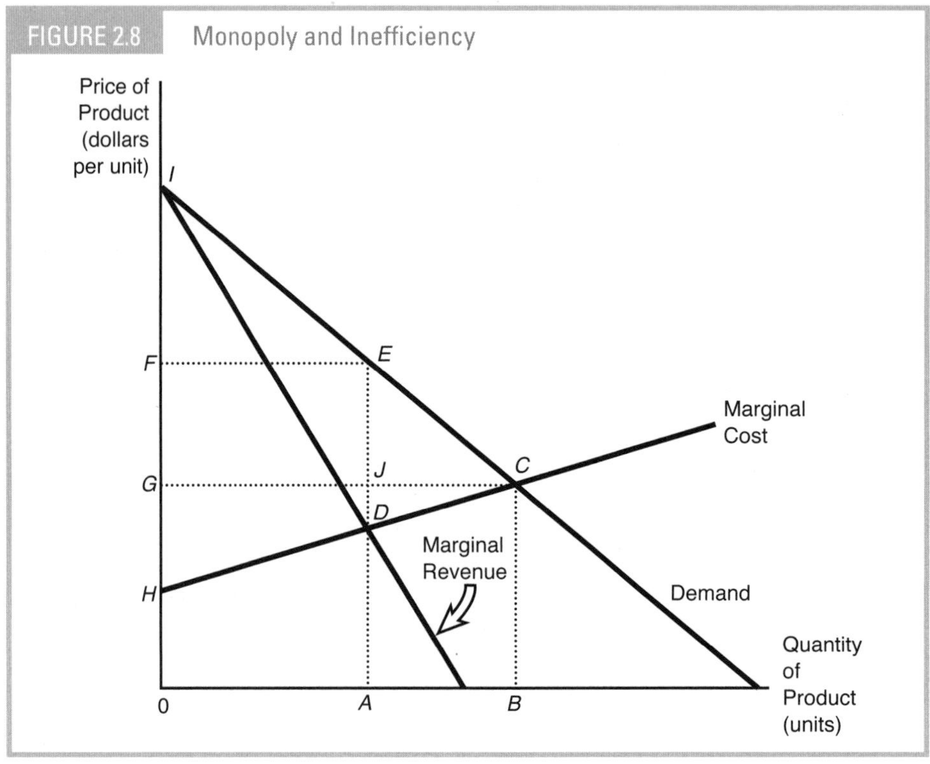

Asymmetric Information

When all parties to a specific situation or transaction have access to the same amount of information about that situation, the information is said to be symmetrically distributed. If, however, one or more parties have more information than the others, the information distribution is said to be asymmetric.

Asymmetic information creates problems for the market when it results in a decision maker knowing too little to make an efficient choice. Suppose, for example, a consumer had a preference for organic food, but didn't know what food choices were truly organic. Since it would be relatively easy for producers to claim their produce was organically grown even if it were not, consumers who could not accurately distinguish produce that truly was organic from produce that (incorrectly) only claimed to be organic, that consumer would tend to be unwilling to pay a higher price for organic produce. As a result both the profits and the output of organic farmers would be inefficiently low. If consumers do not have full information, negative externalities may result. (We shall encounter asymmetric information problems in several chapters, including energy, pollution control, toxic substances, and ecosystem services.)

Government Failure

Market processes are not the only sources of inefficiency. Political processes are fully as culpable. As will become clear in the chapters that follow, some environmental problems have arisen from a failure of political, rather than economic, institutions. To complete our study of the ability of institutions to allocate environmental resources, we must understand this source of inefficiency as well.

Government failure shares with market failure the characteristic that improper incentives are the root of the problem. Special interest groups use the political process to engage in what has become known as *rent seeking*. Rent seeking is the use of resources in lobbying and other activities directed at securing legislation that results in more profitable outcomes for those funding this activity. Successful rent-seeking activity will typically increase the net benefits going to the special interest group, but it will also frequently lower the surplus to society as a whole. In these instances, it is a classic case of the aggressive pursuit of a larger slice of the pie leading to a smaller pie.

Why don't the losers rise up to protect their interests? One main reason is voter ignorance. It is economically rational for voters to remain at least partially ignorant on many issues simply because of the high cost of keeping fully informed and the low probability that any single vote will be decisive. In addition, it is difficult for diffuse groups of individuals, each of whom is affected only to a small degree, to organize a coherent, unified opposition. Successful opposition is, in a sense, a public good, with its attendant tendency for free riding. Opposition to special interests would normally be underfunded.

Rent seeking can take many forms. Producers can seek protection from competitive pressures brought by imports or can seek price floors to hold prices above their efficient levels. Consumer groups can seek price ceilings on goods or special subsidies to transfer part of their costs to the general body of taxpayers.

Rent seeking is not the only source of inefficient government policy. Sometimes governments act without full information and establish policies that are ultimately very inefficient. For example, some time ago, one technological strategy chosen by the government to control motor vehicle pollution involved adding a chemical substance (MTBE) to gasoline. Designed to promote cleaner combustion, this additive turned out to create a substantial water pollution problem.

Governments may also pursue social policy objectives that have the side effect of causing an environmental inefficiency. For example, looking back at Figure 2.5, suppose that the government, when pressured by lobbyists, decides to subsidize the production of steel. Figure 2.9 illustrates the outcome. The private marginal cost curve shifts down and to the right causing a further increase in production, lower prices, and even more pollution produced. Thus, the subsidy moves us even further away from where surplus is maximized at Q^*. The shaded triangle A shows the deadweight loss (inefficiency) without the subsidy. With the subsidy, the deadweight loss grows to areas $A + B + C$. This social policy has the side effect of increasing an environmental inefficiency.

In another example, in Chapter 7, we shall see how the desire to hold down natural gas prices for consumers led to subsequent shortages. These examples provide

FIGURE 2.9 The Market for Steel Revisited

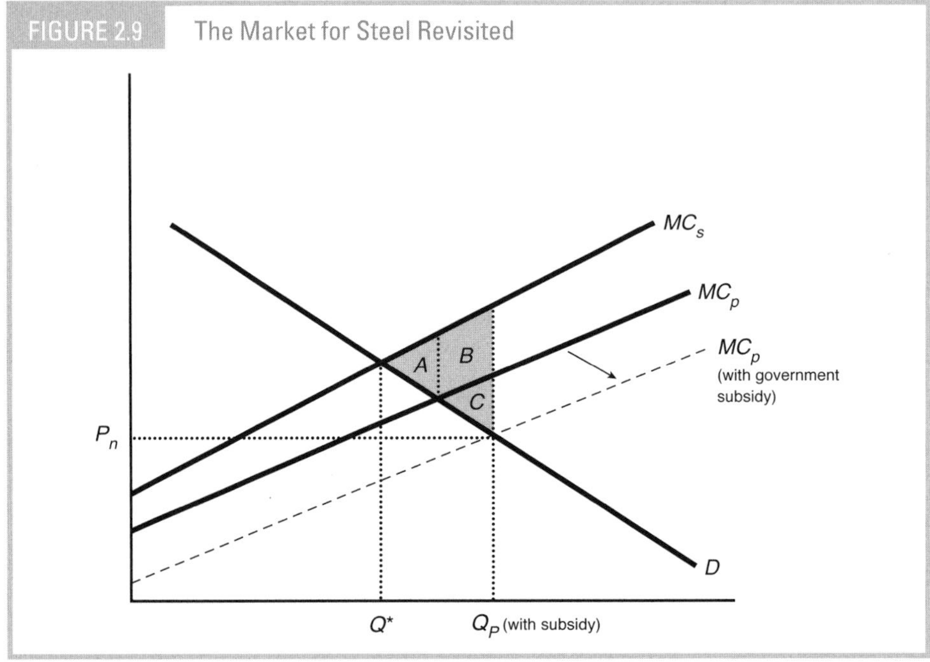

a direct challenge to the presumption that more direct intervention by the government automatically leads to either greater efficiency or greater sustainability.

These cases illustrate the general economic premise that environmental problems arise because of a divergence between individual and collective objectives. This is a powerful explanatory device because not only does it suggest why these problems arise, but also it suggests how they might be resolved—by realigning individual incentives to make them compatible with collective objectives. As self-evident as this approach may be, it is controversial when people disagree about whether the problem is our improper values or the improper translation of our quite proper values into action.

Economists have always been reluctant to argue that values of consumers are warped, because that would necessitate dictating the "correct" set of values. Both capitalism and democracy are based on the presumption that the majority knows what it is doing, whether it is casting ballots for representatives or dollar votes for goods and services.

The Pursuit of Efficiency

We have seen that environmental problems can arise when property rights are ill defined, and when these rights are exchanged under something other than competitive conditions. We can now use our definition of efficiency to explore possible remedies, such as private negotiation, judicial remedies, and regulation by the legislative and executive branches of government.

Private Resolution through Negotiation—Property, Liability and the Coase Theorem

The simplest means to restore efficiency occurs when the number of affected parties is small, making negotiation feasible. Suppose, for example, we return to the case used earlier in this chapter to illustrate an externality—the conflict between the polluting steel company and the downstream resort.

Figure 2.10 allows us to examine how this negotiation might take place. If the resort offers a payment of $C + D$ to the steel company, they would be better off if the steel firm responded by decreasing its production from Q_m to Q^*. Let's assume that the payment is equal to this amount. Would the steel company be willing to reduce production to the desired level? If they refused the compensation, their producer surplus would be $A + B + D$. If they accepted, their producer surplus would be $A + B$ plus the payment, so their total return would be $A + B + C + D$. Clearly, they are better off by C if they accept the payment. Further the sum of producer and producer surplus is better off by amount C as well since the economic surplus from Q_m is $A - C$ and the economic surplus for Q^* is A.

FIGURE 2.10 Efficient Output with Pollution Damage

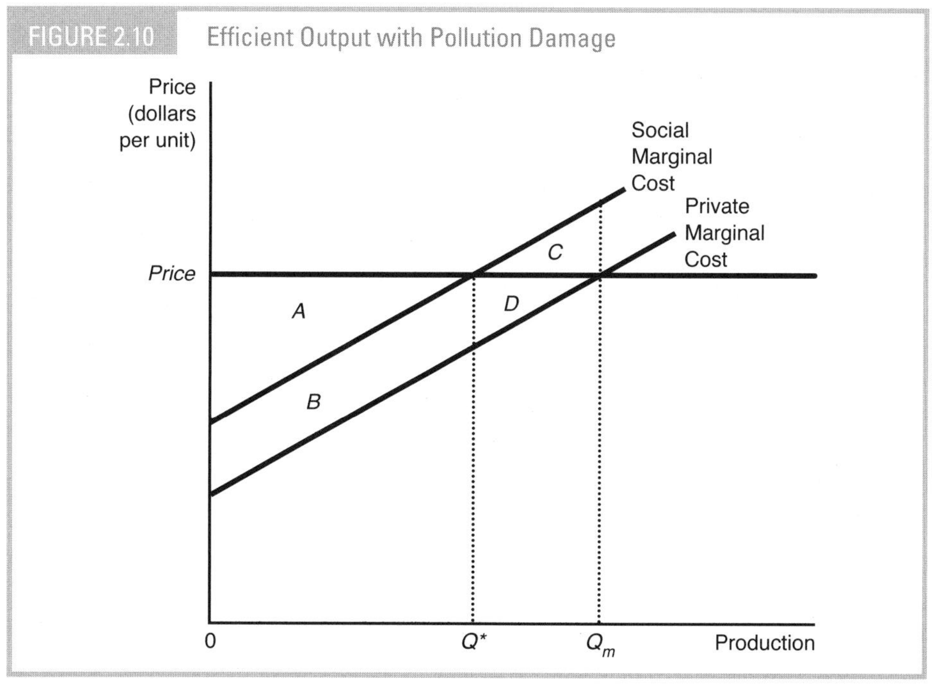

Our discussion of individual negotiations raises two questions: (1) Should the property right always belong to the party who held it first (in this case the steel company)? (2) How can environmental risks be handled when prior negotiation is clearly impractical? These questions are routinely answered by the court system.

The court system can respond to environmental conflicts by imposing either property rules or liability rules. Property rules specify the initial allocation of the entitlement or property right. The entitlements at conflict in our example are, on one hand, the right to add waste products to the river and, on the other, the right to an attractive river. In applying property rules, the court merely decides which right is preeminent and places an injunction against violating that right. The injunction is removed only upon obtaining the consent of the party whose right was violated. Consent is usually obtained in return for an out-of-court monetary settlement achieved via negotiation.

Note that in the absence of a court decision, the entitlement is naturally allocated to the party that can most easily seize it. In our example, the natural allocation would give the entitlement to the steel company. The courts must decide whether to overturn this natural allocation.

How would they decide? And what difference would their decision make? The answers may surprise you.

In a classic article, economist Ronald Coase (1960) held that as long as negotiation costs are negligible and affected consumers can negotiate freely with each other (when the number of affected parties is small), the court could allocate the entitlement to *either* party, and an efficient allocation would result. The only effect of the court's decision would be to change the distribution of surplus among the affected parties. This remarkable conclusion has come to be known as the *Coase theorem*.

Why is this so? In Figure 2.10, we showed that if the steel company has the property right, it is in the resort's interest to offer a payment that results in the desired level of output. Suppose, now, that the resort has the property right instead. To pollute in this case, the steel company must pay the resort. Suppose it could pollute only if it compensated the resort for all damages. (In other words, it would agree to pay the difference between the two marginal cost curves up to the level of output actually chosen.) As long as this compensation was required, the steel company would choose to produce Q^* since that is the level at which its producer's surplus, given the compensation, is maximized. (Note that, due to the compensation, the curve the steel company uses to calculate its producer surplus is now the higher marginal cost curve.)

The difference between these different ways of allocating property rights lies in how the cost of obtaining the efficient level of output is shared between the parties. When the property right is assigned to the steel company, the cost is borne by the resort (part of the cost is the damage and part is the payment to reduce the level of damage). When the property right is assigned to the resort, the cost is borne by the steel company (it now must compensate for all damage). In either case, the efficient level of production results. The Coase theorem shows that the very existence of an inefficiency triggers pressures for improvements. Furthermore, the existence of this pressure does not depend on the assignment of property rights.

This is an important point, but the importance of this theorem should not be overstated. As we shall see in succeeding chapters, private efforts triggered by inefficiency can frequently prevent the worst excesses of environmental degradation. However, both theoretical and practical objections can be raised. The chief theoretical qualification concerns the assumption that wealth effects do not matter. The decision to confer the property right on a particular party results in a transfer of wealth to that party. This transfer might shift the demand curve for either steel or resorts out, as long as higher incomes result in greater demand. Whenever wealth effects are significant, the type of property rule issued by the court does affect the outcome.

Wealth effects normally are small, so the zero-wealth-effect assumption is probably not a fatal flaw. Some serious practical flaws, however, do mar the usefulness of the Coase theorem. The first involves the incentives for polluting that result when the property right is assigned to the polluter. Since pollution would become a profitable activity with this assignment, other polluters might be encouraged to increase production and pollution in order to earn the payments. That certainly would not be efficient.

Negotiation is also difficult to apply when the number of people affected by the pollution is large. You may have already noticed that in the presence of several affected parties, pollution reduction is a public good. The free-rider problem would make it difficult for the group to act cohesively and effectively for the restoration of efficiency.

When individual negotiation is not practical for one reason or another, the courts can turn to liability rules. These are rules that award monetary damages, after the fact, to the injured party. The amount of the award is designed to correspond to the amount of damage inflicted. Thus, returning to Figure 2.10, a liability rule would force the steel company to compensate the resort for all damages incurred. In this case, it could choose any production level it wanted, but it would have to pay the resort an amount of money equal to the area between the two marginal cost curves from the origin to the chosen level of output. In this case the steel plant would maximize its producer's surplus by choosing Q^*. (Why wouldn't the steel plant choose to produce more than that? Why wouldn't the steel plant choose to produce less than that?)

The moral of this story is that appropriately designed liability rules can also correct inefficiencies by forcing those who cause damage to bear the cost of that damage. Internalizing previously external costs causes profit-maximizing decisions to be compatible with efficiency. As we shall see in subsequent chapters, this "internalizing externalities" principle plays a large role in the design of efficient policy in many areas of environmental and natural resource policy.

Liability rules are interesting from an economics point of view because early decisions create precedents for later ones. Imagine, for example, how the incentives to prevent oil spills facing an oil company are transformed once it has a legal obligation to clean up after an oil spill and to compensate fishermen for reduced catches. It quickly becomes evident that in this situation, accident prevention can become cheaper than retrospectively dealing with the damage once it has occurred.

This approach, however, also has its limitations. It relies on a case-by-case determination based on the unique circumstances for each case. Administratively, such a determination is very expensive. Expenses, such as court time, lawyers' fees, and so on, fall into a category called *transaction costs* by economists. In the present context, these are the administrative costs incurred in attempting to correct the inefficiency. The Coase theorem relies on an assumption that transactions costs are low. In reality though, this is rarely the case. Transactions costs in many cases can be quite high. When the number of parties involved in a dispute is large and the circumstances are common, we are tempted to correct the inefficiency by statutes or regulations rather than court decisions.

Legislative and Executive Regulation

These remedies can take several forms. The legislature could dictate that no one produce more steel or pollution than Q^*. This dictum might then be backed up with sufficiently large jail sentences or fines to deter potential violators. Alternatively, the legislature could impose a tax on steel or on pollution. A per-unit tax equal to the vertical distance between the two marginal cost curves would work (see Figure 2.10).

Legislatures could also establish rules to permit greater flexibility and yet reduce damage. For example, zoning laws would establish separate areas for steel plants and resorts. This approach assumes that the damage can be substantially reduced by keeping nonconforming uses apart.

They could also require the installation of particular pollution control equipment (as when catalytic converters were required on automobiles), or deny the use of a particular production ingredient (as when lead was removed from gasoline). In other words, they can regulate outputs, inputs, production processes, emissions, and even the location of production in their attempt to produce an efficient outcome. In subsequent chapters, we shall examine the various options policymakers have not only to show how they can modify environmentally destructive behavior, but also to establish the degree to which they can promote efficiency.

Payments are, of course, not the only means victims have at their disposal for lowering pollution. When the victims also consume the products produced by the polluters, consumer boycotts are possible. When the victims are employed by the polluter, strikes or other forms of labor resistance are also possible.

Legislation and/or regulation can also help to resolve the asymmetric information problem. Because the fundamental problem is that one or more of the parties do not have sufficient crucial, trustworthy information, the obvious solution involves providing that information. How should that information be provided?

Labeling is one attempt to provide more information to consumers. Examples of labeling for food products includes notifying consumers about products containing genetically modified organisms, and identifying organically grown crops and fair trade products.

A recent source of encouragement for organic farms has been the demonstrated willingness of consumers to pay a premium for organically grown fruits and vegetables. To allow consumers to discern which products are truly organic, growers need a reliable certification process. Additionally, fear of lost access to important foreign markets, such as the European Union, led to an industry-wide push in the United States for *mandatory* labeling standards that would provide the foundation for a national uniform seal. (*Voluntary* US certification programs had proved insufficient to assure access to European markets, since they were highly variable by state.)

In response to these pressures, the Organic Foods Production Act (OFPA) was enacted in the 1990 Farm Bill.[4] Title 21 of that law states the following objectives:

> *(1) to establish national standards governing the marketing of certain agricultural products as organically produced; (2) to assure consumers that organically produced products meet a consistent standard; and (3) to facilitate interstate commerce in fresh and processed food that is organically produced.*[5]

The USDA National Organic Program, established as part of this Act, is responsible for a mandatory certification program for organic production. The Act also established the National Organic Standards Board (NOSB) and charged it with defining the "organic" standards. The new rules, which took effect in October 2002, require certification by the USDA for labeling. Foods labeled as "100 percent organic" must contain only organic ingredients. Foods labeled as "organic" must contain at least 95 percent organic agricultural ingredients, excluding water and salt. Products labeled as "Made with Organic Ingredients" must contain at least 70 percent organic agricultural ingredients. Only half of all producers use the "USDA organic" label. For large producers, those whose sales are over $5 million per year, this figure rises to 83 percent. Lack of a dependable supply of organic ingredients—in particular, grains and sugars—has been an issue for producers.[6]

Certification allows socially conscious consumers to make a difference. As Example 2.4 demonstrates, eco-certification for coffee seems to be one such case.

---

[4]The European Union has followed a similar, but by not identical, policy.

[5]Golan et al. (2001)

[6]Organic Trade Association Manufacturer's Survey, 2008 http://www.ota.com/pics/documents/01a_OTAExecutiveSummary.pdf

EXAMPLE 2.4

Can Eco-Certification Make a Difference? Organic Costa Rican Coffee

Environmental problems associated with agricultural production for export in developing countries can be difficult to tackle using conventional regulation because producers are typically so numerous and dispersed, while regulatory agencies are commonly inadequately funded and staffed. In principle, eco-certification of production could circumvent these problems by providing a means for the socially conscious consumer to identify environmentally superior products, thereby providing a basis for paying a price premium for them. These premiums, in turn, would create financial incentives for producers to meet the certification standards.

Do socially conscious buyers care enough to actually pay a price premium that is high enough to motivate changes in the way the products are produced? Apparently, for Costa Rican coffee at least, they are.

One study examined this question for certified organic coffee grown in Turrialba, Costa Rica, an agricultural region in the country's central valley, about 40 miles east of San José, the capital city. This is an interesting case because Costa Rican farmers face significant pressure from the noncertified market to lower their costs, a strategy that can have severe environmental consequences. In contrast, organic production typically not only involves higher labor costs, but the conversion from chemically-based production can also reduce yields. In addition, the costs of initial certification and subsequent annual monitoring and reporting are significant.

The authors found that organic certification did improve coffee growers' environmental performance. Specifically, they found that certification significantly reduced use of pesticides, chemical fertilizers, and herbicides, and increased the use of organic fertilizer. In general, their results suggest that organic certification has a stronger causal effect on preventing negative practices than on encouraging positive ones. The study notes that this finding comports with anecdotal evidence that local inspectors tend to enforce the certification standards prohibiting negative practices more vigorously than the standards requiring positive ones.

Source: Blackman, A., & Naranjo, M.A. (2012).Does eco-certification have environmental benefits? Organic coffee in Costa Rica. *Ecological Economics*, *83*(November), 58–66.

An Efficient Role for Government

While the economic approach suggests that government action could well be used to restore efficiency, it also suggests that inefficiency is not a sufficient condition to justify government intervention. Any corrective mechanism involves transaction costs. If these transaction costs are high enough, and the surplus to be derived from correcting the inefficiency is small enough, then it is best simply to live with the inefficiency.

Consider, for example, the pollution problem. Wood-burning stoves, which were widely used for cooking and heat in the late 1800s in the United States, were sources of pollution, but because of the enormous capacity of the air to absorb the emissions, no regulation resulted. More recently, however, the resurgence of demand for wood-burning stoves, precipitated in part by high oil prices, has resulted in strict regulations for wood-burning stove emissions because the population density is so much higher.

As society has evolved, the scale of economic activity and the resulting emissions have increased. Cities are experiencing severe problems from air and water pollutants because of the clustering of activities. Both the increase in the number of emitters and their clustering have increased the amount of emissions per unit volume of air or water. As a result, pollutant concentrations have caused perceptible problems with human health, vegetation growth, and aesthetics.

Historically, as incomes have risen, the demand for leisure activities has also risen. Many of these leisure activities, such as canoeing and backpacking, take place in unique, pristine environmental areas. With the number of these areas declining as a result of conversion to other uses, the value of remaining areas has increased. Thus, the value derived from protecting some areas have risen over time until they have exceeded the transaction costs of protecting them from pollution and/or development.

The level and concentration of economic activity, having increased pollution problems and driven up the demand for clean air and pristine areas, have also created the preconditions for government action. Can government respond or will rent seeking prevent efficient political solutions? We devote much of this book to pinning down the answer to that question.

Summary

How producers and consumers use the resources making up the environmental asset depends on the nature of the entitlements embodied in the property rights governing resource use. When property rights systems are exclusive, transferable, and enforceable, the owner of a resource has a powerful incentive to use that resource efficiently, since the failure to do so results in a personal loss.

The economic system will not always sustain efficient allocations, however. Specific circumstances that could lead to inefficient allocations include externalities, improperly defined property rights systems (such as open-access resources and public goods), imperfect markets for trading the property rights to the resources (monopoly), and asymmetric information. When these circumstances arise, market allocations do not maximize the surplus.

Due to rent-seeking behavior by special interest groups or the less-than-perfect implementation of efficient plans, the political system can produce inefficiencies as well. Voter ignorance on many issues, coupled with the public-good nature of any results of political activity, tends to create a situation in which maximizing an individual's private surplus (through lobbying, for example) can be at the expense of a lower economic surplus for all consumers and producers.

The efficiency criterion can be used to assist in the identification of circumstances in which our political and economic institutions lead us astray. It can also assist in the search for remedies by facilitating the design of regulatory, judicial, or legislative solutions.

Discussion Questions

1. In a well-known legal case, *Miller v. Schoene* (287 U.S. 272), a classic conflict of property rights was featured. Red cedar trees, used only for ornamental purposes, carried a disease that could destroy apple orchards within a radius of 2 miles. There was no known way of curing the disease except by destroying the cedar trees or by ensuring that apple orchards were at least 2 miles away from the cedar trees. Apply the Coase theorem to this situation. Does it make any difference to the outcome whether the cedar tree owners are entitled to retain their trees or the apple growers are entitled to be free of them? Why or why not?
2. In primitive societies, the entitlements to use land were frequently possessory rights rather than ownership rights. Those on the land could use it as they wished, but they could not transfer it to anyone else. One could acquire a new plot by simply occupying and using it, leaving the old plot available for someone else. Would this type of entitlement system cause more or less incentive to conserve the land than an ownership entitlement? Why? Would a possessory entitlement system be more efficient in a modern society or a primitive society? Why?

Self-Test Exercises

1. Suppose the state is trying to decide how many miles of a very scenic river it should preserve. There are 100 people in the community, each of whom has an identical inverse demand function given by $P = 10 - 1.0q$, where q is the number of miles preserved and P is the per-mile price he or she is willing to pay for q miles of preserved river. (a) If the marginal cost of preservation is \$500 per mile, how many miles would be preserved in an efficient allocation? (b) How large is the economic surplus?
2. Suppose the market demand function (expressed in dollars) for a normal product is $P = 80 - q$, and the marginal cost (in dollars) of producing it is $MC = 1q$, where P is the price of the product and q is the quantity demanded and/or supplied.
   a. How much would be supplied by a competitive market?
   b. Compute the consumer surplus and producer surplus. Show that their sum is maximized.
   c Compute the consumer surplus and the producer surplus assuming this same product was supplied by a monopoly. (*Hint*: The marginal revenue curve has twice the slope of the demand curve.)
   d Show that when this market is controlled by a monopoly, producer surplus is larger, consumer surplus is smaller, and the sum of the two surpluses is smaller than when the market is controlled by competitive industry.
3. Suppose you were asked to comment on a proposed policy to control oil spills. Since the average cost of an oil spill has been computed as \$X, the proposed

policy would require any firm responsible for a spill immediately to pay the government $X. Is this likely to result in the efficient amount of precaution against oil spills? Why or why not?

4. "In environmental liability cases, courts have some discretion regarding the magnitude of compensation polluters should be forced to pay for the environmental incidents they cause. In general, however, the larger the required payments the better." Discuss.
5. Label each of the following propositions as descriptive or normative and defend your choice:
   a. Energy efficiency programs have created jobs.
   b. Money spent on protecting endangered species is wasted.
   c. Fisheries must be privatized to survive.
   d. Raising transport cost lowers suburban land values.
   e. Birth control programs are counterproductive.
6. Identify whether each of the following resource categories is a public good, a common-pool resource, or neither and defend your answer:
   a. A pod of whales in the ocean to whale hunters.
   b. A pod of whales in the ocean to whale watchers.
   c. The benefits from reductions of greenhouse gas emissions.
   d. Water from a town well that excludes nonresidents.
   e. Bottled water.

Further Reading

Lueck, D. (2002). The extermination and conservation of the American bison. *Journal of Legal Studies*, *31*(S2), s609–s652. A fascinating look at the role property rights played in the fate of the American bison.

Mason, C. F. (2012). The economics of eco-labeling: Theory and empirical implications. *International Review of Environmental and Resource Economics*, *6*, 341–372. A survey of the growing literature on eco-labeling.

Ostrom, E., Dietz, T., Dolsak, N., Stern, P., Stonich, S., & Weber, E.U. (Eds.). (2002). *The Drama of the Commons.* Washington, DC: National Academy Press. A compilation of articles and papers on common pool resources.

Ostrom, E. (1992). *Crafting Institutions for Self-Governing Irrigation Systems.* San Francisco: ICS Press. A classic book by a Nobel prize laureate that demonstrates that in favorable circumstances, common-pool problems can sometimes be solved by voluntary organizations, rather than by a coercive state; among the cases considered are communal tenure in meadows and forests, irrigation communities, and fisheries.

Stavins, R. (2012). *The Economics of the Environment: Selected Readings*, 6th ed. New York: W.W. Norton and Company. A carefully selected collection of readings that would complement this text.

Additional References and Historically Significant References are available on this book's Companion Website: http://www.routledgetextbooks.com/textbooks/9780133479690

3 Evaluating Trade-Offs: Benefit-Cost Analysis and Other Decision-Making Metrics

No sensible decision can be made any longer without taking into account not only the world as it is, but the world as it will be . . .

—Isaac Asimov, US science fiction novelist and scholar (1920–1992)

Introduction

In the last chapter we noted that economic analysis has both positive and normative dimensions. The normative dimension helps to separate the policies that make sense from those that don't. Since resources are limited, it is not possible to undertake all ventures that might appear desirable so making choices is inevitable.

Normative analysis can be useful in public policy in several different situations. It might be used, for example, to evaluate the desirability of a proposed new pollution control regulation or a proposal to preserve an area currently scheduled for development. In these cases, the analysis helps to provide guidance on the desirability of a program before that program is put into place. In other contexts, it might be used to evaluate how an already-implemented program has worked out in practice. Here the relevant question is: Was this a wise use of resources? In this chapter, we present and demonstrate the use of several decision-making metrics that can assist us in evaluating options.

Normative Criteria for Decision Making

Normative choices can arise in two different contexts. In the first context, we need simply to choose among options that have been predefined, while in the second we try to find the optimal choice among all the possible choices.

Evaluating Predefined Options: Benefit-Cost Analysis

If you were asked to evaluate the desirability of some proposed action, you would probably begin by attempting to identify both the gains and the losses from that action. If the gains exceed the losses, then it seems natural to support the action.

That simple framework provides the starting point for the normative approach to evaluating policy choices in economics. Economists suggest that actions have both benefits and costs. If the benefits exceed the costs, then the action is desirable. On the other hand, if the costs exceed the benefits, then the action is not desirable. (Comparing benefits and costs across time will be covered later in the Chapter.)

We can formalize this in the following way. Let B be the benefits from a proposed action and C be the costs. Our decision rule would then be

$$\text{if } B > C, \text{ support the action.}$$

Otherwise, oppose the action.[1]

As long as B and C are positive, a mathematically equivalent formulation would be

$$\text{if } B/C > 1, \text{ support the action.}$$

Otherwise, oppose the action.

So far so good, but how do we measure benefits and costs? In economics, the system of measurement is anthropocentric, which simply means human centered. All benefits and costs are valued in terms of their effects (broadly defined) on humanity. As shall be pointed out later, that does *not* imply (as it might first appear) that ecosystem effects are ignored unless they *directly* affect humans. The fact that large numbers of humans contribute voluntarily to organizations that are dedicated to environmental protection provides ample evidence that humans place a value on environmental preservation that goes well beyond any direct use they might make of it. Nonetheless, the notion that humans are doing the valuing is a controversial point that will be revisited and discussed in Chapter 4 and 13 along with the specific techniques for valuing these effects.

In benefit-cost analysis, benefits are measured simply as the relevant area under the demand curve since the demand curve reflects consumers' willingness to pay. Total costs are measured by the relevant area under the marginal cost curve.

It is important to stress that environmental services have costs even though they are produced without any human input. All costs should be measured as opportunity costs. To firm up this notion of opportunity cost, consider an example. Suppose a particular stretch of river can be used either for white-water canoeing or to generate electric power. Since the dam that generates the power would flood the rapids, the two uses are incompatible. The opportunity cost of producing power is the foregone net benefit that would have resulted from the white-water canoeing. The *marginal opportunity cost curve* defines the additional cost of producing another unit

[1]Actually if $B = C$, it wouldn't make any difference if the action occurs or not; the benefits and costs are a wash.

of electricity resulting from the associated incremental loss of net benefits due to reduced opportunities for white-water canoeing.

Since net benefit is defined as the excess of benefits over costs, it follows that net benefit is equal to that portion of the area under the demand curve that lies above the supply curve.

Consider Figure 3.1, which illustrates the net benefits from preserving a stretch of river. Suppose that we are considering preserving a 4-mile stretch of river and that the benefits and costs of that action are reflected in Figure 3.1. Should that stretch be preserved? Why or why not? Hold your answer because we will return to this example later.

Finding the Optimal Outcome

In the preceding section, we examined how benefit-cost analysis can be used to evaluate the desirability of specific actions. In this section, we want to examine how this approach can be used to identify "optimal," or best, approaches.

In subsequent chapters, which address individual environmental problems, the normative analysis will proceed in three steps. First, we will identify an optimal outcome. Second, we will attempt to discern the extent to which our institutions produce optimal outcomes and, where divergences occur between actual and optimal outcomes, to attempt to uncover the behavioral sources of the problems. Finally, we can use both our knowledge of the nature of the problems and their underlying behavioral causes as a basis for designing appropriate policy solutions. Although applying these three steps to each of the environmental problems must

FIGURE 3.1 The Derivation of Net Benefits

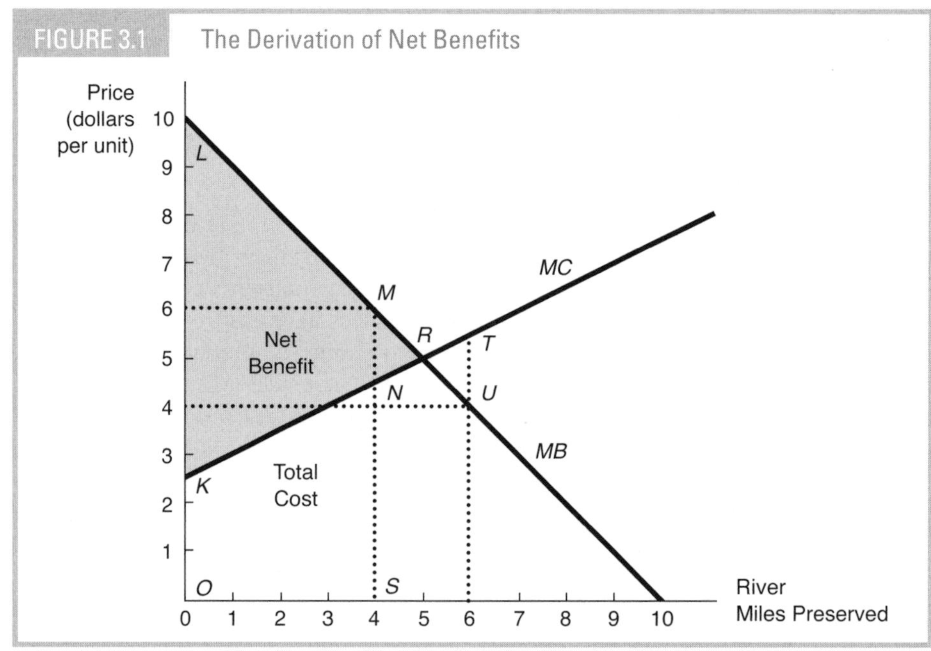

reflect the uniqueness of each situation, the overarching framework used to shape that analysis remains the same.

To provide some illustrations of how this approach is used in practice, consider two examples: one drawn from natural resource economics and another from environmental economics. These are meant to be illustrative and to convey a flavor of the argument; the details are left to upcoming chapters.

Consider the rising number of depleted ocean fisheries. Depleted fisheries, which involve fish populations that have fallen so low as to threaten their viability as commercial fisheries, not only jeopardize oceanic biodiversity, but also pose a threat to both the individuals who make their living from the sea and the communities that depend on fishing to support their local economies.

How would an economist attempt to understand and resolve this problem? The first step would involve defining the optimal stock or the optimal rate of harvest of the fishery. The second step would compare this level with the actual stock and harvest levels. Once this economic framework is applied, not only does it become clear that stocks are much lower than optimal for many fisheries, but also the reason for excessive exploitation becomes clear. Understanding the nature of the problem has led quite naturally to some solutions. Once implemented, these policies have allowed some fisheries to begin the process of renewal. The details of this analysis and the policy implications that flow from it are covered in Chapter 12.

Another problem involves solid waste. As local communities run out of room for landfills in the face of an increasing generation of waste, what can be done?

Economists start by thinking about how one would define the optimal amount of waste. The definition necessarily incorporates waste reduction and recycling as aspects of the optimal outcome. The analysis not only reveals that current waste levels are excessive, but also suggests some specific behavioral sources of the problem. Based upon this understanding, specific economic solutions have been identified and implemented. Communities that have adopted these measures have generally experienced lower levels of waste and higher levels of recycling. The details are spelled out in Chapter 8.

In the rest of the book, similar analysis is applied to energy, minerals, water, pollution, and a host of other topics. In each case, the economic analysis helps to point the way toward solutions. To initiate that process, we must begin by defining "optimal."

Relating Optimality to Efficiency

According to the normative choice criterion introduced earlier in this chapter, desirable outcomes are those where the benefits exceed the costs. It is therefore a logical next step to suggest that optimal polices are those that maximize net benefits (benefits minus costs). The concept of *static efficiency*, or merely *efficiency*, was introduced in Chapter 2. An allocation of resources is said to satisfy the static efficiency criterion if the economic surplus from the use of those resources is maximized by that allocation. Notice that the net benefits area to be maximized in an "optimal outcome" for public policy is identical to the "economic surplus" that is maximized in an efficient allocation. Hence, efficient outcomes are also optimal outcomes.

Let's take a moment to show how this concept can be applied. Previously, we asked whether an action that preserved four miles of river was worth doing (Figure 3.1). The answer is yes because the net benefits from that action are positive. (Can you see why?)

Static efficiency, however, requires us to ask a rather different question, namely, what is the optimal (or efficient) number of miles to be preserved? We know from the definition that the optimal amount of preservation would maximize net benefits. Does preserving 4 miles maximize net benefits? Is it the efficient outcome?

We can answer that question by establishing whether it is possible to increase the net benefit by preserving more or less of the river. If the net benefit can be increased by preserving more miles, clearly, preserving 4 miles could not have maximized the net benefit and, therefore, could not have been efficient.

Consider what would happen if society were to choose to preserve 5 miles instead of 4. Refer back to Figure 3.1. What happens to the net benefit? It increases by area *MNR*. Since we can find another allocation with greater net benefit, 4 miles of preservation could not have been efficient. Could 5? Yes. Let's see why.

We know that 5 miles of preservation convey more net benefits than 4. If this allocation is efficient, then it must also be true that the net benefit is smaller for levels of preservation higher than five. Notice that the additional cost of preserving the sixth unit (the area under the marginal cost curve) is larger than the additional benefit received from preserving it (the corresponding area under the demand curve). Therefore, the triangle *RTU* represents the reduction in net benefit that occurs if 6 miles are preserved rather than 5.

Since the net benefit is reduced, both by preserving less than five and by preserving more than five, we conclude that five units is the preservation level that maximizes net benefit (the shaded area). Therefore, from our definition, preserving 5 miles constitutes an efficient or optimal allocation.[2]

One implication of this example, which will be very useful in succeeding chapters, is what we shall call the "first equimarginal principle":

> *First Equimarginal Principle (the "Efficiency Equimarginal Principle"): Social net benefits are maximized when the social marginal benefits from an allocation equal the social marginal costs.*

The social marginal benefit is the increase in social benefits received from supplying one more unit of the good or service, while social marginal cost is the increase in cost incurred from supplying that additional unit of the good or service.

This criterion helps to minimize wasted resources, but is it fair? The ethical basis for this criterion is derived from a concept called *Pareto optimality*, named after the Italian-born Swiss economist Vilfredo Pareto, who first proposed it around the turn of the twentieth century.

> *Allocations are said to be Pareto optimal if no other feasible allocation could benefit at least one person without any deleterious effects on some other person.*

---

[2]The monetary worth of the net benefit is the sum of two right triangles, and it equals (1/2)($5)(5) + (1/2)($2.50)(5) or $18.75. Can you see why?

Allocations that do not satisfy this definition are suboptimal. Suboptimal allocations can always be rearranged so that some people can gain net benefits without the rearrangement causing anyone else to lose net benefits. Therefore, the gainers could use a portion of their gains to compensate the losers sufficiently to ensure they were at least as well off as they were prior to the reallocation.

Efficient allocations are Pareto optimal. Since net benefits are maximized by an efficient allocation, it is not possible to increase the net benefit by rearranging the allocation. Without an increase in the net benefit, it is impossible for the gainers to compensate the losers sufficiently; the gains to the gainers would necessarily be smaller than the losses to the losers.

Inefficient allocations are judged inferior because they do not maximize the size of the pie to be distributed. By failing to maximize net benefit, they are forgoing an opportunity to make some people better off without harming others.

Comparing Benefits and Costs across Time

The analysis we have covered so far is very useful for thinking about actions where time is not an important factor. Yet many of the decisions made now have consequences that persist well into the future. Time is a factor. Exhaustible energy resources, once used, are gone. Biological renewable resources (such as fisheries or forests) can be overharvested, leaving smaller and possibly weaker populations for future generations. Persistent pollutants can accumulate over time. How can we make choices when the benefits and costs occur at different points in time?

Incorporating time into the analysis requires an extension of the concepts we have already developed. This extension provides a way for thinking not only about the magnitude of benefits and costs, but also about their timing. In order to incorporate timing, the decision rule must provide a way to compare net benefits received in different time periods. The concept that allows this comparison is called *present value*. Therefore, before introducing this expanded decision rule, we must define present value.

Present value explicitly incorporates the time value of money. A dollar today invested at 10 percent interest yields \$1.10 a year from now (the return of the \$1 principal plus \$0.10 interest). The present value of \$1.10 received one year from now is therefore \$1, because given \$1 now, you can turn it into \$1.10 a year from now by investing it at 10 percent interest. We can find the present value of any amount of money (X) received one year from now by computing $X/(1 + r)$, where r is the appropriate interest rate (10 percent in our above example).

What could your dollar earn in two years at r percent interest? Because of compound interest, the amount would be $\$1(1 + r)(1 + r) = \$1(1 + r)^2$. It follows then that the present value of X received two years from now is $X/(1 + r)^2$.

By now the pattern should be clear. The present value of a *one-time* net benefit received n years from now is

$$PV[B_n] = \frac{B_n}{(1 + r)^n}$$

The present value of a stream of net benefits $\{B_0, \ldots, B_n\}$ received over a period of n years is computed as

$$PV[B_0, \ldots, B_n] = \sum_{i=0}^{n} \frac{B_i}{(1 + r)^i}$$

where r is the appropriate interest rate and B_0 is the amount of net benefits received immediately. The process of calculating the present value is called *discounting*, and the rate r is referred to as the discount rate.

The number resulting from a present-value calculation has a straightforward interpretation. Suppose you were investigating an allocation that would yield the following pattern of net benefits on the last day of each of the next 5 years: $3,000, $5,000, $6,000, $10,000, and $12,000. If you use an interest rate of 6 percent ($r = 0.06$) and the above formula, you will discover that this stream has a present value of $29,205.92 (see Table 3.1). Notice how each amount is discounted back the appropriate number of years to the present and then these discounted values are summed.

What does that number mean? If you put $29,205.92 in a savings account earning 6 percent interest and wrote yourself checks, respectively, for $3,000, $5,000, $6,000, $10,000, and $12,000 on the last day of each of the next 5 years, your last check would just restore the account to a $0 balance (see Table 3.2). Thus, you should be indifferent about receiving $29,205.92 now or in the specific 5-year stream of benefits totaling $36,000; given one, you can get the other. Hence, the method is called present value because it translates everything back to its current worth.

It is now possible to show how this analysis can be used to evaluate actions. Calculate the present value of net benefits from the action. If the present value is greater than zero, the action can be supported. Otherwise it should not.

TABLE 3.1 Demonstrating Present Value Calculations

Year	1	2	3	4	5	Sum
Annual Amounts	$3,000	$5,000	$6,000	$10,000	$12,000	$36,000
Present Value ($r = 0.06$)	$2,830.19	$4,449.98	$5,037.72	$7,920.94	$8,967.10	$29,205.92

TABLE 3.2 Interpreting Present Value Calculations

Year	1	2	3	4	5	6
Balance at Beginning of Year	$29,205.92	$27,958.28	$24,635.77	$20,113.92	$11,320.75	$0.00
Year-End Fund Balance before Payment ($r = 0.06$)	$30,958.28	$29,635.77	$26,113.92	$21,320.75	$12,000.00	
Payment	$3,000	$5,000	$6,000	$10,000	$12,000	

Dynamic Efficiency

The static efficiency criterion is very useful for comparing resource allocations when time is not an important factor. How can we think about optimal choices when the benefits and costs occur at different points in time?

The traditional criterion used to find an optimal allocation when time is involved is called *dynamic efficiency*, a generalization of the static efficiency concept already developed. In this generalization, the present-value criterion provides a way for comparing the net benefits received in one period with the net benefits received in another.

An allocation of resources across *n* time periods satisfies the dynamic efficiency criterion if it maximizes the present value of net benefits that could be received from all the possible ways of allocating those resources over the *n* periods.[3]

Applying the Concepts

Having now spent some time developing the concepts we need, let's take a moment to examine some actual studies in which they have been used.

Pollution Control

Benefit-cost analysis has been used to assess the desirability of efforts to control pollution. Pollution control certainly confers many benefits, but it also has costs. Do the benefits justify the costs? That was a question the US Congress wanted answered, so in Section 812 of the Clean Air Act Amendments of 1990, it required the US Environmental Protection Agency (EPA) to evaluate the benefits and costs of the US air pollution control policy initially over the 1970–1990 period and subsequently over the 1990–2020 time period (see Example 3.1).

In responding to this congressional mandate, the EPA set out to quantify and monetize the benefits and costs of achieving the emissions reductions required by US policy. Benefits quantified by this study included reduced death rates and lower incidences of chronic bronchitis, lead poisoning, strokes, respiratory diseases, and heart disease as well as the benefits of better visibility, reduced structural damages, and improved agricultural productivity.

We shall return to this study later in the book for a deeper look at how these estimates were derived, but a couple of comments are relevant now. First, despite the fact that this study did not attempt to value all pollution damage to ecosystems that was avoided by this policy, the net benefits are still strongly positive. While presumably the case for controlling pollution would have been even stronger had all such avoided damage been included, the desirability of this form of control is evident even with only a partial consideration of benefits. An inability to monetize everything does not necessarily jeopardize the ability to reach sound policy conclusions.

---

[3]The mathematics of dynamic efficiency are presented in the appendix to Chapter 5.

Although these results justify the conclusion that pollution control made economic sense, they do not justify the stronger conclusion that the policy was efficient. To justify that conclusion, the study would have had to show that the present value of net benefits was maximized, not merely positive. In fact, this study did not attempt to calculate the maximum net benefits outcome and if it had, it would have almost certainly discovered that the policy during this period was not optimal. As we shall see in Chapters 15 and 16, the costs of the chosen policy approach were higher than necessary to achieve the desired emissions reductions. With an optimal policy mix, the net benefits would have been even higher.

Estimating Benefits of Carbon Dioxide Emission Reductions

Benefit-cost analysis is frequently complicated by the estimation of benefits and costs that are difficult to quantify. (Chapter 4 takes up the topic of nonmarket valuation in detail.) One such value is the benefit of reductions in carbon emissions.

EXAMPLE 3.1

Does Reducing Pollution Make Economic Sense? Evidence from the Clean Air Act

In its 1997 report to Congress, the EPA presented the results of its attempt to discover whether the Clean Air Act had produced positive net benefits over the period 1970–1990. The results suggested that the present value of benefits (using a discount rate of 5 percent) was $22.2 trillion, while the costs were $0.523 trillion. Performing the necessary subtraction reveals that the net benefits were therefore equal to $21.7 trillion. According to this study, US air pollution control policy during this period made very good economic sense.

Soon after the period covered by this analysis, substantive changes were made in the Clean Air Act Amendments of 1990 (the details of those changes are covered in later chapters). Did those additions also make economic sense?

In August of 2010, the US EPA issued a report of the benefits and costs of the Clean Air Act from 1990 to 2020. This report suggests that the costs of meeting the 1990 Clean Air Act Amendment requirements are expected to rise to approximately $65 billion per year by 2020 (2006 dollars). Almost half of the compliance costs ($28 billion) arise from pollution controls placed on cars, trucks, and buses, while another $10 billion arises from reducing air pollution from electric utilities.

These actions are estimated to cause benefits (from reduced pollution damage) to rise from roughly $800 billion in 2000 to almost $1.3 trillion in 2010, ultimately reaching approximately $2 trillion per year (2006 dollars) by 2020! For persons living in the United States, a cost of approximately $200 per person by 2020 produces approximately a $6,000 gain in benefits from the improvement in air quality. Many of the estimated benefits come from reduced risk of early mortality due to exposure to fine particulate matter. Table 3.3 provides a summary of the costs and benefits and includes a calculation of the benefit/cost ratio.

TABLE 3.3 Summary Comparison of Benefits and Costs from the Clean Air Act-1990–2020 (Estimates in Million 2006$)

	Annual Estimates			Present Value Estimate
	2000	2010	2020	1990–2020
Monetized Direct Costs:				
Low[1]				
Central	$20,000	$53,000	$65,000	$380,000
High[1]				
Monetized Direct Benefits:				
Low[2]	$90,000	$160,000	$250,000	$1,400,000
Central	$770,000	$1,300,000	$2,000,000	$12,000,000
High[2]	$2,300,000	$3,800,000	$5,700,000	$35,000,000
Net Benefits:				
Low	$70,000	$110,000	$190,000	$1,000,000
Central	$750,000	$1,200,000	$1,900,000	$12,000,000
High	$2,300,000	$3,700,000	$5,600,000	$35,000,000
Benefit/Cost Ratio:				
Low[3]	5/1	3/1	4/1	4/1
Central	39/1	25/1	31/1	32/1
High[3]	115/1	72/1	88/1	92/1

[1]The cost estimates for this analysis are based on assumptions about future changes in factors such as consumption patterns, input costs, and technological innovation. We recognize that these assumptions introduce significant uncertainty into the cost results; however, the degree of uncertainty or bias associated with many of the key factors cannot be reliably quantified. Thus, we are unable to present specific low and high cost estimates.

[2]Low and high benefit estimates are based on primary results and correspond to 5th and 95th percentile results from statistical uncertainty analysis, incorporating uncertainties in physical effects and valuation steps of benefits analysis. Other significant sources of uncertainty not reflected include the value of unquantified or unmonetized benefits that are not captured in the primary estimates and uncertainties in emissions and air quality modeling.

[3]The low benefit/cost ratio reflects the ratio of the low benefits estimate to the central costs estimate, while the high ratio reflects the ratio of the high benefits estimate to the central costs estimate. Because we were unable to reliably quantify the uncertainty in cost estimates, we present the low estimate as "less than X" and the high estimate as "more than Y," where X and Y are the low and high benefit/cost ratios, respectively.

Sources: US Environmental Protection Agency. (1997). *The Benefits and Costs of the Clean Air Act, 1970 to 1990.* Washington, DC: Environmental Protection Agency, Table 18, p. 56; US Environmental Protection Agency Office of Air and Radiation, *The Benefits and Costs of the Clean Air Act, 1990 to 2020—Summary Report, 8/16/2010.* Full Report available at http://www.epa.gov/oar/sect812/prospective2.html (accessed on 12/31/2010).

Executive Order 12866 requires government agencies "to assess both the costs and the benefits of the intended regulation and, recognizing that some costs and benefits are difficult to quantify, propose or adopt a regulation only upon a reasoned determination that the benefits of the intended regulation justify its costs" (Interagency Working Group on Social Cost of Carbon, 2013). In order to include benefits from reducing carbon dioxide emission, agencies use what is called the "social cost of carbon" to reflect what those damages would have been in the absence of the reductions. The social cost of carbon is the marginal increase in the present value (in dollars) of the economic damages (e.g., sea level rise, floods, changes in agricultural productivity, and altered ecosystem services) resulting from a small increase (usually 1 metric ton) in carbon dioxide emissions. Since the social cost of carbon is a present value calculation both the timing of the emission reduction and the discount rate play an important role.

The Interagency Working Group on Social Cost of Carbon presented the first set of estimates for the social cost of carbon in 2010. In 2013, these estimates were revised upwards with the estimate for the social cost of carbon increasing from $22 to approximately $37 per ton of carbon using a discount rate of 3 percent. Table 3.4 illustrates the revised social cost of carbon dioxide using 2.5, 3 and 5 percent discount rates for selected years. The 4th column, presents the extreme case (95th percentile) using a 3% discount rate. Notice the importance of the discount rate in determining what value is used. (Can you explain why?)

The social cost of carbon is useful in making sure that the calculated benefits of carbon reductions reflect the reduced damages that can be expected. Example 3.2 demonstrates one way the social cost of carbon has been used in policy.

TABLE 3.4 Revised Social Cost of CO_2, 2010–2050 (in 2007 dollars per metric ton of CO_2)

		Discount	Rates	
Year	5% Avg	3% Avg	2.5% Avg	3% 95th
2010	11	32	51	89
2015	11	37	57	109
2020	12	43	64	128
2025	14	47	69	143
2030	16	52	75	159
2035	19	56	80	175
2040	21	61	86	191
2045	24	66	92	206
2050	26	71	97	220

Source: http://www.whitehouse.gov/sites/default/files/omb/assets/inforeg/technical-update-social-cost-of-carbon-for-regulator-impact-analysis.pdf. Accessed1/3/2014.

EXAMPLE 3.2

Using the Social Cost of Capital: The DOE Microwave Oven Rule

In 2013, the Department of Energy (DOE) announced new rules for energy efficiency for microwave ovens in standby mode. By improving the energy efficiency of these ovens, this rule would reduce carbon emissions by reducing the amount of electrical energy needed to power them. In the regulatory impact analysis associated with this rule, it was necessary to value the reduced damages from this lower level of emissions. The social cost of carbon was used to provide this information.

Using the 2010 social cost of carbon produced a present value of net benefits for the microwave oven rule over the next 30 years of $4.2 billion. Since this value is positive, it means that implementing this rule would increase efficiency.

We know that using the revised 2013 number would increase the present value of net benefits, but by how much? According to the DOE, using the 2013 instead of the 2010 social cost of carbon increases the present value of net benefits to $4.6 billion. In this case the net benefits were large enough both before and after the new SCC estimates to justify implementing the rule, but it is certainly possible that in other cases these new estimates would justify rules that prior to the change would not have been justified.

Note that microwave purchasers will bear the cost of this set of rules (as prices rise to reflect the higher production costs), but they will not receive all of the benefits (those reflecting a reduction in external costs). However the DOE notes that due to the increased energy efficiency of the appliances subject to these rules (and the resulting lower energy costs for purchasers), the present value of savings to consumers is estimated to be $3.4 billion over the next 30 years (DOE 2013), an amount that is larger than the costs. In this case the rules represent a win for both microwave consumers and the planet.

Sources: http://energy.gov/articles/new-energy-efficiency-standards-microwave-ovens-save-consumers-energy-bills Technical update of the social cost of carbon for regulatory impact analysis—Under Executive Order 12866. (May 2013). *Interagency Working Group on Social Cost of Carbon, United States Government,*

Issues in Benefit Estimation

The analyst charged with the responsibility for performing a benefit-cost analysis encounters many decision points requiring judgment. If we are to understand benefit-cost analysis, the nature of these judgments must be clear in our minds.

Primary versus Secondary Effects. Environmental projects usually trigger both primary and secondary consequences. For example, the primary effect of cleaning a lake will be an increase in recreational uses of the lake. This primary effect will cause a further ripple effect on services provided to the increased number of users of the lake. Are these secondary benefits to be counted?

The answer depends upon the employment conditions in the surrounding area. If this increase in demand results in employment of previously unused resources, such as labor, the value of the increased employment should be counted. If, on the other hand, the increase in demand is met by a shift in previously employed resources from one use to another, it is a different story. In general, secondary employment benefits should be counted in high unemployment areas or when the particular skills demanded are underemployed at the time the project is commenced. They should not be counted when the project simply results in a rearrangement of productively employed resources.

Accounting Stance. The accounting stance refers to the geographic scale at which the benefits are measured. Scale matters because in a benefit-cost analysis only the benefits or costs affecting that specific geographic area are counted. Suppose, for example, that the federal government picks up many of the costs, but the benefits are received by only one region. Even if the benefit-cost analysis shows this to be a great project for the region, that will not necessarily be the case for the nation as a whole. Once the national costs are factored in, the national project benefits may not exceed the national project costs.

Aggregation. Related to accounting stance are challenges of aggregation. Estimates of benefits and costs must be aggregated in order to derive total benefits and total costs. How many people benefit and how many people incur costs are very important in any aggregation, but additionally, *how* they benefit might impact that aggregation. Suppose, for example, those living closer to the project received more benefits per household than those living farther away. In this case these differences should be accounted for.

With and Without Principle. The "with and without" principle states that only those benefits that would result from the project should be counted, ignoring those that would have accrued anyway. Mistakenly including benefits that would have accrued anyway would overstate the benefits of the program.

Tangible versus Intangible Benefits. *Tangible benefits* are those that can reasonably be assigned a monetary value. *Intangible benefits* are those that cannot be assigned a monetary value, either because data are not available or reliable enough or because it is not clear how to measure the value even with data.[4] Quantification of intangible benefits is the primary topic of the next chapter.

How are intangible benefits to be handled? One answer is perfectly clear: they should not be ignored. To ignore intangible benefits is to bias the results. That benefits are intangible does not mean they are unimportant.

Intangible benefits should be quantified to the fullest extent possible. One frequently used technique is to conduct a sensitivity analysis of the estimated benefit values derived from less than perfectly reliable data. We can determine, for example, whether or not the outcome is sensitive, within wide ranges, to the value of this benefit. If not, then very little time has to be spent on the problem. If the outcome is

---

[4]The division between tangible and intangible benefits changes as our techniques improve. Recreation benefits were, until the advent of the travel-cost model, treated as intangible. The travel cost model will be discussed in the next chapter.

sensitive, the person or persons making the decision bear the ultimate responsibility for weighing the importance of that benefit.

Approaches to Cost Estimation

Estimating costs is generally easier than estimating benefits, but it is not easy. One major problem for both derives from the fact that benefit-cost analysis is forward-looking and thus requires an estimate of what a particular strategy *will* cost, which is much more difficult than tracking down what an existing strategy *does* cost.

Two approaches have been developed to estimate these costs.

The Survey Approach. One way to discover the costs associated with a policy is to ask those who bear the costs, and presumably know the most about them, to reveal the magnitude of the costs to policymakers. Polluters, for example, could be asked to provide control-cost estimates to regulatory bodies. The problem with this approach is the strong incentive not to be truthful. An overestimate of the costs can trigger less stringent regulation; therefore, it is financially advantageous to provide overinflated estimates.

The Engineering Approach. The engineering approach bypasses the source being regulated by using general engineering information to catalog the possible technologies that could be used to meet the objective and to estimate the costs of purchasing and using those technologies. The final step in the engineering approach is to assume that the sources would use technologies that minimize cost. This produces a cost estimate for a "typical," well-informed firm.

The engineering approach has its own problems. These estimates may not approximate the actual cost of any particular firm. Unique circumstances may cause the costs of that firm to be higher, or lower, than estimated; the firm, in short, may not be typical.

The Combined Approach. To circumvent these problems, analysts frequently use a combination of survey and engineering approaches. The survey approach collects information on possible technologies, as well as special circumstances facing the firm. Engineering approaches are used to derive the actual costs of those technologies, given the special circumstances. This combined approach attempts to balance information best supplied by the source with that best derived independently.

In the cases described so far, the costs are relatively easy to quantify and the problem is simply finding a way to acquire the best information. This is not always the case, however. Some costs are not easy to quantify, although economists have developed some ingenious ways to secure monetary estimates even for those costs.

Take, for example, a policy designed to conserve energy by forcing more people to carpool. If the effect of this is simply to increase the average time of travel, how is this cost to be measured?

For some time, transportation analysts have recognized that people value their time, and a large amount of literature has now evolved to provide estimates of how valuable time savings or time increases would be. The basis for this valuation is opportunity cost—how the time might be used if it weren't being consumed in travel. Although the results of these studies depend on the amount of time involved, individuals seem to value their travel time at a rate not more than half their wage rates.

The Treatment of Risk

For many environmental problems, it is not possible to state with certainty what consequences a particular policy will have, because scientific estimates themselves often are imprecise. Determining the efficient exposure to potentially toxic substances requires obtaining results at high doses and extrapolating to low doses, as well as extrapolating from animal studies to humans. It also requires relying upon epidemiological studies that infer a pollution-induced adverse human health impact from correlations between indicators of health in human populations and recorded pollution levels.

For example, consider the potential damages from climate change. While most scientists now agree on the potential impacts of climate change, such as sea level rise and species losses, the timing and extent of those losses are not certain.

The treatment of risk in the policy process involves two major dimensions: (1) identifying and quantifying the risks, and (2) deciding how much risk is acceptable. The former is primarily scientific and descriptive, while the latter is more evaluative or normative.

Benefit-cost analysis grapples with the evaluation of risk in several ways. Suppose we have a range of policy options *A*, *B*, *C*, *D* and a range of possible outcomes *E*, *F*, *G* for each of these policies depending on how the economy evolves over the future. These outcomes, for example, might depend on whether the demand growth for the resource is low, medium, or high. Thus, if we choose policy *A*, we might end up with outcomes *AE*, *AF*, or *AG*. Each of the other policies has three possible outcomes as well, yielding a total of 12 possible outcomes.

We could conduct a separate benefit-cost analysis for each of the 12 possible outcomes. Unfortunately, the policy that maximizes net benefits for *E* may be different from that which maximizes net benefits for *F* or *G*. Thus, if we only knew which outcome would prevail, we could select the policy that maximized net benefits; the problem is that we do not. Furthermore, choosing the policy that is best if outcome *E* prevails may be disastrous if *G* results instead.

When a dominant policy emerges, this problem is avoided. A *dominant policy* is one that confers higher net benefits for every outcome. In this case, the existence of risk concerning the future is not relevant for the policy choice. This fortuitous circumstance is exceptional rather than common, but it can occur.

Other options exist even when dominant solutions do not emerge. Suppose, for example, that we were able to assess the likelihood that each of the three possible outcomes would occur. Thus, we might expect outcome *E* to occur with probability 0.5, *F* with probability 0.3, and *G* with probability 0.2. Armed with this information, we can estimate the expected present value of net benefits. The *expected present value of net benefits* for a particular policy is defined as the sum over outcomes of the present value of net benefits for that policy where each outcome is weighted by its probability of occurrence. Symbolically this is expressed as

$$EPVNB_j = \sum_{i=0}^{I} P_i PVNB_{ij}, \qquad j = 1, \ldots, J,$$

where

$EPVNB_j$ = expected present value of net benefits for policy j,
P_i = probability of the ith outcome occurring,
$PVNB_{ij}$ = present value of net benefits for policy j if outcome i prevails,
J = number of policies being considered,
I = number of outcomes being considered.

The final step is to select the policy with the highest expected present value of net benefits.

This approach has the substantial virtue that it weighs higher probability outcomes more heavily. It also, however, makes a specific assumption about society's preference for risk. This approach is appropriate if society is risk-neutral. *Risk-neutrality* can be defined most easily by the use of an example. Suppose you were allowed to choose between being given a definite $50 or entering a lottery in which you had a 50 percent chance of winning $100 and a 50 percent chance of winning nothing. (Notice that the expected value of this lottery is $50 = 0.5($100) + 0.5($0).) You would be said to be risk-neutral if you would be indifferent between these two choices. If you view the lottery as more attractive, you would be exhibiting *risk-loving* behavior, while a preference for the definite $50 would suggest *risk-averse* behavior. Using the expected present value of net benefits approach implies that society is risk-neutral.

Is that a valid assumption? The evidence is mixed. The existence of gambling suggests that at least some members of society are risk-loving, while the existence of insurance suggests that, at least for some risks, others are risk-averse. Since the same people may gamble and own insurance policies, it is likely that the type of risk may be important.

Even if individuals were demonstrably risk-averse, this would not be a sufficient condition for the government to forsake risk-neutrality in evaluating public investments. One famous article (Arrow & Lind, 1970) argues that risk-neutrality is appropriate since "when the risks of a public investment are publicly borne, the total cost of risk-bearing is insignificant and, therefore, the government should ignore uncertainty in evaluating public investments." The logic behind this result suggests that as the number of risk bearers (and the degree of diversification of risks) increases, the amount of risk borne by any individual diminishes to zero.

When the decision is irreversible, as demonstrated by Arrow and Fisher (1974), considerably more caution is appropriate. Irreversible decisions may subsequently be regretted, but the option to change course will be lost forever. Extra caution also affords an opportunity to learn more about alternatives to this decision and its consequences before acting. Isn't it comforting to know that occasionally procrastination can be optimal?

There is a movement in national policy in both the courts and the legislature to search for imaginative ways to define acceptable risk. In general, the policy approaches reflect a case-by-case method. We shall see that current policy reflects a high degree of risk aversion toward a number of environmental problems.

Distribution of Benefits and Costs

Many agencies are now required to consider the distributional impacts of costs and benefits as part of any economic analysis. For example, the US EPA provides guidelines on distributional issues in its "Guidelines for Preparing Economic Analysis." According to the EPA, distributional analysis "assesses changes in social welfare by examining the effects of a regulation across different sub-populations and entities." Distributional analysis can take two forms: *economic impact analysis* and *equity analysis*. Economic impact analysis focuses on a broad characterization of who gains and who loses from a given policy. Equity analysis examines impacts on disadvantaged groups or sub-populations. The latter delves into the normative issue of equity or fairness in the distribution of costs and benefits. Loomis (2011) outlines several approaches for incorporating distribution and equity into benefit-cost analysis. Some issues of the distribution of benefits and costs related to energy efficiency rules for appliances were highlighted in Example 3.2.

Choosing the Discount Rate

The discount rate can be defined conceptually as the social opportunity cost of capital. This cost of capital can be divided further into two components: (1) the riskless cost of capital and (2) the risk premium. The choice of the discount rate can influence policy decisions. Recall that discounting allows us to compare all costs and benefits in current dollars, regardless of when the benefits accrue or costs are charged. Suppose a project will impose an immediate cost of $4,000,000 (today's dollars), but the $5,500,000 benefits will not be earned until 5 years out. Is this project a good idea? On the surface it might seem like it is, but recall that $5,500,000 in 5 years is not the same as $5,500,000 today. At a discount rate of 5 percent, the present value of benefits minus the present value of costs is positive. However, at a 10 percent discount rate, this same calculation yields a negative value, since the present value of costs exceeds the benefits. Can you reproduce the calculations that yield these conclusions?

As Example 3.3 indicates, this has been, and continues to be, an important issue. When the public sector uses a discount rate lower than that in the private sector, the public sector will find more projects with longer payoff periods worthy of authorization. And, as we have already seen, the discount rate is a major determinant of the allocation of resources among generations as well.

Traditionally, economists have used long-term interest rates on government bonds as one measure of the cost of capital, adjusted by a risk premium that would depend on the riskiness of the project considered. Unfortunately, the choice of how large an adjustment to make has been left to the discretion of the analysts.

EXAMPLE 3.3

The Importance of the Discount Rate

Let's begin with a historical example. For years the United States and Canada had been discussing the possibility of constructing a tidal power project in the Passamaquoddy Bay between Maine and New Brunswick. This project would have heavy initial capital costs, but low operating costs that presumably would hold for a long time into the future. As part of their analysis of the situation, a complete inventory of costs and benefits was completed in 1959.

Using the same benefit and cost figures, Canada concluded that the project should not be built, while the United States concluded that it should. Because these conclusions were based on the same benefit-cost data, the differences can be attributed solely to the use of different discount rates. The United States used 2.5 percent while Canada used 4.125 percent. The higher discount rate makes the initial cost weigh much more heavily in the calculation, leading to the Canadian conclusion that the project would yield a negative net benefit. Since the lower discount rate weighs the lower future operating costs relatively more heavily, Americans saw the net benefit as positive.

In a more recent illustration of why the magnitude of the discount rate matters, on October 30, 2006, economist Nicholas Stern from the London School of Economics issued a report using a discount rate of 0.1 percent that concluded that the benefits of strong, early action on climate change would considerably outweigh the costs. Other economists, such as William Nordhaus of Yale University, who prefer a discount rate around 6 percent, believe that optimal economic policies to slow climate change involve only modest rates of emissions reductions in the near term, followed by sharp reductions in the medium and long term.

In this debate, the desirability of strong current action is dependent (at least in part) on the size of the discount rate used in the analysis. Higher discount rates reduce the present value of future benefits from current investments in abatement, implying a smaller marginal benefit. Since the costs associated with those investments are not affected nearly as much by the choice of discount rate (remember that costs occurring in the near future are discounted less), a lower present value of marginal benefit translates into a lower optimal investment in abatement.

Far from being an esoteric subject, the choice of the discount rate is fundamentally important in defining the role of the public sector, the types of projects undertaken, and the allocation of resources across generations.

Sources: Stokey, E., & Zeckhauser, R. (1978). *A Primer for Policy Analysis*. New York: W. W. Norton, 164–165; Mikesell, R. (1977). *The Rate of Discount for Evaluating Public Projects*. Washington, DC: The American Enterprise Institute for Public Policy Research, 3–5; the Stern Report: http://webarchive.nationalarchives.gov.uk/ and /http://www.hm-treasury.gov.uk/sternreview_index.htm; Nordhaus, W. A review of the Stern Review on the economics of climate change. *Journal of Economic Literature, XLV*(September 2007), 686–702.

This ability to affect the desirability of a particular project or policy by the choice of discount rate led to a situation in which government agencies were using a variety of discount rates to justify programs or projects they supported. One set of hearings conducted by Congress during the 1960s discovered that, at one time, agencies were using discount rates ranging from 0 to 20 percent.

During the early 1970s, the Office of Management and Budget published a circular that required, with some exceptions, all government agencies to use a discount rate of 10 percent in their benefit-cost analysis. A revision issued in 1992 reduced the required discount rate to 7 percent. This circular also includes guidelines for benefit-cost analysis and specifies that certain rates will change annually.[5] This standardization reduces biases by eliminating the agency's ability to choose a discount rate that justifies a predetermined conclusion. It also allows a project to be considered independently of fluctuations in the true social cost of capital due to cycles in the behavior of the economy. On the other hand, when the social opportunity cost of capital differs from this administratively determined level, the benefit-cost analysis will not, in general, define the efficient allocation.

Example 3.3 highlights the importance of the choice of the discount rate for decision making. Most recently, the debate has turned to the question of whether or not discount rates should decline over time. Debate 3.1 explores this question.

Divergence of Social and Private Discount Rates

Earlier we concluded that producers, in their attempt to maximize producer surplus, also maximize the present value of net benefits under the "right" conditions, such as the absence of externalities, the presence of properly defined property rights, and the presence of competitive markets within which the property rights can be exchanged.

Now let's consider one more condition. If resources are to be allocated efficiently, firms must use the same rate to discount future net benefits as is appropriate for society at large. If firms were to use a higher rate, they would extract and sell resources faster than would be efficient. Conversely, if firms were to use a lower-than-appropriate discount rate, they would be excessively conservative.

Why might private and social rates differ? The social discount rate is equal to the social opportunity cost of capital. This cost of capital can be separated into two components: the risk-free cost of capital and the risk premium. The *risk-free cost of capital* is the rate of return earned when there is absolutely no risk of earning more or less than the expected return. The *risk premium* is an additional cost of capital required to compensate the owners of this capital when the expected and actual returns may differ. Therefore, because of the risk premium, the cost of capital is higher in risky industries than in no-risk industries.

One difference between private and social discount rates may stem from a difference in social and private risk premiums. If the risk of certain private decisions is different from the risks faced by society as a whole, then the social and private risk premiums may differ. One obvious example is the risk *caused* by the government.

---

[5]Annual rates can be found at http://www.whitehouse.gov/omb/. 2010 rates can be found at http://www.whitehouse.gov/omb/circulars_a094/a94_appx-c.

Discounting over Long Time Horizons: Should Discount Rates Decline?

DEBATE 3.1

As you are now probably starting to recognize, the choice of the discount rate can significantly alter the outcome of a benefit-cost analysis. This effect is exacerbated over long-time horizons and can become especially influential in decisions about spending now to mitigate damages from climate change, which may be uncertain in both magnitude and timing. What rate is appropriate? Recent literature and some evidence argue for declining rates of discount over long-time horizons? Should a declining rate schedule be utilized? A blue-ribbon panel of experts recently gathered to debate this and related questions (Arrow et al., 2012).

An unresolved debate in the economics literature revolves around the question of whether discount rates should be positive ("descriptive"), reflecting actual market rates, or normative ("prescriptive"), reflecting ethical considerations. Those who argue for the descriptive approach prefer to use market rates of return since expenditures to mitigate climate change are investment expenditures. Those who argue for the alternative prescriptive approach argue for including judgments about intergenerational equity. These rates are usually lower than those found in actual markets (Griffiths, et al. 2012).

In the United States, the Office of Management and Budget (OMB) currently recommends a constant rate of discount for project analysis. The recommendation is to use 3 percent and 7 percent real discount rates in sensitivity analysis (OMB, 2003) with options for lower rates if future generations are impacted. The United Kingdom and France utilize discount rate schedules that decline over time. Is one of these methods better than the other for discounting over long time-horizons? If a declining rate is appropriate, how fast should that rate decline?

The blue-ribbon panel agreed that theory provides strong arguments for a "declining certainty-equivalent discount rate" (Arrow et al., 2012, p. 21). Although the empirical literature also supports a rate that is declining over time (especially in the presence of uncertainty about future costs and/or benefits), the results from the empirical literature vary widely depending on the model assumptions and underlying data. If a declining rate schedule were to be adopted in the United States, this group of experts recommends that the EPA's Science Advisory Board be asked to develop criteria that could be used as the common foundation for determining what the schedule should look like.

Sources: Arrow, K., Maureen, J., Cropper, L., Gollier, C., Groom, B., Heal, G.M., et al. (December 2012). How should benefits and costs be discounted in an intergenerational context: The views of an expert panel. *RFF DP 12–53.*; Griffiths, C., Kopits, E., Marten, A., Moore, C., Newbold, S., & Wolverton, A. (2012). The social cost of carbon: Valuing carbon reductions in policy analysis. In Parry, de Mooij, & Keen (Eds.). *Fiscal Policy to Mitigate Climate Change: A Guide for Policy Makers.* International Monetary Fund; OMB (Office of Management and Budget). Circular A-4: Regulatory Analysis. Washington, DC Executive Office of the President. http://www.whitehouse.gov/omb/circulars/

If the firm is afraid its assets will be taken over by the government, it may choose a higher discount rate to make its profits before nationalization occurs. From the point of view of society—as represented by government—this is not a risk and, therefore, a lower discount rate is appropriate. When private rates exceed social rates, current production is higher than is desirable to maximize the net benefits to society. Both energy production and forestry have been subject to this source of inefficiency.

Another divergence in discount rates may stem from different underlying rates of time preference. Such a divergence in time preferences can cause not only a divergence between private and social discount rates (as when firms have a higher rate of time preference than the public sector), but even between otherwise similar analyses conducted in two different countries.

Time preferences would be expected to be higher, for example, in a cash-poor, developing country than in an industrialized country. Since the two benefit-cost analyses in these two countries would be based upon two different discount rates, they might come to quite different conclusions. What is right for the developing country may not be right for the industrialized country and vice versa.

Although private and social discount rates do not always diverge, they may. When those circumstances arise, market decisions are not efficient.

A Critical Appraisal

We have seen that it is sometimes, but not always, difficult to estimate benefits and costs. When this estimation is difficult or unreliable, it limits the value of a benefit-cost analysis. This problem would be particularly disturbing if biases tended to increase or decrease net benefits systematically. Do such biases exist?

In the early 1970s, Robert Haveman (1972) conducted a major study that shed some light on this question. Focusing on Army Corps of Engineers water projects, such as flood control, navigation, and hydroelectric power generation, Haveman compared the *ex ante* (before the fact) estimate of benefits and costs with their *ex post* (after the fact) counterparts. Thus, he was able to address the issues of accuracy and bias. He concluded that

> *In the empirical case studies presented, ex post estimates often showed little relationship to their ex ante counterparts. On the basis of the few cases and the a priori analysis presented here, one could conclude that there is a serious bias incorporated into agency ex ante evaluation procedures, resulting in persistent overstatement of expected benefits. Similarly in the analysis of project construction costs, enormous variance was found among projects in the relationship between estimated and realized costs. Although no persistent bias in estimation was apparent, nearly 50 percent of the projects displayed realized costs that deviated by more than plus or minus 20 percent from ex ante projected costs.*[6]

In the cases examined by Haveman, at least, the notion that benefit-cost analysis is purely a scientific exercise was clearly not consistent with the evidence; the biases of the analysts were merely translated into numbers.

Does their analysis mean that benefit-cost analysis is fatally flawed? Absolutely not! It does, however, highlight the importance of calculating an accurate value and

---

[6]A more recent assessment of costs (Harrington et al., 1999) found evidence of both overestimation and underestimation, although overestimation was more common. The authors attributed the overestimation mainly to a failure to anticipate technical innovation.

of including all of the potential benefits and costs (e.g., nonmarket values). It also serves to remind us, however, that benefit-cost analysis is not a stand-alone technique. It should be used in conjunction with other available information. Economic analysis including benefit-cost analysis can provide useful information, but it should not be the only determinant for all decisions.

Another shortcoming of benefit-cost analysis is that it does not really address the question of who reaps the benefits and who pays the cost. It is quite possible for a particular course of action to yield high net benefits, but to have the benefits borne by one societal group and the costs borne by another. This admittedly extreme case does serve to illustrate a basic principle—ensuring that a particular policy is efficient provides an important, but not always the sole, basis for public policy. Other aspects, such as who reaps the benefit or bears the burden, are also important.

In summary, on the positive side, benefit-cost analysis is frequently a very useful part of the policy process. Even when the underlying data are not strictly reliable, the outcomes may not be sensitive to that unreliability. In other circumstances, the data may be reliable enough to give indications of the consequences of broad policy directions, even when they are not reliable enough to fine-tune those policies. Benefit-cost analysis, when done correctly, can provide a useful complement to the other influences on the political process by clarifying what choices yield the highest net benefits to society.

On the negative side, benefit-cost analysis has been attacked as seeming to promise more than can actually be delivered, particularly in the absence of solid benefit information. This concern has triggered two responses. First, regulatory processes have been developed that can be implemented with very little information and yet have desirable economic properties. The recent reforms in air pollution control, which we cover in Chapter 15, provide one powerful example.

The second approach involves techniques that supply useful information to the policy process without relying on controversial techniques to monetize environmental services that are difficult to value. The rest of this chapter deals with the two most prominent of these—cost-effectiveness analysis and impact analysis.

Even when benefits are difficult or impossible to quantify, economic analysis has much to offer. Policymakers should know, for example, how much various policy actions will cost and what their impacts on society will be, even if the efficient policy choice cannot be identified with any certainty. Cost-effectiveness analysis and impact analysis both respond to this need, albeit in different ways.

Cost-Effectiveness Analysis

What can be done to guide policy when the requisite valuation for benefit-cost analysis is either unavailable or not sufficiently reliable? Without a good measure of benefits, making an efficient choice is no longer possible.

In such cases, frequently it is possible, however, to set a policy target on some basis other than a strict comparison of benefits and costs. One example is pollution control. What level of pollution should be established as the maximum acceptable level? In many countries, studies of the effects of a particular pollutant on human health have been used as the basis for establishing that pollutant's maximum acceptable concentration. Researchers attempt to find a threshold level below which no damage seems to occur. That threshold is then further lowered to provide a margin of safety and that becomes the pollution target.

Approaches could also be based upon expert opinion. Ecologists, for example, could be enlisted to define the critical numbers of certain species or the specific critical wetlands resources that should be preserved.

Once the policy target is specified, however, economic analysis can have a great deal to say about the cost consequences of choosing a means of achieving that objective. The cost consequences are important not only because eliminating wasteful expenditures is an appropriate goal in its own right, but also to assure that they do not trigger a political backlash.

Typically, several means of achieving the specified objective are available; some will be relatively inexpensive, while others turn out to be very expensive. The problems are frequently complicated enough that identifying the cheapest means of achieving an objective cannot be accomplished without a rather detailed analysis of the choices.

Cost-effectiveness analysis frequently involves an *optimization procedure*. An optimization procedure, in this context, is merely a systematic method for finding the lowest-cost means of accomplishing the objective. This procedure does not, in general, produce an efficient allocation because the predetermined objective may not be efficient. All efficient policies are cost-effective, but not all cost-effective policies are efficient.

In Chapter 2 we introduced the efficiency equimarginal principle. According to that principle, net benefits are maximized when the marginal benefit is equal to the marginal cost.

A similar, and equally important, equimarginal principle exists for cost-effectiveness:

> *Second Equimarginal Principle (the Cost-Effectiveness Equimarginal Principle): The least-cost means of achieving an environmental target will have been achieved when the marginal costs of all possible means of achievement are equal.*

Suppose we want to achieve a specific emissions reduction across a region, and several possible techniques exist for reducing emissions. How much of the control responsibility should each technique bear? The cost-effectiveness equimarginal principle suggests that the techniques should be used such that the desired reduction is achieved and the cost of achieving the last unit of emissions reduction (in other words, the marginal control cost) should be the same for all sources.

To demonstrate why this principle is valid, suppose that we have an allocation of control responsibility where marginal control costs are much higher for one set of techniques than for another. This cannot be the least-cost allocation since we could lower cost while retaining the same amount of emissions reduction. Costs could be lowered by allocating more control to the lower marginal cost sources and less to the high marginal cost sources. Since it is possible to find a way to lower cost, then clearly the initial allocation could not have minimized cost. Once marginal costs are equalized, it becomes impossible to find any lower-cost way of achieving the same degree of emissions reduction; therefore, that allocation must be the allocation that minimizes costs.

In our pollution control example, cost-effectiveness can be used to find the least-cost means of meeting a particular standard and its associated cost. Using this cost as a benchmark case, we can estimate how much costs could be expected to increase from this minimum level if policies that are not cost effective are implemented. Cost-effectiveness analysis can also be used to determine how much compliance costs can be expected to change if the EPA chooses a more stringent or less stringent standard. In Chapters 15 and 16, we shall examine in detail the current movement toward cost-effective polices, a movement triggered in part by studies showing that the cost reductions can be substantial.

Impact Analysis

What can be done when the information needed to perform a benefit-cost analysis or a cost-effectiveness analysis is not available? The analytical technique designed to deal with this problem is called *impact analysis.* An impact analysis, regardless of whether it focuses on economic impact or environmental impact or both, attempts to quantify the consequences of various actions.

In contrast to benefit-cost analysis, a pure impact analysis makes no attempt to convert all these consequences into a one-dimensional measure, such as dollars, to ensure comparability. In contrast to cost-effectiveness analysis, impact analysis does not necessarily attempt to optimize. Impact analysis places a large amount of relatively undigested information at the disposal of the policy maker. It is up to the policy maker to assess the importance of the various consequences and act accordingly.

On January 1, 1970, President Nixon signed the National Environmental Policy Act of 1969. This act, among other things, directed all agencies of the federal government to

> *include in every recommendation or report on proposals for legislation and other major Federal actions significantly affecting the quality of the human environment, a detailed statement by the responsible official on—*
>
> *i. the environmental impact of the proposed action,*
>
> *ii. any adverse environmental effects which cannot be avoided should the proposal be implemented,*
>
> *iii. alternatives to the proposed action,*
>
> *iv. the relationships between local short-term uses of man's environment and the maintenance and enhancement of long-term productivity; and*
>
> *v. any irreversible and irretrievable commitments of resources which would be involved in the proposed action should it be implemented.*[7]

This was the beginning of the environmental impact statement, which is now a familiar, if controversial, part of environmental policy making.

---

[7] 83 Stat. 853.

Current environmental impact statements are more sophisticated than their early predecessors and may contain a benefit-cost analysis or a cost-effectiveness analysis in addition to other more traditional impact measurements. Historically, however, the tendency had been to issue huge environmental impact statements that are virtually impossible to comprehend in their entirety.

In response, the Council on Environmental Quality, which, by law, administers the environmental impact statement process, has set content standards that are now resulting in shorter, more concise statements. To the extent that they merely quantify consequences, statements can avoid the problem of "hidden value judgments" that sometimes plague benefit-cost analysis, but they do so only by bombarding the policymakers with masses of noncomparable information.

Summary

Finding a balance in the relationship between humanity and the environment requires many choices. Some basis for making rational choices is absolutely necessary. If not made by design, decisions will be made by default.

Normative economics uses benefit-cost analysis for judging the desirability of the level and composition of provided services. Cost-effectiveness analysis and impact analysis offer alternatives to benefit-cost analysis. All of these techniques offer valuable information for decision making and all have shortcomings.

A static efficient allocation is one that maximizes the net benefit over all possible uses of those resources. The dynamic efficiency criterion, which is appropriate when time is an important consideration, is satisfied when the outcome maximizes the present value of net benefits from all possible uses of the resources. Later chapters examine the degree to which our social institutions yield allocations that conform to these criteria.

Because benefit-cost analysis is both very powerful and very controversial, in 1996 a group of economists of quite different political persuasions got together to attempt to reach some consensus on its proper role in environmental decision making. Their conclusion is worth reproducing in its entirety:

> *Benefit-cost analysis can play an important role in legislative and regulatory policy debates on protecting and improving health, safety, and the natural environment. Although formal benefit-cost analysis should not be viewed as either necessary or sufficient for designing sensible policy, it can provide an exceptionally useful framework for consistently organizing disparate information, and in this way, it can greatly improve the process and, hence, the outcome of policy analysis. If properly done, benefit-cost analysis can be of great help to agencies participating in the development of environmental, health and safety regulations, and it can likewise be useful in evaluating agency decision-making and in shaping statutes.*[8]

[8]From Kenneth Arrow et al. "Is There a Role for Benefit-Cost Analysis in Environmental, Health and Safety Regulation?" *Science* Vol. 272 (April 12, 1996), 221–222. Reprinted with Permission from AAAS.

Even when benefits are difficult to calculate, however, economic analysis in the form of cost-effectiveness can be valuable. This technique can establish the least expensive ways to accomplish predetermined policy goals and to assess the extra costs involved when policies other than the least-cost policy are chosen. What it cannot do is answer the question of whether those predetermined policy goals are efficient.

At the other end of the spectrum is impact analysis, which merely identifies and quantifies the impacts of particular policies without any pretense of optimality or even comparability of the information generated. Impact analysis does not guarantee an efficient outcome.

All three of the techniques discussed in this chapter are useful, but none of them can stake a claim as being universally the "best" approach. The nature of the information that is available and its reliability make a difference.

Discussion Questions

1. Is risk-neutrality an appropriate assumption for benefit-cost analysis? Why or why not? Does it seem more appropriate for some environmental problems than others? If so, which ones? If you were evaluating the desirability of locating a hazardous waste incinerator in a particular town, would the Arrow–Lind rationale for risk-neutrality be appropriate? Why or why not?
2. Was the executive order issued by President George W. Bush mandating a heavier use of benefit-cost analysis in regulatory rule making a step toward establishing a more rational regulatory structure, or was it a subversion of the environmental policy process? Why?

Self-Test Exercises

1. Suppose a proposed public policy could result in three possible outcomes: (1) present value of net benefits of $4,000,000, (2) present value of net benefits of $1,000,000, or (3) present value of net benefits of –$10,000,000 (i.e., a loss). Suppose society is risk-neutral and the probability of occurrence of each of these three outcomes are, respectively, 0.85, 0.10, and 0.05, should this policy be pursued or trashed? Why?
2. a. Suppose you want to remove ten fish of an exotic species that have illegally been introduced to a lake. You have three possible removal methods. Assume that q_1, q_2, and q_3 are, respectively, the amount of fish removed by each method that you choose to use so that the goal will be accomplished by any combination of methods such that $q_1 + q_2 + q_3 = 10$. If the marginal costs of each removal method are, respectively, 10q_1$, 5q_2$, and 2.5q_3$, how much of each method should you use to achieve the removal cost-effectively?

b. Why isn't an exclusive use of method 3 cost effective?
c. Suppose that the three marginal costs were constant (not increasing as in the previous case) such that $MC_1 = \$10$, $MC_2 = \$5$, and $MC_3 = \$2.5$. What is the cost-effective outcome in that case?

3. Consider the role of discount rates in problems involving long time horizons such as climate change. Suppose that a particular emissions abatement strategy would result in a $500 billion reduction in damages 50 years into the future. How would the maximum amount spent now to eliminate those damages change if the discount rate is 2 percent, rather than 10 percent?

Further Reading

Freeman, A. Myrick III. (2003). *The Measurement of Environmental and Resource Values*, 2nd ed. Washington, DC: Resources for the Future, Inc. A comprehensive and analytically rigorous survey of the concepts and methods for environmental valuation.

Hanley, N., & Spash, C.L. (1994). *Cost-Benefit Analysis and the Environment.* Brookfield, VT: Edward Elgar Publishing Company. An up-to-date account of the theory and practice of this form of analysis applied to environmental problems. Contains numerous specific case studies.

Norton, B., & Minteer, B.A. (2002). From environmental ethics to environmental public philosophy: Ethicists and economists: 1973–future. In T. Tietenberg and H. Folmer (Eds.). *The International Yearbook of Environmental and Resource Economics: 2002/2003.* Cheltenham, UK: Edward Elgar, 373–407. A review of the interaction between environmental ethics and economic valuation.

Scheraga, J. D., & Sussman, F.G. (1998). Discounting and environmental management. In T. Tietenberg and H. Folmer (Eds.). *The International Yearbook of Environmental and Resource Economics 1998–1999.* Cheltenham, UK: Edward Elgar, 1–32. A summary of the "state of the art" for the use of discounting in environmental management.

Additional References and Historically Significant References are available on this book's Companion Website: http://www.routledgetextbooks.com/textbooks/9780133479690

Valuing the Environment: Methods

4

For it so falls out; That what we have we prize not to the worth; Whiles we enjoy it, but being lack'd and lost; Why, then we rack the value; then we find; The virtue that possession would not show us; Whiles it was ours.

—William Shakespeare, *Much Ado About Nothing*

Introduction

Soon after the *Exxon Valdez* oil tanker ran aground on the Bligh Reef in Prince William Sound off the coast of Alaska on March 24, 1989, spilling approximately 11 million gallons of crude oil, the Exxon Corporation (now Exxon Mobil) accepted the liability for the damage caused by the leaking oil. This liability consisted of two parts: (1) the cost of cleaning up the spilled oil and restoring the site insofar as possible, and (2) compensation for the damage caused to the local ecology. Approximately \$2.1 billion was spent in cleanup efforts and Exxon also spent approximately \$303 million to compensate fishermen whose livelihoods were greatly damaged for the 5 years following the spill.[1] Litigation on environmental damages settled with Exxon agreeing to pay \$900 million over 10 years. The punitive damages phase of this case began in May 1994. In January 2004, after many rounds of appeals, the U.S. District Court for the State of Alaska awarded punitive damages to the plaintiffs in the amount of \$4.5 billion.[2] This amount was later cut almost in half to \$2.5 billion and in 2008 the Supreme Court ruled that even those punitive damages were excessive based on maritime law and further argued that the punitive damages should not exceed the \$507 million in compensatory damages already paid.[3]

In the spring of 2010, the Deepwater Horizon, a BP well in the Gulf of Mexico, exploded and began spewing an *Exxon Valdez*-sized oil spill every 4–5 days. By the time the leaking well was capped in August 2010, more than 200 million gallons had been spread through the Gulf of Mexico, almost 20 times greater than the *Exxon Valdez* spill. In 2013, BP announced that the overall net cost for the spill to

[1]U.S. District Court for the State of Alaska, Case Number A89-0095CV, January 28, 2004.

[2]Ibid.

[3]*Exxon Shipping Company v. Baker.*

the company was expected to be $42.4 billion—a sum that includes clean-up costs as well as all potential penalties and damage claims.

How can the economic damages from spills like these that caused substantial economic and environmental harm be calculated? Thousands of birds have been found dead in the Gulf since the BP spill, for example. Interestingly, the *Exxon Valdez* spill triggered pioneering work focused on providing monetary estimates of environmental damages, setting the stage for what is today considered standard practice for *nonmarket valuation*—the monetization of goods and services without market prices.

In Chapter 3, we examined the basic concepts economists use to calculate these damages. Yet implementing these concepts is far from a trivial exercise. While the costs of cleanup are fairly transparent, estimating the damage is far more complex. For example, how was the $900 million in damages in the Exxon case determined?

In this chapter, we explore how we can move from the general concepts to the actual estimates of compensation required by the courts. A series of special techniques has been developed to value the benefits from environmental improvement or, conversely, to value the damage done by environmental degradation. Special techniques are necessary because most of the normal valuation techniques that have been used over the years cannot be applied to environmental resources. Benefit-cost analysis requires the monetization of all relevant benefits and costs of a proposed policy or project, not merely those where the values can be derived from market transactions As such, it is also important to monetize those environmental goods and services that are not traded in any market. Even more difficult to grapple with are those nonmarket benefits associated with values unrelated to use, topics explored below.

Why Value the Environment?

While it may prove difficult, if not impossible, to place a completely accurate value on certain environmental amenities, not making the attempt leaves us valuing them at $0. Will valuing them at $0 lead us to the best policy decisions? Probably not, but that does not prevent controversy from arising over attempts to replace $0 with a more appropriate value (Debate 4.1).

Many federal agencies depend on benefit-cost analyses for decision making. Ideally, the goal is to choose the most economically desirable projects, given limited budgets. Estimation of benefits and costs is used for such diverse actions as follows:

- Natural resources damage assessments, such as for oil spills (National Oceanic and Atmospheric Administration);
- For the designation of critical habitat under the Endangered Species Act, (US Fish and Wildlife Service) ; and
- Dam relicensing applications (The Federal Energy Regulatory Commission).

These analyses, however, frequently fail to incorporate important nonmarket values. If the analysis does not include all the appropriate values, the results will be flawed. Is this exercise worth it?

Should Humans Place an Economic Value on the Environment?

DEBATE 4.1

Arne Naess, the late Norwegian philosopher, used the term *deep ecology* to refer to the view that the nonhuman environment has "intrinsic" value, a value that is independent of human interests. Intrinsic value is contrasted with "instrumental" value in which the value of the environment is derived from its usefulness in satisfying human wants.

Two issues are raised by the Naess critique: (1) what is the basis for the valuing of the environment? and (2) how is the valuation accomplished? The belief that the environment may have a value that goes beyond its direct usefulness to humans is in fact quite consistent with modern economic valuation techniques. As we shall see in this chapter, economic valuation techniques now include the ability to quantify a wide range of "nonuse" values as well as the more traditional "use" values.

Controversies over how the values are derived are less easily resolved. As described in this chapter, economic valuation is based firmly upon human preferences. Proponents of deep ecology, on the other hand, would argue that allowing humans to determine the value of other species would have no more moral basis than allowing other species to determine the value of humans. Rather, deep ecologists argue, humans should only use environmental resources when necessary for survival; otherwise, nature should be left alone. And, because economic valuation is not helpful in determining survival necessity, deep ecologists argue that it contributes little to environmental management.

Those who oppose all economic valuation face a dilemma: when humans fail to value the environment, it may be assigned a default value of zero in calculations designed to guide policy. A value of zero, however derived, will tend to justify a great deal of environmental degradation that could not be justified with proper economic valuation. As a 1998 issue of *Ecological Economics* demonstrated, a number of environmental professionals now support economic valuation as a way to demonstrate the enormous value of the environment to modern society. At the very least, support seems to be growing for the proposition that economic valuation can be a very useful means of demonstrating when environmental degradation is senseless, even when judged from a limited anthropomorphic perspective.

Sources: R. Costanza et al., The value of ecosystem services: Putting the issues in perspective. *Ecological Economics*, Vol. 25, No. 1 (1998), pp. 67–72; Daily, Gretchen, & Ellison, Katherine. (2003). *The New Economy of Nature: The Quest to Make Conservation Profitable.* Washington, DC: Island Press.

Valuation

While the valuation techniques we shall cover can be applied to both the damage caused by pollution and the services provided by the environment, each context offers its own unique aspects. We begin our investigation of valuation techniques by exposing some of the special challenges posed by one of those contexts, pollution control.

In the United States, damage estimates are not only used in the design of policies, but, as indicated in the opening paragraphs of this chapter, they have also become important in the courts. Some basis for deciding the magnitude of liability awards is necessary.[4]

The damage caused by pollution can take many different forms. The first, and probably most obvious, is the effect on human health. Polluted air and water can cause disease when ingested. Other forms of damage include loss of enjoyment from outdoor activities and damage to vegetation, animals, and materials.

Assessing the magnitude of this damage requires (1) identifying the affected categories, (2) estimating the physical relationship between the pollutant emissions (including natural sources) and the damage caused to the affected categories, (3) estimating responses by the affected parties toward averting or mitigating some portion of the damage, and (4) placing a monetary value on the physical damages. Each step is often difficult to accomplish.

Because the data used to track down causal relationships do not typically come from controlled experiments, identifying the affected categories is a complicated matter. Obviously we cannot run large numbers of people through controlled experiments. If people were subjected to different levels of some pollutant, such as carbon monoxide, so that we could study the short-term and long-term effects, some might become ill and even die. Ethical concern precludes human experimentation of this type.

This leaves us essentially two choices. We can try to infer the impact on humans from controlled laboratory experiments on animals, or we can do statistical analysis of differences in mortality or disease rates for various human populations living in polluted environments to see the extent to which they are correlated with pollution concentrations. Neither approach is completely acceptable.

Animal experiments are expensive, and the extrapolation from effects on animals to effects on humans is tenuous at best. Many of the significant effects do not appear for a long time. To determine these effects in a reasonable period of time, test animals are commonly subjected to large doses for relatively short periods. The researcher then extrapolates from the results of these high-dosage, short-duration experiments to estimate the effects of low-dose, long-duration exposure to pollution on a human population. Because these extrapolations move well beyond the range of experimental experience, many scientists disagree on how the extrapolations should be accomplished. There are ethical concerns with animal experiments as well.

Statistical studies, on the other hand, deal with human populations subjected to low doses for long periods, but, unfortunately, they have another set of problems—correlation does not imply causation. To illustrate, the fact that death rates are higher in cities with higher pollution levels does not prove that the higher pollution caused the higher death rates. Perhaps those same cities averaged older populations, which would tend to lead to higher death rates. Or perhaps they had more smokers. The existing studies have been sophisticated enough to account for many of these

---

[4]The rules for determining these damages are defined in Department of Interior regulations. See 40 Code of Federal Regulations 300:72–74.

other possible influences but, because of the relative paucity of data, they have not been able to cover them all.

The problems discussed so far arise when identifying whether a particular observed effect results from pollution. The next step is to estimate how strong the relationship is between the effect and the pollution concentrations. In other words, it is necessary not only to discover *whether* pollution causes an increased incidence of respiratory disease, but also to estimate *how much* reduction in respiratory illness could be expected from a given reduction in pollution.

The nonexperimental nature of the data makes this a difficult task. It is not uncommon for different researchers analyzing the same data to come to remarkably different conclusions. Diagnostic problems are compounded when the effects are synergistic—that is, when the effect depends, in a nonadditive way, on contributing factors such as the victims' smoking habits or the presence of other harmful substances in the air or water.

Once physical damages have been identified, the next step is to place a monetary value on them. It is not difficult to see how complex an undertaking this is. Think about the difficulties in assigning a value to extending a human life by several years or to the pain, suffering, and grief borne by both a cancer victim and the victim's family.

How can these difficulties be overcome? What valuation techniques are available not only to value pollution damage, but also to value the large number of services that the environment provides?

Types of Values

Economists have decomposed the total economic value conferred by resources into three main components: (1) use value, (2) option value, and (3) nonuse or passive-use values. *Use value* reflects the direct use of the environmental resource. Examples include fish harvested from the sea, timber harvested from the forest, water extracted from a stream for irrigation, even the scenic beauty conferred by a natural vista. If you used one of your senses to experience the resource—sight, sound, touch, taste, or smell—then you have *used* the resource. Pollution can cause a loss of use value, such as when air pollution increases the vulnerability to illness, an oil spill adversely affects a fishery, or when smog enshrouds a scenic vista.

Option value reflects the value people place on a future ability to use the environment. It reflects the willingness to pay to preserve the option to use the environment in the future even if one is not currently using it. Whereas use value reflects the value derived from current use, option value reflects the desire to preserve the potential for possible future use. Are you planning to go to Yellowstone National Park next summer? Perhaps not, but would you like to preserve the option to go someday?

Passive-use or *nonconsumptive use values* arise when the resource is not actually used up (consumed) in the process of experiencing it. These types of values reflects the common observation that people are more than willing to pay for improving or preserving resources that they will never use. One type of nonuse value is a *bequest value.* Bequest value is the willingness to pay to ensure a resource is available for your children and grandchildren. A second type of nonuse value, a pure nonuse value, is called *existence value*. Existence value is measured by the willingness to pay to ensure that a resource continues to exist in the absence of any interest in future use. The term existence value was coined by economist John Krutilla in his now-famous quote, "There are many persons who obtain satisfaction from mere knowledge that part of wilderness North America remains even though they would be appalled by the prospect of being exposed to it."[5]

When the Bureau of Reclamation began looking at sites for dams near the Grand Canyon, groups such as the Sierra Club rose up in protest of the potential loss of this unique resource. When Glen Canyon was flooded by Lake Powell, even those who never intended to visit recognized this potential loss. Because this value does not derive either from direct use or potential use, it represents a very different category of value.

These categories of value can be combined to produce the total willingness to pay (TWP):

$$\text{TWP} = \text{Use Value} + \text{Option Value} + \text{Nonuse Value}$$

Since nonuse or passive use values are derived from motivations other than personal use, they are obviously less tangible than use values. Total willingness to pay estimated without nonuse values, however, will be less than the minimum amount that would be required to compensate individuals if they are deprived of this environmental asset. Furthermore, estimated nonuse values can be quite large. Therefore, it is not surprising that they are controversial. Indeed when the U.S. Department of Interior drew up its regulations on the appropriate procedures for performing natural resource damage assessment, it prohibited the inclusion of nonuse values unless use values for the incident under consideration were zero. A subsequent 1989 decision by the District of Columbia Court of Appeals (880 F. 2nd 432) overruled this decision and allowed nonuse values to be included as long as they could be measured reliably.

Classifying Valuation Methods

Typically, the researcher's goal is to estimate the total willingness to pay for the good or service in question. This is the area under the demand curve up to the quantity consumed (recall discussion from Chapter 2). For a market good, this calculation is relatively straightforward. However, nonmarket goods and services, the focus of this chapter, require the estimation of willingness to pay either through examining behavior, drawing inferences from the demand for related goods, or through responses to surveys. And, as highlighted above, capturing all components of value is challenging.

This section will provide a brief overview of some of the methods available to estimate these values and to convey some sense of the range of possibilities and how they are related. Subsequent sections will provide more specific information about how they are actually used.

---

[5]Krutilla, John V. "Conservation Reconsidered," first published in *American Economic Review* Vol. 57 (1967).

Valuation methods can be separated into two broad categories: stated preference and revealed preference methods. Each of these broad categories of methods includes both indirect and direct techniques. The possibilities are presented in Table 4.1. Revealed preference methods are based on actual observable choices that allow resource values to be directly inferred from those choices. For example, in calculating how much local fishermen lost from the oil spill, the revealed preference method might calculate how much the catch declined and the resulting diminished value of the catch. In this case, prices are directly observable, and their use allows the direct calculation of the loss in value. Or, more indirectly, in calculating the value of an occupational environmental risk (such as some exposure to a substance that could pose some health risk), we might examine the differences in wages across industries in which workers take on different levels of risk.

Compare this with the direct stated preference case that might be used when the value is not directly observable, such as the value of preserving a species. Analysts derive this value by using a survey that attempts to elicit the respondents' willingness to pay (their "stated preference") for preserving that species.

Stated Preference Methods

Stated preference methods use survey techniques to elicit willingness to pay for a marginal improvement or for avoiding a marginal loss. The most direct approach, called *contingent valuation*, provides a means of deriving values that cannot be obtained in more traditional ways. The simplest version of this approach merely asks respondents what value they would place on an environmental change (such as the loss of a wetlands or increased exposure to pollution) or on preserving the resource in its current state. Typically this question is framed as, "What is the maximum you are willing to pay for the change?" Alternative versions ask a "yes" or "no" question such as whether or not the respondent would pay \$*X* to prevent the change or preserve the species. The answers reveal either an upper bound (in the case of a "no" answer) or a lower bound (in the case of a "yes" answer).

The contingent valuation survey approach creates a hypothetical market and asks respondents to consider a willingness-to-pay question *contingent* on the existence of

TABLE 4.1 Economic Methods for Measuring Environmental and Resource Values

Methods	Revealed Preference	Stated Preference
Direct	Market Price	Contingent Valuation
	Simulated Markets	
Indirect	Travel Cost	Attribute-Based Models
	Hedonic Property Values	Conjoint Analysis
	Hedonic Wage Values	Choice Experiments
	Avoidance Expenditures	Contingent Ranking

Source: Modified by the authors from Mitchell and Carson, 1989.

this market. Contingent valuation questions come with their own set of challenges. The major concern with the use of the contingent valuation method has been the potential for survey respondents to give biased answers. Five types of potential bias have been the focus of a large amount of research: (1) strategic bias, (2) information bias, (3) starting-point bias, (4) hypothetical bias, and (5) the observed discrepancy between willingness to pay (WTP) and willingness to accept (WTA).

Strategic bias arises when the respondent intentionally provides a biased answer in order to influence a particular outcome. If a decision to preserve a stretch of river for fishing, for example, depends on whether or not the survey produces a sufficiently large value for fishing, the respondents who enjoy fishing may be tempted to provide an answer that ensures a high value, rather than the lower value that reflects their true valuation.

Information bias may arise whenever respondents are forced to value attributes with which they have little or no experience. For example, the valuation by a recreationist of a loss in water quality in one body of water may be based on the ease of substituting recreation on another body of water. If the respondent has no experience using the second body of water, the valuation could be based on an entirely false perception. Consider another example. Visual aides have been shown to reduce uncertainty and unfamiliarity with the good or service being valued. Labao et al. (2008) found that colored photographs, as opposed to black-and-white photographs, influenced respondent willingness to pay for the Philippine Eagle. The colored photographs resulted in a higher willingness to pay than black-and-white photos. Why? The authors suggest that the higher willingness to pay could be explained by photographs in color simply providing more information or by "enhancing respondents' ability to assimilate information." In any case, the nature of the visual aide seems important for revealing preferences.

Starting-point bias may arise in those survey instruments in which a respondent is asked to check off his or her answers from a predefined range of possibilities. How that range is defined by the designer of the survey may affect the resulting answers. A range of $0–$100 may produce a valuation by respondents different from, for example, a range of $10–$100, even if no responses are in the $0–$10 range. Ladenburg and Olsen (2008), in a study of willingness to pay to protect nature areas in Denmark from new highway development, found that the starting-point bias in their choice experiment was gender specific, with female respondents exhibiting the greatest sensitivity to the starting point.

Hypothetical bias can enter the picture because the respondent is being confronted by a contrived, rather than an actual, set of choices. Since he or she will not actually have to pay the estimated value, the respondent may treat the survey casually, providing ill-considered answers. One early survey (Hanemann, 1994) found ten studies that directly compared willingness-to-pay estimates derived from surveys with actual expenditures. Although some of the studies found that the willingness-to-pay estimates derived from surveys exceeded actual expenditures, the majority of those found that the differences were not statistically significant. More recently, Ehmke, Lusk, and List (2008) tested whether hypothetical bias depends on location and/or culture. In a study based on student experiments in China, France, Indiana, Kansas, and Niger, they found significant differences in bias across locations. Given that policymakers frequently rely on existing benefits estimates from other locations when making decisions, this finding should not be taken lightly. The strengths and weaknesses of using estimates derived in one setting to infer benefits in another, a technique known as *benefit transfer*, are discussed below.

Increasingly, environmental economists are using these types of experiments to try to determine the severity of some of these biases as well as to learn how to reduce bias. Some of these experiments are conducted in a laboratory setting, such as a computer lab or a classroom designed for this purpose. In one such experiment on voluntary provision of public goods (donations), Landry et al. (2006) found that for door-to-door interviews, an increase in physical attractiveness of the interviewer led to sizable increases in giving. Interestingly, physical attractiveness also led to increases in response rates, particularly by male households.

The final source of bias addresses observed gaps between two supposedly closely related concepts—willingness to pay (WTP) and willingness to accept (WTA) compensation. Respondents to contingent valuation surveys tend to report much higher values when asked for their willingness to accept compensation for a specified loss of some good or service than if asked for their willingness to pay for a specified increase of that same good or service. Economic theory suggests the two should be equal. Debate 4.2 explores some of the reasons offered for the difference.

Measuring willingess to pay or willingness to accept in the presence of price changes makes two new concepts relevant—compensating variation and equivalent variation. *Compensating variation* is the amount of money it would take to *compensate* for a price increase in order to make a consumer just as well off as she was before the price increase. How much was the consumer "hurt" by the price increase can be measured by the compensating variation. *Equivalent variation*, on the other hand, is the amount of money it would take to make a consumer indifferent (same income) between the money and the price increase. In other words, how much money would she pay to avoid the price increase.

If the compensating variation is greater than zero, that amount represents willingness to pay. If it is negative, it represents willingness to accept. In other words, for increases in environmental quality, compensating variation should be positive (WTP). For decreases in environmental quality, it should be negative (WTA). Equivalent variation is just the opposite—the amount of money the household would need to be given to be just as well off as before the environmental change. Equivalent variation will be positive for increases in environmental quality (WTA) and negative for decreases (WTP). In the absense of any income effects, in theory these measures (along with consumer surplus) should be equivalent.

Much experimental work has been done on contingent valuation to determine how serious a problem biases may present. One early survey (Carson et al., 1994) had already uncovered 1,672 contingent valuation studies and a much more recent one gives annotations for more than 7,500 studies in 130 countries (Carson, 2011)! Are the results from these surveys reliable enough for the policy process?

DEBATE 4.2 Willingness to Pay versus Willingness to Accept: Why So Different?

Many contingent valuation studies have found that respondents tend to report much higher values for questions that ask what compensation the respondent would be willing to accept (WTA) to give something up than for questions that ask for the willingness to pay (WTP) for an incremental improvement in the same good or service. Economic theory suggests that differences between WTP and WTA should be small, but experimental findings both in environmental economics and in other microeconomic studies have found large differences. Why?

Some economists have attributed the discrepancy to a psychological endowment effect; the psychological value of something you own is greater than something you do not. In other words, you would require more compensation to be as well off without it than you would be willing to pay to get that same good, and as such, you would be less willing to give it up (WTA > WTP) (Kahneman, Knetsch, & Thaler, 1990). This is a form of what behavioral economists call loss aversion—the psychological premise that losses are more highly valued than gains.

Others have suggested that the difference is explainable in terms of the market context. In the absence of good substitutes, large differences between WTA and WTP would be the expected outcome. In the presence of close substitutes, WTP and WTA should not be that different, but the divergence between the two measures should increase as the degree of substitution decreases (Hanemann, 1991; Shogren et al., 1994).

The characteristics of the good may matter as well. In their review of the evidence provided by experimental studies, Horowitz and McConnell (2002) find that for "ordinary goods" the ratio of WTA /WTP is smaller than the ratio of WTA/WTP for public and nonmarket goods. Their results support the notion that the nature of the property rights involved are not neutral.

The moral context of the valuation may matter as well. Croson et al. (Draft 2005) show that the amount of WTA compensation estimated in a damage case increases with the culpability of the party causing the damage as long as that party is also paying the damages. If, however, a third party is paying, WTA is insensitive to culpability. This difference suggests that the valuation implicitly includes an amount levied in punishment for the party who caused the damage (the valuation becomes the lost value plus a sanction).

It may also be the case, that in dynamic settings, respondents are uncertain about the value of the good. Zhao and Kling (2004) argue that in intertemporal settings, the equivalence of compensating variation/equivalent variation and WTP/WTA breaks down, in part because WTP and WTA have a behavioral component and the timing of a decision will be impacted by the consumer's rate of time preference and willingness to take risks. A buyer or seller, by commiting to a purchase or sale, must forgo opportunities for additional information. These "commitment costs" reduce WTP and increase WTA. The larger the commitment costs, the larger is the divergence between the two measures.

Ultimately, the choice of which concept to use in environmental valuation comes down to how the associated property right is allocated. If someone owns the right to the resource, asking how much compensation they would take to give it up is the appropriate question. If the respondent does not have the right, using WTP to estimate the value of acquiring it is the right approach. However, as Horowitz and McConnell point out, since the holders and nonholders of "rights" value them differently, the initial allocation of property rights can have strong influence on valuation decisions for environmental amenities. And as Zhao and Kling note, the timing of the decision can also be an important factor.

Sources: R. Croson, Rachlinski, J. J., & Johnston, J. Culpability as an explanation of the WTA-WTP discrepancy in contingent valuation (Draft 2005).; Hanemann, W. M. (1991). Willingness to pay and willingness to accept: How much can they differ? *American Economic Review, 81*, 635–647; Horowitz, J. K., & McConnell, K. E. (2002). A review of WTA/WTP studies. *Journal of Environmental Economics and Management, 44*. 426–447; Kahneman, D., Knetsch, J., & Thaler, R. (1990). Experimental tests of the endowment effect and the coase theorem. *Journal of Political Economy, 98*, 1325–1348; Shogren, J. F., Shin, Senung Y., Hayes, D. J., & Kliebenstein, J. B. (1994). Resolving differences in willingness to pay and willingness to accept. *American Economic Review, 84*(1), 255–270; Zhao, Jinhua, & Kling, Catherine. (2004). Willingness to pay, compensating variation, and the cost of commitment. *Economic Inquiry, 42*(3), 503–517.

Faced with the need to compute damages from oil spills, the National Oceanic and Atmospheric Administration (NOAA) convened a panel of independent economic experts (including two Nobel Prize laureates) to evaluate the use of contingent valuation methods for determining lost passive-use or nonuse values. Their report, issued on January 15, 1993 (58 FR 4602), was cautiously supportive.

The committee made clear that it had several concerns with the technique. Among those concerns, the panel listed (1) the tendency for contingent valuation willingness-to-pay estimates to seem unreasonably large; (2) the difficulty in assuring the respondents have understood and absorbed the issues in the survey; and (3) the difficulty in assuring that respondents are responding to the specific issues in the survey rather than reflecting general warm feelings about public spiritedness, known as the "warm glow" effect.[6]

But the panel also made clear its conclusion that suitably designed surveys could eliminate or reduce these biases to acceptable levels and it provided, in an appendix, specific guidelines for determining whether a particular study was suitably designed. The panel suggested that when practitioners follow these guidelines, they

> *can produce estimates reliable enough to be the starting point of a judicial process of damage assessment, including lost passive-use values. . . . [A well-constructed contingent valuation study] contains information that judges and juries will wish to use, in combination with other estimates, including the testimony of expert witnesses.*

Specifically, they suggested the use of referendum-type (yes/no) willingness-to-pay questions, personal interviews when possible, clear scenario descriptions, and follow-up questions.

---

[6]A more detailed description of the methodological issues and concerns with contingent valuation with respect to the actual *Exxon Valdez* contingent valuation survey can be found in Mitchell (2002).

These guidelines have been influential in shaping more recent studies. For example, Example 4.1 shares the results of a large contingent valuation survey, designed to estimate the value of preventing future spills.

EXAMPLE 4.1

Leave No Behavioral Trace: Using the Contingent Valuation Method to Measure Passive-Use Values

Until the *Exxon Valdez* tanker spilled 11 million gallons of crude oil into Prince William Sound in Alaska, the calculation of nonuse (or passive-use) values was not a widely researched topic. However, following the 1989 court ruling in *Ohio v. U.S. Department of the Interior* that said lost passive-use values could now be compensated within natural resources damages assessments and the passage of the Oil Pollution Act of 1990, the estimation of nonuse and passive-use values became not only a topic of great debate, but also a rapidly growing research area within the economics community.

One study (Carson et al., 2003) discusses the design, implementation, and results of a large survey designed to estimate the passive-use values related to large oil spills. In particular, the survey asked respondents their willingness to pay to prevent a similar disaster in the future by funding an escort ship program that would help prevent and/or contain a future spill. The survey was conducted for the State of Alaska in preparation for litigation in the case against *Exxon Valdez*.

The survey followed the recommendations made by the NOAA panel for conducting contingent valuation surveys and for ensuring reliable estimates. It relied upon face-to-face interviews and the sample was drawn from the national population. The study used a binary discrete-choice (yes/no) question where the respondent was asked whether he or she would be willing to pay a specific amount, with the amount varying across four versions of the survey. A one-time increase in taxes was the chosen method of payment. They also avoided potential embedding bias (where respondents may have difficulty valuing multiple goods) by using a survey that valued a single good. The survey also contained pictures, maps, and background information to make sure the respondent was familiar with the good he/she was being asked to value.

Using the survey data, the researchers were able, statistically, to estimate a valuation function by relating the respondent's willingness to pay to respondent characteristics. After multiplying the estimate of the median willingness to pay by the population sampled, they reported aggregate lost passive-use values at $2.8 billion (in 1990 dollars). They point out that this number is a lower bound, not only because willingness-to-accept compensation would be a more appropriate measure of actual lost passive use from the spill (see Debate 4.2), but also because their median willingness to pay was less than the mean.

The *Exxon Valdez* spill sparked a debate about the measurement of nonuse and passive-use values. Laws put into place after the spill have ensured that passive-use values will be included in natural resource damage assessments. Should other parts of the world follow suit?

Source: Carson, Richard T., Mitchell, Robert C., Hanemann, Michael, Kopp, Raymond J., Presser, Stanley, & Ruud, Paul A. (2003). Contingent valuation and lost passive use: Damages from the *Exxon Valdez* oil spill." *Environmental and Resource Economics*, *25*, 257–286.

The NOAA panel report has created an interesting dilemma. Although it has legitimized the use of contingent valuation for estimating passive-use (nonconsumptive use) and nonuse values, the panel has also set some rather rigid guidelines that reliable studies should follow. The cost of completing an "acceptable" contingent valuation study could well be so high that they will only be useful for large incidents, those for which the damages are high enough to justify their use. Yet, due to the paucity of other techniques, the failure to use contingent valuation may, by default, result in passive-use values of zero. That is not a very appealing alternative.[7]

A final category, indirect hypothetical methods, includes several attribute-based methods. Attribute-based methods, such as choice-based, conjoint models (or, equivalently, choice experiments), are useful when project options have multiple levels of different attributes. Like contingent valuation, choice experiments are also survey based, but instead of asking respondents to state a willingness to pay, respondents are asked to choose among alternate bundles of goods. Each bundle has a set of attributes and the levels of each attribute vary across bundles. Since one of the attributes in each bundle is a price measure, willingness to pay can be identified.

Consider an example (Boyle et al., 2001) that surveyed Maine residents on their preferences for alternative forest-harvesting practices. The State of Maine was considering purchasing a 23,000-acre tract of forest land to manage. Attributes used in the survey included the number of live trees, management practice for dead trees, percent of land set aside, and a tax payment. Three levels of each management attribute and 13 different tax prices were considered. Table 4.2 reproduces the attributes and levels.

TABLE 4.2 Attributes in the Maine Forest Harvesting Conjoint Analysis

Attribute	Level
Live Trees after Harvesting	No trees (clear-cut)
	153 trees/acre
	459 trees/acre
Dead Trees after Harvesting	Remove all
	5 trees/acre
	10 trees/acre
Percent of Forest Set aside from Harvest	20%
	50%
	80%

Source: Boyle et al., 2001 and Holmes and Adamovicz, 2003.

[7]Whittington (2002) examines the reasons why so many contingent valuation studies in developing countries are unhelpful. Poorly designed or rapidly implemented surveys could result in costly policy mistakes on topics that are very important in the developing world. The current push for cheaper, quicker studies is risky and researchers need to be very cautious.

Respondents were given a choice set of four different alternative management plans and the status quo (no purchase). Table 4.3 demonstrates a sample survey question. This type of survey has evolved from both contingent valuation and marketing studies. This approach allows the respondent to make a familiar choice (choose a bundle) and allows the researcher to derive marginal willingness to pay for an attribute from that choice.

Contingent ranking, another survey method, also falls within this final category. Respondents are given a set of hypothetical situations that differ in terms of the environmental amenity available (instead of a bundle of attributes) and are asked to rank-order them. These rankings can then be compared to see the implicit trade-offs between more of the environmental amenity and less of the other characteristics. When one or more of these characteristics is expressed in terms of a monetary value, it is possible to use this information and the rankings to impute a value to the environmental amenity.

Sometimes more than one of these techniques may be used simultaneously. In some cases, using multiple techniques is necessary to capture the total economic value; in other cases, it may be used to provide independent estimates of the value being sought as a check on the reliability of the estimate.

Revealed Preference Methods

Revealed preference methods are "observable" because they involve actual behavior and expenditures and "indirect" because they infer a value rather than estimate it directly. Suppose, for example, a particular sport fishery is being threatened by pollution, and one of the damages caused by that pollution is a reduction in sportfishing. How is this loss to be valued when access to the fishery is free?

Travel-Cost Method. One way to derive this loss is through *travel-cost* methods. Travel-cost methods may infer the value of a recreational resource (such as a sport fishery, a park, or a wildlife preserve where visitors hunt with a camera) by using

TABLE 4.3 A Sample Conjoint Analysis Survey Questionnaire

Attribute	Alternatives				
	A	B	C	D	No change
Live Trees Remaining	No trees	459/acre	No trees	153/acre	
Dead Trees Remaining	Remove all	Remove all	5/acre	10/acre	
Percent Set Aside	80%	20%	50%	20%	
Tax	$40	$200	$10	$80	
I would vote for (please check off)	—	—	—	—	—

Source: Holmes, Thomas P., & Adamowicz, Wiktor L. (2003). Attribute-based methods. *A Primer on Nonmarket Valuation*, Ian Bateman, ed. New York: Kluwer Academic Publishers.

information on how much the visitors spent in getting to the site to construct a demand curve representing willingness to pay for a "visitor day."

Freeman (2003) identifies two variants of this approach. In the first, analysts examine the number of trips visitors make to a site. In the second, the analysts examine whether people decide to visit a site and, if so, which site. This second variant includes using a special class of models, known as random utility models, to value quality changes.

The first variant allows the construction of a travel cost demand function. The value of the flow of services from that site is the area under the estimated demand curve for those services or for access to the site, aggregated over all who visit the site. Using this variant, individual consumer surplus can be estimated. The area below the demand curve, but above the travel cost (price) is the consumer surplus.

The second variant allows the analysis of how specific site characteristics influence choice and, therefore, indirectly how valuable those characteristics are. Knowledge of how the value of each site varies with respect to its characteristics allows the analyst to value how degradation of those characteristics (e.g., from pollution) would lower the value of the site.

Travel cost models have been used to value national parks, mountain climbing, recreational fishing, and beaches. Travel cost models have also been used to value losses from events such as beach closures during oil spills, fish consumption advisories, and the cost of development that has eliminated a recreation area. The methodology for both variants is detailed in Parsons (2003).

In the random utility model, a person choosing a particular site takes into consideration site characteristics and its price (trip cost). Characteristics affecting the site choice include ease of access and environmental quality. Each site results in a unique level of utility and a person is assumed to choose the site giving the highest level of utility to that person. Welfare losses from an event such as an oil spill can then be measured by the resulting change in utility should the person have to choose an alternate, less desirable site.

Example 4.2 looks at the use of travel cost methods to estimate the economic impacts of beach closures due to oil spills in Minorca, Spain.

One interesting paradox that arises with the travel cost model is that those who live closest to the site and may actually visit frequently, will have low travel costs. These users will appear to have a lower value for that site even if their (unmeasured) willingness to pay for the experience is very high. Another challenge in this model is how to incorporate the opportunity cost of time. Usually, this is represented by wages, but that approach is not universally accepted.

Hedonic Property Value and Hedonic Wage Methods. Two other revealed preference methods are known as *the hedonic property value* and *hedonic wage* approaches. They share the characteristic that they use a statistical technique, known as multiple regression analysis, to "tease out" the environmental component of value in a related market. For example, it is possible to discover that, all other things being equal, property values are lower in polluted neighborhoods than in clean neighborhoods. (Property values fall in polluted neighborhoods because they are less desirable places to live.)

EXAMPLE 4.2

Using the Travel Cost Method to Estimate Recreational Value: Beaches in Minorca, Spain

Minorca, an island in the Mediterranean Sea, is a very popular tourist destination. Minorca's population doubles in the summer months from about 80,000 year-round residents to between 150,000 and 175,000 in the summer. The island's beaches are a major attraction.

Just how valuable are those beaches? To provide an estimate, researchers considered a hypothetical scenario in which an oil spill resulted in closure of certain beaches on the island. The analysis involved using a random utility model based upon survey data to estimate the economic impacts of these closures.

In 2008, 573 face-to-face individual surveys were conducted at 51 different beaches on the island using a discrete choice travel cost survey. Respondents were asked some typical travel cost survey questions such as where the trip originated, how they got to the site, how many people were they traveling with and what were their ages, and some questions to collect socio-economic demographics on the respondents. After being asked about their attitudes toward different beach attributes, they completed a questionnaire on the characteristics of the beach they were visiting. The characteristics included a measure of how urban the area was, the type of sand, how clean the beach was, how crowded it was, whether or not there was a toilet, presence of drink vendors, water temperature, calmness of the water, environmental quality, presence of a life guard, the direction the beach faced, and whether or not nudism was present on the beach. Travel costs included the cost of fuel and tolls plus travel time. Travel time varied by mode of transportation—using average walking and average driving speeds.

The random utility model allowed researchers to estimate the impacts on utility of the various beach characteristics identified by the surveys. Those characteristics positively affecting utility included north facing, presence of a life guard, presence of toilets and drink vendors, thin sand, the presence of nudism, warm water temperatures, and good environmental quality. Characteristics negatively affecting utility included non-northern beaches, urban beaches, crowding, algae, and calm water.

Because some beach attributes were more highly valued than others, the range of estimates was dramatically affected by the details in the scenario. For example, for a closure affecting beaches on the west coast, the willingness to pay to avoid this loss was .24 euros (2008) per day per person with peak visitation of 25,000 visitors. Aggregating the per-visitor value across visitors produced a daily welfare loss from these closures of 6,000 euros. On the other extreme, a spill forcing closure of the more valuable northern beaches would cause the welfare loss to rise to 1.73 euros per day per person for a total of 43,250 euros during peak visitation.

It is easy to take highly enjoyable recreational sites for granted since they are freely provided by nature. As a result they may not be given their due when resources are allocated for their protection and enhancement. The travel cost method can help to inform policy not only by demonstrating how truly valuable they are, but also by allowing useful distinctions to be made among various recreation resources.

Source: Pere, Riera, McConnell, Kenneth E., Giergiczny, Marek, & Mahieu, Pierre-Alexandre. (2011). Applying the travel-cost method to Minorca beaches: Some policy results. *International Handbook on Non-Market Environmental Valuation,* (Jeff Bennett, Ed.), Edward Elgar, 60–73.

Hedonic property value models use market data (house prices) and then break down the house sales price into its components, including the house characteristics (e.g., number of bedrooms, lot size, and features), the neighborhood characteristics (e.g., crime rates, school quality, and so on), and environmental characteristics (e.g., air quality, percentage of open space nearby, distance to a local landfill, etc.).

Hedonic models allow for the measurement of the marginal willingness to pay for discrete changes in an attribute. Numerous studies have utilized this approach to examine the effect on property value of things such as distance to a hazardous waste site (Michaels & Smith, 1990), large farm operations (Palmquist et al., 1997), open space and land use patterns (Bockstael, 1996; Geoghegan et al., 1997; Acharya & Bennett, 2001), dams and rivers (Bohlen & Lewis 2008), brownfields (Mihaescu & vom Hofe, 2012), and shale oil production facilities (Gopalakrishnan & Klaiber 2013). This approach has become commonplace with the use of geographic information systems (discussed below).[8]

Hedonic wage approaches are similar except that they attempt to isolate the environmental risk component of wages, which serves to isolate the amount of compensation workers require in order to work in risky occupations. It is well known that workers in high-risk occupations demand higher wages in order to be induced to undertake the risks. When the risk is environmental (such as exposure to a toxic substance), the results of the multiple regression analysis can be used to construct a willingness to pay to avoid this kind of environmental risk. Additionally, the compensating wage differential can be used to calculate the value of a statistical life (Taylor, 2003). Techniques for valuing reductions in life-threatening risks will be discussed later in this chapter.

Benefit Transfer and Meta Analysis

One key to resolving the dilemma created by the possible expense of implementing the NOAA panel's recommendations may be provided by a technique called benefit transfer. Since original studies are time consuming and expensive, benefit transfer allows the estimates for the site of interest to be based upon estimates from other sites or from an earlier time period to provide the foundation for a current estimate.

Benefit transfer methods can take one of three forms: value transfers, benefit function transfers, or meta-analysis. Sometimes the actual benefit values derived from point estimates can simply be directly transferred from one context to another, usually adjusted for differences between the study site and the policy site. Function transfer involves using a previously estimated benefit function that relates site characteristics to site values. In this case, the differentiating characteristics of the site of interest are entered into the previously derived benefit function in order to derive newer, more site-specific values (Johnston et al., 2006).

Most recently, meta-analysis has been utilized. *Meta-analysis*, sometimes called the "analysis of analyses," takes empirical estimates from a sample of studies, statistically relates them to the characteristics of the studies, and calculates the degree

[8]There are many examples in this category. These are just a few.

to which the reported differences can be attributed to differences in location, subject matter, or methodology. For example, meta analysis has been used with cross sections of contingent valuation studies as a basis for isolating and quantifying the determinants of nonuse value. Once these determinants have been isolated and related to specific policy contexts, it may be possible to transfer estimates from one context to another by finding the value consistent with the new context without incurring the time and expense of conducting new surveys each time.

Benefit transfer methods have been widely used in situations for which financial, time, or data constraints preclude original analysis. Policymakers frequently look to previously published studies for data that could inform a prospective decision. Benefit transfer has the advantage of being quick and inexpensive, but the accuracy of the estimates deteriorates as the new context deviates (either temporally or spatially) further from the context used to derive the estimates.[9] Additionally, as we noted previously for contingent valuation estimates, Ehmke, Lusk, and List (2008) find that hypothetical bias varies considerably across countries.

Benefit transfer has not escaped controversy. Johnston and Rosenberger (2010) outline some of the potential problems with the use of benefit transfer, including a lack of studies that are both of sufficiently high quality and policy relevant. Additionally, many of the published studies do not provide enough information on the attributes to allow an assessment of how they might have affected the derived value.

In response to some of these concerns, a valuation inventory database has emerged. The Environmental Valuation Reference Inventory (EVRI) is an online searchable database of empirical studies on the economic value of environmental benefits and human health effects. It was specifically developed as a tool for use in benefit transfer.[10]

Using Geographic Information Systems to Enhance Valuation

Geographic information systems (GIS) are computerized mapping models and analysis tools. A GIS map is made up of layers such that many variables can be visualized simultaneously using overlays. Use of GIS to inform economic analysis is a relatively recent addition to the economist's tool kit. GIS offers a powerful collection of tools for depicting and examining spatial relationships. Most simply, GIS can be used to produce compelling measurements and graphics that communicate the spatial structure of data and analytic results with a force and clarity otherwise impossible. But the technology's real value lies in the potential it brings to ask novel questions and enrich our understanding of social and economic processes

[9]Several examples of the use of meta-analysis and benefit transfer are given in Florax et al. (2002). A critique and alternative to benefits transfer is offered in Smith et al. (2002).

[10]The database can be accessed at http://www.evri.ca/Global/HomeAnonymous.aspx.

by explicitly considering their spatial structure. Models that address environmental externalities have, almost by definition, a strong spatial component.[11]

Hedonic property valuation models have recently incorporated GIS technology. Fundamentally spatial in nature, use of GIS in hedonic property models is a natural fit. Housing prices vary systematically and predictably from neighborhood to neighborhood. Spatial characteristics, from air quality to the availability of open space, can influence property values of entire neighborhoods; if one house enjoys abundant open space or especially good air quality, it is highly likely that its neighbors do as well.

In a 2008 paper, Lewis, Bohlen, and Wilson use GIS and statistical analysis to evaluate the impacts of dams and dam removal on local property values. In a unique "experiment," they collected data on property sales for 10 years before and after the Edwards Dam on the Kennebec River in Maine was removed. The Edwards Dam was the first federally licensed hydropower dam in the United States to be removed primarily for the purpose of river restoration. They also collected data on property sales approximately 20 miles upstream where two dams were still in place. GIS technology enhanced this study by facilitating the calculation of the distance from each home to both the river and the nearby dams. Lewis et al., 2008 found that homeowners pay a price penalty for living close to a dam. In other words, willingness to pay for identical housing is higher the further away from the dam the house is located. They also found that the penalty near the Edwards Dam site dropped to nearly zero after the dam was removed. Interestingly, the penalty upstream also dropped significantly. While a penalty for homes close to the dams upstream remains, it falls after the downstream dam was removed. Can you think of reasons why? [12]

Example 4.3 shows how the use of GIS can enable hedonic property value models to investigate how the view from a particular piece of property might affect its value.

Averting Expenditures. A final example of an indirect observable method involves examining "averting or defensive expenditures." Averting expenditures are those designed to reduce the damage caused by pollution by taking some kind of averting or defensive action. An example would be to install indoor air purifiers in response to an influx of polluted air or to rely on bottled water as a response to the pollution of local drinking water supplies. Since people would not normally spend more to prevent a problem than would be caused by the problem itself, averting expenditures can provide a lower-bound estimate of the damage caused by pollution. They also cause a disproportionate hardship on poor households that cannot affort such coping expenditures. Example 4.4 illustrates the impact of coping or averting expenditures on residents of Kathmandu, Nepal.

---

[11]For examples see Bateman et al., (2002) who describe the contributions of GIS in incorporating spatial dimensions into economic analysis, including benefit-cost analysis and Clapp et al., (1997) who discuss the potential contributions GIS can make for urban and real estate economics.

[12]Interestingly, after this study was complete, one of the two upstream dams, the Fort Halifax Dam, was removed in July 2008 after years of litigation about its removal.

EXAMPLE 4.3

Using GIS to Inform Hedonic Property Values: Visualizing the Data

GIS offer economists and others powerful tools for analyzing spatial data and spatial relationships. For nonmarket valuation, GIS has proven to be especially helpful in enhancing hedonic property value models by incorporating both the proximity of environmental characteristics and their size or amount. GIS studies have also allowed for the incorporation of variables that reflect nearby types and diversity of land use.

Geo-coding housing transactions assign a latitude and longitude coordinate to each sale. GIS allows other spatial data, such as land use, watercourses, and census data, to be "layered" on top of the map. By drawing a circle around each house of the desired circumference, GIS can help us to calculate the amount of each amenity that is in that circle as well as the density and types of people who live there. Numerous census data are available on variables such as income, age, education, crime rates, and commuting time. GIS also makes it relatively easy to calculate straight-line distances to desired (or undesired) locations, such as parks, lakes, schools, or landfills.

In a 2002 paper entitled "Out of Sight, Out of Mind? Using GIS to Incorporate Visibility in Hedonic Property Value Models," Paterson and Boyle use GIS to measure the extent to which visibility measures affect house prices in Connecticut. In their study, visibility is measured as the percentage of land visible within one kilometer of the property, both in total and broken out for various land use categories. Finally, they added variables that measured the percentage of area in agriculture or in forest, or covered by water within one kilometer of each house.

They find that visibility is indeed an important environmental variable in explaining property values, but the nature of the viewshed matters. While simply having a view is not a significant determinant of property values, viewing certain types of land uses is. Proximity to development reduces property values only if the development is visible, for example, suggesting that out of sight, really does mean out of mind! They conclude that any analysis that omits variables that reflect nearby environmental conditions can lead to misleading or incorrect conclusions about the impacts of land use on property values. GIS is a powerful tool for helping a researcher include these important variables.

Source: Paterson, Robert, & Boyle, Kevin. (2002). Out of sight, out of mind? Using GIS to incorporate visibility in hedonic property value models." *Land Economics, 78*(3), 417–425.

Challenges

Aggregation. As you have probably figured out by now, nonmarket valuation faces several challenges. One challenge involves the aggregation of estimated values into a total value that can be used in benefit-cost analysis. How large is the relevant population? Do benefits change with distance to the resource in question? Debate 4.3 explores some of these challenging issues.

EXAMPLE 4.4

Valuing the Reliability of Water Supplies: Coping Expenditures in Kathmandu Valley, Nepal

Nepal, like many other poor developing countries, experiences chronic shortages of safe drinking water. The Kathmandu Valley is no exception. The National Water Supply Corporation serves 70% of the population, but the public water supply is neither reliable nor safe. Shortages are frequent and the water quality is frequently contaminated with fecal coliform and nitrogen-ammonia (Pattanyak, et al. 2005).

How much should be invested in improving water quality depends on how valuable clean water is to this population. Quantifying those benefits requires establishing how much residents would be willing to pay for cleaner water. One pathway for quantifying willingness to pay in this context can be found in analyzing how much households spend to cope with the unreliable water supply. It turns out they purchase water from water vendors, collect water from public taps, invest in wells or storage tanks, purchase filtration systems, and/or boil water. All of these coping mechanisms have both financial cost and a cost associated with the time devoted to coping. Using coping costs as a proxy for willingness to pay can serve as the basis for constructing a lower-bound estimate of the demand curve for water provision in settings where other more direct valuation strategies are simply not practical to implement.

In a survey of 1500 households in five municipalities, researchers found that for households in the Kathmandu Valley, coping or averting behaviors cost the average household about 1 percent of monthly income, most of this attributed to the time spent collecting water. The authors note that these coping costs are almost twice as much as the current monthly bills paid to the water utility.

Some demographic factors were found to have influenced household coping expenditures.

- Wealthier households were found to have higher coping expenditures. As the authors note, this confirms the intuition that relatively rich households have more resources and therefore invest more in water treatment, storage, and purchases.
- More educated respondents also had higher coping costs, perhaps because these households better understood the risks of contaminated water.

If, as suggested by these two findings, the poor face higher financial and educational barriers in their quest for cleaner water, water policy in this region faces an environmental justice issue as well as an efficiency issue.

Even though averting expenditures represent only a lower bound of willingness to pay for water supply, they can provide valuable information for the estimation of benefits of water provision. In addition, these data imply that the common assertion that in poor countries the costs of supplying clean water are so high that they necessarily exceed the benefits received by water users may be a misconception—the value of water in this valley was found to be at least twice the current per unit charge even when the lower bound estimating technique was used.

Source: Pattanayak, Subhrendu K., Yang, Jui-Chen, Whittington, Dale, & Bal Kumar, K.C. (2005). Coping with unreliable public water supplies: Averting expenditures by households in Kathmandu, Nepal. *Water Resources Research, 41*(2), doi:10.1029/2003WR002443.

DEBATE 4.3 Distance Decay in Willingness to Pay: When and How Much Does Location Matter?

One challenge in performing benefit-cost analysis is accurately choosing the "extent of the market." The extent of the market refers to ***who benefits*** from the resource in question. Loomis (1996) argues that not accounting for the full extent of the market (i.e., including everyone who gains some benefit) can lead to **under**estimates of willingness to pay and aggregate value.

On the other hand, a more inclusive design might include respondents with vastly lower willingness to pay simply because of their location. For some resources, distant respondents have a lower willingness to pay for its improvement. It seems reasonable to expect, for example, that the benefits from a reduction in river pollution to an individual household would probably depend on its proximity to the river. Those closest to the river place the highest value on the improvement. In other words, since it seems reasonable to expect that some types of values do experience a "distance decay," in aggregating benefits this deterioration should certainly be taken into account.

Bateman et al. (2006) argue that not accounting for distance decay can lead to **over**estimates of willingness to pay. Those who are further away still benefit and should be counted, but at some kind of decreasing rate. Recently, the number of state preference studies (contingent valuation and choice experiments) that focus on distance decay has increased so we have learned more about it.

What do these studies say about the circumstances that give rise to distance decay?

Interestingly, the empirical evidence suggests that both the type of value being measured (use or non-use value) as well as the type of willingness to pay question (compensating versus equivalent variation) matter. Hanley et al. (2003) and Bateman et al. (2006) both find that distance decay does arise for use value, but very little or not at all for nonuse values. If, however, some of the current nonusers become users under the proposed scenario, their valuation would experience some distance decay. This result follows the intuition that if the willingness to pay question is framed as a marginal improvement in quality (compensating variation), then some of the nonusers might become users and that possibility would be reflected in their valuations. If the question is framed as equivalent variation (willingness to pay to avoid loss), nonuser valuations experience no distance decay, since they will remain nonusers.

These studies suggest that spatial patterns in nonmarket values have important implications not only for how benefit-cost analysis should be conducted and interpreted but also for how that analysis affects the policy evaluations. Different design choices as to the extent of the market and whether to aggregate across particular political or economic jurisdiction can lead to very different results. As Schaafsma et al. (2012) suggest, these spatial patterns should be taken into account both when drawing samples for willingness to pay surveys, and when aggregating the results.

Sources: Batemen, Ian, Day, Brett H., Georgiou, Stavros, & Lake, Ian. (September 2006). The aggregation of environmental benefit values: Welfare measures, distance decay and total WTP. Discussion paper; Hanley, Nick, Schlapfer, Felix, & Spurgeon, James (2003). Aggregating the benefits of environmental improvements: distance-decay functions for use and nonuse values. *Journal of Environmental Management, 68*, 297–304; Loomis, John B. (1996). How large is the extent of the market for public goods: evidence from a nationwide contingent valuation survey. *Applied Economics,* 28, 779–782; Schaafsma, Marije, Brouwer, Roy, & John Rose. (2012). Directional heterogeneity in WTP models for environmental valuation. *Ecological Economics, 79*(1), 21–31

Partial Values. Another large challenge for nonmarket valuation is that most studies only capture a portion of the total value of an environmental good or service. For example, ecosystems are bundles of values, but the methods outlined in this chapter are only capable of capturing a portion of the value.

Figure 4.1 illustrates the different methods environmental economists use to capture different types of value. Each of these methods relies on different data and, many times, different experts. Rarely is the available time or money sufficient to apply all methods to a particular question.

Debate 4.4 illustrates the challenges and importance of attempts to capture the total economic value by examining a specific case study—polar bears in Canada.

Valuing Human Life

One fascinating public policy area where these various approaches have been applied is in the valuation of human life. Many government programs, from those controlling hazardous pollutants in the workplace or in drinking water, to those improving nuclear power plant safety, are designed to save human life as well as to reduce illness. How resources should be allocated among these programs depends crucially on the value of human life. In order to answer this question, an estimate of the value of that life to society is necessary and federal regulations require such estimates for benefit-cost analysis. How is life to be valued?

The simple answer, of course, is that life is priceless, but that turns out to be not very helpful. Because the resources used to prevent loss of life are scarce, choices must be made. The economic approach to valuing lifesaving reductions in

FIGURE 4.1 Different Methods, Different Experts, Different Data

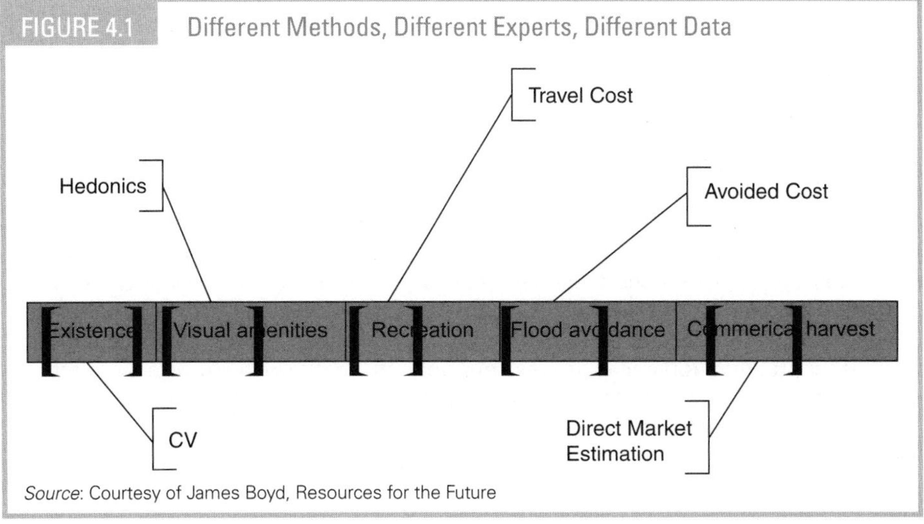

Source: Courtesy of James Boyd, Resources for the Future

DEBATE 4.4 What Is the Value of a Polar Bear?

Because polar bears are such a charismatic species, they have obviously attracted lots of popular support, but exactly how valuable are they? In 2011, the Canadian government issued a report in which it attempted to estimate the different socio-economic values of polar bears in Canada.

They commissioned the study in part to determine the economic impact of adding the polar bear to a list of at-risk species. This study represents one of the few studies to try to estimate the value of polar bears and the only one that tries to do it in a comprehensive fashion.

The authors tried to capture active use values (subsistence and sport hunting, polar bear viewing, and value in scientific research), as well as passive use values (existence and bequest values). Multiple nonmarket valuation methods were used in this study including travel cost (viewing), market prices (hunting), meta-analysis and benefit transfer (passive-use values). Time and budgetary constraints precluded the use of stated preference methods such as contingent valuation or choice experiments. The summary of their findings is reproduced in the figure below. Note that the direct use values actually comprise a relatively small portion of the total value.

An effort to document the value of a species like this produces a value that is no doubt much closer to the truth than the default value of zero, but how close are these numbers to the true value? There are several caveats to consider:

- Consider the calculation of the value of polar bear meat. For this the cost of the next best substitute, which in this case was beef (for humans) and dog food was used. One could certainly argue for alternatives.
- Sport values were estimated using the benefit transfer method. Recall the challenges for using benefit transfer, in particular for a unique species like the polar bear. The study closest to this one was conducted in 1989 and focused on big game and grizzly bear hunting. For the polar bear study, the 1989 values were translated into 2009 dollars. The authors suggest their number might be an underestimate since hunting for a polar bear is such a unique experience. On the other hand, they also acknowledge that the number could just as easily be an overestimate if the charismatic image of the polar bear reduces willingness to pay for hunting.
- Finally, passive-use values were also calculated using benefit transfer. Since no study has been done on the preservation value of the polar bear in Canada, the researchers used a meta-analysis of species at risk (Richardson & Loomis 2009). While that study calculated a total economic value, for the polar bear study the benefit transfer was specifically designed to capture only preservation value. It was relatively straightforward to remove direct uses (visitors) from the transferred value, but not the indirect use benefits such as scientific value.

Using any of these values as inputs into others creates a potential to double count, a common mistake that will be discussed further in Chapter 13. In fact,

FIGURE 4.2 Monetary Values Associated with Polar Bears in Canada, by Value Category (Aggregate Amounts for Canada)

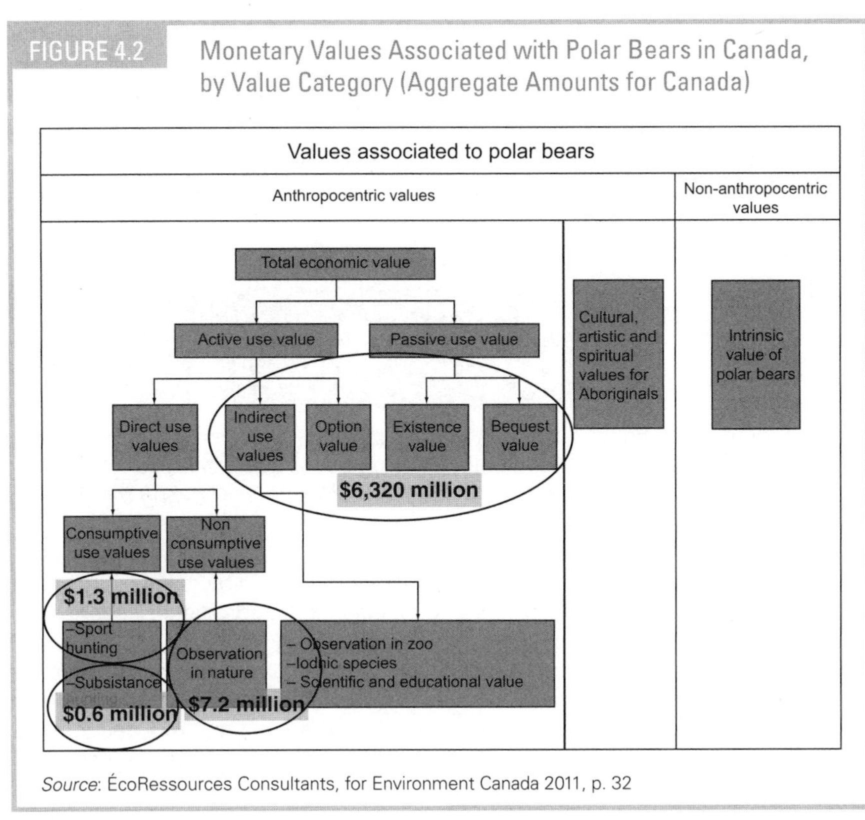

Source: ÉcoRessources Consultants, for Environment Canada 2011, p. 32

scientific values were calculated separately for the polar bear study as well as being included in the preservation value estimated via benefit transfer. As such, these numbers could overestimate the value.

What would you be willing to pay to protect the polar bear? As we have seen in this chapter, these types of questions are challenging to answer.

Source: ÉcoRessources Consultants, "Evidence of the Socio-Economic Importance of Polar Bears for Canada," for Environment Canada, 2011. Full report is accessible at http://www.registrelep.gc.ca/document/default_e.cfm?documentID=2307; Richardson, Leslie, & Loomis, John. Total economic valuation of endangered species: A summary and comparison of the United States and the rest of the world estimates. *Conserving and Valuing Ecosystem Services and Biodiversity: Economic, Institutional and Social Challenges*, K. N. Ninan, ed., Earthscan, 2009.

environmental risk is to calculate the change in the probability of death resulting from the reduction in environmental risk and to place a value on the change. Thus, it is not life itself that is being valued, but rather a reduction in the probability that some segment of the population could be expected to die earlier than otherwise. This *value of statistical life* (VSL) represents an individual's willingness to pay for small changes in mortality risks. It does not represent a willingness to pay to prevent certain death. It is measured as the "marginal rate of substitution between mortality risk and money (i.e., other goods and services)" (Cameron 2011). Debate 4.5 examines the controversy associated with valuing changes in these mortality risks.

It is possible to translate the value derived from this procedure into an "implied value of human life." This is accomplished by dividing the amount each individual is willing to pay for a specific reduction in the probability of death by

DEBATE 4.5 Is Valuing Human Life Immoral?

In 2004, economist Frank Ackerman and lawyer Lisa Heinzerling teamed up to write a book that questions the morality of using benefit-cost analysis to evaluate regulations designed to protect human life. In *Priceless: On Knowing the Price of Everything and the Value of Nothing* (2004), they argue that benefit-cost analysis is immoral because it represents a retreat from the traditional standard that all citizens have an absolute right to be free from harm caused by pollution. When it justifies a regulation that will allow some pollution-induced deaths, benefit-cost analysis violates this absolute right.

Economist Maureen Cropper responds that it would be immoral not to consider the benefits of lifesaving measures. Resources are scarce and they must be allocated so as to produce the greatest good. If all pollution were reduced to zero, even if that were possible, the cost would be extremely high and the resources to cover that cost would have to be diverted from other beneficial uses. Professor Cropper also suggests that it would be immoral to impose costs on people about which they have no say—for example, the costs of additional pollution controls—without at least trying to consider what choices people would make themselves. Like it or not, hard choices must be made.

Cropper also points out that people are always making decisions that recognize a trade-off between the cost of more protection and the health consequences of not taking the protection. Thinking in terms of trade-offs should be a familiar concept. She points out that people drive faster to save time, thereby increasing their risk of dying. They also decide how much money to spend on medicines to lower their risk of disease or they may take jobs that pose morbidity or even mortality risks.

In her response to Ackerman and Heinzerling, Cropper acknowledges that benefit-cost analysis has its flaws and that it should never be the only decision-making guide. Nonetheless, she argues that it does add useful information to the process and throwing that information away could prove to be detrimental to the very people that Ackerman and Heinzerling seek to protect.

Sources: Ackerman, Frank, & Heinzerling, Lisa. (2004). *Priceless: On Knowing the Price of Everything and the Value of Nothing.* New York: The New Press; Ackerman, Frank. (2004). Morality, cost-benefit and the price of life. *Environmental Forum, 21*(5), 46–47; Maureen Cropper. (2004). Immoral not to weigh benefits against costs. *Environmental Forum, 21*(5), 47–48.

the probability reduction. Suppose, for example, that a particular environmental policy could be expected to reduce the average concentration of a toxic substance to which one million people are exposed. Suppose further that this reduction in exposure could be expected to reduce the risk of death from 1 out of 100,000 to 1 out of 150,000. This implies that the number of expected deaths would fall from 10 to 6.67 in the exposed population as a result of this policy. If each of the one million persons exposed is willing to pay $5 for this risk reduction (for a total of $5 million), then the implied value of a statistical life is approximately $1.5 million ($5 million divided by 3.33). Or alternatively, the VSL can be calculated using the change in WTP divided by the change in risk. For this example, that would be $5 divided by the change in risk of death (1/100,000–1/150,000), or $1.5 million. Thus, the VSL is capturing the rate of trade-off between money and a very small risk of death.

What actual values have been derived from these methods? One early survey (Viscusi, 1996) of a large number of studies examining reductions in a number of life-threatening risks found that most implied values for human life (in 1986 dollars) were between $3 million and $7 million. This same survey went on to suggest that the most appropriate estimates were probably closer to the $5 million estimate. In other words, all government programs resulting in risk reductions costing less than $5 million per life saved would be justified in benefit-cost terms. Those costing more might or might not be justified, depending on the appropriate value of a life saved in the particular risk context being examined.

In a meta-analysis, Mrozek and Taylor (2002) found much lower values for VSL. Using over 40 labor market studies, their research suggests that a range of $1.5 million to $2.5 million for VSL is more appropriate. What about age? Does the VSL change with age? Apparently so. Aldy and Viscusi (2008) find an inverted U-shape relationship between VSL and age. Specifically, using the hedonic wage model, they estimate a VSL of $3.7 million for persons ages 18–24, $9.7 million for persons ages 35–44, and $3.4 million for persons ages 55–62. According to their study, VSL rises with age, peaks, and then declines.

What about the value of statistical life across populations or countries with different incomes? Most agencies in the United States use VSLs between $5 million and $8 million. These estimates are based largely on hedonic wage studies that have been conducted in the United States or in other high-income countries.[13] How might those results be translated into settings featuring populations with lower incomes?

Adjustments for income are typically derived using an estimate of the income elasticity of demand. Recall that income elasticity is the percent change in consumption given a 1 percent change in income. Hammitt and Robinson (2011) note that applying income elasticities, derived for countries like the United States, might result in nonsensical VSL estimates if blindly applied to lower-income countries. While US agencies typically assume a 0.4 to 0.6 percent change in

[13]Many labor market estimates of VSL average near $7 million (Viscusi, 2008).

VSL for a 1 percent change in real income over time, elasticities closer to 1.0 or higher are more realistic for transfers of these values between high- and low-income countries. Using the higher income elasticity number is merited since willingness to pay for mortality risk reduction as a percentage of income drops at very low incomes; what limited income is available in poorer households is reserved for basic needs.

How have health, safety, and environmental regulations lived up to this recommendation? As Table 4.4 suggests, not very well. A very large number of regulations listed in that table could be justified only if the value of a life saved were much higher than the upper value of $7 million.

TABLE 4.4 The Cost of Risk-Reducing Regulations

	Agency Year and Status	Initial Annual Risk	Annual Lives Saved	Cost Per Life Saved (Millions of 1984 $)
Unvented Space Heaters	CPSC 1980 F	2.7 in 10^5	63.000	$.10
Cabin Fire Protection	FAA 1985 F	6.5 in 10^8	15.000	.20
Passive Restraints/Belts	NHTSA 1984 F	9.1 in 10^5	1,850.000	.30
Seat Cushion Flammability	FAA 1984 F	1.6 in 10^7	37.000	.60
Floor Emergency Lighting	FAA 1984 F	2.2 in 10^8	5.000	.70
Concrete and Masonry Construction	OSHA 1988 F	1.4 in 10^5	6.500	1.40
Hazard Communication	OSHA 1983 F	4.0 in 10^5	200.000	1.80
Benzene/Fugitive Emissions	EPA 1984 F	2.1 in 10^4	0.310	2.80

	Agency Year and Status	Initial Annual Risk	Annual Lives Saved	Cost Per Life Saved (Millions of 1984 $)
Radionuclides/ Uranium Mines	EPA 1984 F	1.4 in 10^4	1.100	6.90
Benzene	OSHA 1987 F	8.8 in 10^4	3.800	17.10
Asbestos	EPA 1989 F	2.9 in 10^5	10.000	104.20
Benzene/Storage	EPA 1984 R	6.0 in 10^7	0.043	202.00
Radionuclides/ DOE Facilities	EPA 1984 R	4.3 in 10^6	0.001	210.00
Radionuclides/ Elemental Phosphorous	EPA 1984 R	1.4 in 10^5	0.046	270.00
Benzene/ Ethylbenzenol Styrene	EPA 1984 R	2.0 in 10^6	0.006	483.00
Arsenic/Low-Arsenic Copper	EPA 1986 R	2.6 in 10^4	0.090	764.00
Benzene/Maleic Anhydride	EPA 1984 R	1.1 in 10^6	0.029	820.00
Land Disposal	EPA 1988 F	2.3 in 10^8	2.520	3,500.00
Formaldehyde	OSHA 1987 F	6.8 in 10^4	0.010	72,000.00

Note: In the "Agency Year and Status" column, R and F represent Rejected and Final rule, respectively. "Initial Annual Risk" indicates annual deaths per exposed population; an exposed population of 10^3 is 1000, 10^4 is 10,000, and so on.

Source: Data from Tables 1 and 2 from "Economic Foundation of the Current Regulatory Reform Efforts" by W. Kip Viscusi, from *Journal of Economic Perspectives, 10*(3) Summer 1996, pp. 119–134.

Summary: Nonmarket Valuation Today

In this chapter, we have examined the most prominent, but certainly not the only techniques available to supply policymakers with the information needed to implement efficient policy. Finding the total economic value of the service flows requires estimating three components of value: (1) use value, (2) option value, and (3) nonuse or passive-use value.

Our review of these various techniques included direct observation, contingent valuation, contingent choice experiments, travel cost, hedonic property and wage studies, and averting or defensive expenditures. When time or funding precludes original research, benefits transfer or meta-analysis provides alternate methods for estimation of values. Examples of actual studies using these techniques were presented.

In January 2011, a panel of experts gathered at the annual meeting of the American Economics Association to reflect on nonmarket valuation 20 years after the *Exxon Valdez* spill and, unknown to any of them when the panelists were asked to participate, 8 months after the *Deepwater Horizon* spill. The panelists had all worked on estimation of damages from the *Exxon Valdez* spill. The consensus among panelists was that while many of the issues with bias have been addressed in the literature, many unanswered questions remain and some areas still need work. While they all agreed that it is "hard to underestimate the powerful need for values" (i.e., some number is definitely better than no number), and we now have in place methods that can be easily utilized by all researchers, they also emphasized several problem areas. First, the value of time in travel cost models has not been resolved. What is the opportunity cost of time if you are unemployed, for example?

Second, in discussing other revealed preference methods, they asked the question, "How do the recent numerous foreclosures in the real estate market affect hedonic property value model assumptions?"[14] Third, choice experiments do not resolve all of the potential problems with contingent valuation. While choice experiments do seem to better represent actual market choices, some of the issues that arise in contingent valuation, such as the choice of the payment vehicle, also arise with choice experiments. In addition, some new challenges, such as how the sequencing of choices in choice experiments might affect outcomes, arise. The panel highlighted how this area of research has been enhanced by the field of behavioral economics, an emerging research area that combines economics and psychology to examine human behavior. And finally, they suggested that the NOAA panel recommendations be updated to reflect the body of new research.

Discussion Questions

1. Certain environmental laws prohibit the EPA from considering the costs of meeting various standards when the levels of the standards are set. Is this a good example of "putting first things first" or simply an unjustifiable waste of resources? Why?

---

[14]This question was taken up by another panel of experts at the 2012 Association of Environmental and Resource Economics annual conference and later published by Boyle et al. (2012).

Self-Test Exercises

1. In Mark A. Cohen, "The Costs and Benefits of Oil Spill Prevention and Enforcement," *Journal of Environmental Economics and Management* Vol. 13 (June 1986), an attempt was made to quantify the marginal benefits and marginal costs of US Coast Guard enforcement activity in the area of oil spill prevention. His analysis suggests (p. 185) that the marginal per-gallon benefit from the current level of enforcement activity is $7.50, while the marginal per-gallon cost is $5.50. Assuming these numbers are correct, would you recommend that the Coast Guard increase, decrease, or hold at the current level their enforcement activity? Why?
2. In Table 4.4, Professor Kip Viscusi estimates that the cost per life saved by current government risk-reducing programs ranges from $100,000 for unvented space heaters to $72 billion for a proposed standard to reduce occupational exposure to formaldehyde.
   a. Assuming these values to be correct, how might efficiency be enhanced in these two programs?
   b. Should the government strive to equalize the marginal costs per life saved across all lifesaving programs?
3. a. Suppose that hedonic wage studies indicate a willingness to pay $50 per person for a reduction in the risk of a premature death from an environmental hazard of 1/100,000. If the exposed population is four million people, what is the implied value of a statistical life?
   b. Suppose that an impending environmental regulation to control that hazard is expected to reduce the risk of premature death from 6/100,000 to 2/100,000 per year in that exposed population of four million people. Your boss asks you to tell her what is the maximum this regulation could cost and still have the benefits be at least as large as the costs. What is your answer?

Further Reading

Bateman, Ian J., Lovett, Andrew A., & Brainard. Julii S. *Applied Environmental Economics: A GIS Approach to Cost-Benefit Analysis* (Cambridge: Cambridge University Press, 2005). Uses GIS to examine land use change and valuation.

Bennett, Jeff (Ed.). *The International Handbook on Non-Market Envrironmental Valuation*, Edward Elgar, 2011. An excellent compilation on nonmarket valuation.

Boardman, Anthony E., Greenberg, David H., Vining, Aidan R., & Weimer, David L. (2005). *Cost-Benefit Analysis: Concepts and Practice*, 3rd ed. Upper Saddle River, NJ: Prentice-Hall. An excellent basic text on the use of cost-benefit analysis.

Champ, Patricia A., Boyle, Kevin J., & Brown, T. C. (2003). *A Primer on Nonmarket Valuation*. Dordrecht: Kluwer Academic Publishers. A thorough overview of nonmarket valuation methods.

Costanza, R. et al. (1998). "The Value of the World's Ecosystem Services and Natural Capital" (Reprinted from *Nature* Vol. 387, p. 253, 1997), *Ecological Economics*, Vol. 25, No. 1: 3–15. An ambitious, but ultimately flawed, attempt to place an economic value on ecosystem services. This issue of *Ecological Economics* also contains a number of articles that demonstrate some of the flaws.

Mitchell, Robert Cameron, & Carson, Richard T. (1989). *Using Surveys to Value Public Goods: The Contingent Valuation Method.* Washington, DC: Resources for the Future. A comprehensive examination of contingent valuation research with brief summaries of representative studies and recommendations for survey design.

Whitehead, John, Haab, Tim, & Huang, Ju-Chin (Eds). (2011). *Preference Data for Environmental Valuation: Combining Revealed and Stated Approaches*, Taylor and Francis. A compilation of articles that use more than one valuation method or novel applications of data combinations written by nonmarket valuation economists.

Additional References and Historically Significant References are available on this book's Companion Website: http://www.routledgetextbooks.com/textbooks/9780133479690

Dynamic Efficiency and Sustainable Development

5

We usually see only the things we are looking for—so much so that we sometimes see them where they are not.

—Eric Hoffer, *The Passionate State of Mind* (1993)

Introduction

In previous chapters, we have developed two specific means for identifying environmental problems. The first, static efficiency, allows us to evaluate those circumstances where time is not a crucial aspect of the allocation problem. Typical examples might include allocating resources such as water or solar energy where next year's flow is independent of this year's choices. The second, more complicated criterion, dynamic efficiency, is suitable for those circumstances where time is a crucial aspect. The combustion of depletable resources such as oil would be a typical example, since supplies used now are unavailable for future generations.

After defining these criteria and showing how they could be operationally invoked, we demonstrated how helpful they can be. They are useful not only in identifying environmental problems and ferreting out their behavioral sources, but also in providing a basis for identifying types of remedies. These criteria even help design optimal policy instruments for restoring some sense of balance between the economy and the environment.

But the fact that these are powerful and useful tools in the quest for a sense of balance does not imply that they are the only criteria in which we should be interested. In a general sense, the efficiency criteria are designed to prevent wasteful use of environmental and natural resources. That is a desirable attribute, but it is not the only possible desirable attribute. We might care, for example, not only about the value of the environment (the size of the pie), but also how this value is shared (the size of each piece to recipients). In other words, fairness or justice concerns should accompany efficiency considerations.

In this chapter, we investigate one particular fairness concern—the treatment of future generations. We begin by considering a specific, ethically challenging situation—the allocation of a depletable resource over time.

Specifically we shall trace out the temporal allocation of a depletable resource that satisfies the dynamic efficiency criterion and show how this allocation is affected by changes in the discount rate. To lay the groundwork for our evaluation of fairness, we define what we mean by intertemporal fairness. Finally, we consider not only how this theoretical definition can be made operationally measurable, but also how it relates to dynamic efficiency. To what degree is dynamic efficiency compatible with intergenerational fairness?

A Two-Period Model

Dynamic efficiency balances present and future uses of a depletable resource by maximizing the present value of the net benefits derived from its use. This implies a particular allocation of the resource across time. We can illustrate the properties of this allocation with the aid of a simple numerical example. We begin with the simplest of models—deriving the dynamic efficient allocation across two time periods. In subsequent chapters, we show how these conclusions generalize to longer time periods and to more complicated situations.

Assume that we have a fixed supply of a depletable resource to allocate between two periods. Assume further that the demand function is the same in each of the two periods, the marginal willingness to pay is given by the formula $P = 8 - 0.4q$ and marginal cost of supplying that resource is constant at $2 per unit (see Figure 5.1).

Note that if the total supply were 30 or greater, and we were concerned only with these two periods, an efficient allocation would produce 15 units in each period, *regardless of the discount rate*. Thirty units would be sufficient to cover the demand in both periods; the consumption in Period 1 would not reduce the consumption in Period 2. In this case the static efficiency criterion is sufficient because the allocations are not temporally interdependent.

FIGURE 5.1 The Allocation of an Abundant Depletable Resource: (a) Period 1 and (b) Period 2

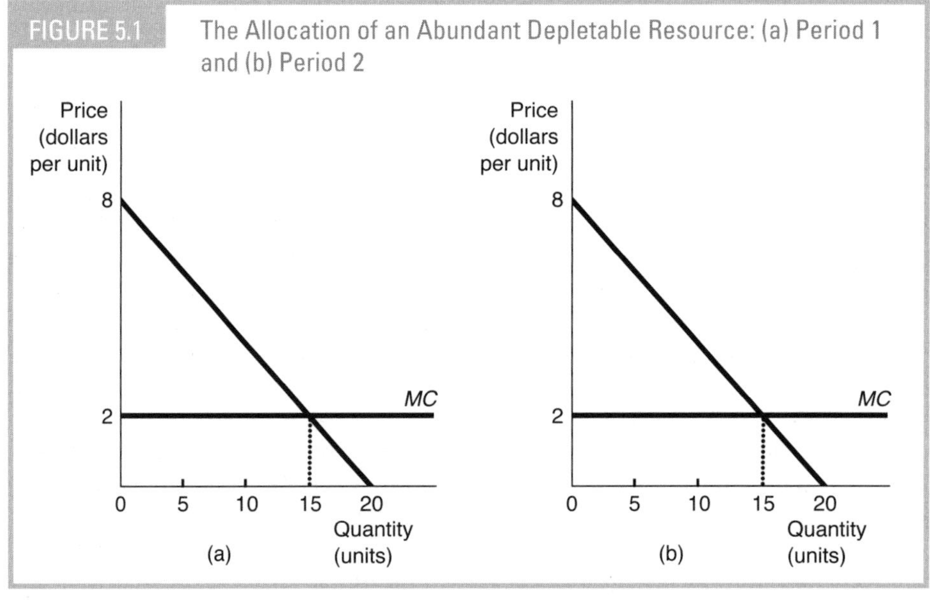

Examine, however, what happens when the available supply is less than 30. Suppose it equals 20. How do we determine the efficient allocation? According to the dynamic efficiency criterion, the efficient allocation is the one that maximizes the present value of the net benefit. The present value of the net benefit for both periods is simply the sum of the present values in each of the two periods. To take a concrete example, consider the present value of a particular allocation: 15 units in the first period and 5 in the second. How would we compute the present value of that allocation?

The present value in the first period would be that portion of the geometric area under the demand curve that is over the supply curve—$45.00.[1] The present value in the second period is that portion of the area under the demand curve that is over the supply curve from the origin to the five units produced multiplied by $1/(1 + r)$. If we use $r = 0.10$, then the present value of the net benefit received in the second period is $22.73,[2] and the present value of the net benefits for the 2 years is $67.73.

Having learned how to find the present value of net benefits for any allocation, how does one find the allocation that *maximizes* present value? One way, with the aid of a computer, is to try all possible combinations of q_1 and q_2 that sum to 20. The one yielding the maximum present value of net benefits can then be selected. That is tedious and, for those who have the requisite mathematics, unnecessary.

The dynamically efficient allocation of this resource has to satisfy the condition that the present value of the marginal net benefit from the last unit in Period 1 equals the present value of the marginal net benefit in Period 2 (see appendix at the end of this chapter). Even without mathematics, this principle is easy to understand, as can be demonstrated with the use of a simple graphical representation of the two-period allocation problem.

Figure 5.2 depicts the present value of the marginal net benefit for each of the two periods. The net benefit curve for Period 1 is to be read from left to right. The net benefit curve intersects the vertical axis at $6; demand would be zero at $8 and the marginal cost is $2, so the difference (marginal net benefit) is $6. The marginal net benefit for the first period goes to zero at 15 units because, at that quantity, the willingness to pay for that unit exactly equals its cost.

The only challenging aspect of drawing the graph involves constructing the curve for the present value of net benefits in Period 2. Two aspects are worth noting. First, the zero axis for the Period 2 net benefits is on the right, rather than the left, side. Therefore, increases in Period 2 are recorded from right to left. By drawing it this way, all points along the horizontal axis yield a total of 20 units allocated between the two periods. Any point on that axis picks a unique allocation between the two periods.[3]

Second, the present value of the marginal benefit curve for Period 2 intersects the vertical axis at a different point than does the comparable curve in Period 1.

---

[1]The height of the triangle is $6 [$8–$2] and the base is 15 units. The area is therefore (1/2)($6)(15) = $45.

[2]The undiscounted net benefit is $25. The calculation is $(6 - 2) \times 5 + 1/2(8 - 6) \times 5 = \$25$. The discounted net benefit is therefore $25/1.10 = 22.73$.

[3]Note that the sum of the two allocations in Figure 5.2 is always 20. The left-hand axis represents an allocation of all 20 units to Period 2 and the right-hand axis represents an allocation entirely to Period 1.

FIGURE 5.2 The Dynamically Efficient Allocation

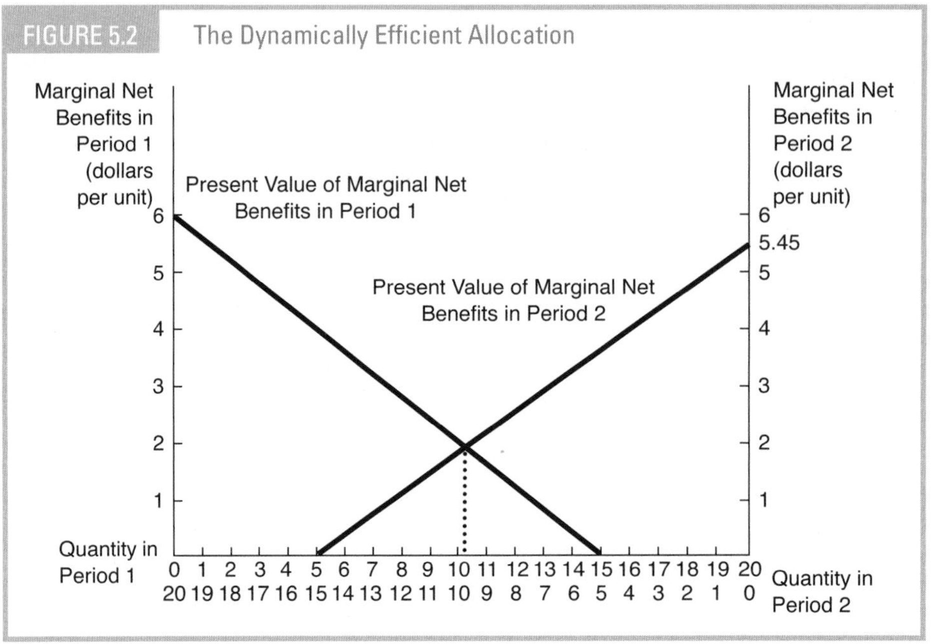

Can you see why? This intersection is lower because the marginal benefits in the second period need to be discounted (multiplied by $1/(1 + r)$) to convert them into present value form since they occur 1 year later. Thus, with the 10 percent discount rate we are using, the marginal net benefit is \$6 and the present value is \$6/1.10 = \$5.45. Note that larger discount rates ($r > .10$) would rotate the Period 2 marginal benefit curve around the point of zero net benefit ($q_1 = 5, q_2 = 15$) toward the right-hand axis. We shall use this fact in a moment.

The efficient allocation is now readily identifiable as the point where the two curves representing present value of marginal net benefits cross (since that is the allocation where the two marginal present values of net benefits for the two periods are equal). The total present value of net benefits is then the area under the marginal net benefit curve for Period 1 up to the efficient allocation, plus the area under the present value of the marginal net benefit curve for Period 2 from the right-hand axis up to its efficient allocation. Because we have an efficient allocation, the sum of these two areas is maximized.[4]

Since we have developed our efficiency criteria independent of an institutional context, these criteria are equally appropriate for evaluating resource allocations generated by markets, government rationing, or even the whims of a dictator. While *any* efficient allocation method must take scarcity into account, the details of precisely how that is done depend on the context.

---

[4]Demonstrate that this point is the maximum by first allocating slightly more to Period 2 (and therefore less to Period 1) and showing that the total area decreases. Conclude by allocating slightly less to Period 2 and showing that, in this case as well, total area declines.

Intertemporal scarcity imposes an opportunity cost that we henceforth refer to as the *marginal user cost*. When resources are scarce, greater current use diminishes future opportunities. The marginal user cost is the present value of these forgone opportunities at the margin. To be more specific, uses of those resources, which would have been appropriate in the absence of scarcity, may no longer be appropriate once scarcity is present. Using large quantities of water to keep lawns lush and green may be wholly appropriate for an area with sufficiently large replenishable water supplies, but quite inappropriate when it denies drinking water to future generations. Failure to take the higher scarcity value of water into account in the present would lead to inefficiency due to the additional cost resulting from the increased scarcity imposed on the future. This additional marginal value created by scarcity is the marginal user cost.

We can illustrate this concept by returning to our numerical example. With 30 or more units, each period would be allocated 15 units, the resource would not be scarce, and the marginal user cost would be zero.

With 20 units, however, scarcity emerges. No longer can 15 units be allocated to each period; each period will have to be allocated less than would be the case without scarcity. Due to this scarcity, the marginal user cost for this case is not zero. As can be seen from Figure 5.2, the present value of the marginal user cost, the additional value created by scarcity, is graphically represented by the vertical distance between the quantity (horizontal) axis and the intersection of the two present-value curves. Notice that the present value of the marginal net benefit for Period 1 is equal to the present value of the marginal net benefit for Period 2. This common value can either be read off the graph or determined more precisely, as demonstrated in the chapter appendix, to be \$1.905.

We can make this concept even more concrete by considering its use in a market context. An efficient market would have to consider not only the marginal cost of extraction for this resource but also the marginal user cost. Whereas in the absence of scarcity, the price would equal only the marginal cost of extraction, with scarcity, the price would equal the sum of marginal extraction cost and marginal user cost.

To see this, solve for the prices that would prevail in an efficient market facing scarcity over time. Inserting the efficient quantities for the two periods (10.238 and 9.762, respectively) into the willingness-to-pay function ($P = 8 - 0.4q$) yields $P_1 = 3.905$ and $P_2 = 4.095$. The corresponding supply-and-demand diagrams are given in Figure 5.3. Compare Figure 5.3 with Figure 5.1 to see the impact of scarcity on price. Note that in the absence of scarcity, marginal user cost is zero.

In an efficient market, the marginal user cost for each period is the difference between the price and the marginal cost of extraction. Notice that it takes the value \$1.905 in the first period and \$2.095 in the second. In both periods, the present value of the marginal user cost is \$1.905. In the second period, the actual marginal user cost is \$1.905$(1 + r)$. Since $r = 0.10$ in this example, the marginal user cost for the second period is \$2.095.[5] Thus, while the *present value* of marginal user cost is equal in both periods, the actual marginal user cost rises over time.

[5]You can verify this by taking the present value of \$2.095 and showing that it equals \$1.905.

FIGURE 5.3 The Efficient Market Allocation of a Depletable Resource: The Constant-Marginal-Cost Case: (a) Period 1 and (b) Period 2

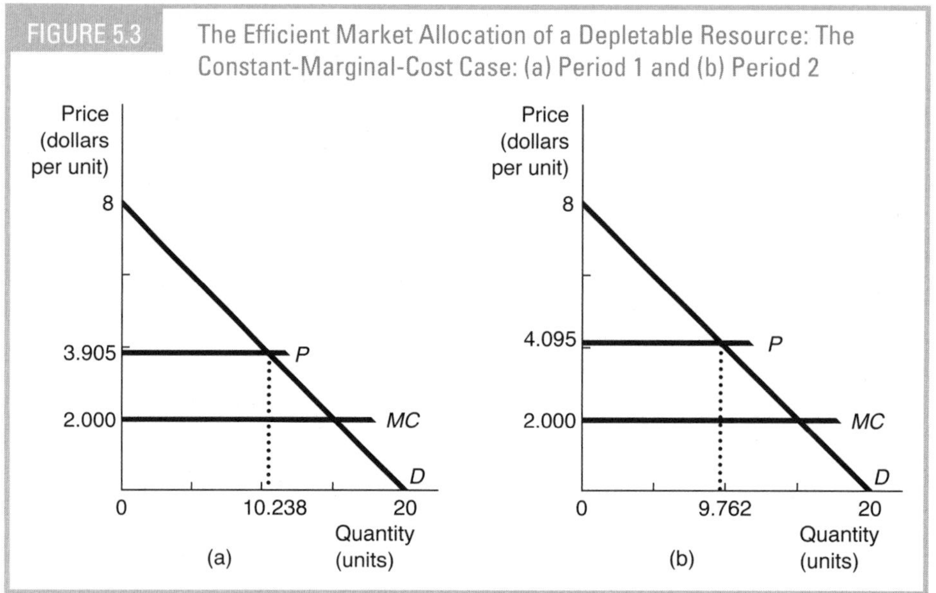

Both the size of the marginal user cost and the allocation of the resource between the two periods is affected not only by the degree of scarcity, but also by the discount rate. In Figure 5.2, because of discounting, the efficient allocation allocates somewhat more to Period 1 than to Period 2. A discount rate larger than 0.10 would be incorporated in this diagram by rotating (not shifting) the Period 2 curve an appropriate amount toward the right-hand axis, holding fixed the point at which it intersects the horizontal axis. (Can you see why?) The larger the discount rate, the greater the amount of rotation required.

The implication is clear—the amount allocated to the second period would be necessarily smaller with larger discount rates. The general conclusion, which holds for all models we consider, is that higher discount rates tend to skew resource extraction toward the present because they give the future less weight in balancing the relative value of present and future resource use. The choice of what discount rate to use, then, becomes a very important consideration for decision makers.

Defining Intertemporal Fairness

While no generally-accepted standards of fairness or justice exist, some have more prominent support than others. One such standard concerns the treatment of future generations. What legacy should earlier generations leave to later ones? This is a particularly difficult issue because, in contrast to other groups for which we may want to ensure fair treatment, future generations cannot articulate their wishes, much less negotiate with current generations. ("We'll accept your radioactive wastes if you leave us plentiful supplies of titanium.")

One starting point for intergenerational equity is provided by philosopher John Rawls in his monumental work *A Theory of Justice*. Rawls suggests that one way to derive general principles of justice is to place, hypothetically, all people into an original position behind a "veil of ignorance." This veil of ignorance would prevent them from knowing their eventual position in society. Once behind this veil, people would be asked to decide on rules to govern the society that they would, after the decision, be forced to inhabit.

In our context, this approach would suggest a hypothetical meeting of all members of present and future generations to decide on rules for allocating resources among generations. Because these members are prevented by the veil of ignorance from knowing the generation to which they will belong after the rules are defined, they will not be excessively conservationist (lest they turn out to be a member of an earlier generation) or excessively exploitative (lest they become a member of a later generation).

What kind of rule would emerge from such a meeting? One possibility is the sustainability criterion. The *sustainability criterion* suggests that, at a minimum, future generations should be left no worse off than current generations. Allocations that impoverish future generations in order to enrich current generations are, according to this criterion, patently unfair.

In essence, the sustainability criterion suggests that earlier generations are at liberty to use resources that would thereby be denied to future generations as long as the well-being of future generations remains just as high as that of all previous generations. On the other hand, diverting resources from future use would violate the sustainability criterion if it reduced the well-being of future generations below the level enjoyed by preceding generations.

One of the implications of this definition of sustainability is that it is possible for the current generation to use resources (even depletable resources) as long as the interests of future generations could be protected. Do our institutions provide adequate protection for future generations? We begin with examining the conditions under which efficient allocations satisfy the sustainability criterion. Are all efficient allocations sustainable?

Are Efficient Allocations Fair?

In the numerical example we have constructed, it certainly does not appear that the efficient allocation satisfies the sustainable criterion. In the two-period example, more resources are allocated to the first period than to the second. Therefore, net benefits in the second period are lower than in the first. Sustainability does not allow earlier generations to profit at the expense of later generations, and this example certainly appears to be a case where that is happening.

Yet appearances can be deceiving. Choosing this particular extraction path does not prevent those in the first period from saving some of the net benefits for those in the second period. If the allocation is dynamically efficient, it will always be possible to set aside sufficient net benefits accrued in the first period for those in the second period, so that those in both periods will be at least as well off as they would have been with any other extraction profile and one of the periods will be better off.

We can illustrate this point with a numerical example that compares a dynamic efficient allocation with sharing to an allocation where resources are committed equally to each generation. Suppose, for example, you believe that setting aside half (10 units) of the available resources for each period would be a better allocation than the dynamic efficient allocation. The net benefits to each period from this alternative scheme would be $40. Can you see why?

Now let's compare this to an allocation of net benefits that could be achieved with the dynamic efficient allocation. For the dynamic efficient allocation to satisfy the sustainability criterion, we must be able to show that it can produce an outcome such that each generation would be at least as well off as it would be with the equal allocation and one will be better off. Can that be demonstrated?

In the dynamic efficient allocation with no sharing, the net benefits to the first period were 40.466, while those for the second period were 39.512.[6] Clearly, in the absence of sharing between the periods, this example would violate the sustainability criterion; the second generation is worse off than it would be with equal sharing. (While it would receive 40.00 from equal resource allocation across the two periods, it receives only 39.512 from the dynamic efficient allocation in the absence of any benefit sharing.)

But suppose the first generation was willing to share some of the net benefits from the extracted resources with the second generation. If the first generation keeps net benefits of $40 (thereby making it just as well off as if equal amounts were extracted in each period) and saves the extra $0.466 (the $40.466 net benefits earned during the first period in the dynamic efficient allocation minus the $40 reserved for itself) at 10 percent interest for those in the next period, this savings would grow to $0.513 by the second period [0.466(1.10)]. Add this to the net benefits received directly from the dynamic efficient allocation ($39.512), and the second generation would receive $40.025. Those in the second period would be better off by accepting the dynamic efficient allocation with sharing than they would if they demanded that resources be allocated equally between the two periods.

This example demonstrates that although dynamic efficient allocations do not automatically satisfy sustainability criteria, they could be compatible with sustainability, even in an economy relying heavily on depletable resources. The possibility that the second period can be better off is not a guarantee; the required degree of

[6]The supporting calculations are (1.905)(10.238) + 0.5(4.095)(10.238) for the first period and (2.095)(9.762) + 0.5(3.905)(9.762) for the second period.

EXAMPLE 5.1

The Alaska Permanent Fund

One interesting example of an intergenerational sharing mechanism currently exists in the State of Alaska. Extraction from Alaska's oil fields generates significant income, but it also depreciates one of the state's main environmental assets. To protect the interests of future generations as the Alaskan pipeline construction neared completion in 1976, Alaska voters approved a constitutional amendment that authorized the establishment of a dedicated fund: the Alaska Permanent Fund. This fund was designed to capture a portion of the rents received from the sale of the state's oil to share with future generations. The amendment requires:

> *At least 25 percent of all mineral lease rentals, royalties, royalty sales proceeds, federal mineral revenue-sharing payments and bonuses received by the state be placed in a permanent fund, the principal of which may only be used for income-producing investments.*

The principal of this fund cannot be used to cover current expenses without a majority vote of Alaskans.

The fund is fully invested in capital markets and diversified among various asset classes. It generates income from interest on bonds, stock dividends, real estate rents, and capital gains from the sale of assets. To date, the legislature has used some of these annual earnings to provide dividends to every eligible Alaska resident, while retaining the rest in the fund in order to increase the size of the endowment, thereby assuring that it is not eroded by inflation. As of 2012, the market value of the fund was $42.154 billion and the dividend to every resident in that year was $878.00

Although this fund does preserve some of the revenue for future generations, two characteristics are worth noting. First, the principal could be used for current expenditures if a majority of current voters agreed. To date, that has not happened, but it has been discussed. Second, only 25 percent of the oil revenue is placed in the fund; assuming that revenue reflects scarcity rent, full sustainability would require dedicating 100 percent of it to the fund. Because the current generation not only gets its share of the income from the permanent fund, but also receives 75 percent of the proceeds from current oil sales, this sharing arrangement falls short of full sustainability.

Source: The fund is managed by the Alaska Permanent Fund Corporation. http://www.apfc.org/home/Content/home/index.cfm

The Alaska Permanent Fund Website: http://www.pfd.state.ak.us/

sharing must take place. Example 5.1 points out that this sharing does sometimes take place, although, as we shall see, such sharing is more likely to be the exception rather than the norm. In subsequent chapters, we shall examine both the conditions under which we could expect the appropriate degree of sharing to take place and the conditions under which it would not.

Applying the Sustainability Criterion

One of the difficulties in assessing the fairness of intertemporal allocations using this version of the sustainability criterion is that it is so difficult to apply. Discovering whether the well-being of future generations would be lower than that of current generations requires us not only to know something about the allocation of resources over time, but also to know something about the preferences of future generations (in order to establish how valuable various resource streams are to them). That is a tall (impossible?) order!

Is it possible to develop a version of the sustainability criterion that is more operational? Fortunately it is, thanks to what has become known as the "Hartwick Rule." In an early article, John Hartwick (1977) demonstrated that a constant level of consumption could be maintained perpetually from an environmental endowment if all the scarcity rent derived from resources extracted from that endowment were invested in capital. That level of investment would be sufficient to assure that the value of the total capital stock would not decline.

Two important insights flow from this reinterpretation of the sustainability criterion. First, with this version, it is possible to judge the sustainability of an allocation by examining whether or not the value of the total capital stock is declining—a declining capital stock violates the rule. That test can be performed each year without knowing anything about future allocations or preferences. Second, this analysis suggests the specific degree of sharing that would be necessary to produce a sustainable outcome, namely, all scarcity rent must be invested.

Let's pause to be sure we understand what is being said and why it is being said. Although we shall return to this subject later in the book, it is important now to have at least an intuitive understanding of the implications of this analysis. Consider an analogy. Suppose a grandparent left you an inheritance of $10,000 and you put it in a bank where it earns 10 percent interest.

What are the choices for allocating that money over time and what are the implications of those choices? If you withdrew exactly $1,000 per year, the amount in the bank would remain $10,000 and the income would last forever; you would be spending only the interest, leaving the principal intact. If you spend more than $1,000 per year, the principal would necessarily decline over time and eventually the balance in the account would go to zero. In the context of this discussion, spending $1,000 per year or less would satisfy the sustainability criterion, while spending more would violate it.

What does the Hartwick Rule mean in this context? It suggests that one way to tell whether an allocation (spending pattern) is sustainable or not is to examine what is happening to the value of the principal over time. If the principal is declining, the allocation (spending pattern) is not sustainable. If the principal is increasing or remaining constant, the allocation (spending pattern) is sustainable.

How do we apply this logic to the environment? In general, the Hartwick Rule suggests that the current generation has been given an endowment. Part of the endowment consists of environmental and natural resources (known as "natural capital") and another part consists of physical capital (such as buildings, equipment, schools, and roads). Sustainable use of this endowment implies that we should keep the principal (the value of the natural and physical endowment) intact and live off only the flow of services provided. We should not, in other words, chop down all the trees and use up all the oil, leaving future generations to fend for themselves. Rather we need to assure that the value of the total capital stock is maintained, not depleted.

The desirability of this version of the sustainability criterion depends crucially on how substitutable the two forms of capital are. If physical capital can readily substitute for natural capital, then maintaining the value of the sum of the two is sufficient. If, however, physical capital cannot completely substitute for natural capital, investments in physical capital alone may not be enough to assure sustainability.

How tenable is the assumption of complete substitutability between physical and natural capital? Clearly, it is untenable for certain categories of environmental resources. Although we can contemplate the replacement of natural breathable air with universal air-conditioning in domed cities, both the expense and the artificiality of this approach make it an absurd compensation device. Obviously, intergenerational compensation must be approached carefully (see Example 5.2).

Recognizing the weakness of the constant total capital definition in the face of limited substitution possibilities has led some economists to propose a new, additional definition. According to this new definition, an allocation is sustainable if it maintains the value of the stock of *natural* capital. This definition assumes that it

EXAMPLE 5.2

Nauru: Weak Sustainability in the Extreme

The weak sustainability criterion is used to judge whether the depletion of natural capital is offset by sufficiently large increases in physical or financial capital so as to prevent total capital from declining. It seems quite natural to suppose that a violation of that criterion does demonstrate *unsustainable* behavior. But does fulfillment of the weak sustainability criterion provide an adequate test of *sustainable* behavior? Consider the case of Nauru.

Nauru is a small Pacific island that lies some 3000 kilometers northeast of Australia. It contains one of the highest grades of phosphate ever discovered. Phosphate is a prime ingredient in fertilizers.

Over the course of a century, first colonizers and then, after independence, the Nauruans decided to extract massive amounts of this deposit. This decision has simultaneously enriched the remaining inhabitants (including the creation of a trust fund believed to contain over $1 billion) and destroyed most of the local ecosystems. Local needs are now mainly met by imports financed by the sales of the phosphate.

However wise or unwise the choices made by the people of Nauru were, they could not be replicated globally. Everyone cannot subsist solely on imports financed with trust funds; every import must be exported by someone! The story of Nauru demonstrates the value of complementing the weak sustainability criterion with other, more demanding criteria. Satisfying the weak sustainability criterion may be a necessary condition for sustainability, but it is not always sufficient.

Source: Gowdy, J. W., & McDaniel, C. N. (1999). The physical destruction of Nauru: An example of weak sustainability. *Land Economics*, 75(2), 333–338.

is natural capital that drives future well-being and further assumes that little or no substitution between physical and natural capital is possible. To differentiate these two definitions, the maintenance of the value of total capital is known as the "weak sustainability" (less restrictive) definition, while maintaining the value of natural capital is known as the "strong sustainability" (more restrictive) definition.

A final, additional definition, known as "environmental sustainability," requires that certain *physical flows* of certain key *individual* resources be maintained. This definition suggests that it is not sufficient to maintain the *value* of an *aggregate.* For a fishery, for example, this definition would require catch levels that did not exceed the growth of the biomass for the fishery. For a wetland, it would require the preservation of the specific ecological functions.

Implications for Environmental Policy

In order to be useful guides to policy, our sustainability and efficiency criteria must be neither synonymous nor incompatible. Do these criteria meet that test?

They do. As we shall see later in the book, not all efficient allocations are sustainable and not all sustainable allocations are efficient. Yet some sustainable allocations are efficient and some efficient allocations are sustainable. Furthermore, market allocations may be either efficient or inefficient and either sustainable or unsustainable.

Do these differences have any policy implications? Indeed they do. In particular they suggest a specific strategy for policy. Among the possible uses for resources that fulfill the sustainability criterion, we choose the one that maximizes either dynamic or static efficiency as appropriate. In this formulation the sustainability criterion acts as an overriding constraint on social decisions. Yet by itself, the sustainability criterion is insufficient because it fails to provide any guidance on which of the infinite number of sustainable allocations should be chosen. That is where efficiency comes in. It provides a means for maximizing the wealth derived from all the possible sustainable allocations.

This combination of efficiency with sustainability turns out to be very helpful in guiding policy. Many unsustainable allocations are the result of inefficient behavior. Correcting the inefficiency can either restore sustainability or move the economy a long way in that direction. Furthermore, and this is important, correcting inefficiencies can frequently produce win-win situations. In win-win changes, the various parties affected by the change can all be made better off after the change than before. This contrasts sharply with changes in which the gains to the gainers are smaller than the losses to the losers.

Win-win situations are possible because moving from an inefficient to an efficient allocation increases net benefits. The increase in net benefits provides a means for compensating those who might otherwise lose from the change. Compensating losers reduces the opposition to change, thereby making change more likely. Do our economic and political institutions normally produce outcomes that are both efficient and sustainable? In upcoming chapters we will provide explicit answers to this important question.

Summary

Both efficiency and ethical considerations can guide the desirability of private and social choices involving the environment. Whereas the former is concerned mainly with eliminating waste in the use of resources, the latter is concerned with assuring the fair treatment of all parties.

Previous chapters have focused on the static and dynamic efficiency criteria. Chapter 19 will focus on the environmental justice implications of environmental degradation and remediation for members of the current generation. The present chapter examines one globally important characterization of the obligation previous generations owe to those generations that follow and the policy implications that flow from acceptance of that obligation.

The specific obligation examined in this chapter—sustainable development—is based upon the notion that earlier generations should be free to pursue their own well-being as long as in so doing they do not diminish the welfare of future generations. This notion gives rise to three alternative definitions of sustainable allocations:

Weak Sustainability. Resource use by previous generations should not exceed a level that would prevent subsequent generations from achieving a level of well-being at least as great. One operational implication of this definition is that the value of the capital stock (natural plus physical capital) should not decline. Individual components of the aggregate could decline in value as long as other components were increased in value (normally through investment) sufficiently to leave the aggregate value unchanged.

Strong Sustainability. According to this interpretation, the value of the remaining stock of natural capital should not decrease. This definition places special emphasis on preserving natural (as opposed to total) capital under the assumption that natural and physical capital offer limited substitution possibilities. This definition retains two characteristics of the previous definition, namely it preserves value (rather than a specific level of physical flow) and it preserves an aggregate of natural capital (rather than any specific component).

Environmental Sustainability. Under this definition, the *physical* flows of *individual* resources should be maintained, not merely the *value* of the *aggregate*. For a fishery, for example, this definition would emphasize maintaining a constant fish catch (referred to as a sustainable yield), rather than a constant value of the fishery. For a wetland, it would involve preserving specific ecological functions, not merely their aggregate value.

It is possible to examine and compare the theoretical conditions that characterize various allocations (including market allocations and efficient allocations) to the necessary conditions for an allocation to be sustainable under these definitions. According to the theorem that is now known as the "Hartwick Rule," if all of the scarcity rent from the use of scarce resources is invested in capital, the resulting allocation will satisfy the first definition of sustainability.

In general, not all efficient allocations are sustainable and not all sustainable allocations efficient. Furthermore, market allocations can be (1) efficient, but not sustainable; (2) sustainable, but not efficient; (3) inefficient and unsustainable; and (4) efficient and sustainable. One class of situations, known as "win-win" situations, provides an opportunity to increase simultaneously the welfare of both current and future generations.

We shall explore these themes much more intensively as we proceed through the book. In particular, we shall inquire into when market allocations can be expected to produce allocations that satisfy the sustainability definitions and when they cannot. We shall also see several specific examples of how the skillful use of economic incentives can allow policymakers to exploit "win-win" situations to promote a transition onto a sustainable path for the future.

Discussion Question

1. The environmental sustainability criterion differs in important ways from both strong and weak sustainability. Environmental sustainability frequently means maintaining a constant physical flow of individual resources (e.g., fish from the sea or wood from the forest), while the other two definitions call for maintaining the *aggregate value* of those service flows. When might the two criteria lead to different choices? Why?

Self-Test Exercises

1. In the numerical example given in the text, the inverse demand function for the depletable resource is $P = 8 - 0.4q$ and the marginal cost of supplying it is \$2. (a) If 20 units are to be allocated between two periods, in a dynamic efficient allocation how much would be allocated to the first period and how much to the second period when the discount rate is zero? (b) Given this discount rate, what would be the efficient price in the two periods? (c) What would be the marginal user cost in each period?
2. Assume the same demand conditions as stated in Problem 1, but let the discount rate be 0.10 and the marginal cost of extraction be \$4. How much would be produced in each period in an efficient allocation? What would be the marginal user cost in each period? Would the static and dynamic efficiency criteria yield the same answers for this problem? Why?
3. Compare two versions of the two-period depletable resource model that differ only in the treatment of marginal extraction cost. Assume that in the second version, the constant marginal extraction cost is lower in the second period than the first (perhaps due to the anticipated arrival of a new, superior extraction technology). The constant marginal extraction cost is the same in both periods in the first version and is equal to the marginal extraction cost in the first period of the second version. In a dynamic efficient allocation, how would the extraction profile in the second version differ from the first? Would relatively more or less be allocated to the second period in the second version

than in the first version? Would the marginal user cost be higher or lower in the second version? Why?

4. a. Consider the general effect of the discount rate on the dynamic efficient allocation of a depletable resource across time. Suppose we have two versions of the two-period model discussed in this chapter. The two versions are identical except for the fact that the second version involves a higher discount rate than the first version. What effect would the higher discount rate have on the allocation between the two periods and the magnitude of the present value of the marginal user cost?
   b. Explain the intuition behind your results.
5. a. Consider the effect of population growth on the allocation on the dynamic efficient allocation of a depletable resource across time. Suppose we have two versions of the two-period model, discussed in this chapter, that are identical except for the fact that the second version involves a higher demand for the resource in the second period (the demand curve shifts to the right due to population growth) than the first version. What effect would the higher demand in the second period have on the allocation between the two periods and the magnitude of the present value of the marginal user cost?
   b. Explain the intuition behind your results.

Further Reading

Heal, G. (2012). Reflections—Defining and measuring sustainability. *Review of Environmental Economics and Policy*, *6*(1), 147–163. An examination of the concept of sustainability and the possibility of quantifying it.

Kiron, D., Kruschwitz, N., Haanæs, K., & Velken, I. V. S. (2012). Sustainability nears a tipping point. *MIT Sloan Management Review*, *53*(2), 69–74. What is the role for the private sector in sustainable development? Is concern over the "bottom line" consistent with the desire to promote sustainable development?

Lopez, R., & Toman, M.A. (Eds.). (2006). *Economic development and environmental sustainability.* New York: Oxford University Press. Thirteen essays that explore how the principles of sustainability can be implemented in the context of reducing poverty through development.

Pezzey, J. V. C., & Toman. M. A. (2002). Progress and problems in the economics of sustainability. In T. Tietenberg & H. Folmer (Eds.). *The international yearbook of environmental and resource economics: A survey of current issues*. Cheltenham, UK: Edward Elgar, 165–232. An excellent technical survey of the economics literature on sustainable development.

World Bank. (2011). *The changing wealth of nations: Measuring sustainable development in the new millennium.* Washington, DC: World Bank. This study presents, for the first time, a set of "wealth accounts" for over 150 countries for 1995, 2000, and 2005. This set of accounts allows a longer-term assessment of global, regional and country performance within the weak sustainability context.

Additional References and Historically Significant References are available on this book's Companion Website: http://www.routledgetextbooks.com/textbooks/9780133479690

Appendix

The Simple Mathematics of Dynamic Efficiency

Assume that the demand curve for a depletable resource is linear and stable over time. Thus, the inverse demand curve in year t can be written as

$$P_t = a - bq_t$$

The total benefits from extracting an amount q_t in year t are then the integral of this function (the area under the inverse demand curve):

$$(\text{Total benefits})_t = \int_0^{qt} (a - bq)dq$$

$$= aq_t - \frac{b}{2}q_t^2$$

Further assume that the marginal cost of extracting that resource is a constant c and therefore the total cost of extracting any amount q_t in year t can be given by

$$(\text{Total cost})_t = cq_t$$

If the total available amount of this resource is $\bar{Q}$, then the dynamic allocation of a resource over n years is the one that satisfies the maximization problem:

$$\text{Max}_q \sum_{i=1}^{n} \frac{aq_i - bq_i^2/2 - cq_i}{(1 + r)^{i-1}} + \lambda\left[\bar{Q} - \sum_{i=1}^{n} q_i\right]$$

Assuming that $\bar{Q}$ is less than would normally be demanded, the dynamic efficient allocation must satisfy

$$\frac{a - bq_i - c}{(1 + r)^{i-1}} - \lambda = 0, i = 1, \ldots, n$$

$$\bar{Q} - \sum_{i=1}^{n} q_i = 0$$

An implication of Equation 5 is that $(P - MC)$ increases over time at rate r. This difference, which is known as the marginal user cost, will play a key role in our thinking about allocating depletable resources over time.

An exact solution to the two-period model can be illustrated using these solution equations and some assumed values for the parameters.

The following parameter values are assumed by the two-period example:

$$a = 8, c = 2, b = 0.4, Q = 20, \text{ and } r = 0.10.$$

Inserting these parameters into the two equations (one for each period) described in equation set (5), we obtain

$$8 - 0.4q_1 - 2 - \lambda = 0,$$

$$\frac{8 - 0.4q_2 - 2}{1.10} - \lambda = 0$$

$$q_1 + q_2 = 20.$$

It is now readily verified that the solution (accurate to the third decimal place) is

$$q_1 = 10.238, \; q_2 = 9.762, \; \lambda = 1.905.$$

We can now demonstrate the propositions discussed in this text.

1. Verbally, Equation (7) states that in a dynamic efficient allocation, the present value of the marginal net benefit in Period 1 $(8 - 0.4q_1 - 2)$ has to equal λ. Equation (8) states that the present value of the marginal net benefit in Period 2 should also equal λ. Therefore, they must equal each other. This demonstrates the proposition shown graphically in Figure 5.2.
2. The present value of marginal user cost is represented by λ. Thus, Equation (7) states that price in the first period $(8 - 0.4q_1)$ should be equal to the sum of marginal extraction cost ($2) and marginal user cost ($1.905). Multiplying λ by $1 + r$, it becomes clear that price in the second period $(8 - 0.4q_2)$ is equal to the marginal extraction cost ($2) plus the higher marginal user cost $[\lambda\,(1 + r) = (1.905)\,(1.10) = \$2.095]$ in Period 2. These results show why the graphs in Figure 5.3 have the properties they do. They also illustrate the point that, in this case, marginal user cost rises over time.

6 Depletable Resource Allocation: The Role of Longer Time Horizons, Substitutes, and Extraction Cost

The whole machinery of our intelligence, our general ideas and laws, fixed and external objects, principles, persons, and gods, are so many symbolic, algebraic expressions. They stand for experience; experience which we are incapable of retaining and surveying in its multitudinous immediacy. We should flounder hopelessly, like the animals, did we not keep ourselves afloat and direct our course by these intellectual devices. Theory helps us to bear our ignorance of fact.

—George Santayana, *The Sense of Beauty* (1896)

Introduction

How do societies react when finite stocks of depletable resources become scarce? Is it reasonable to expect that self-limiting feedbacks would facilitate the transition to a sustainable, steady state? Or is it more reasonable to expect that self-reinforcing feedback mechanisms would cause the system to overshoot the resource base, possibly even precipitating a societal collapse?

We begin to seek answers to these questions by studying the implications of both efficient and profit-maximizing decision making. What kinds of feedback mechanisms are implied by decisions motivated by efficiency and by profit maximization? Are they compatible with a smooth transition or are they more likely to produce overshoot and collapse?

We approach these questions in several steps, beginning by defining and discussing a simple but useful *resource taxonomy* (classification system), as well as explaining the dangers of ignoring the distinctions made by this taxonomy. We initiate the analysis by defining an efficient allocation of an exhaustible resource over time in the absence of any renewable substitute and explore the conditions any efficient allocation must satisfy. Numerical examples illustrate the implications of these conditions.

Renewable resources are integrated into the analysis by relying on the simplest possible case—the resource is assumed to be supplied at a fixed, abundant rate and can be accessed at a constant marginal cost. Solar energy and replenishable surface water are two examples that seem roughly to fit this characterization. Integrating a renewable resource backstop into our basic depletable resource model allows us to characterize efficient extraction paths for both types of resources, assuming that they are perfect substitutes. We also explore how these efficient paths are affected by changes in the nature of the cost functions as well as by the presence or absence of externalities. Succeeding chapters will use these principles to examine the allocation of such diverse resources as energy, minerals, land, and water and to provide a basis for developing more elaborate models of renewable biological populations, such as fisheries and forests.

A Resource Taxonomy

Three separate concepts are used to classify the stock of depletable resources: (1) *current reserves*, (2) *potential reserves*, and (3) *resource endowment*. The U.S. Geological Survey (USGS) has the official responsibility for keeping records of the U.S. resource base and has developed the classification system described in Figure 6.1.

Note the two dimensions—one economic and one geological. A movement from top to bottom represents movement from cheaply extractable resources to those extracted at substantially higher costs. By contrast, a movement from left to right represents increasing geological uncertainty about the size of the resource base.

Current reserves (shaded area in Figure 6.1) are defined as known resources that can profitably be extracted at current prices. The magnitude of these current reserves can be expressed as a number.

Potential reserves, on the other hand, are most accurately defined as a function rather than a number. The amount of reserves potentially available depends upon the price people are willing to pay for those resources—the higher the price, the larger the potential reserves. Higher prices unleash not only more expensive measures to recover more of the resource from conventional sources (such as steam injection), but also measures to extract resources from previously untapped sources (such as oil from tar sands).

The *resource endowment* represents the natural occurrence of resources in the earth's crust. Since prices have nothing to do with the size of the resource endowment, it is a geological, rather than an economic, concept. This concept is important because it represents an upper limit on the availability of terrestrial resources.

The distinctions among these three concepts are significant. One common mistake in failing to respect these distinctions is using data on current reserves as if they represented the maximum potential reserves. This fundamental error can cause a huge understatement of the time until exhaustion.

A second common mistake is to assume that the entire resource endowment can be made available as potential reserves at a price people would be willing to pay. Clearly, if an infinite price were possible, the entire resource endowment could be exploited, but don't hold your breath until the arrival of infinite prices.

FIGURE 6.1 A Categorization of Resources

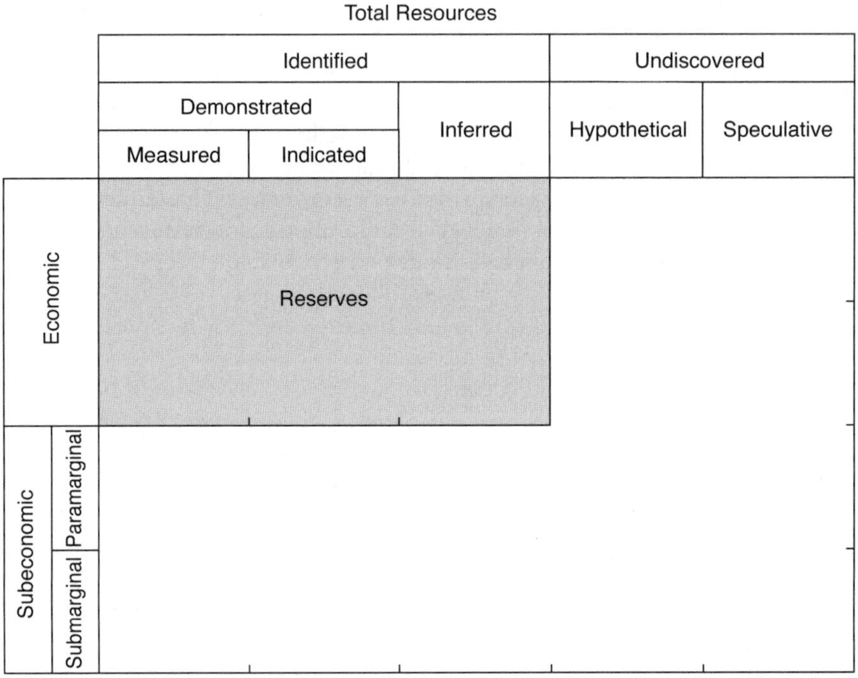

Total Resources

		Identified			Undiscovered	
		Demonstrated		Inferred	Hypothetical	Speculative
		Measured	Indicated			
Economic		Reserves				
Subeconomic	Paramarginal					
	Submarginal					

Terms

Identified resources: specific bodies of mineral-bearing material whose location, quality, and quantity are known from geological evidence, supported by engineering measurements.

Measured resources: material for which quantity and quality estimates are within a margin of error of less than 20 percent, from geologically well-known sample sites.

Indicated resources: material for which quantity and quality have been estimated partly from sample analyses and partly from reasonable geological projections.

Inferred resources: material in unexplored extensions of demonstrated resources based on geological projections.

Undiscovered resources: unspecified bodies of mineral-bearing material surmised to exist on the basis of broad geological knowledge and theory.

Hypothetical resources: undiscovered materials reasonably expected to exist in a known mining district under known geological conditions.

Speculative resources: undiscovered materials that may occur in either known types of deposits in favorable geological settings where no discoveries have been made, or in yet unknown types of deposits that remain to be recognized.

Source: U.S. Bureau of Mines and the U.S. Geological Survey. (1976). Principle of the Mineral Resource Classification System of the U.S. Bureau of Mines and the U.S. Geological Survey. *Geological Survey Bulletin*, 1450-A.

Other distinctions among resource categories are also useful. The first category includes all depletable, recyclable resources, such as copper. A *depletable resource* is one for which the natural replenishment feedback loop can safely be ignored. The rate of replenishment for these resources is so low that it does not offer a potential for augmenting the stock in any reasonable time frame.

A *recyclable resource* is one that, although currently being used for some particular purpose, exists in a form allowing its mass to be recovered once that original purpose is no longer necessary or desirable. For example, copper wiring from an automobile can be recovered after the car has been shipped to the junkyard. The degree to which a resource is recycled is determined by economic conditions, a subject covered in Chapter 8.

The current reserves of a depletable, recyclable resource can be augmented by economic replenishment, as well as by recycling. Economic replenishment takes many forms, all sharing the characteristic that they turn previously unrecoverable resources into recoverable ones. One obvious stimulant for this replenishment is price. As price rises, producers find it profitable to explore more widely, dig more deeply, and use lower-concentration ores.

Higher prices also stimulate technological progress. Technological progress simply refers to an advancement in the state of knowledge that allows us to expand the set of feasible possibilities. Harnessing nuclear power and the advent of both horizontal drilling and hydraulic fracturing are two obvious examples. (Both are discussed in Chapter 7.)

The potential reserves of depletable, recyclable resources, however, can be exhausted. The depletion rate is affected by the demand for and the durability of the products built with the resource, and the ability to reuse the products. Except where demand is totally price-inelastic (i.e., insensitive to price), higher prices tend to reduce the quantity demanded. Durable products last longer, reducing the need for newer ones. Reusable products (e.g., rechargeable batteries or products sold at flea markets) provide a substitute for new products.

For some resources, the size of the potential reserves depends explicitly on our ability to store the resource. For example, helium is generally found commingled with natural gas in common fields. As the natural gas is extracted and stored, unless the helium is simultaneously captured and stored, it diffuses into the atmosphere. This diffusion results in such low atmospheric concentrations that extraction of helium from the air is not economical at current or even likely future prices. Thus, the useful stock of helium depends crucially on how much we decide to store.

Not all depletable resources can be recycled or reused. Depletable energy resources such as coal, oil, and gas are consumed as they are used. Once combusted and turned into heat energy, the heat dissipates into the atmosphere and becomes nonrecoverable.

The endowment of depletable resources is of finite size. Current use of depletable, nonrecyclable resources precludes future use; hence, the issue of how they should be shared among generations is raised in the starkest, least forgiving form.

Depletable, recyclable resources raise this same issue, though somewhat less starkly, since recycling and reuse make the useful stock last longer, all other things being equal. It is tempting to suggest that depletable, recyclable resources could last forever with 100 percent recycling, but unfortunately the physical theoretical upper limit on recycling is less than 100 percent—an implication of a version of the entropy law defined in Chapter 2. Some of the mass is always lost during recycling or use.

Because less than 100 percent of the mass is recycled, the useful stock must eventually decline to zero. Therefore even for recyclable, depletable resources, the cumulative useful stock is finite, and current consumption patterns still have an effect on future generations.

Renewable resources are differentiated from depletable resources primarily by the fact that natural replenishment augments the flow of renewable resources at a non-negligible rate. Solar energy, water, and biological populations are all examples of renewable resources. For this class of resources it is possible, though not inexorable, that a flow of these resources could be maintained perpetually.[1]

For some renewable resources, the continuation and volume of their flow depend crucially on humans. Soil erosion and nutrient depletion reduce the flow of food. Excessive fishing reduces the stock of fish, which in turn reduces the rate of natural increase of the fish population. What other examples can you come up with?

For other renewable resources, such as solar energy, the flow is independent of humans. The amount consumed by one generation does not reduce the amount that can be consumed by subsequent generations.

Some renewable resources can be stored; others cannot. For those that can, storage provides an additional way to manage the allocation of the resource over time. We are not left simply at the mercy of natural ebbs and flows. Food, without proper care, perishes rapidly, but under the right conditions stored food can be used to feed the hungry in times of famine. Unstored solar energy radiates off the earth's surface and dissipates into the atmosphere. While solar energy can be stored in many forms, the most common natural form of storage occurs when it is converted to biomass by photosynthesis.

Storage of renewable resources usually provides a different service than storage of depletable resources. Storing depletable resources extends their economic life; storing renewable resources, on the other hand, can serve as a means of smoothing out the cyclical imbalances of supply and demand. Surpluses can be stored for use during periods when deficits occur. Familiar examples include food stockpiles and the use of dams to store water to be used for hydropower.

Managing renewable resources presents a different challenge from managing depletable resources, although an equally significant one. The challenge for depletable resources involves allocating dwindling stocks among generations while meeting the ultimate transition to renewable resources. In contrast, the challenge for

---

[1]Even renewable resources are ultimately finite because their renewability depends on energy from the sun and the sun is expected to serve as an energy source for only the next five or six billion years. Because the finiteness of renewable resources is sufficiently far into the future, the distinction between depletable and renewable resources remains useful.

managing renewable resources involves the maintenance of an efficient, sustainable flow. Chapters 7 through 13 deal with how the economic and political sectors have responded to these challenges for particularly significant types of resources.

Efficient Intertemporal Allocations

If we are to judge the adequacy of market allocations, we must define what is meant by efficiency in relation to the management of depletable and renewable resource allocations. Because allocation over time is the crucial issue, dynamic efficiency becomes the core concept. The dynamic efficiency criterion assumes that society's objective is to maximize the present value of net benefits coming from the resource. For a depletable, nonrecyclable resource, this requires a balancing of the current and subsequent uses of the resource. In order to refresh our memories about how the dynamic efficiency criterion defines this balance, we shall begin with recalling and elaborating on the very simple two-period model developed in Chapter 5. We can then proceed to demonstrate how conclusions drawn from that model generalize to longer planning horizons and more complicated situations.

The Two-Period Model Revisited

In Chapter 5 we defined a situation involving the allocation over two periods of a finite resource that could be extracted at constant marginal cost. With a stable demand curve for the resource, an efficient allocation meant that more than half of the resource was allocated to the first period and less than half to the second period. How the resources were divided between the two periods was affected by the marginal cost of extraction, the marginal user cost and the discount rate.

Due to the fixed and finite supplies of depletable resources, use of a unit today precludes use of that unit tomorrow. Therefore, production decisions today must take forgone future net benefits into account. Marginal user cost is the opportunity cost measure that allows intertemporal balancing to take place.

In the two-period model, the marginal cost of extraction is assumed to be constant, but the value of the marginal user cost was shown to rise over time. In fact, as was demonstrated mathematically in the appendix to Chapter 5, when the demand curve is stable over time and the marginal cost of extraction is constant, the rate of increase in the current value of the marginal user cost is equal to r, the discount rate. Thus, in Period 2, the marginal user cost would be $1 + r$ times as large as it was in Period 1.[2] Marginal user cost rises at rate r in an efficient allocation in order to preserve the balance between present versus future production.

In summary, our two-period example suggests that an efficient allocation of a finite resource with a constant marginal cost of extraction involves rising marginal user cost and falling quantities consumed. We can now generalize to longer time periods and different extraction circumstances.

---

[2]The condition that marginal user cost rises at rate r is true only when the marginal cost of extraction is constant. Later in this chapter we show how the marginal user cost is affected when marginal extraction cost is not constant.

The *N*-Period Constant-Cost Case

We begin this generalization by retaining the constant-marginal-extraction-cost assumption while extending the time horizon within which the resource is allocated. In the numerical example shown in Figures 6.2a and 6.2b, the demand curves and the marginal cost curve from the two-period case are retained. The only changes in this numerical example from the two-period case involve spreading the allocation over a larger number of years and increasing the total recoverable supply from 20 to 40. (The specific mathematics behind this and subsequent examples is presented in the appendix at the end of this chapter, but we shall guide you through the intuition that follows from that analysis in this section.)

Figure 6.2a demonstrates how the efficient quantity extracted varies over time, while Figure 6.2b shows the behavior of the marginal user cost and the marginal cost of extraction. Total marginal cost refers to the sum of the two. The marginal cost of extraction is represented by the lower line, and the marginal user cost is depicted as the vertical distance between the marginal cost of extraction and the total marginal cost. To avoid confusion, note that the horizontal axis is defined in terms of time, not the more conventional designation—quantity.

Several trends are worth noting. First of all, in this case, as in the two-period case, the efficient marginal user cost rises steadily in spite of the fact that the marginal cost of extraction remains constant. This rise in the efficient marginal user cost reflects increasing scarcity and the accompanying rise in the opportunity cost of current consumption (reflecting forgone future opportunities) as the remaining stock dwindles.

In response to these rising costs over time, the extracted quantity falls over time until it finally goes to zero, which occurs precisely at the moment when the total marginal cost becomes \$8. At this point, total marginal cost is equal to the highest

FIGURE 6.2 (a) Constant Marginal Extraction Cost with No Substitute Resource: Quantity Profile (b) Constant Marginal Extraction Cost with No Substitute Resource: Marginal Cost Profile

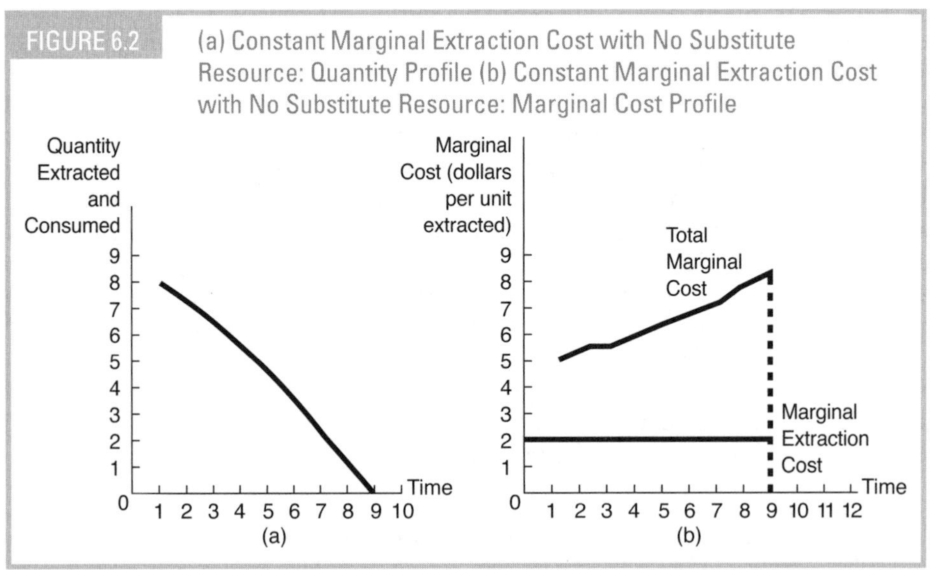

price anyone is willing to pay, so demand and supply simultaneously equal zero. Thus, even in this challenging case involving no increase in the cost of extraction, an efficient allocation envisions a smooth transition to the exhaustion of a resource. The resource does not "suddenly" run out (because prices have signaled the increasing scarcity), although in this case it does run out.

Transition to a Renewable Substitute

So far we have discussed the allocation of a depletable resource when no substitute is available to take its place. Suppose, however, we consider the nature of an efficient allocation when a substitute renewable resource is available at constant marginal cost. This case, for example, could describe the efficient allocation of oil or natural gas with a solar or wind substitute or the efficient allocation of exhaustible groundwater with a surface-water substitute. How could we define an efficient allocation in this circumstance?

Since this problem is very similar to the one already discussed, we can use what we have already learned as a foundation for mastering this new situation. The depletable resource would be exhausted in this case, just as it was in the previous case, but in this case the exhaustion will pose less of a problem, since we'll merely switch to the renewable one at the appropriate time. For the purpose of our numerical example, assume the existence of a perfect substitute for the depletable resource that is infinitely available at a cost of $6 per unit. The transition from the depletable resource to this renewable resource would ultimately transpire because the renewable resource marginal cost ($6) is less than the maximum willingness to pay ($8). (Can you figure out what the efficient allocation would be if the marginal cost of this substitute renewable resource was $9, instead of $6?)

The total marginal cost for the depletable resource in the presence of a $6 perfect substitute would never exceed $6, because society could always use the renewable resource instead, whenever it was cheaper. Thus, while the maximum willingness to pay ($8, the *choke price*) sets the upper limit on total marginal cost when no substitute is available, the marginal cost of extraction of the substitute ($6 in our example) sets the upper limit as long as the perfect substitute is available at a marginal cost lower than the choke price. The efficient path for this situation is given in Figures 6.3a and 6.3b.

In this efficient allocation, the transition is once again smooth. Quantity extracted per unit of time is gradually reduced as the marginal user cost rises until the switch is made to the substitute. No abrupt change is evident in either marginal cost or quantity profiles.

Because the renewable resource is available, more of the depletable resource would be extracted in the earlier periods than was the case without a renewable resource. As a result, the depletable resource would be exhausted sooner than it would have been without the renewable resource substitute. In this example, the switch is made during the sixth period, whereas in the last example the last units were exhausted at the end of the eighth period. That seems consistent with common sense. When a substitute is available, the need to save some of the depletable resource for the future is certainly less pressing (in other words, the opportunity cost has fallen).

FIGURE 6.3 (a) Constant Marginal Extraction Cost with Substitute Resource: Quantity Profile (b) Constant Marginal Extraction Cost with Substitute Resource: Marginal Cost Profile

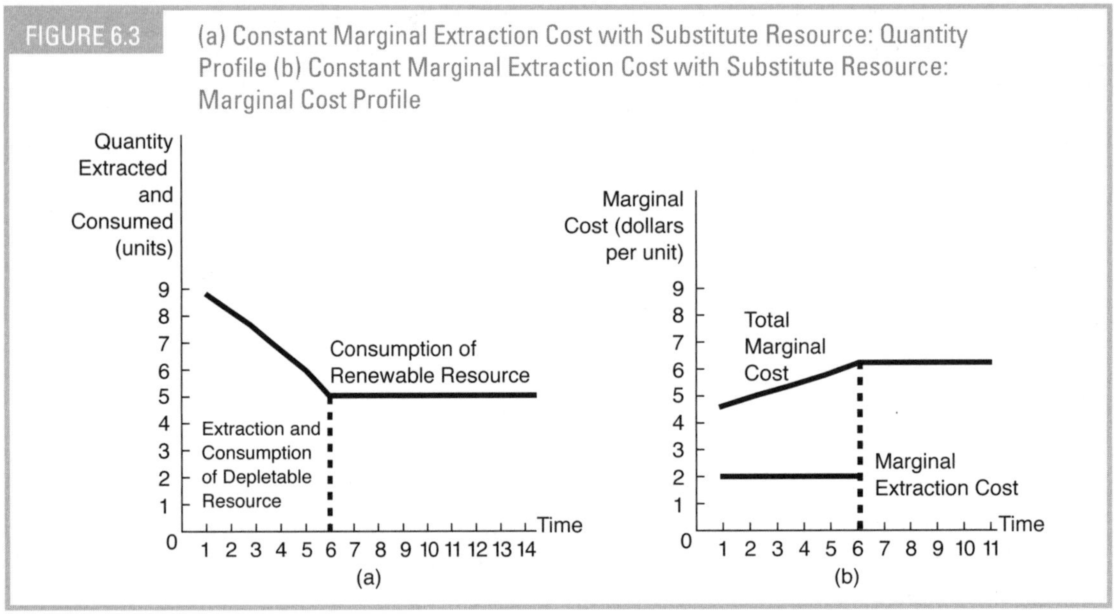

At the transition point, called the switch point, consumption of the renewable resource begins. Prior to the switch point, only the depletable resource is consumed, while after the switch point, only the renewable resource is consumed. This sequencing of consumption pattern results from the cost patterns. Prior to the switch point, the depletable resource is cheaper. At the switch point, the marginal cost of the depletable resource (including marginal user cost) rises to meet the marginal cost of the substitute, and the transition occurs. Due to the availability of the substitute resource, after the switch point consumption never drops below five units in any time period. This level is maintained because five is the amount that maximizes the net benefit when the marginal cost equals $6 (the price of the substitute). (Convince yourself of the validity of this statement by substituting $6 into the willingness-to-pay function and solving for the quantity demanded.)

We shall not show the numerical example here, but it is not difficult to see how an efficient allocation would be defined when the transition is from one constant marginal-cost depletable resource to another depletable resource with a constant, but higher, marginal cost (see Figure 6.4). The total marginal cost of the first resource would rise over time until it equaled that of the second resource at the time of transition (T^*). In the period of time prior to transition, only the cheapest resource would be consumed; all of it would have been consumed by T^*.

A close examination of the total-marginal-cost path reveals two interesting characteristics worthy of our attention. First, even in this case, the transition is a smooth one; total marginal cost never jumps to the higher level. Second, the slope of the total marginal cost curve over time is flatter after the time of transition.

The first characteristic is easy to explain. The total marginal costs of the two resources have to be equal at the time of transition. If they weren't equal, the

FIGURE 6.4 The Transition from One Constant-Cost Depletable Resource to Another

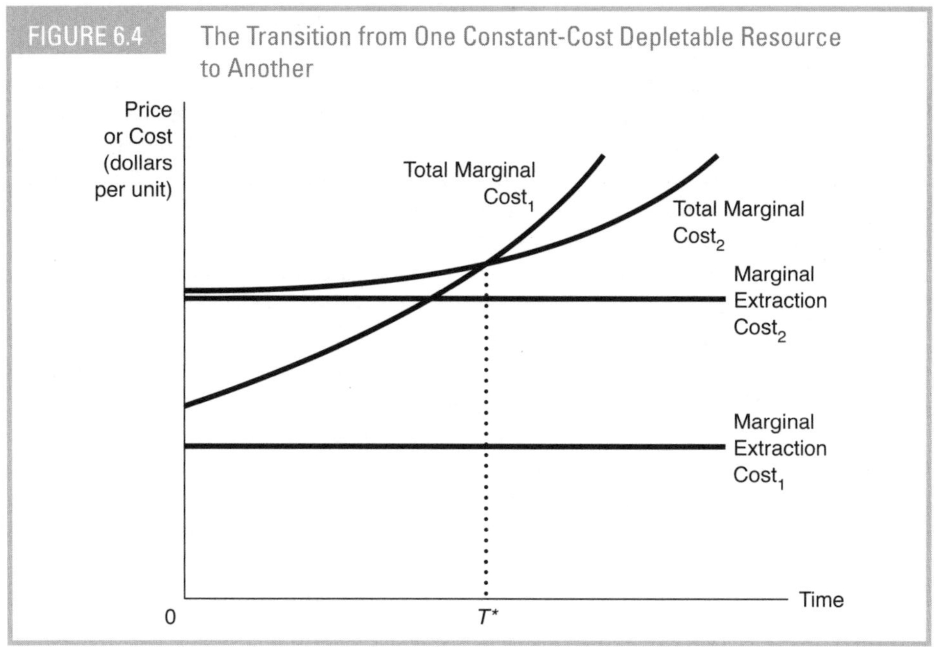

net benefit could be increased by switching to the lower-cost resource from the more expensive resource. Total marginal costs are not equal in the other periods. In the period before transition, the first resource is cheaper and therefore used exclusively, whereas after transition the first resource is exhausted, leaving only the second resource.

The slope of the marginal cost curve over time is flatter after transition simply because the component of total marginal cost that is growing (the marginal user cost) represents a smaller portion of the total marginal cost of the second resource than of the first. The total marginal cost of each resource is determined by the marginal extraction cost plus the marginal user cost. In both cases the marginal user cost is increasing at rate r, and the marginal cost of extraction is constant. As seen in Figure 6.4, the marginal cost of extraction, which is constant, constitutes a much larger proportion of total marginal cost for the second resource than for the first. Hence, total marginal cost rises more slowly for the second resource, at least initially.

Increasing Marginal Extraction Cost

We have now expanded our examination of the efficient allocation of depletable resources to include longer time horizons and the availability of other depletable or renewable resources that could serve as perfect substitutes. As part of our trek toward increasing realism, we will consider a situation in which the marginal cost of extracting the depletable resource rises with the cumulative amount extracted.

This is commonly the case, for example, with minerals, where the higher-grade ores are extracted first, followed by an increasing reliance on lower-grade ones.

Analytically, this case is handled in the same manner as the previous case, except that the function describing the marginal cost of extraction is slightly more complicated.[3] It increases with the cumulative amount extracted. The dynamic efficient allocation of this resource is found by maximizing the present value of the net benefits, using this modified cost of extraction function. The results of that maximization are portrayed in Figures 6.5a and 6.5b.

The most significant difference between this case and the others lies in the behavior of marginal user cost. In the previous case we noted that marginal user cost rose over time at rate r. When the marginal cost of extraction increases with the cumulative amount extracted, marginal user cost *declines* over time until, at the time of transition to the renewable resource, it goes to zero. Can you figure out why?

Remember that marginal user cost is an opportunity cost reflecting forgone future marginal net benefits. In contrast to the constant marginal-cost case, in the increasing marginal-cost case every unit extracted now raises the cost of future extraction. Therefore, as the current marginal cost rises over time, the sacrifice made by future generations (as an additional unit is consumed earlier) diminishes; the net benefit that would be received by a future generation, if a unit of the resource were saved for them, gets smaller and smaller as the marginal extraction cost of that resource gets larger and larger. By the last period, the marginal extraction cost is so high that earlier consumption of one more unit imposes virtually no sacrifice at all. At the switch point, the opportunity cost of current extraction

FIGURE 6.5 (a) Increasing Marginal Extraction Cost with Substitute Resource: Quantity Profile (b) Increasing Marginal Extraction Cost with Substitute Resource: Marginal Cost Profile

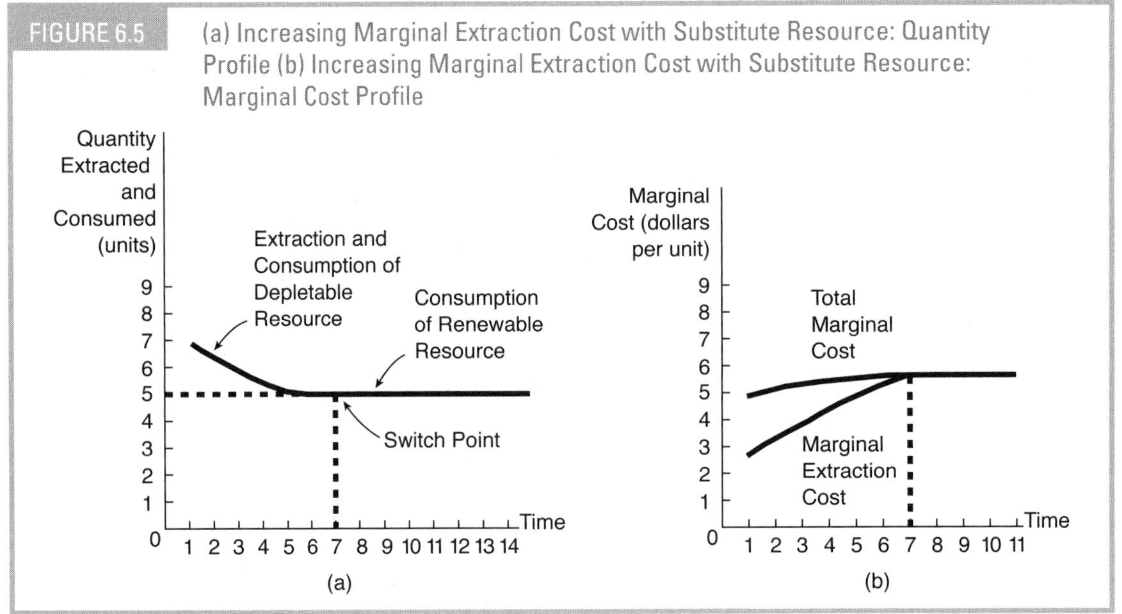

[3]The new marginal cost of extraction is $MCt = \$2 + 0.1Q_t$ where Q_t is cumulative extraction to date.

(as reflected in the marginal user cost) drops to zero, and total marginal cost equals the marginal extraction cost.[4]

The increasing-cost case differs from the constant-cost case in another important way as well. In the constant-cost case, the depletable resource reserve is ultimately completely exhausted. In the increasing-cost case, however, the reserve is not exhausted; some is left in the ground because it is more expensive than the substitute.

Up to this point in our analysis, we have examined how an efficient allocation would be defined in a number of circumstances. First, we examined a situation in which a finite amount of a resource is extracted at constant marginal cost. Despite the absence of increasing extraction cost, an efficient allocation involves a smooth transition to a substitute, when one is available, or to abstinence, when one is not. The complication of increasing marginal cost changes the time profile of the marginal user cost, but it does not alter the basic finding of declining consumption of depletable resources coupled with rising total marginal cost.

Can this analysis be used as a basis for judging whether current extraction profiles are efficient? As a look at the historical record reveals, the consumption patterns of most depletable resources have involved increases, not decreases, in consumption over time. Is this prima facie evidence that the resources are not being allocated efficiently?

Exploration and Technological Progress

Using the historical patterns of increasing consumption to conclude that depletable resources are not being allocated efficiently would not represent a valid finding. As we have noted earlier, the conclusions of any model depend on the structure of that model. The models considered to this point have not yet included a consideration of the role of population and income growth, which could cause consumption to rise over time, or of the exploration for new resources or technological progress—historically significant factors in the determination of actual consumption paths.[5]

The search for new resources is expensive. As easily discovered resources are exhausted, searches are initiated in less rewarding environments, such as the bottom of the ocean or locations deep within the earth. This suggests the *marginal cost of exploration*, which is the marginal cost of finding additional units of the resource, should be expected to rise over time, just as the marginal cost of extraction does.

As the total marginal cost for a resource rises over time, society should actively explore possible new sources of that resource. Larger increases in the marginal cost of extraction for known sources trigger larger potential increases in net benefits from finding new sources that previously would have been unprofitable to extract.

---

[4]Total marginal cost cannot be greater than the marginal cost of the substitute. Yet, in the increasing marginal extraction cost case, at the time of transition the marginal extraction cost also must equal the marginal cost of the substitute. If that weren't true, it would imply that some of the resource that was available at a marginal cost lower than the substitute would not be used. This would clearly be inefficient, since net benefits could be increased by simply using less of the more expensive substitute. Hence, at the switch point, in the rising marginal-cost case, the marginal extraction cost has to equal total marginal cost, implying a zero marginal user cost.

[5]To derive how a rising demand curve over time due to either rising income or population growth would affect the extraction profile complete self-test exercise (2) at the end of this chapter.

Some of this exploration would be successful; new sources of the resource would be discovered. If the marginal extraction cost of the newly discovered resources is low enough, these discoveries could lower, or at least delay, the increase in the total marginal cost of production. As a result, the new finds would tend to encourage more consumption. Compared to a situation with no exploration possible, the model with exploration would show a smaller and slower decline in consumption, while the rise in total marginal cost would be dampened.

It is also not difficult to expand our concept of efficient resource allocations to include *technological progress*, the general term economists give to advances in the state of knowledge. In the present context, technological progress would be manifested as reductions over time in the cost of extraction. For a resource that can be extracted at constant marginal cost, a one-time breakthrough lowering the marginal cost of extraction would hasten the time of transition. Furthermore, for an increasing-cost resource, more of the total available resource would be recovered in the presence of technological progress than would be recovered without it. (Why?)

The most pervasive effects of technological progress involve continuous downward shifts in the cost of extraction over some time period. The total marginal cost of the resource could actually fall over time if the cost-reducing nature of technological progress became so potent that, in spite of increasing reliance on inferior ore, the marginal cost of extraction decreased (see Example 6.1). With a finite amount of this resource, the fall in total marginal cost would be transitory, since ultimately it would have to rise, but, as we shall see in the next few chapters, this period of transition can last quite a long time.

Market Allocations of Depletable Resources

In the preceding sections, we have examined in detail how the efficient allocation of substitutable, depletable, and renewable resources over time would be defined in a variety of circumstances. We must now address the question of whether actual markets can be expected to produce an efficient allocation. Can the private market, involving millions of consumers and producers each reacting to his or her own unique preferences, ever result in a dynamically efficient allocation? Is profit maximization compatible with dynamic efficiency?

Appropriate Property Rights Structures

The most common misconception of those who believe that even a perfect market could never achieve an efficient allocation of depletable resources is based on the idea that producers want to extract and sell the resources as fast as possible, since that is how they derive the value from the resource. This misconception makes people see markets as myopic and unconcerned about the future.

As long as the property rights governing natural resources have the characteristics of exclusivity, transferability, and enforceability (Chapter 2), the markets in which those resources are bought and sold will not necessarily lead to myopic

EXAMPLE 6.1

Historical Example of Technological Progress in the Iron Ore Industry

The term *technological progress* plays an important role in the economic analysis of mineral resources. Yet, at times, it can appear abstract, even mystical. It shouldn't! Far from being a blind faith detached from reality, technological progress refers to a host of ingenious ways in which people have reacted to impending shortages with sufficient imagination that the available supply of resources has been expanded by an order of magnitude and at reasonable cost. An interesting case from economic history illustrates how concrete a notion technological progress is.

In 1947, the president of Republic Steel, C. M. White, calculated the expected life of the Mesabi Range of northern Minnesota (the source of some 60 percent of iron ore consumed during World War II) as being in the range from 5 to 7 years. By 1955, only 8 years later, *U.S. News and World Report* concluded that worry over the scarcity of iron ore could be forgotten. The source of this remarkable transformation of a problem of scarcity into one of abundance was the discovery of a new technique of preparing iron ore, called *pelletization*.

Prior to pelletization, the standard ores from which iron was derived contained from 50 to more than 65 percent iron in crude form. A significant percentage of taconite ore containing less than 30 percent iron in crude form was available, but no one knew how to produce it at reasonable cost.

Pelletization, a process by which these ores are processed and concentrated at the mine site prior to shipment to the blast furnaces, allowed the profitable use of the taconite ores. While expanding the supply of iron ore, pelletization reduced its cost in spite of the inferior grade being used.

There were several sources of the cost reduction. First, substantially less energy was used; the shift in ore technology toward pelletization produced net energy savings of 17 percent in spite of the fact that the pelletization process itself required more energy. The reduction came from the discovery that the blast furnaces could be operated much more efficiently using pelletization inputs. The process also reduced labor requirements per ton by some 8.2 percent while increasing the output of the blast furnaces. A blast furnace owned by Armco Steel in Middletown, Ohio, which had a rated capacity of approximately 1500 tons of molten iron per day, was able, by 1960, to achieve production levels of 2700–2800 tons per day when fired with 90 percent pellets. Pellets nearly doubled the blast furnace productivity!

Sources: Kakela, P. J. (1978). Iron ore: Energy labor and capital changes with technology. *Science, 202*(December 15, 1978), 1151–1157; Kakela, P. J. Iron ore: From depletion to abundance. *Science, 212* (April 10, 1981), 132–136.

choices for the simple reason that myopia would reduce profits. By taking marginal user cost into account, the producer maximizes profits by acting efficiently.

A resource in the ground has two potential sources of value to its owner: (1) a use value when it is sold (the only source considered by those diagnosing inevitable myopia) and (2) an asset value when it remains in the ground. As long as the price of a resource continues to rise, the resource in the ground is becoming more valuable. The owner of this resource accrues this capital gain, however, only if the resource is conserved for later sale. A producer who sells all resources in the earlier periods loses the chance to take advantage of higher prices in the future.

A profit-maximizing producer attempts to balance present and future production in order to maximize the value of the resource. Since higher prices in the future provide an incentive to conserve, a producer who ignores this incentive would not be maximizing the value of the resource. Resources sold by a myopic producer would be bought by someone willing to delay extraction so as to maximize its value. As long as social and private discount rates coincide, property rights structures are well defined, and reliable information about future prices is available, a producer who pursues maximum profits simultaneously provides the maximum present value of net benefits for society.

The implication of this analysis is that, in competitive resource markets, the price of the resource equals the total marginal cost of extracting and using the resource. Thus, Figures 6.2a through 6.5b can illustrate not only an efficient allocation but also the allocation produced by an efficient market. When used to describe an efficient market, the total marginal cost curve describes the time path that prices could be expected to follow.

Environmental Costs

Not all actual situations, however, satisfy the conditions necessary for this harmonious outcome. One of the most important situations in which property rights structures may not be well defined occurs when the extraction of a natural resource imposes an environmental cost on society that is not internalized by the producers. The aesthetic costs of strip mining, the health risks associated with uranium tailings, and the acids leached into streams from mine operations are all examples of associated environmental costs. Not only is the presence of environmental costs empirically important, but also it is conceptually important, since it forms one of the bridges between the traditionally separate fields of environmental economics and natural resource economics.

Suppose, for example, that the extraction of the depletable resource caused some damage to the environment that was not adequately reflected in the costs faced by the extracting firms. This would be, in the context of discussion in Chapter 2, an external cost. The cost of getting the resource out of the ground, as well as processing and shipping it, is borne by the resource owner and considered in the calculation of how much of the resource to extract. The environmental damage, however, may not be borne by the owner and, in the absence of any outside attempt to internalize that external cost, will not be part of the extraction decision. How would the market allocation, based on only the costs born by the owner, differ from the efficient allocation, which is based on all costs, regardless of whom ultimately bears them?

We can examine this issue by modifying the numerical example used earlier in this chapter. Assume the environmental damage can be represented by increasing the marginal cost by $1.[6] The additional dollar reflects the cost of the environmental damage caused by producing another unit of the resource. What effect do you think this would have on the efficient time profile for quantities extracted?

The answers are given in Figures 6.6a and 6.6b. The result of including environmental cost on the timing of the switch point is especially interesting because it involves two different effects that work in opposite directions. On the demand side, the inclusion of environmental costs results in higher prices, which tend to dampen demand. This lowers the rate of consumption of the resource, which, all other things being equal, would make it last longer.

All other things are not equal, however. The higher marginal cost also means that a smaller cumulative amount of the depletable resource would be extracted in an efficient allocation. (Can you see why?) In our example shown in Figures 6.6a and 6.6b, the efficient cumulative amount extracted would be 30 units instead of the 40 units extracted in the case where environmental costs were not included. This supply-side effect tends to hasten the time when a switch to the renewable resource is made, all other things being equal.

Which effect dominates—the rate of consumption effect or the supply effect? In our numerical example, the supply-side effect dominates and, as a result, the time of transition for an efficient allocation is sooner than for the market allocation. In general, the answer depends on the shape of the marginal-extraction-cost function. With constant marginal cost, for example, there would be no supply-side effect

FIGURE 6.6 (a) Increasing Marginal Extraction Cost with Substitute Resource in the Presence of Environmental Costs: Quantity Profile (b) Increasing Marginal Extraction Cost with Substitute Resource in the Presence of Environmental Costs: Price Profile (Solid Line—without Environmental Costs; Dashed Line—with Environmental Costs)

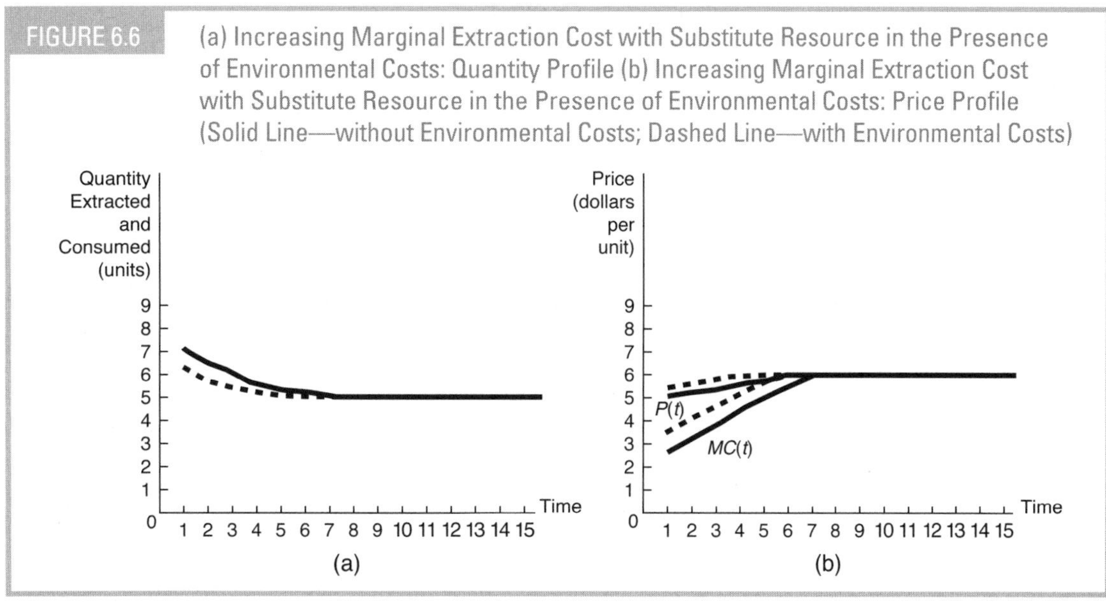

[6]Including environmental damage, the marginal cost function would be raised to $3 + 0.1Q$ instead of $2 + 0.1Q$.

and the market would unambiguously transition later. If the environmental costs were associated with the use of the renewable resource, rather than the depletable resource, the time of transition for the efficient allocation would have been later than the market allocation. Can you see why?

What can we learn from this analysis of the increasing cost case about the allocation of depletable resources over time when environmental side effects are not borne by the agent determining the extraction rate? Ignoring external costs leaves the price of the depletable resource too low, too much of the resource would be extracted and the rate at which it would be extracted would be too high.

Since policies that internalize these external costs can affect both the quantity extracted and price profiles, they can sometimes produce unexpected outcomes (see Example 6.2).

EXAMPLE 6.2

The Green Paradox

Common sense indicates that when pollution taxes or subsides to promote non-polluting technology are imposed, they would lower emissions and improve welfare. In an intriguing article Sinn (2008) argues that in the case of global warming these demand-reducing policies could trigger (under certain conditions) price effects that could actually reduce welfare. Because this analysis suggests that polices designed to internalize an externality could actually result in lower economic welfare, this outcome was labeled "the green paradox."

The basic logic behind this finding is easily explained in terms of the depletable resource models developed in this chapter. The specific policy case examined by Sinn was a carbon tax rate that rises over time faster than the rate of interest. This carbon tax design changes the relative prices between current and future sales, increasing the relative profitability of earlier extraction. (Remember one reason for delaying extraction was the higher prices extractors would gain in the future. With this specific tax profile the after-tax return is falling, not rising.) This policy would not only change the profit-maximizing extraction profile so that more is extracted earlier, but the present value of net benefits could fall.

Notice that this result depends on *earlier*, not *larger* cumulative damages. In the constant MEC model cumulative extraction (and hence, cumulative damages) are fixed so these polices would affect the timing, but not the magnitude, of the cumulative emissions. In the increasing cost MEC case, however, the cumulative emissions would actually be less; the imposition of the carbon tax would ultimately result in more of the depletable resource being left in the ground.

Is the Green Paradox a serious obstacle to climate policy? The early verdict seems to be no (van der Ploeg, 2013), but the dearth of empirical evidence pointing either one way or the other leaves the door ajar.

Source: Sinn, H.-W. (2008). Public policies against global warming: A supply side approach. *International Tax and Public Finance, 15*, 360–394; van der Ploeg, F. Cumulative carbon emissions and the Green Paradox. *Oxford Centre for the Analysis of Resource Rich Economies Research Paper 110*. University of Oxford Retrieved from www.oxcarre.ox.ac.uk/files/OxCarreRP2013110(1).pdf

This once again shows the interdependencies among the various decisions we have to make about the future. Environmental and natural resource decisions are intimately and inextricably linked.

Summary

The efficient extraction profiles for depletable and renewable resources depend on the circumstances. When the resource can be extracted at a constant marginal cost, the efficient quantity of the depletable resource extracted declines over time. If no substitute is available, the quantity declines smoothly to zero. If a renewable constant-cost substitute is available, the quantity of the depletable resource extracted will decline smoothly to the quantity available from the renewable resource. In each case, all of the available depletable resource would be eventually used up and marginal user cost would rise over time, reaching a maximum when the last unit of depletable resource was extracted.

The efficient allocation of an increasing marginal-cost resource is similar in that the quantity extracted declines over time, but differs with respect to the behavior of marginal user cost and the cumulative amount extracted. Whereas marginal user cost typically rises over time when the marginal cost of extraction is constant, it declines over time when the marginal cost of extraction rises. Furthermore, in the constant-cost case the cumulative amount extracted is equal to the available supply; in the increasing-cost case it depends on the relationship between the marginal extraction cost function and the cost of the substitute.

Introducing technological progress and exploration activity into the model tends to delay the transition to renewable resources. Exploration expands the size of current reserves, while technological progress keeps marginal extraction cost from rising as fast as it otherwise would. If these effects are sufficiently potent, marginal cost could actually decline for some period of time, causing the quantity extracted to rise.

When property rights structures are properly defined, market allocations of depletable resources can be efficient. In this case self-interest and efficiency can be compatible.

When the extraction of resources imposes an external environmental cost, however, generally market allocations will not be efficient. The market price of the depletable resource would be too low, the rate of extraction would be excessive, and too much of the resource would ultimately be extracted.

In an efficient market allocation, the transition from depletable to renewable resources is smooth and exhibits no overshoot-and-collapse characteristics. Whether the actual market allocations of these various types of resources are efficient remains to be seen. To the extent markets negotiate an efficient transition, a laissez-faire policy would represent an appropriate response by the government. On the other hand, if the market is not capable of yielding an efficient allocation, then some form of government intervention may be necessary. In the next few chapters, we shall examine these questions for a number of different types of depletable and renewable resources.

Discussion Question

1. One current practice is to calculate the years remaining for a depletable resource by taking the prevailing estimates of current reserves and dividing it by current annual consumption. How useful is that calculation? Why?

Self-Test Exercises

1. To anticipate subsequent chapters where more complicated renewable resource models are introduced, consider a slight modification of the two-period depletable resource model. Suppose a biological resource is renewable in the sense that any of it left unextracted after Period 1 will grow at rate k. Compared to the case where the total amount of a constant-*MEC* resource is fixed, how would the efficient allocation of this resource over the two periods differ? (*Hint*: It can be shown that $MNB_1/MNB_2 = (1 + k)/(1 + r)$, where *MNB* stands for marginal net benefit.)
2. Consider an increasing marginal-cost depletable resource with no effective substitute. (a) Describe, in general terms, how the marginal user cost for this resource in the earlier time periods would depend on whether the demand curve for that resource was stable or shifting outward over time. (b) How would the allocation of that resource over time be affected?
3. Many states are now imposing severance taxes on resources being extracted within their borders. In order to understand the effect of these on the allocation of the mineral over time, assume a stable demand curve. (a) How would the competitive allocation of an increasing marginal-cost depletable resource be affected by the imposition of a per-unit tax (e.g., $4 per ton) if there exists a constant-marginal-cost substitute? (b) Comparing the allocation without a tax to one with a tax, in general terms, what are the differences in cumulative amounts extracted and the price paths?
4. For the increasing marginal-extraction-cost model of the allocation of a depletable resource, how would the ultimate cumulative amount taken out of the ground be affected by (a) an increase in the discount rate, (b) the extraction by a monopolistic, rather than a competitive, industry, and (c) a per-unit subsidy paid by the government for each unit of the abundant substitute used?
5. Suppose you wanted to hasten the transition from a depletable fossil fuel to solar energy. Compare the effects of a per-unit tax on the depletable resource to an equivalent per-unit subsidy on solar energy. Would they produce the same switch point? Why or why not?

Further Reading

Andre, F., & Cerda, E. (2006). On the dynamics of recycling and natural resources. *Environmental & Resource Economics, 33*(2),199–221. This article provides a formal examination of how the recyclability of depletable resources affects extraction profiles and sustainability.

Conrad, J. M., & Clark, C.W., (1987). *Natural Resource Economics: Notes and Problems.* Cambridge: Cambridge University Press. Reviews techniques of dynamic optimization and shows how they can be applied to the management of various resource systems.

Fischer, C., & Laxminarayan, R. (2005). Sequential development and exploitation of an exhaustible resource: Do monopoly rights promote conservation? *Journal of Environmental Economics and Management, 49*(3), 500–515. Examines the conditions under which a monopolist would extract a depletable resource more quickly or more slowly than a competitive industry.

Strand, J. (2010). Optimal fossil-fuel taxation with backstop technologies and tenure risk. *Energy Economics, 32*(2), 418–422. This article examines the time paths for optimal taxes and extraction profiles for a depletable resource that creates a negative stock externality (think climate change), involves increasing marginal extraction cost, and is subject to competition from an unlimited backstop resource causing no externality.

Additional References and Historically Significant References are available on this book's Companion Website: http://www.routledgetextbooks.com/textbooks/9780133479690

Appendix

Extensions of the Constant Extraction Cost Depletable Resource Model: Longer Time Horizons and the Role of an Abundant Substitute

In the appendix to Chapter 5, we derived a simple model to describe the efficient allocation of a constant-marginal-cost depletable resource over time and presented the numerical solution for a two-period version of that model. In this appendix, the mathematical derivations for the extension to that basic model will be documented, and the resulting numerical solutions for these more complicated cases will be explained.

The *N*-Period, Constant-Cost, No-Substitute Case

The first extension involves calculating the efficient allocation of the depletable resource over time when the number of time periods for extraction is unlimited. This is a more difficult calculation because how long the resource will last is no longer predetermined; the time of exhaustion must be derived as well as the extraction path prior to exhaustion of the resource.

The equations describing the allocation that maximizes the present value of net benefits are

$$\frac{a - bq_t - c}{(1 + r)^{t-1}} - \lambda = 0, t = 1, \ldots, T \tag{1}$$

$$\sum_{t=1}^{T} q_t = \bar{Q} \tag{2}$$

The parameter values assumed for the numerical example presented in the text are

$$a = \$8, b = 0.4, c = \$2, \bar{Q} = 40, \text{and } r = 0.10$$

The allocation that satisfies these conditions is

$q_1 = 8.004$	$q_4 = 5.689$	$q_7 = 2.607$	$T = 9$
$q_2 = 7.305$	$q_5 = 4.758$	$q_8 = 1.368$	$\lambda = 2.7983$
$q_3 = 6.535$	$q_6 = 3.733$	$q_9 = 0.000$	

The optimality of this allocation can be verified by substituting these values into the above equations. (Due to rounding, these add to 39.999, rather than 40.000.)

Practically speaking, solving these equations to find the optimal solution is not a trivial matter, but neither is it very difficult. One method of finding the solution for those without the requisite mathematics involves developing a computer algorithm (computation procedure) that converges on the correct answer. One such algorithm for this example can be constructed as follows: (1) assume a value for λ; (2) using Equation set (1) solve for all q's based upon this λ; (3) if the sum of the calculated q's exceeds $\bar{Q}$, adjust λ upward or if the sum of the calculated q's is less than $\bar{Q}$, adjust λ downward (the adjustment should use information gained in previous steps to ensure that the new trial will be closer to the solution value); (4) repeat steps (2) and (3) using the new λ; (5) when the sum of the q's is sufficiently close to $\bar{Q}$ stop the calculations. As an exercise, those interested in computer programming might construct a program to reproduce these results.

Constant Marginal Cost with an Abundant Renewable Substitute

The next extension assumes the existence of an abundant, renewable, perfect substitute, available in unlimited quantities at a cost of \$6 per unit. To derive the dynamically efficient allocation of both the depletable resource and its substitute, let q_t be the amount of a constant-marginal-cost depletable resource extracted in year t and q_{st} the amount used of another constant-marginal-cost resource that is perfectly substitutable for the depletable resource. The marginal cost of the substitute is assumed to be \$$d$.

With this change, the total benefit and cost formulas become

$$\text{Total benefit} = \sum_{t=1}^{T} a(q_t + q_{st}) - \frac{b}{2}(q_t + q_{st})^2 \tag{3}$$

$$\text{Total cost} = \sum_{t=1}^{T} (cq_t + dq_t) \tag{4}$$

The objective function is thus

$$PVNB = \sum_{t=1}^{T} \frac{a(q_t + q_{st}) - \frac{b}{2}\left(q_t^2 + q_{st}^2 + 2q_t q_{st}\right) - cq_t - dq_{st}}{(1 + r)^{t-1}} \tag{5}$$

subject to the constraint on the total availability of the depletable resource

$$\bar{Q} - \sum_{t=1}^{T} q_t \geq 0 \tag{6}$$

Necessary and sufficient conditions for an allocation maximizing this function are expressed in Equations (7), (8), and (9):

$$\frac{a - b(q_t + q_{st}) - c}{(1 + r)^{t-1}} - \lambda \leq 0, t = 1, \ldots, T \tag{7}$$

Any member of Equation set (7) will hold as an equality when $q_t > 0$ and will be negative when

$$a - b(q_t + q_{st}) - d \leq 0, t = 1, \ldots, T \tag{8}$$

Any member of Equation set (8) will hold as an equality when $q_{st} > 0$ and will be negative when $q_{st} = 0$

$$\bar{Q} - \sum_{t=1}^{T} q_t \geq 0 \tag{9}$$

For the numerical example used in the test, the following parameter values were assumed: $a = \$8, b = 0.4, c = \$2, d = \$6, Q = 40$, and $r = 0.10$. It can be readily verified that the optimal conditions are satisfied by

$$q_1 = 8.798 \quad q_3 = 7.495 \quad q_5 = 5.919$$

$$q_2 = 8.177 \quad q_4 = 6.744$$

$$q_{s6} = 2.137 \quad q_{st} = \begin{cases} 5.000 \text{ for } t > 6 \\ 0 \text{ for } t < 6 \end{cases}$$

$$q_6 = 2.863 \quad \lambda = 2.481$$

The depletable resource is used up before the end of the sixth period and the switch is made to the substitute resource at that time. From Equation set (8), in competitive markets the switch occurs precisely at the moment when the resource price rises to meet the marginal cost of the substitute.

The switch point in this example is earlier than in the previous example (the sixth period rather than the ninth period). Since all characteristics of the problem except for the availability of the substitute are the same in the two numerical examples, the difference can be attributed to the availability of the renewable substitute.

Energy: The Transition from Depletable to Renewable Resources

7

If it ain't broke, don't fix it!

—Old Maine proverb

Introduction

Energy is one of our most critical resources; without it, life would cease. We derive energy from the food we eat. Through photosynthesis, the plants we consume—both directly and indirectly when we eat meat—depend on energy from the sun. The materials we use to build our houses and produce the goods we consume are extracted from the earth's crust, and then transformed into finished products with expenditures of energy.

Currently, many industrialized countries depend on oil and natural gas for the majority of their energy needs. According to the International Energy Agency (IEA), these resources together supply 59 percent of all primary energy consumed worldwide. (Adding coal, another fossil fuel resource, increases the share to 86 percent of the total.) Fossil fuels are depletable, nonrecyclable sources of energy.

Kenneth Deffeyes (2001) and Campbell and Laherrere (1998) estimated that *global* oil production would peak early in the twenty-first century. As Example 7.1 points out, however, due to the methodology used, these predictions of the timing of the peak are controversial.

Even if we cannot precisely determine when the fuels on which we currently depend so heavily will run out, we still need to think about the process of transition to new energy sources. New science now makes it clear that holding climate change in check will require a transition to renewable fuels well before the depletable fossil fuels are exhausted so the time of exhaustion is a less important concept than it used to be.

According to depletable resource models, oil and natural gas would be used until the marginal cost of further use exceeded the marginal cost of substitute resources—either more abundant depletable resources such as coal, or renewable sources such as solar energy.[1] In an efficient market path, the transition to these alternative sources would be smooth and harmonious. Have the allocations of the last several decades been efficient or not? Is the market mechanism flawed in its

[1]When used for other purposes, oil can be recyclable. Waste lubricating oil is now routinely recycled.

EXAMPLE 7.1

Hubbert's Peak

When can we expect production of oil to peak? It's a simple question with a complex answer. In 1956 geophysicist M. King Hubbert, then working at the Shell research lab in Houston, predicted that U.S. oil production would reach its peak in the early 1970s. Though Hubbert's analysis failed to win much acceptance from experts either in the oil industry or among academics, his prediction came true in the early 1970s. With some modifications, this methodology has since been used to predict the timing of a downturn in global annual oil production as well as the timing of when we might run out of oil.

These forecasts and the methods that underlie them were controversial, in part because they ignored such obvious economic factors as prices and technical progress that affects extraction costs. The Hubbert model assumes that the annual rate of production follows a bell-shaped curve, regardless of what is happening in oil markets; in this approach market forces don't matter. It seems reasonable to believe, however, from the analysis in the previous chapter that by affecting the incentive to explore new sources and to develop new technologies, market forces should affect the shape of the production curve.

A study by Kaufman and Cleveland (2001) confirms that forecasting with a Hubbert-type model is fraught with peril.

> *Our results indicate that Hubbert was able to predict the peak in US production accurately because real oil prices, average real cost of production, and [government decisions] co-evolved in a way that traced what appears to be a symmetric bell-shaped curve for production over time. A different evolutionary path for any of these variables could have produced a pattern of production that is significantly different from a bell-shaped curve and production may not have peaked in 1970. In effect, Hubbert got lucky. [p. 46]*

What about the recent evidence? Does the Hubbert methodology accurately predict US oil production after the peak? Actually it doesn't. According to the International Energy Agency domestic crude oil production recently has been increasing so much due to the introduction of a technological change known as fracking (explored more fully below) that they expect the United States to overtake Saudi Arabia as the world's largest oil producer by 2020. That expectation is certainly not consistent with a bell-shaped curve.

Clearly we have to be cautious when interpreting forecasts of production peaks as well as the timing of the transition to other sources of energy.

Sources: Kaufman, R., & Cleveland, C. (2001). Oil production in the lower 48 states: Economic, geological, and institutional determinants. *Energy Journal, 22*(1), 27–49; International Energy Agency, *World Energy Outlook*: 2012 (Paris).

allocation of depletable, nonrecyclable resources? If so, is it a fatal flaw? If not, what caused the inefficient allocations? Are the problems correctable?

In this chapter we shall examine some of the major issues associated with the allocation of energy resources over time and explore how economic analysis can clarify our understanding of both the sources of the problems and their solutions.

Natural Gas: From Price Controls to Fracking

The Role of Price Controls in the History of Natural Gas

In the United States, during the winter of 1974 and early 1975, serious shortages of natural gas developed. Customers who had contracted for and were willing to pay for natural gas were unable to get as much as they wanted. The shortage (or curtailments, as the Federal Energy Regulatory Commission [FERC] calls them) amounted to two trillion cubic feet of natural gas in 1974–1975, which represented roughly 10 percent of the marketed production in 1975. In an efficient allocation, shortages of that magnitude would never have materialized. What happened?

The simple answer is regulation. The regulation of natural gas began in 1938 with the passage of the Natural Gas Act. This act transformed the Federal Power Commission (FPC), which subsequently become FERC, into a federal regulatory agency charged with maintaining "just" prices. In 1954 a Supreme Court decision forced the FPC to extend their price control regulations beyond pipeline companies to include producers as well.

Because the process of setting price ceilings proved cumbersome, the hastily conceived initial "interim" ceilings remained in effect for almost a decade before the Commission was able to impose more carefully considered ceilings. What was the effect of this regulation?

By returning to our models in the previous section, we can anticipate the havoc this would raise. The ceiling would prevent prices from reaching their normal levels. Since price increases are the source of the incentive to conserve, the lower future prices would cause more of the resource to be used in earlier years. Consumption levels in the earlier years would be higher under price controls than without them.

Effects on the supply side would also be expected to be significant. Producers would produce the resource only when they could do so profitably. Once the marginal cost rose to meet the price ceiling, no more would be produced, regardless of the demand for the resource at that price. Thus, as long as price controls were permanent, less of the resource would be produced with controls than without and production and consumption would be skewed toward the earlier years.

The combined impact of these demand-and-supply effects would be to distort the allocation significantly (see Figures 7.1a and 7.1b). While a number of

FIGURE 7.1 (a) Increasing Marginal Extraction Cost with Substitute Resource in the Presence of Price Controls: Quantity Profile (b) Increasing Marginal Extraction Cost with Substitute Resource in the Presence of Price Controls: Price Profile

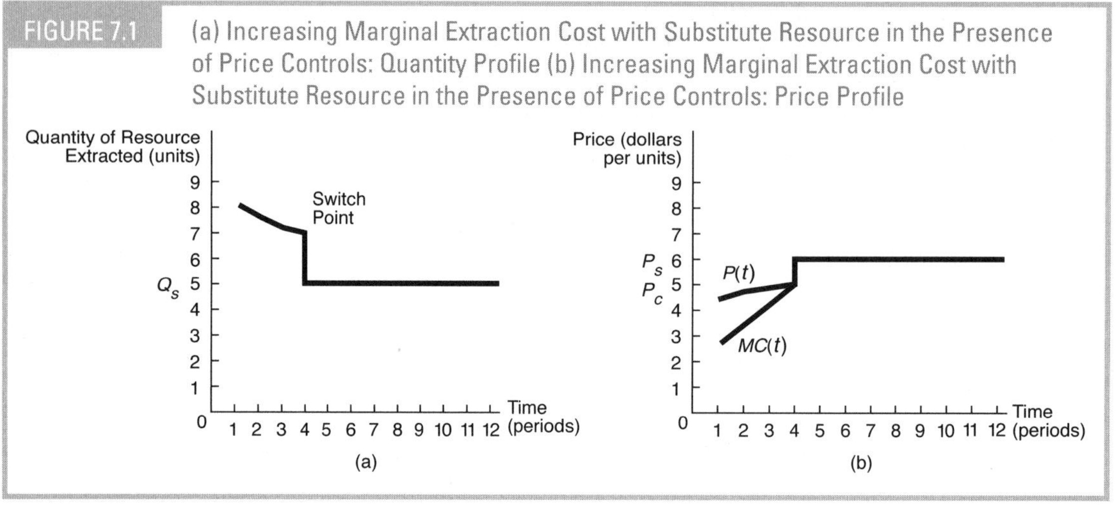

aspects differentiate this allocation from an efficient one, several are of particular importance: the market would react to price controls by (1) leaving more of the resource in the ground, (2) increasing the rate of consumption, (3) causing the time of transition to be earlier, and (4) creating an abrupt transition, with prices suddenly jumping to new, higher levels. All are detrimental. The first effect means we would not be using all of the natural gas available at prices consumers were willing to pay. Because price controls would cause prices to be lower than efficient, the resource would be depleted too fast. These two effects would cause an earlier and abrupt transition to the substitute possibly before the technologies to use it were adequately developed.

The discontinuous jump to a new technology, which results from the fact that price controls eliminate price flexibility, can place quite a burden on consumers. Attracted by artificially low prices, consumers would invest in equipment to use natural gas, only to discover—after the transition—that natural gas was no longer available.

One interesting characteristic of price ceilings is that they affect behavior even before they are binding.[2] This effect is clearly illustrated in Figures 7.1a and 7.1b in the earlier years. Even though the price in the first year is lower than the price ceiling, it is not equal to the efficient price. (Can you see why? Think what effect price controls have on the marginal user cost faced by producers.) The price ceiling causes a reallocation of resources toward the present, which, in turn, reduces prices in the earlier years.

It seems fair to conclude that, by sapping the economic system of its ability to respond to changing conditions, price controls on natural gas created a significant

---

[2]For a complete early recognition of this point, see Lee (1978).

amount of turmoil. When this kind of political control occurs, the overshoot and collapse scenario can have some validity. In this case, however, it would be caused by government actions rather than any pure market behavior. If so, the adage that opens this chapter becomes particularly relevant!

Politicians may view scarcity rent as a possible source of revenue to transfer from producers to consumers. As we have seen, however, scarcity rent is an opportunity cost that serves a distinct purpose—the protection of future consumers. When a government attempts to reduce this scarcity rent through price controls, the result is an overallocation to current consumers and an underallocation to future consumers. Thus, what appears to be a financial transfer from producers to consumers is, in large part, also a transfer of the affected commodity from future consumers to present consumers. Since current consumers mean current votes and future consumers may not know whom to blame by the time shortages appear, price controls are politically attractive. Unfortunately, they are also inefficient; the losses to future consumers and producers are greater than the gains to current consumers. Because controls distort the allocation toward the present, they are also unfair. Thus, markets in the presence of price controls are indeed myopic, but the problem lies with the controls, not the market per se.

After long debating the price control issue, Congress passed the Natural Gas Policy Act on November 9, 1978. This act initiated the eventual phased decontrol of natural gas prices. By January 1993, no sources of natural gas were subject to price controls.

Fracking[3]

Natural gas production remained relatively stable from the mid-1970s until the middle of the first decade of the twenty-first century when a new technology dramatically changed the cost of accessing new sources of natural gas in shale, a type of sedimentary rock. Hydraulic fracturing, or fracking as it is known popularly, is a form of technical progress that combines horizontal drilling with an ability to fracture deep shale deposits using a mixture of high pressure water, sand, and chemicals. Not only does the fractured shale release large quantities of natural gas, but this extraction process also costs less than accessing more conventional sources.

The introduction of this new technology has increased production dramatically in the United States and fracked gas is likely to play an even larger role over the next few decades according to the Energy Information Agency, the statistical arm of the US Department of Energy. If ever there were an example of the profound effect a technical change can have, this is it!

[3]Although we focus here on the role of fracking in natural gas production from shale, as noted in Example 7.1, it is also being used to increase oil production from shale.

While this production is dramatically changing the energy situation in the United States, that change comes with some controversy (see Debate 7.1).

DEBATE 7.1

Does the Advent of Fracking Increase Net Benefits?

While fracking will no doubt lower US dependency on energy imports (the subject of the next section) and provide an economic boost by lowering energy costs in the United States as it displaces more expensive fuels, it also comes with some costs. The main short-term concerns involve water contamination (fracking chemicals leaking into local wells), water depletion (the extraction process uses large quantities of water), air quality issues (some of the toxic fracking chemicals can escape into the surrounding air) and "leakage" (methane, one of the primary components of natural gas and a powerful greenhouse gas that contributes to climate change, can leak into the atmoshpere as a result of the fracking process). Further over the longer run, according to the International Energy Agency, an excessive reliance on natural gas would be incompatible with reaching the proposed climate policy goals.

So if fracking comes with high benefits *and* high costs, does it make economic sense? The simple answer is that we don't know yet. For one thing, as Chapter 3 reminds us, it would depend on the accounting stance (geographic scope) of the analysis. The geographic regions that benefit may not be the same regions that bear the costs. So difference accounting stances could produce different results.

More fundamentally, even if a national benefit-cost analysis could be revealing, many of the components of that analysis are not known yet with sufficient certainty to provide much confidence in the answers this early in the game. To take just one example of our ignorance if the leakage rate exceeds 3.2%, natural gas is apparently no better for the climate than coal or oil, but we have a firm grasp on the leakage rate for only a few specially studied wells. Furthermore, the expected costs from the associated water and air contamination are not yet fully known either. Finally, even if we were able to derive a reasonable answer for the current period prior to much regulation, the answer is likely to be much more favorable to fracking once a regulatory framework to reduce the problems is in place.

Fortunately, studies are underway to fill in the information gaps and regulations that control the most negative net benefit aspects of the industry are likely to follow. Stay tuned.

Source: Alvarez, R. A., Pacala, S. W., Winebrake, J. J., Chameides, W. L., & Hamburg, S. P. (2012). Greater focus needed on methane leakage from natural gas infrastructure. *PNAS, 109*(176435-6440).

Oil: The Cartel Problem

Most of the world's oil is currently still produced by a cartel called the Organization of Petroleum Exporting Countries (OPEC). The members of this organization collude to exercise power over oil production and prices. As established in Chapter 2, seller power over resources due to a lack of effective competition leads to an inefficient allocation. When sellers have market power, they can restrict supply and thus force prices higher than otherwise.

Though these conclusions were previously derived for nondepletable resources, they are valid for depletable resources as well. A monopolist can extract more scarcity rent from a depletable resource base than competitive suppliers simply by restricting supply. The monopolistic transition results in a slower rate of production and higher prices.[4] The monopolistic transition to a substitute, therefore, occurs later than a competitive transition. While monopolistic exploitation raises the net present value of profits to the sellers, it reduces the net present value of net benefits to society.

The cartelization of the oil suppliers has apparently historically been quite effective (Smith, 2005). Why? Are the conditions that make it profitable unique to oil, or could oil cartelization be the harbinger of a wave of natural resource cartels? What is the outlook for the oil cartel in the future? To answer these questions, we must isolate those factors that make cartelization possible and profitable. Although many factors are involved, four stand out: (1) the price elasticity of demand in both the long run and the short run; (2) the income elasticity of demand; (3) the supply responsiveness of the producers who are not cartel members; and (4) the compatibility of interests among members of the cartel.

Price Elasticity of Demand

The price elasticity of demand is an important ingredient because it determines how responsive demand is to price. When demand elasticities are between 0 and –1 (i.e., when the percent quantity response is smaller than the percent price response), price increases lead to increased revenue. Exactly how much revenue would increase when prices increase depends on the magnitude of the elasticity. Generally, the smaller is the absolute value of the price elasticity of demand (the closer it is to 0.0), the larger are the gains to be derived from forming a cartel.

The price elasticity of demand depends on the opportunities for conservation, as well as on the availability of substitutes. As storm windows cut heat losses, the same temperature can be maintained with less heating oil. Smaller, more fuel-efficient automobiles reduce the amount of gasoline needed to travel a given distance. The larger the set of these opportunities and the smaller the cash outlays required to exploit them, the more price-elastic the demand. This suggests that demand will be more price-elastic in the long run (when sufficient time has passed to allow adjustments) than in the short run.

The availability of substitutes is also important because it limits the degree to which prices can be profitably raised by a producer cartel. Abundant quantities of relatively inexpensive fuels that could substitute for oil can set an upper limit on the cartel price. Unless the cartel controls those alternative sources as well—and in oil's case it doesn't—any attempts to raise prices above those limits would cause the consuming nations to simply switch to these alternative sources; the cartel would have priced itself out of the market.

---

[4]The conclusion that a monopoly would extract a resource more slowly than a competitive mining industry is not perfectly general. It is possible to construct demand curves such that the extraction of the monopolist is greater than or equal to that of a competitive industry. As a practical matter, these conditions seem unlikely. That a monopoly would restrict output, while not inevitable, is the most likely outcome.

Income Elasticity of Demand

The income elasticity of demand is important because it indicates how sensitive demand for the cartel's product is to growth in the world economy. As income grows, demand should grow. This continual increase in demand fortifies the ability of the cartel to raise its prices.

The income elasticity of demand is also important, however, because it registers how sensitive demand is to the business cycle. The higher the income elasticity of demand, the more sensitive demand is to periods of rapid economic growth or to recessions. Economic downturns led to a weakening of the oil cartel in 1983 as well as to a significant fall in oil prices starting in late 2008. Conversely, whenever the global economy recovers, the cartel benefits disproportionately.

Non-Member Suppliers

Another key factor in the ability of producer nations to exercise power over a natural resource market is their ability to prevent new suppliers, not part of the cartel, from entering the market and undercutting the price. Prior to fracking OPEC produced about 45 percent of the world's oil, but that is likely to change due to the increase in production from fracked oil. When non-OPEC producers expand their supply dramatically, prices can be expected to fall along with OPEC's market share. If this supply response is large enough, the cartelized allocation of oil would approach the competitive allocation.

Recognizing this impact, the cartel must take the nonmembers into account when setting prices. Salant (1976) proposed an interesting model of monopoly pricing in the presence of a fringe of small nonmember producers that serves as a basis for exploring this issue. His model includes a number of suppliers. Some form a cartel. Others, a smaller number, form a "competitive fringe." The cartel is assumed to set its price so as to maximize its collective profit, taking the competitive fringe production into account. The competitive fringe cannot directly set the price, but, since it is free to choose the level of production that maximizes its own profits, its output does affect the cartel's pricing strategy by increasing the available supply.

What conclusions does this model yield? The model concludes first of all that a resource cartel would set different prices in the presence of a competitive fringe than in its absence. With a competitive fringe, it would set the initial price somewhat lower than the pure monopoly price and allow price to rise more rapidly. This strategy maximizes cartel profits by inducing the competitive fringe to produce more in the earlier periods (in response to higher demand) and eventually to exhaust their supplies. Once the competitive fringe has depleted its reserves, the cartel would raise the price and thereafter prices would increase much more slowly.

Thus, the optimal strategy, from the point of view of the cartel, is to hold back on its own sales during the initial period, letting the other suppliers exhaust their supplies. Sales and profits of the competitive fringe, in this optimal cartel strategy, decline over time, while sales and profits of the cartel increase over time as prices rise and the cartel continues to capture a larger share of the market.

Another fascinating implication of this model is that the formation of the cartel raises the present value of competitive fringe profits by an even greater percentage than it raises the present value of cartel profits. Those without the power gain more in percentage terms than those with the power!

Though this may seem counterintuitive, it is actually easily explained. The cartel, in order to keep the price up, must cut back on its own production level. The competitive fringe, however, is under no such constraint and is free to take advantage of the high prices caused by the cartel's withheld production without cutting back its own production. Thus, the profits of the competitive fringe are higher in the earlier period, which, in present value terms, are discounted less. All the cartel can do is wait until the competitive suppliers become less of a force in the market. The implication of this model is that the presence of a competitive fringe matters, even if it controls as little as one-third of the production.

The impact of this competitive fringe on OPEC behavior was dramatically illustrated by events in the 1985–1986 period. In 1979, OPEC accounted for approximately 50 percent of world oil production, while in 1986 this had fallen to approximately 30 percent. When the recession cut global demand by 10%, the cartel's attempts to keep prices as high as possible by reducing its own production were thwarted by a competitive fringe that simply kept producing. The real cost of crude oil imports in the United States fell from $34.95 per barrel in 1981 to $11.41 in 1986. OPEC simply was not able to hold the line on prices because the necessary reductions in its own production were too large for the cartel members to sustain in the face of continuing supplies from the competitive fringe.

With global economic growth, however, the tide was turned. In the summer of 2008, the price of crude oil soared above $138 per barrel. Strong worldwide demand was coupled with restricted supply from Iraq because of the war. However, these high prices also promoted the major oil companies' search for more unconventional sources of oil including the tar sands in Canada and the use of fracking to extract oil from shale in the United States. Once again the cartel's power was subject to limits, this time imposed by non-member suppliers.

Compatibility of Member Interests

The final factor we shall consider in determining the potential for cartelization of natural resource markets is the internal cohesion of the cartel. With only one seller, the objective of that seller can be pursued without worrying about alienating others who could undermine the profitability of the enterprise. In a cartel composed of many sellers, that freedom is no longer as wide ranging. The incentives of each member and the incentives of the group as a whole may diverge.

Cartel members have a strong incentive to cheat. A cheater, if undeterred by the other members, could lower its price and steal a larger share of the market. Formally speaking, the price elasticity of demand facing an individual member is substantially higher than that for the group as a whole, because some of the increase in individual sales at a lower individual price represents sales reductions for other members. When producers face markets characterized by high price elasticities, lower prices maximize profits. Thus, successful cartelization presupposes a means for detecting cheating and enforcing the collusive agreement.

In addition to cheating, however, cartel stability is also threatened by the degree to which members fail to agree on pricing and output decisions. Oil provides an excellent example of how these dissensions can arise. Since the 1974 rise of OPEC as a world power, Saudi Arabia has frequently exercised a moderating influence on the pricing decisions of OPEC. Why?

One highly significant reason is the size of Saudi Arabia's oil reserves. Saudi Arabia's reserves are larger than those of any other member. Hence, Saudi Arabia has an incentive to preserve the value of those resources. Setting prices too high would undercut the future demand for its oil. As previously stated, the demand for oil in the long run is more price-elastic than in the short run. Countries with smaller reserves, such as Nigeria, know that in the long run their reserves will be gone and therefore these countries are more concerned about the near future. Countries with small reserves want to extract as much rent as possible now, but countries with large reserves want to preserve future rent.

This examination of the preconditions for successful cartelization suggests two things: (1) creating a successful cartel is not an easy path for natural resource producers to pursue, and (2) it is quite likely that OPEC's difficulties in exercising control over the market will only increase in the future.

Fossil Fuels: National Security Considerations

Vulnerable strategic imports such as oil have an added cost that is not reflected in the marketplace. National security is a classic public good. No individual importer correctly represents our collective national security interests in making a decision on how much to import. Hence, leaving the determination of the appropriate balance between imports and domestic production to the market generally results in an excessive dependence on imports due to both climate change and national security considerations (see Figure 7.2).

In order to understand the interaction of these factors, five supply curves are relevant. Domestic supply is reflected by two options. The first, S_{d1}, is the long-run domestic supply curve without considering the climate change damages resulting from burning more oil, while the second, S_{d2}, is the domestic supply curve that includes these per-unit damages.

All fossil fuels contain carbon. When these fuels are combusted, unless the resulting carbon is captured, it is released into the atmosphere as carbon dioxide, a contributor to climate change. Climate change is the subject of Chapter 16. As can be seen from Table 7.1, among the fossil fuels, coal contains the most carbon per unit of energy produced and natural gas contains the least.

The upward slopes of these supply curves reflect increasing availability of domestic oil at higher prices, given sufficient time to develop those resources. Imported foreign oil is reflected by three supply curves: P_{w1} reflects the observed world price, P_{w2} includes a "vulnerability premium" in addition to the world price, and P_{w3} adds in the per-unit climate change damages due to consuming more imported oil. The vulnerability premium reflects the additional national security costs caused by imports. All three curves are drawn horizontally to the axis to reflect

FIGURE 7.2 The National Security Problem

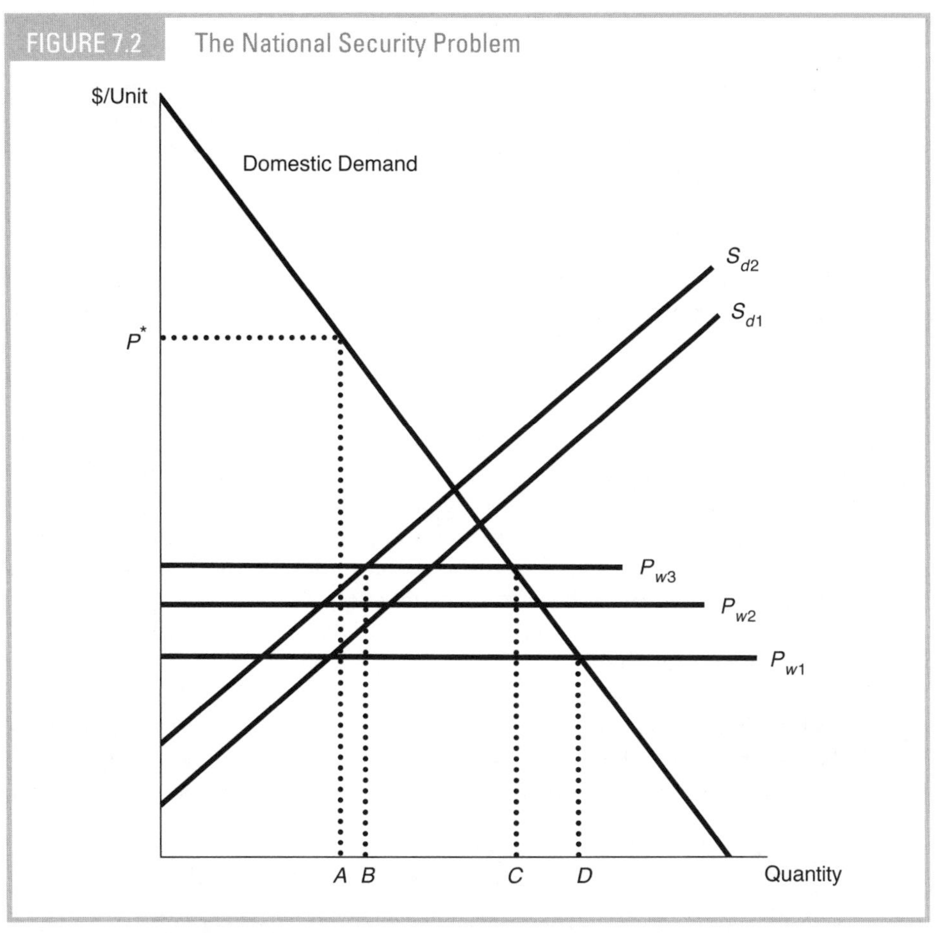

TABLE 7.1 Carbon Content of Fuels

Pounds of CO_2 emitted per million Btu of energy for various fuels

Fuel	Pounds
Coal (anthracite)	227
Coal (bituminous)	205
Coal (lignite)	215
Coal (subbituminous)	213
Diesel fuel & heating oil	161
Gasoline	156
Propane	139
Natural gas	117

Source: Energy Information Administration. Retrieved from http://www.eia.gov/tools/faqs/faq.cfm?id=73&t=11

the assumption that any single importing country's action on imports is unlikely to affect the world price for oil.

As shown in Figure 7.2, in the absence of any correction for national security and climate change considerations, the market would generally demand and receive *D* units of oil. Of this total amount, *A* would be domestically produced and *D–A* would be imported. Why?

In an efficient allocation, incorporating the national security and climate change considerations, only *C* units would be consumed. Of these, *B* would be domestically produced and *C-B* would be imported. Note that because national security and climate change are externalities, the market in general tends to consume too much oil and vulnerable imports exceed their efficient level.

What would happen during an embargo? Be careful! At first glance, you would guess that we would consume where domestic supply equals domestic demand, but that is not right. Remember that S_{d1} is the domestic supply curve, *given enough time to develop the resources*. If an embargo hits, developing additional resources cannot happen immediately (multiple year time lags are common). Therefore, in the short run, the supply curve becomes perfectly inelastic (vertical) at *A*. The price will rise to P^* to equate supply and demand. As the graph indicates, the loss in consumer surplus during an embargo can be very large indeed.

How can importing nations react to this inefficiency? As Debate 7.2 shows, several strategies are available.

The importing country might be able to become self-sufficient, but should it? If the situation is adequately represented by Figure 7.2, then the answer is clearly no. The net benefit from self-sufficiency (the allocation where domestic supply S_{d1} crosses the demand curve) is clearly lower than the net benefit from the efficient allocation (*C*).

DEBATE 7.2 How Should Countries Deal with the Vulnerability of Imported Oil?

Historically, the United States, like many other countries, has imported most of its oil. Since oil is a strategic material, how can the resulting vulnerability to import disruption be addressed?

One vision focuses on a strategy of increasing domestic production, not only of oil, but also of natural gas and coal. This vision includes opening up new oil fields in such places as coastal waters and the Arctic National Wildlife Refuge as well as expanding the production of newer sources such as tar sands or oil shale, Tax incentives and subsidies could be used to promote domestic production.

Another vision emphasizes energy efficiency and energy conservation. Pointing out that expanded domestic production could exacerbate environmental problems (including climate change), this vision promotes such strategies as mandating standards for fuel economy in automobiles, enacting energy efficiency standards for appliances and making buildings much more energy efficient.

Using economic analysis, figure out what the effects of these two different strategies would be on (1) oil prices in the short run and the long run, (2) emissions affecting climate change, and (3) U.S. imports in the short run and the long run. If you were in charge of OPEC, which strategy would you like to see chosen by Americans? Why?

Why, you might ask, is self-sufficiency so inefficient when embargoes obviously impose so much damage and self-sufficiency could grant immunity from this damage? Why would we want any imports at all when national security is at stake?

The simple answer is that the vulnerability premium is lower than the cost of becoming self-sufficient, but that response merely begs the question, "why is the vulnerability premium lower?" It is lower for three primary reasons: (1) embargoes are not certain events—they may never occur; (2) steps can be taken to reduce vulnerability of the remaining imports; and (3) expanding current domestic production via subsidies would incur a user cost by lowering the domestic amounts available to future users.

The expected damage caused by one or more embargoes depends on the likelihood of occurrence, as well as the intensity and duration. This means that the P_{w2} curve will be lower for imports having a lower likelihood of being embargoed. Imports from countries less hostile to our interests are more secure and the vulnerability premium on those imports is smaller.[5]

For any remaining vulnerable imports, we can adopt certain contingency programs to reduce the damage an embargo would cause. The most obvious measure is to develop a domestic stockpile of oil to be used during an embargo. The United States has taken this route. The stockpile, called the *strategic petroleum reserve*, was originally designed to contain one billion barrels of oil (see Example 7.2). A 1 billion barrel stockpile would replace 3 million barrels a day for slightly less than 1 year or a larger number of barrels per day for a shorter period of time. This reserve would serve as an alternative domestic source of supply, which, unlike other oil resources, could be rapidly deployed on short notice. It is, in short, a form of insurance. If this protection can be purchased cheaply, implying a lower P_{w2}, imports become more attractive.

To understand the third and final reason that paying the vulnerability premium would be less costly than self-sufficiency, we must consider vulnerability in a dynamic, rather than static, framework. Because oil is a depletable resource, a user cost is associated with its efficient use. To reorient the extraction of that resource toward the present, as a self-sufficiency strategy would do, reduces future net benefits. Thus, the self-sufficiency strategy tends to be myopic in that it solves the short-term vulnerability problem by creating a more serious one in the future. Paying the vulnerability premium creates a more efficient balance between the present and future, as well as between current imports and domestic production.

We have established the fact that government can reduce our vulnerability to imports, which tends to keep the risk premium as low as possible. Certainly for oil, however, even after the stockpile has been established, the risk premium is not zero; P_{w1} *and* P_{w2} will not coincide. Consequently, the government must also concern itself with achieving both the efficient level of consumption and the efficient share of that consumption borne by imports. Let's examine some of the policy choices.

As noted in Debate 7.2, energy conservation is one popular approach to the problem. One way to accomplish additional conservation is by means of a tax on fossil fuel consumption. Graphically, this approach would be reflected as a shift inward of the after-tax demand curve. Such a tax could reduce energy consumption

---

[5]It is this fact that explains the tremendous U.S. interest in Canadian and Latin American oil, in spite of the fact that, historically, it has not necessarily been cheaper.

EXAMPLE 7.2

Strategic Petroleum Reserve

The US strategic petroleum reserve (SPR) is the world's largest supply of emergency crude oil. The federally owned oil stocks are stored in huge underground salt caverns along the coastline of the Gulf of Mexico.

Decisions to withdraw crude oil from the SPR are made by the president under the authority of the Energy Policy and Conservation Act. In the event of an "energy emergency," SPR oil would be distributed by competitive sale. In practice what constitutes an energy emergency goes well beyond embargoes. The SPR has been used only four times and no drawdown involved protecting against an embargo.

- During Operation Desert Storm in 1991, sales of 17.3 million barrels were used to stabilize the oil market in the face of supply disruptions arising from the war.
- After Hurricane Katrina caused massive damage to the oil production facilities, terminals, pipelines, and refineries along the Gulf regions of Mississippi and Louisiana in 2005, sales of 11 million barrels were used to offset the domestic shortfall.
- A series of emergency exchanges conducted after Hurricane Gustav, followed shortly thereafter by Hurricane Ike, reduced the level by 5.4 million barrels.
- During 2011, 30.59 million barrels were sold in response to sustained interruptions in global supplies due to civil unrest in Libya. President Obama authorized the sale as part of a larger coordinated release of petroleum by International Energy Agency countries.

The Strategic Petroleum Reserve has never reached the original 1 billion barrel target, but the Energy Policy Act of 2005 directed the Secretary of Energy to bring the reserve to its authorized one billion barrel capacity. Building up the reserve is accomplished by the Royalty-in-Kind program. Under the Royalty-in-Kind program, producers who operate leases on the federally owned Outer Continental Shelf are required to provide from 12.5 to 16.7 percent of the oil they produce to the US government. This oil is either added directly to the stockpile or sold to provide the necessary revenue to purchase oil to add to the stockpile.

Source: US Department of Energy Strategic Petroleum Reserve Website. Retrieved August 1, 2013, from http://energy.gov/fe/services/petroleum-reserves/strategic-petroleum-reserve

and emissions of greenhouse gases to an efficient level. It could not, however, achieve the efficient share of imports, since the tax falls on *all* energy consumption, whereas the security problem involves only imports. While energy conservation may increase the net benefit, it cannot ever be the sole policy instrument used or an efficient allocation will not be attained.

Another strategy, the expansion of domestic supply, is already occurring due to fracking in places such as the Bakken Formation (see Example 7.3).

Diagrammatically, this would be portrayed in Figure 7.2 as a shift of the domestic supply curve to the right. Notice that one effect would be to reduce the share of imports in total consumption (an efficient result) and that is already happening (see Figure 7.3).

EXAMPLE 7.3

Fuel from Shale: The Bakken Formation

According to the US Geological Service, one of the larger domestic discoveries in recent years of unconventional oil can be found in the Bakken Formation in Montana and North Dakota. Parts of the formation extend into the Canadian Provinces of Saskatchewan and Manitoba.

The introduction of hydraulic fracturing technology to the region in 2008 has caused a recent boom in Bakken production. A US Geological Survey assessment, released April 10, 2008, showed some 3–4.3 billion barrels of "technically recoverable" oil in this formation. (Technically, recoverable oil resources are defined as those producible using currently available technology and industry practices.) This estimate represented a 25-fold increase in the estimated amount of recovered oil compared to the agency's 1995 estimate.

The resulting boom in oil production has reduced unemployment, boosted incomes and given the state of North Dakota a billion-dollar budget surplus. But the resulting population boom and activity associated with the increased oil production has also put a strain on resources (such as water) and government services in the small towns and ranches in the area.

Sources: 3 to 4.3 billion barrels of technically recoverable oil assessed in North Dakota and Montana's Bakken formation—25 times more than 1995 estimate. Retrieved from http://www.usgs.gov/newsroom/article.asp?ID=1911; Hydraulic fracturing, Retrieved from http://water.epa.gov/type/groundwater/uic/class2/hydraulicfracturing/index.cfm; Hendricks, D. (2012). The great American oil rush: The economic impact of North Dakota's Bakken oil boom. *National Geographic*. Retrieved October 11, 2012, from http://newswatch.nationalgeographic.com/2012/10/11/the-great-american-oil-rush-the-economic-impact-of-north-dakotas-bakken-oil-boom/

FIGURE 7.3 Total Energy Production and Consumption 1980–2040

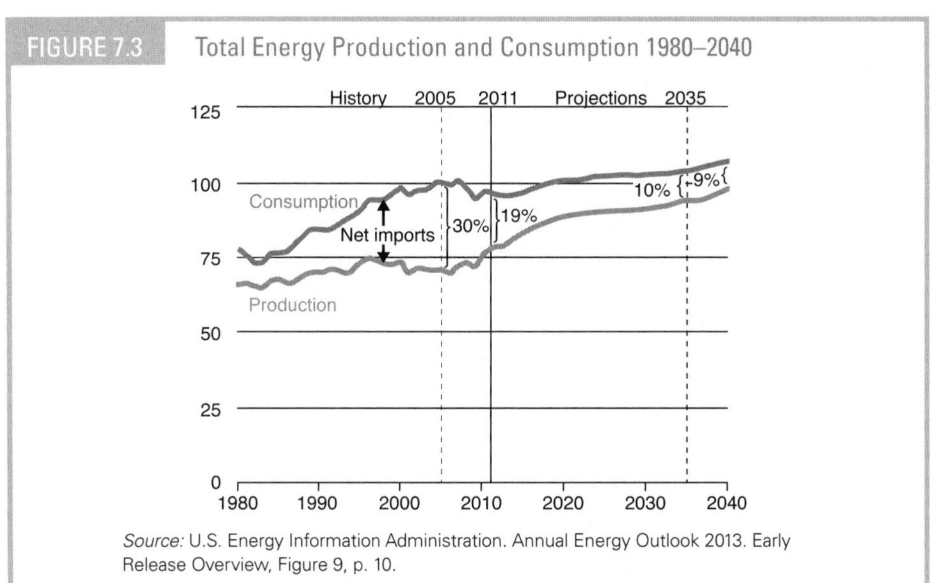

Source: U.S. Energy Information Administration. Annual Energy Outlook 2013. Early Release Overview, Figure 9, p. 10.

It would, however, not reduce climate change emissions (an inefficient result). This strategy also tends to drain domestic reserves faster, which makes the nation more vulnerable in the long run (another inefficient result). The expansion of domestic fossil fuels reduces imports, but it also tends to intensify the climate change problem.

A third approach would tailor the response more closely to the national security problem. One could use either a tariff on imports equal to the vertical distance between P_{w1} *and* P_{w2} or a quota on imports equal to *C–B*. With either of these approaches, the price to consumers would rise to P_1, total consumption would fall to *C*, and imports would be *C–B*. This achieves the appropriate balance between imports and domestic production (an efficient result), but it does not internalize the climate change cost from using domestic production (an inefficient result). Imposing a separate price on carbon would be a necessary component of the package in order to internalize the climate externality.

Electricity: Coal and Nuclear Energy

While the industrialized world currently depends on conventional sources of oil and gas for most of our energy, over the long run, in terms of both climate change and national security issues, the obvious solution involves a transition to domestic renewable sources of energy that do not emit greenhouse gases. What role does that leave for the other depletable resources such as coal, and uranium, which are used primarily to generate electricity?

Although some observers believe the transition to renewable sources of electricity will proceed so rapidly that using these fuels as a bridge will be unnecessary, many others believe that depletable fuels will probably continue to play a significant transition role. Although other contenders do exist, the fuels other than natural gas receiving the most attention (and controversy) as transition fuels are coal, and uranium. Coal, in particular, is abundantly available, both globally and domestically, and its use frees nations with domestic supplies of coal from depending on foreign countries for their energy.

Coal

Although it is a relatively abundant fuel, coal's main drawback is its contribution to air pollution. High sulfur coal is potentially a large source of sulfur dioxide emissions, one of the chief culprits in the acid-rain problem. It is also a major source of particulate emissions and mercury as well as carbon dioxide, one of the greenhouse gases.

Coal is heavily used in electricity generation and the rate of increase in coal use for this purpose is especially high in China. With respect to climate change, the biggest issue for coal is whether it could be used without jeopardizing the international community's ability to reach global greenhouse gas emission targets. As the fossil fuel with the highest carbon emissions per unit of energy supplied, that is a major concern.

Capturing CO_2 emissions from coal-fired plants before they are released into the environment and sequestering the CO_2 in underground geologic formations is one approach that is now technologically feasible. Energy companies have extensive experience in injecting captured carbon dioxide into oil fields as one means to increase the pressure and, hence, the recovery rate from those fields. Whether this practice can be extended to a larger scale and other geologic formations without leakage at reasonable cost is the subject of considerable current research.

Implementing these carbon capture and storage systems requires modifications to existing power plant technologies, modifications that are quite expensive. In the absence of any policy controls on carbon emissions, it is clear that the cost of these large-scale sequestration approaches would rule them out simply because the economic damages imposed by failing to control the gases are externalities. The existence of suitable technologies is not sufficient if the underlying economic forces prevent them from being adopted.

Uranium

Another potential transition fuel used in nuclear electrical-generation stations, uranium, has its own limitations—abundance and safety. With respect to abundance, technology plays an important part. Resource availability is a problem with uranium as long as we depend on conventional reactors. However, as countries move to a new generation of breeder reactors, which can use a wider range of fuel, availability becomes less of an issue. In the United States, for example, on a heat-equivalent basis, domestic uranium resources are 4.2 times as great as domestic oil and gas resources if they are used in conventional reactors. With breeder reactors, the U.S. uranium base is 252 times the size of its oil and gas base.

With respect to safety, two sources of concern stand out: (1) nuclear accidents, and (2) the storage of radioactive waste. Is the market able to make efficient decisions about the role of nuclear power in the energy mix? In both cases, the answer is no, given the current decision-making environment. Let's consider these issues one by one.

The production of electricity by nuclear reactors involves radioactive elements. If these elements escape into the atmosphere and come in contact with humans in sufficient concentrations, they can induce birth defects, cancer, or death. Although some radioactive elements may also escape during the normal operation of a plant, the greatest risk of nuclear power is posed by the threat of nuclear accidents.

As the accident in Fukushima, Japan, in 2011 made clear, nuclear accidents could inject large doses of radioactivity into the environment. Unlike other types of electrical generation, nuclear processes continue to generate heat long after the reactor is turned off. This means that the nuclear fuel must be continuously cooled, or the heat levels will escalate beyond the design capacity of the reactor shield. If, in this case, the reactor vessel fractures, clouds of radioactive gases and particulates would be released into the atmosphere.

An additional concern relates to storing nuclear wastes. The waste-storage issue relates to both ends of the nuclear fuel cycle—the disposal of uranium tailings from the mining process and spent fuel from the reactors—although the latter receives most of the publicity. Uranium tailings contain several elements, the most prominent being thorium-230, which decays with a half-life of 78,000 years to a radioactive, chemically inert gas, radon-222. Once formed, this gas has a very short half-life (38 days).

The spent fuel from nuclear reactors contains a variety of radioactive elements with quite different half-lives. In the first few centuries, the dominant contributors to radioactivity are fission products, principally strontium-90 and cesium-137. After approximately 1000 years, most of these elements will have decayed, leaving the transuranic elements, which have substantially longer half-lives. These remaining elements would remain a risk for up to 240,000 years. Thus, decisions made today affect not only the level of risk borne by the current generation—in the form of nuclear accidents—but also the level of risk borne by a host of succeeding generations (due to the longevity of radioactive risk from the disposal of spent fuel).

Nuclear power has also been beset by economic challenges. New nuclear power plant construction became much more expensive, in part due to the increasing regulatory requirements designed to provide a safer system. As its economic advantage over coal dissipated, the demand for new nuclear plants declined. For example, in 1973, in the United States, 219 nuclear power plants were either planned or in operation. By the end of 1998, that number had fallen to 104; the difference being due primarily to cancellations. More recently, after a period with no new applications, high oil prices, government subsidies, and concern over greenhouse gases had caused some resurgence of interest in nuclear power prior to the Fukushima accident.

Following that accident not all nations have made the same choice with respect to the nuclear option.

- Less than a week into the Fukushima crisis, German Chancellor Angela Merkel temporarily closed seven of Germany's oldest nuclear plants. Later that year she made the temporary closures permanent and announced her intention to permanently close all nine of its remaining nuclear power plants by 2022. This was accompanied by a major commitment to increase electricity production from renewable sources.
- By 2050, India has announced that it expects to satisfy a quarter of its electricity demands with nuclear energy. In 2012, about 20 reactors generated roughly 4 percent of India's electricity.
- In light of the Fukushima disaster, China halted nuclear licensing and construction pending a full safety review. After completing that review in 2012, China's State Council gave approval for projects to proceed. As of January 2013, more nuclear projects were underway in China than in any country.

What future role nuclear power will play in other countries after Fukushima remains to be seen.

Electricity: Transitioning to Renewables

Ultimately our energy needs will have to be fulfilled from renewable energy sources, either because the depletable energy sources have been exhausted or, as is more likely, the environmental costs of using the depletable sources have become so high that renewable sources will be cheaper.

Many of these renewable sources of energy, such as hydroelectric power, wind, photovoltaics, and ocean tidal power are used to generate electricity. These sources not only allow electricity generation to be more sustainable, but they enable other technologies that depend on electricity such as ground-source and air-source heat pumps or plug-in auto battery chargers to be used by consumers to heat homes and power vehicles while reducing their dependence on fossil fuels.

Renewable energy comes in many different forms. It is unlikely that any one source will provide the long-run solution, in part because both the timing (of peak demands and peak supplies) and form (gases, liquids, or electricity) of energy matter. Different sources will have different comparative advantages so, ultimately, a mix of sources will be necessary. As Debate 7.3 suggests the path to greater reliance on renewables is certainly not free of controversy even within the environmental community.

The extent to which these sources will penetrate the market will depend upon their relative cost and consumer acceptance. New systems are usually less reliable and more expensive than old systems. Once they mature, reliability normally increases and cost declines; experience is a good teacher. Table 7.2 presents the

Dueling Externalities: Should the United States Promote Wind Power?

DEBATE 7.3

On the surface the answer seems like a no-brainer, since wind power is a renewable energy source that emits no greenhouse gases, unlike all the fossil fuels it would be likely to replace. Yet some highly visible, committed environmentalists, including Robert F. Kennedy, Jr., have strongly opposed wind projects. Why has this become such a contentious issue?

Opposition to wind power within the environmental community arises for a variety of reasons. Some point out that the turbines can be noisy for those who live, camp, or hike nearby. Others note that these very large turbines can be quite destructive to bats and birds, particularly if they are constructed in migratory pathways. And a number of opponents object to the way the view would be altered by a large collection of turbines on otherwise-pristine mountaintops or off the coast.

Both the benefits from wind power (reduced air pollution including impact on the climate) and the costs (effects on aesthetics, birds, and noise) are typically externalities. This implies that the developers and consumers of wind power will neither reap all of the environmental benefits from reduced impact on the climate, nor will they typically bear the environmental costs. Making matters even more difficult, some of the environmental costs will be concentrated on a relatively few people (those living nearby), while the benefits will be conferred on all global inhabitants, most of whom will bear absolutely none of these costs. Since the presence of externalities typically undermines the ability of a market to produce an efficient outcome, it is not surprising that the permitting process for new wind power facilities is highly regulated. Regulatory processes generally encourage public participation by holding hearings. The concentrated costs imposed on those living nearby may be an effective motivator to attend the public hearings, which are likely to be held near the proposed site, but the diffuse benefits will likely not be.

With environmental externalities lying on both sides of the equation and with many of the environmental costs concentrated on a relatively small number of people, it is understandable that the hearings have become so contentious, and that the opposition to wind power is so well represented.

Sources: Kennedy Jr., R.F. (2005, December 16). An ill wind off Cape Cod (op-ed). *The New York Times*; Felicity Barringer, F. (2006, June 6). Debate over wind power creates environmental rift. *The New York Times*.

2012 best estimates of the Department of Energy on the relative costs of the various fuels used in the generation of electricity.

Since the early producers and consumers, the pioneers, experience both lower reliability and higher costs, procrastination can be an optimal individual strategy. From an individual point of view, waiting until all the bugs have been worked out and costs come down reduces the risk of making the investment.

TABLE 7.2 US Average Levelized Costs (2011 $/megawatthour) for Plants Entering Service in 2018

Plant type	Capacity factor (%)	Levelized capital cost	Fixed O&M	Variable O&M (including fuel)	Transmission investment	Total system levelized cost
Dispatchable Technologies						
Conventional Coal	85	65.7	4.1	29.2	1.2	100.1
Advanced Coal with CCS	85	88.4	8.8	37.2	1.2	135.5
Natural Gas-fired						
Conventional Combined Cycle	87	15.8	1.7	48.4	1.2	67.1
Advanced CC with CCS	87	34.0	4.1	54.1	1.2	93.4
Conventional Combustion Turbine	30	44.2	2.7	80.0	3.4	130.3
Advanced Nuclear	90	83.4	11.6	12.3	1.1	108.4
Geothermal	92	76.2	12.0	0.0	1.4	89.6
Biomass	83	53.2	14.3	42.3	1.2	111.0
Non-Dispatchable Technologies						
Wind	34	70.3	13.1	0.0	3.2	86.6
Wind-Offshore	37	193.4	22.4	0.0	5.7	221.5
Solar PV[1]	25	130.4	9.9	0.0	4.0	144.3
Solar Thermal	20	214.2	41.4	0.0	5.9	261.5
Hydro[2]	52	78.1	4.1	6.1	2.0	90.3

[1]Costs are expressed in terms of net AC power available to the grid for the installed capacity.

[2]As modeled, hydro is assumed to have seasonal storage so that it can be dispatched within a season, but overall operation is limited by resources available by site and season.

Note: These results do not include targeted tax credits such as the production or investment tax credit available for some technologies, which could significantly affect the levelized cost estimate. For example, new solar thermal and PV plants are eligible to receive a 30 percent investment tax credit on capital expenditures if placed in service before the end of 2016, and 10 percent thereafter. New wind, geothermal, biomass, hydroelectric, and landfill gas plants are eligible to receive either: (1) a $22 per MWh ($11 per MWh for technologies other than wind, geothermal and closed-loop biomass) inflation-adjusted production tax credit over the plant's first ten years of service or (2) a 30 percent investment tax credit, if placed in service before the end of 2013, or (2012, for wind only).

Source: U.S. Energy Information Administration, *Annual Energy Outlook 2013*, December 2012, DOE/EIA-0383(2012).

From a social point of view, however, if every producer and consumer procrastinates about switching, the industry will never be able to reach a sufficient scale of operation and will not be able to gain enough experience to produce the reliability and lower cost that will ensure a large, stable market. How can this initial reluctance be overcome?

One strategy subsidizes investments by the pioneers via the tax code.[6] This is commonly done, for example, with production tax credits (say 2.2 cents/kilowatt-hour) or other tax incentives (such as an investment tax credit).

Once the market is sufficiently large that it can begin to take advantage of economies of scale and eliminate the initial sources of unreliability, the subsidies could be eliminated. In the United States, substantial tax credits authorized at both the federal and state levels have been influential in inducing independent producers to accept the financial and engineering risks associated with developing wind power.

The process, however, has not been uniformly effective. Since 1985 the tax credits have elapsed and been reinstated irregularly. In contrast to the "on-again, off-again" nature of the US subsidies, European nations have been steadily increasing the economic incentives for encouraging wind power, with the result that Europe is now dominating the production of wind power.

Another common policy approach for overcoming these obstacles involves combining Renewable Portfolio Standards (RPS) for electricity generation with Renewable Energy Credits (RECs). Renewable portfolio standards stipulate a minimum percentage of the total electricity that must be generated from specified renewable sources such as wind or solar. The generating entity can either meet that standard directly by generating the requisite proportion from the specified renewable sources or indirectly by purchasing renewable energy credits from independent generators.

An independent generator of electricity from a renewable source actually produces two saleable commodities. The first is the electricity itself, which can be sold to the grid, while the second is the renewable energy credit that turns the environmental attributes (such as the fact that it was created by a qualifying renewable source) into a legally recognized form of property that can be sold separately. Generally renewable generators create one REC for every 1,000 kilowatt-hours (or, equivalently, 1 megawatt-hour) of electricity placed on the grid.

By providing this form of flexibility in how the mandate is met, RECs lower the compliance cost, not only in the short run (by allowing the RECs to flow to the areas of highest need), but also in the long run (by making renewable source generation more profitable in areas not under a RPS mandate than it would otherwise be). By 2010 some 38 states and the District of Columbia had a renewable energy standard and a majority of those also had REC programs.

How cost-effective have these polices been and how would cost-effectiveness be affected by using combinations of them? Example 7.4 discusses a study that looks specifically at that question.

Another quite different approach to promoting the use of renewable resources in the generation of electric power is known as a *feed-in tariff.* Heavily used in Europe, especially in Germany, this approach is spreading to the United States.

---

[6]While we focus here on renewable technologies used to generate electricity, in general tax credits and other subsides are also used to promote renewable technologies such as biofuels or solar energy installations used to directly heat buildings.

In April 2012, for example, the Los Angeles City Council approved CLEAN LA, a feed-in tariff program that requires the Los Angeles Department of Water and Power (LADWP) to buy solar power produced from rooftop panels installed by residents, businesses, and public organizations.

The feed-in tariff specifies the prices received by anyone who installs qualified renewable capacity that sells electricity to the grid. The level of this payment (determined in advance by the rules of the program) is based upon the costs of supplying the power and is set sufficiently high so as to assure installers that they will receive a reasonable rate of return on their investment. While in Germany

EXAMPLE 7.4

The Relative Cost-Effectiveness of Renewable Energy Policies in the United States

The United States depends on regional cap-and-trade policies, renewable portfolio standards, and production tax credits to promote renewable resources and reduce carbon emissions. How effective are these polices in pursuing those goals individually and in concert? Using a highly detailed model of regional and interregional electricity markets Palmer et al. (2011) examine this question over a time horizon covering the period from 2010–2035.

The analysis examined a cap-and-trade policy, a renewable portfolio standard with an accompanying renewable energy credit market and a production tax credit all at the national level. These policies were evaluated in terms of their relative effectiveness and cost-effectiveness in reducing carbon emissions, their effectiveness in promoting renewable resource electricity generation, and their effects on electricity prices.

The study found that the cap-and-trade policy would be both the most effective (largest carbon emission reductions) and the most cost-effective (lowest cost per ton reduced). The production tax credit would be the least cost effective with the renewable portfolio standard in the middle of the pack. This relative ranking should not be surprising because, in contrast to the cap-and-trade, which increases the relative cost of using both renewable and nonrenewable higher carbon sources, neither the production tax credit nor the renewable portfolio standard differentiate among nonrenewable technologies; they apply only to renewable sources. Furthermore, because it is a subsidy, the production tax credit is less cost-effective than an renewable portfolio standard since the subsidy leads to lower electricity prices and, hence, greater electricity consumption. Both of the other policies result in higher electricity prices and the resulting lower electricity consumption level is one source of emission reductions.

The cost-effectiveness of reducing CO_2 emissions via a combination of these polices follows directly from the relative cost-effectiveness of the three core policies. Adding a renewable portfolio standard to a cap-and-trade policy or adding a production tax credit to either of the other policies could increase the penetration rate of renewable resources, but all of these combinations tend to reduce cost-effectiveness relative to relying solely on a cap-and-trade policy.

Source: Palmer, K., Paul, A., Woerman, M., & Steinberg. D.C. (2011). Federal policies for renewable electricity: Impacts and interactions. *Energy Policy, 39*(7), 3975–3991.

this incentive payment is guaranteed for 20 years for each installed facility, each year the magnitude of the payment is reduced (typically in the neighborhood of 1–2 percent per year) for newly constructed facilities in order to reflect expected technological improvements and economies of scale.

This approach actually offers two different incentives: (1) it provides a price high enough to promote the desired investment and (2) it guarantees the stability of that price rather than forcing investors to face the market uncertainties associated with fluctuating fossil fuel prices or subsidies that come and go.

Of course when higher prices are paid to renewable investors, these costs must be born by someone. In Germany the higher costs associated with the feed-in tariffs were typically passed along to electricity ratepayers. German electricity rates are, as a result, relatively high.

Spain, however, refused to allow its electric utilities to pass on the increased cost of electricity resulting from the feed-in tariffs. As a result, its electricity system deficit became unsustainable, and in 2013 Spain halted new feed-in tariff contracts for renewable energy. As we have seen so often in other policy circumstances, the implementation details matter.

Energy Efficiency

As the world grapples with creating the right energy portfolio for the future, energy efficiency policy is playing an increasingly prominent role. An activity is said to be *energy efficient* if it is produced with the minimum amount of energy input necessary to produce a given level of that activity. Activities covered by this definition can be as diverse as heating or lighting a building, driving 100 miles or producing a ton of paper. In recent years the amount of both private and public money being dedicated to promoting energy efficiency has increased a great deal.

The role for energy efficiency in the broader mix of energy polices depends, of course, on how large the opportunity is. Estimating the remaining potential is not a precise science, but the conclusion that significant opportunities remain seems inescapable.

The existence of these opportunities can be thought of as a necessary, but not sufficient, condition for government intervention. Depending upon the level of energy prices and the discount rate, the economic return on these investments may be too low to justify intervention. In that case the policy intervention could be so costly as to outweigh any gains that would result.

The strongest case for government intervention flows from the existence of externalities. Markets are not likely to internalize these external costs on their own. The natural security and climate change externalities mentioned above, as well as other external co-benefits such as pollution-induced community health effects, certainly imply that the market undervalues investments in energy efficiency.

The analysis provided by economic research in this area, however, makes it clear that the case for policy intervention extends well beyond externalities. Internalizing externalities is a very important, but incomplete, policy response.

Consider just a few of the other foundations for policy intervention. Inadequately informed consumers can impede rational choice, as can a limited availability of capital (preventing paying the up-front costs for the more energy-efficient choice even when the resulting energy savings would justify the additional expense in present value terms). Perverse incentives can also play a role as in the case of one who lives in a room (think dorm) or apartment where the amount of energy used is not billed directly, resulting in a marginal cost of additional energy use to the occupant that is zero. Another related case of perverse incentives arises for rental housing units (Example 7.5).

EXAMPLE 7.5

Energy Efficiency in Rental Housing Markets

Economic analysis can not only help us understand the empirical finding that rental-housing units are typically less energy efficient than owner-occupied units, but also help us to understand the relative efficacy of policies to promote less energy waste in rental units.

To understand the sources of energy waste, consider the incentives. In an owner-occupied unit the owner bears all the costs (associated with making the unit more energy efficient) and receives all the benefits (the resulting lower energy costs) from an investment in energy efficiency. In a typical rental unit, however, the renter pays for the energy used, while the landlord would pay for any energy efficient investments (such as insulation or an efficient heating system). When prospective renters have no access to credible information on the energy costs associated with this unit (the typical case), the rent for various units would not reflect their energy cost differences. Since the costs of investments to reduce energy waste in the rental unit in this case cannot normally be recovered via higher rents, a landlord would under invest in energy efficiency.

Yet energy efficiency is clearly a cost-effective way not only to reduce waste (by lowering energy costs), but also to lower carbon emissions as well. Can these market barriers be overcome?

A recent experimental economics study addresses this question by examining four policy treatments: (1) mandatory and (2) voluntary energy efficiency ratings for the unit (similar to energy-efficiency stars for appliances), (3) a performance regulatory standard (similar to energy-efficiency standards for appliances), and (4) a cost-sharing arrangement where landlords would be required to pay a fixed percent of their tenant's energy bill.

In the baseline treatment (no policies) the authors confirm the theoretical expectation that owners typical invest more in owner-occupied units than landlords invest in rental units.

In the policy treatments they find that the availability of verified and costless information on rental unit energy costs unequivocally reduces waste, with mandatory information and voluntary information both achieving a high level of efficiency. The regulatory approach was found to result in a higher average investment than the mandatory and voluntary information schemes, but it resulted in fewer properties available in the market; some landlords chose to leave the rental market rather than to comply with the regulation. A cost-sharing policy achieves similar efficiency levels as the regulatory standard, but a significantly lower level of efficiency than the voluntary and mandatory information schemes.

The effectiveness of information strategies found by this study is good news indeed, but two caveats must be kept in mind. First, most actual information strategies are not costless to landlords as they were assumed to be in this study. To the extent that landlords bear some or all of the costs of providing certified information, this study would overestimate (to some unknown degree) the effectiveness of these strategies. Second, experimental economics studies work with participants in a lab, not with data based upon actual market choices. As noted in Chapter 1, lab results are typically informative, but they are not the same as results drawn from actual field experience.

Source: Burfurd, I., Gangadharan, L., & Nemes, V. (2012). Stars and standards: Energy efficiency in rental markets. *Journal of Environmental Economics and Management, 64*(2). 153–168.

A rather large suite of policy options has been implemented to counteract these other sources of deficient levels of investment in energy efficiency. Some illustrations include the following:

- Certification programs such as Energy Star for appliances or LEED (Leadership in Energy and Environmental Design) standards for buildings attempt to provide credible information for consumers to make informed choices on energy efficiency options.
- Minimum efficiency standards (e.g., for appliances) prohibit the manufacture, sale, or importation of clearly inefficient appliances.
- An increased flow of public funds into the market for energy efficiency has led to an increase in the use of targeted investment subsidies. The most common historic source of funding in the electricity sector involved the use of a small mandatory per kilowatt-hour charge (typically called a "system benefit charge" or "public benefit charge") attached to the distribution service bill. The funded services include supplementing private funds for diverse projects such as weatherization of residences for low-income customers to more efficient lighting for commercial and industrial enterprises.

The evidence suggests that none of these policies either by themselves or in concert are completely efficient, but that they have collectively represented a move toward a more efficient use of energy. Not only does the evidence seem to suggest that they have been effective in reducing wasteful energy demand, but also that the programs have been quite cost-effective, with program costs well below the cost of the alternative, namely generating the energy to satisfy that demand.

One further innovation in the electric power industry takes advantage of these energy efficiency opportunities. Known as the forward capacity market[7], this approach uses market forces to facilitate the planning of future electric capacity investment by entities known as independent system operators.

To illustrate how this approach works in practice consider how the program is being used in New England. The Independent System Operator for New England (ISO-NE) is responsible for ensuring the constant availability of electricity, currently and for future generations, in the New England area. ISO-NE meets this obligation part by engaging in comprehensive, regional planning processes.

The objective of the Forward Capacity Market (FCM) run by ISO-NE is to assure that sufficient peak generating capacity for reliable system operation for the future will be

[7]For details on this market, see http://www.iso-ne.com/markets/othrmkts_data/fcm/index.html

available. Since ISO-NE does not itself generate electricity, to assure this future capacity, it solicits bids in a competitive auction for additional generating capacity. It also solicits bids for legally enforceable future reductions in peak demand from energy efficiency, which reduce the need for peak capacity, Soliciting both types of bids allows the ISO-NE to compare the cost of generating the electricity with the cost of reducing the need for that electricity, choosing whichever is cheapest. This system allows strategies for reducing peak demand to complete on a level playing field with strategies to expand capacity.

Summary

We have seen that the relationship between government and the energy market is not always harmonious and efficient. In the past, price controls have tended to reduce energy conservation, to discourage exploration and supply, to cause biases in the substitution among fuel types that penalize future consumers, and to create the potential for abrupt, discontinuous transitions to renewable sources. This important example makes a clear case for less, not more, regulation.

This conclusion is not universally valid, however. Other dimensions of the energy problem, such as climate change and national security issues, suggest the need for some government role. Insecure foreign sources require policies such as tariffs and strategic reserves to reduce vulnerability and to balance the true costs of imported and domestic sources. In addition, government must ensure that the costs of energy fully reflect not only the potentially large environmental costs, including climate change, but also the national security costs associated with our dependence on foreign sources of energy. Government action must also assure that inefficient subsidies do not undermine the transition to sustainable energy resources.

Economic analysis reveals that no single strategy is sufficient to solve the national security and climate change problems simultaneously. Subsidizing domestic supply, for example, would reduce the share of imports in total consumption (an efficient result), but it would reduce neither consumption nor climate change emissions (inefficient results). On the other hand, energy conservation (promoted by a tax on energy, for example) would reduce energy consumption and the associated emissions (efficient outcomes) but would not achieve the efficient share of imports (an inefficient result) since an energy tax falls on all energy consumption, whereas the national security problem involves only imports. It also would fail to produce a fully efficient resolution for climate impacts since it would focus on energy per se, not the harmful emissions emitted by that energy use, a factor that varies widely among fuels. A carbon tax, not an energy tax, would be needed to make this kind of distinction among fuels.

Given the environmental difficulties with all of the depletable transition fuels (tar sands, fracked oil and gas, as well as coal and uranium), energy efficiency and the promotion of renewable sources of energy are now playing (and will continue to play) a larger role.

The menu of energy options as the economy transitions to renewable sources offers a large number of choices. It is far from clear what the ultimate mix will turn out to be, but it is very clear that government policy is a necessary ingredient in any smooth transition to a sustainable-energy future. Since many of the most important costs of energy use are externalities, an efficient transition to these renewable sources will not occur unless the playing field is leveled. The potential for an efficient and sustainable allocation of energy resources by our economic and political institutions clearly exists, even if historically it has not always been pursued.

Discussion Questions

1. Should benefit-cost analysis play the dominant role, a complementary role, or no role in deciding the proportion of electric energy to be supplied by nuclear power? Why or why not?
2. Economist Abba Lerner once proposed a tariff on oil imports equal to 100 percent of the import price. This tariff is designed to reduce dependence on foreign sources as well as to discourage OPEC from raising prices (since, due to the tariff, the delivered price would rise twice as much as the OPEC increase, causing a large subsequent reduction in consumption). Should this proposal become public policy? Why or why not?
3. Does the fact that the strategic petroleum reserve has never been used to offset shortfalls caused by an embargo mean that the money spent in creating the reserve has been wasted? Why or why not?

Self-Test Exercises

1. During a worldwide recession in 1983, the oil cartel began to lose market share. Why would a recession make the cartel more likely to lose market share?
2. Assume the demand and marginal cost conditions given in the second self-test exercise in Chapter 2. In addition, assume that the government imposes a price control at $P = \$80/3$. (a) Find the consumer and producer surplus associated with the resulting allocation. (b) Compare this price control allocation to the monopoly allocation in part (c) of that self-test exercise.
3. Some time ago, a conflict between a paper company and a coalition of environmental groups arose over the potential use of a Maine river for hydroelectric power generation. As one aspect of its case for developing the dam, the paper company argued that without hydroelectric power the energy cost of operating some specific paper machines would be so high that they would have to be shut down. Environmental groups countered that the energy cost was estimated to be too high by the paper company because it was assigning all of the high-cost (oil-fired) power to these particular machines. That was seen as inappropriate because all machines were connected to the same electrical grid and therefore drew power from all sources, not merely the high-cost sources. They suggested, therefore, that the appropriate cost to assign to the machines was the much lower average cost. Revenue from these machines was expected to be sufficient to cover this average cost. Who was right?

4. Peaking plants, those that are only called into service during times of peak demand, are typically cheaper to build (compared to base-load plants), but that they have relatively high operating costs. Explain why it makes sense for utilities to use this lower-capital, high-operating-cost type of plant for peaking and the high-capital, lower-operating-cost type of plant for base load.
5. If OPEC raised the price of oil high enough, would that be sufficient to promote an efficient energy mix?
6. Label the following as *true*, *false*, or *uncertain* and explain your choice. (Uncertain means that it can be either true or false depending upon the circumstances.)
   a. All members of a resource cartel share a common objective, namely increase prices as much and as soon as possible.
   b. By holding prices lower than they would otherwise be, placing a price control on a depletable resource increases both the speed with which the resource is extracted over time and the cumulative amount ultimately extracted.
   c. A price control actually has no influence on the extraction path of a depletable resource until such time as the market price actually reaches the level of the price control.
   d. Forcing companies that drill offshore for oil to compensate victims of any oil spill from one of its facilities would be an efficient requirement.
7. Explain why the existence of a renewable energy credit market would lower the compliance costs for utilities forced to meet a renewable portfolio standard.
8. Using Figure 7.2, show how the level of oil imports and the price level would be affected if the country represented in that figure acted to internalize national security issues, but ignored climate change impacts.

Further Reading

Anthoff, D., & Hahn, R. (2010). Government failure and market failure: On the inefficiency of environmental and energy policy. *Oxford Review of Economic Policy*, *26*(2), 197–224. A selective survey of the literature to highlight what is known about the efficiency of particular kinds of policies, laws, and regulations in managing energy and environmental risk.

Gillingham, K., Newell, R.G., & Palmer, K. (2009). Energy efficiency economics and policy. *Annual Review of Resource Economics*, *1*, 597–620. Reviews economic concepts underlying decision making in energy efficiency and conservation and the related empirical literature.

Schmalensee, R. (2009). Evaluating policies to increase electricity generation from renewable energy. *Review of Environmental Economics and Policy*, *6*, 45–64. Evaluates policies aimed at increasing the generation of electricity from renewable sources based upon on a review of experience in the United States and the European Union (EU).

Additional References and Historically Significant References are available on this book's Companion Website: http://www.routledgetextbooks.com/textbooks/9780133479690

Recyclable Resources: Minerals, Paper, Bottles, and E-Waste

8

Man is endowed with reason and creative powers to increase and multiply his inheritance; yet up to now he has created nothing, only destroyed. The forests grow ever fewer; the rivers parch; the wildlife is gone; the climate is ruined; and with every passing day the earth becomes uglier and poorer.

—Anton Chekhov, *Uncle Vanya*, Act I (1896)

Introduction

Once used, energy resources dissipate into heat. They cannot be recycled. Other resources, in contrast, retain their basic physical and chemical properties during use and under the proper conditions can be recycled or reused. They therefore represent a separate category for us to examine.

What is an efficient amount of recycling? Will the market automatically generate this amount in the absence of government intervention? How does the efficient allocation over time differ between recyclable and nonrecyclable resources? We begin our investigation by looking at the role minerals play in production and the economy. We then move to describing how an efficient market in recyclable, depletable resources would work. We then use this as a benchmark to examine recycling in some detail.

Minerals

Minerals such as copper, iron, aluminum, and metals such as steel and gold are very important in many production processes. Figure 8.1 illustrates the role of non-fuel minerals in the United States. The United States Geological Service keeps extensive data on supply, demand, prices, imports, and exports of production.

As you can see in Figure 8.1, domestic raw materials and recycled materials were utilized in production to create mineral materials valued at $704 billion. These mineral materials, including aluminum, brick, copper, fertilizers, and steel, plus net

FIGURE 8.1 The Role of Nonfuel Minerals in the US Economy

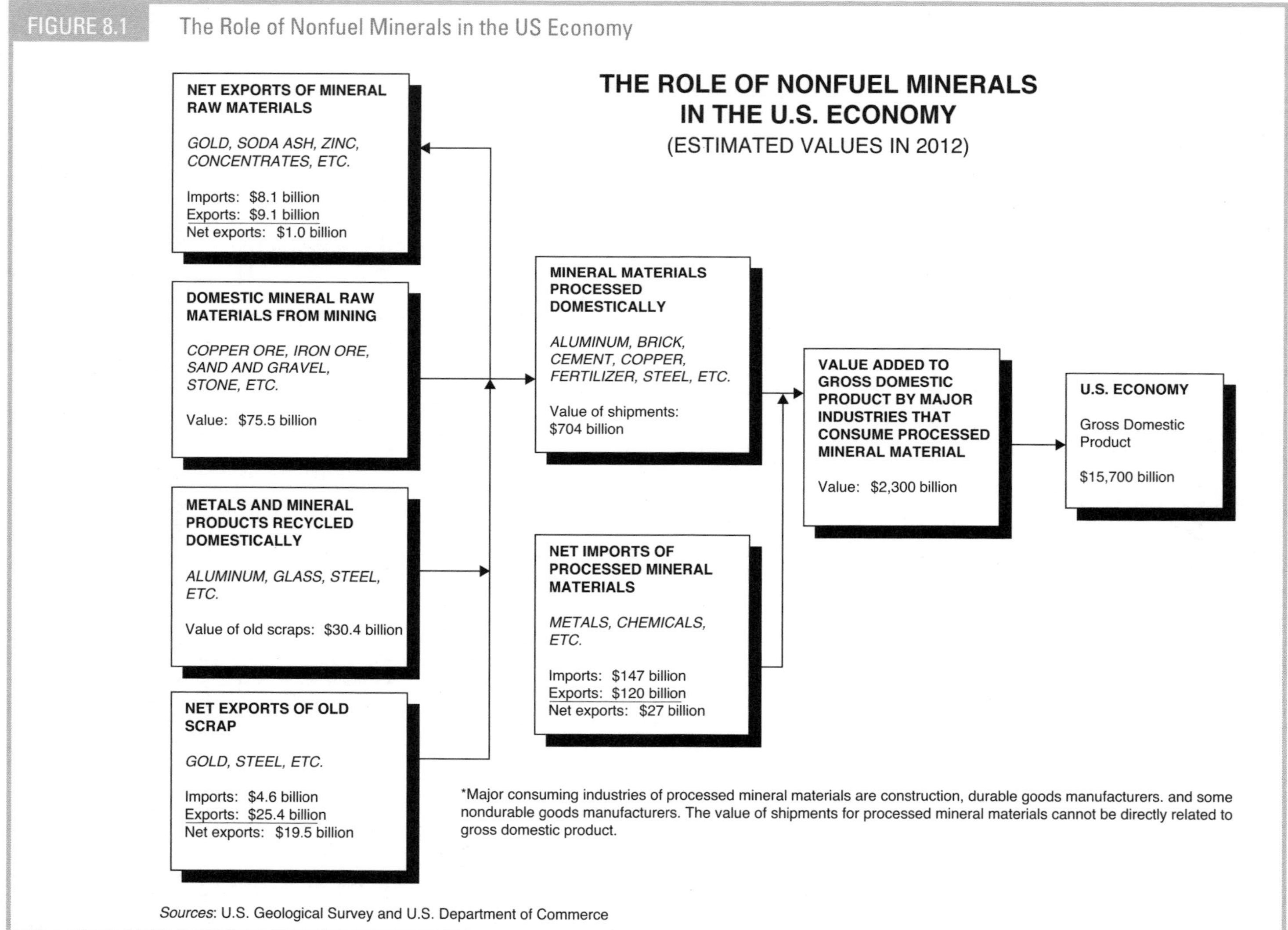

Sources: U.S. Geological Survey and U.S. Department of Commerce

imports of processed mineral materials were, in turn, used by industry adding value of approximately estimated \$2.3 trillion in 2012.

Although minerals and metals are finite, non-renewable resources, stocks can be supplemented through recycling. This point can be illustrated using a simple numerical example. Suppose 100 units of a resource are contained in a product with a useful life of one year. Suppose further that 90 percent of the resource could be recovered and reused after one year. During the first year, the full 100 units could be used. At the end of the second year, 90 percent of the remaining 90 units could once again be recovered, leaving 81 units for the third year, and so on.

How much more of this resource was made available by recycling? Algebraically, if we let the original stock be A, and the recovery rate be a, then the total amount used would be an infinite sum of the form $A + Aa + Aa^2 + Aa^3$... It turns out that the sum of this series as time becomes infinitely long is $A/(1 - a)$.[1] Notice that nonrecyclable resources are represented by the special case where $a = 0$. In this case the sum of resource use equals the available stock. Whenever $a > 0$, however, as it would be when any of the resource was recycled, the sum of the resource flows exceeds the size of the original stock. The closer to 1.0 a is, the larger the sum of the resource flows. For example, if $a = 0.9$, as it was in our example, the sum of the flows is 10 times the size of the stock. The effect of recycling is to increase the size of the available resources by a factor of 10.

An Efficient Allocation of Recyclable Resources

Extraction and Disposal Cost

How would an efficient market, one devoid of any imperfections, allocate a recyclable depletable resource? The models developed in Chapter 6 provide a point of departure for answering this question. In the earliest periods, reliance would generally be exclusively on the virgin ore, because it is cheapest. As more concentrated ores are extracted, the mining industry would turn to the lower-grade ore and to foreign sources for higher-grade ores.

In the presence of technological progress, the increasing reliance on the lower-grade ores would not necessarily precipitate an increase in cost (as shown in Example 6.1), at least initially. Eventually, however, as the sources became increasingly difficult to extract, a point would be reached at which the costs of extraction and prices of the virgin material would begin to rise.

At the same time, the costs of disposing of the products would probably rise as population density became more pronounced and wealth levels supported higher levels of waste. Over the last two centuries, the world has experienced a large

---

[1]Note the similarity of $1/(1 - a)$ to the familiar multiplier used in introductory macroeconomics, $1/(1-MPC)$.

increase in the geographic concentration of people. The attraction of cities and exodus from rural areas led an increasingly large number of people to live in urban or near-urban environments.

This concentration creates waste disposal problems. Historically, when land was plentiful and the waste stream was less hazardous, the remnants could be buried in landfills. But as land became scarce, burial became increasingly expensive. In addition, concerns over environmental effects on water supplies and economic effects on the value of surrounding land have made buried waste less acceptable.

The rising costs of virgin materials and of waste disposal increase the attractiveness of recycling. By recovering and reintroducing materials into the system, recycling not only provides an alternative to virgin ores, but it also reduces the waste disposal load.

Consumers, as well as manufacturers, play a role on both the demand and supply sides of the market. On the demand side, consumers would find that products depending exclusively on virgin raw materials are subject to higher prices than those relying on the cheaper recycled materials. Consequently, consumers would have a tendency to switch to products made with the recycled raw materials, as long as quality is not adversely affected. This powerful incentive is called the *composition of demand effect*.

As long as consumers bear the cost of disposal, they have the additional incentive to return their used recyclable products to collection centers. By doing so they avoid disposal costs and reap financial rewards for supplying a product someone wants.

This highly stylized version of how the market should work has to be complemented by some hard realities that must be faced in setting up actual markets. For the cycle to be complete, it is essential that a demand exist for the recycled products. New markets may ultimately emerge, but the transition may prove somewhat turbulent. Simply returning recycled products to the collection centers accomplishes little if they are simply dumped into a nearby landfill or if the supply is increased so much by mandatory recycling laws that prices for recycled materials fall through the floor (thereby destroying the incentive to continue supplying them).

The purity of the recycled products also plays a key role in explaining the strength of demand for them. One of the reasons for the high rate of aluminum recycling and much lower rate of plastics recycling is the differential difficulty with which a high-quality product can be produced from scrap. Whereas bundles of aluminum cans have a relatively uniform quality, waste plastics tend to be highly contaminated with nonplastic substances or with plastics of very different types, and the plastics manufacturing process has little tolerance for impurities. Remaining contaminants in metals can frequently be eliminated by high-temperature combustion, but plastics are destroyed by high temperatures. Finally, waste that contains hazardous materials, such as mercury and lead, raises additional complexities. The rapidly growing stream of electronic waste (*e*-waste) contains both hazardous waste *and* valuable minerals, creating complicated dilemmas. As we discuss in a subsequent section of this chapter, markets for discarded electronics in industrializing countries may lack good enforcement mechanisms to ensure proper disposal of the hazardous components.

Recycling: A Closer Look

The model in the preceding section would lead us to expect that recycling would increase over time as virgin ore and disposal costs rose. This seems to be the case. Take copper, for example. During 1910, recycled copper accounted for about 18 percent of the total production of refined copper in the United States. Today, approximately 40 percent of the world's copper demand today is met by recycling. And, according to the Bureau of International Recycling, an estimated 70 percent of the copper scrap exported by the United States is used by industries in China. Other new metals being produced using recycled materials include aluminum, lead and zinc, with recycled materials of approximately 33 percent, 35 percent, and 30 percent respectively.

For other materials, recycling rates are on the rise. According to the US EPA, the rate of recycled waste in the United States has risen to 34.7 percent in 2011 (Figure 8.2). For certain materials, the rates are even higher (99 percent for auto batteries, 71 percent for office paper, 48 percent for aluminum beer and soft drink cans, 63 percent for steel packaging). Plastic polyethylene terephthalate (PET) bottles were recovered at a rate of 37 percent, high-density polyethylene (HDPE) bottles at a rate of 28 percent, and glass containers at a rate of 28 percent. According to another indicator, by 2006, over 8600 curbside recycling programs were in existence. Twenty years earlier, only one curbside program was in place.

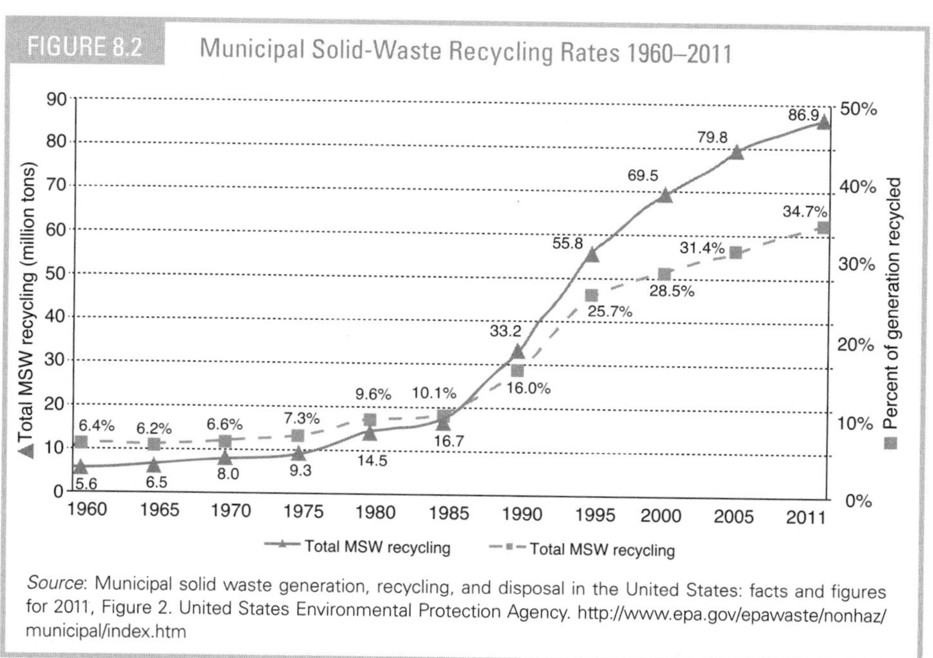

FIGURE 8.2 Municipal Solid-Waste Recycling Rates 1960–2011

Source: Municipal solid waste generation, recycling, and disposal in the United States: facts and figures for 2011, Figure 2. United States Environmental Protection Agency. http://www.epa.gov/epawaste/nonhaz/municipal/index.htm

In most cases recycling is not cheap. While several types of costs are involved, transport and processing costs are usually especially significant. The sources of scrap may be concentrated around cities where most of the products are used, while for historical reasons the processing facilities are near the sources of the virgin ores. The scrap must be transported to the processing facility and the processed scrap to the market.

Labor costs are an important component of the processing costs. Collecting, sorting, and processing scrap is typically very labor intensive. Higher labor costs can make the recycled scrap less competitive in the input market. Recognizing the importance of labor costs raises the possibility that recycling rates would be higher in regions where labor costs are lower, which does seem to be the case. Vibrant markets for scrap have emerged in many developing countries.

Energy costs also matter. According to the Bureau of International Recycling (BIR), recycling offers significant energy savings over production from raw materials. For example, steel recycling expends 74 percent, aluminum 95 percent, copper 85 percent, paper 64 percent, and plastics 80 percent less energy. Additionally, producing materials via recycling results in less water and air pollution. BIR estimates that the production of paper via recycling causes 35 percent less water pollution and 74 percent less air pollution.

And, finally, since the processing of scrap as an input into the production process can produce its own environmental consequences, compliance with environmental regulations can add to the cost of recycled input. In the United States, for example, relatively low world copper prices, coupled with high environmental compliance costs, created a cost squeeze that contributed to the closure of all U.S. secondary smelters and associated electrolytic refineries by 2001.

When recycling markets operate smoothly, however, scrap becomes a cost-competitive input, and rather dramatic changes occur in the manufacturing process. Not only do manufacturers rely more heavily on recycled inputs, but also they begin to design their products to facilitate recycling. Facilitating recycling through product design is already important in industries where the connection between the manufacturer and disposal agent is particularly close. Aircraft manufacturers, which are often asked to scrap old aircraft, may stamp the alloy composition on parts during manufacturing to facilitate recycling. The idea is beginning to spread to other industries. Ski boot manufacturers in Switzerland, for example, are beginning to stamp all individual boot parts with a code to identify their composition.

Recycling and Ore Depletion

How does the efficient allocation of a recyclable resource compare with that of a nonrecyclable resource over time? Thinking back to the models in Chapter 6, perhaps the most important difference occurs in the timing of the switch point. As long as the resource can be recycled at a marginal cost lower than that of the substitute, the market tends to rely on the recyclable resource longer than it does on a nonrecyclable resource with an identical extraction cost curve. This should not be surprising, since one effect of recycling is simply to add more of the resource.

Recall the simple numerical example presented at the beginning of this chapter with the total amount available $= A/(1 - a)$ where A is the stock of the resource available and a is the recycling rate.

This formulation also points out another feature of recycling. Unless the recycling rate is 100 percent ($a = 1.0$), the sum of the resource flows is finite. This means that while some recycled materials can be recycled forever, the amount will become infinitesimally small as time goes on.

An efficient economic system will orchestrate a balance between the consumption of newly mined and recycled materials, between disposing of used products and recycling, and between imports and domestic production. Example 8.1 provides an example of how changing economic circumstances can lead to an increase in recycling.

EXAMPLE 8.1

Lead Recycling

The domestic demand for lead has changed significantly over the last 30 years. In 1972 dissipative, nonrecyclable uses of lead (primarily gasoline additives, pigments in paint, and ammunition) accounted for about 30 percent of reported consumption. And only about 30 percent of all produced lead came from recycled material.

Over the last three decades, however, congressional recognition of lead's negative health effects on children has led to a series of laws limiting the amount of allowable lead in gasoline and paints. This has resulted not only in a decline in the total amount of lead used, but also in the dramatic decline of the dissipative uses (which, by 1997, had fallen to only 13 percent of total demand). A declining role for dissipative uses implies that an increasing proportion of the production is available to be recycled. And, in fact, more is now recycled. By 2012, 80 percent of the domestic lead consumption came from recycled scrap. The lead-acid battery industry continues to be the largest user of lead.

Old (postconsumer) scrap accounts for nearly all the total lead scrap recovered. Used batteries supply about 90 percent of that old scrap. Battery manufacturers have begun entering buyback arrangements with retail outlets, both as a marketing tool for new batteries and as a means of ensuring a supply of inputs to their downstream manufacturing operations. Contrast this with aluminum, for example. In 2012, 53 percent of recycled aluminum came from new (manufacturing) scrap, while only 47 percent was from old scrap (beverage cans and other discarded aluminum products).

Source: U.S. Department of the Interior. *Minerals Yearbook*. Retrieved from http://minerals.usgs.gov/minerals/pubs/mcs/

Factors Mitigating Resource Scarcity

Recycling is promoted by resource scarcity, but resource scarcity is, in turn, affected by a number of other factors. Three alternatives have been particularly important: (1) exploration and discovery, (2) technological progress, and (3) substitution.

Exploration and Discovery

A profit-maximizing firm will undertake exploration activity until the marginal discovery cost equals the marginal scarcity rent received from a unit of the resource sold.[2] Since the marginal scarcity rent—the difference between the price received and the marginal cost of extraction—is the marginal benefit received by the firm engaging in exploration activity, the level of activity should be increased to maximize profits until this marginal benefit is equal to the marginal cost.

An understanding of this relationship between scarcity rent and marginal discovery cost allows us to think about how exploration activity would respond to population and income growth. Since both of these factors contribute to rising demand over time, they raise the marginal user cost and the scarcity rent, stimulating producers to undertake larger marginal discovery costs.

How much this demand pressure is relieved depends upon the amount of exploration activity and the amount of resources discovered per unit of exploration activity undertaken. If the marginal discovery cost curve is flat (implying a large amount of relatively available resources), increases in scarcity rent can stimulate large amounts of successful exploration activity. If the marginal discovery cost curve is steeply sloped (as would be the case when exploration had to take place in increasingly hostile and unproductive environments), increases in scarcity rent stimulate less exploration activity.

Technological Progress

Technological progress reduces the cost of ore by discovering new ways to extract, process, and use it. In Chapter 6, for example, we showed the significant impact of pelletization on the cost of producing steel from iron ore. The effect was so dramatic that production costs actually fell over time in spite of the need to use a lower-grade ore.

It is important to realize that the rate and type of technological progress are influenced by the degree of resource scarcity. Rising extraction costs create new profit opportunities for the development of new technologies. These profit opportunities are largest for technologies that economize on scarce resources and utilize abundant ones. In periods when labor is scarce and capital abundant, new technologies tend to use capital and save labor. If population growth were to reverse the relative scarcity, subsequent technological progress would concentrate on using labor and saving capital. In the past, when fossil-fuel energy was abundant and cheap, newly discovered technologies relied heavily on this energy source. As fossil-fuel supplies decline, technological progress can be expected to economize by increasing the amount of useful energy received per unit of fossil-fuel input and by replacing fossil-fuel energy with forms of renewable energy.

---

[2]This is strictly true only when no uncertainty is associated with exploration.

Substitution

The final way in which adverse consequences of resource scarcity can be mitigated is by substituting abundant resources for scarce ones. The easier the substitution of abundant depletable or renewable resources, the smaller will be the impact of declining availability and rising costs (see Figure 8.3).

In the graph, three isoquants (S_1, F_1, F_2) are plotted. An *isoquant* portrays all the possible combinations of inputs that can produce a given level of output. The two right-angled isoquants (F_1 and F_2) depict the fixed-proportions case, the case in which no input substitution is possible. The fixed-proportions isoquant nearer the origin (F_2) refers to a lower output level than the other fixed-proportion isoquant (F_1). The third isoquant (S_1) does show some possibility for input substitution and is drawn in such a way as to produce the same output level (O_1) as F_1. Naturally it implies a different production technology or set of technologies from F_1.

We can illustrate the significance of input substitution on output using Figure 8.3. Assume that the amount of some input Y (a depletable resource) is reduced from Y_1 to Y_2. If the technology involved is characterized by S_1, the constant output level (O_1) can be maintained by increasing the amount of the other resource used from X_1 to X_3. This increase in X compensates for the reduction in Y, leaving output unaffected.

FIGURE 8.3 Output Levels and the Possibilities for Input Substitution

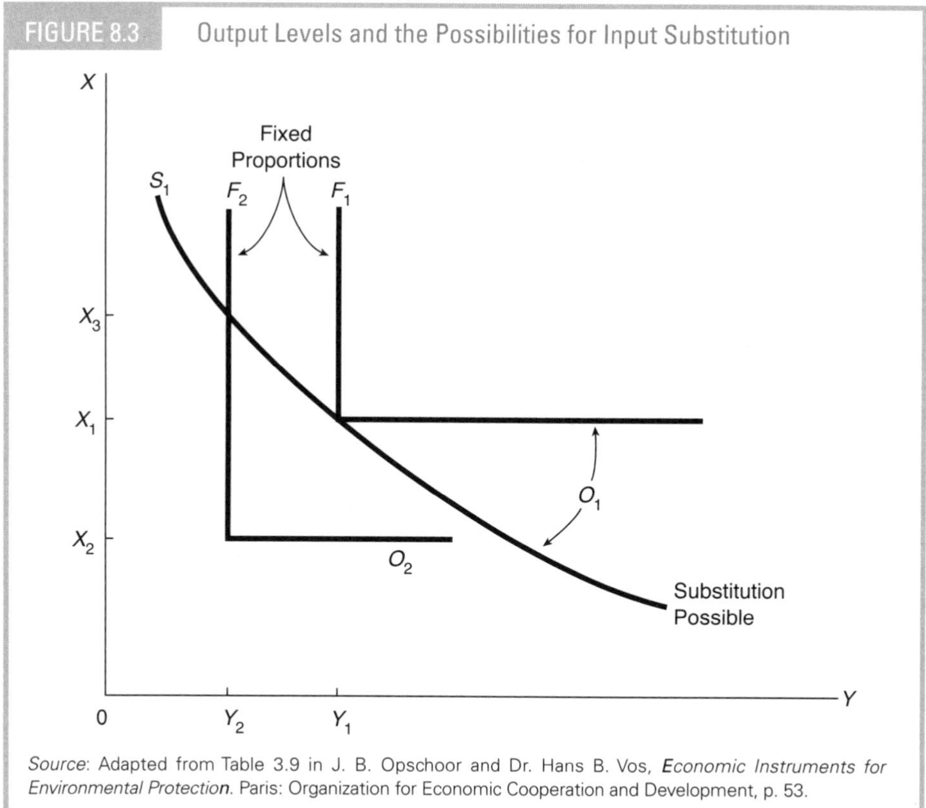

Source: Adapted from Table 3.9 in J. B. Opschoor and Dr. Hans B. Vos, *Economic Instruments for Environmental Protection*. Paris: Organization for Economic Cooperation and Development, p. 53.

Notice what happens, however, when the production process is characterized by F_1 instead of S_1. A reduction in the availability of Y from Y_1 to Y_2 necessitates a reduction in output from O_1 to O_2. No substitution of X for Y is possible. In addition, because inputs must be used in fixed proportions, the amount of X would be reduced from X_1 to X_2. Any more X would be redundant; it would not result in any additional output. These examples serve to illustrate a basic premise—the wider the array of substitution possibilities, the smaller the impact of resource scarcity on output.

This short review suggests that some factors (e.g., rising population and incomes) increase the likelihood of resource scarcity, while others (e.g., exploration and discovery, technological progress, and input substitution) mitigate the seriousness of scarcity. If resource scarcity is increasing in some sense, we should be able to discover that natural resource prices are rising more rapidly than prices in general (see Example 8.2). Resource prices, in turn, affect incentives to recycle as do the marginal costs of disposal.

EXAMPLE 8.2

The Bet

In 1980, each of two distinguished protagonists in the scarcity debate "put his money where his mouth is." Paul Ehrlich, an ecologist with a strong belief in impending scarcity, answered a challenge from Julian Simon, an economist known for his equally strong belief that concerns about impending scarcity were groundless. According to the terms of the bet, Ehrlich would hypothetically invest $200 in each of any five commodities he selected. (He picked copper, chrome, nickel, tin, and tungsten.) Ten years later the aggregate value of the same amounts of those five commodities would be calculated in real terms (after accounting for normal inflation). If the value increased, Simon would send Ehrlich a check for the difference. If the value decreased, Ehrlich would send Simon a check for the difference.

In 1990, Ehrlich performed the calculations and sent Simon a check for $576.07. Real prices for each of the five commodities were lower; some were less than half their former levels. New sources of the minerals had been discovered, substitutions away from these minerals had occurred in many of their uses (particularly computers), and the tin cartel, which had been holding up tin prices, collapsed.

Would the outcome of the Simon-Ehrlich wager have been the same if the bet had covered the entire twentieth century? According to a subsequent analysis of the data on these same minerals by McClintock and Emmett (2005), despite ups and downs in prices over the course of the past century, Simon would also have won even a century-long wager.

Finally, how would Simon have fared in decades other than the one covered by the bet? Was he just lucky to have picked the 1980s? It turns out that to some extent he was lucky. Of the ten decades in that century he would have won in five decades (the 1900s, 1910s, 1940s, 1980s, and 1990s) and lost in the remaining five. He would have lost by a few dollars in the 1950s and by more significant amounts in the other four decades. Does this evidence provide a lesson for the future? You be the judge.

Sources: Tierney, J. (December 2, 1990). Betting the planet. *The New York Times Magazine*, 52–53, 74, 76, 78, 80–81; McClintick, D., & Emmett, R. B. (2005). The Simon-Ehrlich Debate. *PERC Reports, 23*(3), 16–17.

Market Imperfections

As we discovered in the discussion of the role of oil in national security, when mineral imports are critically important and come from risky sources, the market perceives a biased price ratio, one that fails to incorporate some of the social costs of imports. The result would be an inefficient and excessive reliance on imports.

Other market imperfections are apparent as well. An unbalanced treatment of waste by producers and consumers can lead to biases in the market choices between recycling and the use of virgin ores. Since disposal cost is a key ingredient in determining the efficient amount of recycling, the failure of an economic agent to bear the full cost of disposal implies a bias toward virgin materials and away from recycling. We begin by considering how the method of financing the disposal of potentially recyclable waste affects the level of recycling.

Disposal Cost and Efficiency

The efficient level of recycling depends on the marginal cost of disposal. Suppose, for example, it costs a community $20 per ton to recycle a particular waste product that can ultimately be sold to a local manufacturer for $10 per ton. Can we conclude that this is an inefficient recycling venture because it is losing money? No, we can't! In addition to earning the $10 per ton from selling the recycled product, the town is avoiding the cost of disposing of the product. This avoided marginal cost is appropriately considered a marginal benefit from recycling. Suppose the marginal avoided disposal cost was $20 per ton. In this case, the benefits to the town from recycling would be $30 per ton ($20 per ton avoided cost plus $10 per ton resale value) and the cost would be $20 per ton; this would be an efficient recycling venture. Both marginal disposal costs and the prices of recycled materials directly affect the efficient level of recycling.

The Disposal Decision

Potentially recyclable waste can be divided into two types of scrap: old scrap and new scrap. *New scrap* is composed of the residual materials generated during production. For example, as steel beams are formed, the small remnants of steel left over are new scrap. *Old scrap* is recovered from products used by consumers.

To illustrate the relative importance of new scrap and old scrap, consider that in the U.S. aluminum industry, about 40 percent of the recovered aluminum scrap comes from old scrap. The difficulties in recycling new scrap are significantly less than those in recycling old scrap. New scrap is already at the place of production, and with most processes it can simply be reentered into the input stream without transportation costs. Transport costs tend to be an important part of the cost of using old scrap.

Equally important are the incentives involved. Since new scrap never leaves the factory, it remains under the complete control of the manufacturer. Having the joint responsibility of creating a product and dealing with the scrap, the manufacturer now has an incentive to design the product with the use of the new scrap in mind.

It would be advantageous to establish procedures guaranteeing the homogeneity of the scrap and minimizing the amount of processing necessary to recycle it. For all these reasons, it is likely the market for new scrap will work efficiently and effectively.

Unfortunately, the same is not true for old scrap. The market works inefficiently because the product users do not bear the full marginal social costs of disposing of their product. As a result, the market is biased away from recycling old scrap and toward the use of virgin materials.

The key to understanding why these costs are not internalized lies in the incentives facing individual product users. Suppose you had some small aluminum products that were no longer useful to you. You could either recycle them, which usually means driving to a recycling center, or you could toss them into your trash. In comparing these two alternatives, notice that recycling imposes one cost on you (transport cost), while the second imposes another (disposal cost).

It is difficult for consumers to act efficiently because of the way trash collection has traditionally been financed. Urban areas have generally financed trash collection with taxes, if publicly provided, or a flat-rate fee, if privately provided. Neither of these approaches directly relates the size of an individual's payment to the amount of waste. The *marginal* cost to the homeowner of throwing out one more unit of trash is negligible, even when the cost to society is not. The marginal private disposal cost and the cost to society as a whole diverge (see Figure 8.4).

FIGURE 8.4 The Efficient Level of Recycling

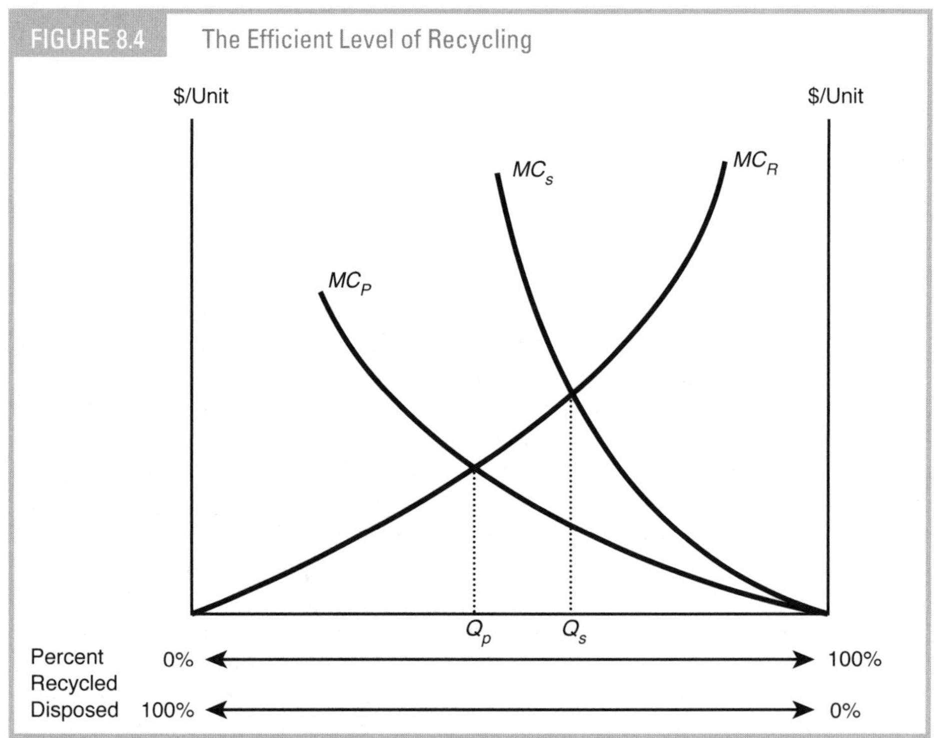

When the private marginal cost of disposal (MC_P) is lower than the marginal social cost of disposal (MC_s), the market level of recycling [where the marginal cost of recycling (MC_R) is equal to the marginal private disposal cost] is inefficient. Only if all social costs are included in the marginal cost of disposal will the efficient amount of recycling (Q_s) be attained.[3]

This point can be reinforced by a numerical example. Suppose your city provides trash pickup for which you pay $150 a year in taxes. Your cost will be $150 regardless (within reasonable limits) of how much you throw out. In that year your additional (marginal) cost from throwing out these items is *zero*. Certainly the marginal cost to society is not zero, and, therefore, the balance between these alternatives as seen by the individual homeowner is biased in favor of throwing things out.[4]

Littering is an extreme example of what we have been talking about. In the absence of some kind of government intervention, the cost to society of littering is the aesthetic loss plus the risk of damage to automobile tires and pedestrians caused by sharp edges of discarded cans or glass. Tossing used containers outside the car is relatively costless for the individual, but costly for society.[5]

Disposal Costs and the Scrap Market

How would the market respond to a policy forcing product users to bear the true marginal disposal cost? The major effect would be on the supply of materials to be recycled. Recycling would now offer consumers a way to avoid disposal costs and possibly even be paid for discarded products. This would cause the diversion of some materials to recycling centers, where they could be reintegrated into the materials process. If this expanded supply allows dealers to take advantage of previously unexploited economies of scale, this expansion could well result in a lower average cost of processing, as well as more recycled materials.

The total consumption of inputs would increase because the price falls. The use of recycled materials increases as well. The amount of virgin ore falls. Thus, the correct inclusion of disposal cost would tend to increase the amount of recycling and extend the useful economic life for depletable, recyclable resources.

Subsidies on Raw Materials

Disposal costs are only part of the story. Inputs derived from recycling can only compete with raw materials if the playing field is level. Subsidies on raw materials are another troubling source of inefficiencies that create a bias away from recycled inputs.

Subsidies can take many forms. One form is illustrated by the US Mining Law of 1872. This law, which was originally passed more than 150 years ago to promote mining on public lands, is still on the books. Under this law, miners can stake lode claims (for subsurface minerals) and placer claims (for surface minerals) for mineral

[3]According to Figure 8.4, would 100 percent recycling normally be efficient? Does that conclusion make sense to you? Why or why not?

[4]The problem is not that $150 is too low; indeed it may be too high! The point is that the cost of waste disposal does not increase with the amount of waste to be disposed.

[5]Using economic analysis, would you expect transients or residents to have a higher propensity to litter? Why?

prospecting on public lands. A claim can be maintained for a payment of only $100 a year. If minerals are discovered in a claim area and at least $500 has been invested in development or extraction, the land could actually be bought for $5 an acre on lode claims or $2.50 an acre on placer claims. In 1999 the US Congress enacted a moratorium on land purchases, but not on staking claims.

These prices for access to public lands are so low relative to market prices that they constitute a considerable implicit subsidy. As a result of this subsidy, taxpayers not only don't receive the true value of the mining services provided by public lands, but the subsidy has the effect of lowering the cost of extracting these raw minerals. As a result, raw materials are artificially cheap and can inefficiently undermine the market for recycled inputs.

Corrective Public Policies

Why are recycling rates so low? No doubt some of the responsibility lies in improper incentives created by inappropriate pricing. Can the misallocation resulting from inefficiently low disposal cost be corrected?

Pricing Trash Disposal. One approach, volume pricing, would impose disposal charges reflecting the true social cost of disposal (see Example 8.3).

EXAMPLE 8.3

An Early Example: Pricing Trash in Marietta, Georgia

In 1994, the people of Marietta, Georgia, participated in a demonstration project that changed the way in which waste was priced. The traditional $15 monthly fee for trash pickup was cut to $8 per month. In addition, half of the residents faced a per-bag price on waste ($0.75 per bag), while the rest faced a monthly fee for pickup that depended on the maximum number of cans per month that the customer wished to have picked up per month. This number was contracted in advance by the customer and did not vary from month to month. The fee was $3 or $4 per can (depending upon the number).

Economic theory suggests that while both plans should reduce waste and increase recycling, the per-bag fee should promote more. (Can you see why?)

And indeed that is what happened. The can program reduced nonrecycled waste by about 20 percent, whereas the bag program reduced it by as much as 51 percent. Both programs had an equally strong effect on encouraging households to recycle. Both programs not only diverted waste into recycling, they also reduced the amount of waste generated.

Could the costs associated with the program be justified in benefit–cost terms? According to the economists who conducted the study, they were. The net benefits for the city were estimated to be $586 per day for the bag program and $234 per day for the can program.

Source: Van Houtven, G. L., & Morris, G. E. (November 1999). Household behavior under alternative pay-as-you-throw systems for solid waste disposal. *Land Economics, 75*(4), 515–537.

A pre-implementation concern about volume pricing was that it might impose a hardship on the poor residents of the area. Strategies based on higher prices always raise the specter that they will end up placing an intolerable burden on the poor. In the case examined by Example 8.3 that concern was apparently misplaced. Under the old system of financing trash collection, every household paid the same fee regardless of how much trash is produced. Since lower-income households produce less trash, they were, in effect, subsidizing wealthier households. Under the new system, lower-income households pay only a flat fee since they don't need to purchase stickers for additional disposal. The expense of these stickers is less than the average cost of disposal, which was the basis for the previous fee. Poor households have turned out to be better off, not worse off, under the new pricing system.

Curbside Recycling. Curbside recycling programs are common in many cities. Economic theory tells us if the marginal cost of recycling is less than the marginal cost of trash disposal, recycling rates will increase. Curbside recycling, especially in combination with pay-as-you go trash disposal attempts to achieve an efficient balance between disposal and recycling. Curbside recycling programs in the United States grew from 1000 programs in 1988 to over 9000 in 2009 (US EPA, 2010). Example 8.4 looks at the demand and supply sides of curbside recycling. Do incentives matter?

EXAMPLE 8.4

Does Packaging Curbside Recyling with Incentives Promote Efficiency?

Municipalities that have landfill constraints or high fees for trash disposal are interested in whether or not they can increase the flow of recyclables (supply) in order to reduce pressure on landfill space. Municipalities considering whether or not to implement curbside recycling programs are also typically interested in which types of incentives are most effective in promoting recycling.

In one interesting experiment, Koford et al. (2012) compare two districts in a municipality in Kentucky; one in which the City provides trash and recycling collection funded via property taxes. In this situation curbside recycling has zero marginal cost. In the other, residents contract privately for trash and recycling services. Districts vote on which service they want.

Koford et al. estimated the demand for curbside recycling using a willingness to pay survey that also asked questions about recycling behavior and motivations for recycling. The survey was mailed to households in both types of districts.

In both samples, 63 percent of households cited an ethical duty when asked what most encouraged them to recycle. Another 37 percent, however, said that monetary incentives would encourage them to recycle.

The survey included a hypothetical curbside recycling service followed by a willingness to pay question in which respndents were asked whether they would be willing to pay a specific dollar amount for the service. The dollar amounts varied, but the average estimated willingness to pay for curbside recycling was $2.29 per month. Interestingly, whether or not the household currently had city service was not significant in influencing willingness to pay.

For the supply side, Koford et al. conducted an experiment to understand how households might respond to both monetary and communication incentives to recycle. They used three monetary incentives ($0, $1, $2) and four different types of communications (none, informational, guilt or feel good) for a total of 12 combinations of incentive and communication. The communications were sent monthly to a random sample of Lexington residents. The weight of their recycled materials was measured during control weeks (no incentive or communication) and experimental weeks.

The experiment had mixed results. The communication strategies were relatively ineffective. When combined (interacted) with the monetary incentives, the information appeal had a significant impact, but the net effect was to reduce recycling! Interestingly, while small monetary payments did have a positive effecct on recycling behavior, the incentives necessary to influence significant behavior changes are likely cost-prohibitive. Their estimate of willingness to pay ($2.29 per household per month) is less than the cost to administer the curbside recycling program (approximately $2.40 per household per month). In this case the benefits do not outweigh the costs.

Are these results specific to Lexington, Kentucky? It appears not. In a study of the Western United States, Aadland and Caplan (2006) find that net social benefits of curbside recycling is equal to zero (costs equal benefits), though the results do vary some by city. The relative ineffectiveness of the personal communications are also consistent with other literature that find that social norms have little impact (Viscusi et al., 2011) unless the appeals include a comparison of to the behaviors of others (Ferraro et al., 2011). However laws that promote recycling via economic incentives that either reduce the time and inconvenience costs of recycling or through bottle deposits can be very influential (Viscusi et al., 2011).

Sources: Aadland, D. M., Caplan, & A. J. (2006). Curbside recycling: Waste resource or waste of resources? *Journal of Policy Analysis and Management, 25*(4), 855–874; Ferraro, P. J., Miranda, J. J., Price, M. K. (2011). The persistence of treatment effects with norm-based policy instruments: Evidence from a randomized environmental policy experiment. *American Economic Review, 101*(3), 318–322; Koford, B. C., Blomquist, G. C., Hardesty, D. M., & Troske, K. (2012). Estimating consumer willingness to supply and willingness to pay for curbside recycling. *Land Economics,* 88(4), 745–763; Viscusi, W. K, Huber, J., & Bell, J. (2011). Promoting recycling: Private values, social norms, and economic incentives. *American Economic Review, 101*(3), 65–70.

Refundable Deposits. Another suggestion for promoting recycling now being applied in many areas is the refundable deposit. Already widely accepted for beverage containers, such deposits could become a remedy for many other products.

A refund system is designed to accomplish two purposes: (1) the initial charge reflects the cost of disposal and produces the desired composition of demand effect; and (2) the refund, attainable upon turning the product in for recycling, helps conserve virgin materials. Such a system is already employed in Sweden and Norway to counter the problem of abandoned automobiles.

The recycling of aluminum beverage cans has been one clear beneficiary of deposit refund schemes.[6] Quite a few countries, including Germany, Finland,

---

[6]A very strong demand for aluminum scrap was also influential. In fact, the price for aluminum scrap went so high in 1988 that pilferers were stealing highway signs and guardrails for their aluminum content.

Norway, Denmark, Sweden, Barbados, Canada, and the state of South Australia, and 11 U.S. states have container deposit refund programs in place. Although not all states have passed bottle bills, over 50 percent of aluminum beverage cans are now recycled in the United States. As a result, aluminum old scrap has become an increasingly significant component of total aluminum supplies. Recycling aluminum saves about 95 percent of the energy that is needed to make new aluminum from ore. The magnitude of these energy savings has had a significant influence on the demand for recycled aluminum as cost-conscious producers search for new ways to reduce energy costs. Debate 8.1 explores why only some states have implemented refundable bottle deposits.

Beverage container deposits also reduce illegal disposal (littering) because an incentive is created to bring the bottle or can to a recycling center. In some cities, scavenging and returning these bottles has provided a significant source of income to the homeless. One Canadian study found that recycling creates six times as many jobs as landfilling.

What about plastic bottles? Only six states currently have bottle deposits that cover plastic bottles. However, plastic waste generated from bottled water consumption has grown from 12 billion bottles in 2000 to 36 billion in 2006. Since bottle deposits offer incentives for nonrecyclers to become recyclers, states with deposits for plastic bottles have higher recycling rates than those without (Viscusi et al., 2012).

Deposit-refund systems are also being used for batteries and tires. New Hampshire and Maine, for example, place a surcharge on new car batteries. Consumers in these states receive a rebate if they trade in their used battery for a new one. Oklahoma places a $1 fee on each new tire sold and then returns $0.50 to certified processing facilities for each tire handled.

Some states in the United States, as well as some developing countries, also use deposit-refund systems to assure that pesticide containers are returned after use. Since these containers usually contain toxic residues after use, which can contaminate water and soil, collecting the containers and either reusing them or properly decontaminating them can eliminate this contamination threat.

Some areas attempt to enlist economic incentives by imposing a disposal or recycling surcharge on the product. Paid at the time of purchase of a new product, this surcharge would normally be designed to recover the costs of recycling the product at the end of its useful life; more-difficult-to-recycle products would have larger fees. These fees would normally be coupled with a requirement that the revenue be used by sellers to set up recycling systems. Assuming these fees correctly internalize the costs of recycling, they will provide consumers with incentives to take the recycling and disposal costs into account, since easier-to-recycle products would have a lower price (including the fee). Note, however, that these recycling surcharges do not provide any incentive against illegal disposal, since the consumer gets no rebate for dropping the product off at a collection center, but they provide no specific incentive for illegal disposal either. Since the surcharge is paid up front, it cannot be avoided by illegal disposal. In this sense, the deposit-refund system is clearly superior to either recycling surcharges or volume pricing of trash.

DEBATE 8.1 "Bottle Bills": Economic Incentives at Work?

Ten U.S. states—California, Connecticut, Hawaii, Iowa, Maine, Massachusetts, Michigan, New York, Oregon, and Vermont—have passed "bottle bill" legislation. One city, Columbia, Missouri, also passed legislation, but it was repealed in 2002. Delaware's bottle-deposit system was repealed in 2010, effective February 2011. Every year, several states either have proposed new legislation or proposed expansions of existing legislation. More often than not, these proposed bills do not pass. Bottle deposits in the United States range from $0.05 to $0.15 and laws vary on which containers are redeemable for deposits.[7]

While on average, U.S. container recycling rates have been below 40 percent, recycling rates in bottle-deposit states are much higher, averaging around 80 percent. Michigan's $0.10 beverage can deposit produced recycling rates close to 100 percent. Statistics on litter reduction show the largest gains in bottle-deposit states.

Although bottle-deposit states have recycling rates double those of states without deposits, that is not sufficient evidence to suggest that it would be efficient for all states to have them.

Economic studies on the efficiency of bottle deposits are limited. Porter (1983) estimated the costs and benefits of the then newly passed Michigan bottle bill. He found that for most estimates of costs and benefits, the bill passed a benefit–cost test. Ashenmiller (2009) finds that bottle deposits increase the numbers of recycled containers and reduce waste stream costs by diverting these containers away from curbside programs. Using survey data from California, she finds between 36 percent and 51 percent of materials at redemption centers would not have been collected using existing curbside programs alone (without the complementary deposit-refund system). Interestingly, however, some of the success of the California program can be attributed to its design—its curbside programs use volume-based pricing for trash. This analysis also notes that curbside programs work best in densely populated areas and that cash recycling programs can be an important income source for the working poor.

Since the efficiency of deposit–refund systems depends on their cost, they may be efficient for some states, but not others. Key determinants of the relative costs of bottle deposits vary from state to state. Disposal costs depend on landfill availability, and return rates depend on population densities and distances to redemption centers. States with bottle deposits may incur the extra expense of illegal returns from bottles purchased in nearby states that do not require a deposit. Enforcement across state lines is costly and imperfect. States with large bottlers like Coca-Cola are usually opposed to bottle deposits. Does your state have a bottle deposit? Does that seem the right choice?

Sources: http://globalwarming.house.gov/mediacenter/pressreleases?id=0126; www.containerrecyclinginstitute.org; Porter, R. C., (1983). Michigan's experience with mandatory deposits on beverage containers. *Land And Economics, 59*; Ashenmiller, B. (August 2009). Cash recycling, waste disposal costs, and the incomes of the working poor: Evidence from California. *Land Economics, 85*(3).

---

[7]Many provinces and territories in Canada also have deposits on beverage containers (www.bottlebill.org).

Taxes, Subsidies, and Other Incentives. The tax system can also be used to promote recycling by taxing virgin materials and by subsidizing recycling activities. The European approach to waste oil recycling, reinforced by the high cost of imported crude oil, was to require both residential and commercial users to recycle all waste oil they generate. Virgin lubricating oils are taxed, and the resulting income is used to subsidize the recycling industry. As a result, many countries collect up to 65 percent of the available waste oil.

In the United States, which does not subsidize waste oil recycling, the waste oil market has been rather less successful, but it is growing. In California in 2005, almost 60 percent of used lubricated oil was recycled. Laws in most states prohibit used oil disposal.

Many areas are now using tax policy to subsidize the acquisition of recycling equipment in both the public and private sectors. Frequently taking the form of sales-tax exemptions or investment tax credits to private industries or loans or grants to local communities, these approaches are designed to get recycling programs off the ground, with the expectation that they will ultimately be self-sustaining. The pioneers are being subsidized.

Examining Oregon's program can serve to illustrate how a tax approach works. From 1981 to 1987, to reduce energy consumption as well as to promote recycling, the Oregon Department of Energy granted tax credits to 163 projects. Being granted this credit allows companies a 5-year period in which to deduct from their taxes an amount equal to 35 percent of the cost of any equipment used solely for recycling. Oregon also offers a broader tax credit that covers equipment, land, and building purchases. Paper companies, the major recipients of both types of credits, have used them to increase the capacity to use recycled newsprint and cardboard in the papermaking process. According to Shea (1988), these incentives helped to raise Oregon's newspaper recycling rate (65 percent) to twice the national average.

Any long-run solution to the solid-waste problem must not only influence consumer choices about purchasing, packaging, and disposal, it must also influence producer choices about product design (to increase recyclability), product packaging, and the use of recycled (as opposed to virgin materials) in the production process. One general approach is called extended producer responsibility, and it involves requiring producers to take back packaging, and even their products, at the end of their useful life (see Example 8.5).

A Summary of Corrective Policies. As we will continue to see in the pollution chapters later in this book, incentives matter. The policies we have examined illustrate that financial incentives such as returnable deposits and time or convenience incentives (curbside recycling) can increase recycling rates. Viscusi et al., 2012 find, however, that "the net effect of recycling policies is less than the marginal effect of each policy introduced separately." Their study focused on plastic water bottles, but is certainly relevant for other types of recycling as well. They suggest that policies should be evaluated at the margin (what is the incremental effect?) rather than on the average performance of the policy. They also find that incentives like bottle deposits increase recycling rates because many nonrecyclers become recyclers. However, as we saw in Example 8.4, economic efficiency requires that the context be carefully considered and that the design be appropriate for that context.

EXAMPLE 8.5

Implementing the "Take-Back" Principle

According to the "take-back" principle, all producers should be required to accept responsibility for their products—including packaging—from cradle to grave by taking them back once they have outlived their useful lives. In principle, this requirement was designed to encourage the elimination of inessential packaging, to stimulate the search for products and packaging that are easier to recycle, and to support the substitution of recycled inputs for virgin inputs in the production process.

Germany has required producers (and retailers as intermediaries) to accept all packaging associated with products, including such different types of packaging as the cardboard boxes used for shipping hundreds of toothbrushes to retailers, to the tube that toothpaste is sold in. Consumers are encouraged to return the packaging by means of a combination of convenient drop-off centers, refundable deposits on some packages, and high disposal costs for packaging that is thrown away.

Producers responded by setting up a new, private, nonprofit corporation, the Duales System Deutschland (DSD), to collect the packaging and to recycle the collected materials. This corporation is funded by fees levied on producers. The fees are based on the number of kilograms of packaging the producers use. The DSD accepts only packaging that it has certified as recyclable. Once certification is received, producers are allowed to display a green dot on their product, signaling consumers that this product is accepted by the DSD system. Other packaging must be returned directly to the producer or to the retailer, who returns it to the producer.

The law has apparently reduced the amount of packaging produced and has diverted a significant amount of packaging away from incineration and landfills. A most noteworthy failure, however, was the inability of the DSD system to find markets for the recycled materials it collected. Some German packaging even ended up in neighboring countries, causing some international backlash. The circumstance where the supply of recycled materials far exceeds the demand is so common—not only in Germany, but in the rest of the world as well—that further efforts to increase the degree of recycling will likely flounder unless new markets for recycled materials are forthcoming.

Despite the initial difficulties with implementing the "take-back" principle, the idea that manufacturers should have ultimate responsibility for their products has a sufficiently powerful appeal that it has moved beyond an exclusive focus on packaging and is now expanding to include the products themselves. In 2002, the European Union (EU) passed a law that makes manufacturers financially responsible for recycling the appliances they produce. In 2004, the European Union's Waste Electrical and Electronic Equipment (WEEE) directive came into effect, making it the responsibility of the manufacturers and importers in EU states to take back their products and to properly dispose of them.

As part of the WEEE program, a pilot study was conducted in Beijing, Delhi, and Johannesburg. This study found that e-waste recycling has developed in all three countries as a market-based activity.

Sources: Rousso, A. S., & Shah, S. P. (September 1994). Packaging taxes and recycling incentives: The German Green Dot Program. *National Tax Journal*, *47*(3), 689–701; Ryan, M. Packaging a Revolution. (September–October 1993). *World Watch*, 28–34; Boerner, C., & Chilton, K. (January/February 1994). False economy: The folly of demand-side recycling. *Environment*, *36*(1), 6–15; Widmer, R., Oswald-Krapf, H., Sinha-Khetriwal, D., Schnellmann, M., & Boni, H. (2005). Global perspectives on e-waste. *Environmental Impact Assessment*, 25, 436–458.

Markets for Recycled Materials

Successful recycling programs depend to a large extent on the existence of markets (buyers) for recycled materials. Consider plastics, for example. Currently, PET bottles are primarily used in carpet fiber and textiles including fleece. Other potential future uses for recycled PET bottles include waterproof shipping containers and coating for paper. HDPE plastics are primarily made into bottles and garden products, such as lawn edging and lawn chairs.

The market for plastics is expanding in some areas where the capacity to process the postconsumer waste and the demand for that material is greater than the amount recovered. As new uses expand, this market can be expected to grow. According to the U.S. EPA, the American Society for Testing and Materials (ASTM) is using new test methods that are facilitating the use of recycled plastics in building materials.

E-Waste

Recognizing the dangers from improperly disposed electronic equipment (e-waste), some states have enlisted economic incentives to promote recycling. Sales of electronics doubled in the 10 years between 1999–2009. Sales of mobile devices grew by nine times. In 2009, 438 million new consumer electronics were sold. An additional 5 million tons were in storage (U.S. EPA, 2009). 2.37 million tons were discarded. Only 25 percent of those were recycled.

Although this represented fewer than 2 percent of the municipal solid-waste stream, electronics waste is a fast-growing segment of it, bringing with it rising concerns about the environmental and health effects of some of this waste. Lead, mercury, cadmium, and brominated flame retardants are all widely used in electronics. All of these substances have been linked to health risks, especially for children, and are considered hazardous waste.

Did you upgrade your cell phone this year? Perhaps you got a new laptop for school. Or maybe you got a new MP3 player or iPad. What happened to the old one? The US Geological Survey (USGS) reports some 1 billion cell phones were in use worldwide in 2002. In the United States alone, the USGS reports that cell phone subscribers increased from 340,000 in 1985 to 180 million in 2004. Moreover, 141 million cell phones were retired in 2009. The US EPA reports that currently fewer than 1 percent of cell phones discarded are recycled (US EPA, 2010). Are the minerals used to make cell phones (primarily copper, iron, nickel, silver, and zinc, with smaller amounts of aluminum, gold, lead, palladium, and tin) valuable? Apparently quite valuable! Table 8.1 shows the estimated value of the metals in cell phones in the United States.

Currently 25 states have enacted e-waste legislation. To take an early example of this legislation, California passed a bill in 2003 that charges consumers a fee for buying computer monitors or televisions and pays recyclers to dispose of the displays safely when users no longer want them. Fees depend on the size of the monitor. In 2009, the fee to dispose of a monitor smaller than 15 inches was \$8, \$16 if the

TABLE 8.1 Weight and Gross Value of Selected Metals in Cell Phones in the United States

The average weight (wt) of a cell phone is estimated to be 113 grams (g), exclusive of batteries and charger (Nokia, 2005). Metal contents are weights in metric tons (t), unless otherwise noted. Values in U.S. dollars are calculated by using the average of prices for 2002–2004 from USGS Mineral Commodity Summaries 2005 (Amey, 2005; Edelstein, 2005; Hilliard, 2005a, 2005b). The gross values do not include costs of recycling. Data may not add to totals shown because of independent rounding.

Metal	Metal Content and Value Estimated for a Typical Cell Phone		Metal Content and Value for 180 Million Cell Phones in Use in 2004[1]		Metal Content and Value for 130 Million Cell Phones Retired in 2005[1]		Metal Content and Value for 500 Million Obsolete Cell Phones in Storage in 2005[1]	
	Wt[2](g)	Value ($)	Wt[3](t)	Value ($ million)	Wt[3](t)	Value ($ million)	Wt[3](t)	Value ($ million)
Copper	16	0.03	2,900	6.2	2,100	4.6	7,900	17
Silver	0.35	0.06	64.1	11	46	7.9	178	31
Gold	0.034	0.40	6.2	72	3.9	52	17	199
Palladium	0.015	0.13	2.7	22.7	2.0	16	7.4	63
Platinum	0.00034	0.01	0.06	1.4	0.04	1	0.18	3.9
Total	2,973			113	2,152	82	8,102	314

[1]Number of cell phones in use in 2004 from Charny (2005). Number of cell phones retired in 2005 from US Environmental Protection Agency, 2005. Number of obsolete cell phones projected to be in storage in 2005 from Most (2003).

[2]Metal content (wt) calculated from weight of a typical cell phone (Nokia, 2005) and data from Rob Bouma, Falconbridge Ltd., written and oral communications, 2005.

[3]Metal content (wt) calculated from data from Rob Bouma, Falconbridge Ltd., written and oral communications, 2005.

Source: Sullivan, D. (2007). Recycled cell phones—A treasure trove of valuable materials. *USGS*. Retrieved from http://pubs.usgs.gov/fs/2006/3097/fs2006-3097.pdf

monitor was 15–35 inches, and $25 for greater than 35 inches. In 2004, California passed a bill that makes it unlawful for retailers to sell mobile phones without the establishment of a collection, reuse, and recycling system for proper disposal of used cell phones. This bill places the responsibility for recycling squarely upon the industry, but leaves the implementation details up to them. While this approach allows the industry to minimize recycling costs, it remains to be seen whether the resulting policy promotes reuse of the materials in a manner that is safe for human health and the environment. The most recent e-waste law was passed by the state of Utah in 2011; however, it is relatively weak in that the legislation contains no land fill bans or recycling goals.

Many of the states with laws have focused on the manufacturer.[8] These states use market share as the basis for allocating responsibility for recycling to the manufacturers of televisions and video games. For example, for 2011 in the state of

[8]Details of each state's program can be found at http://www.electronicsrecycling.org/public/ContentPage.aspx?pageid=14

TABLE 8.2 Electronics Recycling Rates 2009

Management of Used and End-Of-Life Electronics in 2009

	Ready for End-of-Life Management (millions of units)	Disposed (millions of units)	Collected for Recycling (millions of units)	Rate of Collection for Recycling (by weight)
Computers	47.4	29.4	18	38%
Televisions	27.2	22.7	4.6	17%
Mobile Devices	141	129	11.7	8%

Source: http://www.epa.gov/wastes/conserve/materials/ecycling/manage.htm#report

Maine, Samsung had a 19.6 percent share of recycling responsibility. Sony had a 11.3 percent share, Vizio 9.9 percent, etc., all the way to Audiovox with a 0.1 percent share.[9]

Are these laws working? Table 8.2 shows recycling rates for televisions, computer products, and cell phones in 2009. While recycling rates for computers is up to 38%, recycling rates for mobile devices is only 8%. Only 25 percent of all discarded electronics were collected for recycling. It remains to be seen what effect the new laws and market share requirements will have.

Internationally, the Basel Convention regulates the movement of electronic waste across international boundaries (UNEP, 1989), although not all countries have ratified this treaty. One component of the convention would prohibit the export of e-waste from developed to industrializing countries since, in addition to valuable materials, the waste contains hazardous materials, such as lead and mercury.

In their analysis of trends of e-waste, Widmer et al. (2005) find that for countries such as China and India, e-waste is rapidly growing from both domestic sources and illegal imports. Kinnaman and Yokoo (2011) report that levels of air toxins found in and around e-waste dismantling facilities in China are the highest in the world. These countries are just beginning to impose laws to control e-waste imports, but enforcement is lacking and the valuable materials create a business opportunity. Widmer et al. estimates that 50–80 percent of collected domestic e-waste from nonratifying Basel Convention countries, such as the United States, is shipped to China and other Asian countries. This toxic and environmental justice issue will be examined in more detail in Chapter 19.

Pollution Damage

Another situation influences the use of recycled and virgin ores. When environmental damage results from extracting and using virgin materials and not from the use of recycled materials, the market allocation will be biased away from recycling. The damage

[9]http://www.maine.gov/dep/rwm/ewaste/manufacturers.htm

might be experienced at the mine, such as the erosion and aesthetic costs of strip mining, or at the point of processing, where the ore is processed into a usable resource.

Suppose that the mining industry was forced to bear the cost of this environmental damage. What difference would the inclusion of this cost have on the scrap market? The internalizing of this cost results in a leftward shift in the supply curve for the virgin ore. This would, in turn, cause a leftward shift in the total supply curve. The market would be using less of the resource—due to higher price—while recycling more. Thus the correct treatment of these environmental costs would share with disposal costs a tendency to increase the role for recycling.

Disposal also imposes external environmental costs in the form of odors, pests, and contaminants leaching into water supplies; obstruction of visual landscapes; and so on. Kinnaman and Fullerton (2000) note that while the number of landfills in the United States has been decreasing, the aggregate capacity of these landfills has been increasing, as small-town facilities are replaced by large regional sanitary landfills. Since local opposition from potential host communities is likely to rise with landfill size, locating these facilities can be extremely contentious.

While governments now regulate landfills to protect public safety, these regulations rarely eliminate all unpleasant aspects of these landfills for the host communities. As a result, many communities are all for the existence of these facilities as long as they are not located in their community. If every community felt this way, locating new facilities could be difficult, if not impossible.

One technique for resolving this Not In My Back Yard (NIMBY) problem relies on the imposition of host fees. Host fees compensate the local community (and sometimes surrounding communities) for accepting the location of a waste facility within their community. This approach gives local communities veto power over the location, but it also attempts to share the benefits of the regional facility in such a way that makes the net benefits sufficiently positive for them that the communities will accept the facility.

In one example, Porter (2002) reports that a host fee agreement between Browning Ferris Industries and the township of Salem, Michigan, involves sharing with the town 2.5 percent of all landfill revenues and 4 percent of all compost revenues. The town also shares in the revenues derived from the sale of landfill gases (used for energy) and it can use the site free of charge for all town refuse, without limit on volume. These benefits are estimated to be worth about $400 per person per year, apparently enough to overcome local opposition.

Host fees are not a perfect resolution of the siting problem. Note, for example, that the fact that Salem can dispose of its waste free of charge provides no incentive for source reduction. In addition, it is important to ensure that locating these facilities does not raise environmental justice concerns. Although we consider this issue in much greater depth in Chapter 19, let it suffice here to point out that at a minimum, the local community has to be fully informed of the risks it will face from a regional sanitary landfill and must be fully empowered to accept or reject the proposed compensation package. As we shall see, these preconditions frequently did not exist in the past.

Additional complexities arise with hazardous wastes. Because hazardous wastes are more dangerous to handle and to dispose of, special polices have been designed to keep those dangers efficiently low. These policies will be also be treated in Chapter 19.

Summary

One of the most serious deficiencies in both our detection of scarcity and our ability to respond to scarcity is the failure of the market system to incorporate the various environmental costs of increasing resource use, be they radiation or toxics hazards, the loss of genetic diversity or aesthetics, polluted air and drinking water, or climate modification. Without including these costs, our detection indicators give falsely optimistic signals, and the market makes choices that put society inefficiently at risk.

As a result, while market mechanisms automatically create pressures for recycling and reuse that are generally in the right direction, they are not always of the correct intensity. Higher disposal costs and increasing scarcity of virgin materials do create a larger demand for recycling. This is already evident for a number of products, such as those containing copper or aluminum.

Yet a number of market imperfections tend to suggest that the degree of recycling we are currently experiencing is less than the efficient amount. The absence of sufficient stockpiles and the absence of tariffs mean that our national security interests are not being adequately considered. Artificially low disposal costs and tax breaks for ores combine to depress the role that old scrap can, and should, play. Severance taxes could provide a limited if poorly targeted redress for some minerals.

One cannot help but notice that many of these problems—such as pricing municipal disposal services and tax breaks for virgin ores—result from government actions. Therefore, it appears in this area that the appropriate role for government is selective disengagement complemented by some fine-tuning adjustments.

Disengagement is not the prescription, however, for environmental damage due to illegal disposal, air and water pollution, and strip mining. When a product is produced from virgin materials rather than from recycled or reusable materials, and the cost of any associated environmental damage is not internalized, some government action may be called for.

The selective disengagement of government in some areas must be complemented by the enforcement of programs to internalize the costs of environmental damage. The commonly heard ideological prescriptions suggesting that environmental problems can be solved either by ending government interference or by increasing the amount of government control are both simplistic. The efficient role for government in achieving a balance between the economic and environmental systems requires less control in some areas and more in others and the form of that control matters.

Discussion Questions

1. Glass bottles can be either recycled (crushed and re-melted) or reused. The market will tend to choose the cheapest path. Which factors will tend to affect the relative cost of these options? Is the market likely to make the efficient choice? Are the "bottle bills" passed by many of the states requiring deposits on bottles a move toward efficiency? Why?

2. Many areas have attempted to increase the amount of recycled waste lubricating oil by requiring service stations to serve as collection centers or by instituting deposit–refund systems. On what grounds, if any, is government intervention called for? In terms of the effects on the waste lubrication oil market, what differences should be noticed among those states that do nothing, those that require all service stations to serve as collection centers, and those that implement deposit–refund systems? Why?
3. What are the income-distribution consequences of "fashion"? Can the need to be seen driving a new car by the rich be a boon to those with lower incomes who will ultimately purchase a better, lower-priced used car as a result?

Self-Test Exercises

1. Suppose a product can be produced using virgin ore at a marginal cost given by $MC_1 = 0.5q_1$ and with recycled materials at a marginal cost given by $MC_2 = 5 + 0.1q_2$. (a) If the inverse demand curve were given by $p = 10 - 0.5(q_1 + q_2)$, how many units of the product would be produced with virgin ore and how many units with recycled materials? (b) If the inverse demand curve were $p = 20 - 0.5(q_1 + q_2)$, what would your answer be?
2. When the government allows private firms to extract minerals offshore or on public lands, two common means of sharing in the profits are bonus bidding and production royalties. The former awards the right to extract to the highest bidder, while the second charges a per-ton royalty on each ton extracted. Bonus bids involve a single, up-front payment, while royalties are paid as long as minerals are being extracted.
   a. If the two approaches are designed to yield the same amount of revenue, will they have the same effect on the allocation of the mine over time? Why or why not?
   b. Would either or both be consistent with an efficient allocation? Why or why not?
   c. Suppose the size of the mineral deposit and the future path of prices are unknown. How do these two approaches allocate the risk between the mining company and the government?
3. "As society's cost of disposing of trash increases over time, recycling rates should automatically increase as well." Discuss.
4. Suppose a town concludes that it costs on average \$30.00 per household to manage the disposal of the waste generated by households each year. It is debating two strategies for funding this cost: (1) requiring a sticker on every bag disposed of such that the total cost of the stickers for the average number of bags per household per year would be \$30 or (2) including the \$30 fee in each household's property taxes each year.

a. Assuming no illegal disposal, which approach would tend to be more efficient? Why?
b. How would the possibility of rampant illegal disposal affect your answer? Would a deposit–refund on some large components of the trash help to reduce illegal disposal? Why or why not? What are the revenue implications to the town of establishing a deposit–refund system?

Further Reading

Ferrara, I., & Missios, P. (2012). A cross-country study of household waste prevention and recycling: assessing the effectiveness of policy instruments. *Land Economics*, 88(4), 710–744. Using a comprehensive household-level data set involving 10,251 respondents from a cross-section of 10 countries (Australia, Canada, Czech Republic, France, Italy, Korea, Mexico, Netherlands, Norway, and Sweden), this study examines waste policy, recycling behavior, and waste prevention.

Jenkins, R. Salvador, R., Martinez, A., Palmer, K., & Podolsky, M. J. (2003). The determinants of household recycling: A material-specific analysis of recycling program features and unit pricing. *Journal of Environmental Economics and Management*, *45*, 294–318.This study examines a unique, household-level data set representing middle and upper-middle income groups in 20 metropolitan statistical areas across the United States. It contains information on the percent recycled of five different materials: glass bottles, plastic bottles, aluminum, newspaper, and yard waste.

Kellenberg, D. (2012). Trading wastes. (2012). *Journal of Environmental Economics and Management*, *64*, 68–87. Using bilateral waste trade data and an index of environmental stringency for 92 countries, this study finds compelling evidence that waste imports increase for a country whose environmental regulations deteriorate vis-a-vis its trading partner, implying that differences in environmental standards play an important role in international waste trade flows for some country pairs.

Kinnaman, T. C., & Fullerton. D. (2000). The economics of residential solid waste management. In T. Tietenberg & H. Folmer (Eds.). *The International Yearbook of Environmental and Resource Economics 2000/2001*. Cheltenham, UK: Edward Elgar, 100–147. A comprehensive survey of the economic literature devoted to household solid-waste collection and disposal.

Lifset, R., Atasu, A., & Tojo, N. (2013). Extended producer responsibility: National, international, and practical perspectives. *Journal of Industrial Ecology*, *17*(2),162–166. An introductory summary article of a special issue on extended producer responsibility. The articles in this issue provide insights into how and why EPR has evolved into its current form and how it might evolve further.

Porter, R. C. (2002). *The Economics of Waste*. Washington, DC: Resources for the Future, Inc. A highly readable, thorough treatment of how economic principles and policy instruments can be used to improve the management of a diverse range of both business and household waste.

Additional References and Historically Significant References are available on this book's Companion Website: http://www.routledgetextbooks.com/textbooks/9780133479690

9 Water: A Confluence of Renewable and Depletable Resources

When the Well's Dry, We Know the Worth of Water.

—Benjamin Franklin, *Poor Richard's Almanack* (1746)

Introduction

> *To the red country and part of the gray country of Oklahoma, the last rains came gently, and they did not cut the scarred earth. . . . The sun flared down on the growing corn day after day until a line of brown spread along the edge of each green bayonet. The clouds appeared and went away, and in awhile they did not try anymore.*

With these words John Steinbeck (1939) sets the scene for his powerful novel *The Grapes of Wrath*. Drought and poor soil conservation practices combined to destroy the agricultural institutions that had provided nourishment and livelihood to Oklahoma residents since settlement in that area had begun. In desperation, those who had worked that land were forced to abandon not only their possessions but also their past. Moving to California to seek employment, they were uprooted only to be caught up in a web of exploitation and hopelessness.

Based on an actual situation, the novel demonstrates not only how the social fabric can tear when subject to tremendous stress, such as an inadequate availability of water, but also how painful those ruptures can be.[1] Clearly, problems such as these should be anticipated and prevented as much as possible.

Water is one of the essential elements of life. Humans depend not only on an intake of water to replace the continual loss of body fluids, but also on food sources that depend on water to survive. This resource deserves special attention.

In this chapter we examine how our economic and political institutions have allocated this important resource in the past and how they might improve on its allocation in the future. We initiate our inquiry by examining the likelihood and severity of water scarcity. Turning to the management of our water resources, we define the efficient allocation of ground- and surface water over time and compare these allocations to current practice, particularly in the United States. Finally, we examine the menu of opportunities for meaningful institutional reform.

[1]Popular films such as *The Milagro Beanfield War* and *Chinatown* have addressed similar themes.

The Potential for Water Scarcity

The earth's renewable supply of water is governed by the hydrologic cycle, a system of continuous water circulation (see Figure 9.1). Enormous quantities of water are cycled each year through this system, though only a fraction of circulated water is available each year for human use.

Of the estimated total volume of water on earth, only 2.5 percent (1.4 billion km^3) of the total volume is freshwater. Of this amount, only 200,000 km^3, or less than 1 percent of all freshwater resources (and only 0.01 percent of all the water on earth), is available for human consumption and for ecosystems (Gleick, 2000).

If we were simply to add up the available supply of freshwater (total runoff) on a global scale and compare it with current consumption, we would discover that the supply is currently about ten times larger than consumption. Though comforting, that statistic is also misleading because it masks the impact of growing demand and the rather severe scarcity situation that already exists in certain parts of the world. Taken together, these insights suggest that in many areas of the world, including parts of Africa, China, and the United States, water scarcity is already upon us. Does economics offer potential solutions? As this chapter demonstrates, it can, but implementation is sometimes difficult.

FIGURE 9.1 The Hydrologic Cycle

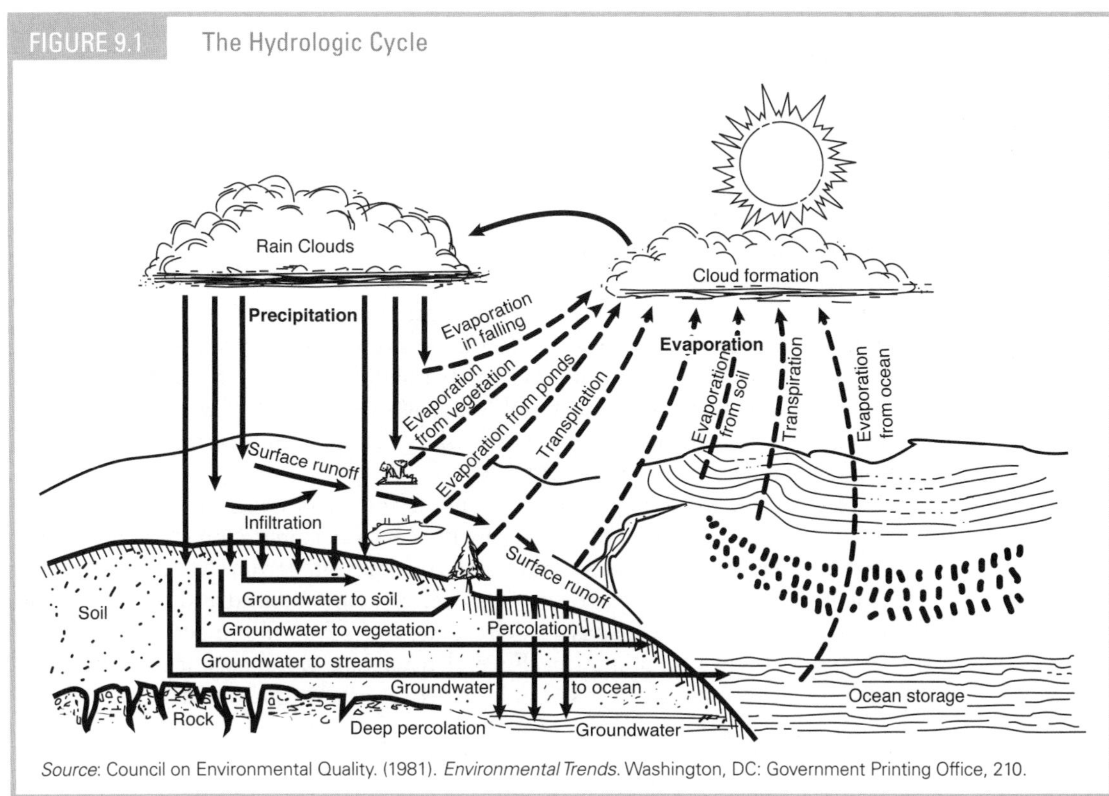

Source: Council on Environmental Quality. (1981). *Environmental Trends*. Washington, DC: Government Printing Office, 210.

Available supplies are derived from two rather different sources—surface water and groundwater. As the name implies, *surface water* consists of the freshwater in rivers, lakes, and reservoirs that collects and flows on the earth's surface. *Groundwater*, by contrast, collects in porous layers of underground rock known as aquifers. Though some groundwater is renewed by percolation of rain or melted snow, most was accumulated over geologic time and, because of its location, cannot be recharged once it is depleted.

According to the UN Environment Program (2002), 90 percent of the world's readily available freshwater resources is groundwater. And only 2.5 percent of this is available on a renewable basis. The rest is a finite, depletable resource.

In 2005 water withdrawals in the United States amounted to 410 billion gallons per day, 349 billion gallons per day or 85 percent of these from freshwater. Of the freshwater withdrawals, approximately 83 billion gallons per day came from groundwater. Water withdrawals, both surface and groundwater, vary considerably geographically. Figure 9.2 shows how surface and groundwater withdrawals for the United States vary by state. California, Texas, Nebraska, Arkansas, and Florida are the states with the largest groundwater withdrawals.

Forty-one percent of all freshwater withdrawals in the United States is used for thermoelectric power generation, most of that from surface water. While irrigation withdrawals account for 37 percent of all freshwater withdrawals, they account for 67% of groundwater withdrawals. Irrigated acreage increased between 2000 and 2005, but increased reliance on micro irrigation systems has prevented further total water withdrawals for irrigation.

While surface water withdrawals in the United States have been relatively constant since 1985, groundwater withdrawals are up 14 percent (Hutson et al., 2004). Globally, annual water withdrawal is expected to grow by 10–12 percent every 10 years. Most of this growth is expected to occur in South America and Africa (UNESCO, 1999).

Tucson, Arizona, demonstrates how some Western communities attempt to cope. Tucson, which averages about 11 inches of rain per year, was (until the completion of the Central Arizona Project, which diverts water from the Colorado River) the largest city in the United States to rely entirely on groundwater. Tucson annually pumped five times as much water out of the ground as nature put back in. The water levels in some wells in the Tucson area had dropped over 100 feet. At those consumption rates, the aquifers supplying Tucson would have been exhausted in less than 100 years. Despite the rate at which its water supplies were being depleted, Tucson continued to grow at a rapid rate.

To head off this looming gap between increasing water consumption and declining supply, a giant network of dams, pipelines, tunnels, and canals, known as the Central Arizona Project, was constructed to transfer water from the Colorado River to Phoenix and Tucson. The project took over 20 years to build and cost $4 billion. While this project has a capacity to deliver Arizona's 2.8 million acre-foot share of the Colorado River (negotiated by Federal Interstate Compact), it is still turning out to not be enough water for Phoenix and Tucson.[2,3] Some of this water is being

[2]One acre-foot of water is the amount of water that could cover 1 acre of land, 1 foot deep.

[3]An Interstate Compact is an agreement negotiated among states along an interstate river. Once ratified by Congress, it becomes a federal law and is one mechanism for allocating water.

FIGURE 9.2 Estimated Use of Water in the United States in 2005, Including Surface Water and Groundwater Withdrawals

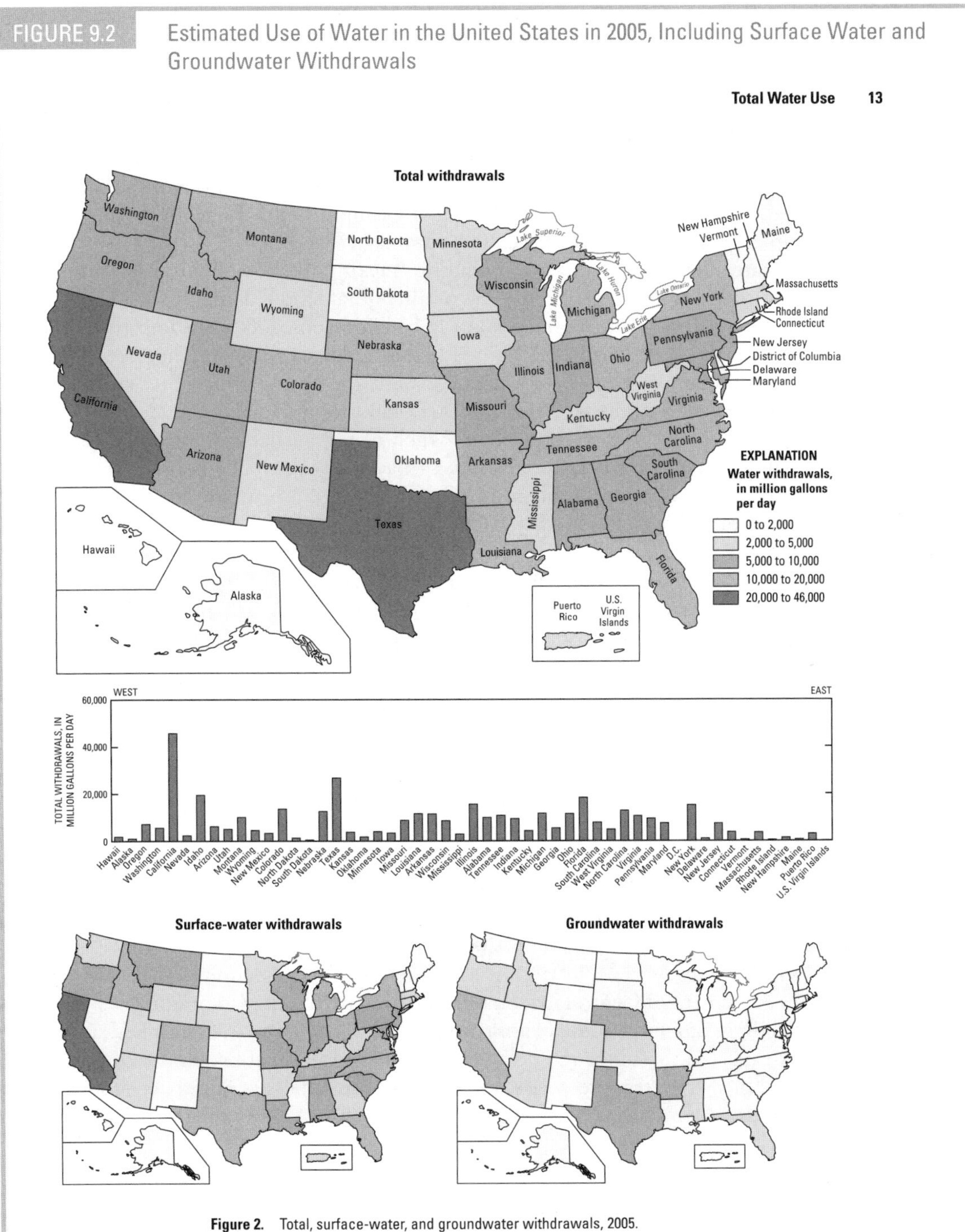

Figure 2. Total, surface-water, and groundwater withdrawals, 2005.

Source: United States Geological Survey (USGS), 2005. Retrieved from http://pubs.usgs.gov/circ/1344/pdf/c1344.pdf

pumped underground in an attempt to recharge the aquifer. While water diversions were frequently used to bring additional water to water stressed regions in the West, they are increasingly unavailable as a policy response to water scarcity.

Globally, access to clean water is a growing problem. Approximately 1.5 billion people in the world depend on groundwater for their drinking supplies. Over 600 million people lack access to clean drinking water—58 percent of those people are in Asia (UNDP, 2006).[4] Relocation of rivers to rapidly growing urban areas is creating local water shortages. China, for example, built a huge diversion project to help ensure water supply at the 2008 summer Olympics.

Water demand for energy, including fracking, is growing at an alarming rate. The International Energy Agency predicts that water demand for energy could double by 2035 (from 2010 levels) to 135 billion cubic meters or four times the size of the largest reservoir in the United States, Lake Mead. That amount is also equal to the amount of household water consumed in the United States over a 3-year period (Lavelle & Grose, 2013; International Energy Agency 2012[5]).

Water quality is also a problem. Much of the available water is polluted with chemicals, radioactive materials, salt, or bacteria. We shall reserve a detailed look at the water pollution problem for Chapter 18, but it is important to keep in mind that water scarcity has an important qualitative dimension that further limits the supply of potable water.

Depletion and contamination of water supplies are not the only problems. Excessive withdrawal from aquifers is a major cause of land subsidence. Land subsidence is a gradual settling or sudden sinking of the earth's surface owing to subsurface movement of the earth's materials, in this case water. Land subsidence has caused millions of dollars in damages in states including California, Texas, and Florida. More than 80 percent of land subsidence in the United States has been caused by human impacts on groundwater.[6]

In Mexico City, land has been subsiding at a rate of 1–3 inches per year. The city has sunk 30 feet over the last century. The Monumento a la Independencia, built in 1910 to celebrate the 100th anniversary of Mexico's War of Independence, now needs 23 additional steps to reach its base. Mexico City, with its population of approximately 20 million, is facing large water problems. Not only is the city sinking, but with an average population growth of 350,000 per year, the city is also running out of water (Rudolph, 2001).

In Phoenix, Arizona, in 1999, it was discovered that a section of the canal that carries 80 percent of Central Arizona Project water from the Colorado River had been subsiding, sinking at a rate of approximately 0.2 feet per year. Continued subsidence was expected to reduce the delivery capacity of the canal by almost 20 percent by 2005. In a short-term response, the lining of the canal was raised. As a longer-term response, Arizona has been injecting groundwater aquifers with surface water to

---

[4]http://www.un.org/apps/news/story.asp?NewsID=17891&Cr=water&Cr1

[5]International Energy Agency World Energy Outlook. http://www.worldenergyoutlook.org/resources/water-energynexus/

[6]http://water.usgs.gov/ogw/pubs/fs00165/

replenish the groundwater tables and to prevent further land subsidence. This process, called artificial recharge, has also been used in other locations to store excess surface water and to prevent saltwater intrusion.[7]

What this brief survey of the evidence suggests is that in certain parts of the world, groundwater supplies are being depleted to the potential detriment of future users. Supplies that for all practical purposes will never be replenished are being "mined" to satisfy current needs. Once used, they are gone. Is this allocation efficient, or are there demonstrable sources of inefficiency? Answering this question requires us to be quite clear about what is meant by an efficient allocation of surface water and groundwater.

The Efficient Allocation of Scarce Water

In defining the efficient allocation of water, whether surface water or groundwater is being tapped is crucial. In the absence of storage, the allocation of surface water involves distributing a fixed renewable supply among competing users. Intergenerational effects are less important because future supplies depend on natural phenomena (such as precipitation) rather than on current withdrawal practices. For groundwater, on the other hand, withdrawing water now does affect the resources available to future generations. In this case, the allocation over time is a crucial aspect of the analysis. Because it represents a somewhat simpler analytical case, we shall start by considering the efficient allocation of surface water.

Surface Water

An efficient allocation of surface water must (1) strike a balance among a host of competing users and (2) supply an acceptable means of handling the year-to-year variability in water flow. The former issue is acute because so many different potential users have legitimate competing claims. Some (such as municipal drinking-water suppliers or farmers) withdraw the water for consumptive use, while others (such as swimmers or boaters) use the water, but do not consume it. The variability challenge arises because surface water supplies are not constant from year to year or month to month. Since precipitation, runoff, and evaporation all change from year to year, in some years less water will be available for allocation than in others. Not only must a system be in place for allocating the average amount of water, but also above-average and below-average flows must be anticipated and allocated.

With respect to allocating among competing users, the dictates of efficiency are quite clear—the water should be allocated so that the marginal net benefit is equalized for all uses. (Remember that the marginal net benefit is the vertical distance between the demand curve for water and the marginal cost of extracting and distributing that water for the last unit of water consumed.)

[7] www.cap-az.com/operations.aspx

To demonstrate why efficiency requires equal marginal net benefits, consider a situation in which the marginal net benefits are not equal. Suppose for example, that at the current allocations, the marginal net benefit to a municipal user is $2,000 per acre-foot, while the marginal net benefit to an agricultural user is $500 per acre-foot. If an acre-foot of water were transferred from the farm to the city, the farm would lose marginal net benefits of $500, but the city would gain $2,000 in marginal net benefits. Total net benefits from this transfer would rise by $1,500. Since marginal net benefits fall with use, the new marginal net benefit to the city after the transfer will be less than $2,000 per acre-foot and the marginal net benefit to the farmer will be greater than $500 (a smaller allocation means moving up the marginal net benefits curve), but until these two are equalized, we can still increase net benefits by transferring water. Because net benefits are increased by this transfer, the initial allocation could not have maximized net benefits. Since an efficient allocation maximizes net benefits, any allocation that fails to equalize marginal net benefits could not have been efficient.

The bottom line is that if marginal net benefits have not been equalized, it is always possible to increase net benefits by transferring water from those users with low net marginal benefits to those with higher net marginal benefits. By transferring the water to the users who value the marginal water more, the total net benefits of the water use are increased; those losing water are giving up less than those receiving the additional water are gaining. When the marginal net benefits are equalized, no such transfer is possible without lowering net benefits. This can be seen in Figure 9.3.

Consider a water supply represented by S_T^0, the amount of water available is Q_T^0. Suppose there are two different users represented by the marginal net benefit curve A

FIGURE 9.3 The Efficient Allocation of Surface Water

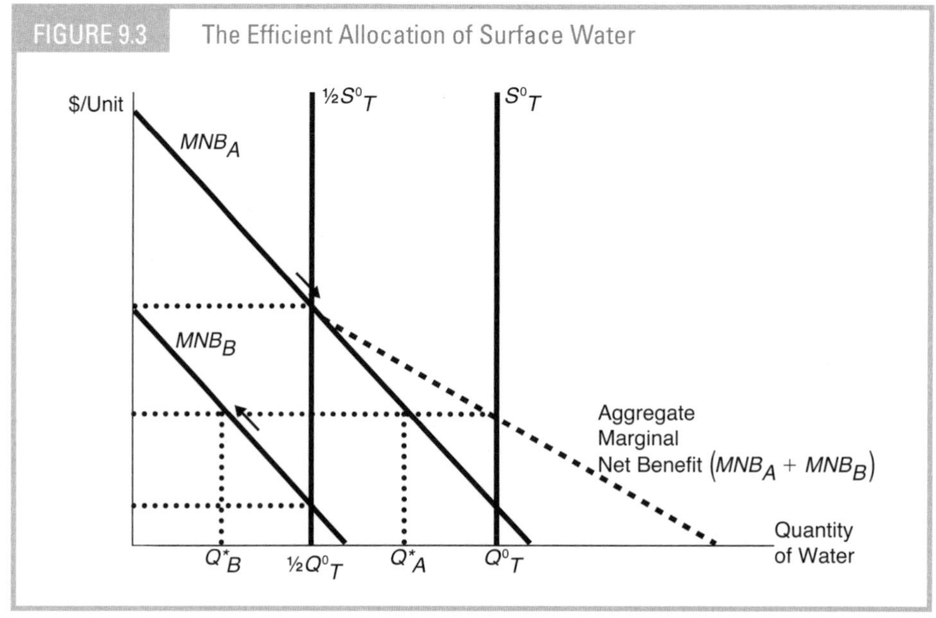

and marginal net benefit curve B.[8] These could be a municipality (A) and an irrigation district (B). In this figure the municipality has higher demand (higher willingness to pay). The total marginal net benefit is the sum of the two demand curves (horizontal summation). Suppose further that the state or water authority decides, for equity or political reasons, to simply divide the available water equally between the two users, giving each an amount $Q_A = Q_B = ½\, Q^0{}_T$. Can you see how this is inefficient? This allocation would result in different marginal net benefits for each user. An efficient allocation would give Q^*_A to user A (the municipality) and Q^*_B to user B. By construction, $Q^*_A + Q^*_B = Q^0_T$. For this optimal allocation, notice that the marginal net benefit is equal for the two users.

Notice also that the marginal net benefit for both users is positive in Figure 9.3. This implies that water sales should involve a positive marginal scarcity rent. Could we draw the diagram so that the marginal net benefit (and, hence, marginal scarcity rent) would be zero? How?

Marginal scarcity rent would be zero if water were not scarce. If the availability of water as presented by the supply curve was greater than the amount represented by the point where the aggregate marginal net benefit curve intersects the axis, water would not be scarce. Both users would get all they wanted; their demands would not be competing with one another. Their marginal net benefits would still be equal, but in this case they would both be zero.

Now let's consider the second problem—dealing with fluctuations in supply. As long as the supply level can be anticipated, the equal marginal net benefit rule still applies, but different supply levels may imply very different allocations among users. This is an important attribute of the problem because it implies that simple allocation rules, such as each user receiving a fixed proportion of the available flow or high-priority users receiving a guaranteed amount, are not likely to be efficient.

Suppose now that we use the same graph in a different way. Suppose in this case the total water supply is equal to $½\, S^0_T$. How should the lower water supply be efficiently allocated between the two users? The answer is that the first user would get it all. Do you see why? With $½\, S^0_T$, use B receives no water, while use A receives it all since A's willingness to pay is everywhere higher than B's. Why does the efficient allocation change so radically between S^0_T and $½\, S^0_T$ The answer lies in the shape of the two demand curves for water.

The marginal net benefit curve for water in use A lies above that for B, implying that as supplies diminish, the cost (the forgone net benefits) of doing without water is much higher for A than for B. To minimize this cost, more of the burden of the shortfall is allocated to B than A. In an efficient allocation, users who can most easily find substitutes or conserve water receive proportionately smaller allocations when supplies are diminished than those who have few alternatives. In practice, this can be handled using a spot market (Zarnikau, 1994).

Groundwater

Extending this analysis to encompass groundwater requires that the depletable nature of groundwater supplies be explicitly taken into account. When withdrawals exceed recharge from a particular aquifer, the resource will be mined over time

[8]Remember that the marginal net benefit curve for an individual would be derived by plotting the vertical distance between the demand curve and the marginal cost of getting the water to that individual.

until either supplies are exhausted or the marginal cost of pumping additional water becomes prohibitive. The similarity of this case to the increasing-cost, depletable-resource model discussed in Chapter 6 allows us to exploit that similarity to learn something about the efficient allocation of groundwater over time.

The first transferable implication is that a marginal user cost is associated with mining groundwater, reflecting the opportunity cost associated with the unavailability in the future of any unit of water used in the present. An efficient allocation considers this user cost.

When the demand curve is stable over time (not shifting out due to population or income increases), the efficient extraction path involves temporally declining use of groundwater. The marginal extraction cost (the cost of pumping the last unit to the surface) would rise over time as the water table fell. Pumping would stop either when (1) the water table ran dry or (2) the marginal cost of pumping was either greater than the marginal benefit of the water or greater than the marginal cost of acquiring water from some other source.

Abundant surface water in proximity to the location of the groundwater could serve as a substitute for groundwater, effectively setting an upper bound on the marginal cost of extraction. The user would not pay more to extract a unit of groundwater than it would cost to acquire another source of water. Unfortunately, in many parts of the country where groundwater overdrafts are particularly severe, the competition for surface water is already keen; a cheap source of surface water doesn't exist.

In efficient groundwater markets, the water price would rise over time. The rise would continue until the point of exhaustion, the point at which the marginal pumping cost becomes prohibitive or when the marginal cost of pumping becomes equal to the next-least-expensive source of water. At that point, the marginal pumping cost and the price would be equal. In all three cases, the net price, the difference between the price of the water and the marginal extraction cost, would decline over time, reaching zero at the switch point (if a substitute were available) or the point of exhaustion (if it were not).

In some regions, groundwater and surface water supplies are not physically separate. For example, due to the porous soils in the Arkansas River Valley, groundwater withdrawals in the region affect surface water flows near the Colorado–Kansas border (Bennett, 2000). Lack of conjunctive use management led the State of Kansas to sue the State of Colorado for depleted surface water flows at the border. (*Conjunctive use* refers to the combined management of surface- and groundwater resources to optimize their joint use and to minimize adverse effects of excessive reliance on a single source.) The hydrologic nature of the water source must be taken into consideration when designing a water allocation scheme if interstate conflicts like this are to be avoided.

The Current Allocation System

Regardless of source, economically efficient allocations have not resulted for most water-sharing situations due to the legal and institutional frameworks governing water resources.

Riparian and Prior Appropriation Doctrines

Within the United States, the means of allocating water differ from one geographic area to the next, particularly with respect to the legal doctrines that govern conflicts. In this section, we shall focus on the allocation systems that prevail in the arid Southwest, which must cope with the most potentially serious and imminent scarcity of water.

In the earliest days of settlement in the American Southwest and West, the government had a minimal presence. Residents were pretty much on their own in creating a sense of order. Property rights played a very important role in reducing conflicts in this potentially volatile situation.

As water was always a significant factor in the development of an area, the first settlements were usually oriented near bodies of water. The property rights that evolved, called *riparian rights*, allocated the right to use the water to the owner of the land adjacent to the water. This was a practical solution because by virtue of their location, these owners had easy access to the water. Furthermore, enough sites provided access to water that virtually all who sought water could be accommodated.

With population growth and the consequent rise in the demand for land, this allocation system became less appropriate. As demand increased, the amount of land adjacent to water became scarce, forcing some spillover onto land that was not adjacent to water. The owners of this land began to seek means of acquiring water to make their land more productive.

About this time, with the discovery of gold in California, mining became an important source of employment. With the advent of mining came a need to divert water away from streams to other sites. Unfortunately, riparian property rights made no provision for water to be diverted to other locations. The rights to the water were tied to the land and could not be separately transferred.

As economic theory would predict, this situation created a demand for a change in the property rights structure from riparian rights to one that was more congenial to the need for transferability. The waste resulting from the lack of transferability became so great that it outweighed any transition costs of changing the system of property rights. The evolution that took place in the mining camps became the forerunner of what has become known as the *prior appropriation doctrine*.

The miners established the custom that the first person to arrive had the superior (or *senior*) claim on the water. Later claimants hold *junior* (or subordinate) claims. In practice, this severed the relationship that had existed under the riparian doctrine between the rights to land and the rights to water. As this new doctrine became adopted in legislation, court rulings, and seven state constitutions, widespread diversion of water based on prior appropriation became possible. Stimulated by the profits that could be made in shifting water to more valuable uses, private companies were formed to construct irrigation systems, and to transport water from surplus to deficit areas. Agriculture flourished.

Although prior to 1860, the role of the government was rather minimal, it began to change—slowly at first, but picking up momentum as the twentieth century began. The earliest incursions involved establishing the principle that the ownership of water properly belonged to the state. Claimants were accorded a right to use, known as a *usufructuary right*, rather than an ownership right. The establishment of this principle of public ownership was followed in short order by the establishment of state control over the rates charged by the private irrigation companies, by imposing restrictions on the ability to transfer water out of the district, and by creating a centralized bureaucracy to administer the process.

This was only the beginning. The demand for land in the arid West and Southwest was still growing, creating a complementary demand for water to make the desert bloom. The tremendous profits to be made from large-scale water diversion created the political climate necessary for federal involvement.

The federal role in water resources originated in the early 1800s, largely out of concern for the nation's regional development and economic growth. Toward these ends, the federal government built a network of inland waterways to provide transportation. Since the Reclamation Act of 1902, the federal government has built almost 700 dams to provide water and power to help settle the West.

To promote growth and regional development, the federal government has paid an average of 70 percent of the combined construction and operating costs of such projects, leaving states, localities, and private users to carry the remaining 30 percent. Such subsidies have even been extended to cover some of the costs of providing marketable water services. For example, according to a 1996 General Accounting Office report, irrigators were repaying only approximately 47 cents for every dollar of construction costs. Interest-free loans and cheap water are additional subsidies. Farmers using Central Valley Project water pay approximately $17 per acre-foot of water, while urban users pay up to 10 times that amount. While the size of these subsidies may, on the surface, seem enormous, the regional benefits are still large enough to allow some projects, like the Central Valley Project, to pass a benefit–cost test. (Recall the accounting stance from Chapter 3.)

This, in a nutshell, is the current situation for water in the southwestern United States. Both the state and federal governments play a large role. State laws vary considerably, especially with respect to groundwater withdrawal and the role of instream flows. Though the prior appropriation doctrine stands as the foundation of this allocation system, it is heavily circumscribed by government regulations and direct government appropriation of a substantial amount of water.

Sources of Inefficiency

The current system is not efficient. The prime source of inefficiency involves restrictions that have been placed on water transfers, preventing their gravitation to the highest-valued use, though other sources, such as charging inefficiently low prices, must bear some of the responsibility.

Restrictions on Transfers. To achieve an efficient allocation of water, the marginal net benefits would have to be equalized across all uses (including nonconsumptive instream uses) of the water (Figure 9.3). With a well-structured system of water property rights, efficiency can be a direct result of the transferability of the rights. Users receiving low marginal net benefits from their current allocation would trade their rights to those who would receive higher net benefits. Both parties would be better off. The payment received by the seller would exceed the net benefits forgone, while the payment made by the buyer would be less than the value of the water acquired.

Unfortunately, the existing mixed system of prior appropriation rights coupled with quite restrictive federal and state laws have diminished the degree of transferability that can take place. Diminished transferability in turn reduces the market pressures toward equalization of the marginal net benefits. By itself this indictment is not sufficient to demonstrate the inefficiency of the existing system. If it could be shown that this regulatory system were able to substitute some bureaucratic process for finding and maintaining this equalization, efficiency would still be possible. Unfortunately, that has not been the case, as can be seen by examining in more detail the specific nature of these restrictions. The allocation is inefficient.

One of the earliest restrictions required users to fully exercise their water rights or else they would lose them. The principle of "beneficial use" was typically applied to offstream consumptive uses. It is not difficult to see what this "use it or lose it" principle does to the incentive to conserve. Particularly careful users who, at their own expense, discover ways to use less water would find their allocations reduced accordingly. The regulations strongly discourage conservation.

A second restriction, known as "preferential use," attempts to establish bureaucratically a value hierarchy of uses. With this doctrine, the government attempts to establish allocation priorities across categories of water. Within categories (irrigation for agriculture, for example), the priority is determined by prior appropriation ("first in time—first in right"), but among categories the preferential-use doctrine governs.

The preferential-use doctrine supports three rather different kinds of inefficiencies. First, it substitutes a bureaucratically determined set of priorities for market priorities, resulting in a lower likelihood that marginal net benefits would be equalized. Second, it reduces the incentive to make investments that complement water use in lower-preference categories for the simple reason that their water could be involuntarily withdrawn as the needs in higher-level categories grow. Finally, it allocates the risk of shortfalls in an inefficient way.

Although the first two inefficiencies are rather self-evident, the third merits further explanation. Because water supplies fluctuate over time, unusual scarcities can occur in any particular year. With a well-specified system of property rights, damage caused by this risk would be minimized by allowing those most damaged by a shortfall to purchase a larger share of the diminished amount of water available during a drought from those suffering the increased shortfall with smaller consequences.

By diminishing, and in some cases eliminating, the ability to transfer rights from so-called "high preferential use" categories to "lower preferential use" categories during times of acute need, the damage caused by shortfalls is higher than necessary. In essence, the preferential-use doctrine fails to adequately consider the marginal damage caused by temporary shortfalls, something a well-structured system of property rights would do automatically.

Another factor that makes water difficult to transfer is the fact that only a portion of the water withdrawn from a stream is typically consumed. As long as the withdrawal gets put to a use in the same river basin, a portion of that water returns to the stream eventually in the form of *return flow*. Crops grown with irrigated water, for example, use only a portion of water put on the field; called the *consumptive use* portion. The remainder either evaporates or flows through the soil, eventually finding its way back to the original water source (such as a river or irrigation ditch). Typically a farmer (or another user) downstream owns the right to this return flow. Since transfers of water cannot, as a matter of law, adversely affect a downstream owner of that water, water courts in the Southwest are very busy and cases can take several years before a ruling is issued.

Inhibiting transfers has very practical implications. Due to low energy costs and federal subsidies, agricultural irrigation became the dominant use of water in the West. Yet, the marginal net benefits from agricultural uses are lower, sometimes substantially lower, than the marginal net benefits of water use by municipalities and industry. A transfer of water from irrigated agriculture to these other uses would raise net benefits. It is therefore not surprising that transfers from agriculture to municipalities are becoming more common.

Federal Reclamation Projects and Agricultural Water Pricing. By providing subsidies to approved projects, federal reclamation projects have diverted water to these projects even when the net benefits were negative. Why was this done? What motivated the construction of inefficient projects?

Some early work by Howe (1986) provides a possible explanation. He examined the benefits and costs of constructing the Big Thompson Project in northeastern Colorado. With this project, the water is pumped to an elevation that allows it to flow through a tunnel to the eastern side of the mountains. On that side, electric power is produced at several points. At lower elevations, the water is channeled into natural streams and feeder canals for distribution to irrigation districts and front-range cities.

Howe calculated that the national net benefits for this project, which include all benefits and costs, were either –$341.4 million or –$237.0 million, depending on the number of years included in the calculations. The project cost substantially more to construct than it returned in benefits. However, regional net benefits for the geographic region served by the facility were strongly positive ($766.9 million or $1,187 million, respectively). This facility was an extraordinary boon for the local area because a very large proportion of the total cost had been passed on to national taxpayers. The local political pressure was sufficient to secure project approval despite its inherent inefficiency. This study is still one of the few that looks at costs and benefits *ex-post*, or after the project was completed.

While the very existence of these facilities underwritten by the federal government is a source of inefficiency, the manner in which the water is priced is another. The subsidies have been substantial. Frederick (1989) reported on some work done by the Natural Resources Defense Council to calculate the subsidies to irrigated agriculture in the Westlands Water District, one of the world's richest agricultural areas located on the west side of California's San Joaquin Valley. The Westlands Water District paid about $10–$12 per acre-foot, less than 10 percent of the unsubsidized cost of delivering water to the district. The resulting subsidy was estimated to be $217 per irrigated acre or $500,000 per year for the average-sized farm.

Municipal and Industrial Water Pricing. The prices charged by water distribution utilities do not promote efficiency of use either. Both the level of prices and the rate structure are at fault. In general, the price level is too low and the rate structure does not adequately reflect the costs of providing service to different types of customers.

Water utilities apply a variety of fees and charges to water. Some are better at reflecting cost than others. Water fees and charges reflect the costs of storage, treatment, and distribution of the water to customers. Rarely, however, does the rate reflect the actual value of water.

In part, perhaps because water is considered an essential commodity, the prices charged by public water companies are typically too low. For surface water, the rates are too low for two rather distinct reasons: (1) historic average costs are used to determine rates and (2) marginal scarcity rent is rarely included.

Efficient pricing requires the use of marginal, not average, cost. In order to adequately balance conservation with use, the customer should be paying the marginal cost of supplying the last unit of water. Yet regulated utilities are typically allowed to charge prices just high enough to cover the costs of running the operation, as revealed by figures from the recent past. Water utilities are capital intensive with very large fixed costs in the short run. This means that short-run average costs will be falling, implying a marginal cost that falls below average cost. In this circumstance, marginal-cost pricing would cause the utility to fail to generate enough revenue to cover costs. (Can you see why?)

Circumstances may be changing, however. Now, long-run costs may be rising since new supplies are typically much more expensive to develop and the old supplies are limited by their fixed capacity.

The second source of the problem is the failure of regulators overseeing the operations of water distribution companies to allow a scarcity rent to be incorporated in the calculation of the appropriate price, a problem that is even more severe when groundwater is involved. For a nonrenewable resource, an efficient price should equal marginal cost plus marginal user cost (recall the two-period model from Chapter 5). One study found that due to a failure to include a user cost, rates in Tucson, Arizona were about 58 percent too low at that time, despite recent increases (Martin et al., 1984). Debate 9.1 illustrates the inconsistencies in both agricultural and municipal pricing.

Both low pricing and ignoring the marginal scarcity rent promote an excessive demand for water. Simple actions, such as fixing leaky faucets or planting non-native lawn grasses, are easy to overlook when water is excessively cheap. Yet in a city such as New York, leaky faucets can account for a significant amount of wasted water.

Instream Flows. Conflicts between offstream and instream uses of water are not uncommon. Since instream flows are *nonconsumptive* uses, instream flows are not covered by traditional prior appropriation rights.

DEBATE 9.1 What Is the Value of Water?

As mentioned earlier in this chapter, the Colorado-Big Thompson (C-BT) Project moves water from the Colorado River to the eastern slope of Colorado. The Northern Colorado Conservancy District distributes the approximately 250,000 acre-feet of water per year to irrigators, towns, cities, and industries in northeastern Colorado. Irrigators with original rights pay approximately \$3.50 per share. (A share is, on average, 0.7 acre-foot per year.) Cities pay approximately \$7 per share if they hold original rights.

Shares of C-BT water are transferable and are actively traded in the district. Market prices have been at a minimum of \$1,800 per share, which translates to approximately \$2,600 per acre-foot for perpetual supply or about \$208 per year using an 8 percent discount rate. Prices have also risen as high as \$22,000 per share! Additionally, water is available for rent (for users who want to sell or buy water on a 1-year basis). As you would expect those prices tend to be much lower and frequently range from \$7.50 to \$25 per acre-foot.

The cities that use the water charge a variety of prices to their customers. Boulder utilizes an increasing block rate structure with an initial block at \$ 2.32 per thousand gallons for the first zero to 60 percent of the average monthly water budget, \$3.09 per thousand gallons for the next 61 to 100 percent, \$6.18 per thousand gallons for 101 percent to 150 percent, \$9.27 for 151 percent to 200 percent, and \$15.45 for any usage over 200 percent of the average monthly water budget. Ft. Collins has some unmetered customers, who pay a fixed monthly fee, but no marginal cost for additional use. Its metered customers pay a fixed charge of \$14.99 plus water charges determined by an increasing block rate. In the first block the charge is \$2.32 per thousand gallons for the first 7000 gallons, \$2.67 per thousand gallons for the usage between 7001 and 13,000 gallons. The highest block rate in Ft. Collins is \$3.07 for users consuming more than 13,000 gallons per month. Longmont has both metered and unmetered customers and utilizes an *increasing* block rate for its residential customers and a *decreasing* block rate for its small commercial customers.

Economic theory not only makes clear that the marginal net benefits for all uses and users of a given water project should be equal, but also that the common marginal net benefit metric provides a useful indication of the value of the marginal water unit to all users of this resource.

What do we make of the huge variation in these prices? From an efficiency perspective the only difference in observed prices should be a difference in the marginal cost of delivering water to those customers (since marginal net benefit should be the same for all users). The prices from the C-BT project exhibit much more variation than could be explained by marginal conveyance cost, so they clearly are not only inefficient, but they are also sending very mixed signals about the value of this water.

Source: Howe, C. (1998). Forms and functions of water pricing: An overview. *Urban Water Demand Management and Planning* (Baumann, Boland, and Hanneman, Eds.). McGraw-Hill, Inc.: New York, Rate information from the cities of Boulder, Longmont, and Ft. Collins, Colorado, and the Northern Colorado Conservancy District (2004). Updated prices and rates from www.watercolorado.com and https://bouldercolorado.gov/water/utility-rates

Consider an important historical case. In 2001, the federal government cut off water to farmers in the Klamath River Basin to protect threatened coho salmon, which are protected under the Federal Endangered Species Act. Farmers responded by forcing open irrigation gates and forming a bucket brigade to dump water on their fields. Secretary of the Interior Gale Norton subsequently decided to resume the traditional diversion of water to the more than 1400 farmers using Klamath River water. Six months later, a huge fish kill (estimated to be at least 35,000 salmon) was blamed on the low flows in the river. This dispute, which continues to this day, provides an illustration of one type of problem that can arise with the current legal and institutional structures governing water resources. Without formal recognition of instream flow rights, the value of species, including salmon, cannot be properly incorporated into the allocation decision.

The presumption would probably be that diverting water to protect species necessarily lowers measured net benefits, but that is not always the case. A study on the Rio Grande River in New Mexico found that diverting water from upstream agriculture in order to provide minimum instream flows for an endangered minnow species, *increased* net benefits by making more water available for high-valued downstream uses (Ward & Booker, 2003). Other studies have found the recreational value of water (another instream use) to be higher than that for irrigation water.

Common Property or Open-Access Problems. The allocation of groundwater must confront one additional problem. When many users tap the same aquifer, that aquifer can become an open-access resource. Tapping an open-access resource will tend to deplete it too rapidly; users lose the incentive to conserve. The marginal scarcity rent will be ignored.

The incentive to conserve a groundwater resource in an efficient market is created by the desire to prevent pumping costs from rising too rapidly and the desire to capitalize on the higher prices that could reasonably be expected in the future. With open-access resources, neither of these desires translates into conservation for the simple reason that water conserved by one party may simply be used by someone else because the conserver has no exclusive right to the water that is saved. Water saved by one party to take advantage of future higher prices can easily be pumped out by another user before the higher prices ever materialize.

For open-access resources, economic theory suggests several direct consequences. Pumping costs would rise too rapidly, initial prices would be too low, and too much water would be consumed by the earliest users. The burden of this waste would not be shared uniformly. Because the typical aquifer is bowl shaped, users on the periphery of the aquifer would be particularly hard-hit. When the water level declines, the edges go dry first, while the center can continue to supply water for substantially longer periods. Future users would also be hard-hit relative to current users. For coastal aquifers, salt water intrusion is an additional potential cost of pumping out the aquifer too rapidly.

Potential Remedies

Economic analysis points the way to a number of possible means of remedying the current water situation in the southwestern United States. These reforms would promote efficiency of water use while affording more protection to the interests of future generations of water users.

Water Transfers, Water Markets, and Water Banks

The first reform would reduce the number of restrictions on water transfers. The "use it or lose it" component that often accompanies the prior appropriation doctrine can promote the extravagant use of water and discourage conservation. Typically, water saved by conservation is forfeited. Allowing users to capture the value of water saved by permitting them to sell it would stimulate water conservation and allow the water to flow to higher-valued uses (see Example 9.1).

Water markets and water banks are being increasingly utilized to transfer water seasonally via short-term leases or on a long-term basis, either by multiple-year leases or permanent transfers. Water markets are one institutional structure that can enhance efficiency by allowing water to flow to its highest valued use. While most markets and banks are restricted to certain geographic areas, water is allowed to move to its higher-valued uses to some extent. Buyers and sellers are brought together through bulletin boards, water brokers, and electronic computer networks. Electronic bulletin boards have been used for water sales in California and Colorado, for example. Drought-year banks have been successful in California. Arizona established a water bank in 1996 that allows Central Arizona Project water to be directly injected into the aquifer underlying Tucson and Phoenix as "in lieu recharge," which can later be withdrawn. Water-stressed southern Nevada has signed the Interstate Banking Agreement (2001, amended 2004), in which the Arizona Water Bank stores 1.25 million acre-feet of long-term storage rights to be sold to Nevada. Nevada pays Arizona $100 million plus storage and recovery costs for these rights (Kenney et al., 2013).

One unique water market in Colorado is explored in Example 9.2. The transfer of water, however, can incur high transaction costs, both in the time necessary for approval (up to 2 years in some cases) and in potential downstream impacts. One reason for the success of the Colorado-Big Thompson Project market is low transactions costs due to the structure of the water rights and the availability of infrastructure. An electronic bank also aids in the transparency of sales. The Website www.watercolorado.com operates like a "Craigslist" for water, bringing buyers and sellers together.

Brookshire et al. (2004) compare three markets including the two described above and find that Colorado's well-developed market allows for prices that can rise and respond to market conditions, while the Arizona market is the least well-developed with very few trades. A third market, in New Mexico, falls somewhere in between with lower prices, but some ability to respond to supply and demand.

Internationally, water marketing is gaining traction in many areas. Example 9.3 assesses water markets in Australia, Chile, South Africa, and the United States in terms of economic efficiency, equity, and environmental sustainability.

EXAMPLE 9.1

Using Economic Principles to Conserve Water in California

In 1977, when then-California Governor Jerry Brown negotiated a deal to settle one of the state's perennial water fights by building a new water diversion project, environmental groups were opposed. The opposition was expected. What was not expected was the form it took. Rather than simply block every imaginable aspect of the plan, the Environmental Defense Fund (EDF) set out to show project supporters how the water needs could be better supplied by ways that put no additional pressure on the environment.

According to this strategy, if the owners of the agricultural lands to the west of the water district seeking the water could be convinced to reduce their water use by adopting new, water-saving irrigation techniques, the conserved water could be transferred to the district in lieu of the project. But the growers had no incentive to conserve because conserving the water required the installation of costly new equipment and as soon as the water was saved, it would be forfeited under the "use it or lose it" regulations. What could be done?

On January 17, 1989, largely through the efforts of the EDF, a historic agreement was negotiated between the growers association, a major user of irrigation water, and the Metropolitan Water District (MWD) of California, a public agency that supplies water to the Los Angeles area. Under that agreement, the MWD bears the capital and operating costs, as well as the indirect costs (such as reduced hydropower), of a huge program to reduce seepage losses as the water is transported to the growers and to install new water-conserving irrigation techniques in the fields. In return, the MWD will get all of the conserved water. Everyone stands to gain: the district gets the water it needs at a reasonable price; the growers retain virtually the same amount of irrigation benefits without being forced to bear large additional expenditures.

Because the existing regulatory system created a very large inefficiency, moving to a more efficient allocation of water necessarily increased the net benefits. By using those additional net benefits in creative ways, it was possible to eliminate a serious environmental threat.

The success of this agreement has spawned others. For example, two water-transfer agreements, finalized in October 2003, provide an additional 200,000 acre-feet of water annually to the San Diego region as a result of conservation measures taken in the Imperial Valley and financed by the municipal payments for the water.

Sources: Taylor, R. E. (1990). *Ahead of the Curve: Shaping New Solutions to Environmental Problems*. New York: Environmental Defense Fund.; San Diego County Water Authority. Retrieved from http://www.sdcwo.org/manage/pdf/QSA_2004.pdf

Water Markets in Australia. Australia has a well-established system of water markets as highlighted in Example 9.3. The Council of Australian Governments facilitated the transition to water marketing starting in 1993 with water reforms that allowed water and land entitlements to be separated. This "unbundling" has improved the efficiency and cost-effectiveness of water trading by allowing more flexibility for users in terms of water deliveries. Unbundling has created two primary types of

EXAMPLE 9.2

Water Transfers in Colorado: What Makes a Market for Water Work?

The Colorado-Big Thompson Project, highlighted in Debate 9.1, pumps water from the Colorado River on the west side of the Rocky Mountains uphill and through a tunnel under the Continental Divide where it finds its way into the South Platte River. With a capacity of 310,000 acre-feet, an average of 270,000 acre-feet of water is transferred annually through an extensive system of canals and reservoirs. Shares in the project are transferable and the Northern Colorado Water Conservancy District (NCWCD) facilitates the transfer of these C-BT shares among agricultural, industrial, and municipal users. An original share of C-BT water in 1937 cost $1.50. Permanent transfers of C-BT water for municipal uses have traded for $2,000–$2,500 (Howe & Goemans, 2003). Prices rose as high as $22,000 per share in 2012 (www.watercolorado.com).

This market is unique because shares are homogeneous and easily traded; the infrastructure needed to move the water around exists and the property rights are well defined (return flows do not need to be accounted for in transfers since the water comes from a different basin). Thus, unlike most markets for water, transactions costs are low. This market has been extremely active and is the most organized water market in the West. When the project started, almost all shares were used in agriculture. By 2000, over half of C-BT shares were used by municipalities. Howe and Goemans (2003) compare the NCWCD market to two other markets in Colorado to show how different institutional arrangements affect the size and types of water transfers. They examine water transfers in the South Platte River Basin and the Arkansas River Basin. For most markets in the West, traditional water rights fall under the appropriation doctrine and as such are difficult to transfer and water does not easily move to its highest-valued use. They find that the higher transactions costs in the Arkansas River Basin result in fewer, but larger, transactions than for the South Platte and NCWCD. They also find that the negative impacts from the transfers are larger in the Arkansas River Basin, given the externalities associated with water transfers (primarily out-of-basin transfers) and the long court times for approval. Water markets can help achieve economic efficiency, but only if the institutional arrangements allow for relative ease of transfer of the rights. They suggest that the set of criteria used to evaluate the transfers be expanded to include secondary economic and social costs imposed on the area of origin.

Sources: http://www.ncwcd.org/project_features/cbt_main.asp; *The Water Strategist 2006*. Retrieved from www.waterstrategist.com; Howe, C.W., & Goemans, C. (2003), Water transfers and their impacts: Lessons from three Colorado water markets. *Journal of the American Water Resources Association*, 1055–1065.

water; tradeable water access entitlements, which are shares of water from a specified consumptive pool sold in perpetuity; and tradable water allocations, which refer to a volume of water allocated in a given season (National Water Commission, 2013). Currently, Australia has eight mechanisms for trading water that include posted water markets, auctions, and the "water exchange," which allows interstate trade and forward contracts (Tisdell, 2011). Most of the trading occurs in the Murray-Darling Basin.

EXAMPLE 9.3

Water Market Assessment: Australia, Chile, South Africa, and the United States

Water markets are gaining importance as a water allocation mechanism. Do they succeed in moving water to higher-valued uses, thus helping to equate marginal benefits across uses?

Grafton et al. (2011) utilize 26 criteria to evaluate four established water markets—Australia's Murray-Darling Basin, Chile's Limari Valley, South Africa, and the western United States—and a new one in China, which due to its limited experience, we do not include in this example. Eight of the criteria relate to economic efficiency, eight relate to institutional underpinnings, five relate to equity, and the remaining five relate to environmental sustainability. These 26 criteria are then melded into a four-point scale.

Focusing on the economic efficiency criteria, water markets should be able to transfer water from low-valued to higher-valued uses. Defining the size of the market as the volume traded as a percentage of total water rights, Grafton et al. find that in Chile and Australia, for example, market size is 30 percent—very high. To provide some context for those numbers, gains from trade in Chile are estimated to be between 8 and 32 percent of agricultural contribution to GDP.

They also define some qualitative variables that they believe capture some of the institutional characteristics, such as the size and scope of the market, that ultimately could affect how well the market operates by impacting transactions costs, as well as the predictability and transparency of prices. Australia performs best on these qualitative measures, followed by Chile. South Africa and the US West have mixed performance.

One insight that arises from their analysis is that water markets can generate "substantial gains for buyers and sellers that would not otherwise occur, and these gains increase as water availability declines." But they also point out, as have others, that markets need to be flexible enough to accommodate changes in benefits and instream uses over time. The specific structure of water rights plays a role. Whereas in the western United States the doctrine of prior appropriation restricts transfers, in Australia a system of rights defined by statute, not tradition, makes transfers easier.

Ultimately, economic efficiency is an important objective in these water markets, but they point out that in some basins tradeoffs between equity and efficiency are necessary in both their design and operation. Economic efficiency might not even be the primary goal or the main motivation for why a water market developed. Finally, they point out that Australia has crafted a system within which environmental sustainability goals do not compromise economic efficiency goals. These two goals can be compatible.

Source: Grafton, R. Q., Landry, C., Libecap, G. D., McGlennon, S., & O'Brien, R. (2011). An integrated assessment of water markets: A cross country comparison. *Review of Environmental Economics and Policy*, *5*(2), 210–239.

Since 2008, the volume of trades of both entitlements and allocations has risen dramatically in the southern Murray-Darling River system. Prices, however, have fallen, in part due to the return to high water availability after severe drought.

The decision to sell water allocations in any given time period is influenced by economic factors such as the price elasticity of demand for water, water prices, and input prices, as well as noneconomic factors including water availability, soil moisture, storage, and forecasts. Water entitlements are similarly influenced, but less so; the prices for entitlements have fluctuated much less than the prices for allocations (National Water Commission, 2013). Can you explain why?

Instream Flow Protection

Achieving a balance between instream and consumptive uses is not easy. As the competition for water increases, the pressure to allocate larger amounts of the stream for consumptive uses increases as well. Eventually the water level becomes too low to support aquatic life and recreation activities.

Although they do exist, water rights for instream flow maintenance are few in number relative to rights for consumptive purposes. Those few instream rights that typically exist have a low priority relative to the more senior consumptive rights. As a practical matter this means that in periods of low water flow, the instream rights lose out and the water is withdrawn for consumptive uses. As long as the definition of "beneficial use" requires diversion to consumptive uses, as it does in many states, water left for fish habitat or recreation is undervalued.

Yet laws that supersede seniority and allow water to remain instream have caused considerable controversy. Attempts to protect instream water uses must confront two problems. First, any acquired rights are usually public goods, implying that others can free ride on their provision without contributing to the cause. Consequently, the demand for instream rights will be inefficiently low. The private acquisition of instream rights is not a sufficient remedy. Second, once the rights have been acquired, their use to protect instream flows may not be considered "beneficial use" (and therefore could be confiscated and granted to others for consumptive use) or they could be so junior as to be completely ineffective in times of low flow, the times when they would most be needed. However, in some cases, instream flows do have a priority right if the flows are necessary to protect endangered species. As Example 9.4 demonstrates, reserving water for instream uses has created controversy on more than one occasion. Undervaluation of instream uses is not inevitable.

In England and Scotland, markets are relied upon to protect instream uses more than they are in the United States. Private angling associations have been formed to purchase fishing rights from landowners. Once these rights have been acquired, the associations charge for fishing, using some of the revenues to preserve and improve the fish habitat. Since fishing rights in England sell for as much as \$220,000, the holders of these rights have a substantial incentive to protect their investments. One of the forms this protection takes is illustrated by the Anglers Cooperative Association, which has taken on the responsibility of monitoring the streams for pollution and alerting the authorities to any potential problems.

Water Prices

Getting the prices right is another avenue for reform. Recognizing the inefficiencies associated with subsidizing the consumption of a scarce resource, the US Congress passed the Central Valley Project Improvement Act in 1992. The act raises prices that the federal government charges for irrigation water, though the full-cost rate is imposed only on the final 20 percent of water received. Collected

EXAMPLE 9.4

Reserving Instream Rights for Endangered Species

The Rio Grande River, which has its headwaters in Colorado, forms the border between Texas and Mexico. Water-sharing disputes have been common in this water-stressed region where demand exceeds supply in most years. In 1974, the Rio Grande silvery minnow was listed as an endangered species by the US Fish and Wildlife Service. Once the most abundant fish in the basin, its habitat had been degraded significantly by diversion dams that restrict the minnow's movement.

What impact would its protection have? Ward and Booker (2006) compare the benefits from two cases: (1) the case where no special provision is made for instream flow for the minnow and (2) the case when adequate flows are maintained using an integrated model of economics, hydrology, and the institutions governing water flow. Interestingly, they find positive economic impacts to New Mexico agriculture from protecting the minnow's habitat. Losses to central New Mexico farmers and to municipal and industrial users are more than offset by gains to farmers in southern New Mexico due to increased flows. For example, losses to agriculture above Albuquerque are approximately $114,000 per year, and below Albuquerque $35,000 per year. Losses to municipal and industrial users is $24,000 per year. Agricultural gains in the southern portion of the basin, however, are approximately $217,000 per year. Both agricultural and municipal users in Texas gain. Overall, a policy to protect the minnow was estimated to provide average annual net benefits of slightly more than $200,000 per year to Texas agriculture, plus an additional $1 million for El Paso municipal and industrial users.

The story is different for the delta smelt, a tiny California fish. In 2007, an interim order issued by a California judge to protect the threatened delta restricts water exports from the Delta to agricultural and municipal users. In the average year, this means a reduction of 586,000 acre-feet of water to agriculture and cities. One study (Sunding et al., 2008) finds that this order causes economic losses of more than $500 million per year (or as high as $3 billion in an extended drought). The authors note that long-run losses would be less ($140 million annually) if investments in recycling, conservation, water banking, and water transfers were implemented. Protests by farmers about water diversions being halted to protect this species received so much attention in 2009 that the story about the trade-offs between these consumptive and nonconsumptive uses even made it to comedian Jon Stewart's *The Daily Show*.

Instream flows become priority "uses" when endangered species are involved, but not everyone shares that sense of priority.

Sources: Ward, F. A., & Booker, J. F. (2006). Economic impacts of instream flow protection for the Rio Grande silvery minnow in the Rio Grande Basin. *Review in Fisheries Science, 14*, 187–202.; Sunding, D., Ajami, N., Hatchet, S., Mitchell, D., & Zilberman, D. (2008). Economic impacts of the Wanger interim order for delta smelt. Berkeley Economic Consulting.

revenues will be placed in a fund to mitigate environmental damage in the Central Valley. The act also allows water transfers to new uses.

Dinar et al. (2004) review and evaluate actual pricing practices for irrigation water in developing countries. Table 9.1 summarizes their findings with respect to both the types and properties of pricing systems they discovered. As the table reveals, they found some clear trade-offs between what efficiency would dictate and what was possible, given the limited information available to water administrators.

Two-part charges and volumetric pricing, while quite efficient, require information on the amount of water used by each farmer and are rarely used in developing countries. (The two-part charge combines volume pricing with a monthly fee that doesn't vary with the amount of water consumed. The monthly fee is designed to help recover fixed costs.) Individual-user water meters can provide information on the volume of water used, but they are relatively expensive. Output pricing (where the charge for water is linked to agricultural output, not water use), on the other hand, is less efficient, but only requires data on each water user's production. Input-based pricing is even easier because it doesn't require monitoring either water use or output. Under input pricing, irrigators are assessed taxes on water-related inputs, such as a per-unit charge on fertilizer. Block-rate or tiered pricing is most common when demand has seasonal peaks. Tiered pricing examples can be found in Israel and California. Area pricing is probably the easiest to implement since the only information necessary is the amount of irrigated land and the type of crop produced on that land. Although this method is the most common, it is not efficient since the marginal cost of extra water use is zero.

Dinar et al. (2004) propose a set of water reforms for developing countries, including pricing at marginal cost where possible and using block-rate prices to transfer wealth between water suppliers and farmers. This strategy would put the burden of fixed costs on the relatively wealthier urban populations, who would, in turn, benefit from less expensive food.

For water distribution utilities, the traditional practice of recovering only the costs of distributing water and treating the water itself as a free good should be abandoned. Instead, utilities should adopt a pricing system that reflects increasing marginal cost and that includes a scarcity value for groundwater. Scarce water is not,

TABLE 9.1 Pricing Methods and their Properties

Column1	Column2	Column3
	Pricing Scheme	**Characteristics**
First Best	Volumetric	Difficult to implement, by easy to control demand
	Tiered Block Rates	Less Difficult to implement, somewhat easy to control demand
	Two-Part Pricing	Same as tiered rates, but longer time horizon to efficiency
	Water Markets	Extremely difficult to implement
Second-Best	Output	Relatively easy to implement, somewhat easy to control demand
	Input	Easy to implement, somewhat easy to control demand
None	Per Area	Easiest to implement, not efficient, hard to control demand

Source: Adapted from Dinar et al. (2004)

in any meaningful sense, a free good. Only if the user cost of that water is imposed on current users will the proper incentive for conservation be created and the interests of future generations of water users be preserved.

Including this user cost in water prices is rather more difficult than it may first appear. Water utilities are typically regulated because they have a monopoly in the local area. One typical requirement for the rate structure of a regulated monopoly is that it earns only a "fair" rate of return. Excess profits are not permitted. Charging a uniform price for water to all users where the price includes a user cost would generate profits for the seller. (Recall the discussion of scarcity rent in Chapter 2.) The scarcity rent accruing to the seller as a result of incorporating the user cost would represent revenue in excess of operating and capital costs.

Water utilities have a variety of options to choose from when charging their customers for water. Figure 9.4 illustrates the most common volume-based price

FIGURE 9.4 Overview of the Various Variable Charge Rate Structures

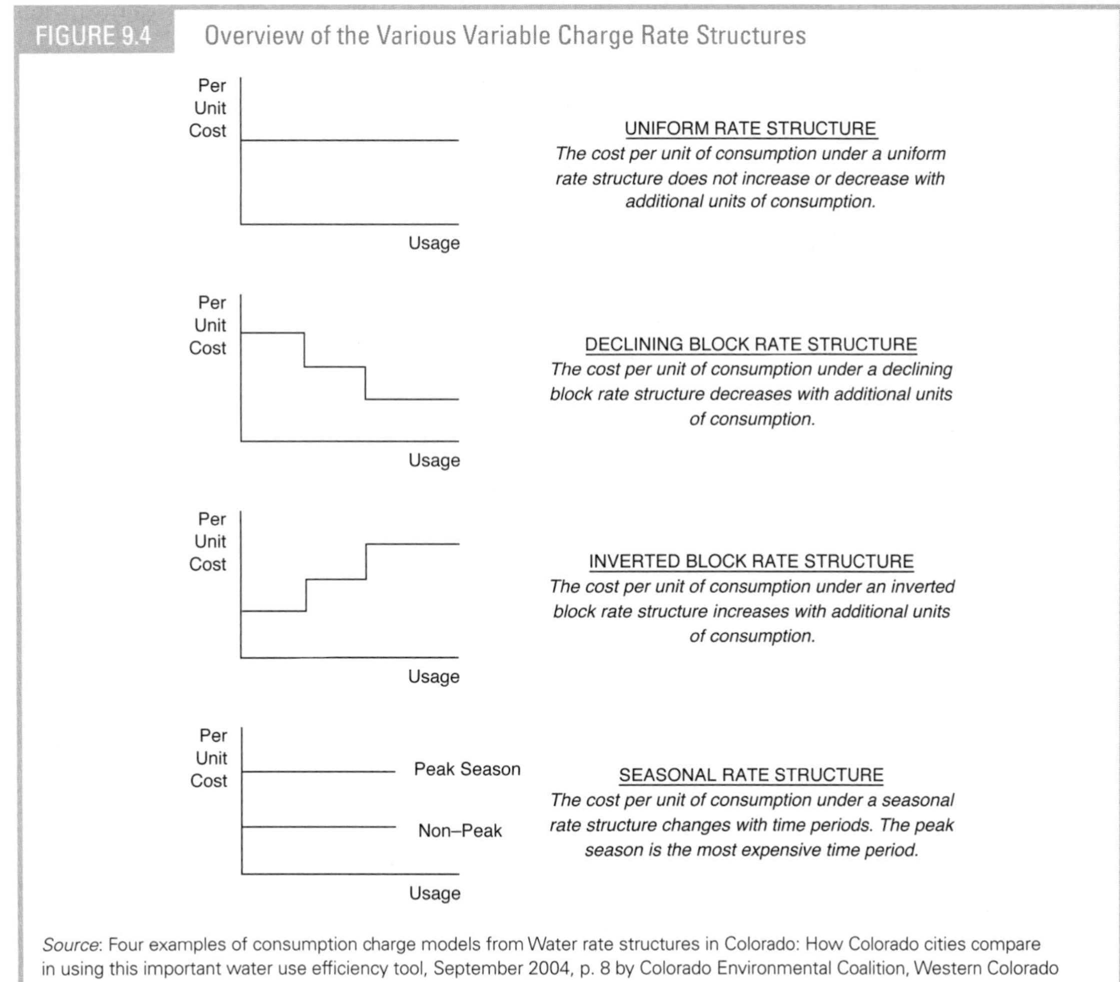

Source: Four examples of consumption charge models from Water rate structures in Colorado: How Colorado cities compare in using this important water use efficiency tool, September 2004, p. 8 by Colorado Environmental Coalition, Western Colorado Congress, and Western Resource Advocates. Copyright © 2004 by Western Resource Advocates. Reprinted with permission.

structures. Some US utilities still use a flat fee, which, from a scarcity point of view, is the worst possible form of pricing. Since a flat fee is not based on volume, the marginal cost of additional water consumption is zero. ZERO! Water use by individual customers is not even metered.

While more complicated versions of a flat-fee system are certainly possible, they do not solve the incentive-to-conserve problem. At least up until the late 1970s, Denver, Colorado, used eight different factors (including number of rooms, number of persons, and number of bathrooms) to calculate the monthly bill. Despite the complexity of this billing system, because the amount of the bill was unrelated to actual volume used (water use was not metered), the marginal cost of additional water consumed was still zero.

Volume-based price structures require metering and some include a fixed fee plus the consumption-based rate and some may include minimum consumption. Three common types of volume-based structures are uniform (or linear or flat) rates, declining block rates, and inverted (increasing) block rates.

Uniform or flat-rate pricing structures are extremely common due to their simplicity. By charging customers a flat marginal cost for all levels of consumption suggests that the marginal cost of providing water is constant. Although this rate does incorporate the fact that the marginal cost of water is not zero, it is still inefficient.

Declining block rate pricing, another inefficient pricing system, has historically been much more prevalent than increasing block pricing. Declining block rates were popular in cities with excess capacities, especially in the eastern United States, because they encouraged higher consumption as a means of spreading the fixed costs more widely. Since utilities with excess capacity are typically natural monopolies with high fixed costs, decreasing block rates reflect the decreasing average and marginal costs of this industry structure. Additionally, municipalities attempting to attract business may find this rate appealing. However, as demand rises with population growth or increased use, costs will eventually rise, not fall, with increased use and this rate is inefficient.

By charging customers a higher marginal cost for low levels of water consumption and a lower marginal cost for higher levels, regulators are also placing an undue financial burden on low-income people who consume little water, and confronting high-income people with a marginal cost that is too low to provide adequate incentives to conserve. As such, many cities have moved away from decreasing block rate structure (Table 9.2).

One way that water utilities are attempting to respect the rate of return requirement while promoting water conservation is through the use of an inverted (increasing) block rate. Under this system, the price per unit of water consumed rises as the amount consumed rises.

This type of structure encourages conservation by ensuring that the marginal cost of consuming additional water is high. At the margin, where the consumer makes the decision of how much extra water to be used, quite a bit of money can be saved by being frugal with water use. However, it also holds revenue down by charging a lower price for the first units consumed. This has the added virtue that those who need some water, but cannot afford the marginal price paid by more extravagant users, can have access to water without placing their budget in as much jeopardy as would be the case with a uniform price. For example, in Durban, South Africa, the first block is actually free (Loftus, 2005). Many utilities base the first block on average winter (indoor) use. As long as the quantity of the first block is not so large such that all users remain in the first block, this rate will promote efficiency as well as send price signals about the scarcity of water.

How many US utilities are using increasing block pricing? As Table 9.2 indicates, the number of water utilities using increasing block rates is on the rise, but the increase has been slow. In Canada, the process of moving to volumetric pricing has been slow, but growing (see Example 9.5). Without a water meter, volume charges are impossible.

What about internationally? Global Water International's 2012 tariff survey suggests that worldwide the trend is moving toward increasing block rates (Table 9.3).

TABLE 9.2 Pricing Structures for Public Water Systems in the United States (1982–2008)

	1982	1987	1991	1998	2002	2004	2006	2008	2010	2012/13
	%	%	%	%	%	%	%	%	%	%
Flat Fee	1	—	3	—	—	—	—	—	—	—
Uniform Volume Charge	35	32	35	34	37	39	40	32	31	30
Decreasing Block	60	51	45	35	31	25	24	28	19	18
Increasing Block	4	17	17	31	32	36	36	40	49	52
Total	100	100	100	100	100	100	100	100	100	100

Source: *Raftelis Rate Survey, Raftelis Financial Consulting.*

TABLE 9.3 World Cities and Rate Structures 2012

Rate Type	Number of Cities	Percentage
Fixed fee	5	1.6
Flat rate	142	45.7
Increasing block rate	150	48.2
Declining block rate	7	2.3
Other	7	2.3
Total	311	100

Source: Global Water International, 2012 Tarrif survey, http://www.globalwaterintel.com/tariff-survey/

EXAMPLE 9.5

Water Pricing in Canada

Water meters allow water pricing to be tied to actual use. Several pricing mechanisms suggested in this chapter require volume to be measured. Households with water meters typically consume less water than households without meters. However, in order to price water efficiently, user volume must be measured. In 1999 only 56 percent of Canada's population was metered. By 2009 this percentage had risen to 72%. Of the urban population 27.9 percent received water for which the perceived marginal cost of additional use was zero. Most of the non-metered customers pay a flat fee.

Increasing block rates grew in popularity between 1991–2004, but have fallen steadily since. In 2009 only about 20 percent of residents were charged an increasing block rate. Toronto, which represented 53 percent of the population with increasing block rates, switched to a uniform or constant unit charge in 2006.

Volumetric rates have also risen faster than constant fee pricing. As expected, customers that pay through volumetric pricing consumed much less water per capita. The survey found water use was 52 percent higher for customers with nonvolumetric prices (fees not based on consumption) than those paying volumetric rates. Volumetric rates did serve as a disincentive to consume. The more you use, the more you pay.

As metering becomes more extensive, some municipalities are also beginning to meter return flows to the sewer system. Separate charges for water and sewer better reflect actual use. Several studies have shown that including sewage treatment in rate calculations generates greater water savings. A number of Canadian municipalities are adopting full-cost pricing mechanisms. Full-cost pricing seeks to recover not only the total cost of providing water and sewer services but also the costs of replacing older systems.

Source: http://www.ec.gc.ca/Publications/992156D4-2599-4026-9B4C-47855D26CCB8/2011MunicipalWaterPricingReport2009Statistics.pdf

Since their last survey in 2010, the number of increasing or inverted block rates dropped slightly (from 51.3 percent, but is still the leader in terms of pricing structures. Just about all the cities that reported have some sort of volumetric pricing, mostly flat and increasing block rates. Interestingly, five out of the seven declining block rates are in US cities.

Other aspects of the rate structure are important as well. Efficiency dictates that prices equal the marginal cost of provision (including marginal user cost when appropriate). Several practical corollaries follow from this theorem. First, prices during peak demand periods should exceed prices during off-peak periods. For water, peak demand is usually during the summer. It is peak use that strains the capacity of the system and therefore triggers the needs for expansion. Therefore, seasonal users should pay the extra costs associated with the system expansion by being charged higher rates. Few current water pricing systems satisfy this condition in practice though some cities in the Southwest are beginning to use seasonal rates. For example, Tucson, Arizona, has a seasonal rate for the months of May–September.

Also, for municipalities using increasing block rates with the first block equal to average winter consumption, one could argue that this is essentially a seasonal rate for the average user. The average user is unlikely to be in the second or third blocks, except during summer months. The last graph in Figure 9.4 illustrates a seasonal uniform rate.

In times of drought, seasonal pricing makes sense, but is rarely politically feasible. Under extreme circumstances, such as severe drought, however, cities are more likely to be successful in passing large rate changes that are specifically designed to facilitate coping with that drought. During the period from 1987 to 1992, Santa Barbara, California, experienced one of the most severe droughts of the century. To deal with the crisis of excess demand, the city of Santa Barbara changed both its rates and rate structure ten times between 1987 and 1995 (Loaiciga & Renehan, 1997). In 1987, Santa Barbara utilized a flat rate of $0.89 per ccf. By late 1989, they had moved to an increasing block rate consisting of four blocks with the lowest block at $1.09 per ccf and the highest at $3.01 per ccf. Between March and October of 1990, the rate rose to $29.43 per ccf (748 gallons) in the highest block! Rates were subsequently lowered, but the higher rates were successful in causing water use to drop almost 50 percent. It seems that when a community is faced with severe drought and community support for using pricing to cope is apparent, major changes in price are indeed possible.

Another corollary of the marginal-cost pricing theorem is that when it costs a water utility more to serve one class of customers than another, each class of customers should bear the costs associated with its respective service. Typically, this implies that those farther away from the source or at higher elevations (requiring more pumping) should pay higher rates. In practice, utility water rates make fewer distinctions among customer classes than would be efficient. As a result, higher-cost water users are in effect subsidized; they receive too little incentive to conserve and too little incentive to locate in parts of the city that can be served at lower cost.

Regardless of the choice of price structure, do consumers respond to higher water prices by consuming less? The examples from Canada in Example 9.5 suggest they do.

A useful piece of information for utilities, however, is *how much* their customers respond to given price increases. Recall from microeconomics that the price elasticity of demand measures consumer responsiveness to price increases. Municipal water use is expected to be price inelastic, meaning that for a 1 percent increase in price, consumers reduce consumption, but by less than 1 percent. A meta-analysis of 24 water demand studies in the United States (Espey, Espey, & Shaw, 1997) found a range of price elasticities with a mean of –0.51. Omstead and Stavins (2007) find similar results in their summary paper. These results suggest that municipal water demand responds to price, but is not terribly price sensitive.

It also turns out that the price elasticity of demand is related to the local climate. Residential demand for water turns out to be more price elastic in arid climates than in wet ones. Why do you think this is true?

Desalination

Until recently, desalinized seawater has been prohibitively expensive and thus not a viable option outside of the Middle East. However, technological advances in reverse osmosis, nanofiltration, and ultrafiltration methods have reduced the price of desalinized water, making it a potential new source for water-scarce regions. Reverse osmosis works by pumping seawater at high pressure through permeable membranes. As of 2005, more than 10,000 desalting plants had been installed or contracted worldwide. Since 2000, desalination capacity has been growing at approximately 7 percent per year. Over 130 countries utilize some form of desalting technology (Gleick, 2006).

According to the World Bank, the cost of desalinized water has dropped from \$1 per cubic meter to an average of \$0.50 per cubic meter in a period of 5 years (World Bank, 2004). Costs are expected to continue to fall, though not as rapidly. However, many projects are being built at extraordinary cost. Example 9.6 looks the feasibility of desalination in northern China.

In the United States, Florida, California, Arizona, and Texas have the largest installed capacity. However, actual production has been mixed. In Tampa Bay, for example, a large desalination project was contracted in 1999 to provide drinking water. This project, while meant to be a low cost (\$0.45/m^3) state-of-the-art project, was hampered by difficulties. Although the plant became fully operational at the end of 2007, projected costs were \$0.67/m^3 (Gleick, 2006). In 1991, Santa Barbara, California, commissioned a desalination plant in response to the previously described drought that would supply water at a cost expected to be

EXAMPLE 9.6

Moving Rivers or Desalting the Sea? Costly Remedies for Water Shortages

In most of northern China, freshwater is extremely scarce. China has been pursuing immense engineering projects in order to bring new water sources to this desperately dry, yet rapidly growing region. One three-phase project involves the diversion of water from the Yangzi River basin through hundreds of kilometers of canals and pipelines at extraordinary cost (\$34 billion so far). The project is only partially complete. The other is a \$4.1 billion power and desalination plant in the port city of Tianjin. The Beijing Power and Desalination Plant began operating in 2009. The capacity of the desalination plant will satisfy only a small portion of China's demand for water.

As of 2013, water from the plant cost 8 yuan per cubic meter (about \$1.30) to produce. Diverted water from the Yangzi is expected to cost about 10 yuan. Both of these are at least 60 percent higher than what households currently pay, though water rates are rising. Even if higher water prices were imposed on consumers, prices would be unlikely to cover the true cost of either source. Desalination is very energy intensive. In China, that energy comes mainly from burning dirty coal. Diverting water is not without external costs either. Diverting water deprives southern China of the water needed to combat drought. Developing scarcity in a crucial resource like water can force some tough choices!

Source: Removing salt from seawater might help slake some of northern China's thirst, but it comes at a high price. *Economist*, February 9, 2013.

$\$1.22/m^3$. Shortly after construction was completed, however, the drought ended and the plant was never operated. In 2000, the city sold the plant to a company in Saudi Arabia. It has been decommissioned, but remains available should current supplies run out. While desalination holds some appeal as an option in California, it is only currently economically feasible for coastal cities, and concerns about the environmental impacts, such as energy usage and brine disposal, remain to be addressed.

In early 2011, a large desalination project in Dubai and another in Israel were scrapped mid-construction due to lower-than-expected demand growth and cost, respectively. These two projects represented 10 percent of the desalination market.[9]

Privatization

One strategy that has received more attention in the last couple of decades is the privatization of water supplies. The controversies that have arisen around this strategy are intense (see Debate 9.2).

Should Water Systems Be Privatized? DEBATE 9.2

Faced with crumbling water supply systems and the financial burden from water subsidies, many urban areas in both industrialized and developing countries have privatized their water systems. Generally this is accomplished by selling the publicly owned water supply and distribution assets to a private company. The impetus behind this movement is the belief that private companies can operate more efficiently (thereby lowering costs and, hence, prices) and do a better job of improving both water quality and access by infusing these systems with new investment.

The problem with this approach is that water suppliers in many areas can act as a monopoly, using their power to raise rates beyond competitive levels, even if those rates are, in principle, subject to regulation. What happened in Cochabamba, Bolivia, illustrates just how serious a problem this can be.

After privatization in Cochabamba, water rates increased immediately, in some cases by 100–200 percent. The poor were especially hard-hit. In January 2000, a 4-day general strike in response to the water privatization brought the city to a total standstill. In February the Bolivian government declared the protests illegal and imposed a military takeover on the city. Despite over 100 injuries and one death, the protests continued until April when the government agreed to terminate the contract.

Is Cochabamba typical? It certainly isn't the only example of privatization failure. Failure (in terms of a prematurely terminated privatization contract) also occurred in Atlanta, Georgia, for example. The evidence is still out on its overall impact in other settings and whether we can begin to extract preconditions for its successful introduction, but it is very clear that privatization of water systems is no panacea and can be a disaster.

---

[9] *Global Water Intelligence*, *12*(1), http://www.globalwaterintel.com/archive/12/1/need-to-know/desal-misery.html

However, it is important to distinguish between the different types of privatization since they can have quite different consequences. Privatization of water supplies creates the possibility of monopoly power and excessive rates, but privatization of access rights (such as discussed in Example 9.1 and Debate 9.2) does not.

Whereas privatization of water supplies turns the entire system over to the private sector, privatization of access rights only establishes specific quantified rights to use the publicly supplied water. As discussed earlier in this chapter, privatization of access rights is one way to solve the excesses that follow from the free-access problem, since the amount of water allocated by these rights would be designed to correspond to the amount available for sustainable use. And if these access rights are allocated fairly (a big if!) and if they are enforced consistently (another big if!), the security that enforceability provides can protect users, including poor or indigenous users, from encroachment. The question then becomes, "Are these rights allocated fairly and enforced consistently?" When they are, privatization of access rights can become beneficial for all users, not merely the rich.

GIS and Water Resources

Allocation of water resources is complicated by the fact that water moves! Water resources do not pay attention to jurisdictional boundaries. Geographic information systems (GIS) help researchers use watersheds and water courses as organizing tools. For example, Hascic and Wu (2006) use GIS to help examine the impacts of land use changes in the United States on watershed health, while Lewis, Bohlen, and Wilson (2008) use GIS to analyze the impacts of dams and rivers on property values in Maine. This enormously powerful tool is making economic analysis easier and the visualizing of economic and watershed data in map form helps in the communication of economic analysis to noneconomists. Check out the EPA's *Surf Your Watershed* site at http://cfpub.epa.gov/surf/locate/index.cfm for GIS maps of your watershed, including stream flow, water use, and pollution discharges, or USGS.gov for surface- and groundwater resources maps.

Summary

On a global scale, the amount of available water exceeds the demand, but at particular times and in particular locations, water scarcity is already a serious problem. In a number of locations, the current use of water exceeds replenishable supplies, implying that aquifers are being irreversibly drained.

In general, any solution to water scarcity should involve more widespread adoption of the principles of marginal-cost pricing. More-expensive-to-serve users should pay higher prices for their water than their cheaper-to-serve counterparts. Similarly, when new, much-higher-cost sources of water are introduced into a water system to serve the needs of a particular category of user, those users should pay the marginal cost of that water, rather than the lower average cost of all water supplied. Finally, when a rise in the peak demand triggers a need for expanding either the water supplies or the distribution system, the peak demanders should pay the higher costs associated with the expansion.

These principles suggest a much more complicated rate structure for water than merely charging everyone the same price. However, the political consequences of introducing these changes may be rather drastic.

Efficiency dictates that replenishable water be allocated so as to equalize the marginal net benefits of water use even when supplies are higher or lower than normal.

The efficient allocation of groundwater requires that the user cost of that depletable resource be considered. When marginal-cost pricing (including marginal user cost) is used, water consumption patterns strike an efficient balance between present and future uses. Typically, the marginal pumping cost would rise over time until either it exceeded the marginal benefit received from that water or the reservoir runs dry.

In earlier times in the United States, markets played the major role in allocating water. But more recently governments have begun to play a much larger role in allocating this crucial resource.

Several sources of inefficiency are evident in the current system of water allocation in the southwestern United States. Transfers of water among various users are restricted so that the water remains in low-valued uses while high-valued uses are denied. Instream uses of water are actively discouraged in many western states. Prices charged for water by public suppliers typically do not cover costs, and the rate structures are not designed to promote efficient use of the resource. For groundwater, user cost is rarely included, and for all sources of water, the rate structure does not usually reflect the cost of service. These deficiencies combine to produce a situation in which we are not getting the most out of the water we are using and we are not conserving sufficient amounts for the future.

Reforms are possible. Allowing conservers to capture the value of water saved by selling it would stimulate conservation. Creating separate fishing rights that can be sold or allowing environmental groups to acquire and retain instream water rights would provide some incentive to protect streams as fish habitats. More utilities could adopt increasing block pricing as a means of forcing users to realize and to consider all of the costs of supplying the water.

Water scarcity is not merely a problem to be faced at some time in the distant future. In many parts of the world, it is already a serious problem and unless preventive measures are taken, it will get worse. The problem is not insoluble, though to date the steps necessary to solve it have proved insufficient.

Discussion Questions

1. What pricing system is used to price the water you use at your college or university? Does this pricing system affect your behavior about water use (length of showers, etc.)? How? Could you recommend a better pricing system in this circumstance? What would it be?

2. In your hometown what system is used to price the publicly supplied water? Why was that pricing system chosen? Would you recommend an alternative?
3. Suppose you come from a part of the world that is blessed with abundant water. Demand never comes close to the available amount. Should you be careful about the amount you use or should you simply use whatever you want whenever you want it? Why?

Self-Test Exercises

1. Suppose that in a particular area the consumption of water varies tremendously throughout the year, with average household summer use exceeding winter use by a great deal. What effect would this have on an efficient rate structure for water?
2. Is a flat-rate or flat-fee system more efficient for pricing scarce water? Why?
3. One major concern about the future is that water scarcity will grow, particularly in arid regions where precipitation levels may be reduced by climate change. Will our institutions provide for an efficient response to this problem?

   To think about this issue, let's consider groundwater extraction over time using the two-period model as our lens.

   a. Suppose the groundwater comes from a well you have drilled upon your land that taps an aquifer that is not shared with anyone else. Would you have an incentive to extract the water efficiently over time? Why or why not?
   b. Suppose the groundwater is obtained from your private well, which is drilled into an aquifer that is shared with many other users who have also drilled private wells. Would you expect that the water from this common aquifer be extracted at an efficient rate? Why or why not?
4. Water is an essential resource. For that reason moral considerations exert considerable pressure to assure that everyone has access to at least enough water to survive. Yet it appears that equity and efficiency considerations may conflict. Providing water at zero cost is unlikely to support efficient use (marginal cost is too low), while charging everyone the market price (especially as scarcity sets in) may result in some poor households not being able to afford the water they need. Discuss how block rate pricing attempts to provide some resolution to this dilemma. How would it work?

Further Reading

Colby, B. G., & D'Estree, T. P. (2000). Economic evaluation of mechanisms to resolve water conflicts. *Water Resources Development*, *16*, 239–251. Examines the costs and benefits of various water dispute resolution mechanisms.

Easter, K. W., Rosegrant, M. W., & Dinar, A. (Eds.). (1998). *Markets for Water: Potential and Performance.* Dordrecht: Kluwer Academic Publishers. Not only develops the necessary conditions for water markets and illustrates how they can improve both water management and economic efficiency, but also provides an up-to-date picture of what we have learned about water markets in a wide range of countries, from the United States to Chile to India.

Grafton, Q. R. (Ed.). (2009). *The Economics of Water Resources,* Elgar Reference Collection. International Library of Critical Writings in Economics, vol. 234. Cheltenham, U.K. and Northampton, Mass.: Elgar. An excellent compilation of articles on topics from water pricing to water markets.

Shaw, W. D. (2005). *Water Resource Economics and Policy: An Introduction.* Cheltenham, UK: Edward Elgar; and Griffen, R. C. (2006). *Water Resource Economics: The Analysis of Scarcity, Policies, and Projects.* Cambridge, MA: MIT Press. Two excellent texts that focus exclusively on water resource economics.

Von Weizsäcker, E.U. Young, O. R., et al. (Eds.). (2005). *Limits to Privatization: How to Avoid too Much of a Good Thing.* London, UK: Earthscan. Case studies on attempts at privatization (including, but not limited to, privatization of water supplies) that assess the factors associated with success or failure.

Young, R. A. (2005). *Determining the Economic Value of Water: Concepts and Methods.* Washington, DC: Resources for the Future, Inc. A detailed survey and synthesis of theory and existing studies on the economic value of water in various uses.

Additional References and Historically Significant References are available on this book's Companion Website: http://www.routledgetextbooks.com/textbooks/9780133479690

10 A Locationally Fixed, Multipurpose Resource: Land

Buy land, they're not making it anymore.

—Mark Twain, *American Humorist*

A land ethic . . . reflects the existence of an ecological conscience, and this in turn reflects a conviction of individual responsibility for the health of the land. Health is the capacity of the land for self-renewal. Conservation is our effort to understand and preserve this capacity.

—Aldo Leopold, *Sand County Almanac*

Introduction

Land occupies a special niche not only in the marketplace, but also deep in the human soul. In its role as a resource, land has special characteristics that affect its allocation. Topography matters, of course, but so does its location, especially since in contrast to many other resources, land's location is fixed. It matters not only *absolutely* in the sense that the land's location directly affects its value, but also *relatively* in the sense that the value of any particular piece of land is also affected by the uses of the land around it. In addition, land supplies many services, including providing habitat for all terrestrial creatures, not merely humans.

Some contiguous uses of land are compatible with each other, but others are not. In the case of incompatibility, conflicts must be resolved. Whenever the prevailing legal system treats land as private property, as in the United States, the market is one arena within which those conflicts are resolved.

How well does the market do? Are the land-use outcomes and transactions efficient and sustainable? Do they adequately reflect the deeper values people hold for land? Why or why not?

In this chapter, we shall begin to investigate these questions. How does the market allocate land? How well do market allocations fulfill our social criteria? Where divergences between market and socially desirable outcomes occur, what policy instruments are available to address the problems? How effective are they? Can they restore conformance between goals and outcomes?

The Economics of Land Allocation

Land Use

In general, as with other resources, markets tend to allocate land to its highest-valued use, as reflected by the users' willing to pay or willingness to accept payment. Consider Figure 10.1, which graphs three hypothetical land uses—residential development, agriculture, and wilderness.[1] The left-hand side of the horizontal axis represents the location of the marketplace where agricultural produce is sold. Moving to the right on that axis reflects an increasing distance away from the market.

The vertical axis represents net benefits per acre. Each of the three functions, known in the literature as *bid rent functions*, records the relationship between distance to the center of the town or urban area and the net benefits per acre received from each type of land use. A bid rent function expresses the maximum net benefit per acre that could be achieved by that land use as a function of the distance from the center. All three functions are downward sloping because the cost of transporting both goods and people lowers net benefits per acre more for distant locations.

FIGURE 10.1 The Allocation of Land

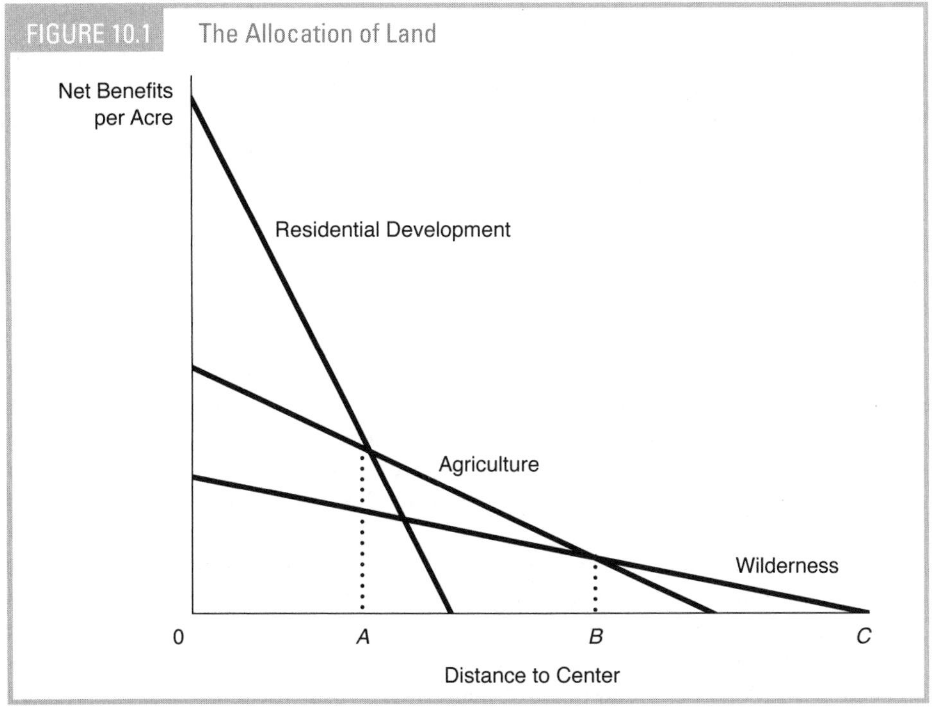

[1]For our purposes in this thought experiment, wilderness is a large, uncultivated tract of land that has been left in its natural state.

According to Figure 10.1, a market process that allocates land to its highest-valued use would allocate the land closest to the center to residential development (a distance of *A*), agriculture would claim the land with the next best access (*A* to *B*), and the land farthest away from the market would remain wilderness (from *B* to *C*). This allocation maximizes the net benefits society receives from the land.

Although very simple, this model also helps to clarify both the processes by which land uses change over time and the extent to which market processes are efficient, subjects we explore in the next two sections.

Land-Use Conversion

Conversion from one land use to another can occur whenever the underlying bid rent functions shift, and apparently in the United States they have shifted a great deal. According to the Economic Research Service of the US Department of Agriculture, "Urban land acreage quadrupled from 1945 to 2007, increasing at about twice the rate of population growth over this period."

Conversion of nonurban land to residential development could occur when the bid rent function for urban development shifts up, the bid rent function for nonurban land uses shifts down, or any combination of the two. Two sources of the conversion of land to urban uses in the United States stand out: (1) increasing urbanization and industrialization rapidly shifted upward the bid rent functions for urban land, including residential, commercial, industrial, and even associated transportation (airports, highways, etc.) and recreational (parks, etc.) uses; (2) rising productivity of the agricultural land allowed the smaller amount of land to produce a lot more food. Less agricultural land was needed to meet the rising food demand than would otherwise have been the case.

Agricultural Land: A Closer Look. While the amount of total land in the United States dedicated to farming has dropped considerably over time since 1920, irrigated acreage has been rising.

It seems unlikely that simple extrapolation of the decline in agricultural land of the magnitude since 1920 into the future would be accurate. Since the middle of the 1970s, the urbanization process has diminished to the point that some urban areas (in the United States) are experiencing declining population. This shift is not merely explained by suburbia spilling beyond the boundaries of what was formerly considered urban.

Furthermore, as increases in food demand are accompanied by increased prices of food, the value of agricultural land should increase. Higher food prices would tend to slow conversion.

What about agricultural land that is still used for agriculture, but not used for growing food? A recent trend in conversion of land to grow corn solely to be used in the production of ethanol has contributed to rising food prices.

In late 2007, Congress passed a new energy bill that included, among other things, a mandate for renewable fuels, including 5 billion gallons of ethanol made from grains, primarily corn, by 2022. Under that legislation ethanol currently carries a sizable subsidy, inducing more farmers to grow corn for ethanol rather than for food or livestock feed.

While some 14 percent of corn use went to ethanol production in the 2005–2006 crop year, according to the US Department of Agriculture's Economic Research Service that share rose to 42.4% by 2013. Even though ethanol represents a very small share of the overall gasoline market, its impacts on the agricultural sector are large.

As the use of corn for ethanol production continued to grow, corn prices have responded with rapid increases. Corn prices have risen from about $1.80 per bushel in 2000–2001 to more than $6 per bushel in 2013! Rising corn prices due to this expansion have caused land previously used to grow soybeans to be converted to corn production, and land previously used to grow corn for feed grains is now being used to grow corn for ethanol. The resulting price increases for corn and soybeans, as well as for meats and other foods using corn or soybeans, have been dramatic.

What about irrigation? Irrigated acreage is on the rise, both domestically and worldwide, although the rate of increase has been falling. Irrigation can increase yields of most crops by 100–400 percent and hence increase the value of the land on which these corps are grown. The FAO estimates that over the next 30 years, 70 percent of the gains in cereal production will come from irrigated land, and by 2030 irrigated land in the developing countries will increase by 27 percent.

However, irrigation, a traditional source of productivity growth, is also running into limits, particularly in the western United States. Some traditionally important underground sources used to supply water are not being replenished at a rate sufficient to offset the withdrawals. Encouraged by subsidies that transfer the cost to the taxpayers, consumption levels are sufficiently high that these water supplies are being exhausted.

Contamination of the remaining water is also an issue. Irrigation of soils with water containing naturally occurring salts causes the salts to concentrate near the surface. This salty soil is less productive and, in extreme cases, kills the crops.

The Rise of Organic Food. The markets have not only been affected by shifts in agricultural land use, they have also been affected by the type of agriculture being practiced. The organic foods industry is the fastest-growing US food segment. Certified organic cropland acreage between 2002 and 2008 averaged 15 percent annual growth. However, in 2008, it still only represented about 0.7 percent of all US cropland, while certified organic pasture only represented 0.5 percent of all US pasture.

Aided by the price premiums that buyers of organic food were willing to pay, US sales of organic food and beverages have grown from $1 billion in 1990 to $26.7 billion in 2010. Organic food and beverage sales represented approximately 4 percent of overall food and beverage sales in 2010. Leading were organic fruits and vegetables, now representing over 11 percent of all US fruit and vegetable sales.

Sources of Inefficient Use and Conversion

In the absence of any government regulation, are market allocations of land efficient? In some circumstances they are, but certainly not in all, or even most, circumstances.

We shall consider several sets of problems associated with land-use inefficiencies that commonly arise in the industrialized countries: sprawl and leapfrogging, the effects of taxes on land-use conversion, incompatible land uses, undervaluation of environmental amenities, and market power. While some of these also plague developing countries, we follow with a section that looks specifically at some of the special problems developing countries face.

Sprawl and Leapfrogging

Two problems associated with land use that are receiving a lot of current attention are *sprawl* and *leapfrogging*. From an economic point of view, sprawl occurs when land uses in a particular area are inefficiently dispersed, rather than efficiently concentrated. The related problem of leapfrogging refers to a situation in which new development continues not on the very edge of the current development, but farther out. Thus, developers "leapfrog" over contiguous, perhaps even vacant, land in favor of land that is farther from the center of economic activity.

Several environmental problems are intensified with dispersed development. Trips to town to work, shop, or play become longer. Longer trips not only mean more energy consumed, but also frequently they imply a change from the least polluting modes of travel (such as biking or walking) to automobiles, a much more polluting source. When the cars used for commuting are fueled by gasoline internal combustion engines, dispersal drives up the demand for oil (including imported oil), results in higher air-pollutant emissions levels (including greenhouse gases), and increases the need for more steel, glass, and other raw materials to supply the increase in the number of vehicles demanded.

The Public Infrastructure Problem. To understand why inefficient levels of sprawl and leapfrogging might be occurring, we must examine the incentives faced by developers and how those incentives affect location choices.

One set of inefficient incentives can be found in the pricing of public services. New development beyond the reach of existing public sewer and water systems may necessitate extending those facilities if the new development is to be served. The question is, "who pays for this extension and how does that choice affect location decisions?"

If the developer is forced to pay for the extension as a means of internalizing the cost, he or she will automatically consider this as part of the cost of locating farther out. When those costs are passed on to the buyers of the newly developed properties, they will also face a higher marginal cost of living farther out.

Suppose, however, as is commonly the case, that the extensions of these services are financed by metropolitan-wide taxes. When the development costs are subsidized by all taxpayers in the metropolitan area, both the developers and potential buyers of the newly developed property find living farther out to be artificially cheap. This bias prevents developers from efficiently considering the trade-off between developing the land in currently served areas more densely and building upon the less developed land outside those areas, thereby promoting inefficient levels of sprawl.

Development farther from the center of economic activity can also be promoted either by transportation subsidies or negative externalities. As potential residential buyers choose where to live, transportation costs matter. Living farther out may mean a longer commute or longer shopping trips. Implicitly, when living farther out means more and/or longer trips, these transport costs should figure into the decision of where to live; higher transportation costs increase the relative net benefits of living closer to the center.

The implication is that if transportation costs are inefficiently low due to subsidies or uninternalized negative travel externalities, the resulting bias will inefficiently favor more distant locations. Finding examples of inefficiently low transportation costs is not difficult. While we reserve a full discussion of this topic for Chapter 17 on mobile-source pollution, for our current purpose, consider just two examples: pollution externalities and parking subsidies.

- When the social cost associated with pollution from car exhaust is not fully internalized, the marginal cost of driving an extra mile is inefficiently low. This implies not only that an excessive number of miles will be driven, but also that dispersed development would become inefficiently attractive.
- Many employers provide free employee parking even though providing that parking is certainly not free to the employer. Free parking represents a subsidy to the auto user and lowers the cost of driving to work. Since commuting costs (including parking) are typically an important portion of total local transportation costs, free parking creates a bias toward more remote residential developments and encourages sprawl.

While these factors can promote sprawl, they don't completely explain why developers skip over land that is closer in. Economic analysis (Irwin & Bockstael, 2007) has identified some of the factors that promote leapfrogging. These include features of the terrain (including its suitability for development), land-use externalities (such as access to scenic bodies of water), and government policy (such as road building and urban large lot zoning).

Incompatible Land Uses

As mentioned earlier in this chapter, the value of a parcel of land will be affected not only by its location, but also by the character of the nearby land. This interdependence can be another source of inefficiency.

We know from previous discussions in this book that even in the presence of fully defined property rights, private incentives and social incentives can diverge in the presence of externalities. When any decision confers external costs on another party, the allocation that maximizes net benefits for the decision maker may not be the allocation that maximizes net benefits for society as a whole.

Negative externalities are rather common in land transactions. Many of the costs associated with a particular land use may not accrue exclusively to the landowner, but will fall on the owner of nearby parcels. For example, houses near the airport are affected by the noise and neighborhoods near a toxic waste facility may face higher health risks.

One current controversial example involves an ongoing battle over the location of large industrial farms where hogs are raised for slaughter. Some of the costs of these farms (e.g., odors and water pollution from animal waste) fall on the neighbors. Since these costs are externalized, they tend to be ignored or undervalued by unregulated hog farm owners in decisions about the land, creating a bias. In terms of Figure 10.1, the private net benefit curve for hog farms would lie above the social net benefit curve, resulting in an inefficiently high allocation of land to hog farms.[2]

One traditional remedy for the problem of incompatible land uses involves a legal approach known as *zoning*. Enacted via an ordinance, zoning creates districts or zones with allowable land uses specified for each of those zones. Land uses in each district are commonly regulated according to such characteristics as type of use (such as residential, commercial, and industrial), density, structure height, lot size, and structure placement, among others. One aspect of the theory behind zoning is that by locating similar land uses together, negative externalities can be limited or at least reduced.

One major limitation of zoning is that it can actually promote urban sprawl. By setting stringent standards for all property (such as requiring a large lot for each residence and prohibiting multifamily dwellings), zoning can mandate a lower density. By reducing the allowed residential density, it can actually contribute to urban sprawl by forcing more land to be used to accommodate a given number of people.[3]

Undervaluing Environmental Amenities

Positive externalities represent the mirror image of the negative externalities described above. Many of the beneficial ecosystem goods and services associated with a particular land use may also not accrue exclusively to the landowner either. Hence, that particular use may be undervalued by the landowner.

Consider, for example, a large farm that provides both beautiful vistas of open space for neighbors (or even for travelers on an adjoining road) and habitat for wildlife in its forests, streams, and rangelands. The owner would be unlikely to reap all the benefits from providing the vistas because travelers could not always be excluded from enjoying them, despite the fact that they contribute nothing to their preservation.[4] In the absence of exclusion, the owners receive only some of the total benefits, thereby creating a bias in decisions. Specifically, in this case, land uses

---

[2]For an economic analysis of the magnitude of this impact, see Herriges et al. (2005).

[3]For evidence on the empirical relevance of this point, see McConnell et al. (2006a).

[4]Note that the aesthetic value from open space is a public good. In many, if not most, cases, exclusion is either impossible or impractical (perhaps simply too expensive) and the benefits from the view are indivisible.

that involve more of the undervalued activities will lose out to activities that convey more benefits to the landowner even when, from society's perspective, that choice is clearly inefficient.

Consider the implication of these insights in terms of Figure 10.1. In the presence of externalities, a farmer's decision whether to preserve agricultural land that provides a number of external benefits or sell it to a developer is biased toward development. The owner's private net benefit curve for agriculture would be lower than the social net benefit curve. The implication of this bias is that the allocation of land to agriculture would inefficiently contract and the allocation to residential development would expand.

One remedy for environmental amenities that are subject to inefficient conversion due to the presence of positive externalities involves direct protection of those assets by regulation or statute. In one common example wetlands help protect water quality in lakes, rivers, streams, and wells by filtering pollutants, nutrients, and sediments, and they reduce flood damage by storing runoff from heavy rains and snow melts. They also provide essential habitat for wildlife. Regulations help to preserve those functions by restricting activities that are likely to damage these ecological services. For example, draining, dredging, filling, and flooding are frequently prohibited in shoreland wetlands.

As Debate 10.1 points out, however, regulations designed to protect social values may diminish the value of the landowner's property and that creates controversy about their use.

The Influence of Taxes on Land-Use Conversion

Many governments use taxes on land (and facilities on that land) as a significant source of revenue. For example, state and federal governments tax estates (including the value of land) at the time of death and local governments depend heavily on property taxes to fund such municipal services as education. In addition to raising revenue, however, taxes also can create incentives to convert land from one use to another, even when such conversions would not be efficient.

The Property Tax Problem. In the United States, the *property tax*, a tax imposed on land and facilities on that land, is typically the primary source of funding for local governments. A property tax has two components: the tax rate and the tax base. The tax base (the value of the land) is usually determined either by the market value, as reflected in a recent sale, or as estimated by a professional estimator called an assessor.

For our purposes, the interesting aspect of this system is that the assessment is normally based upon perceived market value, which can be quite different from the value of the land in its current use. This distinction implies that when a land-intensive activity, such as farming, is located in an area under significant development pressure, the tax assessment may reflect the development potential of the land, not its value in farming. Since the value of developable land is typically higher, potentially much higher, the tax payments required by this system may raise farming cost (and lower net income) sufficiently as to promote a conversion of farmland to development, a

DEBATE 10.1 Should Landowners Be Compensated for "Regulatory Takings"?

When environmental regulations, such as those protecting wetlands, are imposed, they tend to restrict the ability of the landowner to develop the land subject to the regulation. This loss of development potential frequently diminishes the value of the property and is known in the common law as a "regulatory taking." Should the landowner be compensated for that loss in value?

Proponents say that compensation would make the government more likely to regulate only when it was efficient to do so. According to this argument, requiring governments to pay the costs of the regulation would force them to balance those costs against the societal benefits, making them more likely to implement the regulation only where the benefits exceeded the costs. Proponents also argue that it is unfair to ask private landowners to bear the costs of producing benefits for the whole society; those costs should be funded via broad-based taxes on the beneficiaries.

Opponents argue that forcing the government to pay compensation in the face of the severe budget constraints, which most of them face, would result in many (if not most) of these regulations not being implemented despite their efficiency. They also argue that fairness does not dictate compensation when the loss of property value is due to simply preventing a landowner from causing societal damage (such as destroying a wetland); landowners do not have an unlimited right to inflict social damage. Furthermore, landowners are typically not expected to compensate the government when regulation increases the value of their land.

Current judicial decisions tend to award compensation only when the decline of value is so severe as to represent a virtual confiscation of the property (100 percent loss in value). Lesser declines are typically not compensated.

Disagreeing with this set of rulings, voters in Oregon in 2004 approved Measure 37, which allowed individual landowners to claim compensation from the local community for any decrease in property value due to planning, environmental, or other government regulations. After witnessing the effects of that measure, voters passed Measure 49 in 2007, which had the effect of narrowing the impact of Measure 37.

Which sets of arguments do you find most compelling? Why?

conversion that would not occur with current use taxation. When the tax does not actually reflect the current activity's use of the government services funded by that tax, this funding mechanism can create a bias against land-intensive activities.

The Inheritance Tax Problem. The death of someone who has been engaging in land-intensive activities (such as farming) also poses a specific tax problem to those who inherit the estate. Depending on the size of the estate, the heirs may owe a considerable *estate tax*, a type of tax levied on the value of the assets held by the deceased at the time of death. Since the inherited land may not produce a sufficient cash flow to pay the taxes, part or all of the land might have to be sold to raise the necessary funds. In this case, the conversion of the land would be dictated by tax-driven liquidity considerations, not efficiency considerations.

The inheritance tax can apparently be an empirically significant factor in land conversion, at least in some countries. For example, Motohiro and Patel (1999) find a rather large effect of the inheritance tax in motivating the conversion of agricultural land to development among older landowners in Japan.

Market Power

For all practical purposes, the total supply of land is fixed. Furthermore, since the location of each parcel is unique, an absence of good substitutes can sometimes give rise to market power problems. Because market power allows the seller to charge inefficiently high prices, market power can frustrate the ability of the market to achieve efficiency by preventing transfers that would increase social value. One example of this problem is when market power inhibits government acquisitions to advance some public purpose.

The "Frustration of Public Purpose" Problem. One of the functions of government is to provide certain services, such as parks, potable drinking water, sanitation services, public safety, and education. In the course of providing these services, it may be necessary to convert land that is being used for a private purpose to a public use, such as creating a new public park or building a new road.

Efficiency dictates that this conversion should take place only if the benefits from the conversion exceed its costs. The public sector could simply buy the land from its current owner of course and that approach has much to recommend it. Not only would the owner be adequately compensated for giving up ownership, but an outright purchase would make sure that the opportunity cost of this land (represented by the inability of the previous owner to continue its current use) would be reflected in the decision to convert the land to public purpose. If the benefits from the conversion were lower than the cost (including the loss of benefits from the previous use as a result of the conversion), the conversion would not (and from an efficiency point of view should not) take place.

Suppose, however, the owner of the private land recognizes that his or her ownership of the specific parcel of land most suited for this public purpose creates an opportunity to become a monopolist seller. To capitalize on this opportunity, he or she could hold out until such time as the public sector paid a monopoly price for the land. If and when this occurs, it could represent an inefficient frustration of the public purpose by raising its cost to an inefficiently high level.[5] Sellers with market power could inefficiently limit the amount of land acquired

---

[5]Although we are focusing here on a public-sector action, the same logic would apply to a developer trying to buy several pieces of land to build a new large development. One of the potential sellers could hold out for an inflated price, recognizing that their parcel was necessary for the development to go forward, but only the public sector is entitled to condemn property by eminent domain. For this reason private developers try to get local governments to act on their behalf. See Debate 10.2.

by the public sector to provide public access to such amenities as parks, bike paths, and nature trails.

The main traditional device for controlling the "frustration of public purpose" problem is the legal doctrine known as eminent domain. Under eminent domain, the government can legally acquire private property for a "public purpose" by condemnation as long as the landowner is paid "just compensation."

Two characteristics differentiate an eminent domain condemnation from a market transaction. First, while the market transfer would be voluntary, the transfer under eminent domain is mandatory—the landowner cannot refuse. Second, the compensation to the landowner in an eminent domain proceeding is determined not by agreement of both the public and private parties, but by a legal determination of a fair price.

Notice that while this approach can effectively eliminate the "holdout" problem and force the public sector to pay for (and hence, recognize) the opportunity cost of the land, it will only be efficient if the conversion is designed to fulfill a legitimate public purpose and the payment does, in fact, reflect the true opportunity cost of the land. Not surprisingly, both aspects have come under considerable legal scrutiny.

The eminent domain determination of just compensation typically involves one or more appraisals of the property provided by disinterested experts who specialize in valuing property. In the case of residential property, appraisals are commonly based on recent sales prices of comparable properties in the area, suitably adjusted to consider the unique characteristics of the parcel being transferred. Since in reasonable circumstances (e.g., a farm in the family for generations), this inferred value may not reflect a specific owner's true valuation,[6] it is not surprising that landowners frequently do not agree that the compensation that they are ultimately awarded by this process is "fair"; appeals are common.

Controversy also is associated with the issue of determining what conversions satisfy the "public purpose" condition (see Debate 10.2).

Special Problems in Developing Countries

Insecure Property Rights. In many developing countries, property rights to land are either informal or nonexistent. In these cases land uses may be determined on a first-come, first-served basis and the occupiers do not actually hold title to the land. Rather, taking advantage of poorly defined or poorly enforced property rights, they acquire the land simply by occupying it, not by buying or leasing it. In this case the land is acquired for free, but the holders run the risk of eviction if someone else ultimately produces an enforceable claim for the land and mounts a successful action to enforce that claim.

The lack of clear property rights can introduce both efficiency and equity problems. The efficiency aspect is caused by the fact that a first-come, first-served system of allocating land affects both the nature of the land use and incentives to preserve its value. Early occupiers of the land determine the use and, since the land cost them

---

[6]In this case, "true valuation" means a price that would have been accepted in a voluntary transaction in the absence of monopoly considerations.

What Is a "Public Purpose"?

DEBATE 10.2

The US Constitution only allows the eminent domain power to be used to accomplish a "public purpose." What exactly is a public purpose?

Although acquiring land for typical facilities, such as parks and jails, is settled legal terrain, recent decisions that justify the use of eminent domain to condemn private neighborhoods to facilitate urban renewal by private developers are much more controversial.

For example, in *Kelo v. City of New London, Conn. 125 S.Ct. 2655* (2005), the court upheld the city's development authority's right to use eminent domain to acquire parcels of land that it planned to lease to private developers in exchange for their agreement to develop the land according to the terms of a development plan.

Those who support this decision point out that large-scale private developments face many of the same market power obstacles (such as "holdouts") faced by the public sector. Furthermore, since large-scale private developments of this type provide such societal benefits as jobs and increased taxes to the community, eminent domain is seen as justified to prevent inefficient barriers that inhibit development.

Opponents suggest that this is merely using governmental power to favor one set of private landowners (the developers) over others (the current owners of the land).

From an economic point of view should publicly regulated private development such as this be allowed to fulfill the "public purpose" test? When it is allowed, should the developers be under any special requirements to assure that public benefits are forthcoming?

nothing to acquire, the opportunity cost associated with other potentially more socially valuable uses is never considered. Hence, low-valued uses could dominate high-valued uses by default. This means, for example, extremely valuable forests or biologically diverse land could be converted to housing or agriculture even when other locations might be much more efficient.

Does a first-come, first-served allocation provide incentives to preserve the value of the land or to degrade it? Because occupiers with firm property rights could sell the land to others, the ability to resell provides an incentive to preserve its value to achieve the best possible price. If, on the other hand, any movement off the land causes a loss of all rights to the land, as would be the case with an occupier who does not hold a land title, those incentives can be diminished.

This conflict also has an important equity dimension, since the absence of property rights gives occupiers no legal defense against competing claims. Suppose, for example, that some indigenous people have sustainably used a piece of land for a very long period of time, but any implicit property rights they hold are simply unenforceable, because they hold no legal title to that land. If marketable natural resources are discovered on "their" land, enormous political pressure will be exerted to evict the occupants with few protections afforded to their interests so the resource can be exploited.

Efficiency mandates that land-use conversion should take place only if the net benefits of the new use are larger than the net benefits of the old. The traditional means of determining when that test has been satisfied is to require that the current owners be sufficiently compensated that they would voluntarily give up their land. If their rights are not enforceable and, hence, can simply be ignored, the land can be converted and they can be involuntarily displaced even when it is efficient to preserve the land in its current use. With formal enforceable property rights, current users could legally defend their interests. The questionable enforceability of informal rights would make current users much more vulnerable.

The Poverty Problem. In many developing counties, poverty may constrain choices to the extent that degradation of the land can dominate sustainable use, simply as a matter of survival. Even when the present value of sustainable choices is higher, a lack of income or other assets may preclude taking advantage of the opportunity.

As Barbier (1997) points out, poor rural households in developing countries generally only have land and unskilled labor as their principal assets, and thus few human, financial or physical capital assets. The unfortunate consequence of this situation is that poor households with limited holdings often face important labor, land, and cash constraints on their ability to invest in land improvements. Barbier relates the results of a study he conducted with Burgess in Malawi:

> *In Malawi female-headed households make up a large percentage (42 percent) of the "core-poor" households. They typically cultivate very small plots of land (<0.5 ha) and are often marginalized onto the less fertile soils and steeper slopes . . . They are often unable to finance agricultural inputs such as fertilizer, to rotate annual crops, to use "green manure" crops or to undertake soil and water conservation. As a result, poorer female headed households generally face declining soil fertility and crop yields, further exacerbating their poverty and increasing their dependence upon the land.*

This degradation of land, due to inadequate investment in maintaining it, can cause farmers to migrate from that degraded land to other marginal land, only to have it suffer the same fate. For similar reasons, poverty can exacerbate tropical deforestation, promote overgrazing, and hasten the inefficient conversion of land to agriculture.

Government Failure. While both property rights and poverty can be sources of the inefficient allocation of land, government actions can be a source as well. Government failure occurs when the public policies have the effect of distorting land-use allocations. A common example involves building roads into previously preserved land, rendering that land suitable (by increasing access and lowering transportation costs) for a number of new land uses. In this case, by lowering transportation costs, the government makes the bid rent functions flatter and, coupled with the undervaluation of environmental amenities, this could lead to an inefficient conversion of land.

Innovative Market-Based Policy Remedies

The previous section has identified a number of sources of market and public sector failure in the allocation of land to its various uses. One way to deal with those failures is to establish some kind of complementary role between the economy and the government. If the policy remedies are to be efficient, however, they must be able to rectify the failures without introducing a new set of inefficiencies—no small task as we shall see.

Establishing Property Rights

Merely establishing enforceable property rights can rectify some market inefficiencies, but the circumstances must be right for the outcome to be efficient. In an early, highly influential article, Harold Demsetz (1967) pointed out that the efficient system of property rights tends to evolve over time in the face of changing circumstances.

The establishment of property rights systems can mitigate or avoid the problems of overexploitation that can occur when land is merely allocated on a first-come, first-served basis, but establishing a legally enforceable system of private property rights is a costly venture. In cases where land uses are relatively homogeneous and the land is abundant relative to the demand for it, any inefficiency associated with the absence of property rights could well be smaller than the significant cost associated with establishing a property rights system. As societies mature, however, a point will normally be reached when the inefficiencies associated with the absence of a property rights system become so large that bearing the additional administrative costs of establishing it becomes justified. By establishing secure, enforceable, transferable claims, adequate property rights systems can encourage both efficient transfer and efficient maintenance of the value of the property, since in both cases the seller would benefit directly. In the absence of the specific circumstances giving rise to the inefficiencies noted in this chapter, establishing secure property rights can cause private and social incentives to coincide.

Transferable Development Rights

Owners of land that efficiency suggests should be preserved are typically opposed to zoning ordinances designed to promote preservation because (as noted in Debate 10.1) they bear the costs of preservation while society as a whole reaps the benefits. One approach, transferable development rights (TDR), changes that dynamic.

TDR programs are a method for shifting residential development from one portion of a community to another without putting all of the costs on the owner of the land designated for preservation. Local units of government identify *sending areas* (areas where development is to be prohibited or discouraged) and *receiving areas* (areas where development is to be encouraged).

Landowners in sending areas are allocated *development rights* based on criteria identified in adopted plans. Generally, the allocation depends upon the number and quality of developable sites available on their property.

Landowners seeking to develop in a receiving area must first buy a certain amount of development rights from landowners in a sending area. In principle, the revenue from selling these rights compensates the sending area owners for their inability to develop their land and, hence, makes them more likely to support the restrictions.[7] It seeks to preserve land without burdening either the public budget or the owners of the preserved land (see Example 10.1).

Grazing Rights[8]

Farmers have been allowed to graze their livestock on public lands since the early 1900s. The Taylor Grazing Act of 1934 attempted to prevent overgrazing by assuring that the amount of grazing was consistent with the carrying capacity of the land.

The law set up a system that involved the issuance of grazing permits to farmers. Each permit authorized a certain amount of livestock to be grazed on a specific piece of land for a specified period of time. The permits are denominated in animal unit months (AUM). An AUM is the amount of feed or forage required to maintain

EXAMPLE 10.1

Controlling Land Development with TDRs

How transferable development rights (TDRs) work in practice can be illustrated with an example. The New Jersey Pinelands is a largely undeveloped, marshy area in the southeastern part of the state encompassing approximately one million acres. This area provides habitat for several endangered species. In an effort to direct development to the least environmentally sensitive areas, the Pinelands Development Commission created Pineland Development Credits (PDCs), a form of transferable development rights.

Landowners in environmentally sensitive areas received 1 PDC in exchange for every 39 acres of existing preserved farmland, 1 PDC for every 39 acres of preserved upland, and 0.2 PDC for every 39 acres of wetlands. To create a demand for these credits, developers seeking to increase the standard density on land in the receiving area, which is specifically zoned for development, were required to acquire 1 PDC for every 4 units of increase. The price of credits was set by the market.

To assure that the market would be vigorous enough, the commission also established a Pinelands Development Credit Bank to act as a purchaser of last resort for PDCs at the statutory price of $10,000 per credit. In 1990 the bank auctioned its inventory at the price of $20,200 per PDC. By 1997 developers had used well over 100 PDCs. As of 2013 the average price per PDC had risen to $37,872.34.

Source: Anderson, R. C., & Lohof, A. Q. (1997). *The United States Experience with Economic Incentives in Environmental Pollution Control Policy*. Washington, DC: Environmental Law Institute.; New Jersey Pinelands Development Commission Website. Retrieved from http://www.state.nj.us/pinelands/pdcbank/

[7]For an analysis of how a program in Calvert County, Maryland, has worked, see McConnell et al. (2006).

[8]Bureau of Land Management's Grazing Rights Website. Retrieved from http://www.blm.gov/or/resources/rangelands/index.php

one animal unit (e.g., a 1000 lb cow and calf) for one month. The number of issued permits is based upon the carrying capacity of the land (in terms of available forage). A grazing fee is charged for each AUM to help to fund the program.

Conservation Easements

One popular approach to preserving land is known as a *conservation easement*. A conservation easement is a legal agreement between a landowner and private or public agency that limits uses of the land (in many cases in perpetuity) in order to protect its conservation values.

Once created, conservation easements can be either sold or donated. If a donation benefits the public by permanently preserving important resources and meets other federal tax code requirements, it can qualify as a charitable tax deduction. The tax deductible amount is the difference between the land's value with or without the easement.

From an economic point of view, a conservation easement allows the bundle of rights associated with land ownership to be treated as separable transferable units. Separating out the development rights and allowing them to flow to the highest-valued use (conservation in this case) may allow the value of the entire bundle of rights the land to be increased, while simultaneously preserving the land. The value of the bundle of unseparated entitlements would only be maximized if the owner of the property happened to be the one who placed the highest value on each and every entitlement—an unlikely possibility.

Suppose, for example, a landowner wants to continue to harvest timber from her land, but does not want to convert it to housing. In the absence of a conservation easement, the owner is likely to face property taxes on the land that are based on highest-valued use (development) rather than its current use (timber harvest). If, however, the owner executes an agreement with a public or private entity that can legally administer a conservation easement, property taxes will fall (since the assessed value is now lower), and he or she will either get a substantial income tax break (in the case of a charitable donation of the easement) or the revenue (in the case of a sale of the easement). Meanwhile the land is protected in perpetuity from development, and the current owner can use the land for all purposes except those explicitly precluded by the easement agreement.

Conservation easements have much to recommend them. Since they are voluntary transactions, no one is forced to part with the development rights; consent is required for any transfer. This approach also allows land to be protected from unwanted uses much more cheaply than would be possible if the only option for protection were to purchase the land itself, rather than just specific rights contained in the easement.

Easements, however, can also introduce problems. Land uses affected by the conservation easement must be monitored to ensure that the terms of the agreement continue to be upheld and, if they are not, to bear the costs of a legal action to enforce compliance with the agreement. These legal actions are not cheap. In addition, the perpetual nature of conservation easements could become a problem if and when, in the far distant future, development became the universally preferred use.

Land Trusts

What kinds of entities can take on the monitoring and enforcement burdens associated with assuring compliance with the easement agreement, keeping in mind that these duties may last forever? In some cases government performs this role, but increasingly, legal entities, known as conservation *land trusts*, have been created for this purpose. A conservation land trust is a nonprofit organization that, as all or part of its mission, actively works to conserve land using a variety of means. It can purchase land for permanent protection or accept donations or bequests of either land or easements. Because they are organized as charitable organizations under federal tax laws, donations of easements or land to a land trust can entitle the donor to a charitable deduction on their income tax.

Development Impact Fees

Development impact fees are charges imposed on a developer to offset the additional public-service costs of new development. Normally applied at the time a developer receives a building permit, the revenues are dedicated to funding the additional services, such as water and sewer systems, roads, schools, libraries, and parks and recreation facilities, made necessary by the presence of new residents in the development. Since the costs arising from those fees are presumably passed on to those buying houses in the development, in principle they protect against the public infrastructure problem by internalizing the costs of extending services. Internalizing that externality restores the incentives associated with choosing the location of residential development and reduces one distortion that could otherwise promote inefficient leapfrogging and sprawl.

Property Tax Adjustments

Several states offer programs to discount property taxes as a means to protect a socially desired current use, particularly when undiscounted taxes are seen as an inefficient bias against that use. When property taxes are based upon market value, rather than current use, the tax structure can put pressure on the owner to convert the land. This would be particularly true if the current activities are land intensive (farming or a preserved forest, for example) and the land could be sold for a new residential development. This pressure can be inefficient to the extent that it ignores all the positive externalities.

Under schemes to try to counteract this tax bias, eligible property owners seen as conferring uncompensated external benefits on the community are offered specified reductions in their assessed value. Programs are typically available to the property owner through an application process run by the local municipality. Certain criteria must be met for each program in order for a parcel of land to be eligible and any future changes in the eligibility of the land enrolled in this tax relief programs are subject to disqualification and a penalty.[9]

[9]In the farmland program, for example, if the property no longer qualifies as a farmland tract, then the assessed penalty would be an amount equal to the taxes that would have been paid in the last 5 years if it had not been in the farmland, less the taxes that were originally assessed, plus any interest on that balance.

Although different states have different programs, the general approach can be illustrated by considering Maine's Open Space program. To qualify for the program, land must be either preserved or restricted in use so as to provide a public benefit. Benefits specifically recognized for eligibility include public recreation, scenic resources, game management, and wildlife habitat. The valuation (against which the tax is levied) placed on land qualifying for the open space designation is typically accomplished by first determining how many of the four categories of public benefits identified by the law the land qualifies for. The percentage reductions associated with each of the applicable categories are then cumulated and the fair market value is reduced by this cumulative percentage. Those categories and their associated percentage reductions are as follows:

- Ordinary open space—20 percent reduction
- Permanently protected—30 percent reduction
- Forever wild—20 percent reduction
- Public access—25 percent reduction

The owner of any property satisfying all four of these benefit conditions (through selling or donating a conservation easement, for example) could, therefore, receive a cumulative reduction of up to 95 percent on the property taxes associated with the eligible land.

Summary

Land is an important environmental resource not only in its own right, but also as a complement to many related ecosystems. By providing a habitat for wildlife, recharge areas for aquifers, and the foundation for such land-intensive activities as forestry and agriculture, the allocation of land lies at the core of a harmonious relationship between humans and the environment.

The market, which tends to allocate land to the land use that maximizes its value, supports land conversion as the relative values of the various land uses change. For example, in the United States the amount of land allocated to agriculture has declined over time, while the allocations within types of agriculture have changed as well. In particular, relatively more agricultural land is now dedicated to the production of fuel (ethanol), due to a policy mandate, and more has been allocated to certified organic farms due to the price premium their produce can command.

While in principle, the market allocates land to its highest and best use, in practice, several attributes of land and the allocation process can result in inefficient, unsustainable, and/or unjust outcomes. Sources of these problems include not only market problems such as poorly specified property rights, market power, and externalities, but also public sector problems associated with inefficient tax and user fee structures. Furthermore, by constraining choices poverty can also lead to both inefficient and unfair allocations of land.

A number of policy instruments, some quite novel, are available to counteract some of these socially undesirable outcomes. They include the formalization of property rights to protect users from intrusion, transferable development rights, conservation easements, and land trusts to both reduce the cost and increase the likelihood that efficient preservation can take place. In terms of the public sector policy options include changes in property and inheritance tax structures and development impact fees to eliminate inefficient incentives, thereby and promoting efficient land-use decisions. While this collection of policy options can correct some of the imbalances in the land-allocation system, most represent, at best, a movement in the right direction, not the full restoration of efficiency or sustainability.

Discussion Questions

1. Air pollution officials in California's Central Valley have opened a new front in the war against urban sprawl, and regulators and environmental advocates throughout the state are watching closely. Starting in March 2006, the San Joaquin Valley Air Pollution Control District in California became the first regulatory body in the country to impose fees on new residential and commercial development specifically focused on reducing air pollution. Critics argue that this is an ineffective way to control pollution and will mainly drive up housing prices, making housing less affordable for the poor. Is this policy a good idea? (For more details on this program see http://www.valleyair.org/ISR/ISRHome.)

Self-Test Exercises

1. Suppose a city finds that its express highways into the city are congested and it is considering two remedies: (1) imposing a congestion charge on all users of its expressways during the peak periods and (2) adding a couple of lanes to the existing expressways. Would these be expected to have the same effects on residential land use? Why or why not?
2. With respect to strategies used by land conservation groups to preserve land, conservation easements seem to be expanding more rapidly than buying land for preservation. In what respect might conservation easements be relatively more attractive to land conservation groups than acquiring land outright? What is the economic incentive for landowners to donate land or conservation easements to the conservation organizations?
3. Suppose a state was trying to decide whether to fund primary and secondary education with either a property tax or an income tax. What implications might this choice have for land use in the state?

4. Changing preferences can also affect changes in land use. In the United States, the proportion of the population in the 65-and-older age bracket is growing. What effects might this have on the location and the nature of the residential housing stock?
5. In the United States, the production of ethanol fuel from corn is subsidized. Use bid rent function analysis to suggest what effects this subsidy might be expected to have on land use.
6. Increasingly sophisticated communications technology is allowing more people to work at home. What effect do you think this might have on land-use patterns, specifically the density of residential development?

Further Reading

Bell, K. P., Boyle, K. J., & Rubin, J. (2006). *Economics of Rural Land-Use Change*. Aldershot, UK: Ashgate. Presents an overview of the economics of rural land-use change; includes theoretical and empirical work on both the determinants and consequences of this change.

Hascic, I., & Wu, J. (2012). The cost of land use regulation versus the value of individual exemption: Oregon ballot measures 37 and 49. *Contemporary Economic Policy, 30*(2), 195–214. Examines the effects on land values of the zoning regulations that gave rise to Measure 37, the Oregon program mentioned in Debate 10.1.

Irwin, E. G., Bell, K. P., Bockstael, N. E., Newburn, D. A., Partridge, M. D., & Wu, J. J. (2009). The economics of urban-rural space. *Annual Review of Resource Economics, 1*, 435–459. Changing economic conditions, including waning transportation and communication costs, technological change, rising real incomes, and changing tastes for natural amenities, have led to new forms of urban–rural interdependence. This paper reviews the literature on urban land-use patterns, highlighting research on environmental impacts and the efficacy of growth controls and land conservation programs that seek to manage this growth.

Johnston, R. J., & Swallow, S. K. (Eds.). (2006). *Economics and Contemporary Land Use Policy*. Washington, DC: Resources for the Future, Inc. Explores the causes and consequences of rapidly accelerating land conversions in urban-fringe areas, as well as implications for effective policy responses.

Magliocca, N., McConnell, V., Walls, M., & Safirova, E. (2012). Zoning on the urban fringe: Results from a new approach to modeling land and housing markets. *Regional Science and Urban Economics, 42*(1–2): 198–210. This paper examines the effects of large-lot zoning on land conversion, land prices, and the spatial configuration and density of new development over a 20-year period.

McConnell, V., & Walls, M. (2009). US experience with transferable development rights. *Review of Environmental Economics and Policy, 3*(2), 288–303. This article summarizes the key elements in the design of TDR programs and reviews a number of existing markets to identify which have performed well and which have not.

Additional References and Historically Significant References are available on this book's Companion Website: http://www.routledgetextbooks.com/textbooks/9780133479690

11 Storable, Renewable Resources: Forests

There is nothing more difficult to carry out, nor more doubtful of success, nor more dangerous to handle, than to initiate a new order of things. For the reformer has enemies in all who profit by the old order, and only lukewarm defenders in all those who would profit from the new order. The lukewarmness arises partly from fear of their adversaries who have law in their favor; and partly from the incredulity of mankind, who do not truly believe in anything new until they have had actual experience of it.

—Niccolò Machiavelli, *The Prince* (1513)

Introduction

Forests provide a variety of products and services. The raw materials for housing, wood products and paper are extracted from the forest. In many parts of the world, wood is an important fuel. Trees cleanse the air by absorbing carbon dioxide and adding oxygen. Forests provide shelter and sanctuary for wildlife and they play an important role in maintaining the watersheds that supply much of our drinking water.

Although the contributions that trees make to our everyday life are easy to overlook, even the most rudimentary calculations indicate their significance. Almost one-third of the land in the United States is covered by forests, the largest category of land use with the exception of pasture and grazing land. In Maine, an example of a heavily forested state, 95 percent of the land area is covered by forest. In 2005 the comparable figure for the world was 30.7 percent.

Managing these forests is no easy task. In contrast to crops such as cereal grains, which are planted and harvested on an annual cycle, trees mature very slowly. The manager must decide not only how to maximize yields on a given amount of land but also when to harvest and whether to replant. In addition, a delicate balance must be established among the various possible uses of forests. Since harvesting the resource diminishes other values (such as protecting the aesthetic value of forested vistas or providing habitat for shade-loving species), establishing the proper balance requires some means of comparing the value of potentially conflicting uses. The efficiency criterion is one obvious method.

One serious problem, deforestation, has intensified climate change, decreased biodiversity, caused agricultural productivity to decline, increased soil erosion and desertification, and precipitated the decline of traditional cultures of people indigenous to the forests. Instead of forests being used on a sustainable basis to provide for the needs of both current and subsequent generations, some forests are being "cashed in."

In its "Global Forest Land-use Change 1990–2005," the Food and Agricultural Organization of the United Nations reports that due to a shift from forest land use to other land uses, overall global forest area registered a net decrease of 1.7 percent between 1990 and 2005 at an annual rate of change of 0.11 percent. These data suggest that current forestry practices may be violating both the sustainability and efficiency criteria.[1] How serious is the problem and what can be done about it?

In the remainder of this chapter, we shall explore how economics can be combined with forest ecology to assist in efficiently managing this important resource. We begin by characterizing what is meant by an efficient allocation of the forest resource when the value of the harvested timber is the only concern. Starting simply, we first model the efficient decision to cut a single stand or cluster of trees with a common age by superimposing economic considerations on a biological model of tree growth. This model is then refined to demonstrate how the multiple values of the forest resource should influence the harvesting decision and how the problem is altered if planning takes place over an infinite horizon, with forests being harvested and replanted in a continual sequence. Turning to matters of institutional adequacy, we shall then examine the inefficiencies that have resulted or can be expected to result from both public and private management decisions and strategies for restoring efficiency.

Characterizing Forest Harvesting Decisions

Special Attributes of the Timber Resource

While timber shares many characteristics with other living resources, it also has some unique aspects. Timber shares with many other animate resources the characteristic that it is both an output and a capital good. Trees, when harvested, provide a salable commodity, but left standing they are a capital good, providing for increased growth the following year. Each year, the forest manager must decide whether or not to harvest a particular stand of trees or to wait for the additional growth. In contrast to many other living resources, however, the time period

[1]In this context, sustainability refers to harvesting no more than would be replaced by growth; sustainable harvest would preserve the interests of future generations by assuring that the volume of remaining timber was not declining over time. This is consistent with the environmental sustainability criterion discussed in Chapter 5, but is stronger than needed to satisfy the weak sustainability criterion. Conceivably, the weak sustainability criterion could be satisfied even if the volume of wood were declining over time by providing a compensating amount of some commodity or service that is valued even more.

between initial investment (planting) and recovery of that investment (harvesting) is especially long. Intervals of 25 years or more are common in forestry, but not in many other industries. Finally, forestry is subject to an unusually large variety of externalities, which are associated with either the standing timber or the act of harvesting timber. These externalities not only make it difficult to define the efficient allocation, but also they play havoc with incentives, making it harder for institutions to manage efficiently.

The Biological Dimension

Tree growth is conventionally measured on a volume basis, typically cubic feet, on a particular site. This measurement is taken of the stems, exclusive of bark and limbs, between the stump and a 4-inch top. For larger trees, the stump is 24 inches from the ground. Only standing trees are measured; those toppled by wind or age are not included. In this sense, the volume is measured in net, rather than gross, terms.

Based on this measurement of volume, the data reveal that tree stands go through distinct growth phases. Initially, when the trees are very young, growth is rather slow in volume terms, though the tree may experience a considerable increase in height. A period of sustained, rapid growth follows, with volume increasing considerably. Finally, slower growth sets in as the stand fully matures, until growth stops or decline sets in.

The actual growth of a stand of trees depends on many factors, including the weather, the fertility of the soil, susceptibility to insects or disease, the type of tree, the amount of care devoted to the trees, and vulnerability to forest fire or air pollution. Thus, tree growth can vary considerably from stand to stand. Some of these growth-enhancing or growth-retarding factors are under the influence of foresters; others are not.

Abstracting from these differences, it is possible to develop a hypothetical but realistic biological model of the growth of a stand of trees. Our model, as shown in Figure 11.1 is based on the growth of a stand of Douglas fir trees in the Pacific Northwest.[2] Notice that the figure is consistent with the growth phases listed above, following an early period of limited growth in its middle ages, with growth ceasing after 135 years.

The Economics of Forest Harvesting

When should this stand be harvested? From the definition of efficiency, the optimal harvest time (age) would maximize the present value of the net benefits from the wood. The size of the net benefits from the wood depends on whether the land will be perpetually committed to forestry or left to natural processes after harvest.

---

[2]The numerical model in the text is based loosely on the data presented in Marion Clawson. "Decision Making in Timber Production, Harvest, and Marketing," Research Paper R-4 (Washington, DC: Resources for the Future, 1977), 13, Table 1. The mathematical function relating volume to age stand in Figure 12.1 is a third-degree polynomial of the form $v = a + bt + ct^2 + dt^3$, where v = volume in cubic feet, t = the age of the stand in years, and a, b, c, and d are parameters that take on the values 0, 40, 3.1, and −0.016, respectively.

FIGURE 11.1 Model of Tree Growth in a Stand of Douglas Fir

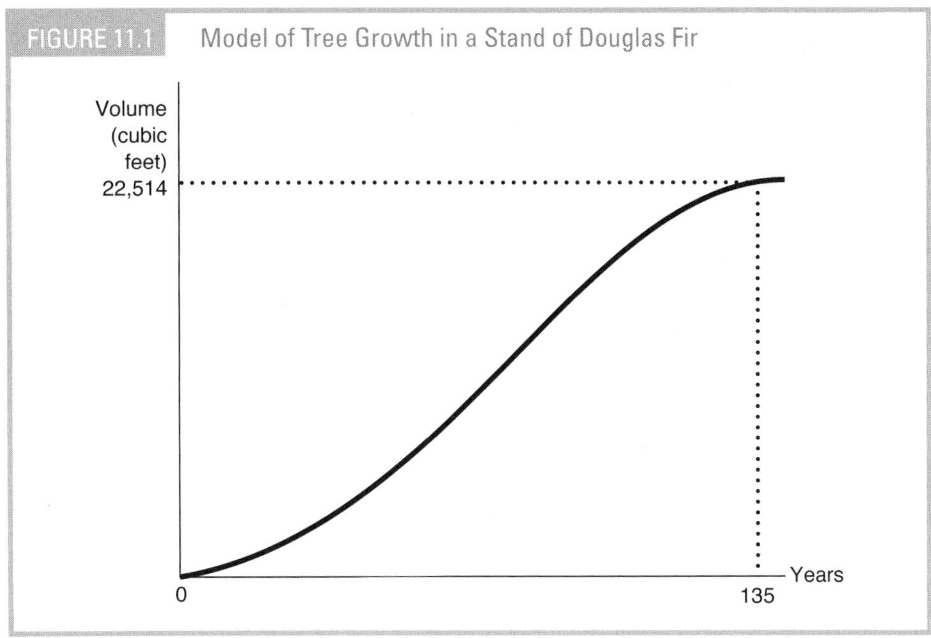

For our first model, we shall assume that the stand will be harvested once and the land will be left as is following the harvest. We also shall assume that neither the price (assumed to be $1) nor the harvesting costs per cubic meter ($0.30) vary with time. The cost of planting this forest is assumed to be $1,000. This model illustrates how the economic principles of forestry can be applied to the simplest case, while providing the background necessary to move to more complicated and more realistic examples.

Planting costs and harvesting costs differ in one significant way—the time at which they are borne. Planting costs are borne immediately, while harvesting costs are borne at the time of harvest. In a present-value calculation, harvesting costs are discounted (as is the value of the wood) because they are paid (costs) or received (revenue) in the future, whereas planting costs are not discounted because they are paid immediately.

Having specified these aspects of the model, it is now possible to calculate the present value of net benefits that would be derived from harvesting this stand at various ages (see Table 11.1). The net benefits are calculated by subtracting the present value of costs from the present value of the timber at that age. Three different discount rates are used to illustrate the influence of discounting on the harvesting decision. The undiscounted calculations ($r = 0.0$) simply indicate the actual values that would prevail at each age, while the positive discount rate takes the time value of money into account.

Some interesting conclusions can be gleaned from Table 11.1. First, discounting shortens the timing of the efficient harvest. Notice that the maximum undiscounted net benefits occur at an age of 135 years, when the volume is maximized. However,

TABLE 11.1 Economic Harvesting Decision: Douglas Fir

Age (years)	10	20	30	40	50	60	68	70	80	90	100	110	120	130	135
Volume (cubic feet)	694	1,912	3,558	5,536	7,750	10,104	12,023	12,502	14,848	17,046	19,000	20,614	21,792	22,438	22,514
Undiscounted ($r = 0.0$)															
Value of Timber ($)	694	1,912	3,558	5,536	7,750	10,104	12,023	12,502	14,848	17,046	19,000	20,614	21,792	22,438	22,514
Cost ($)	1,208	1,574	2,067	2,661	3,325	4,031	4,607	4,751	5,454	6,114	6,700	7,184	7,538	7,731	7,754
Net Benefits ($)	–514	338	1,491	2,875	4,425	6,073	7,416	7,751	9,394	10,932	12,300	13,430	14,254	14,707	14,760
Discounted ($r = 0.01$)															
Value of Timber ($)	628	1,567	2,640	3,718	4,712	5,562	6,112	6,230	6,698	6,961	7,025	6,899	6,603	6,155	5,876
Cost ($)	1,188	1,470	1,792	2,115	2,414	2,669	2,833	2,869	3,009	3,088	3,107	3,070	2,981	2,846	2,763
Net Benefits ($)	–560	97	848	1,603	2,299	2,893	3,278	3,361	3,689	3,873	3,917	3,830	3,622	3,308	3,113
Discounted ($r = 0.02$)															
Value of Timber ($)	567	1,288	1,964	2,507	2,879	3,080	3,128	3,126	3,046	2,868	2,623	2,334	2,024	1,710	1,449
Cost ($)	1,170	1,386	1,589	1,752	1,864	1,924	1,938	1,938	1,914	1,860	1,787	1,700	1,607	1,513	1,435
Net Benefits ($)	–603	–98	375	755	1,015	1,156	1,190	1,188	1,132	1,008	836	634	417	197	14
Discounted ($r = 0.04$)															
Value of Timber ($)	469	873	1,097	1,153	1,091	960	835	803	644	500	376	276	197	137	113
Cost ($)	1,141	1,262	1,329	1,346	1,327	1,288	1,251	1,241	1,193	1,150	1,113	1,083	1,059	1,041	1,034
Net Benefits ($)	–672	–389	–232	–193	–237	–328	–415	–438	–549	–650	–737	–807	–862	–904	–921

Value of timber = price × volume/$(1 + r)^t$

Cost = \$1,000 + (\$0.30 × volume)/$(1 + r)^t$

Net benefits = value of timber – cost

Price = \$1

when a discount rate of only 0.02 is used, the maximum net benefits occur at an age of 68 years, roughly half the age of the undiscounted case.

Second, under these specific assumptions, the optimal harvest age is insensitive to changing the magnitude of the planting and harvesting costs. You can see this by comparing the age that yields the maximum value in the "value of timber" row and age that yields the maximum value in the "net benefit" row. Notice that for all discount rates, these two maxima occur at the same age. Even if both types of costs were zero, the optimal harvesting age would not be affected. The age that maximizes the value of the timber remains the same.

Third, with high enough discount rates, replanting may not be efficient. Note that with $r = 0.04$, the present value of net benefits is uniformly negative due to the assumed \$1,000 planting cost. The harvest age that maximizes the present value of net benefits from a standing forest in this case would occur when the trees were about 40 years old, but the present value of costs of replanting would exceed the present value of the benefits so it would not be efficient to replant the harvested forest.

Higher discount rates imply younger harvesting ages because they are less tolerant of the slow timber growth that occurs as the stand reaches maturity. The use of a positive discount rate implies a direct comparison between the increase in the value of nonharvested timber and the increase in value that would occur if the forest were harvested and the money from the sale invested at rate r. In the undiscounted case, using an r of zero implies that the opportunity cost of capital is zero, so it pays to leave the money invested in trees as long as some growth is occurring. As long as r is positive, however, the trees will be harvested as soon as the growth rate declines sufficiently that more will be earned by harvesting the trees and putting the proceeds in higher-yielding financial investments (in other words, when g, the growth rate in the volume of wood, becomes less than r).

The fact that neither harvesting nor planting costs affect the harvesting period in this model is easy to explain. Because they are paid immediately, the present value of planting costs is equal to the actual expenditure; it does not vary with the age at which the stand is harvested. Essentially, a constant is being subtracted from the value of timber at every age so it does not change the age at which the maximum occurs.

Harvesting costs do not affect the age of harvest for a different reason. Since total harvesting costs are assumed proportional to the amount of timber harvested (\$0.30 for each cubic foot), neither the price nor the marginal cost of a cubic foot of wood varies with age; they are also constants. In the case of our numerical example, this constant net value before discounting is \$0.70 (the \$1 price minus the \$0.30 marginal harvest cost). Regardless of the numerical value assigned to the marginal cost of harvesting, this net value before discounting is a constant that is multiplied by the volume of timber at each age divided by $(1 + r)^t$. Its role is merely to raise or lower the net benefits curve; it does not change its shape, including the location of the maximum point. Therefore, net benefits will be maximized at the same age of the stand, regardless of the value of the marginal harvesting cost, as long as marginal harvesting cost is less than the price received; a rise in the marginal cost of harvesting will not affect the optimal age of harvest. (What is the optimal harvesting strategy if the marginal cost of harvesting is larger than the price?)

What effect could policy have on the harvesting age? Consider the effect of a \$0.20 tax levied on each cubic foot of wood harvested in this simple model. Since this tax would raise the after-tax marginal cost of harvesting from \$0.30 per cubic foot to \$0.50 per cubic foot, it would have the same effect as a rise in harvesting cost. As we have already demonstrated, this implies that the tax would leave the optimal harvesting age unchanged.

The final conclusion that can be drawn from this numerical example relates to the interaction between discount rates and planting costs on the decision to replant. When high discount rates combine with high replanting costs, planting trees for commercial harvest would be less likely to yield positive net benefits than would be the case with lower discount rates. (Notice, for example, in Table 11.1, that replanting would be economically desirable only for discount rates lower than $r = 0.04$.) With high discount rates, tree growth is simply too slow to justify the planting expense; profit-maximizing foresters would favor cutting down an existing forest, but not replanting it.

Extending the Basic Model

This basic model is somewhat unrealistic in several respects. Perhaps, most importantly, it considers the harvest as a single event rather than a part of an infinite sequence of harvesting and replanting. Typically in the infinite planning horizon model, harvested lands are restocked and the sequence starts over again in a never-ending cycle.

At first glance, it may appear that this is really no different from the case just considered. After all, can't one merely use this model to characterize the efficient interval between planting and harvest for each period? The mathematics tells us (Bowes & Krutilla, 1985) that this is *not* the correct way to think about the problem, and with a bit of reflection, it is not difficult to see why.

The single-harvest model we developed would be appropriate for an infinite planning period if and only if all periods were independent (meaning that decisions in any period would be unaffected by anything that went on in the other periods). If interdependencies exist among time periods, however, the harvesting decision must reflect those interdependencies.

Interdependencies do exist. The decision to delay a harvest imposes an additional cost in an infinite planning model that has no counterpart in our single-harvest model—the cost of delaying the onset of the next planting and harvesting cycle. In our single-harvest model, the optimum age to harvest occurs when the marginal benefit of an additional year's growth equals the marginal opportunity cost of capital. In other words, when the capital gains from letting the trees grow another year become equal to the return that could be obtained from harvesting the trees and investing the gains, the stand is harvested. In the infinite-planning horizon case, the opportunity cost of delaying the next cycle, which has no counterpart in the single stand model, must also be covered by the gain in tree growth.

The effect of including the opportunity cost of delay in an infinite horizon model can be rather profound. Assuming that all other aspects of the problem (such as planting and harvesting costs, discount rate, growth function, and price) are the same, the optimal time to harvest (called the *optimal rotation* in the infinite-planning case) is *shorter* in the infinite-planning case than in the single-harvest case. This follows directly from the existence of the opportunity cost of delaying the next harvest. The efficient forester would harvest at an earlier age when he or she is planning to replant the same area than when the plot will be left inactive after the harvest.

This more complicated model also yields some other different conclusions from our original model, a valuable reminder of a point made in Chapter 1—conclusions flow from a specific view of the world and are valid only to the extent that view captures the essence of a problem.

Consider, for example, the effect of a rise in planting costs. In our single-harvest model, they had no effect on the optimal harvest age. In the infinite-horizon case, the optimal rotation is affected because higher planting costs reduce the marginal opportunity cost of delaying the cycle; fewer net benefits are lost by delaying the cycle, compared to the case with lower planting costs. As a result, the optimal rotation (the time between planting and harvesting that crop) would increase as planting costs increase. A similar result would be obtained when harvesting costs are increased. The optimal rotation period would be lengthened in that case as well. (Can you see why?)

Since increased harvesting costs in the infinite-horizon model lengthen the optimal rotation period, a per-unit tax on harvested timber would also lengthen the optimal rotation period in this model. Furthermore, lengthening the rotation period implies that the harvested trees would be somewhat older and, therefore, each harvest would involve a somewhat larger volume of wood.

Another limitation of our basic model lies in its assumption of a constant relative price for the wood over time. In fact, the relative prices of timber have been rising over time. Introducing relative prices for timber that rise at a constant rate in the infinite-horizon model causes the optimal rotation period to increase relative to the fixed-price case. In essence, prices that are rising at a fixed rate act to offset (i.e., diminish) the effect of discounting. Since we have already established that lower discount rates imply longer rotation periods, it immediately follows that rising prices also lead to longer efficient rotation periods.

A final issue with the models as elaborated so far is that they all are concerned solely with the sale of timber as a product. In fact, forests serve several other purposes as well, such as providing habitat for wildlife, supplying recreational opportunities, and stabilizing watersheds. For these uses, additional benefits accrue to the standing timber that are lost or diminished when the stand is harvested.

It is possible to incorporate these benefits into our model to demonstrate the effect they would have on the efficient rotation. Suppose that the amenity benefits conveyed by a standing forest are positively related to the age of the forest. In the infinite horizon case, the optimal rotation would once again occur when the marginal benefit of delay equaled the marginal cost of delay. When amenity values are considered, the marginal benefit of delay (which includes having these amenity values for another year) would be higher than in the models where amenity benefits are not considered. For this reason, considering amenity benefits would lengthen the optimal rotation. If the amenity benefits are sufficiently large, it may even be efficient to leave the forest as a wilderness area and not ever harvest it.

Sources of Inefficiency

The previous section considered the nature of the harvesting decision. In this section, we shall discover sources of inefficiency in that decision. These inefficiencies have the effect of biasing profit-maximizing decisions toward excessive rates of deforestation.

Perverse Incentives for the Landowner

Profit maximization does not produce efficient outcomes when the pattern of incentives facing decision makers is perverse. Forestry provides an unfortunately large number of situations in which perverse incentives produce very inefficient and unsustainable outcomes.

Privately owned forests are a significant force all over the world, but in some countries, such as the United States, they are the dominant force. As described next, private forest decisions are plagued by external costs of various types. Providing a sustainable flow of wood fiber is not the sole *social* purpose of the forest. When the act of harvesting timber imposes costs on other valued aspects of the forest (e.g., watershed maintenance, prevention of soil erosion, and protection of biodiversity), these costs are not borne by the decision maker; these amenity costs normally will not be adequately considered in profit-maximizing decisions.

The fact that the value of the standing forest as wildlife habitat or as a key element in the local ecosystem is an *external* cost can lead to inefficient decisions that threaten biodiversity. Failure to recognize all of the social values of the standing forest provides an incentive not only to harvest an inefficiently large amount of timber in working forests but also to harvest timber even when preservation is the efficient alternative. For example, the controversy that erupted in the Pacific Northwest of the United States between environmentalists concerned with protecting the habitat of the northern spotted owl and loggers can, in part, be explained by the different values these two groups put on habitat destruction. Loggers treat the loss of the northern spotted owl as an external cost; environmentalists treat the loss of timber harvest that results from habitat protection as an external cost.

Government policies can also create perverse incentives for landowners. Historically, the rapid rate of deforestation in the Amazon, for example, was promoted in part by the Brazilian government (Binswager, 1991; Mahar, 1989). When the Brazilian government reduced taxes on income derived from agriculture (primarily cattle ranching), this discriminatory treatment of agricultural income caused agriculture to be overvalued. This overvaluation made it profitable to cut down forests and convert the land to agriculture even when, in the absence of discriminatory tax policy, agriculture in these regions would not have been profitable. This system of taxation encouraged higher-than-efficient rates of conversion of land from forests to pasture (applying the model in Chapter 10) and subsidized an activity that, in the absence of tax discrimination, would not normally have been economically viable. In essence, Brazilian taxpayers were unknowingly subsidizing deforestation that depreciated the value of their natural capital stock.

The Brazilian system of property rights over land also played a role in the early history of deforestation. Acquiring the rights to land simply by occupying it had been formally recognized since 1850. A "squatter" acquired a usufruct right (the right to continue using the land) by (1) living on a plot of unclaimed public land and (2) using it "effectively" for the required period of time. If these two conditions were met for 5 years, the squatter acquired ownership of the land, including the right to transfer it to others. A claimant received a title for an amount of land up to three times the amount cleared of forest. Notice the incentives that this system of property rights created. The more deforestation accomplished by the squatter, the larger the amount of land he or she acquired. In effect, landless peasants could only acquire land by engaging in deforestation; due to this policy, the marginal benefits from clearing land were artificially high.

In recognition of the consequences of these perverse incentives, government policies no longer encourage deforestation by requiring that land be cleared for ownership and the practice of subsidizing cattle has also been abandoned. However, resettlement programs have also promoted the expansion of paved roads, ports, waterways, railways, and hydroelectric power plants into the heavily forested central Amazonia region. All of these government policies radically changed the value of land uses that were competing with preserved forest (remember Chapter 10), and the result was deforestation.

As a result of the resettlement program, many migrants engage in agriculture. Studying the decisions made by these farmers, Caviglia-Harris (2004) found that, as the land conversion model would suggest, the degree to which these farmers contribute to deforestation is impacted by market conditions as well as government policies. Market forces not only affect incentives to expand the scale of operations but also affect incentives to choose particular forms of agriculture. For example, her empirical results show that cattle ownership by migrants significantly increases the percentage of deforestation. Therefore, as the market for cattle and its related products—milk and meat—advanced, deforestation levels also increased.

Even natural conditions affect land conversion since they affect the profitability of agriculture. Chomitz and Thomas (2003), for example, found that the probability that land in Amazonia was used for agriculture or intensively stocked with cattle declined markedly with increasing rainfall, other things equal. This point is significant since it suggests that due to its prevailing high humidity, western Amazonia may be less suitable for agricultural development and therefore could be less vulnerable to the threat posed by the conversion of forested land into agriculture.

In the Far East and in the United States, perverse incentives also take another form. Logging is the major source of deforestation in both regions. Why wouldn't loggers act efficiently? One reason, as noted, is the fact that many amenity values of the standing forest are external to loggers and hence do not play much, if any, role in their decision making.

Another source of inefficiency can be found in the concession agreements, which define the terms under which public forests can be harvested. To loggers, harvesting existing forests has a substantial advantage over planting new forests: old growth can be harvested immediately for profit. By virtue of the commercial value of larger, older trees, considerable economic rent (called *stumpage value* in the industry) is associated with a standing forest.

In principle, governments have a variety of policy instruments at their disposal to capture this rent from the concessionaires, but they have typically given out the concessions to harvest this timber without capturing anywhere near all of the rent.[3] As a result, the cost of harvesting is artificially reduced and loggers can afford to harvest much more forest than is efficient. The failure of government to capture this rent also means that the wealth tied up in these forests has typically gone to a few, now-wealthy individuals and corporations rather than to the government to be used for the alleviation of poverty or other worthy social objectives.

The failure to capture the rent from concession agreements is not the only problem. Other contractual terms in these concession agreements have a role to play as well. Because forest concessions are typically awarded for limited terms, concession holders have little incentive to replant, to exercise care in their logging procedures, or even to conserve younger trees until they reach the efficient harvest age. The future value of the forest will not be theirs to capture. The resulting logging practices can destroy much of the younger stock by (1) the construction of access roads, (2) the felling and dragging of the trees, and (3) the elimination of the protective canopy. Although sustainable forestry would be possible for many of these nations, limited-term concession agreements make it unlikely.[4]

Finally, some harvest is simply illegal. Illegal harvesters have no incentive to protect future values and act as if their discount rate were infinite!

The list of losers from inefficient forestry practices frequently includes indigenous peoples who have lived in and derived their livelihood from these forests for a very long time. As the loggers and squatters push deeper and deeper into forests, the indigenous people, who lack the power to stem the tide, are forced to relocate further away from their traditional lands.

Perverse Incentives for Nations

Another source of deforestation involves external costs that transcend national borders, making it unrealistic to expect national policy to solve the problem. Some international action would normally be necessary for these cases.

Biodiversity. Due to species extinction, the diversity of the forms of life that inhabit the planet is diminishing at an unprecedented rate. And the extinction of species is, of course, an irreversible process. Deforestation, particularly the destruction of the tropical rain forests, is a major source of species extinction because it destroys the most biologically active habitats. In particular, Amazonia has been

[3]One way for the government to capture this rent would be to put timber concessions up for bid. Bidders would have an incentive to pay up to the stumpage value for these concessions. The more competitive the bidding was, the higher the likelihood that the government would capture all of the rent. In practice, many of the concessions have been given to those with influence in the government at far-below market rates. See Jeffrey R. Vincent. "Rent Capture and the Feasibility of Tropical Forest Management," *Land Economics* Vol. 66, No. 2 (May 1990), 212–223.

[4]Currently, foresters believe that the sustainable yield for closed tropical rain forests is zero, because they have not yet learned how to regenerate the species in a harvested area once the canopy has been destroyed. Destroying the thick canopy allows the light to penetrate and changes the growing conditions and the nutrient levels of the soil sufficiently that even replanting is unlikely to regenerate the types of trees included in the harvest.

characterized by Norman Myers, the British environmentalist, as the "single richest region of the tropical biome." The quantity of bird, fish, plant, and insect life that is unique to that region is unmatched anywhere else on the planet.

One of the tragic ironies of the situation is that these extinctions are occurring at precisely the moment in history when we would be most able to take advantage of the gene pool this biodiversity represents. Modern techniques now make it possible to transplant desirable genes from one species into another, creating species with new characteristics, such as enhanced disease resistance or pest resistance. But the gene pool must be diverse to serve as a source of donor genes. Tropical forests have already contributed genetic material to increase disease resistance of cash crops, such as coffee and cocoa, and have been the source of some entirely new foods. Approximately one-quarter of all prescription drugs have been derived from substances found in tropical plants. Future discoveries, however, are threatened by deforestation's deleterious effect on habitat.

Climate Change. Deforestation also contributes to climate change. Since trees absorb CO_2, a major greenhouse gas, deforestation eliminates a potentially significant means of ameliorating the rise in CO_2 emissions. Furthermore, burning trees, an activity commonly associated with agricultural land clearing, adds CO_2 to the air, by liberating the carbon sequestered within the trees.

Why is deforestation occurring so rapidly when the benefits conferred by a standing forest are so significant by virtually anyone's reckoning? The concept of externalities provides the key to resolving this paradox. Both the climate change and biodiversity benefits are largely external to both the private harvester and to the nation containing the forest, while the costs of preventing deforestation are largely internal. The loss of biodiversity precipitated by deforestation is perhaps most deeply felt by the industrialized world, not the countries that host the forests. Currently, the technologies to exploit the gene pool this diversity represents are in widest use in the industrialized countries. Similarly, most of the damage from climate change would be felt outside the borders of the country being deforested. Yet stopping deforestation means giving up the jobs and income derived from either harvesting the wood or harvesting the land made available by clearing the forests. Therefore, it is not surprising that the most vociferous opposition to the loss of biodiversity is mounted in the industrialized nations, not the nations hosting tropical forests. With global externalities, we have not only a clear rationale for market failure but also a clear rationale for why host national governments cannot be expected to solve the problem by themselves. While some external costs to individual agents are in fact internalized at the level of the nation (meaning those who bear those costs live in the same nation), global externalities aren't.

Poverty and Debt

Poverty and debt are also major sources of pressure on the forests. Peasants see unclaimed forest land as an opportunity to become landowners. Nations confronted with masses of peasants see unowned or publicly owned forests as a politically more viable source of land for the landless than taking it forcibly from the rich. Without land, peasants descend upon the urban areas in search of jobs in larger numbers than can be accommodated by urban labor markets. Politically explosive tensions, created and nourished by the resulting atmosphere of frustration and hopelessness, force governments to open up forested lands to the peasants or at least to look the other way as peasants stake their claims.

In eastern and southern Africa, positive feedback loops have created a downward cycle in which poverty and deforestation reinforce each other. Most natural forests have long since been cut down for timber and fuelwood and for producing crops from the cleared land. As forests disappear, the rural poor are forced to divert more time toward locating new sources of fuel. Once fuelwood is no longer available, dried animal waste is burned, thereby eliminating it as a source of fertilizer to nourish depleted soils. Fewer trees lead to more soil erosion and soil depletion leads to diminished nutrition. Diminished nutrition reinforces the threats to human health posed by an inability to find or afford enough fuel, wood, or animal waste for cooking and boiling unclean water. Degraded health saps energy, increases susceptibility to disease, and reduces productivity. Survival strategies may necessarily sacrifice long-term goals simply to ward off starvation or death; the forest is typically an early casualty.

At the national level, poverty takes the form of staggering levels of debt. Repaying this debt and the interest payments flowing from it reduces the capacity of a nation to accumulate foreign exchange earnings. In periods of high real interest rates, servicing these debts commands most if not all foreign exchange earnings. Using these foreign exchange earnings to service the debt eliminates the possibility of using them to finance imports for sustainable activities to alleviate poverty.

According to the "debt-resource hypothesis," large debts owed by many developing countries encourage these countries to overexploit their resource endowments to raise the necessary foreign exchange. Timber exports represent a case in point. Although a number of studies find empirical support for this hypothesis, not all do. And the support for extending the hypothesis to natural resources other than forests seems particularly weak. For example, Neumayer (2005) reports:

> *We did not find evidence that countries with higher debt levels or higher debt service burdens have higher exploitation of subsoil fossil fuel and mineral resources or higher production of cash crops than other countries. (p. 138)*

Sustainable Forestry

We have examined three types of decisions by landowners—the harvesting decision, the replanting decision, and the conversion decision—that affect the rate of deforestation. In all three cases, profit-maximizing decisions may not be efficient and these inefficiencies tend to create a bias toward higher rates of deforestation. These cases present both a challenge and an opportunity. The current level of deforestation is the challenge. The opportunity arises from the realization that correcting these inefficiencies can promote both efficiency and sustainability.

Does the restoration of efficiency guarantee sustainable outcomes? Let's suppose that we apply the environmental sustainability definition to forestry. By this definition, sustainable forestry can be realized only when the forests are sufficiently protected that harvests can be maintained perpetually. Also, sustainable forestry would require harvests to be limited to the growth of the forest, leaving the volume of wood unaffected (or nondecreasing) over time.

Efficiency is not necessarily compatible with this definition of sustainable forestry. Maximizing the present value involves an implicit comparison between the increase in value from delaying harvest (largely because of the growth in volume) and the increase in value from harvesting the timber and investing the earnings (largely a function of r, the interest rate earned on invested savings). With slow-growing species, the growth rate in volume is small. Choosing the harvest age that maximizes the present value of net benefits in slow-growing forests may well involve harvest volumes higher than the net growth of the forest.

The search for sustainable forestry practices that are also economically sustainable has led to a consideration of new models of forestry. One involves a focus on planting rapidly growing tree species in plantations. Rapidly growing species raise the economic attractiveness of replanting because the invested funds are tied up for a shorter time. Species raised in plantations can be harvested and replanted at a low cost. Forest plantations have been established for such varied purposes as supplying fuelwood in developing countries and supplying pulp for paper mills in both the industrialized and developing countries.

Plantation forestry is controversial, however. Not only do plantation forests typically involve a single species of tree, which results in a poor wildlife habitat, they also tend to require large inputs of fertilizer and pesticides.

In some parts of the world, the natural resilience of the forest ecosystem is sufficiently high that sustainability is ultimately achieved, despite decades of earlier unsustainable levels of harvest. In the United States, for example, sometime during the 1940s, the net growth of the nation's timberlands exceeded timber removals. Subsequent surveys have confirmed that net growth has continued to exceed harvests, in spite of a rather large and growing demand for timber. The total volume of forest biomass in the United States has been growing since at least World War II; for the country as a whole, harvests during that period have been sustainable, although the harvests of some specific species in some specific areas have not.

Public Policy

One public policy approach involves restoring efficient incentives. The following examples flow naturally from the previous discussion:

- Concessionaires should pay the full cost for their rights to harvest publicly controlled lands, including compensating for damage to the forests surrounding the trees of interest.
- The magnitude of land transferred to squatters should not be a multiple of the amount of cleared forest.
- The rights of indigenous peoples should be respected.

Another approach involves enlisting the power of consumers in the cause of sustainable forestry. The process typically involves the establishment of standards for sustainable forestry, employing independent certifiers to verify compliance with these standards, and allowing certified suppliers to display a label designating compliance (see Example 11.1).

For this system to work well, several preconditions need to be met. The certification process must be reliable and consumers must trust it. Additionally, consumers must be sufficiently concerned about sustainable forestry to pay a price premium (over prices for otherwise-comparable, but uncertified, products) that is large enough to make certification an attractive option for forestry companies. This means that the revenue should be sufficient to at least cover the higher costs associated with producing certified wood. Nothing guarantees that these conditions would be met in general.

Most of these changes could be implemented by individual nations to protect their own forests. And to do so would be in their interests. By definition, inefficient practices cost more than the benefits received. The move to a more efficient set of policies would necessarily generate more net benefits, which could be shared in ways that build political support for the change. But what about the global inefficiencies—those that transcend national boundaries? How can they be resolved?

EXAMPLE 11.1

Producing Sustainable Forestry through Certification

The Forest Stewardship Council (FSC) is an international, not-for-profit organization originally headquartered in Oaxaca, Mexico, with the FSC Secretariat relocating to Bonn, Germany, in 2003.

The FSC was conceived in large part by environmental groups, most notably the World Wide Fund for Nature (WWF). The goal of the FSC is to foster "environmentally appropriate, socially beneficial, and economically viable management of the world's forests." It pursues this goal by being an independent third-party certifier of well-managed forests.

The FSC has developed standards to assess the performance of forestry operations. These standards address environmental, social, and economic issues. Forest assessments require one or more field visits by a team of specialists representing a variety of disciplines, typically including forestry, ecology/wildlife management/biology, and sociology/anthropology. Additionally, the FSC requires that forest assessment reports be subject to independent peer review. Any FSC assessment may be challenged through a formal complaints procedure. FSC-certified products are identified by an on-product label and/or off-product publicity materials. As of April 2013, the FSC had certified 173,973,446 hectares in 79 countries (a hectare equals 2.47105 acres).

Although the FSC is supported by a broad coalition of industry representatives, social justice organizations, and environmental organizations, it is opposed by some mainstream industry groups, particularly in North America, and by some landowners' associations in Europe. One unresolved issue is how to include small and medium-sized landholdings in this certification process since conventional certification is expensive.

Source: The Forest Stewardship Website. Retrieved April 14, 2013, from http://www.fsc.org

Several economic strategies exist. They share the characteristic that they all involve compensating the nations conferring external benefits so as to encourage conservation actions consistent with global efficiency.

Debt–Nature Swaps

One strategy involves reducing the pressure on the forests caused by the international debt owed by many developing countries. One of the more innovative policies that explores common ground in international arrangements has become known as the debt–nature swap. A debt–nature swap involves the purchase (at a discounted value in the secondary debt market) of a developing country debt, frequently by a nongovernmental environmental organization (NGO). The new holder of the debt, the NGO, offers to cancel the debt in return for an environmentally related action on the part of the debtor nation.

In 1998, this approach received a boost with the passage of the Tropical Forest Conservation Act (TFCA). This Act offered eligible developing countries options for reducing certain official debt owed the US government while at the same time generating funds in local currency to support tropical forest conservation activities. The program took advantage of public–private partnerships and the majority of TFCA agreements to date have included funds raised by US-based NGOs.

TFCA is implemented through bilateral agreements with eligible countries. As of December 2011, approximately $202 million in congressionally appropriated funds have been used to conclude 18 TFCA debt treatment agreements with 14 countries.

The first debt–nature swap took place in Bolivia in 1987. Since then debt-for-nature swaps have been arranged or explored in many developing countries, including Ecuador, the Philippines, Zambia, Jamaica, Madagascar, Guatemala, Venezuela, Argentina, Honduras, and Brazil.

A brief examination of the Madagascar case can illustrate how these swaps work. Recognized as a prime source of biodiversity, the overwhelming majority of Madagascar's land mammals, reptiles, and plants are found nowhere else on Earth. Madagascar is also one of the poorest countries in the world, burdened with high levels of external debt. Because of its limited domestic financial resources, Madagascar could not counter the serious environmental degradation it was experiencing.

Between 1989 and 1996, Conservation International, the Missouri Botanical Garden, and the World Wildlife Fund negotiated nine commercial debt-for-nature swaps in Madagascar. These arrangements generated $11.7 million in conservation funds. Agreements signed by Madagascar's government and the participating conservation organizations identified the programs to be funded. One such program trained over 320 nature protection agents, who focused on involving local communities in forest management.

Other arrangements involving different governments and different environmental organizations have since followed this lead. The main advantage of these arrangements to the debtor nation is that a significant foreign exchange obligation can be paid off with domestic currency. Debt–nature swaps offer the realistic possibility to turn what has been a major force for unsustainable economic activity (the debt crisis) into a force for resource conservation.

Extractive Reserves

One strategy specifically designed to protect the indigenous people of the forest as well as to prevent deforestation involves the establishment of extractive reserves. These areas would be reserved for the indigenous people to engage in the traditional hunting–gathering activities.

Extractive reserves have already been established in the Acre region of Brazil. Acre's main activity comes from the thousands of men who tap the rubber trees scattered throughout the forest, a practice dating back 100 years. Under the leadership of Chico Mendes, a leader of the tappers who was subsequently assassinated, four extractive reserves were established in June 1988 by the Brazilian government to protect the rubber tappers from encroaching development.

Conservation Easements and Land Trusts

One private approach to internalizing the forestry benefits that may normally be externalized (and hence undervalued) in deciding how the resource is to be used involves conservation easements. These were discussed at length in Chapter 10, so here it is only necessary to point out that conservation easements provide a means for amenity values to be explicitly considered in forestry decisions. In the right circumstances, they can facilitate efficient preservation of those values (see Example 11.2).

EXAMPLE 11.2

Conservation Easements in Action: The Blackfoot Community Project

Montana's rural and wild Blackfoot Valley has so far escaped the rapid development occurring in many scenic valleys throughout the West. Although it offers huge amenity benefits to the surrounding community, those benefits are externalities to most potential developers and therefore future private transactions could well be biased against them.

Recognizing this potential, The Nature Conservancy (TNC) purchased significant tracts of this land (a total of 69,179 acres as of 2007) from Plum Creek Timber Company, a private landowner. Their objective, however, was not to retain ownership, but to dispose of the acquired land once they could be assured that the new owners would preserve key amenity assets. Since resale provides additional funds to the organization, this acquire-and-dispose strategy allows TNC to protect much more land with the funds at their disposal than would be permitted by retaining ownership of the acquired land.

Some 32,480 acres have been sold to public agencies. For example, a sale in May 2007 transferred 5234 acres of the western Horseshoe Hills, an important wildlife corridor between the Bob Marshall Wilderness and the Blackfoot Clearwater Wildlife Management Area, to the US Forest Service. The Forest Service had previously purchased the adjacent eastern half of the Horseshoe Hills.

The Conservancy apparently intends to sell roughly half of its acquired lands to private landowners once conservation easements protecting the amenity benefits are attached to the deeds.

Source: More than 69,000 acres conserved as part of the Blackfoot Community Project. Retrieved from http://www.nature.org/wherewework/northamerica/states/montana/news/news1803.html

The World Heritage Convention

The *World Heritage Convention* came into being in 1972 with the primary mission of identifying and preserving the cultural and natural heritage of outstanding sites throughout the world, and ensuring their protection through international cooperation. Currently, some 178 countries have ratified the convention.

Ratifying nations have the opportunity to have their natural properties of outstanding universal value added to the World Heritage List. The motivation for taking this step is to gain international recognition for this site, using the prestige that comes from this designation to raise awareness for heritage preservation and the likelihood that the site can be preserved. A ratifying nation may receive both financial assistance and expert advice from the World Heritage Committee as support for promotional activities for the preservation of its properties as well as for developing educational materials.

Responsibility for providing adequate protection and management of these sites falls on the host nations, but a key benefit from ratification, particularly for developing countries, is access to the World Heritage Fund. This fund is financed by mandatory contributions from ratifying nations, calculated at 1 percent of the country's contribution to UNESCO, the administering agency. Annually, about $3 million (US) are made available, mainly to low-income countries to finance technical assistance and training projects, as well as for assistance preparing their nomination proposals or to develop conservation projects. Emergency assistance may also be made available for urgent action to repair damage caused by human-made or natural disasters.

Royalty Payments

A potential source of revenue for biodiversity preservation involves taking advantage of the extremely high degree of interest by the pharmaceutical industry in searching for new drugs derived from these biologically diverse pools of flora and fauna. Establishing the principle that nations containing these biologically rich resources within their borders would be entitled to a stipulated royalty on any and all products developed from genes obtained from these preserves provides both an incentive to preserve the resources and some revenue to accomplish the preservation.

Nations harboring rich, biological preserves have begun to realize their value and to extract some of that value from the pharmaceutical industry. The revenue is in part used for inventorying and learning more about the resource as well as preserving it. For example, in 1996, Medichem Research, an Illinois-based pharmaceutical company, entered into a joint venture with the Sarawak government. The organization created by this joint venture has the right to file exclusive patents on two compounds that offer some promise as cancer treatments.

The agreement specified a 50–50 split from royalties once the drug is marketed. The Sarawak government was given the exclusive right to supply the latex raw material from which the compounds are derived. Furthermore, Sarawak scientists are involved in screening and isolating the compounds and Sarawak physicians are involved in the clinical trials.

This agreement not only provides a strong rationale for protecting the biological source, but also enables the host country to build its capacity for capturing the value of its biodiversity in the future (Laird & ten Kate, 2002). These arrangements are particularly significant because they facilitate transboundary sharing of the costs of preservation. It is unrealistic to expect countries harboring these preserves to shoulder the entire cost of preservation when the richer countries of the world are the major beneficiaries. It may also be unrealistic to assume that pharmaceutical demand is sufficient to fund efficient preservation (see Example 11.3).

Debt–nature swaps, extractive reserves, royalty payments, and conservation easements all involve recognition of the fact that resolving the global externalities component of deforestation requires a rather different approach from resolving the other aspects of the deforestation problem. In general, this approach involves financial transfers from the industrialized nations to the tropical nations, transfers that are constructed so as to incorporate global interests into decisions about the future of tropical forests.

EXAMPLE 11.3

Does Pharmaceutical Demand Offer Sufficient Protection to Biodiversity?

The theory is clear—incentives to protect plants are stronger when the plants are valuable to humans. Is the practice equally clear?

The case of Taxol is instructive. Derived from the slow-growing Pacific yew, Taxol is a substance that has been proved effective in treating advanced forms of breast and ovarian cancers. As of 1998, it was the best-selling anticancer drug ever.

Since the major site for this tree was in the old-growth forests of the Pacific Northwest, the hope of environmental groups was that the rise in the importance of Taxol might provide both sustainable employment and some protection for old-growth forests.

In fact, that is not how it worked out. The Taxol for the chemical trials was derived from the bark of the tree. Stripping the tree of its bark killed it. And supplying enough bark for the chemical trials put a tremendous strain on the resource.

Ultimately, the private company that marketed Taxol, Bristol-Squibb, developed a semi-synthetic substitute that could be made from imported renewable tree parts.

The Pacific yew, the original source of one of the most important medical discoveries in the twentieth century, was left completely unprotected. And the industry that had grown up to supply the bark collapsed. In the end, its value proved transitory and its ability to support a sustainable livelihood in the Pacific Northwest was illusory.

Source: Goodman, J., & Walsh, V. (2001). *The Story of Taxol: Nature and Politics in the Pursuit of an Anti-Cancer Drug*. New York: Cambridge University Press.

Recognizing the limited availability of international aid for the preservation of biodiversity habitat, nations have begun to tap other revenue sources. Tourist revenues have become an increasingly popular source, particularly where the tourism is specifically linked to the resources that are targeted for preservation. Rather than mixing these revenues with other public funds, nations are earmarking them for preservation (see Example 11.4).

EXAMPLE 11.4

Trust Funds for Habitat Preservation

How can local governments finance biodiversity preservation when faced with limited availability of both international and domestic funds? One option being aggressively pursued by the World Wildlife Fund involves trust funds. Trust funds are moneys that are legally restricted to be used for a specific purpose (as opposed to being placed in the general government treasury). They are administered by trustees to assure compliance with the terms of the trust. Most, but not all, trust funds are protected endowments, meaning that the trustees can spend the interest and dividends from the funds, but not the principal. This assures the continuity of funds for an indefinite period.

Where does the money come from? Many nations that harbor biodiversity preserves cannot afford to spend the resources necessary to protect them. One possibility is to tap into foreign demands for preservation. In Belize, the revenue comes from a "conservation fee" charged to all arriving foreign visitors. The initial fee, $3.75, was passed by Belize's parliament in January 1996, raising $500,000 in revenues each year for the trust fund. Similar trust funds have been set up in Mexico, Honduras, and Guatemala.

Income from the trust funds can be used for many purposes, including training park rangers, developing biological information, paying the salaries of key personnel, and conducting environmental education programs, depending on the terms of the trust agreement.

Biodiversity preservation that depends on funds from the general treasury becomes subject to the vagaries of budgetary pressures. When the competition for funds intensifies, the funds may disappear or be severely diminished. The virtue of a trust fund is that it provides long-term, sustained funding targeted for the protection of biodiversity.

In 2004, Belize joined with Mexico, Honduras, and Guatemala to form the Mesoamerican Reef (MAR) fund, a regional financing mechanism. It was created to strengthen the alliance among the four country-specific trust funds. The MAR fund is unique as the first environmental fund in the Western Hemisphere to transcend national boundaries and encompass an entire ecoregion. The fund supports projects related to improving water quality, ecotourism, sustainable fisheries, and strengthening public institutions.

Source: Spergel, B. (April 1996). Trust funds for conservation. *FEEM Newsletter, 1*,13–16.; the World Wildlife Foundation's Website on conservation trust funds. Retrieved November 18, 2010, from http://www.worldwildlife.org/what/howwedoit/conservationfinance/conservationtrustfunds2.html

Summary

Forests represent an example of a storable, renewable source. Typically, tree stands have three distinct growth phases—slow growth in volume in the early stage, followed by rapid growth in the middle years and slower growth as the stand reaches full maturity. The owner who harvests the timber receives the income from its sale, but the owner who delays harvest will receive additional growth. The amount of growth depends on the part of the growth cycle the stand is in.

From an economic point of view, the efficient time to harvest a stand of timber is when the present value of net benefits is maximized—that is, when the marginal gain from delaying the harvest one more year is equal to the marginal cost of the delay. For longer-than-efficient delays, the additional costs outweigh the increased benefits, while for earlier-than-efficient harvests, more benefits (in terms of the increased value of the timber) are given up than costs saved. For many species, the efficient age at harvest is 25 years or older.

The efficient harvest age depends on the circumstances the decision maker faces. When the plot is to be left fallow after the harvest, the efficient harvest occurs later than when the land is immediately replanted to initiate another cycle. With immediate replanting, delaying the harvest imposes an additional cost—the resulting cost of subsequently delaying the next harvest—which, when factored into the analysis, makes it more desirable to harvest earlier.

A number of other factors affect the size of the efficient rotation as well. In general, the larger the discount rate, the earlier the harvest. With an infinite-planning horizon model, increases in planting and harvesting costs tend to lengthen the optimal rotation, while in a single-harvest model, they have no effect on the length of the efficient rotation. If the relative price of timber grows at a constant rate over time, the efficient rotation is longer than if prices remain constant over time. Finally, if standing timber provides amenity services (such as for recreation or wildlife management) in proportion to the volume of the standing timber, the efficient rotation will be longer in an infinite planning model than it would be in the absence of any amenity services. Furthermore, if the amenity value is large enough, efficiency would preclude any harvest of that forest.

Profit maximization can be compatible with efficient forest management under the right circumstances. In particular, in the absence of externalities, distortions caused by government policy, or illegal harvests, profit-maximizing private owners have an incentive to adopt the efficient rotation and to undertake investments that increase the yield of the forest because that strategy maximizes their net benefits.

In reality, not all private firms will follow efficient forest-management practices because they may choose not to maximize profits, they may be operating at too small a scale of operation, or externalities or public policy may create inefficient incentives. Finally, when amenity values are large and not captured by the forest owner, the private rotation period may fail to consider these values, leading to an inefficiently short rotation period or even harvesting forests that should be preserved.

Inefficient deforestation has also been encouraged by a failure to incorporate global benefits from standing forests: concession agreements can provide incentives to harvest too much too soon, and may fail to provide adequate incentives to protect the interests of future generations; land property rights systems can make the amount of land acquired by squatters a multiple of cleared forestland; and tax systems can discriminate against standing forests.

Substantial strides toward restoring efficiency as well as sustainability can be achieved simply by recognizing and correcting the perverse incentives, actions that can be and should be taken by the tropical-forest nations. But these actions will not, by themselves, provide adequate protection for the global interests in the tropical forests. Six schemes designed to internalize some of these transboundary benefits—debt–nature swaps, extractive reserves, royalty payments, forest certification, and conservation easements—have already begun to be implemented.

Discussion Questions

1. Should US national forests become "privatized" (sold to private owners)? Why or why not?
2. In his book, *The Federal Land Revisited*, Marion Clawson proposed what he called the "pullback concept":

   > *Under the pullback concept any person or group could apply, under applicable law, for a tract of federal land, for any use they chose; but any other person or group would have a limited time between the filing of the initial application and granting other lease or the making of the sale in which to "pull back" a part of the area applied for. . . . The user of the pullback provision would become the applicant for the area pulled back, required to meet the same terms applicable to the original application, . . . but the use could be what the applicant chose, not necessarily the use proposed by the original applicant. (p. 216)*

   Evaluate the pullback concept as a means for conservationists to prevent some mineral extraction or timber harvesting on federal lands.

Self-Test Exercises

1. Suppose there are two identical forest plots except that one will be harvested and left to regrow while the second will be cleared after the harvest and turned into a housing development. In terms of efficiency, which one should have the oldest harvest age? Why?
2. In Table 11.1, when $r = 0.02$, the present value of the cost rises for 68 years and then subsequently declines. Why?

3. As our energy structure transitions toward renewable fuels, forest-based biomass fuels benefit from this transition. What are the likely effects of this transition on consumers, producers, and the states that host these resources?
4. Would a private forest owner normally be expected to reach an efficient balance between using his or her forest for recreation and for harvesting wood? Why or why not?
5. Compare forest certification and the certification of organic produce in terms of the relative degree to which each type of certification could, by itself, be expected to produce an efficient outcome.
6. Would a rise in the price of timber make sustainable forest practices more or less likely? Why?

Further Reading

Amacher, G. S., Ollikainen, M., & Koskela, E. A. (2009). *Economics of forest resources*. Cambridge, MA: MIT Press. This book provides an introduction to forest economics and an overview of its development, with focus on the last 25 years.

Araujo, C., Bonjean, C. A., Combes, J-L., Motel, P. C., & Reis, E. J. (2009). Property rights and deforestation in the Brazilian Amazon. *Ecological Economics, 68*(8–9), 2461–2468. This paper focuses on the impact of property rights insecurity on deforestation in the Brazilian Amazon.

Pagiola, S., Bishop, J., & Landell-Mills, N. (2002). *Selling forest environmental services: Market-based mechanisms for conservation and development*. London, UK: Earthscan. Market-based approaches are thought to offer considerable promise as a means to promote forest conservation and to serve as a new source of income for rural communities. Based on extensive research and case studies, this book demonstrates the feasibility and effectiveness of payment systems and their implications for the poor.

VanKooten, G. C., Sedjo, R. A. et al. (1999). Tropical deforestation: Issues and policies. In T. Tietenberg & H. Folmer (Eds.). *The International Yearbook of Environmental and Resource Economics 1999/2000* (198–249). Cheltenham UK: Edward Elgar. A survey of what we have learned about tropical deforestation.

Additional References and Historically Significant References are available on this book's Companion Website: http://www.routledgetextbooks.com/textbooks/9780133479690

Appendix

The Harvesting Decision: Forests

Suppose that an even-aged stand of trees is to be harvested at an age that maximizes the present value of the harvested timber. That age can be found by (1) defining the present value of the harvested timber as a function of the age of the stand, and (2) maximizing the function with respect to age.

$$\text{Present Value} = [PV(t) - C_h V(t)]e^{-rt} - C_p$$

where,

P = the price received per unit of harvested volume
$V(t)$ = the volume of timber harvested at age t
C_h = the per-unit cost of harvesting the timber
t = the age of the timber, and
C_p = the fixed cost of planting

Taking the derivative of the function with respect to age and setting it equal to zero yields*

$$(P - C_h)\frac{dV(t)}{dt} = (P - C_h)V(t)r$$

or rewriting yields

$$\frac{\frac{dV(t)}{dt}}{V(t)} = r$$

Translated into English, this condition implies that the rate of return from letting the stand grow over the last increment of age should be equal to the market rate of return.

Note that the fixed planting cost has no effect on the choice of harvesting age. While it raises or lowers the present value by the exact amount of the cost of planting, it does not change where the function reaches its maximum. If it is high enough, however, it can make the function reach its maximum at a negative number. In this case, not planting trees would maximize the present value even if that meant no future harvest. (A present value of zero would be larger than the present value that would necessarily be negative with planting.)

Note also that neither the price nor the harvesting cost affects the optimal choice. Mathematically, it is because they cancel out in Equation 2. Economically, it is because the value of a harvested unit does not vary with age; therefore, the *change* in present value as the stand ages is due to the change in *volume*, not the change in the *value* of each unit of volume (since the change in value is zero).

---

*If we had used a discrete time framework (i.e., $(1 + r)^t$ were used for discounting instead of e^{-rt}), then the optimal condition would be the same, except r would be replaced by $ln(1 + r)$. You can verify that for the values of r we are using, these two expressions are approximately equal.

12 Common-Pool Resources: Commercially Valuable Fisheries

In an overpopulated (or overexploited) world, a system of the commons leads to ruin. . . . Even if an individual fully perceives the ultimate consequences of his actions he is most unlikely to act in any other way, for he cannot count on the restraint his conscience might dictate being matched by a similar restraint on the part of all others.

—Garrett Hardin, *Carrying Capacity as an Ethical Concept* (1967)

Introduction

In 2009, the World Bank and the Food and Agriculture Organization of the United Nations (FAO) released a report called *The Sunken Billions: The Economic Justification for Fisheries Reform*. According to this report, economic losses in marine fisheries due to overfishing, poor management, and economic inefficiency are approximately $50 billion per year (US$). Over the last 30 years, those losses sum to over $2 trillion! The report goes on to argue that well-managed marine fisheries could provide sustainable economic benefits for millions of fisheries and coastal villages and cities. In this chapter we explore the role of economics in designing well-managed fisheries.

Humans share the planet with many other living species. How those biological populations are treated depends in part on whether they are commercially valuable and whether the institutional framework set up to manage the harvesting of that resource provides sufficient conservation incentives to those who are best positioned to protect the resource.

In this chapter, we consider how the process of fisheries management could be reformed to improve both efficiency and sustainability. A commercially valuable species is like a double-edged sword. On one side, the value of the species to humans provides a strong, current reason for human concern about its future. On the other hand, its value may promote excessive harvest. Commercially exploited biological resources can become depleted to the point of extinction if the population is drawn down beyond a critical threshold.

Extinction, although important, is not the only critical renewable resource-management issue. Since any sustainable level of harvest will avoid extinction, how do we choose among them? What sustainable level of harvest is appropriate?

Biological populations belong to a class of renewable resources we will call *interactive resources*, wherein the size of the resource stock (population) is determined jointly by biological considerations and by actions taken by society. The postharvest size of the population, in turn, determines the availability of resources for the future. Thus, humanity's actions affect the flow of these resources over time. Because this flow is not purely a natural phenomenon, the rate of harvest has intertemporal effects. Tomorrow's harvesting choices are affected by today's harvesting behavior.

Using the fishery as a case study, we begin by examining what is meant by an efficient sustainable level of harvest. We then investigate whether efficiency is a sufficiently strong criterion to avoid extinction. Will efficient harvests always result in sustainable outcomes? Having shown how our two social choice criteria apply to fisheries, we turn to an examination of how well our institutions fulfill those criteria. Are normal incentives compatible with efficient sustainable harvest levels?

Unfortunately, we shall discover that in many cases normal incentives are compatible with neither efficiency nor sustainability. Many commercial fisheries can be classified as open access, common–pool resources (Chapter 2), and as such, suffer from overharvesting. The FAO estimates that over 75 percent of the world's fish stocks are either fully exploited or overexploited (FAO, 2009). When the asset value of the resource cannot be protected by existing institutions, a *tragedy of the commons*[1] can result. As we shall see, with so many fisheries experiencing overfishing, finding solutions that meet both efficiency and sustainability criteria is challenging.

Efficient Allocations

The Biological Dimension

Like many other studies, our characterization of the fishery rests on a biological model originally proposed by Schaefer (1957). The Schaefer model posits a particular average relationship between the growth of the fish population and the size of the fish population. This is an average relationship in the sense that it abstracts from such influences as water temperature and the age structure of the population. The model therefore does not attempt to characterize the fishery on a day-to-day basis, but rather in terms of some long-term average in which these various random influences tend to counterbalance each other (see Figure 12.1).

The size of the population is represented on the horizontal axis and the growth of the population on the vertical axis. The graph suggests that there is a range of population sizes ($\underline{S} - S^*$) where population growth increases as the population increases and a range ($S^* - \overline{S}$) where initial increases in population lead to eventual declines in growth. We can shed further light on this relationship by examining more closely the two points ($\underline{S}$ and $\overline{S}$) where the function intersects the horizontal

[1]Garrett Hardin. "The Tragedy of the Common," *Science* 162 (1968): 1243–1247.

FIGURE 12.1 Relationship between the Fish Population (Stock) and Growth

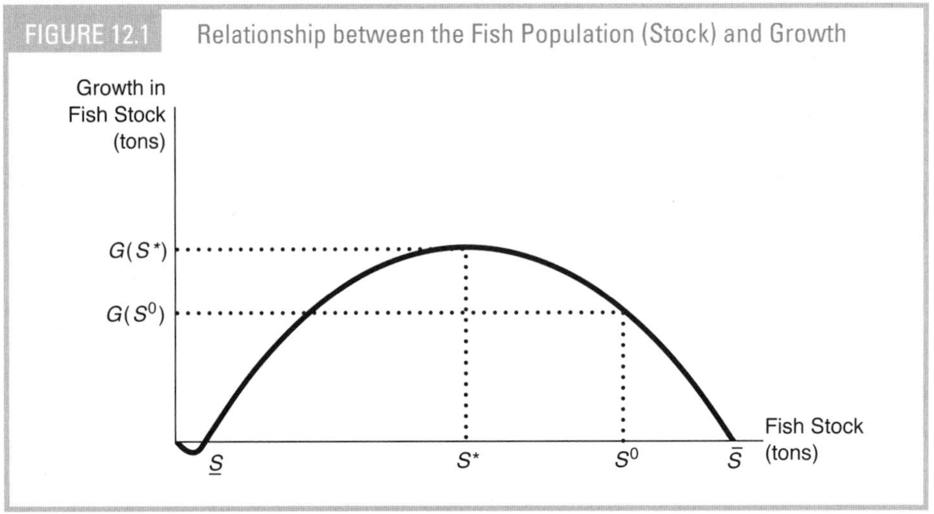

axis and therefore growth in the stock is zero. $\overline{S}$ is known as the natural equilibrium, since this is population size that would persist in the absence of outside influences. Reductions in the stock due to mortality or out-migration would be exactly offset by increases in the stock due to births, growth of the fish in the remaining stock, and in-migration.

This natural equilibrium would persist because it is stable. A *stable equilibrium* is one in which movements away from this population level set forces in motion to restore it. If, for example, the stock temporarily exceeded $\overline{S}$, it would be exceeding the capacity of its habitat (called *carrying capacity*). As a result, mortality rates or out-migration would increase until the stock was once again within the confines of the carrying capacity of its habitat at $\overline{S}$.

This tendency for the population size to return to $\overline{S}$ works in the other direction as well. Suppose the population is temporarily reduced below $\overline{S}$. Because the stock is now smaller, growth would be positive and the size of the stock would increase. Over time, the fishery would move along the curve to the right until $\overline{S}$ is reached again.

What about the other points on the curve? $\underline{S}$, known as the *minimum viable population*, represents the level of population below which growth in population is negative (deaths and out-migration exceed births and in-migration). In contrast to $\overline{S}$, this equilibrium is unstable. Population sizes to the right of $\underline{S}$ lead to positive growth and a movement along the curve to $\overline{S}$ and away from $\underline{S}$. When the population moves to the left of $\underline{S}$, the population declines until it eventually becomes extinct. In this region, no forces act to return the population to a viable level.

A catch level is said to represent a *sustainable yield* whenever it equals the growth rate of the population, since it can be maintained forever. As long as the population size remains constant, the growth rate (and hence the catch) will remain constant as well.

S^* is known in biology as the *maximum sustainable yield population*, defined as the population size that yields the maximum growth; hence, the maximum sustainable yield (catch) is equal to this maximum growth and it represents the largest catch that can be perpetually sustained. Since the catch is equal to the growth, the sustainable yield for any population size (between $\underline{S}$ and $\overline{S}$) can be determined by drawing a vertical line from the stock size of interest on the horizontal axis to the point at which it intersects the function, and drawing a horizontal line over to the vertical axis. The sustainable yield is the growth in the biomass defined by the intersection of this line with the vertical axis. Thus, in terms of Figure 12.1, $G(S^0)$ is the sustainable yield for population size S^0. Since the catch is equal to the growth, population size (and next year's growth) remains the same.

It should now be clear why $G(S^*)$ is the maximum sustainable yield. Larger catches would be possible in the short run, but these could not be sustained; they would lead to reduced population sizes and eventually, if the population were drawn down to a level smaller than $\underline{S}$, to the extinction of the species.

Static Efficient Sustainable Yield

Is the maximum sustainable yield synonymous with efficiency? The answer is no. Recall that efficiency is associated with maximizing the *net* benefit from the use of the resource. If we are to define the efficient allocation, we must include the costs of harvesting as well as the benefits.

Let's begin by defining the efficient sustainable yield without worrying about discounting. The static efficient sustainable yield is the catch level that, if maintained perpetually, would produce the largest annual net benefit. We shall refer to this as the *static efficient sustainable yield* to distinguish it from the *dynamic efficient sustainable yield*, which incorporates discounting. The initial use of this static concept enables us to fix the necessary relationships firmly in mind before dealing with the more difficult role discounting plays. Subsequently, we raise the question of whether or not efficiency always dictates the choice of a sustainable yield as opposed to a catch that changes over time.

We condition our analysis on three assumptions that simplify the analysis without sacrificing too much realism: (1) the price of fish is constant and does not depend on the amount sold, (2) the marginal cost of a unit of fishing effort is constant, and (3) the amount of fish caught per unit of effort expended is proportional to the size of fish population (the smaller the population, the fewer fish caught per unit of effort).

Given these assumptions, we can build the economic model. Under assumption (3), we can overlay harvest-effort functions onto the population function in Figure 12.1. Since the amount of fish caught per unit effort is held constant, the relationship between catch and stock for given levels of effort can be portrayed by the linear functions in Figure 12.2. (For the mathematically inclined, the formula is Equation 3 in the appendix to this chapter). Notice that increasing effort rotates the harvest function up and to the left ($E2 > E1$). The sustained yield associated with each level of effort is the point of intersection of these two curves. If we plot the series of points associated with the possible levels of effort and the sustained yield associated with each effort level, we will have our sustainable yield function defined in terms of effort rather than population as portrayed in Figure 12.3. (Effort could be measured in vessel years, hours of fishing, or some other conventional metric.)

To avoid confusion, notice that increasing fishing effort in Figure 12.2 would result in smaller population sizes and would be recorded as a movement from right to left. Because the variable on the horizontal axis in Figure 12.3 is effort, and not population, an increase in fishing effort is recorded as a movement from left to right.

FIGURE 12.2 Relating Equilibrium Effort, Harvest, and Stock Size

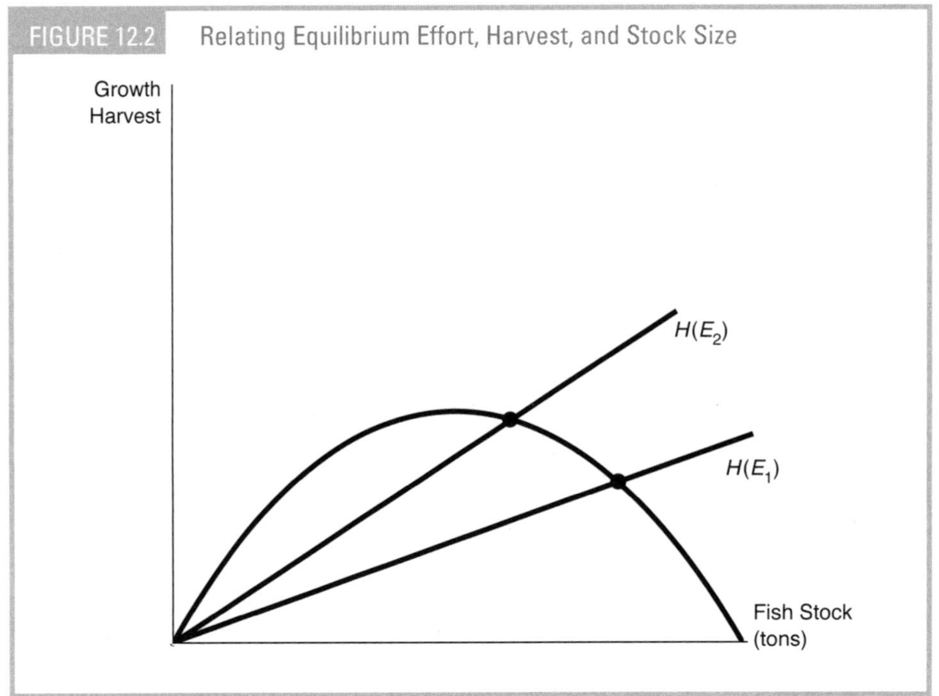

FIGURE 12.3 Sustainable Harvest (Yield)

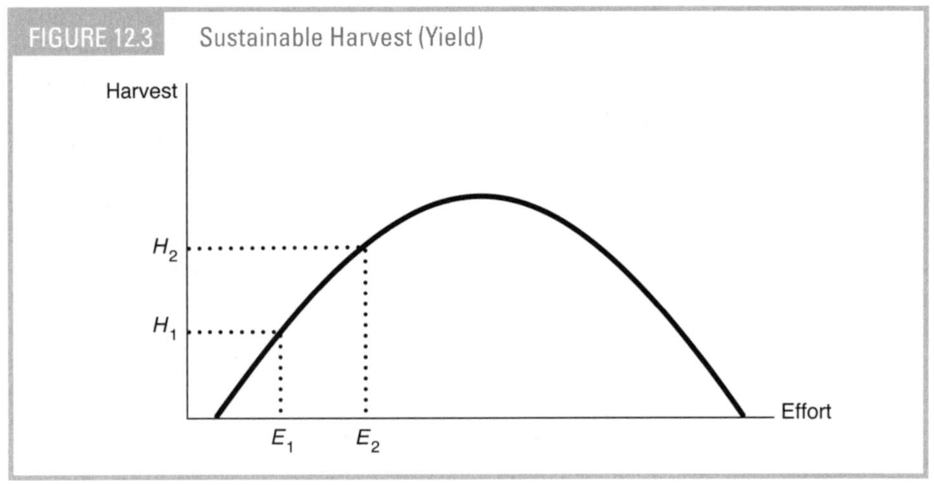

So far so good. To turn this into a complete economic model, we need to determine benefits and costs or, equivalently in this case, total revenue and total costs. From assumption 1 we know that the shape of the biological function dictates the shape of the revenue function. Simply multiplying each sustained yield (harvest) in Figure 12.1 by the constant price, we can turn the physical units (harvest) into monetary units (total revenue). Under assumption 2 we can characterize the final component of our model; the linear function that depicts the total cost is simply calculated as the level of effort times the constant marginal cost of each unit of effort. The resulting figure (12.4) portrays the benefits (revenues) and costs as a function of fishing effort.

In any sustainable yield, annual catches, population, effort levels, and net benefits, by definition, remain constant over time. The static efficient sustainable yield allocation maximizes the constant annual net benefit.

As sustained levels of effort are increased, eventually a point is reached (E^m) at which further effort reduces the sustainable catch (and revenue) for all years. That point, of course, corresponds to the maximum sustainable yield on Figure 12.1 (S^*), meaning that both points reflect the same population and growth levels. Every effort level portrayed in Figures 12.3 and 12.4 corresponds to a specific population level in Figure 12.1.

The net benefit is presented in the diagram as the difference (vertical distance) between benefits (prices times the quantity caught) and costs (the constant marginal cost of effort times the units of effort expended). The efficient level of effort is E^e, that point in Figure 12.4 at which the vertical distance between benefits and costs is maximized.

FIGURE 12.4 Efficient Sustainable Yield for a Fishery

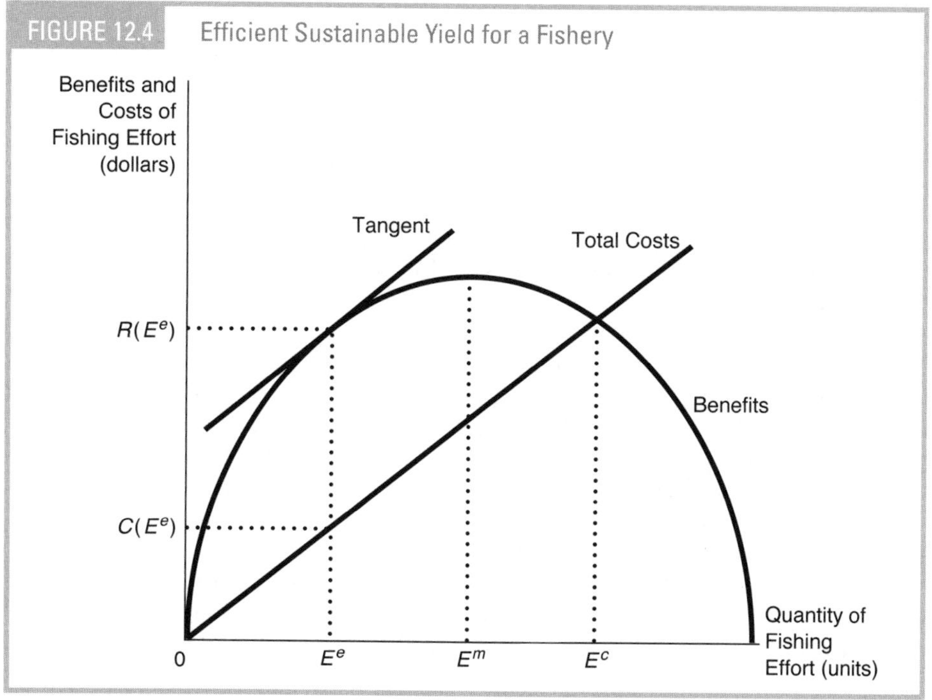

E^e is the efficient level of effort because it is where marginal benefit (which graphically is the slope of the total benefit curve) is equal to marginal cost (the *constant* slope of the total cost curve). Levels of effort higher than E^e are inefficient because the additional cost associated with them exceeds the value of the fish obtained. Can you see why lower levels of effort are also inefficient?

Now we are armed with sufficient information to determine whether or not the maximum sustainable yield is efficient. The answer is clearly no. The maximum sustainable yield would be efficient only if the marginal cost of additional effort were zero. Can you see why? (*Hint*: What is the marginal benefit at the maximum sustainable yield?) Since at E^m the marginal benefit is lower than marginal cost, the efficient level of effort is *less* than that necessary to harvest the maximum sustainable yield. Thus, the static efficient level of effort leads to a *larger* fish population, but a lower annual catch than the maximum sustainable yield level of effort.

To fix these concepts firmly in mind, consider what would happen to the static efficient sustainable yield if a technological change were to occur (e.g., sonar detection) that lowered the marginal cost of fishing. The lower marginal cost would result in a rotation of the total cost curve to the right. With this new cost structure, the old level of effort would no longer be efficient. The marginal cost of fishing (slope of the total cost curve) would now be lower than the marginal benefit (slope of the total benefit curve). Since the marginal cost is constant, the equality of marginal cost and marginal benefit can result only from a decline in marginal benefits. This implies an increase in effort. The new static efficient sustainable yield equilibrium implies more annual effort, a lower population level, a larger annual catch, and a higher net benefit for the fishery.

Dynamic Efficient Sustainable Yield

The static efficient sustainable yield turns out to be the special case of the dynamic efficient sustained yield where the discount rate is zero. It is not difficult to understand why; the static efficient sustained yield is the allocation that maximizes the (identical) net benefit in every period. Any effort levels higher than this would yield temporarily larger catches (and net benefit), but this would be more than offset by a reduced net benefit in the future as the stock reached its new lower level. Thus, the undiscounted net benefits would be reduced.

The effect of a positive discount rate for the management of a fishery is similar to its influence on the allocation of depletable resources—the higher the discount rate, the higher the cost (in terms of forgone current income) to the resource owner of maintaining any given resource stock. When positive discount rates are introduced, the efficient level of effort would be increased beyond that suggested by the static efficient sustained yield with a corresponding decrease in the equilibrium population level.

The increase in the yearly effort beyond the efficient sustained yield level would *initially* result in an increased net benefit from the increased catch. (Remember that the amount of fish caught per unit effort expended is proportional to the size of the population.) However, since this catch exceeds the sustained yield for that population size, the population of fish would be reduced and future population and catch levels would be lower. Eventually, as that level of effort is maintained, a new, lower equilibrium level would be attained when the size of the catch once again equals the growth of the population. Colin Clark (1976) has shown mathematically that in terms of Figure 12.4, as the discount rate is increased, the dynamic efficient level of effort is increased until, with an infinite discount rate, it would become equal to E^c, the point at which net benefits go to zero.

It is easy to see why the use of an infinite discount rate to define the dynamic efficient sustained yield results in allocation E^c. We have seen that temporally interdependent allocations over time give rise to a marginal user cost measuring the opportunity cost of increasing current effort. This opportunity cost reflects the forgone future net benefits when more resources are extracted in the present. For efficient interdependent allocations, the marginal willingness to pay is equal to the marginal user cost plus the marginal cost of extraction.

With an infinite discount rate, this marginal user cost is zero, because no value is received from future allocations. (Do you see why?) This implies that (1) the marginal cost of extraction equals the marginal willingness to pay, which equals the constant price, and (2) total benefits equal total costs.[2] Earlier we demonstrated that the static efficient sustained yield implies a larger fish population than the maximum sustained yield. Once discounting is introduced, it is inevitable that the dynamic efficient sustained yield would imply a smaller fish population than the static efficient sustained yield and it is possible, though not inevitable, that the sustained catch would be smaller. Can you see why? In Figure 12.4 the sustained catch clearly is lower for an infinite discount rate.

The likelihood of the population being reduced below the level supplying the maximum sustainable yield depends on the discount rate. In general, the lower the extraction costs and the higher the discount rate, the more likely it is that the dynamic efficient level of effort will exceed the level of effort associated with the maximum sustainable yield. This is not difficult to see if we remember the limiting case discussed earlier. When the marginal extraction cost is zero, the static efficient sustainable yield and the maximum sustainable yield are equal.

Thus, with zero marginal extraction costs and a positive discount rate, the dynamic efficient level of effort necessarily exceeds not only the static efficient level of effort, but also the level of effort associated with the maximum sustainable yield. Higher extraction costs reduce the static efficient sustainable yield but not

---

[2]This is not difficult to demonstrate mathematically. In our model, the yield (h) can be expressed as $h = qES$, where q is the proportion of the population harvested with one unit of effort, S is the size of the population, and E is the level of effort. One of the conditions a dynamic efficient allocation has to satisfy with an infinite discount rate is $P = a/qS$, where P is the constant price, a is the constant marginal cost per unit of effort, and qS is the number of fish harvested per unit of effort. By multiplying both sides of this equation by h and collecting terms, we obtain $Ph = aE$. The left-hand side is total benefits, while the right is total cost, implying net benefits are zero.

the maximum sustainable yield. (Remember that it is a biological, not an economic, concept.) By reducing efficient effort levels, higher extraction costs reduce the likelihood that discounting would cause the population to be drawn below the maximum sustainable yield level.

Would a dynamically efficient management scheme lead to extinction of the fishery? As Figure 12.4 shows, it would not be possible under the circumstances described here because E^c is the highest dynamically efficient level possible in this model, and that level falls well short of the level needed to drive the population to extinction. However, in more complex models, extinction certainly can be an outcome.

For extinction to occur under a dynamic efficient management scheme, the benefit from extracting the very last unit would have to exceed the cost of extracting that unit (including the costs on future generations). As long as the population growth rate exceeds the discount rate, this will not be the case. If, however, the growth rate is lower than the discount rate, extinction can occur even in an efficient management scheme if the costs of extracting the last unit are sufficiently low.

Why does the biomass rate of growth have anything to do with whether or not an efficient catch profile leads to extinction? Rates of growth determine the productivity of conservation efforts.[3] With high rates of growth, future generations can be easily satisfied. On the other hand, when the rate of growth is very low, it takes a large sacrifice by current generations to produce more fish for future generations. In the limiting case, where the rate of growth is zero, we have a resource with fixed supply and therefore this fishery would become an exhaustible resource. Total depletion would occur whenever the price commanded by the resource is high enough to cover the marginal cost of extracting the last unit.

We have shown that the dynamic efficiency criterion is not automatically consistent with sustaining constant yields perpetually for an interactive renewable resource, since it is mathematically possible for an efficient allocation of a fishery to lead to extinction of the resource. How likely are these criteria to conflict in practice?

It is not as likely as this basic model might imply. Actual fisheries differ from the standard model in two key ways. First, harvesting marginal costs are typically not constant (as they are in the model discussed previously), but rather increase as the remaining stock size diminishes. Second, while the model we discussed holds prices constant, the size of the harvest can affect prices; larger harvests can depress them. Both of these modifications of the basic model suggest additional incentives for conserving the stock.

How empirically important are these incentives? Grafton et al. (2007) examine their importance for four specific fisheries and find not only that extinction is not the efficient outcome in any of the four fisheries but also in general, in this

[3]Note the parallel with the role of the growth rate in efficient timber harvesting in Chapter 11.

reformulated model, the stock level that maximizes the present value of net benefits is actually *larger* than the stock level that supports the maximum sustainable yield. Their results seem to hold both for relatively high discount rates and relatively long-lived fish. (The orange roughy fishery, discussed in more detail below, was one of the four they studied.)

Appropriability and Market Solutions

We have defined an efficient allocation of the fishery over time. The next step is to characterize the normal market allocation and to contrast these two allocations. Where they differ we can entertain the possibility of various public policy corrective means.

Let's first consider the allocation resulting from a fishery managed by a competitive sole owner. A sole owner would have a well-defined property right to the fish. We can establish the behavior of a sole owner by elaborating on Figure 12.4 as is done in Figure 12.5. Note that the two panels share a common horizontal axis, a characteristic that allows us to examine the effect of various fishing effort levels on both graphs.

A sole owner would want to maximize his or her profits. Ignoring discounting for the moment, the owner can increase profits by increasing fishing effort until marginal revenue equals marginal cost. This occurs at effort level E^e, the static efficient sustainable yield, and yields positive profits equal to the difference between $R(E^e)$ and $C(E^e)$.

In ocean fisheries, however, sole owners are unlikely. Ocean fisheries are typically open-access resources—no one exercises complete control over them. Since the property rights to the fishery are not conveyed to any single owner, no fisherman can exclude others from exploiting the fishery.

What problems arise when access to the fishery is completely unrestricted? Open-access resources create two kinds of external costs: a contemporaneous external cost and an intergenerational external cost. The contemporaneous external cost, which is borne by the current generation, involves the overcommitment of resources to fishing—too many boats, too many fishermen, too much effort. As a result, current fishermen earn a substantially lower rate of return on their efforts. The intergenerational external cost, borne by future generations, occurs because overfishing reduces the stock, which, in turn, lowers future profits from fishing.[4]

[4]This will result in fewer fish for future generations as well as smaller profits if the resulting effort level exceeds that associated with the maximum sustainable yield. If the open-access effort level is lower than the maximum sustainable yield effort level (when extraction costs are very high), then reductions in stock would increase the growth in the stock, thus supplying more fish (albeit lower net benefits) to future generations.

FIGURE 12.5 Market Allocation in a Fishery

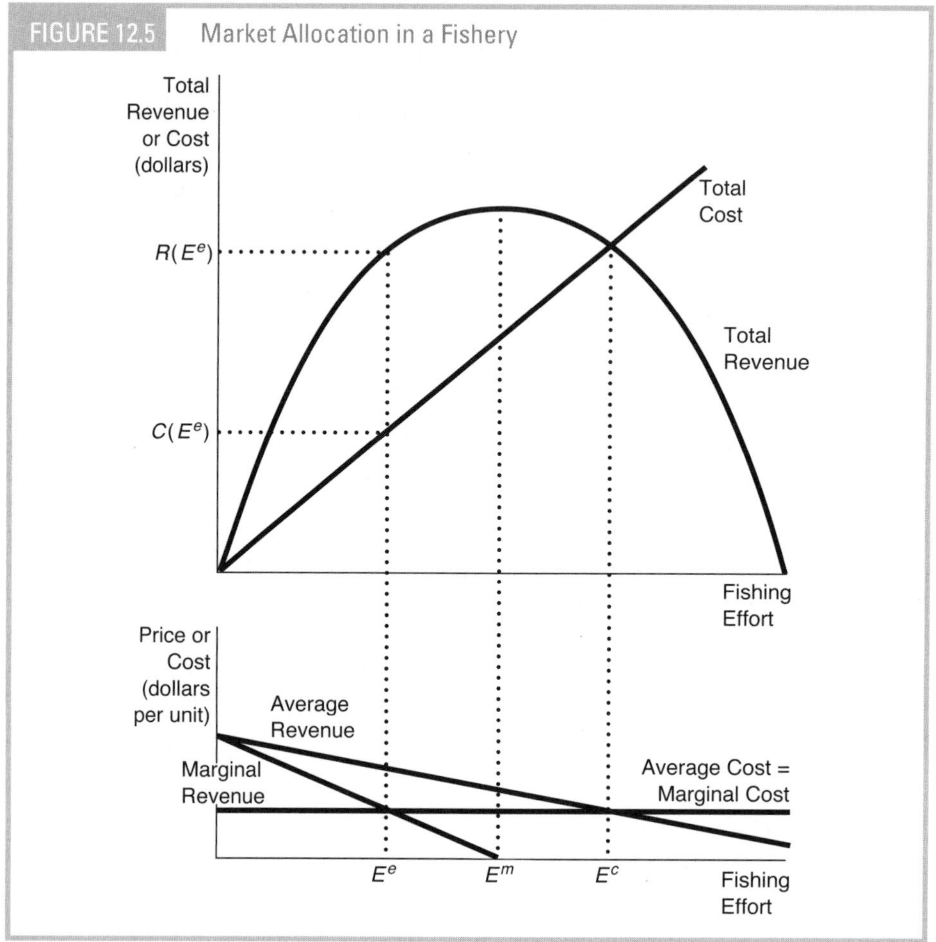

We can use Figure 12.5 to see how these external costs arise.[5] Once too many fishermen have unlimited access to the same common-pool fishery, the property rights to the fish are no longer efficiently defined. At the efficient level, each boat would receive a profit equal to its share of the scarcity rent. This rent, however, serves as a stimulus for new fishermen to enter, pushing up costs and eliminating the rent. Open access results in overexploitation.

The sole owner chooses not to expend more effort than E^e because to do so would reduce the profits of the fishery, resulting in a personal loss to her. When access to the fishery is unrestricted, a decision to expend effort beyond E^e reduces profits to the fishery as a whole but not to that individual fisherman. Most of the decline in profits falls on the other fishermen.

[5]This type of analysis was first used in Gordon (1954).

In an open-access resource, the individual fisherman has an incentive to expend further effort until profits are zero. In Figure 12.5, that point is at effort level E^c, at which average revenue and average cost are equal. It is now easy to see the contemporaneous external cost—too much effort is being expended to catch too few fish, and the cost is substantially higher than it would be in an efficient allocation.

If this point seems abstract, it shouldn't. Many fisheries are currently plagued by precisely these problems. In a productive fishery in the Bering Sea and Aleutian Islands, for example, one study (Huppert, 1990) found significant overcapitalization. While the efficient number of motherships (used to take on and process the catch at sea, so the catch boats do not have to return to port as often) was estimated to be 9, the actual level was 140. As a result, a significant amount of net benefits was lost ($124 million a year). Had the fishery been harvested more slowly, the same catch could have been achieved with fewer boats used closer to their capacity.

In Chapter 2, we stated that the resource owner with exclusive property rights balances the use value against the asset value. When access to the resource is unrestricted, exclusivity is lost. As a result, it is rational for a fisherman to ignore the asset value, since he or she can never appropriate it, and simply maximize the use value. In the process, all the scarcity rent is dissipated. The allocation that results from allowing unrestricted access to the fishery is identical to that resulting from a dynamic efficient sustainable yield when an infinite discount rate is used.

Open-access resources do not automatically lead to a stock lower than (S^*), the one that maximizes the sustained yield. It is possible to draw a cost function with a slope sufficiently steep that it intersects the benefit curve at a point to the left of E^m. Nonetheless, mature, open-access fisheries can be exploited well beyond the point of maximum sustainable yield.

Open-access fishing may or may not pose the threat of species extinction. It depends on the nature of the species and the benefits and costs of an effort level above E^m that would have the effect of driving the stock level below the minimum viable population. Consider the northern bluefin tuna, for example. Considered critically endangered, it is still being harvested at unsustainable levels due to the high market price fishermen receive as a result of its popularity in sushi restaurants. Since the threat of extinction cannot be determined purely from theory, it must be determined by empirical studies on a case-by-case basis.

Are open-access resources and common-pool resources synonymous concepts? They are not. Not all common-pool resources allow unlimited access. Informal arrangements among those harvesting the common-pool resource, which may be fostered by harvester cooperation, can serve to limit access (Example 12.1 presents one such arrangement).

Open-access resources generally violate the efficiency criterion and may violate the sustainability criteria. If these criteria are to be fulfilled, some restructuring of the decision-making environment may be necessary. The next section examines the possible role for government in how that can be accomplished.

EXAMPLE 12.1

Harbor Gangs of Maine and Other Informal Arrangements

Unlimited access to common-pool resources reduces net benefits so drastically that this loss encourages those harvesting the resource to band together to restrict access, if possible. The Maine lobster fishery is one setting where those informal arrangements have served to limit access with some considerable success.

Key among these arrangements is a system of territories that establishes boundaries between fishing areas. Particularly near the off-shore islands, these territories tend to be exclusively harvested by close-knit, disciplined groups of harvesters. These "gangs" restrict access to their territory by various means. (Some methods, although effective, are covert and illegal, such as the practice of cutting the lines to lobster traps owned by new entrants, thereby rendering the traps irretrievable.)

Acheson (2003) found that in every season of the year, the pounds of lobster caught per trap and the size of those lobsters were greater in defended areas. Not only did the larger number of pounds result in more revenue, but also the bigger lobsters brought in a higher price per pound. Informal arrangements were successful in this case, in part, because the Maine lobster stock is also protected by regulations limiting the size of lobsters that can be taken (imposing both minimum and maximum sizes) and prohibiting the harvest of egg-bearing females.

It turns out that many other examples of community *co-management* also offer encouraging evidence for the potential of sustainability. One example, the Chilean abalone (a type of snail called *loco*) is Chile's most valuable fishery. Local fishers began cooperating in 1988 to manage a small stretch (2 miles) of coastline. Today, the co-management scheme involves 700 co-managed areas, 20,000 artisanal fishers, and 2500 miles of coastline.

While it would be a mistake to assume that all common-pool resources are characterized by open access, it would also be a mistake to assume that all informal co-management arrangements automatically provide sufficient social means for producing efficient harvests such that stronger public policy would be unnecessary. A recent study (Gutiérrez et al., 2011) examined 130 fisheries in 44 developed and developing countries. It found that co-management can work, but only in the presence of strong leadership, social cohesion, and complementary incentives such as individual or community quotas. They find that effective community-based co-management can both sustain the resource and protect the livelihoods of nearby fishermen and fishing communities. The existence of nearby protected areas was also found to be an important determinant of success.

Source: Acheson. J. M. (2003). *Capturing the commons: Devising institutions to manage the Maine lobster fishery.* Hanover, NH: University Press of New England.; Gutiérrez, N. L., Hilborn, R., & Omar Defeo, O. (January 5, 2011). Leadership, social capital and incentives promote successful fisheries. *Nature, 470,* 386–389(17 February 2011) doi:10.1038/nature09689. Retrieved from http://www.nature.com/nature/journal/v470/n7334/full/nature09689.html

Public Policy Toward Fisheries

What can be done? A variety of public policy responses is possible. Perhaps it is appropriate to start with circumstances where allowing the market to work can improve the situation.

Raising the Real Cost of Fishing

Perhaps one of the best ways to illustrate the virtues of using economic analysis to help design policies is to show the harsh effects of policy approaches that ignore it. Because the earliest approaches to fishery management had a single-minded focus on attaining the maximum sustainable yield, with little or no thought given to maximizing the net benefit, they provide a useful contrast.

One striking concrete example is the set of policies originally designed to deal with overexploitation of the Pacific salmon fishery in the United States. The Pacific salmon is particularly vulnerable to overexploitation and even extinction because of its migration patterns. Pacific salmon are spawned in the gravel beds of rivers. As juvenile fish, they migrate to the ocean, only to return as adults to spawn in the rivers of their birth. After spawning, they die. When the adults swim upstream, with an instinctual need to return to their native streams, they can easily be captured by traps, nets, or other catching devices.

Recognizing the urgency of the problem, the government took action. To reduce the catch, they raised the cost of fishing. Initially this was accomplished by preventing the use of any barricades on the rivers and by prohibiting the use of traps (the most efficient catching devices) in the most productive areas. These measures proved insufficient, since mobile techniques (trolling, nets, and so on) proved quite capable by themselves of overexploiting the resource. Officials then began to close designated fishing areas and suspend fishing in other areas for certain periods of time. In Figure 12.4, these measures would be reflected as a rotation of the total cost curve to the left until it intersected the total benefits (revenue) curve at a level of effort equal to E^e. The aggregate of all these regulations had the desired effect of curtailing the yield of salmon.

Were these policies efficient? They were not even though they resulted in the efficient catch! This statement may seem inconsistent, but it is not. Efficiency implies not only that the catch must be at the efficient level, but also it must be extracted at the lowest possible cost. It was this condition that was violated by these policies (see Figure 12.6).

Figure 12.6 reflects the total cost in an unregulated fishery (TC_1) and the total cost after these policies were imposed (TC_2). The net benefit received from an efficient policy is shown graphically as the vertical distance between total cost and total benefit. After the policy, however, the net benefit was reduced to zero; the net benefit (represented by vertical distance) was lost to society. Why?

The net benefit was squandered on the use of excessively expensive means to catch the desired yield of fish. Rather than use traps to reduce the cost of catching

FIGURE 12.6 Effect of Regulation

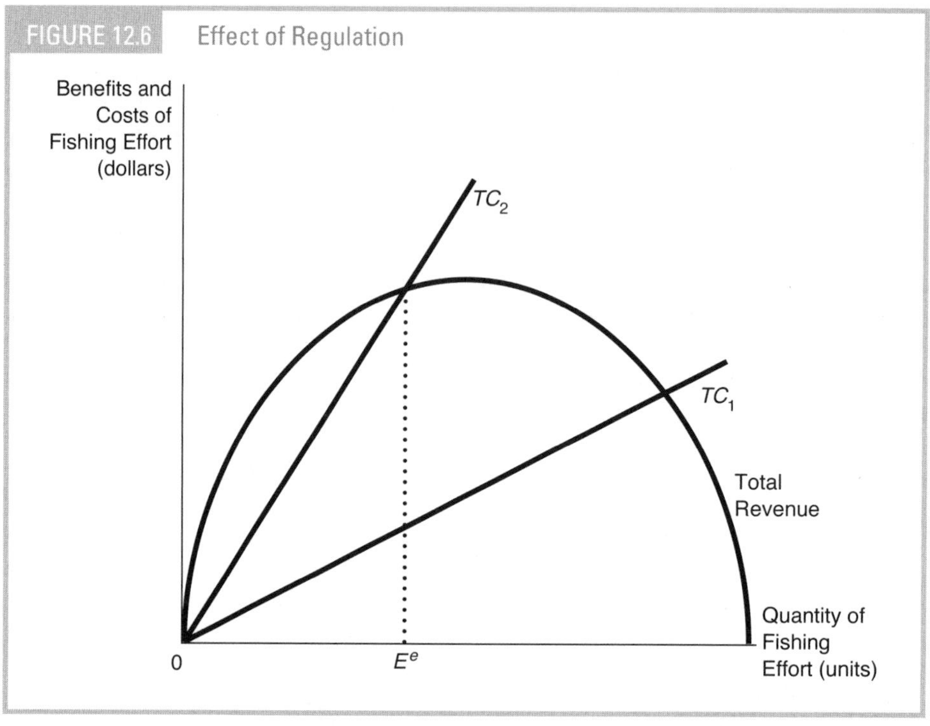

the desired number of fish, traps were prohibited. Larger expenditures on capital and labor were required to catch the same number of fish. This additional capital and labor represent one source of the waste.

The limitations on fishing times had a similar effect on cost. Rather than allowing fishermen to spread their effort out over time so the boats and equipment could be more productively utilized, fishermen were forced to buy larger boats to allow them to take as much as possible during the shorter seasons. (As one extreme example, Tillion (1985) reported that the 1982 herring season in Prince William Sound lasted only four hours and the catch still exceeded the area quota.) Significant overcapitalization produced gross inefficiency.

Regulation imposed other costs as well. It was soon discovered that while the above regulations were adequate to protect the depletion of the fish population, they failed to curb the incentive for individual fishermen to increase their share of the take. Even though the profits would be small because of high costs, new technological change would allow adopters to increase their shares of the market and put others out of business.

To protect themselves, the fishermen were eventually successful in introducing bans on new technology. These restrictions took various forms, but two are particularly noteworthy. The first was the banning of the use of thin-stranded, monofilament net. The coarse-stranded net it would have replaced was visible to the salmon in the daytime and therefore could be avoided by them. As a result, it was useful only at night. By contrast, the thinner monofilament nets could be successfully used during the daylight hours as well as at night. Monofilament nets were banned in Canada and the United States soon after they appeared.

The most flagrantly inefficient regulation was one in Alaska that barred gill netters in Bristol Bay from using engines to propel their boats. This regulation lasted until the 1950s and heightened the public's awareness of the anachronistic nature of this regulatory approach. The world's most technologically advanced nation was reaping its harvest from the Bering Sea in sailboats, while the rest of the world—particularly Japan and the Soviet Union—was modernizing their fishing fleets at a torrid pace!

Time-restriction regulations had a similar effect. Limiting fishing time provides an incentive to use that time as intensively as possible. Huge boats facilitate large harvests within the period and therefore are profitable but are very inefficient; the same harvest could normally be achieved with fewer, smaller (less expensive) boats used to their optimum capacity.

Guided by a narrow focus on biologically determined sustainable yield that ignored costs, these policies led to a substantial loss in the net benefit received from the fishery. Costs are an important dimension of the problem, and when they are ignored, the incomes of fishermen suffer. When incomes suffer, further conservation measures become more difficult to implement, and incentives to violate the regulations are intensified.

Technical change presents a further problem, with attempts to use cost-increasing regulations to reduce fishing effort. Technical innovations can lower the cost of fishing, thereby offsetting the increases imposed by the regulations. In the New England fishery, for example, Jin et al. (2002) report that the introduction of new technologies such as fishfinders and electronic navigation aids in the 1970s and 1980s led to higher catches and declines in the abundance of the stocks despite the extensive controls in place at the time.

Taxes

Is it possible to provide incentives for cost reduction while assuring that the yield is reduced to the efficient level? Can a more efficient policy be devised? Economists who have studied the question believe that more efficient policies are possible.

Consider a tax on effort. In Figure 12.6, taxes on effort would also be represented as a rotation of the total cost line and the after-tax cost to the fishermen would be represented by line TC_2. Since the after-tax curve coincides with TC_2, the cost curve for all those inefficient regulations, doesn't this imply that the tax system is just as inefficient? No! The key to understanding the difference is the distinction between *transfer costs* and *real resource costs.*

Under a regulation system of the type described earlier in this chapter, all of the costs included in TC_2 are real resource costs, which involve utilization of resources. Transfer costs, by contrast, involve transfers of resources from one part of society to another, rather than their dissipation. Transfers do represent costs to that part of society bearing them, but are exactly offset by the gain received by the recipients.

Unlike real resource costs, resources are not used up with transfers. Thus, the calculation of the size of the net benefit should subtract real-resource costs, but not transfer costs, from benefits. For society as a whole, transfer costs are retained as part of the net benefit; only who receives them is affected.

In Figure 12.6, the net benefit under a tax system is identical to that under an efficient allocation. The net benefit represents a transfer cost to the fisherman that is exactly offset by the revenues received by the tax collector. This discussion should not obscure the fact that, as far as the individual fisherman is concerned, tax payments are very real costs. Rent normally received by a sole owner is now received by the government. Since the tax revenues involved can be substantial, fishermen wishing to have the fishery efficiently managed may object to this particular way of doing it. They would prefer a policy that restricts catches while allowing them to keep the rents. Is that possible?

Catch Share Programs

Catch share programs offer this option. The Magnuson Stevens Act authorizes several types of catch share approaches under its "limited access privilege" program. All of them allocate a portion of the total allowable catch to individuals, communities, or cooperatives. Programs in this category include individual fishing quotas (IFQs), individual transferable quotas (ITQs), and territorial use rights fisheries (TURFs).[6] An ITQ program is a specific IFQ program where harvesting privileges can be transferred subsequent to initial allocations, while TURFs grant rights to a geographic area. All of these create a type of harvest entitlement either in the fishery as a whole or in a specific geographic area. By 2012, all U.S. fisheries were covered by annual catch limits.

ITQs. Let's first consider individual transferable quotas. Several of their identifiable characteristics serve to enhance efficiency:

1. The quotas entitle the holder to catch a specified share of the total authorized catch of a specified type of fish.
2. The catch authorized by the quotas held by all fishermen should be equal to the efficient catch for the fishery.
3. The quotas should be freely transferable among fishermen and markets should send appropriate price signals about the value of the fishery.

Each of these three characteristics plays an important role in obtaining an efficient allocation. Suppose, for example, the quota was defined in terms of the right to own and use a fishing boat rather than in terms of catch—not an uncommon type of quota. Such a quota is not efficient because under this type of quota an inefficient incentive still remains for each boat owner to build larger boats, to place extra equipment on them, and to spend more time fishing. These actions would expand the capacity of each boat and cause the actual catch to exceed the target

---

[6]NOAA Catch Share Policy, *Executive Summary, 2013*. Retrieved from http://www.nmfs.noaa.gov/sfa/domes_fish/catchshare/docs/noaa_cs_policy.pdf

(efficient) catch. In a nutshell, the boat quota limits the number of boats fishing but does not limit the amount of fish caught by each boat. If we are to reach and sustain an efficient allocation, it is the catch that must ultimately be limited.

While the purpose of the second characteristic is obvious, the role of transferability deserves more consideration. With transferability, the entitlement to fish flows naturally to those gaining the most benefit from it because their costs are lower. Because it is valuable, the transferable quota commands a positive price. Those who have quotas but also have high costs find they make more money selling the quotas than using them. Meanwhile, those who have lower costs find they can purchase more quotas and still make money.

Transferable quotas also encourage technological progress. Adopters of new cost-reducing technologies can make more money on their existing quotas and make it profitable to purchase new quotas from others who have not adopted the technology. Therefore, in marked contrast to the earlier regulatory methods used to raise costs, both the tax system and the transferable quota system encourage the development of new technologies.

How about the distribution of the rent? In a quota system, the distribution of the rent depends crucially on how the quotas are initially allocated. There are many possibilities with different outcomes. The first possibility is for the government to auction off these quotas. With an auction, government would appropriate all the rent and the outcome would be very similar to the outcome of the tax system. If the fishermen do not like the tax system, they would not like the auction system either.

In an alternative approach, the government could give the quotas to the fishermen, for example, in proportion to their historical catch. The fishermen could then trade among themselves until a market equilibrium is reached. All the rent would be retained by the current generation of fishermen. Fishermen who might want to enter the market would have to purchase the quotas from existing fishermen. Competition among the potential purchasers would drive up the price of the transferable quotas until it reflected the market value of future rents, appropriately discounted.[7]

Thus, this type of quota system allows the rent to remain with the fishermen, but only the current generation of fishermen. Future generations see little difference between this quota system and a tax system; in either case, they have to pay to enter the industry, whether it is through the tax system or by purchasing the quotas.

In 1986, a limited ITQ system was established in New Zealand to protect its deepwater trawl fishery (Newell et al., 2005). Although this was far from being the only, or even the earliest, application of ITQs (see Table 12.1), it is the world's largest and provides an unusually rich opportunity to study how this approach works in practice. Some 130 species are fished commercially in

---

[7]This occurs because the maximum bid any potential entrant would make is the value to be derived from owning that permit. This value is equal to the present value of future rents (the difference between price and marginal cost for each unit of fish sold). Competition will force the purchaser to bid near that maximum value, lest he or she lose the quota.

TABLE 12.1 Countries with Individual Transferable Quota Systems

Country	Number of Species Covered
Argentina	1
Australia	26
Canada	52
Chile	9
Denmark	1
Estonia	2
Falkland Islands	4
Greenland	1
Iceland	25
Italy	1
Morocco	1*
Mozambique	4
Namibia	10
The Netherlands	7
New Zealand	97
Portugal	1*
South Africa	1*
United States	6

*Complete species list unavailable. Norway, Peru, and Russia also use ITQ systems as part of their fisheries management.

Source: Adapted from Chu, C. (2009). Thirty years later: The global growth of ITQs and their influence on stock status in marine fisheries. *Fish and Fisheries, 10,*217–230; Arnason, R. (Summer 2012). Property rights in fisheries: How much can individual transferable quotas accomplish? *Review of Environmental Economics and Policy. 6*(2), 217–236.

New Zealand.[8] The Fisheries Amendment Act of 1986 that set up the program covered 17 inshore species and 9 offshore species. By 2004, it had expanded to cover 70 species. Newell et al. (2005) found that the export value of these species ranged from NZ $700/metric ton for jack mackerel to NZ $40,000/metric ton for rock lobster.[9]

Because this program was newly developed, allocating the quotas proved relatively easy. The New Zealand Economic Exclusion Zone (EEZ) was divided geographically into quota-management regions. The total allowable catches (TACs) for the seven basic species were divided into individual transferable quotas by quota-management regions. By 2000, 275 quota markets were in existence.

[8]Ministry of Fisheries, New Zealand, www.fish.govt.nz.

[9]The New Zealand Ministry of Fisheries reports that the average quota increased in value from $2.7 billion in 1996 to $3.8 billion in 2007.

Quotas were initially allocated to existing firms based on their average catch over the period from 1982 to 1984. The rights to harvest were denominated in terms of a specific amount of fish, but were granted only for a 10-year period. At the same time as the deep-sea fishery policy was being developed, the inshore fishery began to fall on hard times. Too many participants were chasing too few fish. Some particularly desirable fish species were being seriously overfished. While the need to reduce the amount of pressure being put on the population was rather obvious, the means to accomplish that reduction was not at all obvious. Although it was relatively easy to prevent new fishermen from entering the fisheries, it was harder to figure out how to reduce the pressure from those who had been fishing in the area for years or even decades. Because fishing is characterized by economies of scale, simply reducing everyone's catch proportionately wouldn't make much sense. That would simply place higher costs on everyone and waste a great deal of fishing capacity as all boats sat around idle for a significant proportion of time. A better solution would clearly be to have fewer boats harvesting the stock. That way each boat could be used closer to its full capacity without depleting the population. Which fishermen should be asked to give up their livelihood and leave the industry?

The economic-incentive approach addressed this problem by having the government buy back catch quotas from those willing to sell them. Initially, this was financed out of general revenues; subsequently, it was financed by a fee on catch quotas. Essentially, each fisherman stated the lowest price that he or she would accept for leaving the industry; the regulators selected those who could be induced to leave at the lowest price, paid the stipulated amount from the fee revenues, and retired their licenses to fish for this species. It wasn't long before a sufficient number of licenses had been retired and the population was protected. Because the program was voluntary, those who left the industry did so only when they felt they had been adequately compensated. Meanwhile, those who paid the fee realized that this small investment would benefit them greatly in the future as the population recovered. A difficult and potentially dangerous pressure on a valuable natural resource had been alleviated by the creative use of an approach that changed the economic incentives.

Toward the end of 1987, however, a new problem emerged. The stock of one species (orange roughy) turned out to have been seriously overestimated by biologists. Since the total allocation of quotas was derived from this estimate, the practical implication was that an unsustainably high level of quotas had been issued; the stock was in jeopardy. The New Zealand government began buying some quotas back from fishermen, but this turned out to be quite expensive with NZ$45 million spent on 15,000 tons of quotas from inshore fisheries.

Faced with the unacceptably large budget implications of buying back a significant amount of quotas, the government ultimately shifted to a percentage-share allocation of quotas. Under this system, instead of owning quotas defined in terms of a specific quantity of fish, fishermen own percentage shares of a total allowable catch. The total allowable catch is determined annually by the government. In this way the government can annually adjust the total allowable catch, based on the latest stock assessment estimates, without having to buy back (or sell) large amounts of quota.

This approach affords greater protection to the stock but increases the financial risk to the fishermen.

The quota markets in New Zealand have been quite active. By 2000, 140,000 leases and 23,000 sales of quotas had occurred. Newell et al. (2005) found that 22 percent of quota owners participated in a market transaction in the first year of the program. By 2000, this number had risen to 70 percent.

Despite this activity, some implementation problems have emerged. Fishing effort is frequently not very well targeted. Species other than those sought (known as "bycatch") may well end up as part of the catch. If those species are also regulated by quotas and the fishermen do not have sufficient ITQs to cover the bycatch, they are faced with the possibility of being fined when they land the unauthorized fish. Dumping the bycatch overboard avoids the fines, but since the jettisoned fish frequently do not survive, this represents a double waste—not only is the stock reduced, but also the harvested fish are wasted.

Managers have also had to deal with "high-grading," which can occur when quotas specify the catch in terms of weight of a certain species, but the value of the catch is affected greatly by the size of the individual fish. To maximize the value of the quota, fishermen have an incentive to throw back the less valuable (typically smaller) fish, keeping only the most valuable individuals. As with bycatch, when release mortality is high, high-grading results in both smaller stocks and wasted harvests.

One possible strategy is simply banning discarding, but due to the difficulties of monitoring and enforcement, that is not as straightforward a solution as it may seem. Kristoffersson and Rickertsen (2009) examine whether a ban on discarding has been effective in the Icelandic cod fishery. They use a model of a fishery with an ITQ program and apply it to the Icelandic cod fishery. They estimate that longline vessels would discard up to 25 percent of the catch of small cod and gillnet vessels up to 67 percent. Their analysis found that quota price did not seem to be an influencing factor, but the existence of a system of quotas and the size of the hold in which the harvested fish are kept do matter. They suggest that to get the "most bang for the buck," enforcement efforts should be directed at gillnet vessels and on fisheries with small hold capacities.

Some fisheries managers have successfully solved both problems by allowing fishermen to cover temporary overages with allowances subsequently purchased or leased from others. As long as the market value of the "extra" fish exceeds the cost of leasing quotas, the fishermen will have an incentive to land and market the fish and the stock will not be placed in jeopardy.

Worldwide, ITQs are currently used by 22 countries to manage hundreds of different species (Table 12.1). The annual global catch taken under ITQs may be as large as a quarter of the global harvest (Arnason, 2012). The fact that ITQ systems are spreading to new fisheries so rapidly suggests that their potential is being increasingly recognized. This expansion does not mean the absence of any concerns. In 1997, the United States issued a moratorium on the implementation of new ITQ programs, which expired in 2002. Issues about the duration of catch shares, whether shareholders need to be active in the fishery and the distributional implications all remain contentious.

Although ITQ systems are far from perfect, frequently they offer the opportunity to improve on traditional fisheries management (see Example 12.2).

EXAMPLE 12.2

The Relative Effectiveness of Transferable Quotas and Traditional Size and Effort Restrictions in the Atlantic Sea Scallop Fishery

Theory suggests that transferable quotas will produce more cost-effective outcomes in fisheries than traditional restrictions, such as minimum legal size and maximum effort controls. Is this theoretical expectation compatible with the actual experience in implemented systems?

In a fascinating study, economist Robert Repetto (2001) examined this question by comparing Canadian and American approaches to controlling the sea scallop fishery off the Atlantic coast. While Canada adopted a transferable quota system, the United States adopted a mix of size, effort, and area controls. The comparison provides a rare opportunity to exploit a natural experiment since scallops are not migratory and the two countries use similar fishing technologies. Hence, it is reasonable to presume that the differences in experience are largely due to the difference in management approaches.

What were the biological consequences of these management strategies for the two fisheries?

- The Canadian fishery was not only able to maintain the stock at a higher level of abundance but it was also able to deter the harvesting of undersized scallops.
- In the United States, stock abundance levels declined and undersized scallops were harvested at high levels.

What were the economic consequences of these differences?

- Revenue per sea-day increased significantly in the Canadian fishery, due largely to the sevenfold increase in catch per sea-day made possible by the larger stock abundance.
- In the United States, fishery revenue per sea-day fell, due not only to the fall in the catch per day that resulted from the decline in stock abundance, but also to the harvesting of undersized scallops.
- Although the number of Canadian quota holders was reduced from nine to seven over a 14-year period, 65 percent of the quota remained in its original hands. The evidence suggests that smaller players were apparently not at a competitive disadvantage.

What were the equity implications?

- Both US and Canadian fisheries have traditionally operated on the "lay" system, which divides the revenue among crew, captain, and owner according to preset percentages, after subtracting certain operating expenditures. This means that all parties remaining in the fishery after regulation shared in the increasing rents.

In these fisheries at least, it seems that the expectations flowing from the theory were borne out by the experience.

Source: Repetto, R. (2001). A natural experiment in fisheries management. *Marine Policy, 25,* 252–264.

In its 2012 annual report, to Congress, NOAA reported that 32 stocks have been rebuilt. Some 41 stocks (19 percent) are still overfished, but that is down from 45 just a year earlier.

Costello, Gaines, and Lynham (2008) examined the global effectiveness of these polices in over 11,000 fisheries from 1950 to 2003. Fisheries with catch share rules, including ITQs, experienced much less frequent collapse than fisheries without them. In fact, they found that by 2003 the fraction of fisheries with ITQs that had collapsed was only half that of non-ITQ fisheries. They suggest that this might be an underestimate since many fisheries with ITQs have not had them for very long. This large study suggests that well-designed property rights regimes (catch shares or ITQs more specifically) may help prevent fisheries collapse and/or help stocks of some species recover. Chu (2009) examined 20 stocks after ITQ programs were implemented and found that 12 of those had improvements in stock size. Eight, however, continued to decline. Apparently, ITQs can sometimes help, but they are no panacea. In the next chapter we will consider whether ITQs can help to conserve different marine species such as whales.

Territorial Use Rights Fisheries (TURFs). An alternative to ITQs is to allocate rights to a specific area for a specific species or group of species, rather than to a portion of the total allowable catch. Such geographic-based rights systems are called territorial use rights fisheries or TURFs. Like ITQs, TURFs typically grant access rights, not ownership rights, to harvesters.

TURFs can allow access to a layer of the water column (such as the bottom of the ocean or the surface, for example) in a specific zone. They could also allow access to a specific oyster bed or a raft for mollusks. They could be granted to individuals, communities, corporations, or even to nations. An economic exclusion zone (EEZ) is a TURF granted to an individual nation.

Early examples of operating TURFs can be found in Japan. These now well-established TURFs allocate zones to local fisher organizations called Fishery Cooperative Assocations (FCAs). Approximately 1,300 FCAs now operate in Japan (Wilen et al., 2012). They can also be found in Chile. With its 3,000 mile shoreline, Chile has created management and exploitation areas (MEAs) along its nearshore. These TURFs help manage the economically important Chilean abalone and sea urchin (Wilen et al., 2012).

TURFs can allow for more economically efficient use of the fishery resource by creating a form of property right, albeit a different property right from that conveyed by an ITQ. Despite their differences, both types of property rights create incentives to protect the future value of the resource, which in turn can incentivize self-enforcement mechanisms. They also can improve the welfare of small fishing communities.

While TURFs do help reduce the open-access problem, the value of a TURF is complicated by the fact that fish are mobile and therefore do not stay in one location. Since a TURF is site specific, its value is impacted by capture outside of the TURF. Obviously, for stocks that do not migrate far, the value of a TURF is enhanced.

Some researchers have suggested that some combination of TURF and ITQ policies may be most efficient. Debate 12.1 considers this question.

ITQs or TURFs? Species, Space, or Both?

DEBATE 12.1

ITQs and TURFs can improve economic efficiency and help protect fisheries from overexploitation. Is one management method better than another? Can they be usefully combined?

Species-based ITQs have proven very popular and they can, in theory, create efficient harveting and conservation incentives. However, in practice enforcement can be challenging and they suffer from several externalities. Some of the most prominent externalties, including gear impacts on ecosystems, spatial externalities and cross-species interactions, might actually be increased by ITQs. Let's see how.

Typically the total allowable catch (TAC) is divided amongst several, perhaps numerous, owners. Although they do not compete over the size of their catch (since that is fixed by their catch share), they do still compete over the timing of that catch. Timing might matter a great deal when the most productive harvesting periods (in terms of reducing the private effort required per unit catch) turn out to be precisely the periods that impose the largest external costs (say by increasing the likelihood of bycatch or negatively impacting the juvenile stock). As such, they help solve one problem (assuring a sustainable total catch), while creating another (encouraging a harvest timing that increases external costs).

The Coase theorem (Chapter 2) suggests that these ownership rights should, in principle, create incentives to solve the remaining externalities, as well, but in practice, the transactions costs of such negotiations are apparently prohibitively high.

What about TURFs? TURFs help solve the problem of managing harvests over time and space and can help protect sensitive areas given that an individual or group has sole rights to that area. Local cooperatives have the advantage of being able in principle to manage interspecies interactions and habitat destruction, but in practice TURFs tend to suffer from conflict and coordination problems. Another common criticism of TURFs is that the scale must match the range of the species and many TURFs do not (or cannot) achieve this size.

Rather than framing the issue as whether ITQs or TURFs are the best choice, it may be that each has its own niche. Certainly, in developing countries with weak institutional structures, TURFs offer many advantages over species-based ITQs. TURFs also may be most appropriate for small, local populations. On the other hand, ITQs have been used successfully for many marine fisheries. Clearly, one size does not fit all for fisheries policy.

Source: Wilen, J. E., Cancino, J., & Uchida, H. (Summer 2012), The economics of territorial use rights fisheries, or TURFs. *Review of Environmental Economics and Policy*, *6*(2), 237–257.

Aquaculture

Having demonstrated that inefficient management of the fishery results from treating it as an open-access resource, one obvious solution is to allow some fisheries to be privately held. This approach can work when the fish are not very mobile, when they can be confined by artificial barriers, or when they instinctively return to their place of birth to spawn.

The advantages of such a move go well beyond the ability to preclude overfishing. The owner is encouraged to invest in the resource and undertake measures that will increase the productivity (yield) of the fishery. (For example, adding certain nutrients to the water or controlling the temperature can markedly increase the yields of some species.) The controlled raising and harvesting of fish is called *aquaculture*. Probably the highest yields ever attained through aquaculture resulted from using rafts to raise mussels. Some 300,000 kilograms per hectare of mussels, for example, have been raised in this manner in the Galician bays of Spain. This productivity level approximates those achieved in poultry farming, widely regarded as one of the most successful attempts to increase the productivity of farm-produced animal protein.

Japan became an early leader in aquaculture, undertaking some of the most advanced aquaculture ventures in the world. The government has been supportive of these efforts, mainly by creating private property rights for waters formerly held in common. The governments of the prefectures (which are comparable to states in the United States) initiate the process by designating the areas to be used for aquaculture. The local fishermen's cooperative associations then partition these areas and allocate the subareas to individual fishermen for exclusive use. This exclusive control allows the individual owner to invest in the resource and to manage it effectively and efficiently.

Another market approach to aquaculture involves *fish ranching* rather than *fish farming*. Whereas fish farming involves cultivating fish over their lifetime in a controlled environment, fish ranching involves holding them in captivity only for the first few years of their lives.

Fish ranching relies on the strong homing instincts in certain fish, such as Pacific salmon or ocean trout, which permits their ultimate return and capture. The young salmon or ocean trout are hatched and confined in a convenient catch area for approximately 2 years. When released, they migrate to the ocean. Upon reaching maturity, they instinctually return to the place of their births, where they are harvested.

Fish farming has certainly affected the total supply of harvested fish. Aquaculture is currently the fastest-growing animal food production sector. In 1970, it was estimated that 3.9 percent of fish consumed globally were raised on farms. By 2008, this proportion had risen to 46 percent. (Between 1970 and 2008, global per capita supply of farm-raised fish increased from 1.5 pounds to 17.2 pounds.)

In China, growth rates in aquaculture have been even higher and aquaculture represents more than two-thirds of fisheries production. China has become the largest producer (and exporter) of seafood in the world (see Figure 12.7), now producing 62 percent of the global supply of farmed fish. Shrimp, eel, tilapia, sea bass, and carp are all intensively farmed. While the top five producers (in volume) of fish from aquaculture in 2006 were China, India, Vietnam, Thailand, and Indonesia, growth rates in aquaculture production were highest in Uganda, Guatemala, Mozambique, Malawi, and Togo.[10]

Aquaculture is certainly not the answer for all fish. Today, it works well for certain species, but other species will probably never be harvested domestically. Furthermore, fish farming can create environmental problems (see Debate 12.2). Nonetheless, it is comforting to know that aquaculture can provide a safety valve in some regions and for some fish and in the process take some of the pressure off the overstressed natural fisheries. The challenge will be to keep aquaculture sustainable.

FIGURE 12.7 China's Rising Share of Global Aquaculture

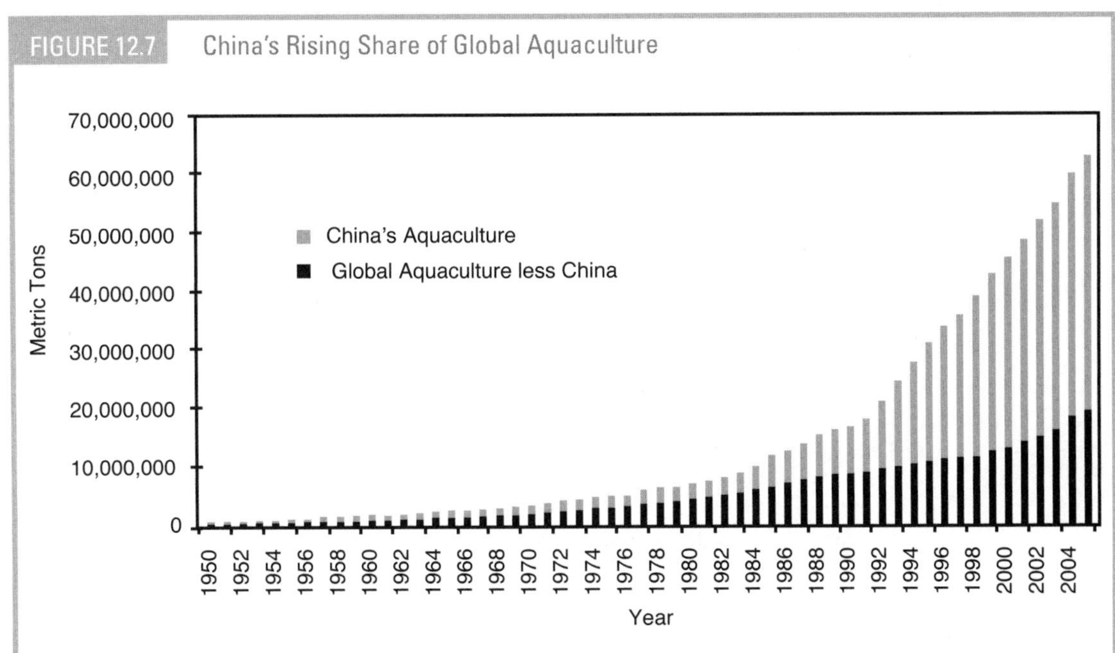

Source: FAO Statistics and Information Service of the Fisheries and Aquaculture Department. 2013. Aquaculture production (Quantities and values) 1950-2011. FISHSTAT Plus - Universal software for fishery statistical time series [online or CD-ROM]. Food and Agriculture Organization of the United Nations. Available at: http://www.fao.org/fishery/statistics/software/fishstat/en.

[10]Food and Agriculture Organization of the United Nations. *State of the World's Fisheries and Aquaculture* (2008) ftp://ftp.fao.org/docrep/fao/011/i0250e/i0250e.pdf.

DEBATE 12.2 Aquaculture: Does Privatization Cause More Problems Than It Solves?

Privatization of commercial fisheries, namely through fish farming, has been touted as a solution to the overfishing problem. For certain species, it has been a great success. Some types of shellfish, for example, are easily managed and farmed through commercial aquaculture. For other species, however, the likelihood of success is not so clear-cut.

Atlantic salmon is a struggling species in the northeastern United States and for several rivers, is listed as "endangered." Salmon farming takes the pressure off of the wild stocks. Atlantic salmon are intensively farmed off the coast of Maine, in northeastern Canada, in Norway, and in Chile. Farmed Atlantic salmon make up almost all of the farmed salmon market and more than half of the total global salmon market. While farmed salmon offer a good alternative to wild salmon and aquaculture has helped meet the demand for salmon from consumers, it is not problem-free.

Farmed fish escapees from the pens threaten native species, pollution that leaks from the pens creates a large externality, and pens that are visible from the coastline degrade the view of coastal residents. The crowded pens also facilitate the prevalence and diffusion of several diseases and illnesses, such as sea lice and salmon anemia. Antibiotics used to keep the fish healthy are considered dangerous for humans. Diseases in the pens can also be transferred to wild stocks. In 2007, the Atlantic Salmon Federation and 33 other conservation groups called on salmon farms to move their pens farther away from sensitive wild stocks.

And the concerns do not end there. Currently, many small species of fish, like anchovies or herring, are being harvested to feed carnivorous farmed fish. Scientists argue that this is not an efficient way to produce protein, since it takes 3–5 pounds of smaller fish to produce 1 pound of farmed salmon.

Pollution externalities associated with the increased production include contaminated water supplies for the fish ponds and heavily polluted wastewater. Some farmers raising their fish in contaminated water have managed by adding illegal veterinary drugs and pesticides to the fish feed, creating food safety concerns. Some tested fish flesh has been found to contain heavy metals, mercury, and flame retardants. In 2007, the United States refused 310 import shipments of seafood; 210 of those were drug-chemical refusals.

While solving some problems, intensive aquaculture has created others. Potential solutions include open-ocean aquaculture (moving pens out to sea), closing pens, monitoring water quality, and improving enforcement. Clearly, sole-ownership to the fishery isn't a silver bullet when externalities are prevalent.

Sources: Atlantic Salmon Federation; Fishstat FAO 2007; Barboza, D. (2007, December 15). China's seafood industry: Dirty water, dangerous fish. *New York Times*.

Subsidies and Buybacks

Excess fleet capacity or overcapitalization is prevalent in many commercial fisheries. Overcapacity encourages overfishing. Many subsidies exacerbate this effect by encouraging overcapacity and overcapitalization. Fuel subsidies, tax exemptions, fish price supports, and grants for new vessels are common forms of subsidies in fisheries. By enhancing profits, these subsides create perverse incentives to continue fishing even while stocks are declining. Over $10 billion in subsidies were provided in 2000, 80 percent of which came from developing countries (World Bank, 2009).

A rather different type of subsidy is intended to discourage overfishing. If vessel owners do not have alternative uses for their vessels, they may resist catch restrictions or other measures meant to help depleted stocks. Management options have included buyback or, equivalently, decommissioning subsidies to reduce fishing capacity. In 2004, the US government spent $100 million to buy out 28 of the 260 Alaskan snow crab fishery vessels. The EU has also proposed spending an additional €272 million on decommissioning (Clark et al., 2005). Payments used to buy out excess fishing capacity are useful subsidies in that they reduce overcapacity, but if additional capacity seeps in over time, they are not as effective as other management measures. Clark et al. (2005) also note that if fishermen come to anticipate a buyback, they may acquire more vessels than they otherwise would have, which would lead to even greater levels of overcapacity.

Marine Protected Areas and Marine Reserves

Regulating only the amount of catch leaves the type of gear that is used and locations where the harvests take place uncontrolled. Failure to control those elements can lead to environmental degradation of the habitat on which the fishery depends even if catch is successfully regulated. Some gear may be particularly damaging, not only to the targeted species (e.g., by capturing juveniles that cannot be sold, but that don't survive capture), but also to nontargeted species (bycatch). Similarly, harvesting in some geographic areas (such as those used for spawning) might have a disproportionately large detrimental effect on the sustainability of the fishery.

Conservation biologists have suggested complementing current policies with the establishment of a system of marine protected areas (MPAs). The US federal government defines MPAs as "any area of the marine environment that has been reserved by federal, state, tribal, territorial, or local laws or regulations to provide lasting protection for part or all of the natural and cultural resources therein."[11] Restrictions range from minimal to full protection. A marine reserve, a marine protected area with full protection, is an area that prohibits harvesting and enjoys a very high level of protection from other threats, such as pollution.

Biologists believe that marine protected areas can perform several maintenance and restorative functions. First, they protect *individual species* by preventing harvest within the reserve boundaries. Second, they reduce *habitat damage* caused by fishing gear or practices that alter biological structures. Third, in contrast to quotas on single species, reserves can promote *ecosystem balance* by protecting against the removal of ecologically pivotal species (whether targeted species or bycatch) that could throw an ecosystem out of balance by altering its diversity and productivity (Palumbi, 2002).

---

[11]For information and maps of marine protected areas of the United States, see www.mpa.gov.

Reducing harvesting in these areas protects the stock, the habitat, and the ecosystem on which it depends. This protection results in a larger population and, ultimately, if the species swim beyond the boundaries of the reserve, larger catches in the remaining harvest areas.

Simply put, reserves promote sustainability by allowing the population to recover. Their relationship to the welfare of current users, however, is less clear. Proponents of MPAs suggest that they can promote sustainability in a win–win fashion (meaning current users benefit as well). This is an important point because users who did not benefit might mount political opposition to marine reserve proposals, thereby making their establishment very difficult.

Would the establishment of a marine protected area maximize the present value of net benefits for fishermen? If MPAs work as planned, they reduce harvest in the short run (by declaring areas previously available for harvest off-limits), but they increase it in the long run (as the population recovers). However, the delay would impose costs. (Remember how discounting affects present value?) To take one concrete example of the costs of delay, harvesters may have to pay off a mortgage on their boat. Even if the bank grants them a delay in making payments, total payments will rise. So, by itself, a future rise in harvests does not guarantee that establishing the reserve maximizes present value unless the rise in catch is large enough and soon enough to compensate for the costs imposed by the delay.[12]

Since the present value of this policy depends on the specifics of the individual cases, a case study can be revealing. In an interesting case study of the California sea urchin industry, Smith and Wilen (2003) state the following:

> *Our overall assessment of reserves as a fisheries policy tool is more ambivalent than the received wisdom in the biological literature. . . . We find . . . that reserves can produce harvest gains in an age-structured model, but only when the biomass is severely overexploited. We also find . . . that even when steady state harvests are increased with a spatial closure, the discounted returns are often negative, reflecting slow biological recovery relative to the discount rate. (p. 204)*

This certainly does not mean that MPAs or marine reserves are a bad idea! In some areas, they may be a necessary step for achieving sustainability; in others, they may represent the most efficient means of achieving sustainability. It does mean, however, that we should be wary of the notion that they always create win–win situations; sacrifices by local harvesters might be required. MPA policies must recognize the possibility of this burden and deal with it directly, not just assume it doesn't exist.

Some international action on marine reserves is taking place as well. The 1992 international treaty, called the Convention on Biological Diversity, lists as one of its goals the conservation of at least 10 percent of the world's ecological regions,

---

[12]The distribution of benefits and costs among current fishermen also matters. Using a case study on the Northeast Atlantic Cod fishery, Sumaila and Armstrong (2006) find that the distributional effects of MPAs depend significantly on the management regime that was in place at the time of the development of the MPA and the level of cooperation in the fishery.

including, but not limited to, marine ecoregions. Progress has been significant for terrestrial ecoregions, but less so for coastal and marine ecoregions. In 2010, however, in one noteworthy event, the United Kingdom created the largest marine reserve in the world by setting aside the Chagos Archipelago, which stretches 544,000 square kilometers in the Indian Ocean, as a protected area.

The 200-Mile Limit

The final policy dimension concerns the international aspects of the fishery problem. Obviously, the various policy approaches to effective management of fisheries require some governing body to have jurisdiction over a fishery so that it can enforce its regulations.

Currently, this is not the case for many of the ocean fisheries. Much of the open water of the oceans is a common-pool resource to governments as well as to individual fishermen. No single body can exercise control over it. As long as that continues to be the case, the corrective action will be difficult to implement. In recognition of this fact, there is now an evolving law of the sea defined by international treaties. One of the concrete results of this law, for example, has been some limited restrictions on whaling. Whether this process ultimately yields a consistent and comprehensive system of management remains to be seen, but it is certainly an uphill battle.

Countries bordering the sea have taken one step by declaring that their ownership rights extend some 200 miles out to sea. Within these areas, the countries have exclusive jurisdiction and can implement effective management policies. These zones are essentially very large TURFs. These "exclusive zone" declarations have been upheld and are now firmly entrenched in international law. Thus, very rich fisheries in coastal waters can be protected, while those in the open waters await the outcome of an international negotiations process.

Preventing Poaching

Poaching (illegal harvesting) can introduce the possibility of unsustainability even when a legal structure to protect the population has been enacted. For example, in 1986 the International Whaling Commission set a ban on commercial whaling, but under a loophole in this law, Japan had continued to kill hundreds of whales each year. In November 2007, a fleet embarked on a 5-month hunt in the Antarctic despite numerous international protests. While originally intending to target humpback whales, in response to the protests, Japan eventually stopped harvesting that species. Since humpback whales are considered "vulnerable," commercial hunts have been banned since 1966, but Japan had claimed that harvests for research were not covered by this ban.

Bluefin tuna is another very valuable commerical species that is threatened and has been brought under international control. The population of bluefin tuna has plummeted 85 percent since 1970, with 60 percent of that loss occurring in the last decade. Japan is the largest consumer of bluefin tuna, which is prized for sushi. Fleets from Spain, Italy, and France are the primary suppliers.

In the United States, the National Marine Fisheries Service has proposed a catch-share program for the US portion of the International Commission for the Conservation of Atlantic Tunas (ICCAT) quota of endangered bluefin tuna. If implemented, it remains to be seen whether this type of program can work well for such a highly migratory species.

A rather different approach to protect the species was also tried in the international forum. In 2009, a petition to ban trade in the Atlantic bluefin tuna went before the U.N. Convention on International Trade in Endangered Species (CITES). This was the first time that a major commercial fishery has been addressed by CITES. While conservationists and biologists supported the CITES listing, many industry groups were opposed. The National Fisheries Institute president, John Connelly, wrote in opposition, "Commercially-exploited aquatic species are fundamentally different from the other species that CITES regulates . . . Unlike these other species, fish and seafood stocks are not generally threatened with biological extinction. While they can and do become overfished, the resulting loss of return on investment for fishermen prevents them from driving commercial fish stocks toward biological extinction" (Gronewold, 2009). In early 2010, CITES voted against the ban. In January 2011, a record price was set for a northern bluefin. A giant 754-pound bluefin brought 32.5 million yen, or nearly $400,000. Do you think this price is a sufficient incentive to protect the bluefin tuna from extinction? Why or why not? See Debate 12.3.

DEBATE 12.3 Bluefin Tuna: Is Its High Price Part of the Problem or Part of the Solution?

The International Commission for the Conservation of Atlantic Tunas (ICCAT) is responsible for the conservation of highly migratory species, including several species of tuna. ICCAT reports fish biomass as well as catch statistics and is responsible for setting total allowable catch by species each year.

Since ICCAT has never successfully enforced their quotas, it is not clear that they have a credible enforcement capability. Monitoring statistics consistently show catch well above the TAC.

Additionally, international pressure from the fishing industry frequently results in a TAC higher than scientists recommend. In 2009, for example, having reviewed the current biomass statistics, which showed the current stock to be at less than 15 percent of its original stock, ICCAT scientists recommended a total suspension of fishing. Ignoring their scientists' recommendation, ICCAT proceeded to set a quota of 13,500 tons. They did, however, also agree to establish new management measures for future years that will allow the stock to rebuild with an estimated 60 percent degree of confidence. While that sounds good, it turns out that if enforcement is less than perfect, and the resulting catch is above 13,500, the probability that the stock will recover cannot reach the 60 percent level by 2022 (Table 12.2).

TABLE 12.2 Probabilities of Stock Rebuilding at SSBF0.1 by Years and TAC Levels

TAC	Percent				
	2010	2013	2016	2019	2022
0	0	2	25	69	99
2,000	0	1	21	62	99
4,000	0	1	18	55	99
6,000	0	1	14	47	97
8,000	0	0	11	40	92
10,000	0	0	9	33	84
12,000	0	0	6	26	73
13,500	0	0	5	21	63
14,000	0	0	4	20	59
16,000	0	0	3	14	46
18,000	0	0	2	10	34
20,000	0	0	1	6	24

Note: Grey color highlights the catch at which the 60 percent probability would not be achieved.

Source: Report of the 2010 Atlantic bluefin tuna stock assessment session (Table 1); ICCAT, www.iccat.int/en

---

Sources: International commission for the conservation of Atlantic tunas 2009 annual iccat meeting press release 16, November 2009; ICCAT, www.iccat.org; Gronewold, G. (October 14, 2009). Is the bluefin tuna an endangered species? *Scientific American,* Retrieved from http://www.scientificamerican.com/article.cfm?id=bluefin-tuna-stocks-threatened-cites-japan-monaco; Draft amendment 7 to the consolidated Atlantic highly migratory species fishery management plan, *National Marine Fisheries Service*, August 2013, Retrieved from http://www.scribd.com/doc/161801821/NOAA-Draft-Bluefin-Tuna-Amendment.

Summary

Unrestricted access to commercially valuable species will generally result in overexploitation. This overexploitation, in turn, results in overcapitalization, depressed incomes for harvesters, and depleted stocks. Even extinction of the species is possible, particularly for populations characterized by easy, low-cost extraction. Where extraction costs are higher, extinction is unlikely, even with unrestricted access.

Both the private and public sectors have moved to ameliorate the problems associated with past mismanagement of commercial fisheries. By reasserting private property rights, many countries have stimulated the development of aquaculture. Governments in Canada and the United States have moved to limit overexploitation of the Pacific salmon. International agreements have been instituted to place limits on whaling. It is doubtful that these programs fully satisfy the efficiency criterion, although it does seem clear that more sustainable catches will result.

Creative strategies for sharing the gains from moving to an efficient level of harvest could prove to be a significant weapon in the arsenal of techniques designed to protect a broad class of biological resources from overexploitation. An increasing reliance on individual transferable quotas (ITQs) and TURFs offers the possibility of preserving stocks without jeopardizing the incomes of those men and women currently harvesting those stocks. Strengthening property rights is a key component in generating both efficient and sustainable harvests.

It would be folly to ignore barriers to further action, such as the reluctance of individual harvesters to submit to many forms of regulation, the lack of a firm policy governing open-ocean waters, and the difficulties of enforcing various approaches. Whether these barriers will fall before the pressing need for effective management remains to be seen.

In this chapter we have focused on fisheries as an example of a renewable biological resource, but the models and the insights that flow from them can be used to think about managing other wildlife populations as well. This topic will be taken up in the next chapter.

Discussion Questions

1. Is the establishment of the 200-mile limit a sufficient form of government intervention to ensure that the tragedy of the commons does not occur for fisheries within the 200-mile limit? Why or why not?
2. With discounting it is possible for the efficient fish population to fall below the level required to produce the maximum sustained yield. Does this violate the sustainability criterion? Why or why not?

Self-Test Exercises

1. Assume that the relationship between the growth of a fish population and the population size can be expressed as $g = 4P - 0.1P^2$, where g is the growth in tons and P is the size of the population (in thousands of tons). Given a price of \$100 a ton, the marginal benefit of smaller population sizes (and hence larger catches) can be computed as $20P - 400$. (a) Compute the population size that is compatible with the maximum sustainable yield. What would be the size of the annual catch if the population were to be sustained at this level? (b) If the marginal cost of additional catches (expressed in terms of the population size) is $MC = 2(160 - P)$, what is the population size that is compatible with the efficient sustainable yield?

2. Assume that a local fisheries council imposes an enforceable quota of 100 tons of fish on a particular fishing ground for one year. Assume further that 100 tons per year is the efficient sustained yield. When 100 tons have been caught, the fishery would be closed for the remainder of the year. (a) Is this an efficient solution to the common property problem? Why or why not? (b) Would your answer be different if the 100-ton quota were divided into 100 transferable quotas, each entitling the holder to catch 1 ton of fish, and distributed among the fishermen in proportion to their historical catch? Why or why not?
3. In the economic model of the fishery developed in this chapter, compare the effect on fishing effort of an increase in cost of a fishing license with an increase in a per-unit tax on fishing effort that raises the same amount of revenue. Assume the fishery is private property. Repeat the analysis assuming that the fishery is a free-access common property resource.
4. When trying to reduce the degree of inefficiency from an open-access fishery, would a regulation that increases the marginal cost of fishing effort by banning certain types of gear or a tax on effort be equally efficient? Why or why not?
5. a. In the typical economic model of an efficient fishery, would a fall in the price of fish generally result in a larger or a smaller sustainable harvest? Why?
   b. Suppose the fishery allowed free access. Would a fall in the price of fish generally result in a larger or a smaller harvest? Why?
6. Suppose that a particular fishery experiences a technological change such that the fixed cost of fishing increases, but the marginal cost of fishing decreases. The change is such that the before and after total cost curves cross at an effort level higher than that associated with the before efficient sustained yield, but lower than the free-access level of effort.
   a. What would the effect of this technological change be on the static efficient level of effort and the size of the static efficient level of harvest? Would they increase or decrease or are the effects ambiguous?
   b. What would the effect of this technological change be on the level of effort and the size of the harvest in a free-access fishery? Would they increase or decrease or are the effects ambiguous?

Further Reading

Acheson, J. M. (2003). *Capturing the commons: Devising institutions to manage the Maine lobster industry*. Hanover, NH: University Press of New England. An impressive synthesis of theory and empirical work, combined with an insider's knowledge of the institutions and the people who run them, makes this a compelling examination of the history of one of America's most important fisheries.

Adler, J. H., & Stewart, N. (2013). Learning how to fish: Catch shares and the future of fisheries conservation. *UCLA Journal of Environmental Law & Policy*, *31*(1). A useful summary of the history, law, and economics of catch shares.

Clark, C. W. (1990). *Mathematical bioeconomics: The optimal management of renewable resources*, 2nd ed. New York: Wiley-Interscience. Careful development of the mathematical models that underlie current understanding of the exploitation of renewable resources under a variety of property rights regimes.

NOAA Catch Share Policy: Executive Summary 2013. Retrieved from http://www.nmfs.noaa.gov/sfa/domes_fish/catchshare/docs/noaa_cs_policy.pdf. A useful review of US Fisheries Policy. Review of Environmental Economics and Policy Volume 6 Issue 2 Sum 2012. Contains several summary articles from the Symposium: Rights-Based Fisheries Management.

Schlager, E., & Ostrom, E. (1992). Property right regimes and natural resources: A conceptual analysis. *Land Economics*, *68*, 249–262. A conceptual framework for analyzing a number of property rights regimes; the authors use this framework to interpret findings from a number of empirical studies.

Additional References and Historically Significant References are available on this book's Companion Website: http://www.routledgetextbooks.com/textbooks/9780133479690

Appendix

The Harvesting Decision: Fisheries

Defining the efficient sustainable yield for a fishery begins with a characterization of the biological relationship between the growth for the biomass and the size of the biomass. The standard representation of this relationship is

$$g = rS\left(1 - \frac{S}{k}\right), \tag{1}$$

where

g = the growth rate of the biomass,
r = the intrinsic growth rate for this species,
S = the size of the biomass, and
k = the carrying capacity of the habitat.

Since we want to choose the most efficient *sustained* yield, we must limit the possible outcomes we shall consider to those that are sustainable. Here we define a sustainable harvest level, h_S, as one that equals the growth of the population. Hence:

$$h_s = rS\left(1 - \frac{S}{k}\right). \tag{2}$$

The next step is to define the size of the harvest as a function of the amount of effort expended. This is traditionally modeled as

$$h = qES, \tag{3}$$

where

q = a constant (known as the "catchability coefficient") and
E = the level of effort.

The next step is to solve for sustained yields as a function of effort. This can be derived using a two-step procedure. First, we express S in terms of E. Then we use this newly derived expression for S along with the relationship in Equation (3) to derive the sustained yield expressed in terms of effort.

To define S in terms of E, we can substitute Equation (3) into Equation (2):

$$qES = rS\left(1 - \frac{S}{k}\right). \tag{4}$$

Rearranging terms yields

$$S = k\left(1 - \frac{qE}{r}\right). \tag{5}$$

Using $S = h/qE$ from Equation (3) and rearranging terms to solve for h yields

$$h_s = qEk - \frac{q^2kE^2}{r}. \tag{6}$$

It is now possible to find the maximum sustainable effort level by taking the derivative of the right-hand side of Equation (6) with respect to effort (E) and setting the result equal to zero.

The maximum condition is

$$qk - 2\frac{q^2kE}{r} = 0. \tag{7}$$

So

$$E_{msy} = \frac{r}{2q}, \tag{8}$$

where

E_{msy} = the level of effort that is consistent with the maximum sustained yield.

Can you see how to solve for the maximum sustainable yield, h_{msy}? (*Hint*: Remember how the maximum sustained yield was defined in terms of effort in Equation (6)?)

To conduct the economic analysis, we need to convert this biological information to a net benefits formulation. The benefit function can be defined by multiplying Equation (6) by P, the price received for a unit of harvest. Assuming a constant marginal cost of effort, a, allows us to define total cost as equal to aE. Subtracting the total cost of effort from the revenue function produces the net benefits function:

$$\text{Net benefits} = PqEk - \frac{Pq^2kE^2}{r} - aE. \tag{9}$$

Since the efficient sustained effort level is the level that maximizes Equation (9), we can derive it by taking the derivative of Equation (9) with respect to effort (E) and setting the derivative equal to zero:

$$Pqk - \frac{2Pkq^2E}{r} - a = 0. \tag{10}$$

Rearranging terms yields

$$E = \frac{r}{2q}\left(1 - \frac{a}{Pqk}\right). \tag{11}$$

Note that this effort level is smaller than that needed to produce the maximum sustainable yield. Can you see how to find the efficient sustainable harvest level? Finally, we can derive the free-access equilibrium by setting the net benefits function in Equation (9) equal to zero and solving for the effort level.

Rearranging terms yields

$$E = \frac{r}{q}\left(1 - \frac{a}{Pqk}\right). \tag{12}$$

Note that this is larger than the efficient sustained level of effort. It may or may not be larger than the level of effort needed to produce the maximum sustained yield. That comparison depends on the specific values of the parameters.

13 Ecosystem Goods and Services: Nature's Threatened Bounty

Bees work for man, and yet they never bruise.
Their Master's flower, but leave it having done,
As fair as ever and as fit to use;
So both the flower doth stay and honey run.

George Herbert - The Church

Introduction

In the previous chapters we have learned that economic activity can pose several different types of threats to the natural world ranging from converting land from wildlife habitat to housing, introducing substances that either intentionally or unintentionally harm wildlife, and overharvesting biological populations to name but a few. We have also seen how economic incentives can play a remedial role in preventing or at least reducing these potentially damaging interactions, particularly for resources that are commercially valuable.

Those commercially valuable resources, however, comprise only a portion of what nature has to offer. Many of the remaining ecological functions and services are not only supplied by natural processes, but nature charges nothing for their use. Examples of these ecological goods and services include pollination by bees, the aquifer recharge services by wetlands, breathable air, biodiversity, nitrogen fixation in the soil, climate regulation through carbon sequestration, as well as aesthetic and recreation services. If these services directly benefit at least one person, they are called *ecosystem services*.

In 1997 a team of researchers attempted to place a monetary global value on ecosystem services (Constanza et al., 1997). Basing their estimates on previously published studies and a few original calculations, they found the (1997) economic value of 17 ecosystem services for 16 biomes, to be in the range of US$16–54 trillion per year, with an average of US$33 trillion per year. This article attracted considerable attention.

However, because the methods they used were controversial, the specific estimated values were controversial as well. What was not controversial was the fact that ecosystems play a very valuable role in the lives of humans.

What role can economic analysis play in assuring that the value provided by these ecosystem services is not only recognized, but also protected from degradation? In this chapter we take up that question, focusing on two specific roles: (1) refining and improving the methods for quantifying the values received from natural services to increase their reliability and to demonstrate their importance, taking care to identify the specific contributions to human welfare, and (2) facilitating the design of private, public, and public–private partnership arrangements as well as incentive mechanisms that can help protect these important components of nature from degradation.

The State of Ecosystem Services

In 2001, U.N. Secretary-General Kofi Annan initiated the Millennium Ecosystem Assessment (MA) with the goal to assess "the consequences of ecosystem change for human well-being and to establish the scientific basis for actions needed to enhance the conservation and sustainable use of ecosystems and their contributions to human well-being."

To examine the connections and the linkages between ecosystems and human well-being, the MA divides ecosystem services into several categories.

- *Provisioning services* provide direct benefits such as water, timber, food and fiber.
- *Regulating services* include flood control, water quality, disease prevention, and climate.
- *Supporting services* consist of such foundational processes as photosynthesis, nutrient cycling, and soil formation.
- *Cultural Services* provide recreational, aesthetic, and spiritual benefits.

In 2005, the Assessment published four main findings.

- Ecosystems have changed rapidly in the last 50 years—at a rate higher than any other time period. Due to the growing demands on the earth's resources and services, some of these high rates of change are irreversible.
- Many of the changes to ecosystems, while improving the well-being of some humans, have been at the expense of ecosystem health. Fifteen of the 24 ecosystems evaluated are in decline.
- If degradation continues, it will be difficult to achieve many of the UN Millennium Development Goals since resources that are vital for certain especially vulnerable groups are being affected.[1] Further degradation not only intensifies current poverty, but it limits options for future generations, thereby creating intergenerational inequity.

[1]The Millennium Development Goals (MDGs) include reducing the world's biodiversity losses and loss of environmental resources, as well as reducing the number of people without access to such services as safe drinking water.

- Finally, the Assessment suggests that reversing the degradation of ecosystems would require significant changes in institutions and policies and it specifically notes that economic instruments can play an important role in this transformation.

Another report, The Economics of Ecosystems and Biodiversity (TEEB), examines the costs of policy inaction on the decline of biodiversity worldwide. It finds that by 2050 under several "business as usual" scenarios, an additional 11 percent of remaining biodiversity could be lost, 40 percent of low-impact agriculture could be converted to intensive agriculture and 60 percent of coral reefs could be gone (perhaps as early as 2030).

Recognizing the importance of ecosystem services the Intergovernmental Platform on Biodiversity and Ecosystem Services (IPBES) was established in April 2012, as an independent intergovernmental body open to all member countries of the United Nations. IPBES provides a forum for synthesizing, reviewing, assessing and critically evaluating relevant information and knowledge generated worldwide on biodiversity and ecosystem services.

Economic Analysis of Ecosystem Services

Ecosystem services are flows that are generated from stocks of natural assets and that benefit humans. Tropical forests, for example, are assets that can provide carbon sequestration, habitat, watershed protection and recreation, but also can provide flows of timber. The harvest of flows can either be sustainable or unsustainable.

Economic analysis is helpful both in identifying sources of economic degradation and in evaluating possible approaches to maintain and restore these services. Both of these tasks are enhanced by careful valuation of the flows in question.

One avenue for using these valuations is benefit-cost analysis and the scope for these analyses is wider than you might expect. They are not limited to traditional evaluation of water or land use projects. Bandara and Tisdell (2004), for example, use the results of a contingent valuation study on saving the Asian elephant to show that the WTP for the conservation of Asian elephants in Sri Lanka more than compensates for the damage caused by elephants.

Demonstrating the Value of Ecosystem Services

The starting point for economic analysis in reversing ecosystem degradation lies in revealing the economic value foregone by the loss of these services. Quantifying those values, even imperfectly, can make it clear just how much their loss or degradation means.

Many of the services explored in this chapter are nonmarket goods or services, which means that we must use a methodology that does not depend on the availability of market prices to derive their value. As discussed in Chapter 4 two main strategies are available for eliciting these values: revealed preference methods—attributing value by observing or measuring what people spend on goods and services that contain attributes we wish to value —and stated preference methods—using surveys to ascertain willingness to pay . Other methods commonly used for valuing ecosystem services including using adjusted market prices, avoidance costs (or averting expenditures), production function methods, or damage costs avoided.[2] Here we will focus specifically on valuing services that ecosystems provide to humans either directly or indirectly.

Consider some specific contexts to illustrate both how these techniques can be applied to the valuation of ecosystem services and why the results matter.

The Value of Reefs

Coral reefs are an integral part of an extensive and vital landscape of coastal ecosystems. Increasingly they are in jeopardy. One of the specific areas benefited by the new field of ecosystems services research is the derivation, not only of better estimates of the value of those ecosystem benefits, but also the identification of the specific sources of that value.

While some of the threat to coral reefs is due to pollution or overfishing, recently coral reef losses have accelerated significantly due to climate change. Specifically, rising water temperatures have induced coral bleaching, and excessive CO_2 dissolution in seawater is causing ocean acidification, which in turn hampers reef regeneration.

What is at stake? Just how valuable are the services provided by coral reefs? And how much do the four different categories of services contribute to the overall value?

One well-known study (TEEB, 2009) provides some relevant estimates to answer these questions by pulling together the existing literature on values of reefs in a global context. Table 13.1, drawn from that study, not only demonstrates that reefs provide valuable ecosystem services, but it also divides up the sources of value into the four categories described at the beginning of this chapter.

Note that this study finds that cultural services (particularly tourism and recreation) make the largest contribution to value. The clear implication is that studies that capture only the provisional services from coral reefs seriously underestimate this value.

One use of this type of estimate would be in calculating the reef degradation damages from climate change, a calculation that would be useful in designing climate change policy. Equivalently, the estimates could be used to derive the benefits from reducing that damage via greenhouse gas mitigation policy.

Because the TEEB study aggregates the results from a number of individual studies, it would be helpful to have some sense of what an underlying individual study might look like. What does it include? What methods are used to derive the

[2]For a description of these approaches and the role they play in ecosystem service evaluation see Bateman et al., (2011).

TABLE 13.1 Benefits from ecosystem services in coral reef ecosystems

CORAL REEFS	Value of ecosystem services (in US$ / ha / year – 2007 values)		
Ecosystem Service	Average	Maximum	Number of Studies
Provisioning services			
Food	470	3,818	22
Raw materials	400	1,990	5
Ornamental resources	264	347	3
Regulating services			
Climate regulation	648	648	3
Moderation of extreme events	25,200	34,408	9
Waste treatment / water purification	42	81	2
Biological control	4	7	2
Cultural Services			
Aesthetic information / Amenity	7,425	27,484	4
Opportunities for recreation and tourism	79,099	1,063,946	29
Information for cognitive development	2,154	6,461	4
Total	**115,704**	**1,139,190**	**83**
Supporting Services			
Maintenance of genetic diversity	13,541	57,133	7

Note: these estimates are based on ongoing analyses for TEEB (TEEB Ecological and Economic Foundations, Chapter 7). As the TEEB data base and value-analysis are still under development, this table is for illustrative purposes only.

Note: ha = hectare, a metric unit of area defined as 10,000 square meters.

Source: TEEB, 2009, Climate Issues Updated (September) Table 1, p. 7.

estimates? What uses are anticipated for these estimates? Example 13.1 provides some insights from one study that helps to answer these questions.

Damage Assessments: Loss of Ecosystem Services

Another area where the quantification of ecosystem valuation can, and has, played a significant role is in assessing the magnitude of damage to ecosystems caused by human activities.

Oil spills are a case in point. In Chapter 4 we mentioned the 2010 Deepwater Horizon spill in the Gulf of Mexico. Prior to that spill, the Oil Pollution Act of 1990 had established a formal legal framework for determining when an oil spill results in

EXAMPLE 13.1

The Value of Coral Reefs in the U. S. Virgin Islands

The United States Virgin Islands (USVI) are located approximately 100 miles east of Puerto Rico by air. The four main islands are St. Croix, St. John, Water Island, and St. Thomas.

Recognizing the value of the local coral reefs and needing a baseline to provide a quantitative measure with which to compare possible alternative development/conservation plans, a study was commissioned to derive a total economic value (TEV) for these reefs. A TEV framework attempts to measure value from both use and nonuse values. This information was also felt to be useful in providing an economic basis for advocating for the preservation of these coral reefs, for establishing the basis for any damage compensation, and for determining potential user fees for residents and tourists.

This study focused on valuing the six main uses of coral reefs and adjacent habitats in selected sites on the USVI: (1) fishery value, (2) tourism value, (3) recreational and cultural value, (4) real estate value, (5) the value of shoreline protection, and (6) education/research values.

The study involved a wide range of valuation methodologies including (1) a revealed preference study of the commercial value of the fishery, (2) a local resident survey aimed at estimating the local cultural and recreation attachment to the marine environment, (3) a tourist survey using both travel cost and choice experiment methods to get a comprehensive insight into the importance of the marine environment for visitors to the USVI, (4) an analysis of the coastal protection function of reefs, (5) a hedonic pricing analysis to discern the positive impact of healthy reefs on house prices, (6) a GIS analysis aimed at preparing value maps of the coral reefs of the USVI, and (7) an aggregation of the separate components to produce the estimation of the TEV of these coral reefs.

This study found the TEV to be $187 million per year with the values of the component parts found to be as follows:

- Reef related tourism —$96 million
- Recreation—$48 million
- Amenity—$35 million
- Coastal protection—$6 million
- Support to commercial fisheries—$3 million

Note that tourism and recreation once again comprise the largest sources of value for this individual case as it did for the global total considered previously.

Source: van Beukering, P., Brander, L., van Zanten, B., Verbrugge, E., & Lems, K. (2011). The economic value of the coral reef ecosystems of the United States Virgin Islands: Final report. *IVM Institute for Environmental Studies Report Number: R-11/06.* The Netherlands: Amsterdam (31 August).

a quantifiable adverse change in a natural resource. Through a process known as the Natural Resources Damage Assessment (NRDA), trustees of the affected ecosystem must attempt to quantify the extent of damages caused by a spill in order to seek compensation from the responsible parties.

As a recent report from the National Research Council notes (NRC, 2013), highlighting the relationship between ecosystem services and the economy can heighten public knowledge of and support for protecting those services. That report advocated incorporating a broader ecosystem services approach to assessing damage from the spill rather than focusing only on provisioning services. By encompassing the wider array of services this broader approach could end up identifying restoration projects that would benefit not only the trustees and direct-use parties, but the larger public as well.

That process of widening the scope of assessment is complex and will ultimately take time. As of July 2013, according to its records BP had paid out over $12 billion in claims, but virtually all of that is based upon direct human losses rather than the broader focus suggested by the NRC. One exception, however, involved an oyster reef project in Alabama's Mobile Bay. The restoration project was originally focused on a location that would be convenient for fishermen who lost harvests during the spill, thereby responding directly to their losses. However, the ecosystem services provided by oysters are much greater than their direct value to harvesters. The filtering action of oysters plays an important role not only in removing suspended sediments from the water column but also in cleansing the water of various pollutants. When the broader scope suggested by the NRC was applied, a location that better suited to supply all these ecosystem services was chosen.

Valuing Supporting Services: Pollination

Ecosystem valuation can also help to raise awareness of extremely valuable, but probably underappreciated, ecosystem services, especially when the continuation of those services is threatened. Pollination services supplied by bees is one such valuable ecosystem service. Many valuable agricultural crops rely on bees for pollination.

Some 1,000,000 honeybee hives, or more than 40 percent of all the beehives in the United States, are required just for cross-pollination of the $2 billion almond crop in California. When the almond trees flower, managed honeybee hives are moved by flatbed trucks to the San Joaquin Valley to provide sufficient bees to pollinate the crop (Ratnieks & Carreck, 2010).

The benefits from pollination, however, include not only the direct economic impacts of increasing the productivity of agricultural crops but also such nonmarket impacts as aiding in genetic diversity, improving ecosystem resilience and providing nutrient cycling. Unfortunately these important ecosystem services may be in jeopardy.

In 2006, the popular press began reporting on what has been called Colony Collapse Disorder, an unexplained disappearance of honeybee colonies. Beekeeper surveys suggest that 33 percent of honeybee colonies in the United States died in the winter of 2010. While the exact causes are, as of yet, unknown, multiple causes are likely to blame.

Ratnieks and Carreck speculate about economic impact of potential future losses and ask an important question:

> *Is the future of U.S. commercial beekeeping going to be based on pollinating a few high-value crops? If so, what will be the wider economic cost arising from crops that have modest yield increases from honey bee pollination? These crops cannot pay large pollination fees but have hitherto benefited from an abundance of honey bees providing free pollination.*

The damage caused by loss of pollination services to other parts of the world could be even higher than those in the United States. One study argues that possible future global shortages of pollination services are not only likely to be profound, but have quite different economic impacts around the globe (Example 13.2).

EXAMPLE 13.2

Valuing Pollination Services: Two Illustrations

Wild bees from a nearby tropical forest provide pollination services to aid Costa Rican coffee production. While this coffee (*C. arabica*) can self-pollinate, pollination from wild bees has been shown to increase coffee productivity from 15 to 50 percent.

In one study (Ricketts et al., 2002) examined this relationship and placed an economic value on this particular ecological service. They found that the pollination services from bees living in two specific preserved forest fragments (46 and 111 hectares, respectively) were worth approximately $60,000 per year for one large, nearby Costa Rican coffee farm. As the authors conclude:

> *The value of forest in providing crop pollination service alone is . . . of at least the same order [of magnitude] as major competing land uses, and infinitely greater than that recognized by most governments (i.e., zero).*

Although these estimates only partially capture the value of this forest because they consider only a single farm and a single type of ecological service, they are apparently sufficient, by themselves, to demonstrate the economic value of preserving this particular forest.

Recognizing that this kind of partial analysis, which focuses on an individual case, should be complemented by studies with a more macro focus has encouraged different methodologies with a more global focus. One of these studies, which used a multi-region, computable general equilibrium (CGE) model of agricultural production and trade, examined the global economic impacts of pollinator declines (Bauer & Wing, 2010).

CGE models produce numerical assessments of economy-wide consequences of various events or programs. They include not only the direct effects on the crop sector, but also the indirect, noncrop effects. Using this type of model not only allows the authors to estimate the impacts of a decline in pollination services in different geographic regions but also how these impacts are affected by the presence of different local substitutes for pollination services.

The authors find that the annual global losses to the crop sector attributable to a decline in direct pollination services are estimated to be $10.5 billion, but economy-wide losses (noncrop sectors) are estimated to be much larger, namely $334 billion. Clearly estimates based only a direct services would seriously underestimate the value of pollination services.

They also find that some regions of the world, especially western Africa, are likely to suffer disproportionately. Their enhanced vulnerability is due not only to the larger share that pollinator-dependent crops make up in western Africa's agricultural output, but also to the relatively higher importance of the agriculture sector in the African economy.

Source: Ricketts, T.H. et al. (August 24, 2002). Economic value of tropical forest to coffee production. *PNAS (Proceedings of the National Academy of Science), 101*(34), 12579–12582; Bauer, D.M., & Sing, I. S. (October 2010). Economic consequences of pollinator declines: A synthesis. *Agricultural and Resource Economics Review, 39*(3), 368–383.

Valuing Supporting Services: Forests and Coastal Ecosystems

Valuation methods have been used extensively to value forest ecosystem services, coastal and marine ecosystem services, and biodiversity. In his summary of the literature on coastal and marine ecosystem services (CMEs) valuation, Barbier (2012) notes that losses to fishery nurseries, mangroves that provide storm protection, coral reefs that are a rich source of biodiversity, filtering services of wetlands, and sea grasses have now been measured worldwide. Quantifying the benefits of these services can provide an empirical foundation for decision making and for setting priorities.

The TEEB (2009) presents several other examples that demonstrate the numerous and diverse possible sources of benefits. One such example derives the ecosystem benefits from protecting a forest with high biodiversity in Madagascar. Benefits flowing from that resource include medicines (estimated net present value of $1.57 million US$), erosion control (estimated NPV of $380,000), carbon storage (estimated NPV of $105 million), recreation, and forest products (estimated value of $9.4 million).

This study also notes the complicated scale dimension of ecosystem services by demonstrating how benefits flow from developing countries to a distant city; in this case, London. These transboundary benefits include medicines, fish, coffee, flood control, and existence value. Valuing services that simultaneously affect several different scales (local, regional, global) can be challenging, but not including all scales can produce a serious underestimate.

Challenges and Innovation in Ecosystem Valuation

In order for valuations to be useful, their derivations must be based upon consistent methodologies. Consistency is important not only to assure that various valuation projects can be directly compared but also so that benefit transfers are facilitated.

(Recall from Chapter 4 that benefit transfer involves using values from one study site to provide the basis for valuing services at another policy site.)

Achieving this kind of consistency requires precise definitions of the services as well as agreement on how these services contribute to value. It also requires that the valuation procedures avoid double counting.

For nonmarket goods and services these issues are especially challenging. While market goods have well-defined units based on actual purchases, nonmarket goods and services may offer a large variety of attributes, each of which could have value. If different analysts choose different attributes to value, the result will not only be inconsistent valuations, but inconsistent valuations make policy-relevant benefit transfer impossible (Johnston et al., 2005).

The Millenium Ecosystem Assessment (2005) provides a classification of ecosystem services that has been widely cited, but unfortunately these classifications are vulnerable to double counting. "Water purification" and the "provision of freshwater" are listed as separate services for example (Balmford et al., 2011; Boyd & Banzhaf, 2007). Double counting can also occur if an ecosystem service provides both an intermediate good and a final good. When both are separately valued and simply added together, a common mistake, the resulting values are inflated. On the other hand intermediate services cannot simply be ignored since they are one source of the final value (Johnston & Russell, 2011).

Given these challenges, how do nonmarket valuation methods fare in practice? Because ecosystem service valuation is relatively new, the quest for clean, reliable estimates is still evolving. For example, Boyd and Krupnick (2009) note in their survey of the stated preference literature that a lack of consistency in definitions is still relatively common. Johnston and Russell (2011) also lament the lack of clarity in definitions of final ecosystem goods and services.

Researchers using stated preference methods are beginning to grapple with this aspect of inconsistency—how to distinguish between intermediate and final goods. The specific challenge for economists using stated preference techniques is to design surveys that identify commodities that are both true to the ecological science and meaningful and understandable to respondents (Boyd & Krupnick, 2009; Johnston et al., 2012). This is no easy undertaking.

Distinctions between inputs and ecological endpoints are crucial for valuation. Do people value wetlands themselves (input) or do they value flood control (endpoint)? A common practice in valuation has been to simplify or "map" ecological information into outcomes that respondents have experience with. An early example is the water quality ladder developed by Resources for the Future which was used in a national contingent valuation study (Carson & Mitchell, 1993). This ladder translates water quality measures into the categories "boatable," "fishable," and "swimmable." This attempt to make the specific services being valued understandable to respondents answering the surveys actually creates another problem. Since these terms have no precise ecological definition, it becomes unclear how to interpret the resulting willingness to pay measure (Boyd & Krupnick 2009).

Stated preference methods are further challenged when respondents have little experience or knowledge of the service being valued. Researchers have tried to overcome this problem by simplifying the scenarios, but many times simplicity is achieved at the expense of ecological precision. Johnston et al. (2012) note some examples where terms like "low," "medium," and "high" are used to characterize levels of biodiversity, but those terms have no specific connection to a precise level of biodiversity. Their assumed meanings would likely not only vary from respondent to respondent but it is also not clear what the results would actually mean for specific levels of biodiversity.

For revealed preference methods the challenge of properly treating intermediate and final goods is smaller because those methods typically deal only with final goods; they rarely attempt to measure intermediate ecological inputs (Johnston, 2014). However, revealed preference methods are only available for a subset of ecosystem services, namely those where purchases actually occur. Additionally, with revealed preference methods, even when final goods have been demonstrated to have value, it is sometimes difficult to know the specific underlying source of that value. For example, if a hedonic property value study finds that being near beaches raises land value, which attributes of the beaches are the source of that value. Is it the beach width? The sand quality? Both?

One emerging solution to this dilemma involves combining stated and revealed preference data. (Note that the study in Example 13.1 uses both.) By combining the two methods, the source of the revealed preference value can be explored in greater depth using the more specific stated preferences of the respondent. The downside is that implementing two studies is obviously more expensive than one.

Moore et al. (2011) provide a useful example of how an attribute-based study can bring greater clarity to the question of *what* is being valued. In their study aimed at estimating marginal values of forest protection programs, they utilized a stated preference survey that asked respondents to consider two different types of conservation sites—one with distinct use values like recreation and easy access, versus another with high ecological values like a richer biodiversity or providing habitat for endangered species. Identifying and valuing these specific attributes, as opposed to deriving only an overall value for the site, allows for the estimation of the marginal value of each type of service. Note that estimating separate marginal values for specific ecosystem services also facilitates more precise benefit transfers.

One response to the high cost of conducting new site-specific studies for each ecosystem service is to use meta-analysis, the technique (discussed in Chapter 4) that can draw insights from a large number of previously completed studies. This approach has the advantage that not only will the service value be based upon a large number of studies but it can also identify the study characteristics that seem to play a role in the resulting value. In one example of this approach, Brander et al. (2006) conducted a meta-analysis of approximately 190 valuation studies of wetlands. They found the most significant determinants of value included socio-economic variables such as income and population density of the surrounding community. Interestingly, they found that certain attributes, such as water quality, had the highest value, but they found a negative relationship between size of the wetland and its value.

Despite the challenges, the role for nonmarket valuation is already clear and numerous studies have highlighted the benefits of protection of one or more ecosystem service in ways that have made for better policy.

Institutional Arrangements and Mechanisms for Protecting Nature's Services

Valuation is only one of the contributions economic analysis can make to the maintenance and protection of important ecosystem services. Another is using economics to help design institutions and policies that can bring economic incentives to bear.

Payments for Environmental Services

One avenue where economic analysis has been helpful in this regard lies in identifying ways to create institutional arrangements in which the providers of ecosystem services can be compensated for nonmarket services. This would not only create better incentives for maintaining and enhancing those services, but also provide a revenue source that could be used to further that purpose. While we have previously provided some examples of these arrangments,[3] a few additional examples may prove helpful in conveying some sense of the scope of the options.

Costa Rica's Pago por Servicios Ambientales (PSA) Program.[4] One of the earliest examples of this approach can be found in Costa Rica. Built upon an existing forestry law, the PSA program includes four specific environmental services provided by forest ecosystems: (1) greenhouse gas emission mitigation; (2) water services for human consumption, irrigation, and energy production; (3) biodiversity conservation; and (4) scenic beauty for recreation and ecotourism. For our purposes in this chapter the water services component is the most interesting and we shall focus on it.

The program started with voluntary agreements involving payments to private land-owners from water users in return for conserving certain forested areas that served as recharge or purification areas in the watershed. Bottlers, municipal water supply systems, irrigation water users, and hotels have all chosen to participate in these agreements. Whereas early agreements saw water users paying for a quarter of conservation costs (since water services were only one of four services that the law enumerated as provided by forests), in more recent agreements water users are not only paying the entire cost of conservation, but the administrative costs as well. These agreements typically cover a 5-year period.

As the program has matured, a water tariff was added to finance the payments, effectively transforming one aspect of the program from a voluntary one into a

[3]See Example 2.2 (shrimp farming externalities) and Example 3.1 (ecological services from preserved forests).

[4]For a full description of this program and a series of evaluation documents see its World Bank Website at http://web.worldbank.org/WBSITE/EXTERNAL/TOPICS/ENVIRONMENT/EXTEEI/0, contentMDK:21647925~menuPK:1187844~pagePK:210058~piPK:210062~theSitePK:408050~isCURL:Y~isCURL:Y,00.html

mandatory one. Interestingly the voluntary agreements are still occurring not only because the payments made under these agreements are deducted from the amounts owed under the tariff, but the voluntary agreements give somewhat more control to the signatory over exact how his or her payment will be used.

Pagiola (2008) reports that the PSA program has been very popular with landowners, (with requests to participate far outstripping available financing) and that recipients had a higher percentage of their forest under conservation than nonrecipients. He also points out, however, that the program does have some specific inefficiencies. In particular because the PSA program offers a relatively low, undifferentiated, and mostly untargeted payment, it tends to attract participants whose opportunity cost of participation is low or negative. As a result some socially desirable land use practices are not adopted because the payment being offered is insufficient.

This program also provides a good opportunity to discuss an issue of some importance to these types of programs—economic sustainability. Programs will only be successful over the long term if they create the means to sustain themselves financially after the initial enthusiasm. This can either occur because (1) the incentives created by the program are large enough to cause private benefits to be higher than costs for both payees and recipients or (2) sufficient required financing is provided by law.

Indeed some payments for service arrangements (including some in the PAS program) are funded by limited-term grants from international organizations. These are no doubt helpful in setting up the program and providing some initial successes, but many times what happens after these grants run out is not clear. In the case of the PSA water services program the existence of the tariff coupled with the apparent private land-owner interest in participating suggest that outlook for the economic sustainability of this program seems relatively good.

Other Watershed Payment Programs. Investing in watershed services is a broad category that covers payments for watershed services, water quality trading markets (see also Chapter 17), instream buybacks, and water funds. Bennett et al. (2013) report on the state of watershed payments and find 205 active programs in 29 countries as of 2011. Sixty-seven of these are in the United States and 61 are in China. In 2011, $8.17 billion was transacted, though not all payments were in cash. In kind payments, training programs, or agriculture inputs are also included.

Of the programs tracked, 66 of them include the stacking or "bundling" of other benefits. Most of these include co-benefits of biodiversity. Others include the bundling of carbon offsets or aesthetics. Concern for endangered species has also been a primary impetus for many of these programs.

Having users pay for services that they previously received for free can serve to produce an efficient outcome by providing both an incentive and revenue to protect those services. Suppose, however, the provider threatens to cut off supplies of those services unless the desired payments are forthcoming. Is this extortion or simply good business (see Debate 13.1)?

Water is not the only service to be involved in a payments scheme and sometimes the payments can be in kind rather than in cash (see Example 13.3).

Paying for Ecosystem Services or Extortion?: The Case of Yasuni National Park

DEBATE 13.1

Designated a UNESCO Biosphere Reserve in 1989, Yasuni National Park is one of the most biologically diverse places on earth. It is also the location for an estimated 846 million barrels of crude oil, 20% of Ecuador's reserves. As a developing country Ecuador was faced with a classic dilemma—should it preserve the parkland or extract the oil?

To avoid the environmental destruction caused by oil exploration in one of the areas with the greatest biological and cultural diversity of the Amazon, the government proposed permanently forgoing oil production in the Ishpingo-Tambococha-Tiputini (ITT) oil fields, located in Yasuni, if the world community would contribute 50 percent of the forgone income (estimated to be US$3.6 billion over a 13-year period).

Supporters argued that the payments would pay for global climate change benefits resulting from the CO_2 emissions avoided. They calculated 407 million metric tons of CO_2 emissions would be saved due to non-extraction and burning of oil and another 800 million metric tons of CO_2 from avoided deforestation.

Detractors suggested that this was extortion—"pay us or we will destroy the planet."

Regardless of whether it was a good idea or not, it failed. In August 2013, Ecuador's president announced that since the initiative had attracted only a fraction of the cash it had aimed to raise, he ended the initiative.

Sources: Ecuador Yasuni ITT Trust Fund. Retrieved from http://mptf.undp.org/yasuni; Ecuador approves Yasuni park oil drilling in Amazon rainforest. Retrieved from (http://www.bbc.co.uk/news/world-latin-america-23722204

Tradable Entitlement Systems

Another program approach recognizes that not only more land but also land better suited for supplying environmental services could be supplied if those services were treated separately in land titles. Some land may be especially good at providing environmental services while having a low opportunity cost, but other land may have a very high opportunity cost. If all land is required to meet the same environmental service provision requirements, the cost of the program will soar. Suppose, however, that the landowner has to supply those services, but not necessarily on the specific piece of land facing the requirement. This is the premise of a number of programs including wetlands banking and carbon sequestration credits.

Wetlands Banking[5]

Several U. S. administrations, both Republican and Democratic, have pledged that wetlands should experience "no net loss." Despite these bipartisan pledges to

[5]This section benefited from Salzman & Ruhl (2006).

EXAMPLE 13.3

Trading Water for Beehives and Barbed Wire in Bolivia

Amboro National Park in Bolivia supports a very biologically diverse ecosystem. The park and surrounding areas are under intense pressure from illegal land incursions. Migrants from the surrounding highlands, with encouragement from local political leaders, extract timber from the park and clear areas for agriculture. Lack of well-defined property rights for local communities leaves few alternative options. Due to increased timber harvesting and increased agriculture, the Los Neros River dries up earlier than it did in the past, causing suffering among the local communities that depend on the river for irrigation.

Asquit (2006) describes a unique solution to this property rights problem involving payments for environmental services. Natura Bolivia, an environmental group, helped negotiate an agreement through which downstream water users would pay for the protection of native vegetation in the watershed. Instead of financial compensation though, payment would be in the form of one beehive and training in honey production per 10 hectares of cloud forest protected. In 2003, 60 beehives were provided to farmers in exchange for 600 hectares of cloud forest conserved. In 2004, the municipal government provided another 11 hives to farmers. By 2006, 2100 hectares had been protected.

The Los Negros scheme is slowly building a market for environmental services and helping to define property rights in the region. In 2006, when contracts were renewed, some farmers requested barbed wire, instead of beehives, in order to help them strengthen their land claims. Combining a market mechanism (payment for environmental services) with developing a local enforcement mechanism and strengthening local property rights has proven to be a successful scheme so far.

Source: Asquith, N. (December 2006). Bees and barbed wire for water on the Bolivian frontier. *PERC, 24*.

protect wetlands, as the pressure on coastal and shorefront properties has increased, the economic benefits from developing wetlands (and political pressures to remove obstacles to development) have significantly increased as well.

One policy instrument for attempting to preserve wetlands in the face of this pressure is known as Wetlands Mitigation Banking and involves providing incentives for creating off-site "equivalent" wetlands services when adverse impacts on the original site are unavoidable and when on-site compensation is either not practical or use of a mitigation bank is environmentally preferable to on-site compensation. According to the US EPA, "The objective of a mitigation bank is to provide for the replacement of the chemical, physical, and biological functions of wetlands and other aquatic resources which are lost as a result of authorized impacts."

Mitigation banks involve wetlands, streams, or other aquatic resource areas that have been restored, established, enhanced, or (in certain circumstances) specifically preserved for the purpose of providing compensation for unavoidable impacts to aquatic resources. Mitigation banks involve a form of "third-party" compensatory mitigation in which the responsibility for compensatory mitigation implementation and success is assumed by someone other than the party who, by causing an adverse impact to a wetland, is required by law to provide mitigation.

A mitigation bank may be created when a government agency, corporation, nonprofit organization, or other entity undertakes mitigation activities under a formal agreement with a regulatory agency. The value of those activities is defined in "compensatory mitigation credits." In principle, the number of credits available for sale is based upon the use of ecological assessment techniques to certify that the credited areas provide the specified ecological functions.

How has the program performed? As one recent review (Saltzman & Ruhl, 2006) concludes,

> *Despite policies mandating that habitat trading ensure equivalent value and function, the experience is that most programs are not administered this way. In practice, most habitat trades to date in wetlands programs have been approved on the basis of acres, in many instances ensuring equivalence in neither value nor function.*

This experience is instructive. Merely assuring that the compensation involves a similar number of acres falls short of true equivalence unless the replacement ecological functions supplied by those acres are also the same.

Carbon Sequestration Credits

To the extent that landowners do not receive all the benefits of landownership, they may discount or ignore the benefits that accrue to others. Carbon sequestration credits are an attempt to rectify one such imbalance. Is this an efficient remedy?

As will be discussed in Chapter 16, carbon dioxide is a greenhouse gas, which means that excessive concentrations of carbon dioxide in the atmosphere can contribute to climate change. Through photosynthesis, trees absorb (sequester) carbon dioxide, thereby removing it from the atmosphere and lowering its threat to the climate.

Carbon sequestration credits attempt to internalize the carbon-absorption benefit externality by giving forest owners credit for the additional carbon they remove from the atmosphere. They can earn this credit by investing in additional carbon sequestration (by planting new trees, for example). This credit (or offset) can be sold to those who can use these reductions in fulfillment of their legal obligations to meet specified carbon-emissions targets. Some evidence suggests that reducing carbon in this way would be cheaper than many other measures. The Reducing Emissions from Deforestation and Forest Degradation (REDD) program, run by the United Nations, is an example of this approach (see Example 13.4).

Conflict Resolution in Open-Access Resources via Transferable Entitlements

In Chapter 12, we described how individual transferable quotas (ITQs) are used in fisheries management. When marine resources and services suffer from free access problems, ITQs are one option for reducing the overfishing problem.

EXAMPLE 13.4

Reducing Emissions from Deforestation and Forest Degradation (REDD): A Twofer?

According to the United Nations, deforestation and forest degradation, through agricultural expansion, conversion to pastureland, infrastructure development, destructive logging, fires, etc., account for nearly 20 percent of global greenhouse gas emissions, more than the entire global transportation sector and second only to the energy sector. In response, the United Nations has set up a program to reduce these emissions by reducing the forest degradation in developing countries. REDD is an effort to create a financial value for the carbon stored in forests, offering incentives for developing countries to reduce emissions from forested lands and to invest in low-carbon paths to sustainable development. According to this scheme, nations would receive payments for emissions-reduction credits determined on the basis of actual reductions in forest emissions measured against agreed-upon baselines. Although some of the details of this program remain to be worked out, these credits could, in principle, be sold in the international compliance carbon markets (where they could be used in combination with domestic reductions to meet assigned national targets) or voluntary carbon markets (where they could be used to pursue other organizational goals, such as demonstrating carbon neutrality).

The promise of this program is that it offers opportunities to make progress on two goals at once: (1) reducing forest degradation, and (2) reducing emissions that contribute to climate change. The challenges, which are far from trivial, are to establish baselines that are both fair and effective and to assure that monitoring and verification procedures are sufficiently rigorous as to provide reliable, accurate measures of actual emissions reductions. Otherwise the emissions authorized by the credits might exceed the actual emissions reductions that the credits are based upon.

Sources: Government of Norway. (2009). Reducing emissions from deforestation and forest degradation (REDD): An options assessment report. An electronic copy of this report is available at http://www.REDD-OAR.org; and the United Nations REDD Website. Retrieved from http://www.unredd.org/

Arnason (2012) argues that a properly designed ITQ system could also provide another, quite different, benefit, namely facilitating the resolution of marine resource conflicts between recreational and commercial fisheries as well as conflicts between fishing and other marine resource uses. Making the entitlements transferable creates both an economic means and an economic incentive for the entitlements to move to their highest valued use as circumstances change, but careful design and adequate enforcement would be key to achieving success in conflict resolution.

Have ITQs helped to resolve conflicts? Not yet, but some ITQ holders are beginning to coordinate with other users of marine resources. In New Zealand, the scallop fishery has formed an association that coordinates activities not only with other open-water fisheries, but also with aquaculture (Arnason, 2012).

One difficult international area of conflict involves the management of whale populations. Could tradable entitlements possibly help to resolve this conflict (see Debate 13.2)?

Tradable Quotas for Whales?

DEBATE 13.2

The International Whaling Commission banned whaling in 1986. Yet approximately 2000 are still harvested each year —approximately 1000 by Japan for "scientific purposes," 600 by Iceland and Norway, who do not recognize the ban, and 350 for subsistence (Costello et al., 2012). In 2010, some nations proposed allowing limited whaling with the hope that taking this step would reduce the number of whales actually harvested. This proposal never materialized due to disagreements between whaling and non-whaling nations.

Costello et al. (2012) argue that this conflict could be reduced using tradable quotas for whale harvesting thus "creating a market that would be economically, ecologically and socially valuable for whalers and whales alike" (p. 139). Under their scheme both whalers and conservationists could bid for quotas and whalers could earn profits from whaling or from selling their quotas to conservationists. They propose allocating "whale shares" in sustainable numbers to all the member nations of the International Whaling Commission (IWC). (Note that this means that non-whaling nations would also get a share. These shares could only be acquired by the whaling nations by buying them from the non-whaling nations.) Shares would be traded in a global market and could be exercised or retired in perpetuity. The size of the harvest would depend on who bought the shares and could fall between zero (conservationists purchase all) and the sustainable total quota. Since trades are voluntary, in principle this market mechanism has the potential to make all parties better off (including the whales)!

Opponents note that multiple challenges exist including determining the sustainable quota, obtaining agreement on how the shares to this quota would be initially allocated among the parties, and creating a trading system with adequate transparency and enforcement. Additionally those who oppose putting a price tag on whales as a matter of principle certainly are opposed to this idea. However, as Costello et al., point out, this lack of a real price tag could well be what has hindered anti-whaling operations.

What about costs and benefits? Conservation organizations such as Greenpeace spend millions of dollars on anti-whaling campaigns. The authors estimate that Greenpeace USA, Greenpeace International, Sea Shepard Conservation Society, and the World Wildlife Fund spend approximately $25 million annually on anti-whaling activities. The estimated profit from one minke whale is approximately $13,000, while the profit is $85,000 for a fin whale (2012 market prices and costs). Costello et al. estimate that the 350 whales saved by the Sea Sheppard in 2008 could simply have been purchased for less than $4 million.

Instead of spending money on anti-whaling, these groups would have the option to simply purchase the whales, thereby preventing anyone from harvesting them. The authors think it could be a win–win situation! Do you think they are right?

Source: Costello, C., Gaines, S., & Gerber, L. R. (January 12, 2012). Conservation science: A market approach to saving the whales. *Nature, 481*, 139–140.

Ecotourism

Ecotourism provides another prominent example of an activity that attempts to create a revenue stream based upon environmental services that can serve to fund protection of those services.

According to several organizations such as the International Ecotourism Society and International Union for Conservation of Nature, ecotourism can be defined as follows:

> *Environmentally responsible travel to natural areas, in order to enjoy and appreciate nature (and accompanying cultural features, both past and present) that promotes conservation, has a low visitor impact and provides for beneficially active socio-economic involvement of local peoples.*

The theory behind ecotourism is that it rectifies some of the bias against preserved land by providing an income stream from that land. In the language of Chapter 10, it shifts out the private preservation bid rent function, thereby bringing it closer to the social preservation bid rent function.

Not all ecotourism projects turn out to be consistent with this definition. Increasing the number of visitors to sensitive natural areas in the absence of appropriate oversight and control can threaten the integrity of both ecosystems and local cultures (see Debate 13.3). Additionally, the possible instabilities in this revenue source posed by climate fluctuations, volatile exchange rates, and political and social upheaval could make an excessive reliance upon tourism a risky business.

Another major threat to wildlife comes from poaching. Poaching is the illegal taking of game or domestic livestock. Normally we consider adequate enforcement to be the solution to poaching, but in some settings assuring adequate enforcement is easier said than done. Can trophy hunting help?

Consider, for example, how the economics of poaching might be used to enhance enforcement in the case of African wildlife. From an economic point of view, poaching can be discouraged if it is possible to raise the relative cost of illegal activity. In principle that can be accomplished by increasing the sanctions levied against poachers, but it is effective only if monitoring can not only detect the illegal activity but also apply the sanctions to those who engage in it. In many places that is a tall order, given the large size of the habitat to be monitored and the limited budgets for funding enforcement. Example 13.5 shows, however, how economic incentives can be enlisted to promote more monitoring by local inhabitants as well as to provide more revenue for enforcement activity.

Other types of incentives have also proved successful. In Kenya, for example, a compensation scheme has helped Maasai tribesmen to transition from hunting lions to protecting them. Maasai from the Mbirikani ranch are now compensated for livestock killed by predators. They receive $80 for each donkey and $200 for each cow killed. The Mbirikani Predator Fund has compensated herders for the loss

Does Ecotourism Provide a Pathway to Sustainability?

DEBATE 13.3

One of the ways ecotourism can promote conservation is by providing the necessary funds to implement an effective conservation program. Take the example of Bolivia's Eduardo Avaroa Reserve. This diverse landscape includes hot springs and geysers surrounded by volcanoes and majestic mountains. Its freshwater and saltwater lakes provide habitat for year-round flocks of pink flamingos and other birds, while nearby 23 types of mammals and almost 200 species of plants flourish in the desert-like environment. With over 40,000 visitors per year, the park is Bolivia's most visited.

When a conservation planning initiative determined that tourism was a major threat to the reserve, The Nature Conservancy worked with the Bolivian National Park System to develop a visitor-fee system. The program, which reportedly generated over half a million dollars in new funds, allows the reserve to fund efforts to mitigate these tourism-related threats. The visitor-fee approach is now being extended across the Bolivian Park System. It is estimated that the national protected areas system could generate more than $3 million per year in new income for conservation.

Quite a different take on ecotourism is provided by a British academic Rosaleen Duffy. Speaking about the former British colony of Belize—a popular ecotourist destination in Central America—Duffy relates stories of how scuba diving and snorkeling visitors have spoiled fragile corals and otherwise-harassed marine wildlife.

"In their pursuit of reefs, rainforests, and ruins," writes Duffy, "they did not reflect on the environmental impact of the construction of hotels, the use of airlines, the manufacture of diving equipment, the consumption of imported goods or even something as visible as taking a motorboat out to the reef, which polluted the water." As a *Time* article on her book notes, "To Duffy, it seems, the only good tourist is the one who stays home."

Sources: Duffy, D. (2002). A Trip too far—Ecotourism, politics & exploitation. Island Press; Mary Ann Bird, M. A. (2002). Ecotourism or egotourism. *TIME* online. Retrieved May 24, 2007, from http://content.time.com/time/magazine/article/0,9171,338585,00.html; The Nature Conservancy, Ecotourism and Conservation Finance. Retrieved May 24, 2007, from http://www.nature.org/aboutus/travel/ecotourism/about/art14824.html.

of 750 head of livestock each year since the program began in 2003. As an additional collective incentive, if any herder kills a lion, no one gets paid.[6]

Rearranging the economic incentives so that local groups have an economic interest in preservation can provide a powerful means of protecting some biological populations. Open access undermines those incentives.

---

[6]Conservation International June 21, 2007.

EXAMPLE 13.5

Local Approaches to Wildlife Protection: Zimbabwe

In 1989, an innovative program was initiated in Zimbabwe that stands out as a success among other African wildlife protection schemes. It transformed the role of wildlife from a state-owned treasure to be preserved into an active resource controlled and used by both commercial farmers and smallholders in communal lands. The transformation has been good for the economy and the wildlife.

The initiative is called the Communal Areas Management Program for Indigenous Resources (CAMPFIRE). It was originally sponsored by several different agencies in cooperation with the Zimbabwean government, including the University of Zimbabwe's Center for Applied Study, the Zimbabwe Trust, and the Worldwide Fund for Nature (WWF).

Under the CAMPFIRE system, villagers collectively utilize local wildlife resources on a sustainable basis. Trophy hunting by foreigners is perhaps the most important source of revenue, because hunters require few facilities and are willing to pay substantial fees to kill a limited number of large animals. The government sets the prices of hunting permits as well as quotas for the number of animals that can be taken per year in each locality. Individual communities sell the permits and contract with safari operators who conduct photographic and hunting expeditions on community lands.

The associated economic gains accrue to the villages, which then decide how the revenues should be used. The money may either be paid to households in the form of cash dividends, which may amount to 20 percent or more of an average family's income, or they may be used for capital investments in the community, such as schools or clinics. In at least one area, revenues compensate citizens who have suffered property loss due to wild animals. Households may also receive nonmonetary benefits, such as meat from problem animals or culled herds. By consistently meeting their needs from their own resources on a sustainable basis, local communities have become self-reliant. This voluntary program has been steadily expanding since its inception, and now includes about half of Zimbabwe's 55 districts.

Sources: Barbier, E. (1992). Community based development in Africa. In T. Swanson & E. Barbier (Eds.), *Economics for the wilds: Wildlife, diversity, and development* (107–118). Washington, DC: Island Press; Bojö, J. (February 1996). The Economics of wildlife: Case studies from Ghana, Kenya, Namibia and Zimbabwe. *AFTES Working Paper No. 19*. The World Bank; and the Website http://www.Colby.edu/personal/thtieten/end-zim.html

The Special Problem of Protecting Endangered Species

Suppose the survival of a specific species is found to be endangered and listed as such under the US Endangered Species Act (ESA). How can economics help to create incentive-based programs to enhance the likelihood of survival for these species?

Conservation biologists have found that one key to reducing the threat to endangered species is to prevent their habitat from become fragmented into smaller parcels. In response economists have developed programs that attempt to reduce habitat fragmentation.

Conservation Banking

One such program, conservation banking, enlists a tailored transferable credits program into endangered and threatened species conservation. A conservation bank is a parcel of land containing natural-resource values that are conserved and managed, in perpetuity, through a conservation easement (described in Chapter 10) held by an entity responsible for enforcing the terms of the easement. Banks of especially suitable land are established for specified listed species (under the Endangered Species Act) and used to offset impacts to the species occurring on nonbank lands by providing a larger, less fragmented habitat for them.

Access to the habitat services provided by these banks is provided by the creation of saleable quantified "credits," where each credit provides a specified amount of habitat provision designed to satisy the requirements of the ESA. Project proponents are, therefore, able to complete their ESA obligations through a one-time purchase of credits from the conservation bank (see Example 13.6).

EXAMPLE 13.6

Conservation Banking: The Gopher Tortoise Conservation Bank

In rapidly growing Mobile County, Alabama, the gopher tortoise faced survival problems due to the disappearance of its habitat. Since the tortoise is federally listed as a threatened species under the Endangered Species Act (ESA), small landowners were forced to observe some rather severe restrictions on their use of the land. Because these restrictions were quite burdensome for the landowners and the resulting fragmented, patchy habitat proved ineffective in protecting the tortoise, these restrictions created quite a conflict in the community.

A conservation bank established by the Mobile Area Water and Sewer System (MAWSS) in 2001 reduced the conflict, allowing development to continue in other areas while restoring and permanently protecting a much more suitable large tract of the long-leaf pine habitat that the tortoise prefers.

MAWSS owns a 7000-acre forest that buffers and protects the county's water supply. Under the terms of its conservation bank, MAWSS has agreed to set aside 222 acres, forgo any development on that land, and manage it in perpetuity for the benefit of gopher tortoises. Landowners who want to build on tortoise habitat elsewhere in Mobile County can purchase "credits" from the bank, and thereby be relieved of their ESA responsibilities to set aside a small patch of their land. The tortoises benefit because the large tract of contiguous, suitable habitat is vastly superior to a network of small, unconnected patches of land, while the landowners can now develop their land by helping to fund (through the purchase of credits) this tortoise habitat.

Source: Environmental Defense's Center for Conservation Incentives. (February 24, 2003). Gopher tortoise conservation bank: Mobile area landowners and wildlife get help. Retrieved from http://www.environmentaldefense.org

The Agglomeration Bonus

Another strategy to reduce fragmentation, known as the *agglomeration bonus*, has been proposed by Smith and Shogren (2002). The agglomeration bonus is a voluntary incentive mechanism that is designed to protect endangered species and biodiversity by reuniting fragmented habitat across private land in a manner that minimizes landowner resistance.

Many states currently have programs that encourage landowners to conserve land, but how can these owners be further encouraged to give priority to land that connects with other land? Under this bonus payment scheme the landowner receives an additional payment (the bonus) for each retired acre that shares a common border with another retired acre. If both landowners retire land at their common border, both can profit from their neighbor's retired acres. With this bonus each landowner has an explicit incentive to give priority to retiring acres that are adjacent to his neighbor's retired acres. Notice that the agglomeration bonus pays for connected land not any specific piece of land—landowners are free to select any land that shares a common border with other retired land.

This mechanism provides an incentive for landowners to give preference to land that would form a contiguous reserve across their common border. The government agency's role would be to target the critical habitat and to integrate the agglomeration bonus into the compensation package, but the landowners would have the ultimate power to decide whether or not to participate.

An analysis of the properties of this mechanism using experimental economics (Parkhurst et al., 2002) found that in the lab the absence of a bonus always created fragmented habitat, whereas with the bonus players cooperated to establish the optimal habitat reserve.

Safe Harbor Agreements[7]

Safe harbor agreements are a new means of conserving endangered and threatened species on privately owned land. These agreements approach the problem of landowner incentives from a different perspective, mainly seeking to overcome some rather severe unintended consequences that can flow from the Endangered Species Act (ESA).

Under the ESA many landowners are actually inhibited from implementing practices likely to benefit endangered species because of the repercussions that might arise from these apparently benign activities. Under the approach taken by the ESA, the presence of an endangered species on a property may result in new legally imposed restrictions on any activities deemed harmful to that species. Thus, if landowners were simply to restore wildlife habitats on their property, and those habitats attracted endangered animals, they might find themselves faced with many new restrictions on their use of the land. As a result, some landowners are not only

[7]This section benefited from the information in Environmental Defense's Center for Conservation Incentives. For more information on safe harbor agreements, see the Website at http://www.environmentaldefense.org/article.cfm?ContentID=399

unwilling to take such risks, but they may actually actively manage property to prevent endangered species from occupying their land.

Safe harbor agreements overcome these perverse incentive problems. Any landowner who agrees to carry out activities expected to benefit an endangered species is guaranteed that no added ESA restrictions will be imposed as a result. A landowner's ESA responsibilities are effectively frozen at their current levels for a particular species if he or she agrees to restore, enhance, or create habitat for that species. Safe Harbor agreements do not, however, confer a right to harm any endangered species already present when the agreement is entered into (established by the landowner's "baseline" responsibilities). Those responsibilities are unaffected by a safe harbor agreement.

Moving Forward

Ecosystem goods and services may be the ultimate resources that humans rely on. This chapter has highlighted some of the ways that economic analysis can place values on these goods and services to assist policy makers in decision making. We have also looked at multiple examples of economic incentives and mechanisms to encourage the provision of ecosystem goods and services and to reduce their degradation.

As we have seen with these examples the theory is relatively straight forward, but in practice, developing innovative mechanisms like payments for ecosystem services or carbon sequestration credits is challenging, especially in developing countries.

Summary

Ecosystems provide a host of services to humans, but the continued existence of those services is threatened. In this chapter we explore how two different kinds of economic analysis can contribute to protecting, maintaining, and enhancing these ecosystems.

The first step involves providing quantitative estimates of the value of these ecosystem services both to demonstrate their importance in general and to provide metrics that can be included in cost-benefit analyses that are being used for making choices that affect ecosystems. For commercial species such as fish, forests, and commercial resources such as water the valuation task is made somewhat easier by the ready availability of prices.

For other ecosystem services the task is more difficult, but over time some of those barriers are beginning to fall as techniques such as avoided cost, stated preference surveys and travel cost studies are used to value ecosystem services. These methodologies are increasingly being applied to such different problems as valuing pollination services, assessing the economic impact of ecosystem-degrading events such as oil spills, and quantifying the role and economic benefits of natural water purification systems derived from wetlands or stream buffer zones. Newer methods such as computable general equilibrium (CGE) models allow analysts to capture not only the direct values to humans, but the indirect values as well. These studies not only corroborate and quantify the general sense that ecosystems services are valuable and deserve protection but they also identify the many pathways that provide these provisioning, regulating, supporting, and cultural services.

This chapter also examines the other main protection avenue—designing institutions and mechanisms that can eliminate or at least reduce perverse incentives that intensify degradation. Specifically we have examined innovative schemes that provide payments from service users to service providers for historically non-marketed services to assure that the providers have an incentive to refrain from converting the land to some other incompatible use. Another category of approaches focuses on creating new transferable entitlements to service flows. Not only do they give rise to new markets (such as wetlands banking, conservation entitlements for fish, or carbon sequestration credits) that can provide more economic sustainability to these flows by returning revenue to those who protect those services but they also provide a new venue for potentially reducing resource conflicts.

And finally we note how economic incentives can be used to protect those most vulnerable species—those that have already been classified as endangered. Environmental organizations have turned to economic approaches such as conservation banking to provide incentives for the market to preserve more of the most suitable endangered species habitat and safe harbor programs to counteract some of the more perverse habitat-destroying incentives for landowners that were inadvertently created by the Endangered Species Act.

As we point out in this chapter this new subfield is experiencing some growing pains, but early successes and new innovations indicate that its future is promising.

Discussion Questions

1. Consider the issues raised by the debate over Equador's proposal to preserve the Yasuni National Park from oil extraction. What is your view? Is this simply another payment for ecosystem services or was this extortion? Is this case different from some of the other payment for services cases described above? If so, how is it different?
2. Consider the issues raised by the debate over using ecotourism to promote sustainability. What is your view? Is ecotourism always a pathway to sustainability? Never a pathway to sustainability? or Sometimes a pathway to sustainability? Does your view suggest an appropriate role for government in managing ecotourism or should the entire process be left to the private sector? Why?
3. One approach to protecting ecosystem services involves dedicating specific habitat to wildlife (such as parks or reserves), a strategy that prohibits

residential development in those areas. Other strategies (wetlands and conservation banking) accommodate residential development at a specific site, while attempting to offset the adverse effects on that site with requirements for preservation activities at other sites as a condition of allowing development at the original site. In your mind does one of these strategies always dominate the other? Is so, why? If not, does the context matter? How would an economist think about these questions?

Self-Test Exercises

1. Several of the policy options discussed in this chapter rely on transferable entitlements of one kind or another. The prominence of these approaches raises the question of what transferability adds to mix. For each of the following options describe why making the entitlement transferable increases its efficiency.
   (a) Carbon reduction credits
   (b) Conservation banking
2. Suppose that a fishery has two sectors: (1) a commercial fishery that harvests fish to sell them to a processor, and (2) a recreational fishery where boat captains take individuals out to catch some fish for the sport of it. Each sector has a catch share. Suppose further that the demand for sport fishing goes up considerably relative to the commercial fishery. This development would create a conflict because the recreational fishery would no doubt argue that its catch share is now unfairly low. Compare how this conflict might be dealt with depending on whether the catch shares are transferable between sectors or not. Think about how the incentives of each sector to resolve this conflict are affected by the possibility of inter-sector transferability of the catch shares.

Further Reading

Agricultural and Resource Economics Review (continues the Northeastern Journal of Agricultural and Resource Economics) Volume 42, Number 1, April 2013: This special issue is devoted entirely to the economics of ecosystem services valuation, measurement and analysis.

Millennium Ecosystem Assessment. (2005). Ecosystems and human well-being: A synthesis. Washington, DC, Island Press. A summary of the findings of the UN Ecosystem Assessment.

National Research Council of the National Academies of Science (NRC). (2013). *An ecosystem services approach to assessing the impacts of the Deepwater Horizon Oil Spill in the Gulf of Mexico*. Washington, DC: National Academies Press. Discusses the benefits and challenges associated with using an ecosystem services approach to damage assessment, and offers suggestions for areas of future research.

Pattanayak, S. K., Wunder, S., & Ferraro, P.J. (2010). Show me the money: Do payments supply environmental service in developing countries. *Review of Environmental Economics and Policy*, *4*(2), 254–274, Survey of the literature on payments for ecosystem services with a particular emphasis on their use in developing countries.

Ruckelshaus, M., E. McKenzie, H. Taillis, A. Guerry, G. Daily, P. Kareiva, S. Polasky, T. Ricketts, N. Bhagabati, S. Wood and J. Bernhardt. (2013). "Notes from the field: Lessons learned from using ecosystem service approaches to inform real-world decisions." Ecological Economics, http://dxdoi.org/10.1016/j.ecolecon2013.07.009. Offers six lessons from recent assessments of biodiversisty and ecosystem services.

TEEB. (2009). The economics of ecosystems and biodiversity: Climate issues update (September 2009). A report that examines the impacts of climate change on ecosystems and biodiversity with a special emphasis on coral reefs and forests.

Additional References and Historically Significant References are available on this book's Companion Website: http://www.routledgetextbooks.com/textbooks/9780133479690

14 Economics of Pollution Control: An Overview

Democracy is not a matter of sentiment, but of foresight. Any system that doesn't take the long run into account will burn itself out in the short run.

—Charles Yost, *The Age of Triumph and Frustration* (1964)

Introduction

In Chapter 2 we introduced a schematic describing the relationship between the natural and economic systems. One side depicted the flow of mass and energy to the economic system, while the other depicted the flow of waste products back to the environment. In the last few chapters we dealt extensively with different types of natural resources and maintaining efficient and sustainable levels for both stocks and flows of those resources. Now we turn to examining how a balance can be achieved in the reverse flow of waste products back to the environment. Because the waste flows are inexorably intertwined with the flow of mass and energy into the economy, establishing a balance for waste flows will have feedback effects on the input flows as well.

Two questions must be addressed: (1) what is the appropriate level of flow of pollution? and, (2) how should the responsibility for achieving this flow level be allocated among the various sources of the pollutant when reductions are needed?

In this chapter we lay the foundation for understanding the policy approach to controlling the flow of these waste products by developing a general framework for analyzing pollution control. This framework allows us to define efficient and cost-effective allocations for a variety of pollutant types, to compare these allocations to market allocations, and to demonstrate how efficiency and cost-effectiveness can be used to formulate desirable policy responses. This overview is then followed by a series of chapters that apply these principles by examining the policy approaches that have been adopted in the United States and in the rest of the world to establish control over waste flows.

A Pollutant Taxonomy

The amount of waste products emitted determines the load upon the environment. The damage done by this load depends on the capacity of the environment to assimilate the waste products (see Figure 14.1). We call this ability of the environment to absorb pollutants its *absorptive capacity*. If the emissions load exceeds the absorptive capacity, then the pollutant accumulates in the environment.

Pollutants for which the environment has little or no absorptive capacity are called *stock pollutants*. Stock pollutants accumulate over time as emissions enter the environment. Examples of stock pollutants include nonbiodegradable bottles tossed by the roadside; heavy metals, such as lead, that accumulate in the soils near the emissions source; and persistent synthetic chemicals, such as dioxin and PCBs (polychlorinated biphenyls).

Pollutants for which the environment has some absorptive capacity are called *fund pollutants*. For these pollutants, as long as the emissions rate does not exceed the absorptive capacity of the environment, the pollutants do not accumulate. Examples of fund pollutants are easy to find. Many organic pollutants injected into an oxygen-rich stream will be transformed by the resident bacteria into less harmful inorganic matter. Carbon dioxide is absorbed by plant life and the oceans.

The point is *not* that the mass is destroyed; the law of conservation of mass suggests this cannot be the case. Rather, when fund pollutants are injected into the air or water, they may be transformed into substances that are not considered harmful to people or to the ecological system, or they may be so diluted or dispersed that the resulting concentrations are not harmful.

Pollutants can also be classified by their zone of influence, defined both horizontally and vertically. The horizontal dimension deals with the spatial domain over which damage from an emitted pollutant is experienced. The damage caused by *local* pollutants is experienced near the source of emission, while the damage from *regional* pollutants is experienced at greater distances from the source of emission. The limiting case is a *global* pollutant, where the damage affects the entire planet. The categories are not mutually exclusive; it is possible for a pollutant to be in more

FIGURE 14.1 Relationship between Emissions and Pollution Damage

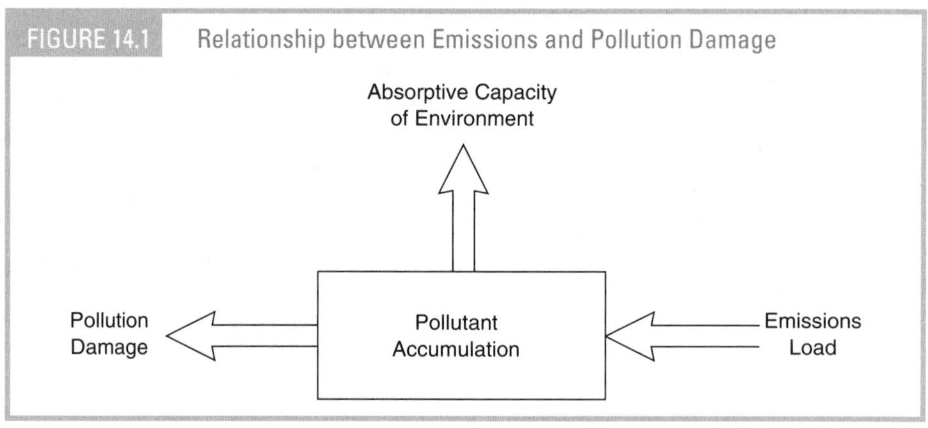

than one category. Sulfur oxides and nitrogen oxides, for example, are both local and regional pollutants.

The vertical zone of influence describes whether the damage is caused mainly by ground-level concentrations of an air pollutant or by concentrations in the upper atmosphere. For some pollutants, such as lead or particulates, the damage caused by a pollutant is determined mainly by concentrations of the pollutant near the earth's surface. For others, such as ozone-depleting substances or greenhouse gases (described in Chapter 16), the damage is related more to their concentrations in the upper atmosphere. This taxonomy will prove useful in designing policy responses to these various types of pollution problems. Each type of pollutant requires a unique policy response. The failure to recognize these distinctions leads to counterproductive policy.

Defining the Efficient Allocation of Pollution

Pollutants are the residuals of production and consumption. These residuals must eventually be recycled or returned to the environment in one form or another. Since their presence in the environment may depreciate the service flows received, an efficient allocation of resources must take this cost into account. What is meant by the efficient allocation of pollution depends on the nature of the pollutant.

Stock Pollutants

The efficient allocation of a stock pollutant must take into account the fact that the pollutant accumulates in the environment over time and that the damage caused by its presence increases and persists as the pollutant accumulates. By their very nature, stock pollutants create an interdependency between the present and the future, since the damage imposed in the future depends on current actions.

The damage caused by pollution can take many forms. At high enough exposures to certain pollutants, human health can be adversely impacted, possibly even leading to death. Other living organisms, such as trees or fish, can be harmed as well. Damage can even occur to inanimate objects, as when acid rain causes sculptures to deteriorate or when particulates cause structures to discolor.

It is not hard to establish what is meant by an efficient allocation in these circumstances using the intuition we gained from the discussion of depletable resource models. Suppose, for example, that we consider the allocation of a commodity that we refer to as X. Suppose further that the production of X involves the generation of a proportional amount of a stock pollutant. The amount of this pollution can be reduced, but that takes resources away from the production of X. The damage caused by the presence of this pollutant in the environment is further assumed to be proportional to the size of the accumulated stock. As long as the stock of pollutants remains in the environment, the damage persists.

The dynamic efficient allocation, by definition, is the one that maximizes the present value of the net benefit. In this case the net benefit at any point in time, t, is equal to the benefit received from the consumption of X minus the cost of the damage caused by the presence of the stock pollutant in the environment.

This damage is a cost that society must bear, and in terms of its effect on the efficient allocation, this cost is not unlike that associated with extracting minerals or fuels. While for minerals the extraction cost rises with the cumulative amount of the depletable resource extracted, the damage cost associated with a stock pollutant rises with the cumulative amount deposited in the environment. The accretion of the stock pollutant is proportional to the production of *X*, which creates the same kind of linkage between the production of *X* and this pollution cost as exists between the extraction cost and the production of a mineral. They both rise over time with the cumulative amount produced. The one major difference is that the extraction cost is borne only at the time of extraction, while damage persists as long as the stock pollutant remains in the environment.

We can exploit this similarity to infer the efficient allocation of a stock pollutant. As discussed in Chapter 6, when extraction cost rises, the efficient quantity of a depletable resource extracted and consumed declines over time.

Exactly the same pattern would emerge for a commodity that is produced jointly with a stock pollutant. The efficient quantity of *X* (and therefore, the addition to the accumulation of this pollutant in the environment) would decline over time as the marginal cost of the damage rises. The price of *X* would rise over time, reflecting the rising social cost of production. To cope with the increasing marginal damage, the amount of resources committed to controlling the pollutant would increase over time. Ultimately, a steady state would be reached where additions to the amount of the pollutant in the environment would cease and the size of the pollutant stock would stabilize. At this point, all further emission of the pollutant created by the production of *X* would be controlled (perhaps through recycling). The price of *X* and the quantity consumed would remain constant. The damage caused by the stock pollutant would persist.

As was the case with rising extraction cost, technological progress could modify this efficient allocation. Specifically, technological progress could reduce the amount of pollutant generated per unit of *X* produced; it could create ways to recycle the stock pollutant rather than injecting it into the environment; or it could develop ways of rendering the pollutant less harmful. All of these responses would lower the marginal damage cost associated with a given level of production of *X*. Therefore, more of *X* could be produced with technological progress than without it.

Stock pollutants are, in a sense, the other side of the intergenerational equity coin from depletable resources. With depletable resources, it is possible for current generations to create a burden for future generations by using up resources, thereby diminishing the remaining endowment. Stock pollutants can create a burden for future generations by passing on damages that persist well after the benefits received from incurring the damages have been forgotten. Though neither of these situations automatically violates the weak sustainability criterion, they clearly require further scrutiny.

Fund Pollutants

To the extent that the emission of fund pollutants exceeds the assimilative capacity of the environment, they accumulate and share some of the characteristics of stock pollutants. When the emissions rate is low enough, however, the discharges can be assimilated by the environment, with the result that the link between present emissions and future damage may be broken.

When this happens, current emissions cause current damage, and future emissions cause future damage, but the level of future damage is independent of current emissions. This independence of allocations among time periods allows us to explore the efficient allocation of fund pollutants using the concept of static, rather than dynamic, efficiency. Because the static concept is simpler, this affords us the opportunity to incorporate more dimensions of the problem without unnecessarily complicating the analysis.

The normal starting point for the analysis would be to maximize the net benefit from the waste flows. However, pollution is more easily understood if we deal with a mathematically equivalent formulation involving the minimization of two rather different types of costs: damage costs and control or avoidance costs.

To examine the efficient allocation graphically, we need to know something about how control costs vary with the degree of control and how the damages vary with the amount of pollution emitted. Though our knowledge in these areas is far from complete, economists generally agree on the shapes of these relationships.

Generally, the marginal damage caused by a unit of pollution increases with the amount emitted. When small amounts of the pollutant are emitted, the incremental damage is quite small. However, when large amounts are emitted, the marginal unit can cause significantly more damage. It is not hard to understand why. Small amounts of pollution are easily diluted in the environment, and the body can tolerate small quantities of substances. However, as the amount in the atmosphere increases, dilution is less effective and the body is less tolerant.

Marginal control costs commonly increase with the amount controlled. For example, suppose a source of pollution tries to cut down on its particulate emissions by purchasing an electrostatic precipitator that captures 80 percent of the particulates as they flow past in the stack. If the source wants further control, it can purchase another precipitator and place it in the stack above the first one. This second precipitator captures 80 percent of the remaining 20 percent, or 16 percent of the uncontrolled emissions. Thus, the first precipitator would achieve an 80 percent reduction from uncontrolled emissions, while the second precipitator, which costs the same as the first, would achieve only a further 16 percent reduction. Obviously each unit of emissions reduction costs more for the second precipitator than for the first.

In Figure 14.2 we use these two pieces of information on the shapes of the relevant curves to derive the efficient allocation. A movement from right to left refers to greater control and less pollution emitted. The efficient allocation is represented by Q^*, the point at which the damage caused by the marginal unit of pollution is exactly equal to the marginal cost of avoiding it.[1]

Greater degrees of control (points to the left of Q^*) are inefficient because the further increase in avoidance costs would exceed the reduction in damages. Hence, total costs would rise. Similarly, levels of control lower than Q^* would result in a

[1]At this point, we can see why this formulation is equivalent to the net benefit formulation. Since the benefit is damage reduction, another way of stating this proposition is that marginal benefit must equal marginal cost. That is, of course, the familiar proposition derived by maximizing net benefits.

FIGURE 14.2 Efficient Allocation of a Fund Pollutant

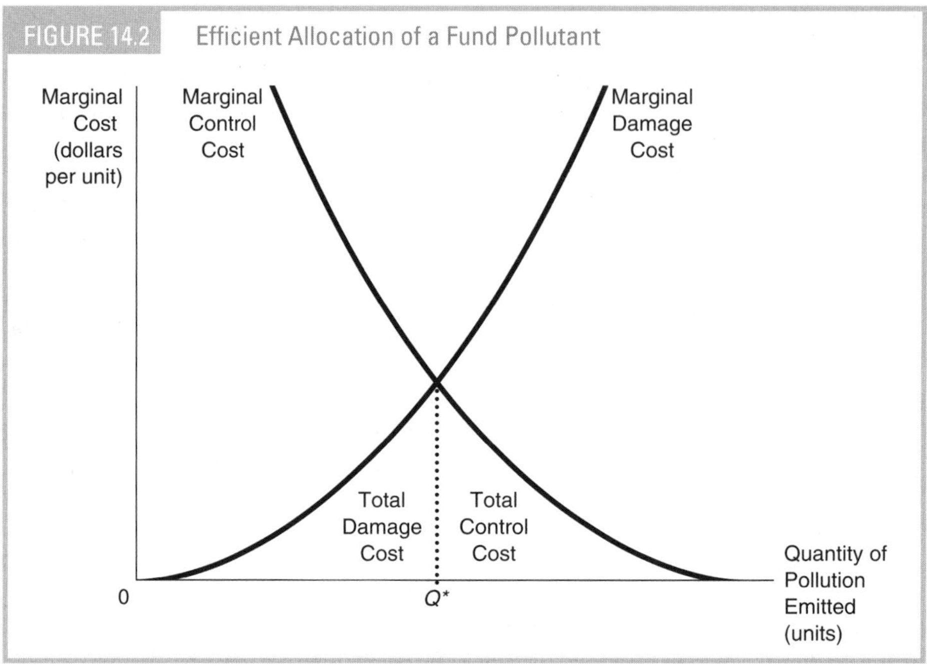

lower cost of control but the increase in damage costs would be even larger, yielding an increase in total cost. Increasing or decreasing the amount controlled causes an increase in total costs. Hence, Q^* must be efficient.

The diagram suggests that under the conditions presented, the optimal level of pollution is not zero. If you find this disturbing, remember that we confront this principle every day. Take the damage caused by automobile accidents, for example. Obviously, a considerable amount of damage is caused by automobile accidents, yet we do not reduce that damage to zero because the cost of doing so would be too high.

The point is *not* that we do not know how to stop automobile accidents. All we would have to do is eliminate automobiles! Rather, the point is that since we value the benefits of automobiles, we take steps to reduce accidents (such as using speed limits) only to the extent that the costs of accident reduction are commensurate with the damage reduction achieved. The efficient level of automobile accidents is not zero.

The second point is that in some circumstances the optimal level of pollution *may* be zero, or close to it. This situation occurs when the damage caused by even the first unit of pollution is so severe that it is higher than the marginal cost of controlling it. This would be reflected in Figure 14.2 as a leftward shift of the damage cost curve of sufficient magnitude that its intersection with the vertical axis would lie above the point where the marginal cost curve intersects the vertical axis. This circumstance seems to characterize the treatment of highly dangerous radioactive pollutants such as plutonium.

Additional insights are easily derived from our characterization of the efficient allocation. For example, it should be clear from Figure 14.2 that the optimal level of pollution generally is not the same for all parts of the country. Areas that have higher population levels or are particularly sensitive to pollution would have a marginal damage cost curve that intersected the marginal control cost curve close to the vertical axis. Efficiency would imply lower levels of pollution for those areas. Areas that have lower population levels or are less sensitive should have higher efficient levels of pollution.

Examples of ecological sensitivity are not hard to find. For instance, some areas are less sensitive to acid rain than others because the local geological strata neutralize moderate amounts of the acid. Thus, the marginal damage caused by a unit of acid rain is lower in those fortunate regions than in other, less tolerant regions. It can also be argued that pollutants affecting visibility are more damaging in national parks and other areas where visibility is an important part of the aesthetic experience than in other more industrial areas.

Market Allocation of Pollution

Since air and water are treated in our legal system as common-pool resources, at this point in the book it should surprise no one that the market misallocates them. Our previously derived conclusion that free-access resources are overexploited certainly also applies here. Air and water resources have been overexploited as waste repositories. However, this conclusion only scratches the surface; much more can be learned about market allocations of pollution.

When firms create products, rarely does the process of converting raw material into outputs use 100 percent of the mass. Some of the mass, called a *residual*, is left over. If the residual is valuable, it is simply reused. However, if it is not valuable, the firm has an incentive to deal with it in the cheapest manner possible.

The typical firm has several alternatives. It can control the amount of the residual by using inputs more completely so that less is left over. It can also produce less output, so that smaller amounts of the residual are generated. Recycling the residual is sometimes a viable option, as is removing the most damaging components of the waste stream and disposing of the rest.

Pollutant damages are commonly externalities.[2] When pollutants are injected into water bodies or the atmosphere, they cause damages to those firms and consumers (as well as to flora and fauna) downstream or downwind of the source, not to the source itself. These costs are *not* borne by the emitting source and hence not considered by it, although they certainly are borne by society at large.[3] As with other services that are systematically undervalued, the disposal of wastes into the air or water becomes inefficiently attractive. In this case the firm minimizes its costs when it chooses not to abate anything, since the only costs it bears are the control costs. What is cheapest for the firm is not cheapest for society.

[2]Note that pollution damage is not inevitably an externality. For any automobile rigged to send all exhaust gases into its interior, those exhaust gases would not be an externality to the occupants.

[3]Actually the source certainly considers some of the costs, if only to avoid adverse public relations. The point, however, is that this consideration is likely to be incomplete; the source is unlikely to internalize all of the damage cost.

In the case of stock pollutants, the problem is particularly severe. Uncontrolled markets would lead to an excessive production of the product that generates the pollution, too few resources committed to pollution control, and an inefficiently large amount of the stock pollutant in the environment. Thus, the burden on future generations caused by the presence of this pollutant would be inefficiently large.

The inefficiencies associated with pollution control and the previously discussed inefficiencies associated with the extraction or production of minerals, energy, and food exhibit some rather important differences. For private property resources, the market forces provide automatic signals of impending scarcity. These forces may be understated (as when the vulnerability of imports is ignored), but they operate in the correct direction. Even when some resources are treated as open-access (fisheries), the possibility for a private property alternative (fish farming) is enhanced. When private property and open-access resources sell in the same market, the private property owner tends to ameliorate the excesses of those who exploit open-access properties. Efficient firms are rewarded with higher profits.

With pollution, no comparable automatic amelioration mechanism is evident.[4] Because this cost is borne partially by innocent victims rather than producers, it does not find its way into product prices. Firms that attempt unilaterally to control their pollution are placed at a competitive disadvantage; due to the added expense, their costs of production are higher than those of their less conscientious competitors. Not only does the unimpeded market fail to generate the efficient level of pollution control, but also it penalizes those firms that might attempt to control an efficient amount. Hence, the case for some sort of government intervention is particularly strong for pollution control.

Efficient Policy Responses

Our use of the efficiency criterion has helped demonstrate why markets fail to produce an efficient level of pollution control as well as trace out the effects of this less-than-optimal degree of control on the markets for related commodities. It can also be used to define efficient policy responses.

In Figure 14.2 we demonstrated that for a market as a whole, efficiency is achieved when the marginal cost of control is equal to the marginal damage caused by the pollution. This same principle applies to each emitter. Each emitter should control its pollution until the marginal cost of controlling the last unit is equal to the marginal damage it causes. One way to achieve this outcome would be to impose a legal limit on the amount of pollution allowed by each emitter. If the limit were chosen precisely at the level of emission where marginal control cost equaled the marginal damage, efficiency would have been achieved for that emitter.

An alternative approach would be to internalize the marginal damage caused by each unit of emissions by means of a tax or charge on each unit of emissions.

[4]Affected parties do have an incentive to negotiate among themselves, a topic covered in Chapter 2. As pointed out there, however, that approach works well only in cases where the number of affected parties is small.

Either this per-unit charge could increase with the level of pollution (following the marginal damage curve for each succeeding unit of emission) or the tax rate could be constant as long as the rate were equal to the marginal social damage at the point where the marginal social damage and marginal control costs cross (see Figure 14.2). Since the emitter is paying the marginal social damage when confronted by these fees, pollution costs would be internalized. The efficient choice would also be the cost-minimizing choice for the emitter.[5]

While the efficient levels of these policy instruments can be easily defined in principle, they are very difficult to implement in practice. To implement either of these policy instruments, we must know the level of emissions at which the two marginal cost curves cross for every emitter. That is a tall order, one that imposes an unrealistically high information burden on control authorities. Control authorities typically have very poor information on control costs and little reliable information on marginal damage functions.

How can environmental authorities allocate pollution control responsibility in a reasonable manner when the information burdens are apparently so unrealistically large? One approach, the choice of several countries including the United States, is to select specific legal levels of pollution based on some other criterion, such as providing adequate margins of safety for human or ecological health. Once these thresholds have been established by whatever means, only half of the problem has been resolved. The other half deals with deciding how to allocate the responsibility for meeting predetermined pollution levels among the large numbers of emitters.

This is precisely where the cost-effectiveness criterion comes in. Once the objective is stated in terms of meeting the predetermined pollution level at minimum cost, it is possible to derive the conditions that any cost-effective allocation of the responsibility must satisfy. These conditions can then be used as a basis for choosing among various kinds of policy instruments that impose more reasonable information burdens on control authorities.

Cost-Effective Policies for Uniformly Mixed Fund Pollutants

Defining a Cost-Effective Allocation

We begin our analysis with uniformly mixed fund pollutants, which analytically are the easiest to deal with. The damage caused by these pollutants depends on the amount entering the atmosphere. In contrast to nonuniformly mixed pollutants, the damage caused by uniformly mixed pollutants is relatively insensitive to where the emissions are injected into the atmosphere. Thus, the policy can focus simply

[5]Another policy choice is to remove the people from the polluted area. The government has used this strategy for heavily contaminated toxic-waste sites, such as Times Beach, Missouri, and Love Canal, New York. See Chapter 19.

on controlling the total amount of emissions in a manner that minimizes the cost of control. What can we say about the cost-effective allocation of control responsibility for uniformly mixed fund pollutants?

Consider a simple example. Assume that two emissions sources are currently emitting 15 units each for a total 30 units. Assume further that the control authority determines that the environment can assimilate is 15 units in total, so that a reduction of 15 units is necessary. How should this 15-unit reduction be allocated between the two sources in order to minimize the total cost of the reduction?

We can demonstrate the answer with the aid of Figure 14.3, which is drawn by measuring the marginal cost of control for the first source from the left-hand axis (MC_1) and the marginal cost of control for the second source from the right-hand axis (MC_2). Note that a total 15-unit reduction is achieved for every point on this graph; each point represents some different combination of reduction by the two sources. Drawn in this manner, the diagram represents all possible allocations of the 15-unit reduction between the two sources. The left-hand axis, for example, represents an allocation of the entire reduction to the second source, while the right-hand axis represents a situation in which the first source bears the entire responsibility. All points in between represent different degrees of shared responsibility. What allocation minimizes the cost of control?

In the cost-effective allocation, the first source cleans up ten units, while the second source cleans up five units. The total variable cost of control for this particular assignment of the responsibility for the reduction is represented by area *A* plus area *B*. Area *A* is the cost of control for the first source; area *B* is the cost of control for the second. Any other allocation would result in a higher total control cost. (Convince yourself that this is true.)

FIGURE 14.3 Cost-Effective Allocation of a Uniformly Mixed Fund Pollutant

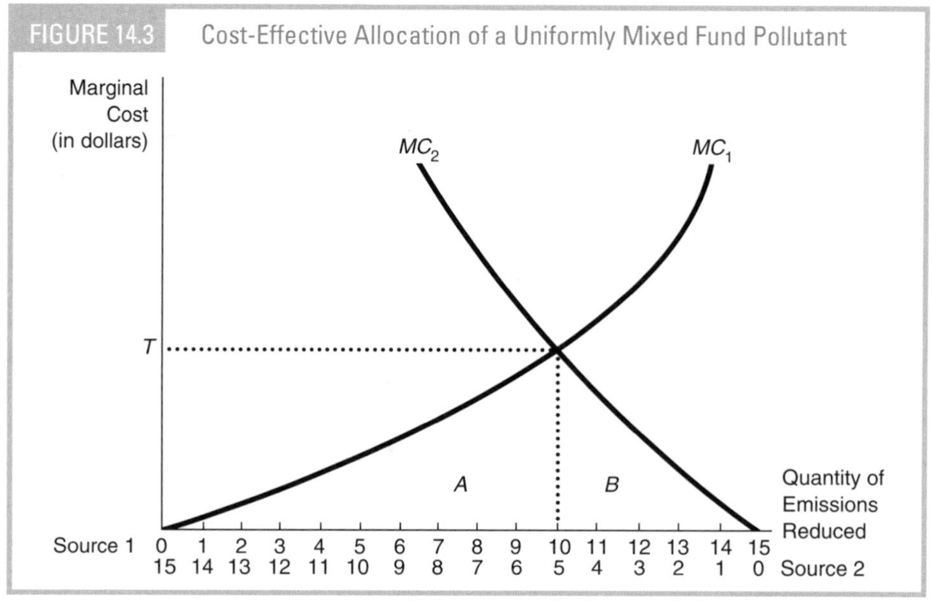

Figure 14.3 also demonstrates the cost-effectiveness equimarginal principle introduced in Chapter 3. *The cost of achieving a given reduction in emissions will be minimized if and only if the marginal costs of control are equalized for all emitters.*[6] This is demonstrated by the fact that the marginal cost curves cross at the cost-effective allocation.

Cost-Effective Pollution Control Policies

This proposition can be used as a basis for choosing among the various policy instruments that the control authority might use to achieve this allocation. Sources have a large menu of options for controlling the amount of pollution they inject into the environment. The cheapest method of control will differ widely not only among industries but also among plants in the same industry. The selection of the cheapest method requires detailed information on the possible control techniques and their associated costs.

Generally, plant managers are able to acquire this information for their plants when it is in their interest to do so. However, the government authorities responsible for meeting pollution targets are not likely to have this information. Since the degree to which these plants would be regulated depends on cost information, it is unrealistic to expect these plant managers to transfer unbiased information to the government. Plant managers would have a strong incentive to overstate control costs in hopes of reducing their ultimate control burden.

This situation poses a difficult dilemma for control authorities. The cost of incorrectly assigning the control responsibility among various polluters is likely to be large. Yet the control authorities do not have sufficient information at their disposal to make a correct allocation. Those who have the information—the plant managers—are not inclined to share it. Can the cost-effective allocation be found? The answer depends on the approach taken by the control authority.

Emissions Standards. We start our investigation of this question by supposing that the control authority pursues a traditional legal approach by imposing a separate emissions limit on each source. In the economics literature this approach is referred to as the "command-and-control" approach. An *emissions standard* is a legal limit on the amount of the pollutant an individual source is allowed to emit. In our example it is clear that the two standards should add up to the allowable 15 units, but it is not clear how, in the absence of information on control costs, these 15 units are to be allocated between the two sources.

The easiest method of resolving this dilemma—and the one chosen in the earliest days of pollution control—would be simply to allocate each source an equal reduction. As is clear from Figure 14.3, this strategy would not be cost effective. While the first source would have lower costs compared to the cost-effective allocation, this cost reduction would be substantially smaller than the cost increase faced

[6]This statement is true when marginal cost increases with the amount of emissions reduced as in Figure 14.3. Suppose that for some pollutants the marginal cost were to decrease with the amount of emissions reduced. What would be the cost-effective allocation in that admittedly unusual situation?

by the second source. Compared to a cost-effective allocation, total costs would increase if both sources were forced to clean up the same amount.

When emissions standards are the policy of choice, there is no reason to believe that the authority will assign the responsibility for emissions reduction in a cost-minimizing way. This is probably not surprising. Who would have believed otherwise?

Surprisingly enough, however, some policy instruments do allow the authority to allocate the emissions reduction in a cost-effective manner even when it has no information on the magnitude of control costs. These policy approaches rely on economic incentives to produce the desired outcome. The two most common approaches are known as emissions charges and emissions trading.

Emissions Charges. An *emissions charge* is a fee, collected by the government, levied on each unit of pollutant emitted into the air or water. The total payment any source would make to the government could be found by multiplying the fee times the amount of pollution emitted. Emissions charges reduce pollution because paying the fees costs the firm money. To save money, the source seeks ways to reduce its pollution.

How much pollution control would the firm choose? A profit-maximizing firm would control, rather than emit, pollution whenever it proved cheaper to do so. We can illustrate the firm's decision with Figure 14.4. The level of uncontrolled emission is 15 units and the emissions charge is *T*. Thus, if the firm were to decide against controlling any emissions, it would have to pay *T* times 15, represented by area 0*TBC*.

Is this the best the firm can do? Obviously not, since it can control some pollution at a lower cost than paying the emissions charge. It would pay the firm to reduce emissions until the marginal cost of reduction is equal to the emissions charge. The firm would minimize its cost by choosing to clean up ten units of pollution and to emit five units. At this allocation the firm would pay control costs equal to area 0*AD*

FIGURE 14.4 Cost-Minimizing Control of Pollution with an Emissions Charge

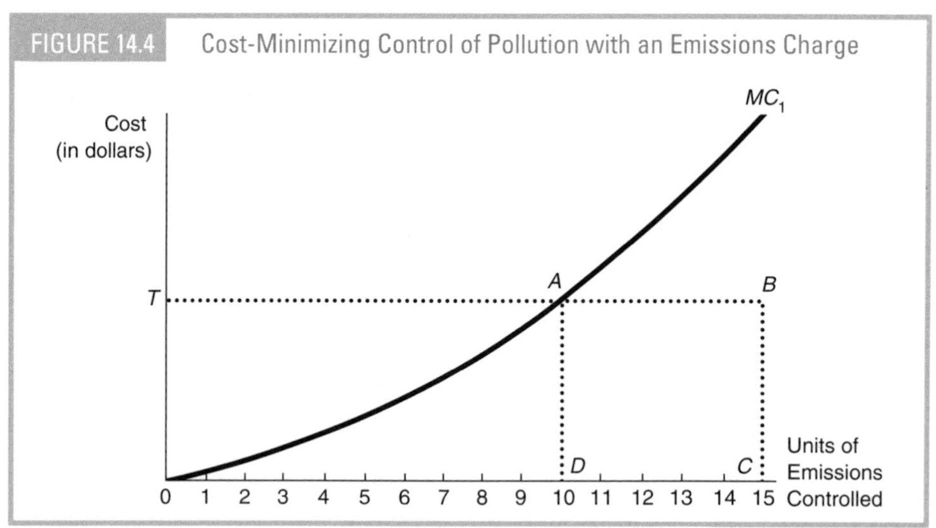

and total emissions charge payments equal to area *ABCD* for a total cost of 0*ABC*. This is clearly less than 0*TBC*, the amount the firm would pay if it chose not to clean up any pollution.

Let's carry this one step further. Suppose that we levied the same emissions charge on both sources discussed in Figure 14.3. Each source would then control its emissions until its marginal control cost equaled the emissions charge. (Faced with an emissions charge *T*, the second source would clean up five units.) Since they both face the same emissions charge, they will *independently* choose levels of control consistent with equal marginal control costs. This is precisely the condition that yields a cost-minimizing allocation.

This is a remarkable finding. We have shown that as long as the control authority imposes the same emissions charge on all sources, the resulting incentives are *automatically* compatible with minimizing the costs of achieving that level of control. This is true in spite of the fact that the control authority may not have sufficient knowledge of control costs.

However, we have not yet dealt with the issue of how the appropriate level of the emissions charge is determined. Each level of a charge will result in *some* level of emissions reduction. Furthermore, as long as each firm minimizes its own costs, the responsibility for meeting that reduction will be allocated in a manner that minimizes control costs for all firms. How high should the charge be set to ensure that the resulting emissions reduction is the *desired* level of emissions reduction?

Without having the requisite information on control costs, the control authority cannot establish the correct tax rate on the first try. It is possible, however, to develop an iterative, trial-and-error process to find the appropriate charge rate. This process is initiated by choosing an arbitrary charge rate and observing the amount of reduction that occurs when that charge is imposed. If the observed reduction is larger than desired, it means the charge should be lowered; if the reduction is smaller, the charge should be raised. The new reduction that results from the adjusted charge can then be observed and compared with the desired reduction. Further adjustments in the charge can be made as needed. This process can be repeated until the actual and desired reductions are equal. At that point the correct emissions charge would have been found.

The charge system not only causes cost-minimizing sources to choose a cost-effective allocation of the control responsibility, it also stimulates the development of newer, cheaper means of controlling emissions, as well as promoting technological progress. This is illustrated in Figure 14.5.

The reason for this is rather straightforward. Control authorities base the emissions standards on specific technologies. As new technologies are discovered by the control authority, the standards are tightened. These stricter standards force firms to bear higher costs. Therefore, with emissions standards, firms have an incentive to hide technological changes from the control authority.

With an emissions charge system, the firm saves money by adopting cheaper new technologies. As long as the firm can reduce its pollution at a marginal cost lower than *T*, it pays to adopt the new technology. In Figure 14.5 the firm saves *A* and *B* by adopting the new technology and voluntarily increases its emissions reduction from Q^0 to Q^1.

With an emissions charge, the minimum cost allocation of meeting a predetermined emissions reduction can be found by a control authority even when it

FIGURE 14.5 Cost Savings from Technological Change: Charges versus Standards

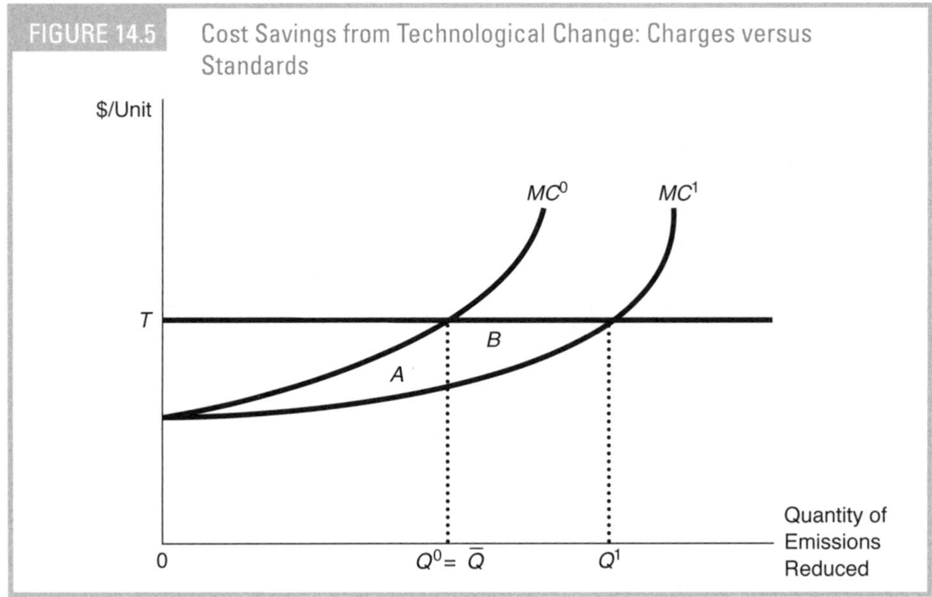

has insufficient information on control costs. An emissions charge also stimulates technological advances in emissions reduction. Unfortunately, the process for finding the appropriate rate takes some experimenting. During the trial-and-error period of finding the appropriate rate, sources would be faced with a volatile emissions charge. Changing emissions charges would make planning for the future difficult. Investments that would make sense under a high emissions charge might not make sense when it falls. From either a policymaker's or business manager's perspective, this process leaves much to be desired.

Cap-and-Trade. Is it possible for the control authority to find the cost-minimizing allocation without going through a trial-and-error process? It is possible if cap-and-trade (or equivalently emissions trading) is the chosen policy. Under this system, all sources face a limit on their emissions and they are allocated (or sold) allowances to emit. Each allowance authorizes a specific amount of emissions (commonly 1 ton). The control authority issues exactly the number of allowances needed to produce the desired emissions level. These can be distributed among the firms either by auctioning them off to the highest bidder or by granting them directly to firms free of charge (an allocation referred to as "gifting"). However they are acquired, the allowances are freely transferable; they can be bought and sold. Firms emitting more than their holdings would buy additional allowances from firms who are emitting less than authorized. Any emissions by a source in excess of those allowed by its allowance holdings at the end of the year would cause the source to face severe monetary sanctions.

Why this system automatically leads to a cost-effective allocation can be seen in Figure 14.6, which treats the same set of circumstances as in Figure 14.3. Consider first the gifting alternative. Suppose that the first source was allocated

FIGURE 14.6 Cost-Effectiveness and Emissions Trading

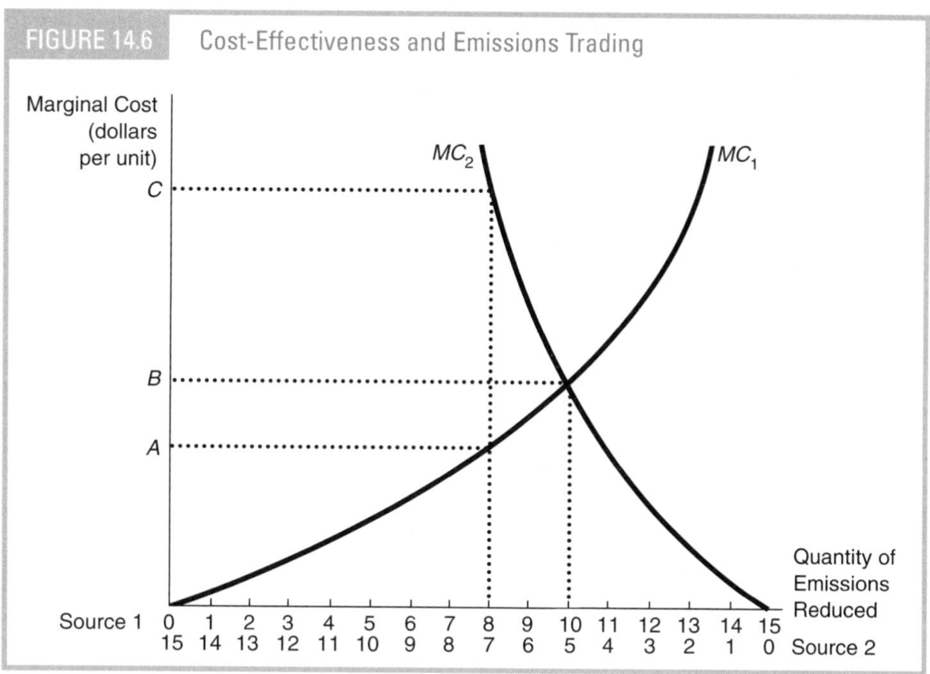

seven allowances (each allowance corresponds to one emission unit). Because it has 15 units of uncontrolled emissions, this would mean it must control eight units. Similarly, suppose that the second source was granted the remaining eight allowances, meaning that it would have to clean up seven units. Notice that both firms have an incentive to trade. The marginal cost of control for the second source (*C*) is substantially higher than that for the first (*A*). The second source could lower its cost if it could buy an allowance from the first source at a price lower than *C*. Meanwhile, the first source would be better off if it could sell an allowance for a price higher than *A*. Because *C* is greater than *A*, grounds for trade certainly exist.

A transfer of allowances would take place until the first source had only five allowances left (and controlled ten units), while the second source had ten allowances (and controlled five units). At this point, the allowance price would equal *B*, because that is the marginal value of that allowance to both sources, and neither source would have any incentive to trade further. The allowance market would be in equilibrium.

Notice that the market equilibrium for an emission-allowance system is the cost-effective allocation! Simply by issuing the appropriate number of allowances (15) and letting the market do the rest, the control authority can achieve a cost-effective allocation without having even the slightest knowledge about control costs. This system allows the government to meet its policy objective, while allowing greater flexibility in how that objective is met.

How would this equilibrium change if the allowances were auctioned off? Interestingly, it wouldn't; both allocation methods lead to the same result. With an auction, the allowance price that clears demand and supply is *B*, and we have already demonstrated that *B* supports a cost-effective equilibrium.

The incentives created by this system ensure that sources use this flexibility to achieve the objective at the lowest possible cost. As we shall see in the next two chapters, this remarkable property has been responsible for the prominence of this type of approach in current attempts to reform the regulatory process.

How far can the reforms go? Can developing countries use the experience of the industrialized countries to move directly into using these market-based instruments to control pollution?

As Debate 14.1 points out, that may be easier said than done.

DEBATE 14.1

Should Developing Countries Rely on Market-Based Instruments to Control Pollution?

Since the case for using market-based instruments seems so strong in principle, some observers, most prominently the World Bank (2000), have suggested that developing countries should capitalize on the experience of the industrialized countries to move directly to market-based instruments to control pollution. The desirability of this strategy is seen as flowing from the level of poverty in developing countries; abating pollution in the least expensive manner would seem especially important to poorer nations. Furthermore, since developing countries are frequently also starved for revenue, revenue-generating instruments (such as emissions charges or auctioned allowances) would seem especially useful. Proponents also point out that a number of developing countries already use market-based instruments.

Another school of thought (e.g., Russell & Vaughan, 2003) suggests that the differences in infrastructure between the developing and industrialized countries make the transfer of lessons from one context to another fraught with peril. To illustrate their more general point, they note that the effectiveness of market-based instruments presumes an effective monitoring and enforcement system, something that is frequently not present in developing countries. In its absence, the superiority of market-based instruments is much less obvious.

Some middle ground is clearly emerging. Russell and Vaughan do not argue that market-based instruments should never be used in developing countries, but rather that they may not be as universally appropriate as the most enthusiastic proponents seem to suggest. They see themselves as telling a cautionary tale. And proponents are certainly beginning to see the crucial importance of infrastructure. Recognizing that some developing countries may be much better suited (by virtue of their infrastructure) to implement market-based systems than others, proponents are beginning to see capacity building as a logical prior step for those countries that need it.

For market-based instruments, as well as for other aspects of life, if it looks too good to be true, it probably is.

Source: World Bank. (2000). *Greening industry: New roles for communities, markets and governments* Washington, DC: World Bank and Oxford University Press; Clifford S. Russell, C. S., & Vaughan, W. J. The choice of pollution control policy instruments in developing Countries: arguments, evidence and suggestions. In H. Folmer & T. Tietenberg (Eds.). *The International Yearbook of Environmental and Resource Economics 2003/2004* (331–371). Cheltenham, UK: Edward Elgar.

Cost-Effective Policies for Nonuniformly Mixed Surface Pollutants

The problem becomes more complicated when dealing with nonuniformly mixed surface pollutants rather than uniformly mixed pollutants. For these pollutants, the policy must be concerned not only with the weight of emissions entering the atmosphere but also with the location and timing of emissions. For nonuniformly mixed pollutants, it is the concentration in the air, soil, or water that counts. The concentration is measured as the amount of pollutant found in a given volume of air, soil, or water at a given location and at a given point in time.

It is easy to see why pollutant concentrations are sensitive to the location of emissions. Suppose that three emissions sources are clustered and emit the same amount as three distant but otherwise-identical sources. The emissions from the clustered sources generally cause higher pollution concentrations because they are all entering the same volume of air or water. Because the two sets of emissions do not share a common receiving volume, those from the dispersed sources result in lower concentrations. This is the main reason why cities generally face more severe pollution problems than do rural areas; urban sources tend to be more densely clustered.

The timing of emissions can also matter in two rather different senses. First, when pollutants are emitted in bursts rather than distributed over time they can result in higher concentrations. Second, the time of year in which some pollutants are emitted can matter. Since ozone, for example, is formed by a photochemical reaction, in the Northeast emissions of the precursor pollutants in the summer result in much higher ozone levels per unit of emission.

Since the damage caused by nonuniformly mixed surface pollutants is related to their concentration levels in the air, soil, or water, it is natural that our search for cost-effective policies for controlling these pollutants focuses on the attainment of ambient standards. *Ambient standards* are legal ceilings placed on the concentration level of specified pollutants in the air, soil, or water. They represent the target concentration levels that are not to be exceeded. A cost-effective policy results in the lowest cost allocation of control responsibility consistent with ensuring that the predetermined ambient standards are met at specified locations called receptor sites.

The Single-Receptor Case

We can begin the analysis by considering a simple case in which we desire to control pollution at one, and only one, receptor location. We know that all units of emissions from sources do not have the same impact on pollution measured at that receptor. Consider, for example, Figure 14.7.

Suppose that we allow each of the four sources individually, at different points in time, to inject ten units of emission into the stream. Suppose further that we measured the pollutant concentration resulting from each of these injections at receptor R. In general, we would find that the emissions from A or B would

FIGURE 14.7 Effect of Location on Local Pollutant Concentration

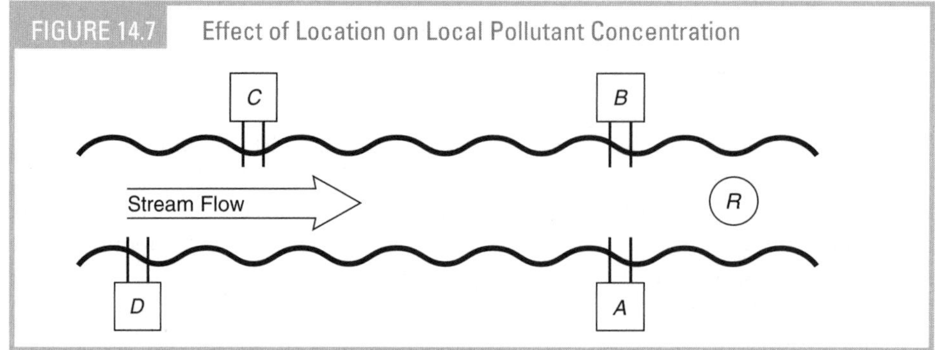

cause a larger rise in the recorded concentration than would those from C and D, even though the same amount was emitted from each source. The reason for this is that the emissions from C and D would be substantially diluted by the time they arrived at R, while those from A and B would arrive in a more concentrated form.

Since emissions are what can be controlled, but the concentrations at R are the policy target, our first task must be to relate the two. This can be accomplished by using a transfer coefficient. A transfer coefficient (a_i) captures the constant amount the concentration at the receptor will rise if source i emits one more unit of pollution. Using this definition and the knowledge that the a_is are constant, we can relate the concentration level at R to emissions from all sources:

$$K_R = \sum_{i=1}^{I} a_i E_i + B \quad (1)$$

where

K_R = concentration at the receptor

E_i = emissions level of the ith source

I = total number of sources in the region

B = background concentration level (resulting from natural sources or sources outside the control region)

We are now in a position to define the cost-effective allocation of responsibility. A numerical example involving two sources is presented in Table 14.1. In this example, the two sources are assumed to have the same marginal cost curves for cleaning up emissions. This assumption is reflected in the fact that the first two corresponding columns of the table for each of the two sources are identical.[7] The main difference between the two sources is their location vis-à-vis the receptor. The first source is closer to the receptor, so it has a larger transfer coefficient than the second (1.0 as opposed to 0.5).

[7]This assumption has no bearing on the results we shall achieve. It serves mainly to illustrate the role location plays on eliminating control-cost difference as a factor.

TABLE 14.1 Cost-Effectiveness for Nonuniformly Mixed Pollutants: A Hypothetical Example

Emissions Units Reduced	Marginal Cost of Emissions Reduction (dollars per unit)	Concentration Units Reduced[1]	Marginal Cost of Concentration Reduction (dollars per unit)[2]
Source 1 ($a_1 = 1.0$)			
1	1	1.0	1
2	2	2.0	2
3	3	3.0	3
4	4	4.0	4
5	5	5.0	5
6	6	6.0	6
7	7	7.0	7
Source 2 ($a_2 = 0.5$)			
1	1	0.5	2
2	2	1.0	4
3	3	1.5	6
4	4	2.0	8
5	5	2.5	10
6	6	3.0	12
7	7	3.5	14

[1]Computed by multiplying the emissions reduction (column 1) by the transfer coefficient (a_i).
[2]Computed by dividing the marginal cost of emissions reduction (column 2) by the transfer coefficient (a_i).

The objective is to meet a given concentration target at minimum cost. Column 3 of the table translates emissions reductions into concentration reductions for each source, while column 4 records the marginal cost of each unit of concentration reduced. The former is merely the emissions reduction times the transfer coefficient, while the latter is the marginal cost of the emissions reduction divided by the transfer coefficient (which translates the marginal cost of *emissions* reduction into a marginal cost of *concentration* reduction).

Suppose the concentration at the receptor has to be reduced by 7.5 units in order to comply with the ambient standard. The cost-effective allocation would be achieved when the marginal costs of concentration reduction (*not* emissions reduction) are equalized for all sources. In Table 14.1, this occurs when the first source reduces six units of emissions (and six units of concentration) and the second source reduces three units of emissions (and 1.5 units of concentration). At this allocation the marginal cost of concentration reduction is equal to $6 for both sources. By adding all marginal costs for each unit reduced, we calculate the total variable cost of this allocation to be $27. From the definition of cost-effectiveness, no other allocation resulting in 7.5 units of concentration reduction would be cheaper.

Policy Approaches for Nonuniformly Mixed Pollutants. This framework can now be used to evaluate various policy approaches that the control authority might use. We begin with the *ambient charge*, the charge used to produce a cost-effective allocation of a nonuniformly mixed pollutant. This charge takes the form following:

$$t_i = a_i F \qquad (2)$$

where t_i is the per-unit charge paid by the *i*th source on each unit emitted, a_i is the *i*th source's transfer coefficient, and F is the marginal cost of a unit of concentration reduction, which is the same for all sources. In our example, F is $6, so the first source would pay a per-unit emissions charge of $6, while the second source would pay $3. *Note that sources will, in general, pay different charges when the objective is to meet an ambient standard at minimum cost because their transfer coefficients differ.* This contrasts with the uniformly mixed pollutant case in which a cost-effective allocation required that all sources pay the same charge.

How can the cost-effective t_i be found by a control authority with insufficient information on control costs? The transfer coefficients can be calculated using knowledge of hydrology and meteorology, but what about F? Here a striking similarity to the uniformly mixed case becomes evident. Any level of F would yield a cost-effective allocation of control responsibility for achieving *some* level of concentration reduction at the receptor. That level might not, however, be compatible with the ambient standard.

We could ensure compatibility by changing F in an iterative process until the desired concentration is achieved. If the actual pollutant concentration is below the standard, the tax could be lowered; if it is above, the tax could be raised. The correct level of F would be reached when the resulting pollution concentration is equal to the desired level. That equilibrium allocation would be the one that meets the ambient standard at minimum cost.

Table 14.1 allows us to consider another issue of significance. The cost-effective allocation of control responsibility for achieving surface-concentration targets places a larger information burden on control authorities; they have to calculate the transfer coefficients. What is lost if the simpler emissions charge system (where each source faces the same charge) is used to pursue a surface-concentration target? Can location be safely ignored?

Let's use our numerical example to find out. In Table 14.1, a uniform emissions charge equal to $5 would achieve the desired 7.5 units of reduction (5 from the first source and 2.5 from the second). Yet the total variable cost of this allocation (calculated as the sum of the marginal costs) would be $30 ($15 paid by each source). This is $3 higher than the allocation resulting from the use of ambient charge discussed earlier. In subsequent chapters we present empirical estimates of the size of this cost increase in actual air and water pollution situations. In general, they show the cost increases to be large; location matters.

Table 14.1 also helps us understand why location matters. Notice that with a uniform emissions charge, 10 units of emission are cleaned up, whereas with the ambient charge, only 9 units are cleaned up. Both achieve the concentration target, but the uniform-emissions charge results in fewer emissions. The ambient charge results in a lower cost allocation than the emissions charge because it results in less emissions control. Those sources having only a small effect on the recorded concentration at the receptor location are able to control less than they would with a uniform charge.

With the ambient charge, we have the same problem that we encountered with emissions charges in the uniformly mixed pollutant case—the cost-effective level can be determined only by an iterative process. Can emissions trading get around this problem when dealing with nonuniformly mixed pollutants?

It can, by designing the allowance trading system in the correct way. An ambient allowance market (as opposed to an emissions allowance market) entitles the owner to cause the concentration to rise at the receptor by a specified amount, rather than allowing the same amount of emissions to each allowance holder. Using ΔK_R to represent this permitted rise and E to indicate the units of emissions allowed to the ith source, we can see from Equation (1) that

$$\frac{\Delta K_R}{a_i} = \Delta E_i. \tag{3}$$

The larger the transfer coefficient (i.e., the closer the source is to the receptor), the smaller the amount of emissions legitimized by the allowances held by that firm. Proximate sources must purchase more allowances than distant sources to legitimize a given level of emissions. In this ambient allowance market, the sources pay the same price for each allowance, but the amount of emissions allowed by each allowance varies from location to location. The market automatically determines this common price, and the resulting allocation of allowances is cost-effective. With respect to Table 14.1, the ambient allowance price would be \$6. This cost-effective system is called an *ambient allowance system* to differentiate it from the *emissions allowance system*, which is used to achieve a cost-effective allocation of control responsibility for uniformly mixed pollutants.

We can reinforce our understanding of what is going on with the ambient allowance system by examining a specific trade. Suppose our two sources in Table 14.1 want to trade permits with the first source buying from the second. To maintain the same concentration level before and after the trade, we must ensure that

$$a_1 \Delta E_1 = a_2 \Delta E_2 \tag{4}$$

where the subscripts refer to the first source and second source and the ΔE_i refers to a change in emissions by the ith source. Solving this for the allowable increase in emissions by the buyer yields

$$\Delta E_1 = \frac{a_2}{a_t} \Delta E_2. \tag{5}$$

For $a_2 = 0.5$ and $a_1 = 1.0$, this equation suggests that for each allowance traded, the buyer (the first source) is allowed to emit only one-half the amount of emissions allowed by that same allowance to the seller. After this trade, the total amount of emissions by both sources goes down.[8] This could not happen in an emissions allowance system, since the design of those allowances causes all trades to leave emissions (but not concentrations!) unchanged.

---

[8]Emissions could rise with ambient allowance trades as well. This would occur whenever the transfer coefficient of the seller was larger than that of the buyer.

The Many-Receptors Case

This analysis generalizes easily to the many-receptors case. The cost-effective ambient charge paid by any source would, in this case, be

$$T_i = \sum_{j=1}^{J} a_{ij}F_j$$

where

T_i = charge paid by the ith source for each unit of emissions

a_{ij} = transfer coefficient that translates emissions by source i into concentration increases at the jth receptor

J = number of receptors

F_j = monetary fee associated with the jth receptor

Thus, the source has to pay a charge that incorporates its effect on all receptors. The control authority could manipulate F_j for each receptor location until the desired concentration level is achieved at that receptor.[9]

The extension of the ambient allowance system to the many-receptor case requires that a separate allowance market be created *for each receptor*. The price prevailing in each of these markets would reflect the difficulty of meeting the ambient standard at that receptor. All other things being equal, ambient allowance markets associated with receptors in heavily congested areas could be expected to sustain higher prices than those affected by relatively few emitters.

Since both the ambient allowance and the ambient charge systems take location into account, when these policies are chosen, the marginal cost of emissions control varies from location to location. Sources located in heavily populated portions of the region would pay higher marginal costs, since their emissions have a greater impact on the receptors of interest. Having control costs depend on location provides incentives for new sources to choose their location carefully. Since heavily polluted areas have high control costs, new firms have some incentive to locate elsewhere, even though pollution control expenditures are only part of the costs a firm considers when deciding where to locate. For nonuniformly mixed pollution problems, where the emissions occur is important and relocation may be one way to approach the least cost allocation. With the ambient allowance and charge systems, this is precisely what occurs.

As a practical matter, however, ambient charge and allowance systems have proved to be excessively complex to implement. As a result, control authorities have developed a number of rule-of-thumb procedures designed to deal adequately with

---

[9]Because any higher F_j reduces concentrations at several locations, not just at the jth receptor, not all selections of F_j that result in the ambient standards being met will result in cost-effective allocations. In the single-receptor case, the charge equilibrium is unique and equal to the cost-effective one. This is a further burden on the control authority of using an emission charge system as opposed to the allowance system where the equilibrium is unique and cost-effective. The allowance system equilibrium is unique because all equilibria other than the cost-effective one involve higher costs and, therefore, further opportunities for trade.

spatial issues while promoting cost effectiveness. One approach allows unrestricted trading within predefined zones on a "one-for-one" basis, but allows trading between zones only after adjusting the trading ratios to take location into account. Another approach allows unrestricted *trading*, but restricts *use*, depending on the conditions around the acquiring source.

Other Policy Dimensions

Two main pollution control policy instruments rely on economic incentives—charges and cap-and-trade. Both of these allow the control authority to distribute the responsibility for control in a cost-effective manner. The major difference between them we have discussed so far is that the appropriate charge can be determined only by an iterative trial-and-error process over time, whereas for the cap-and-trade approach the allowance price can be determined immediately by the market. Can other differences be identified?

The Revenue Effect

One of the differentiating characteristics of these instruments is their ability to raise revenue. Environmental taxes and auctioned allowances raise revenue, but cap-and-trade programs that gift the allowances to users free of charge do not. Does this difference matter?

It does, for at least two reasons.[10] First, a number of authors (Parry & Bento, 2000; Bovenberg & Goulder, 1996; Goulder, 1997; Parry, 1995) have noted that the revenue from environmental taxes or auctioned transferable allowances could be substituted for the revenue from distortionary taxes, thereby reducing those taxes and their associated distortions. When this substitution is made, the calculations indicate that it allows an increase in the present value of net benefits from the application of this instrument, an effect that has been called the "double dividend." This effect creates a preference for instruments that can raise revenue as long as both the implementation of a revenue-raising instrument and the use of this revenue to reduce distortionary taxes are politically feasible.

The second important consideration is that the revenue from taxes or auctions could be used to reduce the burden on low-income households. The empirical evidence suggests that gifting allowances produces a regressive distribution of the control burden. (A regressive distribution is one that places a higher relative cost burden on low-income households or individuals as a percentage of their income than middle- or high-income households or individuals.) That same evidence has also demonstrated that when the revenue from auctions or taxes is targeted appropriately, the regressiveness of the policy can be eliminated.

---

[10]The literature contains a third reason. It suggests that unless emitters cover all external costs via a revenue-raising instrument, the cost of production will be artificially low, production will be artificially high, and the industry will contain too many firms.

A final consequence of raising revenues involves their political feasibility. It seems quite clear that until 2008, using a free-distribution ("gifting") approach for the initial allocation of allowances was a necessary ingredient to build the necessary political support for cap-and-trade legislation to be implemented (Raymond, 2003). Existing users frequently have the power to block implementation, while potential future users do not. This made it politically expedient to allocate a substantial part of the economic rent from these resources to existing users as the price of securing their support, sometimes in creative ways (see Example 14.1).

While this strategy reduces the adjustment costs to existing users, generally it raises them for new users. Interestingly in the climate change case, the empirical

EXAMPLE 14.1

The Swedish Nitrogen Charge

One of the dilemmas facing those who wish to use charges to control pollution is that the amounts of revenue extracted from those subject to the tax can be considerable and that additional expense can produce a lot of political resistance to the policy. This resistance can be lowered if the revenue is rebated to those who pay it, but if all firms know they are getting their money back, the economic incentive to limit emissions is lost. Is it possible to design a system of rebates that will promote political feasibility without undermining abatement incentives?

The Swedish nitrogen charge was designed specifically to resolve this dilemma. Sweden's nitrogen oxide emissions charge was first imposed in 1992 on large energy sources. Some 120 heating plants and industrial facilities with about 180 boilers were subject to the tax.

It was intended from the beginning to have a significant incentive effect, not to raise revenue. Although the charge rate is high by international standards (thereby producing an effective economic incentive), the revenue from this tax is not retained by the government, but rather is rebated to the emitting sources (thereby lowering resistance to the policy by the regulated sources). It is the form of this rebate that makes this an interesting scheme. While the tax is collected on the basis of *emissions*, it is rebated on the basis of *energy production*. In effect, this system rewards plants that emit little per unit of energy and penalizes plants that emit more per unit of energy, thereby providing incentives to reduce emissions per unit of energy produced.

As expected, emissions per unit of energy produced fell rather dramatically. The Swedish Ministry of the Environment and Natural Resources has estimated that the benefits exceeded the costs by a factor of more than 3 to 1. Note, however, that rebating the revenue means that this tax cannot produce a double dividend and it provides no incentives to reduce energy consumption.

Sources: Anderson, R., & Lohof, A. (1997). Foreign Experience with Incentive Systems. Section 11 in *The United States Experience with Economic Incentives in Environmental Pollution Control Policy*. Washington, DC: Environmental Law Institute; Sterner, T. (2003). *Policy Instruments for Environmental and Natural Resource Management*. Washington, DC: Resources for the Future, 286–288.

evidence suggests that only a small fraction of the total revenue would be needed to assure that the profits of carbon suppliers would be unchanged by a switch to a revenue raising approach (Bovenberg & Goulder, 2001). Gifting all allowances therefore may not be inevitable in principle, even if political feasibility considerations affect the design.

Some of the newest programs auction the permits off. On January 1, 2009, the historic tendency to "gift" allowances changed with the implementation of the Regional Greenhouse Gas Initiative (RGGI) in nine Northeastern states, from Maryland to Maine.[11] This cap-and-trade program covers CO_2 emissions from large fossil fuel–fired electricity-generating plants.

A number of RGGI states have chosen to auction nearly 100 percent of these allowances, using a sealed-bid system, with the revenue returned to the states. Most states have chosen to use the revenue to promote energy efficiency (see Example 14.2), although two states—New York and New Hampshire—chose to siphon off some of the money for budget relief. New Jersey also pursued this latter option and subsequently dropped out of RGGI.

Using the revenue from auctions to promote investment in energy efficiency reduces the cost of meeting the carbon targets. Costs are reduced not only because less energy is used (and hence less carbon emitted), but also because the lower demand for energy lowers the price not only of the allowances, but of electricity too. (Can you see why?)

It would be hard to overemphasize what a departure from the previous norm this venture into auctioning represents. Allowing emitters to pollute up to the emissions standard without paying for the right to pollute (the traditional approach) implies that emitters have an implicit property right to pollute already; they don't have to buy it.

A cap-and-trade program with allowance auctions implies, in contrast, that the atmosphere is held in trust for the community. Institutions that use the atmosphere for emissions must therefore pay to acquire that scarce right. Notice that this understanding of who actually holds the property right to the atmosphere completely changes the lens through which this regulation is viewed.

Economic analysis reminds us that putting a price on carbon (as both a carbon tax and cap-and-trade policies do) is a necessary, but not sufficient, component of the efficient path to stabilizing the climate. Pricing carbon is necessary to correct the externality associated with the damages from climate change, but the price is not sufficient because, by itself, it does not promote the efficient level of investment in energy efficiency (remember the discussion in Chapter 7?). While the cap-and-trade program corrects the climate externality whether or not the allowances are auctioned, auctioning the allowances and using the revenue to promote energy efficiency provides a faster transition.

[11]There were 10 original members. New Jersey subsequently dropped out of the program.

EXAMPLE 14.2

RGGI Revenue: The Maine Example

The revenue received by Maine from the quarterly RGGI auctions is received by the Efficiency Maine Trust, a specially created, quasi-independent organization. The enabling statute requires the trustees to spend the RGGI funds on energy efficiency measures such as more efficient lighting, motors, heating and air conditioning, as well as on building weatherization.

For large customers such as paper mills, the money is allocated on a competitive bid basis, where the bids are compared on the basis of the amount of kilowatt-hours reduced (for electricity) or tons of CO_2 reduced (for fossil fuels) *per trust dollar expended.* (Notice how focusing on public dollars, as opposed to the sum of public and private dollars, provides an incentive for cost sharing on the part of bidders—putting more of their own money and less public money into the project raises the ratio of the savings per trust dollar and, hence, increases the competitiveness of their bid.)

As of September 2013, roughly $44.7 million had been raised by RGGI for the EMT. The investments in energy efficiency incentivized by these funds have been very cost effective.

- Data from the EMT show that *saving* one kilowatt/hour of electricity cost, on average, about 3 cents, but *buying* that kilowatt-hour would have cost small businesses or homeowners about 6 cents. In addition the energy homeowners and businesses pay another 6 or 7 cents to have that kilowatt-hour delivered to them, a cost they do not have to bear for the saved energy.
- The Trust's programs to help homeowners save heating fuel through weatherization and upgrading their heating systems have been able to save heating oil at a cost of $1.16 per gallon, or less than a third of the price at that time to purchase a gallon.

The data demonstrate that at the margin saving energy is cheaper than buying it. In other words investing in energy savings actually lowers energy costs. Lower energy costs have made local firms more cost competitive and have saved jobs and bolstered the local economy, while reducing emissions of one of the gases that contributes to climate change.

Sources: Hibbard, P. J. Tierney, S. F., Okie, A. M, & Darling, P. G. (2011). The economic impacts of the regional greenhouse gas initiative on ten northeast and mid-Atlantic states review of the use of RGGI auction proceeds from the first three-year compliance period. Boston, MA: The Analysis Group. Retrieved from http://www.analysisgroup.com/uploadedFiles/Publishing/Articles/Economic_Impact_RGGI_Report.pdf; Efficiency Maine trust (EMT). (2012). *Triennial Plan For Fiscal Years 2014–2016.* Retrieved from http://www.efficiencymaine.com/docs/TriPlan2-11-26-2012.pdf

Responses to Changes in the Regulatory Environment

One major additional difference between charges and allowances concerns the manner in which these two systems react to changes in external circumstances in the absence of further decisions by the control authority. This is an important consideration, because bureaucratic procedures are notoriously sluggish and changes in policies are usually rendered slowly.[12] We consider three such circumstances: growth in the number of sources, inflation, and technological progress.

If the number of sources were to increase in a cap-and-trade program, the demand for allowances would shift to the right. Given a fixed supply of allowances, the price would rise, as would the control costs, but the amount of emissions or pollution concentrations (in the case of the ambient allowance system) would remain the same. If charges were being used, in the absence of additional action by the control authority, the charge level would remain the same. This implies that the amount the existing sources would control would be unchanged by the growth. Therefore, the arrival of new sources would cause a deterioration of air or water quality in the region due to the added emissions by the new sources. The costs of abatement would rise, since the costs of control paid by the new sources must be considered, but by a lesser amount than with cap-and-trade, because of the lower amount of pollution being controlled. If the economy is growing, the allowance system ensures that emissions will not rise. With cap-and-trade, inflation in the cost of control would automatically result in higher allowance prices, but with a charge system it would result in lower control. Essentially, the real charge (the nominal charge adjusted for inflation) declines with inflation if the nominal charge remains the same.

We should not, however, conclude that over time, charges always result in less control than allowances. Suppose, for example, technological progress in designing pollution control equipment were to cause the marginal cost of abatement to fall. With cap-and-trade this would result in lower prices and lower abatement costs, but the same aggregate degree of control. With a charge system, the amount controlled would actually increase (see Figure 14.5) and, therefore, would result in more control than a cap-and-trade program that, prior to the fall in costs, controlled the same amount.

If the control authority were to adjust the charge in each of the above cases appropriately, the outcome would be identical to that achieved by cap-and-trade. The allowance market reacts automatically to these changes in circumstances, while the charge system requires a conscious administrative act to achieve the same result.

Price Volatility

Future abatement costs depend on current investment decisions when the adoption of new technologies is involved. The desirability of current abatement investment depends not only on the level of the price associated with emitting (either the allowance price or the emissions charge), but also on its volatility. Volatility can inhibit investment incentives.

---

[12] This is probably particularly true when the modification involves a change in the rate at which firms are charged for their emissions.

Do these two policies differ in terms of the likelihood that prices will exhibit volatility? They do. Because emissions charges fix the price, price volatility is not an issue with that approach unless the government keeps changing the price. Allowances, however, fix the quantity and leave the price to the market. Large shifts in the demand for allowances, coupled with the fixed supply, can cause prices to vary a lot. In terms of reducing price volatility, charges have the edge.

Instrument Choice under Uncertainty

Another major difference between allowances and charges involves the cost of being wrong. Suppose that we have very imprecise information on damages caused and avoidance costs incurred by various levels of pollution and yet we have to choose either a charge level or an allowance level and live with it. What can be said about the relative merits of allowances versus charges in the face of this uncertainty?

The answer depends on the circumstances. Allowances offer a greater amount of certainty about the quantity of emissions, while charges confer more certainty about the marginal cost of control. Allowance markets allow an ambient standard or an aggregate emissions standard to be met with certainty, but they offer less certainty about marginal costs. When the objective is to minimize total costs (the sum of damage cost and control costs), allowances would be preferred when the costs of being wrong are more sensitive to changes in the quantity of emissions than to changes in the marginal cost of control. Charges would be preferred when control costs were more important. What circumstances give rise to a preference for one or the other?

When the marginal damage curve is steeply sloped and the marginal cost curve is rather flat, certainty about emissions is more important than certainty over control costs. Smaller deviations of actual emissions from expected emissions can cause a rather large deviation in damage costs, whereas control costs would be relatively insensitive to the degree of control. Allowances would prevent large fluctuations in these damage costs and therefore, would yield a lower cost of being wrong than charges.

Suppose, however, that the marginal control cost curve was steeply sloped, but the marginal damage curve was flat. Small changes in the degree of control would have a large effect on abatement costs but would not affect damages very much. In this case it makes sense to rely on charges to give more precise control over control costs, accepting the less dire consequences from possible fluctuations in damage costs.

These cases suggest that a preference either for allowances or for charges in the face of uncertainty is not universal; it depends on the circumstances. Theory is not strong enough to dictate a choice. Empirical studies are necessary to establish a preference for particular situations.

One interesting current application of these insights involves the control of the gases that intensify climate change. The conventional wisdom suggests that the marginal benefits of reducing greenhouse gas (GHG) emissions are likely to be flat, since the damages from climate change are driven by the accumulated concentration of GHGs (e.g., Nordhaus, 2008). The implication is that when marginal costs are quite sensitive to the level of emissions reduction, but the damages from climate change are not, a carbon tax is preferred on efficiency grounds.

The conventional wisdom, however, assumes that the effects of climate change increase steadily as a function of atmospheric concentrations of GHGs. In fact, growing scientific evidence suggests that climatic responses to temperature increases may well be highly nonlinear, characterized by thresholds or abrupt changes. This understanding of the science leads to a greater sensitivity of damages to the level of emissions reduction, shifting the preference toward cap-and-trade (Keohane, 2009). Given these conflicting views, the dominance of one approach over the other in the presence of uncertainty is not clear.

Product Charges: An Indirect Form of Environmental Taxation

The use of emissions charges presumes that it is possible to monitor and keep track of the level of emissions so the appropriate tax can be levied. Sometimes that is either impossible or impractical.

One strategy that has been employed in this circumstance is to tax the commodity that is most directly responsible for the emissions, rather than the emissions themselves. For example, one might tax gasoline rather than attempt to measure (and tax) the emissions from every gasoline-powered vehicle. And several countries tax fertilizer rather than attempt to measure the amount of contamination of groundwater sources from each bag sold. Many countries and states now have a fee or tax on the use of disposable bags (especially plastic bags).[13] One of these programs, the Irish bag levy, will be explored in the water pollution chapter (Example 18.2).

While product charges frequently are simpler to administer, it is important to keep in mind that they are not equivalent to emissions charges. Not every unit of the taxed product may have the same impact on the environment. For example, some purchased fertilizer may be used in sensitive areas (and therefore should be heavily taxed to reflect its high marginal damage), while others may be used in areas with lots of natural buffering (and therefore should not be taxed as heavily). Since the normal product charge would be the same per bag, it would not be able to make these kinds of distinctions. Product charges are most efficient when all purchased units of that product cause exactly the same marginal damage. Although full efficiency is probably rarely achieved by product charges, they may be better (even much better) than doing nothing.

---

[13]For a list of US legislation on disposable bags, see http://www.ncsl.org/issues-research/env-res/plastic-bag-legislation.aspx

Summary

In this chapter we developed the conceptual framework needed to evaluate current approaches to pollution control policy. We have explored many different types of pollutants, and found that context matters. Different policy approaches are appropriate for different circumstances.

Stock pollutants pose the most serious intertemporal problems. The efficient production of a commodity that generates a stock pollutant could be expected to decline over time. Eventually, a point would be reached when all of the pollutant would be recycled. After this point, the amount of the pollutant in the environment would not increase. The amount already accumulated, however, would continue to cause damage perpetually unless some natural process could reduce the amount of the pollutant over time.

The efficient amount of a fund pollutant was defined as the amount that minimizes the sum of damage and control costs. Using this definition, we were able to derive two propositions of interest: (1) the efficient level of pollution would vary from region to region; and (2) the efficient level of pollution would not generally be zero, although in some particular circumstances, it might.

Since pollution is a classic externality, markets will generally produce more than the efficient amount of both fund pollutants and stock pollutants. For both types of pollutants, this will imply higher-than-efficient damages and lower-than-efficient control costs. For stock pollutants, an excessive amount of pollution would accumulate in the environment, imposing a detrimental externality on future generations as well as on current generations.

The market would not provide any automatic ameliorating response to the accumulation of pollution as it would in the case of natural resource scarcity. Firms attempting to unilaterally control their pollution could be placed at a competitive disadvantage. Hence, the case for some sort of government intervention is particularly strong for pollution control.

While policy instruments could, in principle, be defined to achieve an efficient level of pollution for every emitter, it is very difficult in practice because the amount of information required by the control authorities is unrealistically high.

Cost-effectiveness analysis provides a way out of this dilemma. In the case of uniformly mixed-fund pollutants, uniform emissions charges or an allowance system focused purely on emissions (not ambient effects) could be used to attain the cost-effective allocation, even when the control authority has no information whatsoever on either control costs or damage costs. Uniform emissions standards would not, except by coincidence, be cost-effective. In addition, either emissions trading or charges would provide more incentives for technological progress in pollution control than would emissions standards.

Policies to control nonuniformly mixed pollutants must take the location and possibly the timing of the emissions into account as well as the amount. In principle, this can be accomplished with either an appropriately designed ambient allowance trading system or ambient charge; either one can result in a cost-effective allocation of the control responsibility even when the control authority has no information on control costs. A policy based on emissions standards cannot.

Policies ignoring these distinctions are not cost-effective. The use of a uniform emissions charge or emissions trading (which are appropriate for uniformly mixed pollutants) to allocate the responsibility for controlling a nonuniformly mixed surface pollutant will not be cost-effective whenever transfer coefficients differ.

The fact that auctioned allowances or taxes can raise revenue is also an important characteristic. If the revenue from pollution charges or auctioned allowances can be used to reduce revenue from other, more distortionary taxes (such as labor or income taxes), greater welfare gains can be achieved from revenue-raising instruments than instruments that raise no revenue. On the other hand, historically at least, transferring some or all of that revenue back to the sources either by gifting the allowances or including some sort of tax rebate has been an important aspect of securing the political support for implementing the system. Revenue use for this purpose, of course, cannot be used to reduce distortionary taxes or lower the regressive nature of the program.

The allowance approach and the charge approach respond differently to growth in the number of sources, to inflation, to technological change, and to uncertainty. Price volatility is likely to be greater for allowances than for emissions charges. As we shall see in the next few chapters, some countries have chosen to rely on emissions charges, while others have chosen to rely on cap-and-trade.

Discussion Question

1. In his book *What Price Incentives?* Steven Kelman suggests that from an ethical point of view, the use of economic incentives (such as emissions charges or emissions trading) in environmental policy is undesirable. He argues that transforming our mental image of the environment from a sanctified preserve to a marketable commodity has detrimental effects not only on our use of the environment, but also on our attitude toward it. His point is that applying economic incentives to environmental policy weakens and cheapens our traditional values toward the environment.
   a. Consider the effects of economic incentive systems on prices paid by the poor, on employment, and on the speed of compliance with pollution-control laws—as well as the Kelman arguments. Are economic incentive systems more or less ethically justifiable than the traditional regulatory approach?
   b. Kelman seems to feel that because emissions allowances automatically prevent environmental degradation, they are more ethically desirable than emissions charges. Do you agree? Why or why not?

Self-Test Exercises

1. Two firms can control emissions at the following marginal costs: $MC_1 = \$200q_1, MC_2 = \$100q_2$, where q_1 and q_2 are, respectively, the amount of emissions reduced by the first and second firms. Assume that with no control at all, each firm would be emitting 20 units of emissions or a total of 40 units for both firms.
   a. Compute the cost-effective allocation of control responsibility if a total reduction of 21 units of emissions is necessary.
   b. Compute the cost-effective allocation of control responsibility if the ambient standard is 27 ppm, and the transfer coefficients that translate a unit of emissions into a ppm concentration at the receptor are, respectively, $a_1 = 2.0$ and $a_2 = 1.0$.
2. Assume that the control authority wanted to reach its objective in 1(a) by using an emissions charge system.
   a. What per-unit charge should be imposed?
   b. How much revenue would the control authority collect?
3. In a region that must reduce emissions, three polluters currently emit 30 units of emissions. The three firms have the following marginal abatement cost functions that describe how marginal costs vary with the amount of emissions each firm reduces.

Firm Emissions Reduction	Firm 1 Marginal Cost	Firm 2 Marginal Cost	Firm 3 Marginal Cost
1	$1.00	$1.00	$2.00
2	$1.50	$2.00	$3.00
3	$2.00	$3.00	$4.00
4	$2.50	$4.00	$5.00
5	$3.00	$5.00	$6.00
6	$3.50	$6.00	$7.00
7	$4.00	$7.00	$8.00
8	$4.50	$8.00	$9.00
9	$5.00	$9.00	$10.00
10	$5.50	$10.00	$11.00

   Suppose this region needs to reduce emissions by 14 units and plans to do it using a form of cap-and-trade that auctions allowances off to the highest bidder.
   a. How many allowances will the control authority auction off? Why?
   b. Assuming no market power, how many of the allowances would each firm be expected to buy? Why?

c. Assuming that demand equals supply, what price would be paid for those allowances? Why?
d. If the control authority decided to use an emissions tax rather than cap-and-trade, what tax rate would achieve the 14-unit reduction cost-effectively? Why?

Further Reading

Baumol, W. J., & Oates. W. E. (1988). *The theory of environmental policy*, 2nd ed. Cambridge, UK: Cambridge University Press. A classic on the economic analysis of externalities. Accessible only to those with a thorough familiarity with multivariate calculus.

Harrington, W., Morgenstern, R. D., & Sterner, T. (2002). *Choosing environmental policy: Comparing instruments and outcomes in the United States and Europe*. Washington, DC: Resources for the Future. Uses paired case studies from the United States and Europe to contrast the costs and outcomes of direct regulation on one side of the Atlantic with an incentive-based policy on the other.

OECD. (1989). *Economic instruments for environmental protection*. Paris: OECD. A survey of how economic incentive approaches to pollution control have been used in industrialized nations that belong to the OECD.

OECD. (1994). *Environment and taxation: The cases of the Netherlands, Sweden, and the United States*. Paris: OECD. Background case studies for a larger research project seeking to discover the extent to which fiscal and environmental policies could be made not only compatible but also mutually reinforcing.

Rock, M. (2002). *Pollution control in East Asia: Lessons from newly industrializing countries.* Washington, DC: Resources for the Future, Inc. These studies of pollution management in East Asia's newly industrialized economies (NIEs) include successful government responses in Singapore and Taiwan, qualified results in China and Indonesia, and much more limited success in Thailand and Malaysia.

Stavins, R. N. (2003). Experience with market based environmental policy instruments. In K. G. Maler & J. R. Vincent (Eds.). *Handbook of environmental economics, volume 1: Environmental degradation and institutional reponses* (355–435).Amsterdam: Elsevier. A review of what we have learned from our experience with market-based instruments.

Sterner, T. (2003). *Policy instruments for environmental and natural resource management.* Washington, DC: Resources for the Future, Inc. Intended primarily for audiences in developing and transitional countries, this volume compares the accumulated experiences of the use of economic policy instruments in the United States and Europe, as well as in select rich and poor countries in Asia, Africa, and Latin America.

Tietenberg, T. (Ed.) (2001). *Emissions trading programs: Volume I implementation and evolution* and *Volume II theory and design.* International Library of Environmental Economics and Policy. Aldershot, UK: Ashgate. A two-volume collection of the leading published articles on emissions trading, coupled with an editor's introduction that traces the history of our state of knowledge about this policy instrument.

Additional References and Historically Significant References are available on this book's Companion Website: http://www.routledgetextbooks.com/textbooks/9780133479690

Appendix

The Simple Mathematics of Cost-Effective Pollution Control

Suppose that each of N polluters would emit u_n units of emission in the absence of any control. Furthermore, suppose that the pollutant concentration K_R at some receptor R in the absence of control is

$$K_R = \sum_{n=1}^{N} a_n u_n + B \tag{1}$$

where B is the background concentration and a_n is the transfer coefficient. This K_R is assumed to be greater than ϕ, the legal concentration level. The regulatory problem, therefore, is to choose the cost-effective level of control q_n for each of the n sources. Symbolically, this can be expressed as minimizing the following Lagrangian with respect to the Nq_n control variables:

$$\min \sum_{n=1}^{N} C_n(q_n) + \lambda\left[\sum_{n=1}^{N} a_n(u_n - q_n) - \Phi\right] \tag{2}$$

where $C_n(q_n)$ is the cost of achieving the q_n level of control at the nth source and λ is the Lagrangian multiplier.

The solution is found by partially differentiating (2) with respect to λ and the $N\,q_n$'s. This yields

$$\frac{\partial C_n(q_n)}{\partial q} - \lambda^* a_n \geq 0,\ n = 1,\ldots, N, \tag{3}$$

$$\sum_{n=1}^{N} a_n(u_n - q_n) + B - \Phi = 0. \tag{4}$$

Solving these equations produces the N-dimensional vector q^0 and the scalar λ.

Note that this same formulation can be used to reflect both the uniformly mixed and nonuniformly mixed single-receptor case. In the uniformly mixed case, every $a_n = 1$. This immediately implies that the marginal cost of control should be equal for all emitters who are required to engage in some control. (The first N equations would hold as equalities except for any source where the marginal cost of controlling the first unit exceeded the marginal cost necessary to meet the target.) For the nonuniformly mixed single-receptor case, in the cost-effective allocation the control responsibility would be allocated so as to ensure that the ratio of the marginal control costs for two emitters would be equal to the ratio of their transfer coefficients. For J receptors both λ^* and λ^* would become J-dimensional vectors.

Policy Instruments

A special meaning can be attached to λ. If emissions trading were being used, it would be the market-clearing price of an allowance. In the uniformly mixed case, λ would be the price of an allowance to emit one unit of emission. In the nonuniformly mixed case, λ would be the price of being allowed to raise the concentration at the receptor location one unit. In the case of taxes, λ represents the value of the cost-effective tax.

Note how firms choose emissions control when the allowance price or tax is equal to λ. Each firm wants to minimize its costs. Assume that each firm is given allowances of Ω_n, where the regulatory authority ensures that

$$\sum_{n=1}^{N} a_n \Omega_n + B = \Phi \tag{5}$$

for the set of all emitters. Each firm would want to

$$\min \; c_n(q_n) + P^0[a_n(u_n - q_n) - \Omega_n)]. \tag{6}$$

The minimum cost is achieved by choosing the value of $q_n(q_n{}^0)$ that satisfies

$$\frac{\partial C_n(q_n)}{\partial q_n} - P^* a_n = 0. \tag{7}$$

This condition (marginal cost equals the price of a unit of concentration reduction) would hold for each of the N firms. Because P^* would equal λ^* and the number of allowances would be chosen to ensure the ambient standard would be met, this allocation would be cost-effective. Exactly the same result is achieved by substituting T^*, the cost-effective tax rate, for P^*.

15 Stationary-Source Local and Regional Air Pollution

"People are very open-minded about new things - as long as they're exactly like the old ones."

—Charles F. Kettering (American engineer, inventor of the electric starter, 1876–1958)

Introduction

Attaining and maintaining clean air is an exceedingly difficult policy task. In the United States, for example, an estimated 27,000 major stationary sources of air pollution are subject to control as well as hundreds of thousands of more minor sources. Many distinct production processes emit many different types of pollutants. The resulting damages range from minimal effects on plants and vegetation to the modification of the earth's climate.

The policy response to this problem has been continually evolving. The Clean Air Act Amendments of 1970 set a bold new direction that has been retained and refined by subsequent acts. By virtue of 1970 amendments, the federal government assumed a much larger and much more vigorous direct role. The US Environmental Protection Agency (EPA) was created to implement and oversee this massive attempt to control the injection of pollutants into the nation's air. Individually tailored strategies were created to deal with mobile and stationary sources.

Conventional Pollutants

Conventional pollutants are relatively common substances, found in almost all parts of the country, and are thought, on the basis of research, to be dangerous only in high concentrations. In the United States, these pollutants are called *criteria pollutants* because the Act requires the EPA to produce "criteria documents" to be used in setting acceptable standards for these pollutants. These documents summarize and evaluate all of the existing research on the various health and environmental effects associated with these pollutants. The central focus of air pollution control during the 1970s was on criteria pollutants.

The Command-and-Control Policy Framework

In Chapter 14 several possible approaches to controlling pollution were described and analyzed in theoretical terms. The historical approach to air pollution control, known popularly as "command-and-control" (CAC), depended primarily on emissions standards. In this section we outline the specific nature of this approach, analyze its shortcomings from an efficiency and cost-effectiveness perspective, and show how a series of reforms based on the logic advanced in the last chapter has worked to rectify some of these deficiencies.

For each of the conventional pollutants, the typical first step is to establish the National Ambient Air Quality Standards (NAAQS). These standards have to be met everywhere, although as a practical matter they are monitored at a large number of specific locations.

Ambient standards set legal ceilings on the allowable concentration of the pollutant in the outdoor air averaged over a specified time period. The allowable concentrations for many pollutants are defined in terms of both a long-term average (defined frequently as an annual average) and a short-term average (such as a 3-hour average). Compliance with short-term averages usually requires that the allowable concentrations be exceeded no more than once a year. Control costs can be quite sensitive to the level of these short-term averages.

In the United States, two ambient standards have been defined. The *primary standard* is designed to protect human health. It was the first standard to be determined, and had the earliest deadlines for compliance. All pollutants have a primary standard. The primary ambient standards are required by statute to be set at a level sufficient to protect even the most sensitive members of the population without any consideration given to the costs of meeting them.

The *secondary standard* is designed to protect other aspects of human welfare from those pollutants having separate effects. Currently, only two separate secondary standards have been set for sulfur oxides and small particulates. For some other pollutants, the concentration levels allowed by the primary and secondary standards are the same. The secondary standards are designed to protect aesthetics (particularly visibility), physical objects (houses, monuments, and so on), and vegetation. When a separate secondary standard exists, both it and the primary standard must be met.[1]

While the EPA is responsible for defining the ambient standards, the primary responsibility for enforcement falls on the state control agencies. They exercise this responsibility by developing and executing an acceptable state implementation plan (SIP), which must be approved by the EPA. This plan divides the state into separate air-quality-control regions. Special procedures were developed for handling regions that cross state borders, such as metropolitan New York.

The SIP spells out for each control region the procedures and timetables for meeting local ambient standards and for abatement of the effects of locally emitted pollutants on other states. The required degree of control depends on the severity of the pollution problem in each of the control regions. All areas not meeting the deadlines were designated as *nonattainment regions*.

[1]The actual standards can be found at at http://www.epa.gov/air/criteria.html

The areas receiving this designation are subjected to particularly stringent controls. Nonattainment areas have been placed within one of seven categories (basic, marginal, moderate, serious, two categories of severe, and extreme). Each category has its own criteria for compliance with the standard. Generally, the more severe the degree of nonattainment in an area, the more stringent the requirements imposed on it. To prod the states into action, Congress gave the EPA the power to halt the construction of major new or modified pollution sources and to deny federal sewage and transportation grants for any state not submitting a plan showing precisely how and when attainment would be reached.

Recognizing that it is typically much easier and much cheaper to control new sources rather than existing ones, the Clean Air Act established the New Source Review (NSR) Program. This program requires all new major stationary sources (as well as those undergoing major modifications) in both attainment and nonattainment areas to seek a permit for operation. This permit requires compliance with the specified standards (more stringent in nonattainment areas than in attainment areas). The theory was that as old, dirtier plants became obsolete, this program would ensure that their replacements would be significantly less polluting. As Debate 15.1 points out, the New Source Review Program has stimulated some controversy.

The Efficiency of the Command-and-Control Approach

Efficiency presumes that the allowable concentration levels authorized by the ambient standards are set where the marginal benefit equals the marginal cost. To ascertain whether or not the current standards are efficient, it is necessary to inquire into five aspects of the standard-setting process: (1) the threshold concept on which the standards are based, (2) the level of the standard, (3) the choice of uniform standards over standards more tailored to the regions involved, (4) the timing of emissions flows, and (5) the failure to incorporate the degree of human exposure in the standard-setting process.

The Threshold Concept. Since the Clean Air Act prohibits the balancing of costs and benefits, some alternative criterion must be used to set the standard. For the primary (health-related) standard, this criterion is known as the *health threshold*. In principle, this threshold is defined with a margin of safety sufficiently high that no adverse health effects would be suffered by any member of the population as long as the air quality was at least as good as the standard. This approach presumes the existence of a threshold such that concentrations below that level produce no adverse health effects.

If the threshold concept presumption were valid, the marginal damage function would be zero for concentrations under the threshold and would be positive at higher concentrations. In practice, this shape is not consistent with the latest evidence. Adverse health effects can occur at pollution levels lower than the ambient standards. The standard that produces no adverse health effects among the general population (which, of course, includes especially susceptible groups) is probably zero or close to it. It is certainly lower than the established ambient standards. What the standards purport to accomplish and what they actually accomplish are rather different.

Does Sound Policy Require Targeting New Sources via the New Source Review?

DEBATE 15.1

One of the characteristics of the New Source Review program is that it requires large stationary sources that are undergoing major modifications (not just routine maintenance) to meet the same stringent standards as new sources, while maintained, but not modified old sources avoid installing the more stringent control technology. Due to this routine maintenance exemption, a number of older plants have never triggered the major modification threshold and therefore have never been upgraded. As a result, over time these older plants have become responsible for a larger share of the total emissions.

One approach was to take enforcement actions against individual companies, including numerous electric utilities that own and operate coal-fired power plants in the Southeast and Midwest. The lawsuits alleged that plants that should have been retired years earlier were being modified and retained past their normal life under the cover of "routine maintenance." Using this exemption to prop up the plants was seen as an evasion of the principle of improving air quality over time by replacing older plants with modern, less polluting plants.

Opponents of the New Source Review process argue that it has been counterproductive, resulting in worse air quality, not better, and it should be replaced, not merely better enforced. According to this view, not only has New Source Review deterred investment in newer, cleaner technologies, but it has also discouraged companies from keeping power plants adequately maintained, lest they trigger the major modification designation. The solution, they argue, is to use cap-and-trade to create a level-playing field, where all electricity generators (old and new) would face the same emissions constraint. Under this new policy, plant owners would pursue the investment and/or retirement strategies that secured the required emissions reductions at minimum cost. Artificial delay in replacing plants would no longer make any economic sense with the new incentives created by cap-and-trade—private and social goals would be harmonized.

Source: Stavins, R. (2006). Vintage-Differentiated Environmental Regulation. *Stanford Environmental Law, 25*(1), 29–63.

The Level of the Ambient Standard. The absence of a defensible health threshold complicates the analysis (see Debate 15.2). Some other basis must be used for determining the level at which the standard should be established. Efficiency would dictate setting the standard in order to maximize the net benefit, which includes a consideration of costs as well as benefits.

The current policy explicitly excludes costs from consideration in setting the ambient standards. It is difficult to imagine that the process of setting the ambient standard would yield an efficient outcome when it is prohibited from considering one of the key elements of that outcome!

Unfortunately, for reasons that were discussed in some detail in Chapter 4, our current benefit measurements are not sufficiently reliable as to permit the

DEBATE 15.2 The Particulate and Smog Ambient Standards Controversy

During one of its periodic reviews of the ambient air-quality standards, the US EPA concluded that 125 million Americans, including 35 million children, were not adequately protected by the existing standards for ozone and particulates. More stringent standards were estimated to prevent 1 million serious respiratory illnesses each year, and 15,000 premature deaths.

The proposed revisions were controversial because the cost of compliance would be very high. No health threshold existed at the chosen level (some health effects would be noticed at even more stringent levels than those proposed) and the EPA was, by law, prohibited from using a benefit–cost justification. In the face of legal challenge, the EPA found it very difficult to defend the superiority of the chosen standards from slightly more stringent or slightly less stringent standards.

In its ruling on the issues raised in this case, the US Court of Appeals for the District of Columbia Circuit overturned the proposed revisions. In a 2–1 ruling, the three-judge panel rejected the EPA's approach to setting the level of those standards:

> *the construction of the Clean Air Act on which EPA relied in promulgating the NAAQS at issue here effects an unconstitutional delegation of legislative power. . . . Although the factors EPA uses in determining the degree of public health concern associated with different levels of ozone and PM are reasonable, EPA appears to have articulated no "intelligible principle" to channel its application of these factors . . . . EPA's formulation of its policy judgement leaves it free to pick any point between zero and a hair below the concentrations yielding London's Killer Fog.*

Although the threat to the EPA's authority from this decision was ultimately overturned by the US Supreme Court, the dilemma posed by the absence of a compelling health threshold remains unresolved.

identification of the efficient level with any confidence. For example, an early EPA study of the Clean Air Act found that the total monetized benefits of the Clean Air Act realized during the period from 1970 to 1990 ranged from \$5.6 to \$49.4 trillion, with a central estimate of \$22.2 trillion. That is a very large band of uncertainty.

The study further noted the following:

> *The central estimate of 22.2 trillion dollars in benefits may be a significant underestimate due to the exclusion of large numbers of benefits from the monetized benefit estimate (e.g., all air toxics effects; ecosystem effects; numerous human health effects). (p. ES-8)*

The EPA's estimates suggest that a high degree of confidence can be attached to the belief that government intervention to control air pollution in the United States was economically justified; but they provide no evidence whatsoever on whether current policy was, or is, efficient.

Uniformity. The same primary and secondary standards apply to all parts of the country. No account is taken of the number of people exposed, the sensitivity of the local ecology, or the costs of compliance in various areas. All of these aspects of the problem would have some effect on the efficient standard and efficiency would, therefore, dictate different standards for different regions. Uniform ambient standards are inconsistent with an efficient allocation of pollution control resources. Spatially differentiated standards that target the level of control so as to reflect the damage caused would produce more damage reduction per dollar of abatement cost.

Timing of Emissions Flows. Because ambient concentrations are important for criteria pollutants, the timing of emissions is an important policy concern. Emissions concentrated in time are as troublesome as emissions concentrated in space. One circumstance that gives rise to this concern involves those relatively rare, but devastating, occasions when thermal inversions prevent the normal dispersion and dilution of the pollutants. The resulting concentration levels can be quite dangerous. How should these circumstances be handled?

From an economic efficiency point of view, the most obvious approach is to tailor the degree of control to the circumstances. The most stringent control would be exercised when (and only when) meteorological conditions were relatively stagnant; less control would be applied under normal circumstances. A reliance on a constant degree of control, rather than allowing intermittent controls, raises compliance costs substantially, particularly when the required degree of control is high. The strong stand against intermittent controls in the Clean Air Act, however, rules out this approach.

Concentration versus Exposure. Presently ambient standards are defined in terms of pollutant concentrations in the outdoor air. Yet health effects are closely related to human exposure to pollutants and exposure is determined not only by the concentrations of air pollutants in each of the places in which people spend time, but also by the number of people exposed and the amount of time spent in each place. Since in the United States only about 10 percent of the population's person-hours are spent outdoors, indoor air becomes very important in designing strategies to improve the health risk of pollutants. To date, very little attention has been focused on controlling indoor air pollution despite its apparent importance.[2]

Cost-Effectiveness of the Command-and-Control Approach

While empirically determining the magnitude of the inefficiency of the ambient standards is difficult at best, determining their cost-effectiveness is somewhat easier. Although it does not allow us to shed any light on whether a particular ambient

[2]The most obvious major policy response to indoor air pollution has been the large number of states that have passed legislation requiring "smoke-free" areas in public places to protect nonsmokers.

standard is efficient or not, cost-effectiveness does allow us to see whether the ambient standards are being met in the least costly manner possible.

The theory covered in Chapter 14 makes it clear that the CAC strategy will normally not be cost-effective. What the theory does not make clear, however, is the degree to which this strategy diverges from the least-cost ideal. If the divergence is small, the proponents of reform would not likely be able to overcome the inertia of the status quo. If the divergence is large, the case for reform is stronger.

The cost-effectiveness of the CAC approach depends on local circumstances such as prevailing meteorology, the spatial configuration of sources, stack heights, and the degree to which costs vary with the amount controlled. Several simulation models capable of dealing with these complexities have now been constructed for a number of different pollutants in a variety of airsheds (see Table 15.1).

Since for a number of reasons the estimated costs cannot be directly compared across studies, it is appropriate to develop a means of comparing costs that minimizes the comparability problems. One such technique, the one we have chosen, involves calculating the ratio of the CAC allocation (traditional emissions standards) costs to the lowest cost of meeting the same objective for each study. A ratio equal to 1.0 implies that the CAC allocation is cost-effective. By subtracting 1.0 from the ratio in the table and multiplying by 100, it is possible to interpret the remainder as the percentage increase in cost from the least-cost ideal due to relying on the CAC system.

Of the nine reported comparisons, eight find that the CAC policy costs at least 78 percent more than the least-cost allocation. If we omit the Hahn and Noll (1982) study (for reasons discussed in the next two paragraphs), the study involving the *smallest* cost savings (sulfur dioxide control in the Lower Delaware Valley) finds that the CAC allocation would result in abatement costs that are 78 percent higher than necessary to meet the standards. In the Chicago study, the CAC costs were estimated to be 14 times as expensive as necessary, while in the Lower Delaware Valley they were estimated to be 22 times more expensive than necessary.

The Hahn and Noll finding that the CAC strategy was close to being cost-effective was somewhat unique in a couple of respects. Because we can learn something from this study about the conditions under which CAC policies may not be far off the mark, we study it closely.

Los Angeles, the city studied by Hahn and Noll, had a large sulfate problem, necessitating a very high degree of control. In effect, virtually every source was forced to control as much as is economically feasible. When that is true, the possibilities for trade are small or nonexistent. Without the flexibility of trades the possibilities for cost savings are also small or nonexistent so the cost-effectiveness disadvantage of standards in this particular case is small.

As Example 15.1 points out, the command-and-control program to control SO_2 emissions in Germany had a similar outcome (quite cost-effective) for similar reasons (stringent controls resulting in similar marginal control costs). In that case, most of the excessive cost resulted from the policy's lack of temporal flexibility.

TABLE 15.1 Empirical Studies of Air Pollution Control

Study	Pollutants Covered	Geographic Area	CAC Benchmark	Assumed Pollutant Type	Ratio of CAC Cost to Least Cost
Atkinson and Lewis	Particulates	St. Louis Metropolitan Area	SIP Regulations	Nonuniformly Mixed	6.00
Roach et al.	Sulfur Dioxide	Four Corners in Utah, Colorado, Arizona, and New Mexico	SIP Regulations	Nonuniformly Mixed	4.25
Hahn and Noll	Sulfates	Los Angeles	California Emission Standards	Nonuniformly Mixed	1.07
Krupnick	Nitrogen Dioxide	Baltimore	Proposed RACT Regulations	Nonuniformly Mixed	5.96
Seskin, Anderson, and Reid	Nitrogen Dioxide	Chicago	Proposed RACT Regulations	Nonuniformly Mixed	14.40
McGartland	Particulates	Baltimore	SIP Regulations	Nonuniformly Mixed	4.18
Spofford	Sulfur Dioxide	Lower Delaware Valley	Uniform Percentage Reduction	Nonuniformly Mixed	1.78
	Particulates	Lower Delaware Valley	Uniform Percentage Reduction	Nonuniformly Mixed	22.00
Maloney and Yandle	Hydrocarbons	All Domestic DuPont Plants	Uniform Percentage Reduction	Uniformly Mixed	4.15
O'Ryan	Particulates	Santiago, Chile	Uniform Percentage Reduction	Nonuniformly Mixed	1.31

CAC = command and control, the traditional regulatory approach.
SIP = state implementation plan.
RACT = reasonably available control technologies, a set of standards imposed on existing sources in nonattainment areas.

EXAMPLE 15.1

Controlling SO_2 Emissions by Command-and-Control in Germany

Germany and the United States took quite different approaches to controlling SO_2 emissions. Whereas the United States used a version of cap-and-trade, Germany used traditional command-and-control regulation. Theory would lead us to believe that the U.S. approach, due to its flexibility, would achieve its goals at a considerably lower expense. The evidence suggests that it did, but the reasons are a bit more complicated than one might suppose.

Due to the large amount of forest death (Waldsterben) in Germany in which SO_2 emissions were implicated, the pressure was on to significantly reduce SO_2 emission from large combustion sources in a relatively short period of time. Both the degree of control and the mandated deadlines for compliance were quite stringent.

The stringency of the targets meant that sources had very little control flexibility; only one main technology could meet the requirements, so every covered combustion source had to install that technology. Even if firms had been allowed to engage in allowance trading once the equipment was installed, the pretrade marginal costs would have been very similar. Since the purpose of trading is to equalize marginal costs, the fact that they were very similar before trading left little room for cost savings from trade.

The main cost disadvantage to the German system, however, was not found to be due to unequal marginal costs but rather to the temporal inflexibility of the command-and-control regulations. As Wätzold (2004) notes the following:

> *The nearly simultaneous installation of desulfurization equipment in LCPs [Large Combustion Plants] all over Germany led to a surge in demand for this equipment with a resulting increase in prices. Furthermore, because Germany had little experience with the necessary technology, no learning effects were achieved; . . . shortcomings that should have come to light before the systems were introduced in the entire fleet of power stations . . . had to be remedied in all power stations. (p. 35)*

This was quite different from the U.S. experience with its sulfur allowance program. In the U.S. program (described later in this chapter), the ability to bank or save allowances for subsequent use, which provided an incentive for some firms to comply early, and the phased deadline allowed much more flexibility in the timing of the installation of abatement controls; not all firms had to comply at the same time.

Source: Wätzold, F. F. (2004). SO_2 emissions in Germany: Regulations to fight Waldsterben. *Choosing Environmental Policy: Comparing Instruments and Outcomes in the United States And Europe.* In W. Harrington, R. D. Morgenstern, & T. Sterner (Eds.). (23–40). Washington, DC: Resources for the Future.

Air Quality

Each year, the US Environmental Protection Agency publishes air-quality trends using measurements from monitors located across the country. Table 15.2 shows the national improvement in air quality (the pollutant concentrations in the ambient air) that have occurred over the 30 years from 1980 to 2010. Notice that every pollutant experienced improvement and in some cases the improvements were dramatic.

TABLE 15.2 Air-Quality Trend in the United States

	Percent Change in Air Quality		
	1980 vs 2010	1990 vs 2010	2000 vs 2010
Carbon Monoxide (CO)	−82	−73	−54
Ozone (O3) (8-hr)	−28	−17	−11
Lead (Pb)	−90	−83	−62
Nitrogen Dioxide (NO_2) (annual)	−52	−45	−38
PM10 (24-hr)	—	−38	−29
PM2.5 (annual)	—	—	−27
PM2.5 (24-hr)	—	—	−29
Sulfur Dioxide (SO_2) (24-hr)	−76	−68	−48

Notes:
1. —Trend data not available
2. Negative numbers indicate improvements in air quality

Source: USEPA Air Quality Trends Website. Retrieved from http://www.epa.gov/airtrends/aqtrends.html

How typical has the US experience been? Is pollution declining on a worldwide basis? The Global Environmental Monitoring System (GEMS), operating under the auspices of the World Health Organization and the United Nations Environment Program, monitors air quality around the globe. Scrutiny of its reports reveal that the US experience is typical for the industrialized nations, which have generally reduced pollution (both in terms of emissions and ambient outdoor air quality). Some of the reductions achieved in countries such as Japan and Norway have been spectacular. However, the air quality in most developing nations has steadily deteriorated, and the number of people exposed to unhealthy levels of pollution in those countries is frequently very high.[3] Since these countries typically are struggling merely to provide adequate employment and income to their citizens, they cannot afford to waste large sums of money on inefficient environmental policies, especially if the inefficiencies tend to subsidize the rich at the expense of the poor. Some cost-effective, yet fair means of improving air quality that work in the developing country context must be found.

Market-Based Approaches

Fortunately some more cost-effective approaches are available. Since various versions of these approaches have now been implemented around the world, we can learn from the experience gained from their implementation.

[3]For sulfur oxides, for example, the GEMS study estimates that only 30–35 percent of the world's population lives in areas where the air is at least as clean as recommended by World Health Organization guidelines.

Smog Trading (RECLAIM)

Whereas the Clean Air Act transferred a considerable amount of power to the federal government, the newest programs have arisen from state initiatives. Faced with the need to reduce ozone concentrations considerably to come into compliance with the ozone-ambient standard, states have chosen trading programs as a means of facilitating rather drastic reductions in precursor pollutants.

One of the most ambitious of these programs is California's Regional Clean Air Incentives Market (RECLAIM), established by the South Coast Air Quality Management District, the district responsible for the greater Los Angeles area. Under RECLAIM, each of the almost 400 participating industrial polluters is allocated an annual pollution limit for nitrogen oxides and sulfur dioxide, which decrease by 5–8 percent each year for the next decade. Polluters are allowed great flexibility in meeting these limits, including purchasing credits from other firms that have controlled more than their legal requirements.

The cap-and-trade approach has fundamentally changed the nature of the regulatory process as it was practiced in the command-and-control regime. The burden of identifying the appropriate control strategies has shifted from the control authority to the polluter. In part, this shift was a necessity (traditional processes were incapable of identifying enough appropriate technologies to produce sufficiently stringent reductions) and was, in part, motivated by a desire to make the process as flexible as possible.

As a result of this flexibility, many new control strategies began to emerge. Instead of the traditional focus on end-of-pipe control technologies (where the pollution is still created, but it is captured before being emitted into the environment), pollution prevention (where the pollution is not created in the first place) has been given an economic underpinning by this program. All possible pollution-reduction strategies could, for the first time, compete on a level-playing field.

The RECLAIM program also illustrates a couple of potential problems with cap-and-trade markets. Compromises designed to gain enough political support to enact the system may affect the level of the cap, at least initially. This was certainly the case with RECLAIM as initial allocations were inflated (Harrison, 2004). An early evaluation of the program by the EPA concluded that due to these inflated initial allocations in the earlier years of the program fewer emissions had been reduced by RECLAIM than would have been reduced by more traditional regulation.

The second problem with RECLAIM arose from a confluence of adverse forces. Due to electric deregulation and a shortage of imported power, power plants in the RECLAIM area were required to run full tilt. These abnormally high production levels generated an abnormally large amount of emissions. Since the supply of allowances that determined the level of authorized emissions was fixed by the cap, which had been set without anticipating these increases, the price of these allowances shot up to politically unsupportable levels.

The very large price increases triggered the use of a "safety valve" mechanism that had been built into the program. RECLAIM procedures specified that if allowance prices went over some threshold (as it did in this case), the program would be temporarily suspended, and an alternative fee per ton would be imposed until the normal operation of the program could resume. This alternative fee, of course, in essence replaced the unacceptably high market price with a somewhat lower, administratively determined price that was politically acceptable. This fee was designed to retain some financial pressure on the plants to reduce emissions without straining the system beyond its tolerance limits. The revenue was used to secure emissions reductions from other sources.

This experience provides some insights about both the nature of the problem and a potential solution. When prices rise to levels that jeopardize the integrity of the program (due to the fixed supply of allowances), it is possible to switch to a fee-based system until more normal conditions once again prevail. In fact some of the newer cap-and-trade programs now routinely build a safety valve feature into their design.

Emissions Charges

Air pollution emissions charges have been implemented by a number of countries, including Sweden, France, and Japan. The Swedish nitrogen charge was discussed in the previous chapter. The French air pollution charge was designed to encourage the early adoption of pollution control equipment, with the revenues returned to those paying the charge as a subsidy for installing the equipment. In Japan, the emissions charge is designed to raise revenue to compensate victims of air pollution.

The French charge system has been in effect since 1985. Originally designed to operate until 1990, it was renewed and expanded in that year. The charge is levied on all industrial firms having a power-generating capacity of 20 megawatts or more, or industrial firms discharging over 150 metric tons of taxable pollutants. Some 1400 plants were affected. Some 90 percent of the charge revenue was recovered by charge payers as a subsidy for pollution control equipment, while the remaining 10 percent was used for new technological developments.

While data are limited, a few highlights seem clear. The prevailing charge level is too low to have any incentive impact. Analysis suggests that total revenues are only about one-tenth of the revenue that would result from a charge sufficient to bring French industries in line with the air pollution control directives of the European Community (Millock & Sterner, 2004).

Economists typically envision two types of effluent or emissions charges. The first, an efficiency charge, is designed to force the polluter to compensate completely for all damage caused. The second, a cost-effective charge, is designed to achieve a predefined ambient standard at the lowest possible control cost. In practice, the French approach fits neither of these designs.

In Japan, the charge is based upon damages to human health. As a result of four important legal cases where Japanese industries were forced to compensate victims for pollution damages caused, in 1973 Japan passed the Law for the Compensation of Pollution-Related Health Injury. According to this law, victims of designated diseases, upon certification by a council of medical, legal, and other experts, are eligible for medical expenses, lost earnings, and other expenses; they are not eligible for other losses, such as pain and suffering. Two classes of diseases are funded: designated diseases where the specific source is relatively clear, and nonspecific respiratory diseases where all polluters are presumed to have some responsibility.

Victim compensation is funded by an emissions charge on sulfur dioxides and by an automobile weight tax. The level of the charge/tax is determined by the revenue needs of the compensation fund.

In contrast to cap-and-trade where allowance prices respond automatically to changing market conditions, emissions charges have to be determined by an administrative process. When the function of the charge is to raise revenue for a particular purpose, charge rates will be determined by the costs of achieving that purpose; when the costs of achieving the purpose rise, the level of the charge must rise to secure the additional revenue.[4]

Sometimes that process produces an unintended dynamic. In Japan, for example, the charge is calculated on the basis of the amount of compensation paid to victims of air pollution in the previous year. While the amount of compensation has been increasing, the amount of emissions (the base to which the charge is applied) has been decreasing. As a result, unexpectedly high charge rates are necessary in order to raise sufficient revenue for the compensation system and these have quite an incentive effect on emissions reduction.

Regional Pollutants

The primary difference between regional pollutants and local pollutants is the distance they are transported in the air. Although the damage caused by local pollutants occurs in the vicinity of emission, for regional pollutants the damage can occur at significant distances from the emissions point.

The same substances can be both local pollutants and regional pollutants. Sulfur oxides, nitrogen oxides, and ozone, for example, have already been discussed as local pollutants, but they are regional pollutants as well. For example, sulfur emissions, the focal point for most acid rain legislation, have been known to travel some 200–600 miles from the point of emission before returning to the earth. As the substances are being transported by the winds, they undergo a complex series of chemical reactions. Under the right conditions, both sulfur and nitrogen oxides are transformed into sulfuric and nitric acids (see Example 15.2). Nitrogen oxides and hydrocarbons can combine in the presence of sunlight to produce ozone.

In many countries with a federal form of government, such as the United States, the policy focus in the past has been on treating all pollutants as if they were local pollutants, overlooking the adverse regional consequences in the process. By giving local jurisdictions a large amount of responsibility for achieving the desired air quality and by measuring progress at local monitors, the stage was set for making regional pollution worse, rather than better.

In the early days of pollution control, local areas adopted the motto "Dilution is the solution." As implemented, this approach suggested that the way to control local pollutants was to require tall stacks for emissions. By the time the pollutants hit the ground, according to this theory, the concentrations would be diluted, making it easier to meet the ambient standards at nearby monitors.

[4]While it is theoretically possible (depending on the elasticity of demand for pollution abatement) for a rise in the tax to produce less revenue, this has typically not been the case.

EXAMPLE 15.2

The Economics of Adirondack Acidification Control

About 180 lakes in the Adirondack Mountains of New York State, mostly at higher altitudes, which had supported natural or stocked brook trout populations in the 1930s, no longer supported these populations by the 1970s. In some cases, entire communities of six or more fish species had disappeared.

The location of these lakes, some distance east of any local emissions sources, makes it quite clear that most of the acid deposition is coming from outside of the region. These lakes have relatively little capacity to neutralize deposited acid because they are in areas with little or no limestone or other forms of basic rock that might serve to buffer the acid.

This is a prime recreational area, particularly for fishing. Most of the sites are within the boundary of the 6-million acre Adirondack Park, the last substantially undeveloped area of its size in the northeastern United States. Its remoteness, mountainous terrain, and multitude of lakes provide an accessible outdoor recreation experience for the 55 million people who live within a day's traveling distance.

Although the 1990 amendments to the Clean Air Act (described below) resulted in substantial reductions in acid deposition, subsequent legislative proposals encouraged policy-makers to determine if further reduction efforts would be justified in terms of net benefits. Using a contingent valuation method that includes both use and nonuse values, Banzhaf, Burtraw, Evans, and Krupnick (2004) estimated the benefits from further reductions in SO_2 and NO_x and compared them with the costs of achieving those reductions.

Their preferred estimates of the mean willingness to pay (WTP) for ecological improvements ranged from $48 to $107 per year per household in New York state. Multiplying these population-weighted estimates by the approximate number of households in the state yielded benefits ranging from about $336 million to $1.1 billion per year.

Their estimate of the costs of those reductions attributable to Adirondack improvements range from $86 million in 2010 to $126 million in 2020. Since these cost estimates are significantly less than the benefit estimates, the study suggested that further reductions would be economically justified despite the large reductions already achieved.

Source: Banzhaf, S., Burtraw, D., Evans, D., & Krupnick, A. (September 2004). Valuation of natural resource improvements in the Adirondacks. A *Report to the Environmental Protection Agency.* Resources for the Future, Inc.

This approach had several consequences. First, it lowered the amount of emissions reduction necessary to achieve ambient standards; with tall stacks, any given amount of emission would produce lower nearby ground-level concentrations than an equivalent level of emissions from a shorter stack. Second, the ambient standards could be met at a lower cost. Using Cleveland as a case study, Scott Atkinson (1983) has shown that control costs would be approximately 30 percent lower but emissions would be 2.5 times higher if a local, rather than a regional, strategy were followed in a marketable-permit system. In essence, local areas would be able to lower their own cost by exporting emissions to other areas. By focusing its attention on local pollution, the Clean Air Act actually made the regional pollution problem worse.

Crafting a Policy

By the end of the 1980s, it had become painfully clear in the United States that the Clean Air Act was ill-suited to solving regional pollution problems. Revamping the legislation to do a better job of dealing with regional pollutants, such as acid rain, became a high priority.

Politically, that was a tall order. By virtue of the fact that these pollutants are transported long distances, the set of geographic areas receiving the damage is typically not the same as the set of geographic areas responsible for most of the emission causing the damage. In many cases the recipients and the emitters are even in different countries! In this political milieu, it should not be surprising that those bearing the costs of damages should call for a large, rapid reduction in emissions, whereas those responsible for bearing the costs of that cleanup should want to proceed more slowly and with greater caution.

Economic analysis was helpful in finding a feasible path through this political thicket. In particular, a Congressional Budget Office (CBO) study helped to set the parameters of the debate by quantifying the consequences of various courses of action (1986). To analyze the economic and political consequences of various strategies designed to achieve reductions of SO_2 emissions from utilities anywhere from 8 to 12 million tons below the emissions levels from those plants in 1980, the CBO used a computer-based simulation model that related utility emissions, utility costs, and coal-market supply and demand levels to the strategies under consideration.

The results of this modeling exercise will be presented in two segments. The first segment examines the basic available strategies, including both a traditional command-and-control strategy that simply allocates reductions on the basis of a specific formula and an emissions-charge strategy. This analysis demonstrated how sensitive costs were to various levels of emissions reduction and highlighted some of the political consequences of implementing these strategies. The second segment of analysis considers various strategies designed to mitigate the adverse political effects of the basic strategies as a means of ascertaining what would be gained and lost by adopting these compromises.

The first implication of the analysis was that the marginal cost of additional control would rise rapidly, particularly after 10 million tons had been reduced. The cost of reducing a ton of SO_2 was estimated to rise from $270 for an 8-million-ton reduction to $360 for a 10-million-ton reduction, and it would rise to a rather dramatic $779 per ton for a 12-million-ton reduction. Costs would rise much more steeply as the amount of required reduction was increased, because reliance on the more expensive *scrubbers* would become necessary. (Scrubbers involve a chemical process to extract, or "scrub," sulfur gases before they escape into the atmosphere.)

The second insight, one that should be no surprise to readers of this book, is that the emissions charge would be more cost-effective than the comparable CAC strategy. Whereas the CAC strategy could secure a 10-million-ton reduction at about $360 a ton, the emissions charge could do it for $327 a ton. The superiority of the emissions charge was due to the fact that would result in equalized marginal costs, a required condition for cost-effectiveness.

Although the emissions-charge approach may be the most cost-effective policy, it was not the most popular, particularly in states with a lot of old, heavily polluting power plants. With an emissions-charge approach, utilities not only have to pay the higher equipment and operating costs associated with the reductions, but also have to pay the charge on all uncontrolled emissions. The additional financial burden on utilities associated with controlling acid rain by means of an emissions charge would have been significant. Instead of paying the $3.2 billion for reducing 10 million tons under a CAC approach, utilities would be saddled with a $7.7 billion financial burden with an emissions charge. The savings from lower equipment and operating costs achieved because the emissions-charge approach is more cost-effective would have been more than outweighed by the additional expense of paying the emissions charges. The political dilemma posed by this additional financial burden was resolved by adopting an emissions trading system known as the *sulfur allowance trading program*. Adopted as part of the Clean Air Act Amendments of 1990, this approach was designed to complement, not replace, the traditional approach.

Under this program allowances to emit sulfur oxides were allocated to older sulfur-emitting, electricity-generating plants. The number of allowances was restricted in order to assure a reduction of 10 million tons in emissions from 1980 levels by the year 2010.

These allowances, which provide a limited authorization to emit 1 ton of sulfur dioxide (SO_2), are defined for a specific calendar year, but unused allowances can be carried forward into the next year. They are transferable among the affected sources. Any plants reducing emissions more than required by the allowances could transfer the unused allowances to other plants. Emissions in any plant may not legally exceed the levels permitted by the allowances (allocated plus acquired) held by the managers of that plant. An annual year-end audit balances emissions with allowances. Utilities that emit more than authorized by their holdings of allowances must pay an "excess emissions" penalty and are required to forfeit an equivalent number of tons of emissions in the following year (equal to the amount of the excess emissions). The penalty is adjusted annually for inflation.

An important innovation in this program is the establishment of an auction market for the allowances. Each year the EPA withholds an allowance auction reserve of 2.8 percent of the allocated allowances; these go into the sealed bid auction. These withheld allowances are allocated to the highest bidders, with successful buyers paying their bid price (not the market clearing price). The proceeds are refunded to the utilities from whom the allowances were withheld, on a proportional basis. One main advantage of this auction is that it made allowance prices publicly transparent. By providing more information to investors, business investment strategies were facilitated.

Private allowance holders may also offer allowances for sale at these auctions. Potential sellers specify minimum acceptable prices. Once the withheld allowances have been disbursed, the EPA then matches the highest remaining bids with the lowest minimum acceptable prices on the private offerings and matches buyers and sellers until the sum of all remaining bids is less than that of the remaining minimum acceptable prices.

How did the program fare? Rather well in many respects, but not always with the expected outcomes or for the expected reasons (see Example 15.3).

EXAMPLE 15.3

The Sulfur Allowance Program after 20 Years

A recent article conducts a thorough retrospective evaluation of the Sulfur Allowance Program. It found the following:

- The program was environmentally effective, with SO_2 emissions from electric power plants decreasing by 36 between 1990 and 2004, even though electricity generation from coal-fired power plants *increased* 25 percent over the same period.
- The program's long-term annual emissions goal was achieved early. However, it turns out that the ecological benefits of the program, the original focus, were relatively small, largely because it takes much longer than thought to reverse the acidification of ecosystems. In retrospect more than 95 percent of the benefits from this program were associated not with ecological impacts, but rather with human health improvements resulting from reduced levels of small airborne sulfate particles derived from SO_2 emissions.
- Due to effective penalties and continuous monitoring of emissions, compliance was nearly 100 percent.
- Some evidence suggests that the intertemporal allocation of abatement cost (via allowance banking) was at least approximately efficient.
- Although the law was clearly more cost-effective than a traditional command-and-control approach would have been, and it produced savings even much larger than anticipated before the act was enacted, much of this reduced cost was due to an unanticipated consequence—the deregulation of railroad rates in the late 1970s and early 1980s. This event, which clearly preceded the 1990 enactment of this program, allowed more low-sulfur coal to flow eastward at a cheaper price than previously possible.
- In July 2011, the Cross-State Air Pollution Rule (CSAPR), a different regulation resulting from a court decision, allowed for trading only *within* states, a restriction that eliminated the scope for cost-effective interstate trades. The SO_2 market collapsed, with allowance prices falling to record low levels.

The authors note several ironies in this history:

- By enacting an ambitious—and successful—policy to reduce SO_2 emissions in order to curb acid rain, the government essentially did the right thing for the wrong reason.
- Although the program was apparently successful on nearly all dimensions, much of its cost-effectiveness was the unanticipated consequence of the deregulation of railroad rates.
- Although this market-based, cost-effective policy innovation was championed and implemented by Republican administrations from President Ronald Reagan to President George W. Bush, in recent years it has come to be demonized by conservative Republican politicians.
- Finally, court decisions and subsequent responses by the Obama administration have led to the virtual collapse of the SO_2 market, demonstrating that what the government gives, the government can take away.

Source: Schmalensee, R. & Stavins, R. N. "The SO_2 allowance trading system: The ironic history of a grand policy experiment. *Journal of Economic Perspectives. 27*(1), 103–122.

Summary

While air quality has improved in the industrial nations, it has deteriorated in the developing nations. Because the historical approach to air pollution control has been a traditional command-and-control approach, it has been neither efficient nor cost-effective.

The command-and-control policy has not been efficient in part because it has been based on a legal fiction, a threshold below which no health damages are inflicted on any member of the population. In fact, damages occur at levels lower than the ambient standards to especially sensitive members of the population, such as those with respiratory problems. This attempt to formulate standards without reference to control costs has been thwarted by the absence of a scientifically defensible health-based threshold. In addition, the traditional policy failed to adequately consider the timing of emissions flows. By failing to target the greatest amount of control on those periods when the greatest damage is inflicted, the current policy encourages too little control in high-damage periods and excessive control during low-damage periods. Current policy has also failed to pay sufficient attention to indoor air pollution, which may well pose larger health risks than outdoor pollution, at least in developed countries. Unfortunately, because the existing benefit estimates have large confidence intervals, the size of the inefficiency associated with these aspects of the policy has not been measured with any precision.

Traditional regulatory policy has not been cost-effective either. The allocation of responsibility among emitters for reducing pollution has resulted in control costs that are typically several times higher than necessary to achieve the air-quality objective. This has been shown to be true for a variety of pollutants in a variety of geographic settings.

The recent move toward cap-and-trade policies is based on the cost-effective economic incentives they provide. Providing more flexibility in meeting the air-quality goals has reduced both the cost and the conflict between economic growth and the preservation of air quality.

What about the impact of environmental regulation on the diffusion of more environmentally benign technologies? Does the evidence suggest that new technologies with reduced environmental impact are being developed and adopted? As Example 15.4 points out, for chlorine manufacturing, the answer is a definite yes, but not quite in the manner expected.

France and Japan have both introduced emissions charges as part of their approach to pollution control, but neither application fits the textbook model very well. In France, the charge level is too low to have the appropriate incentive effects. In Japan, the charge is designed mainly to raise revenue for compensating victims of respiratory damage caused by pollution. Although the Japanese charge is closer to satisfying the conditions of an efficient charge than the French version (since the level of the charge is based upon the damage caused), it falls short of complete efficiency in that it covers only certain types of damages.

Regional pollutants differ from local pollutants chiefly in the distance they are transported in the air. Whereas local pollutants damage the environment near the

EXAMPLE 15.4

Technology Diffusion in the Chlorine-Manufacturing Sector

Most of the world's chlorine is produced using one of three types of cells: the mercury cell, the diaphragm cell, and the membrane cell. Generally, the mercury-cell technology poses the highest environmental risk, with the diaphragm-cell technology posing the next highest risk.

Over the last 25 years, the mercury-cell share of the total production has fallen from 22 to 10 percent; the diaphragm-cell share has fallen from 73 to 67 percent, and the membrane-cell share has risen from less than 1 percent of the total to 20 percent.

What role did regulation play? One might normally expect that, prodded by regulation, chlorine manufacturers would have increasingly adopted the more environmentally benign production technique. But that is not what happened. Instead, other regulations made it beneficial for users of chlorine to switch to nonchlorine bleaches, thereby reducing the demand for chlorine. In response to this reduction in demand, a number of producers shut down, and a disproportionate share of the plants that remained open were the ones using the cleaner, membrane-cell production.

Source: Snyder, L. D., Miller, N. H., & Stavins, R. N. (2003). The effects of environmental regulation on technology diffusion: The case of chlorine manufacturing. *American Economic Review*, 93(2), 431–435.

emissions site, regional pollutants can cause damage some distance away. Some substances, such as sulfur oxides, nitrogen oxides, and ozone, are both local and regional pollutants.

As the zone of influence of pollutants extends beyond local boundaries, the political difficulties of implementing comprehensive, cost-effective, control measures increase. Pollutants crossing political boundaries impose external costs; neither the emitters nor the nations within which they emit have the proper incentives to institute efficient control measures.

Acid rain is a case in point. Sulfate and nitrate deposition has caused problems both among regions within countries and among countries. In the United States, the Clean Air Act had had a distinctly local focus until 1990. To control local pollution problems, state governments encouraged the installation of tall stacks to dilute the pollution before it hit the ground level. In the process, a high proportion of the emissions were exported to other areas, reaching the ground hundreds of miles from the point of injection. A focus on local control made the regional problem worse.

Finding solutions to the acid rain problem has been very difficult because those bearing the costs of further control are not those who will benefit from the control. In the United States, for example, opposition from the Midwestern and Appalachian states delayed action on acid rain legislation—stumbling blocks included the higher electricity prices that would result from the control and the employment impacts on those states that would suffer losses of jobs in the high-sulfur, coal-mining industry.

These barriers were overcome by the 1990 Clean Air Act Amendments, which instituted the sulfur allowance program. This program placed a cap on total emissions from the utility sector for the first time and implemented a cost-effective way of reducing emissions to the level specified by the cap. The *ex-post* evidence suggests that it was both effective and relatively efficient, but not always for the expected reasons.

Discussion Questions

1. The efficient regulation of hazardous pollutants should take exposure into account—the more persons exposed to a given pollutant concentration, the larger is the damage caused by it and therefore the smaller is the efficient concentration level, all other things being equal. An alternative point of view would simply ensure that concentrations would be held below a uniform threshold regardless of the number of people exposed. For this point of view, the public policy goal is to expose any and all people to the same concentration level—exposure is not used to establish different concentrations for different settings. What are the advantages and disadvantages of each approach? Which do you think represents the best approach? Why?
2. European countries have relied to a much greater extent on emissions charges than has the United States, which seems to be moving toward a greater reliance on cap-and-trade. From an efficiency point of view, should the United States follow Europe's lead and shift the emphasis toward emissions charges? Why or why not?

Self-Test Exercises

1. The marginal control cost curves for two air pollutant sources affecting a single receptor are $MC_1 = \$0.3q_1$ and $MC_2 = \$0.5q_2$, where q_1 and q_2 are controlled emissions. Their respective transfer coefficients are $a_1 = 1.5$ and $a_2 = 1.0$. With no control they would emit 20 units of emission apiece. The ambient standard is 12 ppm.
   a. If an ambient permit system were established, how many permits would be issued and what price would prevail?
   b. How much would each source spend on permits if they were auctioned off? How much would each source ultimately spend on permits if each source were initially given, free of charge, half of the permits?
2. Would imposing the same tax rate on every unit of emissions normally be expected to yield a cost-effective allocation of pollution control responsibility? Does your answer depend on whether the environmental target is an aggregate emissions reduction or meeting an ambient standard? Why or why not?

3. Suppose in an emissions trading system the permits are allocated free of charge to emitters on the basis of how much they have historically emitted. Can that allocation be consistent with cost-effectiveness? Does your answer depend at all on whether this allocation scheme was announced well in advance of its implementation?

Further Reading

Ando, A. W., & Harrington, D. R. (2006). Tradable discharge permits: A student-friendly game. *The Journal of Economic Education (JEE)*, *37*(2), 187–201. A classroom exercise to improve understanding of how tradable permits work.

Blackman, A. (2010). Alternative pollution control policies in developing countries. *Review of Environmental Economics and Policy*, *4*(2), 234–253. This article reviews the effectiveness of the increasing tendency for developing countries to experiment with alternative approaches to control pollution.

Harrington, W., Morgenstern, R. D., & Sterner, T. (Eds.). (2004). *Choosing environmental policy: Comparing instruments and outcomes in the United States and Europe*. Washington, DC: Resources for the Future Inc. A study that compares the evidence on the relative effectiveness of command-and-control and economic incentive polices for controlling pollution in Europe and the United States.

Hendrick, W., & Perry, L. (2010). Policy monitor: Trends in clean air legislation in Europe: Particulate matter and low emission zones," *Review of Environmental Economics and Policy*, *4*(2), 293–308. This article describes recent developments in Europe concerning clean air legislation, focusing in particular on particulate matter (PM).

Hubbel, B. J., Crume, R. V., Evarts, D. M., & Cohen, J. M. (2010). Policy monitor: Regulation and progress under the 1990 clean air act amendments. *Review of Environmental Economics and Policy*, *4*(1), 122–138. This article describes the 1990 CAA Amendments, regulations issued by EPA following their passage, progress made in air-quality management in the nearly 20 years since their enactment, and the likely future direction of US air-quality management programs at the federal level.

Schmalensee, R., Stavins, R. N. (2013). The SO_2 allowance trading system: The ironic history of a grand policy experiment. *The Journal of Economic Perspectives*, 27(1), 103–121. Evaluating the Sulfur Allowance Program after 20 years.

Additional References and Historically Significant References are available on this book's Companion Website: http://www.routledgetextbooks.com/textbooks/9780133479690

Climate Change 16

Everything should be made as simple as possible, but not simpler.

—Albert Einstein

Introduction

As pollutants flow beyond local boundaries, the political difficulties of implementing comprehensive, cost-effective control measures are compounded. Pollutants crossing national boundaries impose external costs; neither emitters nor the political jurisdictions within which they emit have the proper incentives for controlling them.

Compounding the problem of improper incentives is the scientific uncertainty that limits our understanding of these complex problems. Our knowledge about various relationships that form the basis for our understanding of the magnitude of the problems and the effectiveness of various strategies to control them is far from complete. Unfortunately, the problems are so important and the potential consequences of inaction so drastic that procrastination is not usually an optimal strategy. To avoid having to act in the future under emergency conditions when the remaining choices have dwindled, strategies with desirable properties must be formulated now on the basis of the available information, as limited as it may be. Options must be preserved.

The costs of inaction are not limited to the direct damages caused. International cooperation among such traditional allies as the United States, Mexico, and Canada and the countries of Europe has been undermined by disputes over the proper control of transboundary pollution. The potential for conflict is heightened by impending scarcities (water, for example) and the expected border-crossing surge of refugees fleeing extreme weather-related disasters.

In this chapter we survey the scientific evidence on the effectiveness of policy strategies designed to alleviate the problems associated with climate change. We also consider difficulties confronted by the government in implementing solutions and the role of economic analysis in understanding how to circumvent these difficulties.

The Science of Climate Change

One class of global pollutants, greenhouse gases, absorb the long-wavelength (infrared) radiation from the earth's surface and atmosphere, trapping heat that would otherwise radiate into space. The mix and distribution of these gases within the atmosphere is in no small part responsible for both the hospitable climate on the earth and the inhospitable climate on other planets; changing the mix of these gases, however, can modify the climate.

Although carbon dioxide is the most abundant and the most studied of these greenhouse gases, many others have similar thermal radiation properties. These include the chlorofluorocarbons, nitrous oxide, and methane.

The current concern over the effect of this class of pollutants on climate arises not only because emissions of these gases are increasing over time, changing their mix in the atmosphere, but also because many of them have very long residence times in the atmosphere. Emissions entering the atmoshpere now will affect climate for a very long time.

By burning fossil fuels, leveling tropical forests, and injecting more of the other greenhouse gases into the atmosphere, humans are creating a thermal blanket capable of trapping enough heat to raise the temperature of the earth's surface.

The Intergovernmental Panel on Climate Change (IPCC), the body charged with compiling and assessing the scientific information on climate change, reported its findings in 2013 on the sources of climate change. It noted the following:

- Warming of the climate system is unequivocal, and since the 1950s, many of the observed changes are unprecedented over decades to millennia.
- Most aspects of climate change will persist for many centuries even if emissions of CO_2 are stopped.
- It is extremely likely that human influence has been the dominant cause of the observed warming since the mid-20th century....This is evident from the increasing greenhouse gas concentrations in the atmosphere, positive radiative forcing, observed warming, and understanding of the climate system.

Scientists have also uncovered evidence to suggest that climate change may occur rather more abruptly than previously thought. Since the rate of temperature increase is a significant determinant of how well ecosystems can adapt to temperature change, abrupt climate change has become a matter of intensified concern. An example that raises this concern is the large quantities of methane trapped in the frozen tundra of the north. As temperatures warm, the tundra can thaw, releasing the trapped methane. Since methane is a powerful greenhouse gas, this release could accelerate the rate of warming.

These climate changes are expected to result in adverse human health impacts from heat waves and the migration of disease vectors to new areas, in rising sea levels that when coupled with storm surges could inundate coastal areas, in precipitating more intense storms, in triggering an increase in both droughts and floods, and in intensifying ocean acidification, among other impacts.

Negotiations over Climate Change Policy

Characterizing the Broad Strategies

What can be done? Three strategies have been identified: (1) climate engineering, (2) adaptation, and (3) mitigation.

Climate engineering or, alternatively, *geoengineering*, approaches can be divided into two very different categories: carbon dioxide removal and solar-radiation management. While approaches in the former category, such as direct air capture or ocean fertilization, seek to reduce the concentrations of greenhouse gases, approaches in the second category, such as injecting stratospheric aerosols, aim to cool the planet by reflecting a fraction of the incoming sunlight away from Earth. Some propose that one or more of these strategies could provide a cost-effective alternative to mitigation, but recent other reviews have emphasized that such approaches are fraught with uncertainties and may have potential adverse effects and, thus, cannot currently be considered a substitute for comprehensive mitigation until such time as it is too late for conventional policies. Research continues, while the ultimate role for geoengineering remains to be determined.

Adaptation strategies involve efforts to modify natural or human systems in order to minimize harm from climate change impacts. Examples include modifying development planning to increase the resilience of damage-prone areas, such as moving transportation systems and waste treatment facilities away from areas vulnerable to sea-level rise, and preparing public health facilities to handle the larger burdens resulting from the changing disease impacts of a warmer climate.

Mitigation attempts to moderate the temperature rise by using strategies designed to reduce emissions or increase the planet's natural capacity to absorb greenhouse gases.

In this chapter we shall focus mainly on mitigation. The most significant mitigation strategy deals with our use of fossil-fuel energy. Combustion of fossil fuels results in the creation of carbon dioxide. Carbon dioxide emissions can be reduced either by using less energy or by using alternative energy sources (such as wind, photovoltaics, or hydro) that produce less or no carbon dioxide. Any serious reduction in carbon dioxide emissions would involve significant changes in our energy-consumption patterns and those changes could come with an economic cost. Thus, the debate over how vigorously this strategy is to be followed is a controversial public-policy issue.

Another possible strategy involves encouraging activities that increase the amount of carbon that is absorbed by trees or soils. As Debate 16.1 points out, however, the desirability of this approach is heavily debated in current climate change negotiations.

Finding a global solution to climate change is certainly one of the most challenging and pressing problems of our time, but it is not the first global pollutant to be the subject of international negotiations. As we shall examine more closely subsequently in this chapter the negotiations aimed at reducing ozone-depleting gases broke the ice.

DEBATE 16.1 Should Carbon Sequestration in the Terrestrial Biosphere Be Credited?

Both forests and soils sequester (store) a significant amount of carbon. Research suggests that with appropriate changes in practices, they could store much more. Increased *carbon sequestration* in turn would mean less carbon in the atmosphere. Recognition of this potential has created a strong push in the climate change negotiations to give credit in carbon markets or toward carbon taxes for actions that result in more carbon uptake by soils and forests. Whether this should be allowed, and, if so, how it would be done are currently heavily debated.

Proponents argue that this form of carbon sequestration is typically quite cost-effective. Cost-effectiveness not only implies that the given goal can be achieved at lower cost, but also it may increase the willingness to accept more stringent goals with closer deadlines. Allowing credit for carbon absorption may also add economic value to sustainable practices (such as limiting deforestation or preventing soil erosion), thereby providing additional incentives for those practices. Proponents further point out that many of the prime beneficiaries of this increase in value would be the poorest people in the poorest countries.

Opponents say that our knowledge of the science of carbon sequestration in the terrestrial biosphere is in its infancy, so the amount of credit that should be granted is not at all clear. Obtaining estimates of the amount of carbon sequestered could be both expensive (if done right) and subject to considerable uncertainty. Because carbon absorption could be easily reversed at any time (by cutting down trees or changing agricultural practices), continual monitoring and enforcement would be required, adding even more cost. Even in carefully enforced systems, the sequestration is likely to be temporary (even the carbon in completely preserved forests, for example, may ultimately be released into the atmosphere by decay). And finally, the practices that may be encouraged by crediting sequestration will not necessarily be desirable, as when slow-growing old-growth forests are cut down and replaced with fast-growing plantation forests in order to increase the amount of carbon uptake.

Game Theory as a Window on Climate Negotiations

One area of economics that has been used to study the incentives in situations such as this (where participant outcomes are jointly determined) is *game theory*. Outcomes are jointly determined in the sense that the payoff to any nation from its participation in an international agreement or not depends not only on its decisions, but also on the decisions of other nations as well.

One particularly interesting strain of game theory investigates the conditions that support self-enforcing agreements (Barrett, 1994)—namely those where the incentives are sufficient to encourage both joining the agreement and, once a member, continuing to abide by the rules. Since no country can be forced to sign an international agreement, and signatories can always withdraw after signing, self-enforcing agrements are those where the incentives are most likely to create successful, stable coalitions.

The Barrett model assumes that signatories choose their strategies in order to maximize their collective net benefits, In the structure of this game when a country joins the international agreement the other signatories respond by increasing their abatement levels, and hence reward the country for particpating in the agreement; when a country withdraws, the remaining signatories reduce their abatement levels, and hence punish the country for withdrawing from the agreement. These punishments and rewards are credible, because the signatories always choose their levels in order to maximize their collective net benefits. The questions of interest are under what conditions is a stable, successful coalition achieved? and how well do these conditions fit the curent climate negotiations?

The Barrett analysis finds that a stable successful agreement can only be achieved when the difference between the cooperative and noncooperative outcomes is small. Why? The principle barrier to a stable, successful coaltion for climate policy is the free-rider principle. Countries that join an agreement pay all of marginal costs of participation, but get back only a fraction of the marginal benefits of their action (the rest go to the other nations, both signatories and nonsignatories alike). Nonsignatories get the benefits created by the abatement actions of others without having to abate at all. Unfortunately, this analysis demonstrates that in precisely those cases where the gains from cooperation are greatest, the gains from being free riders are also greatest, thereby inhibiting the formation of a stable successful agreement.

More recent work (Barrett, 2013) has focused on whether the existence of a catastrophe threshold (known as a "tipping point") ups the ante sufficiently so that cooperation has a better chance. This analysis finds that when the specifics of a climate catastrophe threshold are known with certainty and the benefits of avoiding catastrophe are high relative to the costs, self-enforcing treaties can coordinate countries' behavior so as to avoid the catastrophe. Where the net benefits of avoiding catastrophe are lower relative to the costs, however, agreements typically fail to avoid catastrophe; only modest cuts in emissions are sustained. This analysis also finds that uncertainty about the magnitude of the temperature rise that would trigger the catastrophic threshold normally causes coordination to collapse as well.

Another game theory study (Jacquet, 2013) reveals even more barriers to cooperation—the nature and timing of the payoffs to cooperation. At the start of this game, which is played with real money for 10 rounds in a lab, each of six participants is allotted a fixed amount of money (40 euros) to invest in a climate account. Each round these players choose how much of their allotted money they want to put into the account.

At the end of 10 rounds, if the climate account grows to 120 euros from the contributions made by the six players over the 10 rounds, the participants in that game are deemed to have won their game (averted "dangerous climate change"). Each participant in a game that averts dangerous climate change receives a bonus in addition to the money they each have leftover after their contributions to the climate account. However, if after 10 rounds the climate account ends up smaller than 120 euros, the participants in that game are deemed to have lost the game and they receive no bonus.

The game was played with three different sets of rules. In the first scenario,where the earned bonus (45 euros) would be received the next day, seven out of 10 groups averted dangerous climate change. In the second scenario, where the earned bonus (still 45 euros) would be received seven weeks later, only four of the 11 groups succeeded. In the final scenario, where the bonus was used to plant oak trees in order to sequester carbon, and thus provide the greatest benefit to future generations, none of the 11 groups reached the target.

Achieving cooperation is more difficult in games featuring not only deferred payoffs, but also payoffs that result in public, rather than private, benefits. Unfortunately that is precisely the nature of the situation facing those seeking international cooperation on climate change policy.

In general these results are very discouraging because they suggest that under precisely the conditions currently prevailing in the climate policy arena, a close examination of the incentives facing nations seeking to form stable, effective agreements to mitigate greenhouse gases suggests that global cooperation is at best an elusive outcome.

Fortunately the current climate arena also includes some aspects of international cooperation that are not included in these models, but that suggest somewhat greater possibilities for success. One such area involves co-benefits, the benefits that are derived from mitigating other nontargeted pollutants in the process of mitigating greenhouse gases. One important example is the reduction in adverse human health impact when low- or no-carbon fuels are substituted for coal. Since all the health benefits from mitigating these local pollutants are received by the mitgating nation, the free-rider effect does not come into play. Co-benefits can add a powerful additional incentive for individual participants receiving those co-beenfits to mitigate.

Another strategy involves "issue linkage" in which countries simultaneously negotiate a climate change agreement and a linked economic agreement. Typical candidates for linkage are agreements on trade liberalization, or cooperation on either research and development (R&D) or international debt. The intuition behind this approach is that some countries gain from resolving the first issue, while others gain from the second. Linking the two issues increases the chances that cooperation may result in mutual gain and, hence, increases the incentives to join and abide by the agreement.

To understand how this works, consider a research-and-development example from Cararro (2002). To counteract the incentive to free ride on the benefits from climate change, suppose only ratifiers of both agreements share in the insights gained from research and development in the ratifying countries. The fact that this benefit can only be obtained by ratifying both the climate change agreement and the R&D agreement provides an incentive to ratify both. Since those nations choosing not to ratify can be excluded from the research-and-development benefits, they would have to join the agreement to benefit.

Another strategy for encouraging participation involves transfers from the gainers to the losers. Some countries have more to gain from an effective agreement than others. If the gainers were willing to share some of those gains with reluctant nations who have more to lose, the reluctant nations could be encouraged to join. Some interesting work (Chandler & Tulkens, 1997) has shown that it is possible to define a specific set of transfers such that each country is better off participating than not participating. That is a powerful, comforting result, but is it practical?

In terms of operationalizing this concept of using transfers as an inducement to join the agreement, the Bali Climate Change Conference in 2007 established a funding mechanism for adaptation, which could generate up to $300 million over 2008–2012. It was established to finance specific adaptation projects and programs in developing countries that are Parties to the Kyoto Protocol (http://www.adaptation-fund.org). The fund, which falls under the auspices of the Global Environmental Facility, is financed primarily from a 2 percent levy on proceeds from Clean Development Mechanism projects. Note that while this fund is directed toward adaptation, rather than mitigation, the fact that it is available only to parties to the agreement provides an incentive for nonsignatories to participate.

As a complementary measure the Parties (COP) to the United Nations Framework Convention on Climate Change (UNFCCC), decided in 2010 to also establish the Green Climate Fund, which would raise significantly more funding. This fund is intended to provide support to developing countries as they limit or reduce their greenhouse gas emissions and as they adapt to the impacts of climate change, focusing especially on those developing countries that are particularly vulnerable to the adverse effects of climate change.

And, finally, choosing cost-effective policies can positively affect the level of participation. Since cost-effective policies reduce the cost, but not the benefits, of participation, those policies should make participation more likely by increasing the net benefits from joining the agreement.

The Precedent: Reducing Ozone-Depleting Gases

In the stratosphere, the portion of the atmosphere lying just above the troposphere, rather small amounts of ozone present have a crucial positive role to play in determining the quality of life on the planet. In particular, by absorbing the ultraviolet wavelengths, stratospheric ozone shields people, plants, and animals from harmful radiation, and by absorbing infrared radiation, it is a factor in determining the earth's climate.

Chlorofluorocarbons (CFCs), which are greenhouse gases, also deplete the stratospheric ozone shield as a result of a complicated series of chemical reactions. These chemical compounds have been used as aerosol propellants and in cushioning foams, packaging and insulating foams, industrial cleaning of metals and electronics components, food freezing, medical instrument sterilization, refrigeration for homes and food stores, and air-conditioning of automobiles and commercial buildings.

The major known health effect of the increased ultraviolet radiation resulting from *tropospheric ozone depletion* is an increase in nonmelanoma skin cancer. Other potential effects, such as an increase in the more serious melanoma form of skin cancer, suppression of human immunological systems, damage to plants, eye cancer in cattle, and an acceleration of degradation in certain polymer materials, are suspected but not as well established.

Responding to the ozone-depletion threat, an initial group of 24 nations signed the *Montreal Protocol* in September 1988. A series of new agreements followed that generally broadened the number of covered substances and established specific schedules for phasing out their production and use. Currently, some 96 chemicals are controlled by these agreements to some degree.

The protocol is generally considered to have been a noteworthy success. As of 2008, more than 95 percent of ozone-depleting substances have been phased out and the ozone layer is expected to return to its pre-1980 levels no later than 2075.

How did this treaty avoid the free-rider pitfalls identified previously? One reason for the success of this approach was an early recognition of the need to solicit the active participation of developing countries. One component of the success in eliciting that participation resulted from offering later phaseout deadlines for developing countries. Another involved the creation of a Multilateral Fund.

In 1990 the parties agreed to establish the *Multilateral Fund*, which was designed to cover the incremental costs that developing countries incur as a result of taking action to eliminate the production and use of ozone-depleting chemicals. Contributions to the Multilateral Fund come from the industrialized countries. The fund has been replenished multiple times. As of April 2013, the contributions made to the Multilateral Fund by some 45 countries (including Countries with Economies in Transition, or CEIT countries) totaled over US$ 3.09 billion.

The fund promotes technical change and facilitates the transfer of more environmentally safe products, materials, and equipment to developing countries. It offers developing countries that have ratified the agreement access to technical expertise, information on new replacement technologies, training and demonstration projects, and financial assistance for projects to eliminate the use of ozone-depleting substances.

The existence of the Multilateral Fund, however, does not deserve all the credit for the success of the Montreal Protocol. The success of ozone protection has been possible in no small measure because producers were able to develop and commercialize alternatives to ozone-depleting chemicals. In many cases the companies that would be forced to stop producing ozone-depleting chemicals were the same companies that would produce the substitutes. Countries and producers ended the use of CFCs faster and cheaper than was originally anticipated due both to the availability of these substitutes and the fact that profit from their sale would offset any losses from stopping production of the ozone-depleting chemicals.

Although the agreements specify national phasedown targets, it is up to the countries to design policy measures to reach those targets. The United States chose a unique combination of product charges and tradable allowances to control the production and consumption of ozone-depleting substances . Most observers believe the flexibility embodied in this combination was highly effective in encouraging the transition away from ozone-depleting substances.

More recently, attempts have been made internationally to use this agreement as the basis for phasing out hydrofluorocarbons (HFCs), one class of chemicals used to replace the CFCs, because they also turn out to be powerful greenhouse gases. Along with Mexico and Canada, the United States has proposed a series of steps to reduce HFC production, with wealthier countries not only facing quicker deadlines than developing nations, but also providing financing for poorer countries to adopt substitutes. The Environmental Protection Agency estimates that adopting the HFC proposal could slow global warming by a decade.

Economics and the Mitigation Policy Choice

Early in climate change negotiations it became clear that mitigation by means of cost-effective strategies was a priority. For reasons explained in Chapter 15, the policy choices quickly narrowed down to a carbon tax and the cap-and-trade version of emissions trading . In general, Europe tended to favor carbon taxes, while the United States preferred cap-and-trade. In practice, as shown in Table 16.1, both

TABLE 16.1 Selected Existing or Scheduled Carbon Markets or Carbon Taxes

Carbon Markets	Carbon Taxes
The Kyoto Protocol's Clean Development and Joint	Finland (1990)
Implementation Mechanisms (2005)	Sweden (1991)
The European Union Emissions Trading Scheme (2005)	Norway (1991)
Regional Greenhouse Gas Initiative US (2009)	United Kingdom (2001)
New Zealand (2010)	Denmark (2005)
California, US (2013)	Alberta, Canada (2007)
Quebec, Canada (2013)	Switzerland (2007)
Australia (2012)	British Columbia, Canada (2008)
Peoples Republic of China Pilot Programs (2013) and	India (2010)
National Program (2015)	Australia (2012)
South Korea (2015)	Japan (2012)

have been adopted. (Australia is in both columns because, as described in the next section, its system started out with a tax-like program, which was intended to evolve into a carbon-market.)

Providing Context: A Brief Look at Three Illustrative Carbon Pricing Programs

To provide some feel for the natures of these programs consider three examples: (1) the British Columbia Carbon Tax, (2) the European Union's Emissions Trading System and (3) the Australian Hybrid System that involves elements of both a carbon tax and a carbon market.

British Columbia Carbon Tax Program. Since 2008, British Columbia has imposed a carbon tax on each metric ton of carbon dioxide equivalent (CO_2–e) emissions from the combustion of fuel. This program affects an estimated 77 percent of British Columbia's total greenhouse gas (GHG) emissions.

Under this program, CO_2–e is defined as the amount of CO_2, methane, and nitrous oxide (N_2O) released into the atmosphere, with the methane and N_2O emission levels adjusted to a CO_2–e basis that accounts for their relative impact on global warming. Certain fuels, such as fuel for commercial aviation and ships, are exempted. To facilitate implementation, the carbon tax is applied and collected at the wholesale level, using the administrative channels established earlier for collecting motor fuel taxes. The cost of the tax is ultimately passed forward to consumers via higher prices.

The carbon tax is revenue neutral (i.e., all revenue generated is returned to British Columbians through cuts in other taxes). To help protect low-income households, the Low Income Climate Action Tax Credit program provides adult residents with lump sum tax credits that are reduced by 2 percent of net family income above specified income thresholds.

After 4 years in effect, BC's per capita consumption of fuels subject to the tax was found to have declined by 19 percent compared to the rest of Canada while its economy kept pace with the rest of Canada.

European Union Emissions Trading System (EU ETS). Launched in 2005, the EU ETS operates in 30 countries and is the largest emissions trading system in the world. The program establishes a cap on the total amount of certain GHGs that can be emitted from installations covered by the system. Under this cap, companies receive emission allowances (EUAs), which they can sell to, or buy from, one another as needed. At the end of the year each company must surrender enough allowances to cover all its emissions or pay penalties on any excess. Companies can bank any spare allowances for future sale or for covering their future needs. The cap (and, hence, the number of allowances) is reduced over time so that total emissions will fall. The installations currently covered by the EU ETS account for almost half of the EU's CO_2 emissions and 40 percent of its total GHG emissions. Although the system currently covers only CO_2 emissions, its scope will soon be expanded to include other sectors and other GHGs.

Australian Hybrid System. The Australian program, which started in 2012, envisions a two-stage transition from a fixed price regime to an emissions trading market:

- In the first stage, emitters face a fixed price for each metric ton of carbon emitted. The price started at $A23 (US$23.8) per metric ton and rises at 2.5 percent per annum in real terms.
- In the second stage, originally scheduled to begin in 2014, the fixed carbon price regime transitions to a fully flexible price regime, with the price determined by an emissions trading market.

While at least half of a source's compliance obligation must be met through the use of domestic permits or credits, during the flexible price period offsets from credible international carbon markets and emissions trading systems may be used to fulfill the remaining obligation.

Although the scope of coverage will be quite broad, it will not be universal. Households, on-road business use of light vehicles, and the agriculture, forestry, and fishery industries will not face a carbon price on the fuel they consume, but will continue to pay fuel excise taxes.

More than 50 percent of the potential revenue generated between 2011 and 2015 is targeted for reducing the cost burden on households. The plan also sets aside some revenue for assisting highly impacted firms.

The Australian scheme is interesting not only for its rather creative and effective design, but also because it indicates how fragile carbon pricing can be. Remember from chapter 14 that in carbon pricing the government sets either the price or an aggregated emissions reduction target and the private sector does the rest. In 2013, in the election for prime minister, carbon pricing became a major issue, and the victor, Tony Abbott, immediately announced his intention to cancel their carbon-pricing program. What the voters can create, the voters can also take away.

Carbon Markets and Taxes: How Have These Approaches Worked in Practice?

Cost Savings. Two types of studies have conventionally been used to assess cost savings: *ex ante* analyses based on computer simulations, and *ex post* analyses, which examine actual implementation experience. A substantial majority, though not all, of the large number of *ex ante* analyses have found that a change from more traditional regulatory measures based upon source-specific limits to more cost effective market-based measures such as emissions trading or pollution taxes could potentially achieve either similar reductions at a much lower cost or much larger reductions at a similar cost. The evidence also suggests that these two instruments typically produce more emissions reduction per unit expenditure than other types of polices such as renewable resource subsidies or mandates.

Although the number of existing detailed *ex post* studies is small, they typically find that the cost savings from shifting to these market-based measures are considerable, but less than would have been achieved if the final outcome had been fully cost-effective. In other words, while both taxes and emissions trading are fully cost-effective in principle, they fall somewhat short of that in practice.

Both tax and emissions trading outcomes can be distorted through political manipulation, but emissions trading is uniquely susceptible to price manipulation arising from market power that could, in principle, reduce the cost savings. However, actual experience with emissions trading has uncovered only one actual case of market power and it resulted directly from a design flaw. Evidence from the Regional Clean Air Incentives Market (RECLAIM), an emissions trading program in California, indicates that some generators manipulated NOx emission permit prices in late 2000 and early 2001 (Kolstad & Wolak, 2008).

The paucity of cases involving market power is perhaps not surprising since most carbon markets have a large number of participants and market power declines with large markets. However, if emissions trading expands to settings where the market is fragmented (and hence limited to relatively few participants), more cases of market power could arise.

Emission Reductions. Emission reductions resulting from carbon taxes are typically in the high single digits. However, the experience has not been uniform. Norway actually reported an emissions increase, apparently due to extensive tax exemptions and relatively inelastic demand in the sectors in which the tax was implemented. Possibly in reaction to this experience, Norway nearly doubled the CO_2 tax rate for its offshore oil and gas production in 2013.

Sweden's carbon tax appears to have caused emission reductions mainly in the residential sector (largely by encouraging district heating) and has diminished the historic trend of increasing emissions in transport. Experts believe that the carbon tax's impact on Swedish industry is probably small due to the many exemptions.

In one study that attempts to control for other factors that could affect emissions outcomes, Lin and Li (2011) compare the change in per capita CO_2 emissions over time between countries that do and do not use a carbon tax. They find that (with the exception of Norway) carbon taxes have reduced emissions, but the role of carbon taxes was statistically significant only for Finland. The authors attributed this lack of statistical significance for the other countries to tax exemption policies on certain energy intensive industries.

Among emissions trading markets the EU ETS reported "reduced annual emission per covered installation" of 8 percent from 2005 to 2010. In the Northeastern U. S. the Regional Greenhouse Gas Initiative (RGGI) emissions from all covered sources were reduced 25.6 percent during the same period despite a rather weak cap. While the recession played some role, the main sources of the RGGI reductions were (1) fuel substitution, aided considerably by lower natural gas prices, and (2) energy efficiency, that reduced the amount of energy used per unit of output.

Not all sources of greenhouse gases end up being regulated, of course, and that raises the specter of leakage. When leakage occurs it means that the actual emissions reductions are smaller than those recorded at the regulated site, because some emissions have been merely transferred to another location, not reduced. Leakage can occur when pressure on the regulated source to reduce emissions results in a diversion of emissions to unregulated, or lesser regulated, sources. Common channels for this diversion involves firms moving their polluting factories to countries with lower environmental standards or consumers increasing their reliance on imported products from countries with unregulated sources. Generally to date, however, the evidence suggests that carbon leakage effects have been rather small.

In principle leakage can be controlled by border adjustment mechanisms, such as import tariffs or requiring importers to buy carbon allowances, but those mechanisms have been subject to court challenges. These issues have already arisen in the EU's attempt to make airlines flying into or departing from the European Union subject to the EU ETS regardless of their country of origin. Only time will tell the ultimate fate of this conflict between trade and environmental objectives.

The Special Role of Natural Gas. The RGGI experience highlights an important aspect of current carbon reductions—the role of natural gas. The advent of fracking, a process described in Chapter 7, has resulted in large increases in the availability of relatively low-cost natural gas. Carbon emissions have declined as electric generators substitute this now-abundant, lower-carbon gas for coal. While thus far the impact of this decline has been felt mostly in the United States, it could well spread, particularly to other countries with large deposits of gas-bearing shale such as Poland and China, if local constraints such as the availability of adequate supplies of water are overcome.

The widespread availability of low-cost natural gas is not an unambiguous victory for the climate or for the environment in general. Methane, which is a powerful GHG, has been found to leak from these wells and from pipelines. These leaks offset to some degree (studies are underway to get a solid handle on the magnitude) the carbon advantages of combusting natural gas rather than coal. Fracking wells can also be a source of both water contamination and local air pollution and the process uses large quantities of water. Finally, the International Energy Agency has shown that relying on natural gas would not be sufficient to reach the carbon reduction targets put forward in international forums; it is, after all, still a fossil fuel that releases carbon when burned.

Another concern is that low natural gas prices might impede the adoption of renewables such as wind or solar because they are substitutes in both electrical generation and heating. Government policies such as feed-in tariffs, renewable portfolio standards, and production subsidies have all played a role in the increased market penetration of solar and wind over the last few years. However, the political durability of these policies is far from certain in light of the cheap natural gas alternative.

A similar concern has been raised about the impact of natural gas prices on the market for energy efficiency. Clearly, the value of an energy efficiency investment rises when the displaced energy is expensive and falls when it is cheaper. Thus, cheaper gas could well undermine some of the demand for energy efficiency. For the moment, the importance of these factors remains an open question.

Two Carbon Pricing Program Design Issues: Offsets and Price Volatility

Offsets. While allowances cover emissions under the cap, offsets allow emission reductions from sources not covered by the cap to be credited against the cap or tax base of the acquiring party. Offsets can also be used to reduce the tax base in carbon taxation. Offsets or offset tax credits perform several roles in pricing GHGs:

- First, by increasing the number of reduction opportunities, they lower the cost of compliance. The cost effects can be dramatic. For example, estimates by the U.S. Environmental Protection Agency suggest that if the American Clean Energy and Security Act of 2009 had become law, its liberal offset provisions would have had the effect of reducing the allowance price by approximately 50 percent.
- Second, lowering the cost in this manner could increase the likelihood of enacting a carbon-pricing program by making compliance easier.
- Third, offsets extend the reach of a program by providing economic incentives for reducing sources that are not covered by the tax or cap.
- Finally, because offset credits separate the source of financing from the source providing the reduction, it secures some reductions (in developing countries, for example) that for affordability reasons might not occur otherwise.

The challenge for establishing an effective offset program is assuring that all three of the primary requirements (namely, that the reductions be quantifiable, enforceable, and additional) are met. One obstacle is the tradeoff between transactions costs and offset validity (assuring valid offsets is not cheap).

In response to concerns over the validity of offsets, most programs now try to limit their use. One historical approach has been to restrict the use of offsets (domestic, foreign, or both) to some stipulated percentage of the total required allowances. In the Regional Greenhouse Gas Initiative (RGGI) in the Northeastern U. S. states, for example, CO_2 offset allowances may be used to satisfy only 3.3 percent of a source's total compliance obligation during a control period, although this may be expanded to 5 percent and 10 percent if certain CO_2 allowance price thresholds are reached. In contrast in 2011, Germany announced that it would not allow any offsets to be used to pursue its reduction goals.

The Role of Price Volatility. A tax system fixes prices, and unless some administrative intervention changes those fixed prices, price volatility is not an issue. This is not the case with emissions trading in either principle or practice.

Experience not only validates the concern that emissions trading can be plagued by volatile prices, but also demonstrates that price volatility is not a rare event. In the EU-ETS case, two early price declines were attributable to inadequate public knowledge of actual emissions relative to the cap and a failure to allow allowances in the first phase to be banked for use in the second phase. A subsequent dramatic price decline in 2012 stemmed from an over-allocation of permits, recession, and long-term uncertainty about climate policy.

This experience demonstrates that the design of an emissions trading system is vulnerable to unstable prices in two rather fundamental ways:

- First, because the cap establishes a fixed supply of allowances, demand shifts (due, for example, to regulatory actions, recessions, or shifts in prices of lower carbon fuels) can trigger large changes in allowance prices (since supply cannot respond).
- Second, the demand for allowances is derived from satisfying compliance obligations. Changing circumstances (due either to external factors or simply greater than anticipated success in lowering carbon emissions) can create a surplus of allowances. This surplus may cause the price to drop precipitously since lower prices do not stimulate any increase in the quantity demanded. Both the RGGI and the EU-ETS markets have experienced precisely this kind of price-dropping surplus.

One promising approach, included in the California program, for dealing with price volatility couples a safety valve price ceiling backed by an allowance reserve with a price floor. Establishing a safety valve ceiling would allow sources to purchase additional allowances from a reserve at a predetermined price, one that is set sufficiently high to make it unlikely to have any effect unless unexpected spikes in allowance prices occur. To prevent these purchases from causing the emissions cap to be exceeded, the reserve would be established from allowances set aside for this purpose from earlier years, an expansion in the availability of domestic or international offsets, or perhaps from allowances borrowed from future allocations.

Controversy: The Morality of Emissions Trading

Emissions trading has not avoided controversy . One element of that controversy raises the rather important question of whether the greenhouse gas trading concept violates conventional norms of international ethics (see Debate 16.2).

DEBATE 16.2 Is Global Greenhouse Gas Trading Immoral?

In a December 1997 editorial in the *New York Times,* Michael Sandel, a Harvard government professor, suggested that greenhouse gas trading is immoral. He argues that treating pollution as a commodity to be bought and sold not only removes the moral stigma that is appropriately associated with polluting but also trading reductions undermines an important sense of shared responsibilities that global cooperation requires. He illustrated the point by suggesting that legitimizing further emission by offsetting it with a credit acquired from a project in a poorer nation would be very different from penalizing the firm for emitting, even if the cost of the credit were equal to the penalty. Not only would the now-authorized emission become inappropriately "socially acceptable" but also the wealthier nation would have met its moral obligation by paying a poorer nation to fulfill a responsibility that should have been fulfilled by a domestic emissions reduction.

Published responses to this editorial countered with several points. First, it was pointed out that since it is voluntary, international emissions trading typically benefits both nations; one nation is not imposing its will on another. Second, the historical use of these programs has resulted in much cleaner air at a much lower cost than would otherwise have been possible, so the ends would seem to justify the means. Third, with few exceptions, virtually all pollution-control regulations allow some emission that is not penalized; this is simply a recognition that zero pollution is rarely either efficient or politically feasible.

Source: Sandel, M. J. (1997, December 17). It's immoral to buy the right to pollute. With replies by Steven Shavell, Robert Stavins, Sanford Gaines, and Eric Maskin. *New York Times*; excerpts reprinted in Stavins, R. N. (Ed.) (2000). *Economics of the environment: Selected readings* (4th ed.) (449–452). New York: W.W. Norton & Company.

Policy Timing

What is the optimal level of current investments in greenhouse gas reduction? In order to answer this question, we must first discover just how serious the problem is and then ascertain the costs of being wrong, either by acting too hastily or by procrastinating. Because uncertainties are associated with virtually every link in the logical chain from human activities to subsequent consequences, we cannot at this juncture state unequivocally how serious the damage will be. We can, however, begin to elaborate the range of possibilities and see how sensitive the outcomes are to the choices before us.

Benefit–cost studies of options for controlling climate change that ignore uncertainties in the state of our knowledge typically suggest a "go slow" or "wait-and-see" policy. The reasons for these results are instructive. First, the benefits from current control are experienced well into the future, while the costs occur now. The present-value criterion in benefit-cost analysis discounts future values more than current values. Second, both energy-using and energy-producing capital are long-lived. Replacing them all at an accelerated pace now would be more expensive than replacing them over time closer to the end of their useful lives. Third, the models anticipate that the number of new emissions-reducing technologies would be larger in the future and, due to this larger menu of options, the costs of reduction would be lower with delay.

The use of benefit-cost analysis in climate change discussion is controversial due to the role of the present-value criterion. Although, as we demonstrated earlier, this approach is not inherently biased against future generations, their interests will only be adequately protected if they are adequately compensated for the damage inflicted on them. Because it is not obvious that growth in per capita well-being would be adequate, the long lead times associated with this particular problem place the interests of future generations in maintaining a stable climate in jeopardy, raising an important ethical concern (Portney & Weyant, 1999).

The reasons for caution have economic merit, but they do not necessarily imply a "wait-and-see" policy. Spreading the capital investment decisions over time implies that some investments take place now as current capital is replaced. Furthermore, the expectation that future technical change can reduce costs will only be fulfilled if the incentives for producing the technical change are in place now. In both cases, waiting simply postpones the process of change.

Another powerful consideration in the debate over the timing of control investments involves uncertainty about both the costs and the benefits of climate change. Governments must act without complete knowledge. How can they respond reasonably to this uncertainty?

As economic analysis points out, the risks of being wrong are clearly asymmetric. If it turns out in retrospect that we controlled more than necessary, current generations would bear a larger-than-necessary cost. On the other hand, if the problem turns out to be as serious as the worst predictions indicate, catastrophic and largely irreversible damage to the planet could be inflicted on future generations.

Yohe, Andronova, and Schlesinger (2004) investigate both consequences of being wrong using a standard, well-respected global climate model. Their model assumed that decision makers would choose global mitigation policies in 2005 that would be in effect for 30 years, but that in 2035 policy makers would be able to modify the policies to take into account the better understanding of climate change consequences that would have afforded by the intervening 30 years. The specific source of uncertainty in their model results from our imperfect knowledge about the relationship between the atmospheric greenhouse gas concentrations and the resulting change in climate impacts. The specific question they examine is "What is the best strategy now?"

They find that a hedging strategy that involves modest reductions now dominates a "wait-and-see" strategy. Not only does current action initiate the capital turnover process and provide incentives for technical change, but also it allows the avoidance of very costly and potentially irreversible mistakes later. Since emissions from the "wait-and-see" strategy would be much higher by 2035, the reductions necessary to meet a given concentration target would have to be not only larger, but also concentrated within a smaller period of time. If in 2035, for example, scientists discover that greenhouse gas concentrations must be stabilized at a more stringent level than previously thought to avoid exceeding important thresholds (such as the methane example discussed previously), that may not only be much more difficult and much more expensive to do later, but it may actually be impossible (because it would be too late).

Summary

The first global pollutant problem confronted by the international community arose when ozone-depleting gases were implicated in the destruction of the stratospheric ozone shield that protects the earth's surface from harmful ultraviolet radiation. Because these are accumulating pollutants, an efficient response to this problem involves reducing their emissions over time. In principle, this could be accomplished by either an emissions charge that rises over time or an allowance system that allows a fixed amount of emissions.

To restrict their accumulation in the atmosphere, the international agreements on ozone-depleting substances created a system of limits on production and consumption. As part of its obligation under the agreements, the United States adopted a transferable allowance system, coupled with a tax on the additional profits generated when the supply of allowances was restricted. Internationally, this system is considered a success in part because the Multilateral Fund and other incentives, such as delayed compliance deadlines, facilitated the participation of developing countries and in part because the losses imposed on producers of ozone-depleting chemcials when those chemicals were phased out were offset by the profits gained by many of the same producers as they produced and sold the substitutes.

Climate change is appropriately considered a more difficult problem to solve than ozone depletion. In addition to the features it shares with ozone depletion, such as the free-rider problem, and the fact that the current generation bears the costs while the benefits accrue in the future, climate change presents some unique challenges. Some countries, for example, may be benefited, not harmed, by climate change, diminishing even further their incentive to control. And in contrast to ozone-depleting substances, which had readily available substitutes, controlling greenhouse gases means controlling energy use from fossil fuels, the lynchpin of modern society.

Fortunately, economic analysis of the climate change problem not only defines the need for action, but also sheds light on effective forms that action might take. The empirical studies suggest that it makes sense to take action now to reduce emissions of greenhouse gases in order to provide insurance against the adverse, possibly irreversible consequences if the damage turns out to be higher than anticipated.

Economics also sheds light on the barriers to effective participation in climate change agreements and some potential solutions as well. Game theory studies reveal that the free-rider effect is a significant barrier to participation as is the long horizon over which the effects of current polices are felt. Game theory studies with a broader scope, however, point out specific strategies (such as international transfers and issue linkage) that can be used to build incentives for participation. Some international cost sharing is likely to be as necessary an ingredient in a successful attack on the climate problem as it was in the ozone-depletion case.

Although progress on international action has stalled, the number of exising regional and national carbon pricing programs is growing. The evidence demonstrates that these programs are achieving emissions reductions in a relatively cost-effective manner, but some issues, such as volatile prices and the approriate role for offsets, are still in the process of being resolved.

During the next few decades, options must not only be preserved, they must be enhanced. Responding in a timely and effective fashion to global and regional pollution problems will not be easy. Our political institutions are not configured in such a way as to make decision making on a global scale simple. International organizations exist at the pleasure of the nations they serve. Only time will tell if the mechanisms of international agreements described in this chapter will prove equal to the task.

Discussion Question

1. Concerned individuals can now seek to reduce their carbon footprint by buying offsets. Air travelers, for example, are now asked if they wish to purchase offsets when they buy their ticket. Is this a complement or substitute for a national climate change policy? Why?

Self-Test Exercises

1. Explain why a climate policy using emissions-charge revenue to provide capital and operating subsidies for carbon capture technologies is less cost-effective than an emissions-charge policy alone.
2. The revenues from an emissions-charge approach to controlling climate change would be unusually large in comparison to other pollutants. What circumstances would lead to high revenues?
3. Label the following as True, False, or Uncertain, and explain your choice. (Uncertain means that it can be either true or false depending upon the circumstances.)
   a. The imposition of a tax on currently uncontrolled greenhouse gas emissions would represent a move toward efficiency.
   b. Relying on a series of regional systems (like the EU ETS), rather a true global system, for controlling greenhouse gases increases the importance of the leakage problem.

4. Suppose two countries with domestic cap-and-trade polices are considering linking their two systems. Country A has a cap of 20 tons of emissions, a domestic marginal cost of abatement of $10 and an uncontrolled emissions level of 60 tons, while Country B has a cap of 40 tons, a domestic marginal cost of abatement of $1q, where q = the tons of emission abatement, and an uncontrolled emissions level of 80 tons.
   a. Before linkage what would be the prices in the two separate markets and how much abatement would each country choose?
   b. If these two markets were linked by allowing each country to buy from and sell allowances to the other, what would be the prices in the two markets? How much would each country abate? Describe the transfer of allowances, if any, that would take place between the two countries.
5. In negotiations over a public good such a as greenhouse gas emission reduction, a cooperative agreement always produces higher aggregate benefits than a noncooperative agreement so cooperation will dominate noncooperation. Discuss.

Further Reading

Agrawala, S., & S. Fankhauser, (2008). *Economics aspects of adaptation to climate change. costs, benefits and policy instrument*. Paris: OECD. A critical assessment of adaptation costs and benefits in key climate sensitive sectors, as well as at national and global levels.

Calvo, E., & Santiago J. R. (2012). Dynamic models of international environmental agreements: A differential game approach. *International Review of Environmental and Resource Economics*, *6*, 289–339. A survey of dynamic models of international environmental agreements.

Lovins, L., Cohen, H., & Cohen, B. (2011). *Climate capitalism: Capitalism in the age of climate change*. New York: Hill and Wang. A manifesto that suggests that innovation is the key for capitalism's profitable transition to the low-carbon economy. Contains hundreds of examples from successful businesses, NGOs and municipalities.

Mendelsohn, R., Dinar, A. et al. (2006). The distributional impacts of climate change on rich and poor countries,. *Environment and Development Economics*, *11*, 159–178. This economic analysis concludes that poor countries will suffer the bulk of the damages from climate change, due primarily to their location.

Metcalf, G. E. (2009). Designing a carbon tax to reduce US greenhouse gas emissions. *Review of Environmental Economics and Policy*, *3*(1), 63–83. Describes considerations for designing a carbon tax to control greenhouse gas emissions in the United States.

Stavins, R. N. (2008). Addressing climate change with a comprehensive US cap-and-trade system. *Oxford Review of Economic Policy*, *24*(2), 298–321. Describes considerations for designing a cap-and-trade policy to control greenhouse gas emissions in the United States.

Stern, N. (2008). The economics of climate change. *American Economic Review*, *98*(2), 1–37. As assessment by the former chief economist of the World Bank.

Tacconi, L., Mahanty, S., & Suich, H. (Eds.) (2011). *Payments for environmental services, forest conservation and climate change: Livelihoods in the REDD?* Cheltenham, UK: Edward Elgar. This collection of essays examines carbon-focused payments for environmental services schemes from three tropical regions.

Tietenberg, T. H. (Summer 2013). Reflections—Carbon pricing in practice. *Review of Environmental Economics and Policy*, 7, 313–329. A review of the existing carbon pricing programs that considers their effectiveness and the emerging design lesssons.

Additional References and Historically Significant References are available on this book's Companion Website: http://www.routledgetextbooks.com/textbooks/9780133479690

17 Mobile-Source Air Pollution

There are two things you shouldn't watch being made, sausage and law.

—Anonymous

Introduction

Although they emit many of the same pollutants as stationary sources, mobile sources require a different policy approach. These differences arise from the mobility of the source, the number of vehicles involved, and the role of the automobile in the modern lifestyle.

Mobility has two major impacts on policy. On the one hand, pollution is partly caused by the temporary location of the source—a case of being in the wrong place at the wrong time. This occurs, for example, during rush hour in metropolitan areas. Since the cars have to be where the people are, relocating them—as might be done with electric power plants—is not a viable strategy. On the other hand, it is more difficult to tailor vehicle emissions rates to local pollution patterns, since any particular vehicle may end up in many different urban and rural areas during the course of its useful life.

Mobile sources are also more numerous than stationary sources. In the United States, for example, while there are approximately 27,000 major stationary sources, well over 250 million motor vehicles have been registered, a number that has been growing steadily since the 1960s when there were 74 million (U.S. Bureau of Transportation Statistics). Enforcement is obviously more difficult as the number of sources being controlled increases. Additionally, in the United States alone, 33 percent of carbon emissions from anthropogenic sources come from the transportation sector, 60 percent of which comes from the combustion of gasoline by motor vehicles. As discussed in Chapter 16, creating incentives to reduce human-induced sources of carbon emissions is a large focus for environmental policy makers. When the sources are mobile, the problem of creating appropriate incentives is even more complex.

Where stationary sources generally are large and run by professional managers, automobiles are small and run by amateurs. Their small size makes it more difficult to control emissions without affecting performance, while amateur ownership makes it more likely that emissions control will deteriorate over time due to a lack of dependable maintenance and care.

These complications might lead us to conclude that perhaps we should ignore mobile sources and concentrate our control efforts solely on stationary sources. Unfortunately, that is not possible. Although each individual vehicle represents a miniscule part of the problem, mobile sources collectively represent a significant proportion of three criteria pollutants—ozone, carbon monoxide, and nitrogen dioxide—as well as a significant source of greenhouse gases.

For two of these—ozone and nitrogen dioxide—the process of reaching attainment has been particularly slow. With the increased use of diesel engines, mobile sources are becoming responsible for a rising proportion of particulate emissions.

Since it is necessary to control mobile sources, what policy options exist? What points of control are possible and what are the advantages or disadvantages of each? In exercising control over these sources, the government must first specify the agent charged with the responsibility for the reduction. The obvious candidates are the manufacturer and the owner-driver. The balancing of this responsibility should depend on a comparative analysis of costs and benefits, with particular reference to such factors as (1) the number of agents to be regulated; (2) the rate of deterioration while in use; (3) the life expectancy of automobiles; and (4) the availability, effectiveness, and cost of programs to reduce emissions at the point of production and at the point of use.

While automobiles are numerous and ubiquitous, they are manufactured by a small number of firms. It is easier and less expensive to administer a system that controls relatively few sources, so regulation at the production point has considerable appeal.

Some problems are associated with limiting controls solely to the point of production, however. If the factory-controlled emissions rate deteriorates during normal usage, control at the point of production may buy only temporary emissions reduction. Although the deterioration of emissions control can be combated with warranty and recall provisions, the costs of these supporting programs have to be balanced against the costs of local control.

Automobiles are durable, so new vehicles make up only a relatively small percentage of the total fleet of vehicles. Therefore, control at the point of production, which affects only new equipment, takes longer to produce a given reduction in aggregate emissions because newer, controlled cars replace old vehicles very slowly. Control at the point of production produces emissions reductions more slowly than a program securing emissions reductions from used as well as new vehicles.

Some possible means of reducing mobile-source pollution cannot be accomplished by regulating emissions at the point of production because they involve choices made by the owner-driver. The point-of-production strategy is oriented toward reducing the amount of emissions per mile driven in a particular type of car, but only the owner can decide what kind of car to drive, as well as when and where to drive it.

These are not trivial concerns. Diesel and hybrid automobiles, buses, trucks, and motorcycles emit different amounts of pollutants than do standard gasoline-powered automobiles. Changing the mix of vehicles on the road affects the amount and type of emissions even if passenger miles remain unchanged.

Where and when the car is driven is also important. Clustered emissions cause higher concentration levels than dispersed emissions; therefore, driving in urban areas causes more environmental damage than driving in rural areas. Local control strategies could internalize these location costs; a uniform national strategy focusing solely on the point of production could not.

Timing of emissions is particularly important because conventional commuting patterns lead to a clustering of emissions during the morning and evening rush hours. Indeed, plots of pollutant concentrations in urban areas during an average day typically produce a graph with two peaks corresponding to the two rush hours.[1] Since high concentrations are more dangerous than low concentrations, some spreading over the 24-hour period could also prove beneficial.

Subsidies and Externalities

Vehicles emit an inefficiently high level of pollution because their owner-drivers are not bearing the full cost of that pollution. This inefficiently low cost, in turn, has two sources: (1) implicit subsidies for road transport and (2) a failure by drivers to internalize external costs.

Implicit Subsidies

Several categories of the social costs associated with transporting goods and people over roads are related to mileage driven, but the private costs do not reflect that relationship. For example:

- Road construction and maintenance costs, which are largely determined by vehicle miles, are mostly funded out of tax dollars. On average, states raise only 38 percent of their road funds from fuel taxes. The marginal private cost of an extra mile driven on road construction and maintenance funded from general taxes is zero, but the social cost is not.
- Despite the fact that building and maintaining parking space is expensive, parking is frequently supplied by employers at no marginal cost to the employee. The ability to park a car for free creates a bias toward private auto travel since other modes receive no comparable subsidy.

Other *transport subsidies* create a bias toward gas-guzzling vehicles that produce inefficiently high levels of emissions. In the United States, one example not long ago was that business owners who purchased large, gas-guzzling sport utility vehicles (SUVs) received a substantial tax break worth tens of thousands of dollars, while purchasers of small energy-efficient cars received none (Ball & Lundegaard, 2002). (Only vehicles weighing over 6000 pounds qualified.)

[1]The exception is ozone, formed by a chemical reaction involving hydrocarbons and nitrogen oxides in the presence of sunlight. Since, for the evening rush-hour emissions, too few hours of sunlight remain for the chemical reactions to be completed, graphs of daily ozone concentrations frequently exhibit a single peak.

This tax break was established 20 years earlier for "light trucks," primarily to benefit small farmers who depended upon the trucks for chores around the farms. More recently, most purchasers of SUVs, considered "light trucks" for tax purposes, have nothing to do with farming.

Externalities

Road users also fail to bear the full cost of their choices because many of the costs associated with those choices are actually borne by others. For example:

- The social costs associated with accidents are a function of vehicle miles. The number of accidents rises as the number of miles driven rises. Generally the costs associated with these accidents are paid for by insurance, but the premiums for these insurance policies rarely reflect the mileage–accident relationship. As a result, the additional private cost of insurance for additional miles driven is typically zero, although the social cost is certainly not zero.
- Road congestion creates externalities by increasing the amount of time required to travel a given distance. Increased travel times also increase the amount of fuel used.
- The social costs associated with greenhouse gas emissions are also a function of vehicle miles. These costs are rarely borne by driver of the vehicle.
- Recent studies have indicated high levels of pollution inside vehicles, caused mainly by the exhaust of cars in front.

Because the social costs of driving are not fully borne by motorists, the number of miles driven is inefficiently high.

To elaborate on the congestion point, consider Figure 17.1. As traffic volumes get closer to the design capacity of the roadway, traffic flow decreases; it takes more

FIGURE 17.1 Congestion Inefficiency

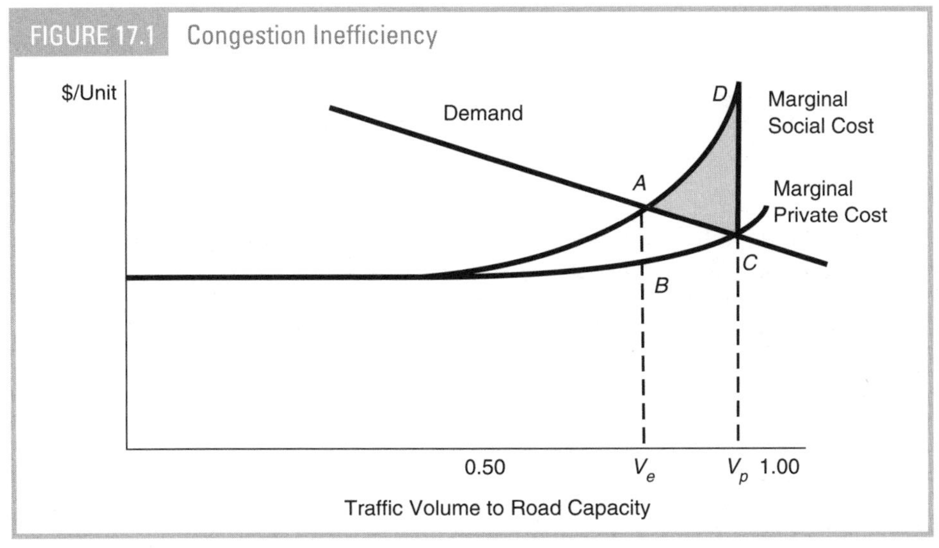

time to travel between two points. At this point, the marginal private and social costs begin to diverge. The driver entering a congested roadway will certainly consider the extra time it will take her to travel that route, but she will not consider the extra time that her presence imposes on everyone else; it is an externality.

The efficient ratio of traffic volume to road capacity (V_e) occurs where the marginal benefits (as revealed by the demand curve) equal the marginal social cost. Because individual drivers do not internalize the external costs of their presence on this roadway, too many drivers will use the roadway and traffic volume will be too high (V_p). The resulting efficiency losses would be measured by the triangle *ACD* (the shaded area). One recent study estimates that highway congestion in 2005 caused 4.2 billion hours of delay, 2.9 billion gallons of additional fuel to be used, resulting in a cost of $78 billion to highway users.[2]

Consequences

Understated road transport costs create a number of perverse incentives. Too many roads are crowded. Too many miles are driven. Too many trips are taken. Transport energy use is too high. Pollution from transportation is excessive. Competitive modes, including mass transit, bicycles, and walking, suffer from an inefficiently low demand.

Perhaps the most pernicious effect of understated transport cost, however, is its effect on land use. Low transport cost encourages dispersed settlement patterns. Residences can be located far from work and shopping because the costs of travel are so low. Unfortunately, this pattern of dispersal creates a path dependence that is hard to reverse. Once settlement patterns are dispersed, it is difficult to justify high-volume transportation alternatives (such as trains or buses). Both need high-density travel corridors in order to generate the ridership necessary to pay the high fixed cost associated with building and running these systems. With dispersed settlement patterns, sufficiently high travel densities are difficult, if not impossible, to generate.

Policy toward Mobile Sources

History

Concern about mobile-source pollution originated in Southern California in the early 1950s, following a path-breaking study by Dr. A. J. Haagen-Smit of the California Institute of Technology. The study by Dr. Haagen-Smit identified motor vehicle emissions as a key culprit in forming the photochemical smog for which Southern California was becoming infamous.

---

[2]2007 Annual Urban Mobility Report, Texas Transportation Institute. http://mobility.tamu.edu/ums/ as cited in "Using Pricing to Reduce Congestion" (2009), Congressional Budget Office.

In the United States, the Clean Air Act Amendments of 1965 set national standards for hydrocarbon and carbon monoxide emissions from automobiles to take effect during 1968. Interestingly, the impetus for this act came not only from the scientific data on the effects of automobile pollution, but also from the automobile industry itself. The industry saw uniform federal standards as a way to avoid a situation in which every state passed its own unique set of emissions standards, something the auto industry wanted to avoid. This pressure was successful in that the law prohibits all states, except California, from setting their own standards.

By 1970 the slow progress being made on air pollution control in general and automobile pollution in particular created the political will to act. In a "get tough" mood as it developed the Clean Air Act Amendments of 1970, Congress required new emissions standards that would reduce emissions by 90 percent below their uncontrolled levels. This reduction was to have been achieved by 1975 for hydrocarbon and carbon monoxide emissions and by 1976 for nitrogen dioxide. It was generally agreed at the time the act was passed that the technology to meet the standards did not exist. By passing this tough act, Congress hoped to force the development of an appropriate technology.

It did not work out that way. The following years ushered in a series of deadline extensions. In 1972 the automobile manufacturers requested a 1-year delay in the implementation of the standards. The administrator of the EPA denied the request and was taken to court. At the conclusion of the litigation in April 1973, the administrator granted a 1-year delay in the 1975 deadline for the hydrocarbon and carbon monoxide standards. Subsequently, in July 1973, a 1-year delay was granted for nitrogen oxides as well.[3] That was not the last deferred deadline.

The US Approach

The overall design of the US approach to mobile-source air pollution has served as a model for mobile-source control in many other countries (particularly in Europe). The US approach represents a blend of controlling emissions at the point of manufacture with controlling emissions from vehicles in use. New car emissions standards are administered through a certification program and an associated enforcement program.

Certification and Enforcement Programs. The certification program tests prototypes of car models for conformity to federal standards. Only engine families with a certificate of conformity are allowed to be sold.

The certification program is complemented by an associated enforcement program that contains assembly-line testing, as well as recall and anti-tampering procedures and warranty provisions. If these tests reveal that more than 40 percent of the cars do not conform to federal standards, the certificate may be suspended or revoked.

[3]The only legal basis for granting an extension was technological infeasibility. Only shortly before the extension was granted, the Japanese Honda CVCC engine was certified as meeting the original standards. It is interesting to speculate on what the outcome would have been if the company meeting the standards was American, rather than Japanese.

The EPA has also been given the power to require manufacturers to recall and remedy manufacturing defects that cause emissions to exceed federal standards. If the EPA uncovers a defect, it usually requests the manufacturer to recall vehicles for corrective action. If the manufacturer refuses, the EPA can order a recall.

Lead Phaseout Program

Section 211 of the US Clean Air Act provides the EPA with the authority to regulate lead and any other fuel additives used in gasoline. Under this provision, gasoline suppliers were required to make unleaded gasoline available. By ensuring the availability of unleaded gasoline, this regulation sought to reduce the amount of airborne lead, as well as to protect the effectiveness of the catalytic converter, which was poisoned by lead.[4]

In the mid-1980s, prior to the issuance of new, more stringent regulations on lead in gasoline, the EPA announced the results of a benefit-cost analysis of their expected impact. The analysis concluded that the proposed 0.01 gram per leaded gallon (gplg) standard would result in $36 billion ($1983) in benefits (from reduced adverse health effects) at an estimated cost to the refining industry of $2.6 billion. These actions followed a highly publicized series of medical research findings on the severe health and developmental consequences, particularly to small children, of even low levels of atmospheric lead. On March 7, 1985, the EPA issued regulations imposing strict new standards on the allowable lead content in refined gasoline. The primary phaseout of lead was completed by 1986.

Although the regulation was unquestionably justified on efficiency grounds, the EPA wanted to allow flexibility in how the deadlines were met without increasing the amount of lead used. While some refiners could meet early deadlines with ease, others could do so only with a significant increase in cost. Recognizing that meeting the goal did not require every refiner to meet every deadline, the EPA initiated an innovative program to provide additional flexibility in meeting the regulations (see Example 17.1). The program was successful in reducing both lead emissions and the concentration of lead in the ambient air. From 1981 to 2001, emissions of lead fell by 93 percent and concentrations of lead in the air fell by 94 percent.

By contrast, European Union (EU) banned leaded gasoline in 2000 and implemented stricter emissions standards for light-duty vehicles in 2005.

Russia, in principle, agreed to follow the example of Western Europe in introducing more stringent emissions controls, but the phaseout of lead has been much slower. By 1995, only eight of Russia's 25 oil refineries manufactured unleaded gasoline. This made up 40 percent of the gasoline produced in Russia. Many former Soviet Union transition economies have permitted lead content in gasoline that is twice the level allowed by the EU. A few, however, have launched initiatives to phase out lead completely. Slovakia phased out leaded gasoline in 1995, moving from a 6 percent market share of unleaded gasoline in 1992 to 100 percent in 1995 (World Bank, 2001). A 2001 World Bank study found that it would cost between

---

[4]Three tanks of leaded gas used in a car equipped with a catalytic converter would produce a 50 percent reduction in the effectiveness of the catalytic converter.

EXAMPLE 17.1

Getting the Lead Out: The Lead Phaseout Program

Under the Lead Phaseout Program, a fixed number of lead rights (authorizing the use of a fixed amount of lead in gasoline produced during the period) were allocated to the 195 or so refineries. (Due to a loophole in the regulations, some new "alcohol blender" refineries were created to take advantage of the program, but their impact was very small.) The number of issued rights declined over time. Refiners who did not need their full share of authorized rights could sell their rights to other refiners.

Initially no banking of rights was allowed (rights had to be created and used in the same quarter), but the EPA subsequently allowed banking. Once banking was initiated, created rights could be used in that period or any subsequent period up to the end of the program in 1987. Prices of rights, which were initially about 0.75 cents per gram of lead, rose to 4 cents after banking was allowed.

Refiners had an incentive to eliminate the lead quickly because early reductions freed up rights for sale. Acquiring these credits made it possible for other refiners to comply with the deadlines, even in the face of equipment failures or acts of God; fighting the deadlines in court, the traditional response, was unnecessary. Designed purely as a means of facilitating the transition to this new regime, the lead banking program ended as scheduled on December 31, 1987.

Sources: Nussbaum, B. D. (1992). Phasing down lead in gasoline in the US: Mandates, incentives, trading and banking. In T. Jones & J. Corfee-Morlot (Eds.). *Climate Change: Designing a Tradeable Permit System* (21–34). Paris: Organisation for Economic Cooperation and Development Publication; Hahn, R. W., & Hester, G. L. Marketable permits: Lessons from theory and practice. *Ecology Law Quarterly, 16*, 361–406.

$0.005 and $0.02 per liter of gasoline to phase out lead at a less modern refinery in Russia. These costs could be cut in half, however, if the refinery's production was modified to meet market demand.[5]

CAFE Standards

The Corporate Average Fuel Economy (CAFE) program, established in 1975, was designed to reduce American dependence on foreign oil by producing more fuel-efficient vehicles. Although it is not an emissions control program, fuel efficiency does affect emissions.

The program requires each automaker to meet government-set miles-per-gallon targets (CAFE standards) for all its car and light truck fleets sold in the United States each year. The unique feature is that the standard is a *fleet average*, not a standard applied to each vehicle. As a result, automakers can sell some low-mileage vehicles as long as they sell enough high-mileage vehicles to raise the average to the standard.

[5]Magdolna Lovei, *Toward an Unleaded Environment: World Bank Support to Transition Economies* (2001), http://www.worldbank.org/html/prddr/trans/m&j96/art5.htm.

The CAFE standards took effect in 1978, mandating a fleet average of 18 miles per gallon (mpg) for automobiles. The standard increased each year until 1985 when it reached 27.5 mpg. The standards were controversial. Most observers believe that the CAFE standards did, in fact, reduce oil imports. During the 1977–1986 period, oil imports fell from 47 to 27 percent of total oil consumption. The CAFE standard remained at 27.5 mpg until 2005 when a new set of rules was announced.

CAFE standards, however, have had their share of problems. When Congress instituted the CAFE standards, light trucks were allowed to meet a lower fuel-economy standard because they constituted only 20 percent of the vehicle market and were used primarily as work vehicles. Light truck standards were set at 17.2 mpg for the 1979 model year and went up to 20.7 mpg in 1996 (combined two-wheel and four-wheel drive). With the burgeoning popularity of SUVs, which are counted as light trucks, trucks now comprise nearly half of the market. In addition, intense lobbying by the auto industry resulted in an inability of Congress to raise the standards from 1985 until 2004. As a result of the lower standards for trucks and SUVs, the absence of any offsetting increase in the fuel tax, and the increasing importance of trucks and SUVs in the fleet of on-road vehicles, the average miles per gallon for all vehicles declined, rather than improved. In 2005 the standard for light trucks saw its first increase since 1996 to 21 miles per gallon.

The standards for all types of vehicles have recently continued this upward trend. Standards for model year 2011 rose to 27.3 miles per gallon. According to Department of Transportation's National Highway Transportation Safety Administration (NHTSA), this increase was expected to save 887 million gallons of fuel and reduce CO_2 emissions by 8.3 million metric tons.

In 2010, new rules were announced for both fuel efficiency and greenhouse gas emissions. These rules cover the 2012–2016 model years and the CAFE standard was set to reach 34.1 miles per gallon by 2016. Medium- and heavy-duty trucks were also subject to new rules. The US EPA and the National Highway Traffic Safety Administration (NHTSA) calculated benefits and costs of the proposed program for medium- and heavy-duty trucks. Using a social cost of carbon of $22/ton and a 3 percent discount rate, they find costs to the industry of $7.7 billion and societal benefits of $49 billion, for a total net benefit of approximately $41 billion.[6] Imagine if they made this calculation using the revised estimate of $37/ton for the social cost of carbon.

New rules were again announced in 2012 with the CAFE standard rising to 54.5 mpg for cars and light trucks by model year 2025.

Since new fuel economy standards only affect new vehicles, overall fuel economy takes a long time to improve—up to 15 years or until all the older cars are off the roads. This combined with the "rebound effect," which says that better fuel economy increases miles driven, raises the question of whether fuel taxation is a more efficient policy than a fuel economy standard (Anderson et al., 2011). Debate 17.1 looks at the evidence.

---

[6]http://www.nhtsa.gov/staticfiles/rulemaking/pdf/cafe/CAFE_2014-18_Trucks_FactSheet-v1.pdf, October 2010.

CAFE Standards or Fuel Taxes?

DEBATE 17.1

Increasing the fuel efficiency of oil consumption could, in principle, be accomplished by increasing either fuel taxes or fuel-efficiency standards. By raising the cost of driving, the former would encourage auto purchasers to seek more fuel-efficient vehicles, while the latter would ensure that the average new vehicle sold was fuel efficient. Does it make a difference which strategy is followed?

It turns out that it does, and economics can help explain why. Think about what each strategy does to the marginal cost of driving an extra mile. Increased fuel taxes raise the marginal cost per mile driven, but fuel-economy standards lower it. In the first case, the marginal cost per mile rises because the tax raises the cost of the fuel. In the second case, the more fuel-efficient cars uses less fuel per mile so the cost has gone down.

Following economic logic leads immediately to the conclusion that even if both strategies resulted in the same fuel economy, the tax would reduce oil consumption by more because it would promote fewer miles driven. On these grounds, a tax is better than a fuel-economy standard.

Austin and Dinan (2005) test these ideas with a simulation model in which they compare an increase in the CAFE standards to a gasoline tax designed to save the same amount of gasoline. Using a highly stylized representation of the US automobile market, they examine policies that would reduce gasoline consumption by 10 percent after the retirement of all existing vehicles (assumed to be 14 years). They estimate that an increase in the CAFE standards by 3.8 miles per gallon would achieve this result. They compare this to a gasoline tax designed to save 10 percent over the same 14-year period. They also estimate the cost savings from allowing fuel-economy credits to be bought and sold by manufacturers. They find that, even with tradable fuel-economy credits that reduce the cost of increasing the fuel-economy standards, a tax is still advantageous. With a tax, the savings occur much earlier than with the standards (while the costs rise gradually), supporting the arguments above. Using a 12 percent discount rate, they estimate that a tax of \$0.30 per gallon would save the same amount of gasoline and do so at a cost that is 71 percent lower than the comparable change in fuel-economy standards!

Supporters of fuel-economy standards, however, counter with a political feasibility argument. They point out that in the United States, sufficiently high gasoline taxes to produce that level of reduction could never have passed Congress, so the fuel-economy standards were better, indeed much better, than no policy at all. Indeed the \$0.30 increase estimated by Austin and Dinan represented a 73 percent increase in the tax on gasoline in the United States.

Source: Austin, D., & Terry Dinan, T. (2005). Clearing the air: The costs and consequences of higher CAFE standards and increased gasoline taxes. *Journal of Environmental Economics and Management, 50*, 562–582.

Fuel Economy Standards in Other Countries

Anderson et al. (2011) summarize fuel economy standards outside of the United States for countries including Japan, China, S. Korea, Australia, and the United States. Japan has some of the most stringent standards with different standards for diesel and gasoline vehicles. China sets fuel consumption standards that are based on weight. The European Union standards are set to rise annually from the 2012 standard of 45 miles per gallon. They also have a carbon dioxide target of 130 grams per kilometer. The European Union also combines standards with very high fuel taxes, which creates a larger demand for small cars (Anderson et al., 2011).

The Netherlands, Norway, Germany, and Sweden used differential tax rates to encourage consumers to purchase (and manufacturers to produce) low-emitting cars before subsequent regulations required all cars to be low emitting. Tax differentiation confers a tax advantage (and, hence, after-tax price advantage) on cleaner cars. The amount of the tax usually depends on (1) the emissions characteristics of the car (heavier taxes being levied on heavily polluting cars), (2) the size of the car (in Germany, heavier cars qualify for larger tax advantages to offset the relatively high control requirements placed upon them), and (3) the year of purchase (the tax differential is declining since all cars will eventually have to meet the standards).

Apparently it worked. In Sweden, 87 percent of the new cars sold qualified for the tax advantage, while in Germany the comparable percentage was more than 90 percent (Opschoor & Vos, 1989).

Europe not only has much higher gasoline prices, but also it has developed strategies to make better use of transportation capital. Its intercity rail system is better developed than the one in the United States, and public transit ridership is typically higher within cities. Europe was also a pioneer in the use of car-sharing arrangements, an idea that the United States has now begun to mimic (see Example 17.2).

External Benefits of Fuel Economy Standards

Fuel economy standards create positive externalities in two ways. First, fuel efficiency also lowers emissions. Lower carbon dioxide emissions as well as reduced dependence on foreign fuels are both positive externalities that flow from better fuel efficiency. These external benefits along with the political feasibility of fuel efficiency makes CAFE standards and appealing options.

Interestingly, in a thorough evaluation of the literature on consumer responses to fuel economy, Helfand and Wolverton (2011) find that automakers do not build in as much fuel economy as consumers are willing to purchase. Although the literature is so far inconclusive as to why this is the case, they posit that uncertainty, attribute bundling and the vehicle design process all play a role. If manufacturers are risk adverse and returns to fuel economy are uncertain, they will provide a lower level of fuel economy. Automakers will also invest more in those attributes for which consumers have already exhibited a strong preference. These attributes include size and performance. Additionally since attributes tend to be bundled, consumers can chose a bundle of attributes including color, features, etc. Fuel economy is not a bundled attribute so it may not be a priorty for manufacturers to vary. Finally, new designs take time and as such manufacturers many not be as responsive to consumer's preferences in the short run (Helfand & Wolverton, 2011).

EXAMPLE 17.2

Car-Sharing: Better Use of Automotive Capital?

One of the threats to sustainable development is the growing number of vehicles on the road. Though great progress has been made since the 1970s in limiting the pollution each vehicle emits per mile of travel, as the number of vehicles and the number of miles increase, the resulting increases in pollution offset much of the gains from the cleaner vehicles.

How to limit the number of vehicles? One strategy that started in Europe and has migrated to America is car-sharing. Car-sharing recognizes that the typical automobile sits idle most of the time, a classic case of excess capacity. (Studies in Germany suggest the average vehicle use per day is 1 hour.) Therefore the car-sharing strategy tries to spread ownership of a vehicle over several owners who share both the cost and the use.

The charges imposed by car-sharing clubs typically involve an upfront access fee plus fees based both on time of actual use and mileage. (Use during the peak periods usually costs more.) Some car-sharing clubs offer touch-tone automated booking, 24-hour dispatchers, and such amenities as child-safety seats, bike racks, and roof carriers.

Swiss and German clubs started in the late 1980s. As of 1998, an estimated 25,000 Germans and 20,000 Swiss belonged to car-sharing groups. The European idea of car-sharing was captured by some US entrepreneurs who started Zipcar, a company that now boasts 400,000 members and fleets of car-sharing vehicles in 50 cities in North America and the United Kingdom. Similar car-sharing companies can now be found in hundreds of cities.

The University of California, Berkeley's Transportation Sustainability Research Center (TSRC) and Susan Shaheen have been tracking car-sharing developments worldwide since 1997. They report that as of January 1, 2013, there were 46 active programs in North America with 1,033,564 members sharing 15,603 vehicles.

What could the contribution of car-sharing be to air pollution control in those areas where it catches on? It probably does lower the number of vehicles and the resulting congestion. Zipcar claims that each Zipcar takes 15–20 personally owned vehicles off the road. In addition, peak-hour pricing probably encourages use at the less polluted periods. On the other hand, it does not necessarily lower the number of miles driven, which is one of the keys to lowering pollution. The contribution of this particular innovation remains to be clarified by some solid empirical research.

Source: Walsh, M. W. (1998, July 23). Car-sharing holds the road in Germany. *Los Angeles Times*, A1; What do you do when you are green, broke and connected? You share. *The Economist*. (October 10, 2010). Retrieved from http://www.economist.com/node/17249322?story_id=17249322&fsrc=rss and www.zipcar.com and http://www.innovativemobility.org/publications/Carsharing_Innovative_Mobility_Industry_Outlook.shtml.

Alternative Fuels and Vehicles

Alternative Fuels. The Clean Air Act Amendments of 1990 required nonattainment areas to use cleaner-burning (oxygenated) automotive fuels during the winter months in some cases and year round (reformulated gasoline) in the worst cases.

Ethanol and methyl tertiary butyl ether (MTBE) were the two additives most widely used to meet the oxygen content standard.

Largely due to cost, most non-Midwestern states opted for gasoline with the additive MTBE, rather than ethanol. MTBE was designed to make gasoline burn cleaner and more efficiently. Unfortunately, once it entered into widespread use, it was discovered to be a source of contaminated groundwater and drinking water. Once in soil or water, MTBE breaks down very slowly while accelerating the spread of other contaminants in gasoline, such as benzene, a known carcinogen. Once these properties became known, several states passed measures to ban or significantly limit the use of MTBE in gasoline.

The MTBE story provides an interesting case study of the problems that can occur with a strategy that relies on a "technical fix" to solve air pollution problems. Sometimes the effects of the "solution" can, in retrospect, turn out to be worse than the original problem.

Even before the MTBE water contamination issue surfaced, questions were also being raised about the cost-effectiveness of using oxygenated fuels. For example, when Rask (2004) compared the oxyfuel smog test results to emissions' improvements resulting from emissions system repairs, he found increased maintenance and repairs to be a much more cost-effective strategy for lowering CO and hydrocarbon emissions than oxyfuels.

In 1989 the South Coast Air Quality Management District identified 120 options for reducing volatile hydrocarbons. The average cost-effectiveness of the 68 measures proposed was a stunning $12,250 per ton. While early estimates such as these should not determine the outcome, they certainly did suggest that some caution against proceeding too rapidly down this path would be appropriate.

Alternative Vehicles. In an attempt to foster the development of alternative vehicles and alternative fuels that would be less damaging to the environment, Congress and some states have passed legislation requiring their increased use. Title II of the Clean Air Act Amendments of 1990 mandates the sale of cleaner-burning reformulated gasoline in certain CO and severe ozone nonattainment regions. In the Energy Policy Act, passed in 1992, Congress requires the federal government (and some private fleet owners) to purchase alternative-fueled vehicles.

California has pushed the envelope even further. In September 1990, the California Air Resources Board (CARB) passed its low emission vehicle (LEV) and zero emission vehicle (ZEV) regulations. The former imposed increasingly stringent emissions standards over time on conventionally fueled vehicles. The latter mandated that a certain percentage of new cars and light trucks sold in the state must be zero emission vehicles (defined as vehicles that directly emit no VOCs, NO_x, or CO; any indirect emissions from producing the electricity are not counted).

When these ZEV regulations were written, the focus was on electric vehicles, but over time the emphasis has come to include hybrids (vehicles powered by a combination of gasoline and electric power) and fuel-cell vehicles. In response to this trend, the California regulations were modified in 2004. Under the new regulations, auto manufacturers can meet their ZEV obligations in one of two ways.

To fulfill the first option, manufacturers must sell a vehicle mix of 2 percent pure ZEVs, 2 percent advanced technology, partial zero emissions vehicles (AT-PZEVs), and 6 percent partial zero emissions vehicles (PZEVs), which are very clean conventional vehicles. The ZEV obligation is based on the number of passenger cars and small trucks a manufacturer sells in California.

Or, manufacturers may choose a new alternative ZEV-compliance strategy, meeting part of their ZEV requirement by producing their sales-weighted market share of approximately 250 fuel-cell vehicles by 2008. The remainder of their ZEV requirements could be achieved by producing 4 percent AT-PZEVs and 6 percent PZEVs. The required number of fuel-cell vehicles (to which the market share is applied) will increase to 2500 from 2009 to 2011, 25,000 from 2012 to 2014, and 50,000 from 2015 to 2017. Automakers are allowed to substitute battery-electric vehicles for up to 50 percent of their fuel-cell vehicles requirements.

Clearly, this is an attempt to force automotive technology using a rather innovative method—mandated sales quotas for clean vehicles. Notice that selling this number of clean vehicles depends not only on how many are manufactured, but also on whether demand for those vehicles is sufficient. If the demand is not sufficient, manufacturers will have to rely on factory rebates or other strategies to promote sufficient demand. Inadequate demand is not a legal defense for failing to meet the deadlines.

How well this strategy works in forcing the development and market penetration of new automotive technologies remains to be seen. Other US states, particularly in the Northeast, have followed suit, so the size of the potential market is growing.

Road Pricing

Fuel Taxes. As controls on manufacturers have become more common and vehicles have become cleaner, attention is increasingly turning to the user. Drivers have little incentive to drive or maintain their cars in a manner that minimizes emissions because the full social costs of road transport have not been internalized by current policy. How far from a full internalization of cost are we? Parry et al. (2007) compile estimates from the literature and find the sum of mileage-related external marginal costs to be approximately $2.10 per gallon.

Mileage-related externalities include local pollution, congestion, and accidents. Fuel external costs, such as oil dependency and climate change, are another $0.18 per gallon. Figure 17.2 illustrates current fuel taxes by country. These data suggest current fuel taxes would have to be much higher in many countries in order to internalize the full social cost of road transport.

But fuel taxes are not the only way to begin to internalize costs, and, by themselves, they would be a blunt instrument anyway because typically they would not take into account when and where the emissions occurred. One way to focus on these temporal and spatial concerns is through congestion pricing.

FIGURE 17.2 2006 Fuel Taxes in Selected Countries

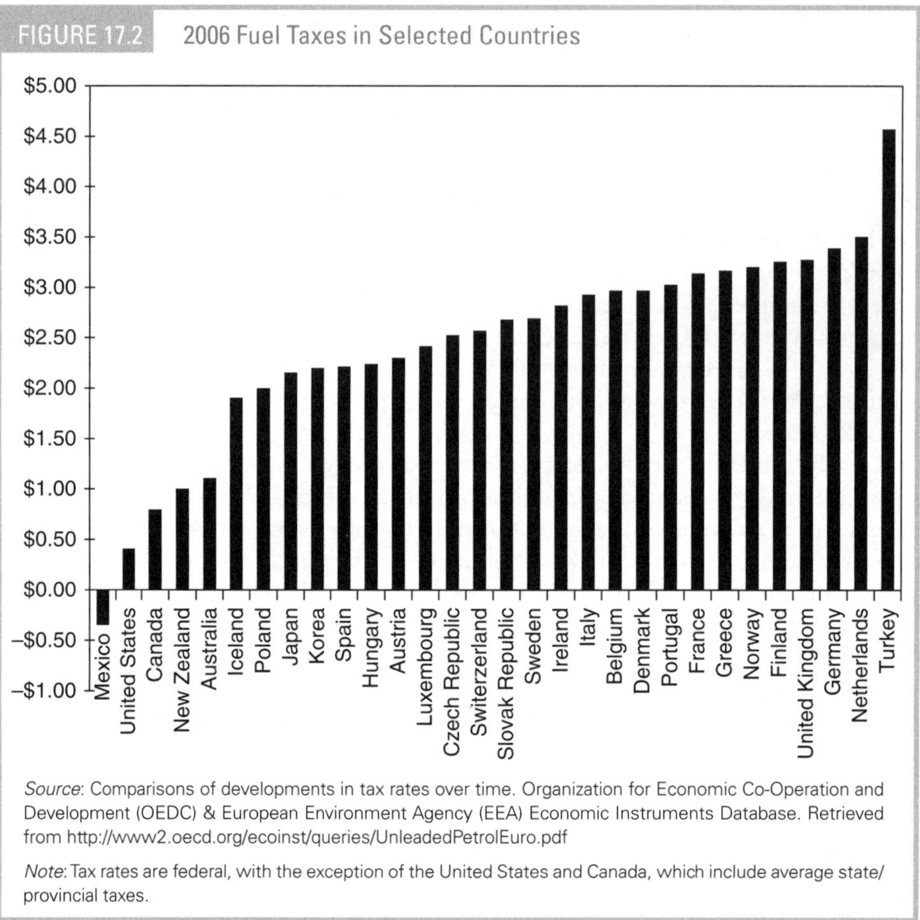

Source: Comparisons of developments in tax rates over time. Organization for Economic Co-Operation and Development (OEDC) & European Environment Agency (EEA) Economic Instruments Database. Retrieved from http://www2.oecd.org/ecoinst/queries/UnleadedPetrolEuro.pdf

Note: Tax rates are federal, with the exception of the United States and Canada, which include average state/provincial taxes.

Congestion Pricing. Congestion is influenced not only by how many vehicle miles are traveled, but also where and when the driving occurs. Congestion pricing addresses the spatial and temporal externalities by charging for driving on congested roads or at congested times. Four different types of congestion pricing mechanisms are in current use (1) cordon (area or zonal) pricing, (2) facilities pricing, (3) pricing lanes, and (4) high occupancy toll (HOT) lanes.[7] Congestion pricing of roads or zones has recently been gaining considerable attention as a targeted remedy for these time- and space-specific pollutant concentrations. Anas and Lindsey (2011) note that truly efficient congestion pricing is challenging to implement because the toll not only varies over time, but it also varies with lane width, travel speed and the types of vehicles on the road. The amount of information necessary to implement fully efficient tolls may be unrealistically high.

---

[7]Congressional Budget Office. (2009). "Using Pricing to Reduce Traffic Congestion," Washington, DC, A CBO Study.

Toll rings have existed for some time in Oslo, Norway, and Milan, Italy. In the United States, electronic toll collection systems are currently in place in many states. Express lanes for cars with electronic meters reduce congestion at toll booths. Reserved express bus lanes during peak hour periods are also common in the United States for congested urban highways. (Reserved lanes for express buses lower the relative travel time for bus commuters, thereby providing an incentive for passengers to switch from cars to buses.) High occupancy vehicle (HOV) lanes have also been established for some highways. During certain hours, vehicles traveling in the HOV lanes must have more than one passenger. Honolulu, Hawaii, has a high occupancy "zipper lane." The zipper lane is in the middle of the highway; in the morning commute hours the traffic travels toward Honolulu and by mid-afternoon the lane is literally zipped up on one side and unzipped on the other, creating an additional lane for the outgoing evening commute.

Several cities have also undertaken some innovative approaches including London, Stockholm, and Singapore. Perhaps the most far-reaching can be found in Singapore (Example 17.3). Bangkok also bars vehicles from transporting goods from certain parts of the metropolitan area during various peak hours, leaving the roads available to buses, cars, and motorized tricycles.

Safirova et al. (2007) compare six different road-pricing instruments all aimed at internalizing the congestion externality. These include three types of cordon pricing schemes (area-based congestion taxes), a distance-based toll on highways, a distance-based toll on metro roads only, and a gas tax. Examining the effectiveness of these instruments for the Washington, DC, metropolitan area in 2000, they explicitly model how residential choice (and hence travel time) could be affected by the type of policy instrument employed. The question they ask is "But how do policies designed to address congestion alone fare, once the many other consequences associated with driving—traffic accidents, air pollution, oil dependency, urban sprawl, and noise, to name a few—are taken into account?"[8] They find that using "social-cost pricing" (incorporating the social costs of driving) instead of simple congestion pricing affects the outcome of instrument choice. Specifically, when the policy goal is solely to reduce congestion, variable time-of-day pricing on the entire road network is the most effective and efficient policy. However, when additional social costs are factored in, the vehicle miles traveled (VMT) tax is almost as efficient.

Private Toll Roads. New policies are also being considered to ensure that road users pay all the costs of maintaining the highways, rather than transferring that burden to taxpayers. One strategy, which has been implemented in Mexico and in Orange County, California, is to allow construction of new private toll roads. The tolls are set high enough to recover all construction and maintenance costs and in some cases may include congestion pricing.

---

[8]http://www.rff.org/rff/News/Releases/2008Releases/MarginalSocialCostTrafficCongestion.cfm

EXAMPLE 17.3

Zonal Mobile-Source Pollution-Control Strategies: Singapore

Singapore has one of the most comprehensive strategies to control vehicle pollution in the world. In addition to imposing very high vehicle-registration fees, this approach also includes the following:

- Central Business District parking fees that are higher during normal business hours than during the evenings and on weekends.
- An area-licensing scheme that requires the display of an area-specific purchased vehicle license in order to gain entry to restricted downtown zones during restricted hours. These licenses are expensive and penalties for not displaying them when required are very steep.
- Electronic peak-hour pricing on roadways. These charges, which are deducted automatically using a "smart card" technology, vary by roadway and by time of day. Conditions are reviewed and charges are adjusted every 3 months.
- An option for people to purchase an "off-peak" car. Identified by a distinctive red license plate that is welded to the vehicle, these vehicles can only be used during off-peak periods. Owners of these vehicles pay much lower registration fees and road taxes.
- Limiting the number of new vehicles that can be registered each year. In order to ensure that they can register a new car, potential buyers must first secure one of the fixed number of licenses by submitting a winning financial bid.
- An excellent mass-transit system that provides a viable alternative to automobile travel.

Has the program been effective? Apparently, it has been quite effective in two rather different ways. First, it has provided a significant amount of revenue for the government, which the government can use to reduce more burdensome taxes. (The revenues go into the General Treasury; they are not earmarked for the transport sector.) Second, it has caused a large reduction in traffic-related pollution in the affected areas. The overall levels of carbon monoxide, lead, sulfur dioxide, and nitrogen dioxide are now all within the human-health guidelines established by both the World Health Organization and the US Environmental Protection Agency.

Source: Chia, N. C., & Phang, S.-Y. (2001). Motor vehicle taxes as an environmental management instrument: The case of Singapore. *Environmental Economics and Policy Studies*, *4*(2), 67–93.

Parking Cash-Outs

Providing parking spaces for employees costs employers money, yet most of them provide this benefit free of charge. This employer-financed subsidy reduces one significant cost of driving to work. Since this subsidy only benefits those who drive to work, it lowers the relative cost of driving vis-à-vis all other transport choices, such as walking, biking, and public transport. Most of those choices create much less air pollution; therefore, the resulting bias toward driving creates an inefficiently high level of pollution.

One way to rectify this bias is for employers to compensate employees who do not use a parking space with an equivalent increase in income. This would transfer the employer's savings in not having to provide a parking spot to the employee and remove the bias toward driving to work.

Pricing Public Transport

The common notion is that public transit reduces vehicle miles and hence reduces both emissions and energy use. That outcome, however, is not inevitable and the fares charged on public transit should reflect the actual situation.

In the absence of congestion, public transportation fees should equal the marginal cost of the service minus a subsidy that reflects the external benefits of taking public transportation (Anas & Lindsey, 2011). If the public transport actually turns out to increase congestion, however, fares should also include a congestion charge.

The level of the external benefits subsidy should also reflect the local situation. Although the subsidy may attract new riders to public transit, the source of these riders is important in structuring the fares. Did they actually come from personal vehicles? Or were they riders that would not otherwise have taken a trip? Subsidies may also attract riders that use public transport (such as light rail) as a complement, rather than a substitute, for driving. Subsides that were designed by assuming that all public transit trips represent shifts from private vehicles will be excessively high to the extent these other trip sources are prevalent (Anas & Lindsey 2011).

Feebates

Some research has found that consumers may undervalue fuel economy. One study found that consumers only consider the first 3 years of fuel savings when choosing a more fuel-efficient vehicle. This understates the value of fuel savings by up to 60 percent (NRC, 2002). To remedy this undervaluation bias among consumers purchasing new vehicles, feebates combine taxes on purchases of new high-emitting (or high-fuel-consumption) vehicles with subsidies for purchases of new low-emitting/low-fuel-consumption vehicles. By raising the relative cost of high-emitting vehicles, it encourages consumers to take the environmental effects of those vehicles into account. Feebate system structures are based on a boundary that separates vehicles charged a tax from those entitled to rebates. The simplest feebate structure uses a constant dollar rate per gallon of fuel consumed (Greene et al., 2005). The revenue from the taxes can serve as the financing for the subsidies, but previous experience indicates that policies such as this are rarely revenue-neutral; the subsidy payouts typically exceed the revenue from the fee.

Feebates are not yet widely used, but Ontario, Canada, and Austria have implemented feebates. Greene et al. (2005) find that feebates achieve fuel economy increases that are two times higher than those achieved by either rebates or gas guzzler taxes alone.

Tax Credits for Electric Vehicles

Tax credits subsidize the purchase of electric vehicles and can be as high as $7,500 per vehicle in the United States. Consumers who purchase electric vehicles not only receive a tax credit but also pay less in gasoline and emit fewer greenhouse gases, both of which have external benefits. However, tax credits also have a downside—they lower tax revenue. The loss of revenue due to tax credits has been estimated to be $7.5 billion through 2019. Additionally, since they help manufacturers reduce their miles per gallon average for new cars, the sales of electric vehicles help them to meet the CAFE standards.[9]

Pay-as-You-Drive (PAYD) Insurance

Another possibility for internalizing an environmental externality associated with automobile travel, thereby reducing both accidents and pollution, involves changing the way car insurance is financed. As Example 17.4 illustrates, small changes could potentially make a big difference.

Accelerated Retirement Strategies

A final reform possibility involves strategies to accelerate the retirement of older, polluting vehicles. This could be accomplished either by raising the cost of holding onto older vehicles (as with higher registration fees for vehicles that pollute more) or by providing a bounty of some sort to those retiring heavily polluting vehicles early.

Under one version of a bounty program, stationary sources were allowed to claim emissions reduction credits for heavily polluting vehicles that were removed from service. Heavily polluting vehicles were identified either by inspection and maintenance programs or remote sensing. Vehicle owners could bring their vehicle up to code, usually an expensive proposition, or they could sell it to the company running the retirement program. Purchased vehicles are usually disassembled for parts and the remainder is recycled. The number of emissions reduction credits earned by the company running the program depends on such factors as the remaining useful life of the car and the estimated number of miles it

---

[9]http:///www.cbo.gov/publication/43633

EXAMPLE 17.4

Modifying Car Insurance as an Environmental Strategy

Although improvements in automobile technology (such as air bags and antilock brakes) have made driving much safer than in the past, the number of road deaths and injuries are still inefficiently high. Since people do not consider the full societal cost of accident risk when deciding how much and how often to drive, the number of vehicle miles traveled is excessive. Although drivers are very likely to take into account the risk of injury to themselves and family members, other risks are likely to be externalized. They include the risk of injury their driving poses for other drivers and pedestrians, the costs of vehicular damage that is covered through insurance claims, and the costs to other motorists held up in traffic congestion caused by accidents. Externalizing these costs artificially lowers the marginal cost of driving, thereby inefficiently increasing the pollution from the resulting high number of vehicle miles.

Implementing PAYD insurance could reduce those inefficiencies. With PAYD insurance, existing rating factors (such as age, gender, and previous driving experience) would be used by insurance companies to determine a driver's per-mile rate, and this rate would be multiplied by annual miles driven to calculate the annual insurance premium. This approach has the effect of drastically increasing the marginal cost of driving an extra mile without raising the amount people spend annually on insurance. Estimates by Harrington and Parry (2004) suggest that calculating these insurance costs on a per-mile basis would have the same effect as raising the federal gasoline tax from $0.184 to $1.50 per gallon for a vehicle that gets 20 miles per gallon. This is a substantial increase and could have a dramatic effect on people's transport choices (and, therefore, the pollution they emit) despite the fact that it imposes no additional financial burden on them.

Source: Harrington, W., & Parry, I. (2004). Pay-as-You-Drive for Car Insurance. In R. Morgenstern & P. Portney (Eds.). New Approaches on Energy and the Environment: Policy Advice for the President (53–56). Washington, DC: Resources of the Future.

would be driven and is controlled so that the transaction results in a net increase in air quality.

Another accelerated retirement approach was undertaken in 2009 as a means to stimulate the economic recovery, while reducing emissions. Example 17.5 explores how well this Cash-for-Clunkers program worked.

We also have learned some things about what doesn't work very well. One increasingly common strategy involves limiting the days any particular vehicle can be used, as a means of limiting miles traveled. As Example 17.6 indicates, this strategy can backfire!

EXAMPLE 17.5

The Cash-for-Clunkers Program: Did It Work?

On July 27, 2009, the Obama administration launched the car allowance rebate system (CARS), known popularly as "Cash for Clunkers." This federal program had two goals: to provide stimulus to the economy by increasing auto sales, and to improve the environment by replacing old, fuel-inefficient vehicles with new, fuel-efficient ones.

Under the CARS program, consumers received a $3,500 or $4,500 discount from a car dealer when they traded in their old vehicle and purchased or leased a new, qualifying vehicle. In order to be eligible for the program, the trade-in passenger vehicle had (1) to be manufactured less than 25 years before the date it was traded in, (2) to have a combined city/highway fuel economy of 18 miles per gallon or less, (3) to be in drivable condition, and (4) to be continuously insured and registered to the same owner for the full year before the trade-in. The end date was set at November 1, 2009, or whenever the money ran out. Since the latter condition prevailed, the program terminated on August 25, 2009.

During the program's nearly 1-month run, it generated 678,359 eligible transactions at a cost of $2.85 billion. Using Canada as the control group, one research group (Li et al., 2010) found that the program significantly shifted sales to July and August from other months.

In terms of environmental effects, this study found that the program resulted in a cost per ton ranging from $91 to $301, even including the benefits from reducing criteria pollutants. This is substantially higher than the per ton costs associated with other programs to reduce emissions, a finding that is consistent with other studies (Knittel, 2009; Gayer and parker, 2013)). In addition, the program was estimated to have created 3676 job-years in the auto assembly and parts industries from June to December of 2009. That effect decreased to 2050 by May 2010.

In summary, this study found mixed results. An increase in sales did occur, but much of it was simply shifting sales that would have occurred either earlier or later into July and August. And while it did produce positive environmental benefits, the approach was not a cost-effective way to achieve those benefits. This case study illustrates a more general principle, namely that trying to achieve two policy objectives with a single policy instrument rarely results in a cost-effective outcome.

Sources: United States Government Accountability Office, Report to Congressional Committees: Lessons Learned from Cash for Clunkers Program Report # GAO-10-486 (2010); Li, S., Linn, J., & Spiller, E. Evaluating 'cash-for-clunkers': Program effect on auto sales, jobs and the environment. Washington, DC: Resources for the Future Discussion Paper 10–39; Knittel, C. R. (August 31, 2009). The implied cost of carbon dioxide under the cash for clunkers program. Retrieved from SSRN: http://ssrn.com/abstract=1630647;Gayer, T., & Parker, E. (October 31, 2013). Cash for clunkers: An evaluation of the car allowance rebate system. Washington, DC: Brookings Institution.

EXAMPLE 17.6

Counterproductive Policy Design

As one response to unacceptably high levels of traffic congestion and air pollution, the Mexico City administration imposed a regulation that banned each car from driving on a specific day of the week. The specific day when the car could not be driven was determined by the last digit of the license plate.

This approach appeared to offer the opportunity for considerable reductions in congestion and air pollution at a relatively low cost. In this case, however, the appearance was deceptive because of the way in which the population reacted to the ban.

An evaluation of the program by the World Bank found that in the short run the regulation was effective. Pollution and congestion were reduced. However, in the long run the regulation not only was ineffective, it was actually counterproductive (paradoxically it increased the level of congestion and pollution). This paradox occurred because a large number of residents reacted by buying an additional car (which would have a different banned day), and once the additional cars became available, total driving actually increased. Policies that fail to anticipate and incorporate behavior reactions run the risk that actual and expected outcomes may diverge considerably.

Source: Eskeland, G. S., & Feyzioglu, T. (December 1995). Rationing can backfire: The 'day without a car program' in Mexico City. *World Bank Policy Research Working Paper 1554*.

Summary

The current policy toward motor vehicle emissions blends point-of-production control with point-of-use control. It began with uniform emissions standards.

Grams-per-mile emissions standards, the core of the current approach in the United States and Europe, have had, in practice, many deficiencies. While they have achieved lower emissions per mile, they have been less effective in lowering aggregate emissions and in ensuring cost-effective reductions.

Aggregate mobile-source emissions have been reduced by less than expected because of the large offsetting increase in the number of miles traveled. Unlike sulfur emissions from power plants, aggregate mobile-source emissions are not capped, so as miles increase, emissions increase.

The efficiency of the emissions standards has been diminished by their geographic uniformity. Too little control has been exercised in highly polluted areas, and too much control has been exercised in areas with air quality that exceeds the ambient standards.

Local approaches, such as targeted inspection and maintenance strategies and accelerated retirement strategies, have had mixed success in redressing this imbalance. Since a relatively small number of vehicles are typically responsible for a disproportionately large share of the emissions, a growing reliance on remote sensing to identify the most polluting vehicles is allowing the policy to target resources where they will produce the largest net benefit.

The historic low cost of auto travel has led to a dispersed pattern of development. Dispersed patterns of development make mass transit a less-viable alternative, which causes a downward spiral of population dispersal and low mass-transit ridership. In the long run, part of the strategy for meeting ambient standards will necessarily involve changing land-use patterns to create the kind of high-density travel corridors that are compatible with effective mass-transit use. Though these conditions already exist in much of Europe, it is likely to evolve in the United States over a long period of time. Ensuring that the true social costs of transportation are borne by those making residential and mode-of-travel choices will start the process moving in the right direction.

A couple of important insights about the conventional environmental policy wisdom can be derived from the history of mobile-source control. Contrary to the traditional belief that tougher laws produce more environmental results, the sanctions associated with meeting the grams-per-mile emissions standards were so severe that, when push came to shove, authorities were unwilling to impose them. Threatened sanctions will only promote the desired outcome if the threat is credible. The largest "club" does not necessarily produce the best incentive.

The second insight confronts the traditional belief that simply applying the right technical fix can solve environmental problems. The gasoline additive MTBE was advanced as a way to improve the nation's air. With the advantage of hindsight, we now know that its pollution effects on groundwater have dwarfed its positive effects on air quality. Though technical fixes can, and do, have a role to play in environmental policy, they also can have large, adverse, unintended consequences.

Looking toward the future of mobile-source air pollution control, two new emphases are emerging. The first involves encouraging the development and commercialization of new, cleaner automotive technologies ranging from gas-electric hybrids to fuel-cell vehicles powered by hydrogen. Policies such as fuel-economy standards, gasoline taxes, feebates, and sales quotas imposed on auto manufacturers for low-emitting vehicles are designed to accelerate their entry into the vehicle fleet.

The second new emphasis focuses on influencing driver choices. The range of available policies is impressive. One set of strategies focuses on bringing the private marginal cost of driving closer to the social marginal cost through such measures as congestion pricing and pay-as-you-drive auto insurance. Others, such as parking cash-outs, attempt to create a more level playing field for choices involving the mode of travel for the journey to work.

Complicating all of these strategies is the increased demand for cars in developing countries. In 2007, Tata Motors, the Indian automaker, introduced "the world's cheapest car," the Tata Nano. The Nano sells for about 100,000 rupees (US $2,500). Tata Motors expects to sell millions of these affordable, stripped-down vehicles. Fuel efficiency of these cars is quite good (over 50 miles per gallon), but the sheer number of vehicles implies sizable increases in the demand for fuel, congestion, and pollution emissions.

Appropriate regulation of emissions from mobile sources requires a great deal more than simply controlling the emissions from vehicles as they leave the factory. Vehicle purchases, driving behavior, fuel choice, and even residential and employment choices must eventually be affected by the need to reduce mobile-source emissions. Affecting the choices facing automobile owners can only transpire if the economic incentives associated with those choices are structured correctly.

Discussion Questions

1. When a threshold concentration is used as the basis for pollution control, as it is for air pollution, one possibility for meeting the threshold at minimum cost is to spread the emissions out over time. To achieve this, one might establish a peak-hour pricing system that charges more for emissions during peak periods.
   a. Would this represent a movement toward efficiency? Why or why not?
   b. What effects should this policy have on mass-transit usage, gasoline sales, downtown shopping, and travel patterns?
2. What are the advantages and disadvantages of using an increase in the gasoline tax to move road transport decisions toward both efficiency and sustainability?

Self-Test Exercises

1. "While gasoline taxes and fuel economy standards can both be effective in increasing the number of miles per gallon in new vehicles, gasoline taxes are superior means of reducing emissions from the vehicle fleet." Discuss.
2. Suppose the nation wishes to reduce gasoline consumption not only to promote national security, but also to reduce the threats from climate change.
   a. How effective is a strategy relying on the labeling of the fuel efficiency of new cars likely to be? What are some of the advantages or disadvantages of this kind of approach?
   b. How effective would a strategy targeting the retirement of old, fuel-inefficient vehicles be? What are some of the advantages or disadvantages of this kind of approach?
   c. Would it make any economic sense to combine either of these polices with pay-as-you-drive insurance? Why or why not?
3. a. If a pay-as-you-drive insurance program is being implemented to cope with automobile related externalities associated with driving, what factors should be considered in setting the premium?
   b. Would you expect a private insurance company to take all these factors into account? Why or why not?

Further Reading

Anas, A., & Lindsey, R. (2011). Reducing urban road transportation externalities: Road pricing in theory and in practice. *Review of Environmental Economics and Policy*, *5*(1), 66–88,. A survey of the literature on road pricing and policy.

Anderson, S. T., Parry, I. W. H., Sallee, J. M., & Fischer, C. (2011). Automobile fuel economy standards: Impacts, efficiency, and alternatives. *Review of Environmental Economics and Policy*, *5*(1), 89–108,. A comprehensive summary and assessment of fuel economy standards.

Harrington, W., & McConnell, V. (2003). Motor vehicles and the environment. In H. Folmer & T. Tietenberg (Eds.) *International Yearbook of Environmental and Resource Economics 2003/2004* (190–268). Cheltenham, UK: Edward Elgar. A comprehensive survey of what we have learned from economic analysis about cost-effective ways to control pollution from motor vehicles.

Additional References and Historically Significant References are available on this book's Companion Website: http://www.routledgetextbooks.com/textbooks/9780133479690

18 Water Pollution

It was the best of times, it was the worst of times, it was the age of wisdom, it was the age of foolishness, it was the epoch of belief, it was the epoch of incredulity . . .

—Charles Dickens, *A Tale of Two Cities* (1859)

Introduction

While various types of pollution share common attributes, important differences are apparent as well. These differences form the basis for the elements of policy unique to each pollutant. We have seen, for example, that although the types of pollutants emitted by mobile and stationary sources are often identical, the policy approaches differ considerably.

Water pollution control has its own unique characteristics as well. The following stand out as having particular relevance for policy:

1. Recreation benefits are much more important for water pollution control than for air pollution control.
2. Large economies of scale in treating sewage and other wastes create the possibility for large, centralized treatment plants as one control strategy, while for air pollution, on-site control is the standard approach.
3. Many causes of water pollution are more difficult to trace to a particular source. Runoff from streets and agriculture as well as atmospheric deposition of pollutants are major diffuse sources of water pollution. Control of these sources adds additional complexities for water pollution control.

These characteristics create a need for yet another policy approach. In this chapter we explore the problems and prospects for controlling this unique and important form of pollution.

Nature of Water Pollution Problems

Types of Waste-Receiving Water

Two primary types of water are susceptible to contamination. The first, *surface water*, consists of the rivers, lakes, and oceans covering most of the earth's surface. Historically, policy makers have focused almost exclusively on preventing and cleaning up lake and river water pollution. Only recently has ocean pollution received the attention it deserves.

Groundwater, once considered a pristine resource, has been shown to be subject to considerable contamination from toxic chemicals. *Groundwater* is water beneath the earth's surface in soils or rocks, or in geological formations that are fully saturated.

Groundwater is a vast natural resource. It has been estimated that the reserves of groundwater are approximately 88 times the annual flow of surface water. Groundwater is used primarily for irrigation and as a source of drinking water.

While surface water also serves as a significant source of drinking water, it has many other uses as well. Recreational benefits, such as swimming, fishing, and boating, are important determinants of surface water policy in areas where the water is not used for drinking.

Sources of Contamination

Whereas some contamination has been accidental, the product of unintended and unexpected waste migration to water supplies, a portion of the contamination was deliberate. Watercourses were simply a convenient place to dump municipal or private sewage and industrial wastes. Along the shoreline of many lakes or rivers, pipes dumping human or industrial wastes directly into the water were a common occurrence before laws limiting this activity were enacted and enforced.

For lake and river pollution policy purposes, it is useful to distinguish between two sources of contamination—point and nonpoint—even though the distinction is not always crystal clear. *Point sources* generally discharge into surface waters at a specific location through a pipe, outfall, or ditch, while *nonpoint sources* usually affect the water in a more indirect and diffuse way. Examples of nonpoint source pollution include the runoff of fertilizers and pesticides from lawns and farms after rainstorms. From the policy point of view, nonpoint sources are more difficult to control because both the source and timing are hard to predict and, as such, they have received little legislative attention until recently. As a result of the gains made in controlling point sources, nonpoint sources now compose over half of the waste load borne by the nation's waters.

Contamination of groundwater occurs when polluting substances leach into a water-saturated region. Many potential contaminants are removed by filtration and adsorption as the water moves slowly through the layers of rock and soil. Toxic organic chemicals are one major example of a pollutant that may not be filtered out during migration. Once these substances enter groundwater, very little, if any, further cleansing takes place. Moreover, since the rate of replenishment for many groundwater sources, relative to the stock, is small, very little mixing and dilution of the contaminants occur.

Three primary sources of ocean pollution are oil spills, ocean dumping, and trash (primarily plastics) that ends up in the ocean. Oil spills from tankers have become less frequent and have decreased in magnitude since 1970 (see Figure 18.1). Spills, however, are still not uncommon, as shown in Table 18.1, which lists the largest spills. Various unwanted by-products of modern life have also been dumped into ocean waters based upon the mistaken belief that the vastness of the oceans allowed them to absorb large quantities of waste without suffering noticeable damage. Dumped materials have included sewage and sewage sludge, unwanted chemicals, trace metals, and even radioactive materials. More recently, vast amounts of plastics have been found in the ocean. Much of this plastic gets ingested by sea life and kills thousands of marine birds and mammals each year.

Types of Pollutants

For our purposes, the large number of water pollutants can be usefully classified by means of the taxonomy developed in Chapter 14.

Fund Pollutants. Fund pollutants are those for which the environment has some assimilative capacity. If the absorptive capacity is high enough relative to the rate

FIGURE 18.1 The Decreasing Frequency of Oil Spills from Tankers and Barges

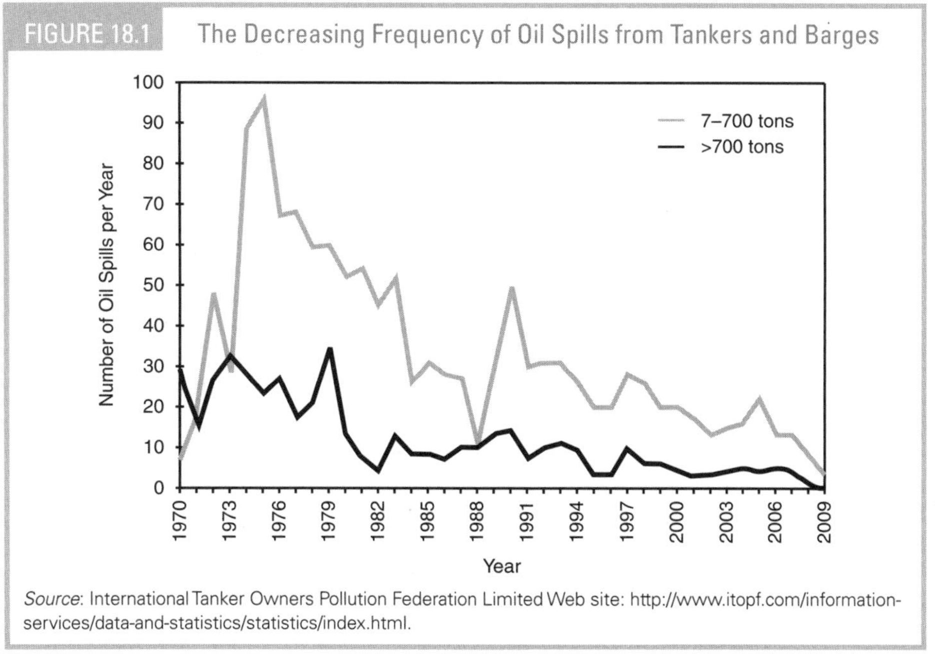

Source: International Tanker Owners Pollution Federation Limited Web site: http://www.itopf.com/information-services/data-and-statistics/statistics/index.html.

TABLE 18.1 Notable Oil Spills from Tankers

Rank	Spill Size (tons)	Ship Name	Year	Location
1	287,000	*Atlantic Empress*	1979	Off Tobago, West Indies
2	260,000	*ABT Summer*	1991	700 nautical miles off Angola
3	252,000	*Castillo de Bellver*	1983	Off Saldanha Bay, South Africa
4	223,000	*Amoco Cadiz*	1978	Off Brittany, France
5	144,000	*Haven*	1991	Genoa, Italy
6	132,000	*Odyssey*	1988	700 nautical miles off Nova Scotia, Canada
7	119,000	*Torrey Canyon*	1967	Scilly Isles, the United Kingdom
8	115,000	*Sea Star*	1972	Gulf of Oman
9	100,000	*Irenes Serenade*	1980	Navarino Bay, Greece
10	100,000	*Urquiola*	1976	La Coruna, Spain
11	95,000	*Hawaiian Patriot*	1977	300 nautical miles off Honolulu
12	94,000	*Independenta*	1979	Bosphorus, Turkey
13	88,000	*Jakob Maersk*	1975	Oporto, Portugal
14	85,000	*Braer*	1993	Shetland Islands, the United Kingdom
15	74,000	*Aegean Sea*	1992	La Coruna, Spain
16	72,000	*Sea Empress*	1996	Milford Haven, the United Kingdom
17	70,000	*Khark 5*	1989	120 nautical miles off Atlantic coast of Morocco
18	70,000	*Nova*	1985	Off Kharg Island, Gulf of Iran
19	66,700	*Katina P*	1992	Off Maputo, Mozambique
	63,000	*Prestige*	*2002*	Off Galicia, Spain
35	37,000	*Exxon Valdez*	1989	Prince William Sound, Alaska, the United States

Source: International Tanker Owners Pollution Federation Limited Website: Updated June 2013, http://www.itopf.com/information-services/data-and-statistics/ statistics/#majoreprinted with permission from ITOPF.

of discharge, they may not accumulate at all. One type of fund water pollutant is called *degradable* because it degrades, or breaks into its component parts, within the water. Degradable wastes are normally organic residuals that are attacked and broken down by bacteria in the stream.

The process by which organic wastes are broken down into component parts consumes oxygen. The amount of oxygen consumed depends upon the magnitude of the waste load. All of the higher life-forms in watercourses are *aerobic*; they require oxygen for survival. As a stream's oxygen levels fall, fish mortality increases, with the less tolerant fish becoming the first to succumb. The oxygen level can become low enough that even the aerobic bacteria die. When this happens, the stream becomes *anaerobic* and the ecology changes drastically. This is an extremely unpleasant circumstance because the stream takes on a dark hue, and the stream water stinks!

To control these waste loads, two different types of monitoring are needed: (1) monitoring the ambient conditions in the watercourse; and (2) monitoring the magnitude of emissions or effluent as it is commonly labeled for water pollutants. One measure commonly used to keep track of ambient conditions for these conventional fund pollutants is *dissolved oxygen* (DO). The amount of dissolved oxygen in a body of water is a function of ambient conditions, such as temperature, stream flow, and the waste load.[1] The measure of the oxygen demand placed on a stream by any particular volume of effluent is called the *biochemical oxygen demand* (BOD).

Using modeling techniques, effluent (measured as BOD) at a certain point can be translated into DO measures at various receptor locations along a stream. This step is necessary in order to implement an ambient permit system or an ambient emissions charge.

If we were to develop a profile of dissolved oxygen readings on a stream where organic effluent is being discharged, that profile would typically exhibit one or more minimum points called *oxygen sags*. These oxygen sags represent locations along the stream where the dissolved oxygen content is lower than at other points. An ambient permit or ambient charge system would be designed to reach a desired DO level at those sag points, while a cap-and-trade or effluent charge system would simply try to hit a particular BOD reduction target. The former would take the location of the emitter into account, while the latter would not. Later in this chapter we examine studies that model these systems on particular watercourses.

A second type of fund pollutant, thermal pollution, is caused by the injection of heat into a watercourse. Typically, *thermal pollution* is caused when an industrial plant or electric utility uses surface water as a coolant, returning the heated water to the watercourse. This heat is dissipated in the receiving waters by evaporation. By raising the temperature of the water near the outfall, thermal pollution lowers the dissolved oxygen content and can result in dramatic ecological changes in that area.

Yet another example is provided by a class of pollutants, such as nitrogen and phosphorus, that are plant nutrients. These pollutants stimulate the growth of aquatic plant life, such as algae and water weeds. In excess, these plants can produce odor, taste, and aesthetic problems. A lake with an excessive supply of nutrients is called *eutrophic*.

The various types of fund pollutants could be ordered on a spectrum. On one end of the spectrum would be pollutants for which the environment has a very large absorptive capacity and on the other end pollutants for which the absorptive capacity is virtually nil. The limiting case, with no absorptive capacity, is stock pollutants.

---

[1]The danger of anaerobic conditions is highest in the late summer and early fall, when temperatures are high and the stream flow is low.

Near the end of that spectrum is a class of inorganic synthetic chemicals called *persistent* pollutants. These substances are called persistent because their complex molecular structures are not effectively broken down in the stream. Some degradation takes place, but so slowly that these pollutants can travel long distances in water in a virtually unchanged form.

These persistent pollutants accumulate, not only in the watercourses, but also in the food chain. The concentration levels in the tissues of living organisms rise with the order of the species. Concentrations in lower life-forms such as plankton may be relatively small, but because small fish eat a lot of plankton and do not excrete the chemical, the concentrations in small fish would be higher. The magnification continues as large fish consume small fish; concentration levels in the larger fish would be even higher.

Because they accumulate in the food chains, persistent pollutants present an interesting monitoring challenge. The traditional approach would involve measurements of pollutant concentration in the water, but that is not the only variable of interest. The damage is related not only to its concentration in the water, but its concentration in the food chain as well. Although monitoring the environmental effects of these pollutants may be more compelling than for other pollutants, it is also more difficult.

Finally, infectious organisms such as bacteria and viruses can be carried into surface water and groundwater by human and animal wastes and by wastes from such industries as tanning and meatpacking. These live organisms may either thrive and multiply in water or their population may decline over time, depending upon how hospitable or hostile the watercourse is for continued growth.

Stock Pollutants. The most troublesome cases of pollution result from stock pollutants, which merely accumulate in the environment. No natural process removes or transforms stock pollutants; the watercourse cannot cleanse itself of them.

Inorganic chemicals and minerals comprise the main examples of stock pollutants. Perhaps the most notorious members of this group are the heavy metals, such as lead, cadmium, and mercury. Extreme examples of poisoning by these metals have occurred in Japan. One ocean-dumping case was responsible for *Minamata disease*, named for the location where it occurred. Some 52 people died and 150 others suffered serious brain and nerve damage. Scientists puzzled for years over the source of the ailments until tracing it to an organic form of mercury that had accumulated in the tissues of fish eaten three times a day by local residents.

In the United States, mercury contamination of fish has led to consumption advisories for many freshwater and migratory fish. Women of childbearing age and children especially are cautioned against eating large amounts of certain species. Debate 18.1 examines the effects of fish consumption advisories on consumer behavior.

In another case, in Japan, known as the *itai itai* (literally, *ouch-ouch*) *disease*, scientists traced the source of a previously undiagnosed, extremely painful bone disease to the ingestion of cadmium. Nearby mines were the source of the cadmium, which apparently was ingested by eating contaminated rice and soybeans.

Toxics in Fish Tissue: Do Fish Consumption Advisories Change Behavior?

DEBATE 18.1

Since mercury persists and bioaccumulates, the concentrations of mercury rise as you move up the food chain. Ingested mercury has been linked to neurological disorders in infants and children. In January 2001, the Food and Drug Administration (FDA) released an advisory on methyl mercury in fish. An updated advisory was issued in 2004 and again in 2006. Part of that advisory reads as follows:

> *However, nearly all fish and shellfish contain traces of mercury. For most people, the risk from mercury by eating fish and shellfish is not a health concern. Yet, some fish and shellfish contain higher levels of mercury that may harm an unborn baby or young child's developing nervous system. The risks from mercury in fish and shellfish depend on the amount of fish and shellfish eaten and the levels of mercury in the fish and shellfish. Therefore, the Food and Drug Administration (FDA) and the Environmental Protection Agency (EPA) are advising women who may become pregnant, pregnant women, nursing mothers, and young children to avoid some types of fish and eat fish and shellfish that are lower in mercury.*[2]

The FDA targeted women planning on becoming pregnant within 6 months, pregnant women, and nursing women to receive information about the new advisory on methyl mercury.

Using the Bureau of Labor Statistics' Consumer Expenditure Survey, Shimshack, Ward, and Beatty (2007) examine the effectiveness of advisories in affecting consumer choices. In particular, they look at the effects of the advisory on the consumption of canned fish during 1999–2002, a time period that includes 2 years before and 2 years after the advisory. They examine whether the groups targeted reduced their consumption of canned fish and what determined the responses.

Comparing target households (those with young children) to nontarget households, they find that targeted consumers significantly reduced their canned fish consumption as a result of the warning. College-educated consumers responded quite strongly. Additionally, they found that newspaper and magazine readership were significant in influencing the postadvisory reduction in fish consumption, but health consciousness was not. Interestingly, they also found evidence of spillover effects; nontargeted consumers also reduced their consumption of canned fish.

Access to information is clearly important to the success of a health advisory. At-risk consumers who were less educated and nonreaders did not significantly reduce consumption. The authors suggest that this particular group is also less likely to be able to withstand negative health shocks.

What is the best way to get information to different population groups? Unequal access to information creates unevenly distributed health risks and might be labeled an environmental justice issue.

Sources: Shimshack, J. P., Ward, M. B., and Beatty, T. K. M. (2007). Mercury advisories: Information, education and fish consumption. *Journal of Environmental Economics and Management*, 53(2), 158–179; www.fda.gov.

---

[2]http://www.cfsan.fda.gov/~dms/admehg3.html

Most recently, medicinal waste has been found in watercourses and in fish tissue. In 2002, the USGS tested 139 rivers in 30 states and found that 80 percent of the streams sampled resulted in evidence of residuals from drugs such as birth-control pills and antidepressants. Residuals from soaps, perfumes, and caffeine were also found. While the magnitude of the damage that will ultimately be caused by these substances is not yet clear, it is certainly a new twist in water pollution control policy.

As is typical with persistent pollutants, some of the stock pollutants are difficult to monitor. Those accumulated in the food chains give rise to the same problem as is presented by persistent pollutants. Ambient sampling must be supplemented by sampling tissues from members of the food chain. To further complicate matters, the heavy metals may sink rapidly to the bottom, remaining in the sediment. While these could be detected in sediment samples, merely drawing samples from the water itself would allow these pollutants to escape detection.

Traditional Water Pollution Control Policy

Water pollution control policies vary around the world. In this section we begin with a somewhat detailed discussion of US policy, which provides a rather rich example of a typical legal approach to regulation. Later in the chapter we will look at the European approach, which has depended more heavily on economic incentives.

US policy for water pollution control predates federal air pollution control. We might suppose that the policy for water pollution control would, therefore, be superior, since authorities had more time to profit from early mistakes. Unfortunately, that is not the case.

Early Legislation

The first federal legislation dealing with discharge into the nation's waterways occurred when Congress passed the 1899 Refuse Act. Designed primarily to protect navigation, this act focused on preventing any discharge that would interfere with using rivers as transport links. All discharges into a river were prohibited unless approved by a permit from the Chief of the US Engineers. Most permits were issued to contractors dredging the rivers, and they dealt mainly with the disposal of the removed material. This act was virtually unenforced for other pollutants until 1970, when this permit program was rediscovered and used briefly (with little success) as the basis for federal enforcement actions.

The Water Pollution Control Act of 1948 represented the first attempt by the federal government to exercise some direct influence over what previously had been a state and local function. A hesitant move, since it reaffirmed that the primary responsibility for water pollution control rested with the states, it did initiate the authority of the federal government to conduct investigations, research, and surveys.

Early hints of the current approach are found in the amendments to the Water Pollution Control Act, which were passed in 1956. Two provisions of this act were especially important: (1) federal financial support for the construction of waste treatment plants, and (2) direct federal regulation of waste discharges via a mechanism known as the *enforcement conference.*

The first of these provisions envisioned a control strategy based on subsidizing the construction of a particular control activity—waste treatment plants. Municipalities could receive federal grants to cover up to 55 percent of the construction of municipal sewage treatment plants. This approach not only lowered the cost to the local governments of constructing these facilities, but also it lowered the cost to users. Since the federal government contribution was a grant, rather than a loan, the fees users were charged did not reflect the federally subsidized construction portion of the cost. The user fees were set at a lower rate that was high enough to cover merely the unsubsidized portion of construction cost, as well as operating and maintenance cost.

The 1956 amendments envisioned a relatively narrow federal role in the regulation of discharges. Initially, only polluters contributing to interstate pollution were included, but subsequent laws have broadened the coverage. By 1961, discharges into all navigable water were covered.

The mechanism created by the amendments of 1956 to enforce the regulation of discharges was the enforcement conference. Under this approach, the designated federal control authority could call for a conference to deal with any interstate water pollution problem, or it could be requested to do so by the governor of an affected state. The fact that this authority was discretionary and not mandatory and that the control authority had very few means of enforcing any decisions reached meant that the conferences simply did not achieve the intended results.

The Water Quality Act of 1965 attempted to improve the process by establishing ambient water quality standards for interstate watercourses and by requiring states to file implementation plans. This sounds like the approach currently being used in air pollution control, but there are important differences. The plans forthcoming from states in response to the 1965 act were vague and did not attempt to link specific effluent standards on discharges to the ambient standards. They generally took the easy way out and called for secondary treatment, which removes 80–90 percent of BOD and 85 percent of suspended solids. The fact that these standards bore no particular relationship to ambient quality made them difficult to enforce in the courts, since the legal authority for them was based on this relationship.

Subsequent Legislation

Point Sources. As discussed in the preceding chapters, an air of frustration regarding pollution control pervaded Washington in the 1970s. As with air pollution legislation, this frustration led to the enactment of a very tough water pollution control law. The tone of the act is established immediately in the preamble, which calls for the achievement of two goals: (1) "… that the discharge of pollutants into the navigable waters be eliminated by 1985"; and (2) "… that wherever attainable, an interim goal of water quality which provides for the protection and propagation of fish, shellfish, and wildlife and provides for recreation in and on the water be achieved by June 1, 1983." The stringency of these goals represented a major departure from previous policy.

This act also introduced new procedures for implementing the law. Permits were required of all dischargers (replacing the 1899 Refuse Act, which, because of its navigation focus, was difficult to enforce). The permits would be granted only when the dischargers met certain technology-based effluent standards. The ambient standards were completely bypassed as these effluent standards were uniformly imposed and, hence, could not depend on local water conditions.[3]

According to the 1972 amendments, the effluent standards were to be implemented in two stages. By 1977, industrial dischargers, as a condition of their permit, were required to meet effluent limitations based on the "best practicable control technology currently available" (BPT). In setting these national standards, the EPA was required to consider the total costs of these technologies and their relation to the benefits received, but not to consider the conditions of the individual source or the particular waters into which it was discharged. In addition, all publicly owned treatment plants were to have achieved secondary treatment by 1977. By 1983, industrial discharges were required to meet effluent limitations based on the presumably more stringent "best available technology economically achievable" (BAT) while publicly owned treatment plants were required to meet effluent limitations that depended on the "best practicable waste treatment technology."

The program of subsidizing municipal water treatment plants, begun in 1956, was continued in a slightly modified form by the 1972 act. Whereas the 1965 act allowed the federal government to subsidize up to 55 percent of the cost of construction of waste treatment plants, the 1972 act raised the ceiling to 75 percent. The 1972 act also increased the funds available for this program. In 1981, the federal share was returned to 55 percent.

The 1977 amendments continued this regulatory approach, but with some major modifications. This legislation drew a more careful distinction between conventional and toxic pollutants, with more stringent requirements placed on the latter, and it extended virtually all of the deadlines in the 1972 act.

For conventional pollutants, a new treatment standard was created to replace the BAT standards. The effluent limitations for these pollutants were to be based on the "best conventional technology," and the deadline for these standards was set at July 1, 1984. In setting these standards, the EPA was required to consider whether the costs of adding the pollution control equipment were reasonable when compared with the improvement in water quality. For unconventional pollutants and toxics (any pollutant not specifically included on the list of conventional pollutants), the BAT requirement was retained but the deadline was shifted to 1984.

Other deadlines were also extended. The date for municipalities to meet the secondary treatment deadline moved from 1977 to 1983. Industrial compliance with the BPT standards was delayed until 1983 when the contemplated system had the potential for application throughout the industry.

The final modification made by the 1977 amendments involved the introduction of pretreatment standards for waste being sent to a publicly owned treatment system. These standards were designed to prevent discharges that could inhibit the

---

[3]Actually, the ambient standards were not completely bypassed. If the uniform controls were not sufficient to meet the desired standard, the effluent limitation would have to be tightened accordingly.

treatment process and to prevent the introduction of toxic pollutants that would not be treated by the waste treatment facility. Existing facilities were required to meet the standards 3 years after the date they were published, while facilities constructed later would be required to meet the pretreatment regulations upon commencement of operations.

Nonpoint Sources. In contrast to the control of point sources, the EPA was given no specific authority to regulate nonpoint sources. This type of pollution was seen by Congress as a state responsibility.

Section 208 of the act authorized federal grants for state-initiated planning that would provide implementable plans for area-wide waste-treatment management. Section 208 further specified that this area-wide plan must identify significant nonpoint sources of pollution, as well as procedures and methods for controlling them. The reauthorization of the Clean Water Act, passed over President Reagan's veto during February 1987, authorized an additional $400 million for a new program to help states control runoff, but it still left the chief responsibility for controlling nonpoint sources to the states.

The main federal role for controlling nonpoint sources has been the Conservation Reserve Program run by the US Department of Agriculture rather than the EPA. Designed to remove some 40–45 million acres of highly erodible land from cultivation, this act provides subsidies to farmers for planting grass or trees. These subsidies are designed to result in reduced erosion and to reduce loadings of nitrogen, phosphorus, and total suspended solids.

Since the late 1980s, efforts focused on nonpoint sources have increased dramatically. Voluntary programs and cost-sharing programs with landowners have been the most common tools. Section 319 of the Clean Water Act specifies guidelines for state implementation of nonpoint source-management plans. In 2003, the EPA devoted a large portion of its Section 319 funds ($100 million) to address areas where nonpoint source pollution has significantly impaired water quality.[4] Another recent role for municipalities has been the separation of storm water and sewer drains so that sewage treatment plants do not overflow during rainstorms. Federal subsidies have also assisted with these projects.

The TMDL Program

In 1999, recognizing the problems with both the technology-based national effluent standards and the growing importance of nonpoint pollution control, the US EPA proposed new rules designed to breathe fresh life into the previously unenforced *Total Maximum Daily Load (TMDL) program* of the Clean Water Act. A TMDL is a calculation of the maximum amount of a pollutant that a water body can receive and still meet water quality standards as well as an allocation of that amount to the pollutant's sources. The calculation must include a margin of safety to ensure that the water body can be used for its designated purpose. The calculation must also account for seasonable variation in water quality.

---

[4] *U.S. Federal Register* Vol. 68, No. 205 (October 2003).

The TMDL program moves water pollution control toward the ambient standard approach long used to control air pollution. Under this program, water quality standards are promulgated by states, territories, and/or tribes. The promulgated standards are tailored to the designated uses for each water body (such as drinking water supply or recreational uses such as swimming and/or fishing). The states must then undertake strategies for achieving the standards, including significantly bringing nonpoint source pollutants under control.

The Safe Drinking Water Act

The 1972 policy focused on achieving water quality sufficiently high for fishing and swimming. Because that quality is not high enough for drinking water, the Safe Drinking Water Act of 1974 issued more stringent standards for community water systems. The primary drinking water regulations set maximum allowable concentration levels for bacteria, turbidity (muddiness), and chemical-radiological contaminants. National secondary drinking water regulations were also established to protect "public welfare" from odor and aesthetic problems that may cause a substantial number of people to stop using the affected water system. The secondary standards are advisory for the states; they cannot be enforced by the EPA.

The 1986 Amendments to the Safe Drinking Water Act required the EPA to (1) issue primary standards within 3 years for 83 contaminants and by 1991 for at least 25 more, (2) set standards based on the BAT, and (3) monitor public water systems for both regulated and unregulated chemical contaminants. Approximately 60,000 public water systems are subject to these regulations. Civil and criminal penalties for any violations of the standards were also increased by the amendments.

More recent drinking water rules and standards cover MTBE, arsenic, radon, lead, microbials, and disinfection by-products. In 2007, the EPA issued a final ruling on lead and copper in drinking water, two contaminants that enter through plumbing materials. Many older homes have faucets or fittings of brass, which contain some lead, lead pipes, or copper pipes with solder.

Ocean Pollution

Oil Spills. The Clean Water Act prohibits discharges of "harmful quantities" of oil into navigable waters. Since the EPA regulations define "harmful" to include all discharges that "violate applicable water quality standards or cause a film or sheen upon the surface of the water," virtually all discharges are prohibited.

Industry responsibilities include complying with Coast Guard regulations (which deal with contingency planning in case of a spill and various accident avoidance requirements) and assuming the financial liability for any accident. If a spill does occur, it must be immediately reported to the Coast Guard or the EPA. Failure to report a spill can result in a fine up to $10,000 and/or imprisonment for up to 1 year.

In addition to giving notice, the discharger must either contain the spill or pay the cost of cleanup by a responsible government agency. The discharger's liability for the government's actual removal cost is limited to $50 million unless willful negligence or willful misconduct can be proved. Successful proof of willful negligence or willful misconduct eliminates the liability limit. In addition to cleanup costs, removal costs also include compensation for damages to natural resources. (Natural resource damages are defined as "any costs or expenses incurred by the federal government or any state government in the restoration or replacement of natural resources damaged or destroyed as a result of a discharge of oil. …")

Ocean Dumping. Except for oil spills, which are covered by the Clean Water Act and the Oil Pollution Act of 1990, discharges to the ocean are covered by the Marine Protection Research and Sanctuaries Act of 1972. This act governs all discharges of wastes to ocean waters within US territorial limits and discharges of wastes in ocean waters by US vessels or persons regardless of where the dumping occurs. With only a few exceptions, no ocean dumping of industrial wastes or sewer sludge is now permitted. Radiological, chemical, and biological warfare agents and high-level radioactive wastes are specifically prohibited by the statute. Under the amended statute, the only ocean-dumping activities permitted are the disposal of dredged soil, fish wastes, human remains, and submerged vessels. This dumping is subject to specific regulations and is approved on a case-by-case basis.

Ocean Trash. Similar to nonpoint source pollution, floating trash found in the ocean comes from a variety of sources and is almost impossible to attribute to a particular location. Marine debris, in particular plastics, are harmful to marine life that frequently mistakes plastics for food. Ingesting the plastic objects, many of which contain toxics, kills thousands of sea birds and other sea life each year. Sea turtles and albatross have both been known to mistake the plastics for food and feed pieces to their young.

The "Great Pacific Garbage Patch" also known as the Pacific Trash Vortex is a giant float mass of marine garbage located in the North Pacific Ocean. Scientists are not sure of its exact size, but all of the estimates are enormous.

Few laws govern ocean trash except for explicit dumping. Some states and countries have bans or fees for the use of plastic bags in grocery stores. Hawaii has a statewide ban on plastic bags, though it is difficult to enforce.[5]

Efficiency and Cost-Effectiveness

Recall that the efficient allocation of uncontaminated water requires marginal benefits to be equalized across all uses (as was illustrated in Figure 9.3). However, if return flows are contaminated, this can alter the efficient allocation.[6]

---

[5]For a full list of legislation on plastic bags, see http://www.ncsl.org/issues-research/env-res/plastic-bag-legislation.aspx

[6]Return flow is a measure of the unused portion of water. For example, in agriculture, water withdrawal is the amount of water taken from a source and applied to a field. Consumptive use is the amount actually used by the plant. Return flow is the unconsumed portion that will eventually return to the watercourse and is frequently claimed by a downstream user. Return flows will bring with them leached contaminants, pesticides, fertilizers, and salts from the soil.

Figure 18.2 demonstrates the effect of return flow contamination on the efficient allocation in the case of two users: an upper basin (*UB*) user and a downstream lower basin (*LB*) user. Efficiency dictates that water should be allocated at the point of equal marginal benefits across the two users. If the two users have identical marginal benefits for uncontaminated water, the two users should receive equal amounts of water (recall Figure 9.3). However, subtracting the effect of contaminated return flows from the upper basin marginal benefit function ($MB_{UB'}$) (internalizing this externality) changes the efficient allocation to one with unequal sharing. In particular, more water would be allocated to the lower basin user ($Q_{LB'}$) and less to the upper basin user ($Q_{UB'}$). (See Bennett (2000) for a more detailed discussion.) Accounting for water quality can be an important and often-overlooked factor in allocation decisions.

Ambient Standards and the Zero-Discharge Goal

The 1956 amendments defined ambient standards as a means of quantifying the objectives being sought. A system of ambient standards allows the control authority to tailor the quality of a particular body of water to its use. Water used for drinking would be subject to the highest standards, swimming the next highest, and so on. Once the ambient standards are defined, the control responsibility could be allocated among sources. Greater efforts to control pollution would be expended where the gap between desired and actual water quality was the largest.

FIGURE 18.2 Economic Efficiency When Return Flows Are Contaminated

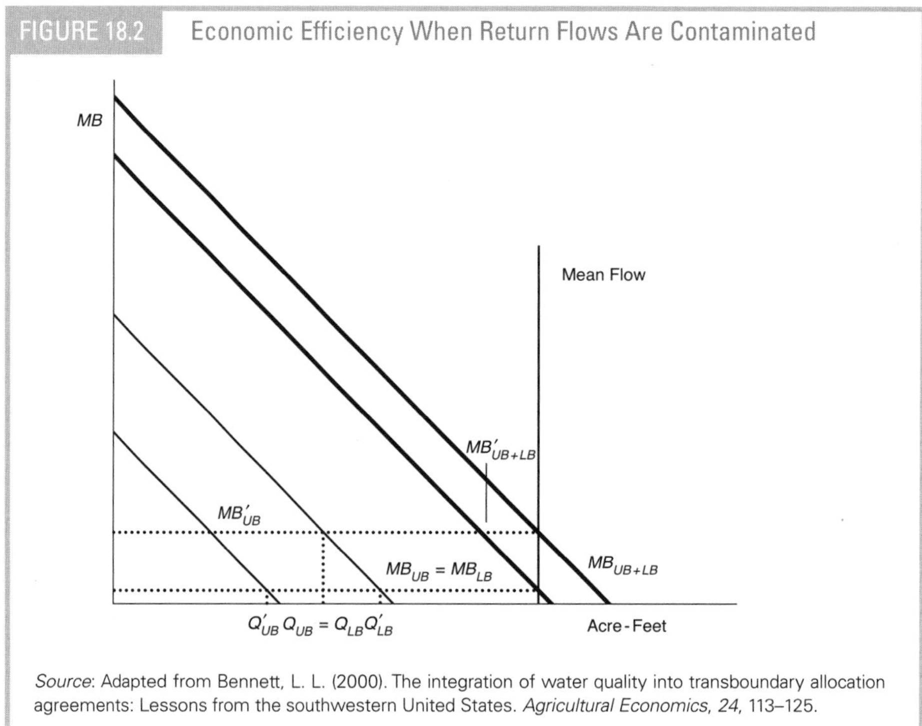

Source: Adapted from Bennett, L. L. (2000). The integration of water quality into transboundary allocation agreements: Lessons from the southwestern United States. *Agricultural Economics, 24,* 113–125.

Unfortunately, the early experience with ambient standards for water was not reassuring. Rather than strengthening the legal basis for the effluent standards, while retaining their connection to the ambient standards, Congress chose to downgrade the importance of ambient standards by specifying a zero-discharge goal. Additionally, the effluent standards were given their own legal status apart from any connection with ambient standards. The wrong inference was drawn from the early lack of legislative success.

In his own inimitable style, Mark Twain (1893) put the essential point rather well:

> *We should be careful to get out of an experience only the wisdom that is in it—and stop there; lest we be like the cat that sits down on a hot stove lid. She will never sit down on a hot stove lid again—and that is well; but also she will never sit down on a cold one anymore. (p. 125)*

The most fundamental problem with the current approach is that it rests on the faulty assumption that the tougher the law, the more that is accomplished. The zero-discharge goal provides one example of a case in which passing a tough standard, in the hopes of actually achieving a weaker one, can backfire. Kneese and Schultze (1975) point out that in the late 1960s, the French experimented with a law that required zero discharge and imposed severe penalties for violations. The result was that the law was never enforced because it was universally viewed as unreasonable. Less control was accomplished under this stringent, but unenforceable law than would have been accomplished with a less stringent but enforceable one.

Is the US case comparable? It appears to be. In 1972, the EPA published an estimate of the costs of meeting a zero-discharge goal, assuming that it was feasible. They concluded that over the decade from 1971 to 1981, removing 85–90 percent of the pollutants from all industrial and municipal effluents would cost $62 billion. Removing all of the pollutants was estimated to cost $317 billion, more than five times as much, and this figure probably understates the true cost (Kneese & Schultze, 1975, 1978).

Is this cost justified? Probably not for all pollutants, though for some it may be. Unfortunately, the zero-discharge goal makes no distinction among pollutant types. For some fund pollutants it seems extreme. Perhaps the legislators realized this because when the legislation was drafted, no specific timetables or procedures were established to ensure that the zero-discharge goal would be met by 1985 or, for that matter, anytime.

National Effluent Standards

The first prong in the two-pronged congressional attack on water pollution was the national effluent standards (the other being subsidies for the construction of publicly owned waste treatment facilities). Deciding on the appropriate levels for these standards for each of the estimated 60,000 sources is not a trivial task. Not surprisingly, difficulties arose.

Enforcement Problems. Soon after the passage of the 1972 amendments, the EPA geared up to assume its awesome responsibility. Relying on a battery of consultants, it began to study the technologies of pollution control available to each industry in order to establish reasonable effluent limits. In establishing the guidelines, the EPA is required to take into account "the age of the equipment and facilities involved, the process employed, the engineering aspects of the application of various types of control techniques, process changes, nonwater quality environmental impact (including energy requirements) and such factors as the Administrator deems appropriate ...."

It is not clear whether this provision means that individual standards should be specified for each source, or general standards for broad categories of sources. Cost-effectiveness would require the former, but in a system relying on effluent standards, the transaction costs associated with that approach would be prohibitively high and the delay unacceptably long. Therefore, the EPA chose the only feasible interpretation available and established general standards for broad categories of sources. While the standards could differ among categories, they were uniformly applied to the large number of sources within each category.

The EPA inevitably fell behind the congressional deadlines. In fact, not one effluent standard was published by the deadline. As the standards were published, they were immediately challenged in the courts. By 1977, some 250 cases had been mounted, challenging the established standards (Freeman, 1978). Some of the challenges were successful, requiring the EPA to revise the standards. All of this took time.

By 1977, the EPA was having so much trouble defining the BPT standards that the deadlines for the BAT standards became completely unreasonable. Furthermore, for conventional pollutants, not only the deadlines but the standards themselves were irrational. Many bodies of water would have met the ambient standards without the BAT standard, while for others, the effluent standards were not sufficient, particularly in areas with large nonpoint pollution problems. In addition, in some cases the technologies required by BPT would not be compatible (or even necessary) once the BAT standards were in effect. The situation was in shambles.

The 1977 amendments changed both the timing of the BAT standards (delaying the deadlines) and their focus (toward toxic pollutants and away from conventional pollutants). As a result of these amendments, the EPA was required to develop industry effluent standards based on the BAT guidelines for control of 65 classes of toxic priority pollutants. In a 1979 survey, the EPA discovered that all primary industries regularly discharge one or more of these toxic pollutants. As of 1980, the EPA had proposed BAT effluent limitations for control of toxic priority pollutants for nine primary industries.

The 1977 amendments certainly improved the situation. Because toxics represent a more serious problem, it makes sense to set stricter standards for those pollutants. Extension of the deadlines was absolutely necessary; there was no alternative.

These amendments have not, however, resulted in a cost-effective strategy. In particular, they tend to retard technological progress and to assign the responsibility for control in an unnecessarily expensive manner.

Allocating Control Responsibility. Because the effluent standards established by the EPA are based upon specific technologies, these technologies are known to the industries. Therefore, in spite of the fact that the industry can choose any technology that keeps emissions under the limitation stated in the standard, in practice industries tend to choose the specific equipment cited by the EPA when it established the standard. This, they reason, minimizes their risk. If anything goes wrong and they are hauled into court, they can simply argue that they did precisely what the EPA had in mind when it set the standard.

The problem with this reaction is that it focuses too narrowly on a particular technology rather than on the real objective, effluent reduction. The focus should be less on the purchase of a specific technology and more on doing what is necessary to hold effluent down, such as maintenance, process changes, and so on. In a field undergoing rapid technological change, tying all control efforts to a particular technology (which may become obsolete well before the standards are revised) is a poor strategy. Unfortunately, technological stagnation has become a routine side effect of the current policy, to the detriment of securing clean water.

In allocating the control responsibility among various sources, the EPA was constrained by the inherent difficulty of making unique determinations for each source and by limitations in the act itself, such as the need to apply relatively uniform standards. We know from Chapter 14 that uniform effluent standards are not cost-effective, but it remains an open question whether or not the resulting increases in cost are sufficiently large to recommend an alternative approach, such as effluent charges or allowances. The fact that the cost increases are largely in the control of stationary-source air pollution does not automatically imply that they are large for water pollution control as well.

A number of early empirical studies investigated how closely the national effluent standards approximate the least-cost allocation (see Tietenberg 1985, p. 46, Table 5). These studies support the contention that EPA standards are not cost-effective, though the degree of cost-ineffectiveness is typically smaller than that associated with the standards used to control air pollution.

Perhaps the most famous study examining the cost-effectiveness of uniform standards in contrast with emissions and ambient charges and permits was conducted on the Delaware Estuary (Kneese & Bower, 1968). This river basin, though small by the standards of the Mississippi or other major basins, drains an area serving a population in excess of 6 million people. It is a highly industrial, densely populated area.

In this study, a simulation model was constructed to capture the effect on ambient dissolved oxygen content of a variety of pollutants discharged by a large number of polluters into the river at numerous locations. In addition, this model was capable of simulating the cost consequences of various methods used to allocate the responsibility for controlling effluent to meet dissolved oxygen standards.

Four specific methods of allocating responsibility were considered. The first was the *least-cost* (LC) method, which would correspond to an ambient charge or ambient permit system. This method takes both locations of the emissions and control costs into account.

The second method was a *uniform treatment* (UT) strategy in which all discharges were faced with an effluent standard requiring them to remove a given percentage of their waste before discharging the remainder into the river. This method mirrors, in a crude way, the EPA strategy in effect at the time.

The third method simulated the allocation attained from the use of a *uniform emission charge* (UEC) or an emissions permit system. This method takes control costs, but not effluent locations, into account. The final case simulates a *zoned effluent charge* (ZEC). For this case, the river basin was subdivided into a series of zones. All dischargers within a zone would face the same emissions charges, while dischargers in different zones could face different emissions charges. This fourth simulation was an intermediate step between the first and third strategies. It allowed location to be more of a factor than in the third method, but less of a factor than in the first method. The first simulation would be identical to the fourth if the zones were sufficiently small that each discharger was in its own unique zone; it would be identical to the third if one zone contained all sources.

For control of water pollution, the UT strategy does increase the cost substantially. For either dissolved oxygen objective, the costs are roughly three times higher. Also of interest is the fact that the zonal system results in costs that are quite close to the minimum for the higher DO objective, while the UEC does not. This result suggests that even rudimentary attempts to take location into account may make a big difference for water pollution just as it does for air pollution.

Despite this evidence, the regulatory reform movement that played such an important role for air pollution control has been much slower to emerge for water pollution control. An early attempt at trading was implemented for the Fox River in Wisconsin, but only one trade was completed in the first 10 years after implementation.

Watershed-Based Trading

More recently, however, watershed-based trading programs are gaining attention. In 1996, the EPA began exploring trading programs for the Tar-Pamlico River in North Carolina, Long Island Sound, Chesapeake Bay, and the Snake and Lower Boise rivers in Idaho. Dozens of small trading programs are now in existence. Worldwide, 57 trading programs are now in existence. All but six of these are in the United States. Of the programs in existence, 26 are active, 21 are under development or under consideration and 10 are now inactive (WRI, 2009). Trading for water pollution control typically involves point source polluters meeting water quality standards by purchasing reductions from other sources (point or nonpoint sources) that have lower marginal costs of abatement.

Most of the markets currently in place focus on either nitrogen or phosphorus trading and are too new to evaluate, but at least 23 US water trading programs have carried out at least one trade (for some examples see Table 18.2). The six trading programs outside of the United States include four in Australia (three of which are active and one under development), one in Canada and one in New Zealand (WRI, 2009).

Ex-ante studies, however, suggest that the economic benefits can be large. Example 18.1 illustrates the potential for tradable effluent cost savings for treating hypoxic (low levels of dissolved oxygen) conditions in Long Island Sound. Allowing firms the flexibility to exploit economies of scale in pollution-control technology can provide for large savings. This point-point trading program has resulted in cheaper *and* faster cleanup.

TABLE 18.2 Summary of NPDES Trading Programs That Have Traded at Least Once as of June 2007

Point-Point Trades	Pollutant(s) Traded	Point-Nonpoint Trades	Pollutant(s) Traded
Long Island Sound, CT	Total Nitrogen	Wayland Center, MA	Total Phosphorus
Bear Creek, CO	Total Phosphorus	Croton Watershed, NY	Total Phosphorus
Neuse River, NC	Total Nitrogen	Pinnacle, DE	Total Nitrogen, Total Phosphorus
Charlotte-Mecklenburg, NC	Total Phosphorus	Rahr Malting, MN	Offset Biological Oxygen Demand with Total Phosphorus
Cobb County, GA	Total Phosphorus	Southern MN Beetsugar Cooperative, MN	Total Phosphorus
City of Newman, GA	Total Phosphorus	Red Cedar River, WI	Total Phosphorus
MN General Permit	Total Phosphorus	Great Miami River, OH	Total Nitrogen, Total Phosphorus
Las Vegas Wash, NV	Total Ammonia, Total Phosphorus	Taos Ski Valley, NM	Total Nitrogen
		Carlota Copper, AZ	Copper
		Clean Water Services, OR	Temperature
		Cherry Creek, CO	Total Phosphorus
		Chatfield Res, CO	Total Phosphorus
		Lake Dillon, CO	Total Phosphorus

Source: Table from Summary of NPDES Trading Programs That Have Traded at Least Once as of June 2007. Retrieved from http://www.ecosystemmarketplace.com/pages/dynamic/article.page.php?page_id=5335§ion=home&eod=1. Reprinted with permission of Ecosystem Marketplace.

The EPA supports market-based programs for certain pollutants if they can help meet Clean Water Act goals. In 2008, the EPA issued a Water Quality Trading Evaluation (US EPA, 2008) and found significant cost savings and nutrient (nitrogen and phosphorus) reductions for the trading programs they evaluated.[7] Comparing across programs is somewhat challenging, however, since they do not all rely on the same trading mechanism. Some trades are case-by-case, while others are open-market trades. Some rely on a broker, while others operate through direct negotiations. And some are not based on market mechanisms at all (US EPA, 2008).[8]

Watershed-based trading is complicated by the difficulties of accounting for spatial distribution of pollutants, thus requiring complicated trading ratios (Olmstead, 2010). A trading ratio ensures the reduction in pollution after a trade is equal to

[7]For a map of current US water-quality trading programs, see www.epa.gov/owow/watershed/trading/tradingmap.html

[8]http://www.epa.gov/evaluate/pdf/wqt.pdf

EXAMPLE 18.1

Effluent Trading for Nitrogen in Long Island Sound

Long Island Sound experiences severe hypoxia (low levels of dissolved oxygen) during the summer months. This *eutrophication* is caused primarily by excess nitrogen discharges from municipal sewage-treatment plants. As discussed earlier in this chapter, most past policies for water pollution control focused on technology standards to control discharges. Economic theory suggests that lower costs can be achieved by providing flexibility to the plants via a permit-trading program. In the late 1990s, Connecticut, New York, and the US EPA began exploring this possibility for sewage-treatment plants with discharges reaching Long Island Sound. The plan targeted trading to certain management zones. The overall goal of this management plan was a 58.5 percent reduction in nitrogen over 15 years, beginning in 1999.

Bennett et al. (2000) estimated the costs associated with the proposed scheme, whereby trading is restricted to the 11 management zones designated by the *Long Island Sound Study*. They then estimate the cost savings of alternative programs that expand the zone of trading to (1) trading among sources and across zones, but within state boundaries, and (2) trading across all sources. For each trading scenario, polluting sources are grouped into trading "bubbles" that are based on geographic location. Trading is allowed to take place within each bubble, but not among bubbles.

Bennett et al. find what economic theory would predict—that cost savings rise (and rise substantially) as the scope of trading expands (meaning, fewer bubbles). Expanding trading across the two state bubbles could save up to 20 percent or $156 million, based on their estimates. The following table is reproduced from their results.

Number of Trading Bubbles	Present Value of Total Costs ($ million)	Cost Savings Relative to 11 Bubbles ($ million)	Percentage Savings
11	781.44	—	—
2	740.55	40.89	5.23
1	625.14	156.30	20.00

Not all discharges have the same impact. In fact, discharges from zones in the eastern portion of Long Island Sound and the northern parts of Connecticut do not have as detrimental effects as those closer to New York City. Despite differences in abatement cost, the proposed management plan recommends that each management zone be responsible for an equal percentage of nitrogen reduction.

While marginal abatement costs vary widely across management zones (suggesting that trades could reduce costs), the marginal contributions to damages also vary widely, thus ruling out a simple system of ton-for-ton effluent trades. (As Chapter 14 pointed out, more complicated ambient trades would be required to achieve cost-effectiveness for this nonuniformly mixed pollutant.) Currently, in recognition of this complexity, trading is not being considered across the boundaries of the 11 management zones despite the apparent potential cost savings.

Between 2002 and 2004, Connecticut's Long Island Sound program reduced more total nitrogen via trading than was needed to meet the TMDL requirement. Between 2002 and 2009, 15.5 million nitrogen credits were exchanged at a total value of $45.9 million. Cost savings through trading are estimated at $300 to $400 million. The credit price in 2002 was $1.65 and rose to $4.54 in 2009. As it turns out, however, the price is set by the state and trades go through the nitrogen credit exchange, so potential gains from trade resulting from allowance price fluctuations are not captured.

Source: Bennett, L. L., Thorpe, S. G., & Guse, A. J. (December 2000). Cost-effective control of nitrogen loadings in Long Island Sound. *Water Resources Research, 36*(12), 3711–3720; Kibler, V., & Kasturi, K. (2007). Status of water quality trading programs today. Katoomba Group's Ecosystem Marketplace. Retrieved from http://www.ecosystemmarketplace.com; Connecticut Department of Environmental Protection. (2010). Retrieved from http://www.ct.gov/dep/lib/dep/water/lis_water_quality/nitrogen_control_program/water_quality_trading_summary_2010.pdf

the required reduction. Important features of the trading ratio are the location of the sources, the distance between buyers and sellers, uncertainty if nonpoint source pollutants are involved and whether or not the pollutant is equivalent after discharge.[9] Complicated trading ratios may be one barrier to trade. Using the Upper Ohio River Basin as a case study, Farrow et al. (2005) demonstrate that social costs can be minimized if trading ratios are based on relative damages between sources. Of course, calculating the damages remains a challenge.

Water quality trading is also complicated by measurement and enforcement challenges (especially for nonpoint sources), abatement cost differentials, sufficient trading volumes, and trading flexibility (Fisher-Vanden & Olmstead, 2013). Where markets are thin (few traders) or when cost differentials are slight, there will be very few feasible trades. Large differences in marginal abatement costs can result in the largest gains from trade; the most significant gains are likely to come from point-nonpoint source trades. Lack of flexibility in trading over time and space has also inhibited water quality trading (Fisher-Vanden & Olmstead, 2013).

Water Quality, Watershed-Based Trading, and GIS.[10] Land use change (see Chapter 10) significantly affects watershed health. Agricultural and urban runoff into rivers, streams, and estuaries is the largest contributor to water pollution. Hascic and Wu (2006) use digital land use maps to examine the relationship between land use and water quality. They find that the levels of nutrient and conventional water pollutants are significantly affected by the amount of land in

---

[9]USEPA Water Quality Trading page, http://water.epa.gov/type/watersheds/trading/tradingfaq.cfm#11

[10]The US EPA maintains digital data by watershed with indicators of conventional ambient water quality, toxic ambient water quality, and other water-quality indicators. See http://www.epa.gov/surf

agriculture and urban development, while the level of toxic pollution is dependent on land in transportation or mining. Their results suggest that water quality trading programs should take into account land uses within the watershed as well as the overall watershed health.

Municipal Wastewater Treatment Subsidies

The second phase of the two-pronged water pollution control program involves subsidies for wastewater treatment plants. This program has run into problems as well, ranging from deficiencies in the allocation of the subsidies to the incentives created by the program.

The Allocation of Funds. Since the available funds were initially allocated on a first-come, first-served basis, it is not surprising that the funds were not spent in areas having the greatest impact. It was not uncommon, for example, for completed treatment plants to dump effluent that was significantly cleaner than the receiving water. Also, federal funds have traditionally been concentrated on smaller, largely suburban communities, rather than on the larger cities with the most serious pollution problems.

The 1977 amendments attempted to deal with this problem by requiring states to set priorities for funding treatment works, while giving the EPA the right, after holding public hearings, to not only veto a state's priority list but also to request a revised list. This tendency to ensure that the funds are allocated to the highest-priority projects was reinforced with the passage of the Municipal Wastewater Treatment Construction Grant Amendments of 1981. Under this act, states were required to establish project priorities for targeting funds to projects with the most significant water quality and public health consequences.

Operation and Maintenance. This approach subsidized the *construction* of treatment facilities but provided no incentive to *operate* them effectively. The existence of a municipal wastewater treatment plant does not by itself guarantee cleaner water. The EPA's annual inspection surveys of operating plants in 1976 and 1977 found only about half of the plants performing satisfactorily. Later surveys found that the general level of wastewater treatment performance had remained substantially unchanged from previous years.

When sewage treatment plants chronically or critically malfunction, the EPA may take a city to court to force compliance with either a direct order or a fine. Because of various constitutional legal barriers, it is very difficult to force a city to pay a fine to the federal treasury. Without an effective and credible sanction, the EPA is in a difficult position to deal with municipalities. Therefore, the end of the treatment-plant malfunction problem cannot yet be pronounced with any assurance.

Capital Costs. Due to the federal subsidies, local areas ended up paying only a fraction of the true cost of constructing these facilities. Since much of the money came from federal taxpayers, local communities had less incentive to hold construction costs down. The Congressional Budget Office (1985) estimated that substantially increasing the local share could reduce capital costs by as much as 30 percent. Local areas would be expected to be more careful with their own money.

Pretreatment Standards

To deal with untreatable hazardous wastes entering municipal wastewater treatment plants, the EPA has defined pretreatment standards regulating the quality of the wastewater flowing into the plants. These standards suffer the same deficiencies as other effluent standards; they are not cost-effective. The control over wastewater flows into treatment plants provides one more aspect of environmental policy where economic incentive approaches offer yet another unclaimed opportunity to achieve equivalent results at a lower cost.

Nonpoint Source Pollution

Nonpoint source pollution has become, in many areas, a significant part of the total problem. In some ways, the government has tried to compensate for this uneven coverage by placing more intensive controls on point sources. Is this emphasis efficient?

It could conceivably be justified on two grounds. If the marginal damages caused by nonpoint sources are significantly smaller than those of point sources, then a lower level of control could well be justified. Since in many cases, nonpoint source pollutants are not the same as point source pollutants, this is a logical possibility.

Or, if the costs of controlling nonpoint sources even to a small degree are very high, this could justify benign neglect as well. Are either of these conditions met in practice?

Costs. Research on economic incentives for nonpoint source pollution control is relatively new as cost information is relatively scarce. Some of the case-specific studies available, however, can give us a sense of the economic analysis. Most of the available studies focus on nonpoint source pollution from agriculture.

McCann and Easter (1999) measured the size of transaction costs associated with various agricultural nonpoint source pollution control policies. Transaction costs (the administrative costs associated with implementing a policy) are an important consideration for nonpoint source pollution control because monitoring costs tend to be much higher than for point sources. The net gain from implementing a policy is the abatement cost savings minus the transaction costs; if the transaction costs are too high, they can offset all or a major part of the abatement cost gains from implementing the policy.

McCann and Easter looked specifically at the Minnesota River, where severe water quality problems made the river "unswimmable, unfishable and uncanoeable" near the Twin Cities. Four policies aimed at reducing agricultural sources of phosphorus were considered: education about best management practices, a conservation tillage requirement, expansion of a program that obtained permanent development rights, and a tax on phosphorus fertilizers. They found that a tax on phosphorus fertilizers had the lowest transaction costs ($0.94 million). Educational programs had the second-lowest transaction costs at $3.11 million. Conservation tillage and expansion of the conservation easement program had the highest transaction costs at $7.85 million and $9.37 million, respectively. In terms of transaction costs, their results suggest a comparative advantage for input taxes relative to the other approaches. However, since the price elasticity of demand for phosphorus fertilizers is low (it has been estimated at between –0.25 and –0.29), a considerable tax increase would be needed to guarantee the desired level of water-quality improvements.

Schwabe (2001) examines various policy options for nonpoint source pollution control for the Neuse River in North Carolina. He compares cost-effectiveness of both the initial and final proposed rules considered by the State of North Carolina. In 1998, nutrient loads in the Neuse River basin were so high that the basin received a *nutrient sensitive waters* classification.[11] In the 2 years prior to his study, two large swine waste spills caused major algal blooms and killed 11 million fish. The State of North Carolina initially proposed a rule requiring all farms with land adjacent to a stream to install vegetative filter strips. This was compared to a uniform rollback that measured loadings by county with the objective of a 30 percent reduction in total nitrogen loadings. Using a least-cost mathematical programming model, Schwabe finds that the uniform rollback is the more cost-effective strategy, especially since the 30 percent reduction target would be unlikely to be met using the vegetative strips. However, the author notes that the dominance of the uniform strategy is specific to this particular setting and should not be taken as a general proposition.

The fact that point and nonpoint sources have received such different treatment from the EPA suggests the possibility that costs could be lowered by a more careful balancing of these control options. Point sources have received the most attention and have cleaned up considerably. Nonpoint sources have received very little attention. This suggests that perhaps the marginal cost of additional abatement for point sources is now significantly high that it justifies moving control toward nonpoint sources. Figure 18.3 portrays the current situation. The marginal cost of abatement of point sources is consistently lower than the marginal cost of abatement of nonpoint sources. However, consider a case in which point sources have already cleaned up 50 percent of their discharges. If nonpoint sources have not cleaned up any, then the marginal cost of the *next* unit of cleanup is actually *lower* for the nonpoint sources! Suppose the regulatory agency is seeking additional cleanup. Can you see how the total cost of this additional abatement would be less for the nonpoint source than the point source? The total cost for the point source of additional cleanup (or area defg) is less than the total cost for the same amount of clean up from the nonpoint source (oabc).

Such a scenario also offers an incentive for point source–nonpoint source trading. One situation like this happened in Colorado. An Industrial Economics, Inc. (1984) study of phosphorus control in the Dillon reservoir in Colorado provides empirical support that such point-nonpoint trading could be more cost-effective.

In this reservoir, four municipalities constitute the only point sources of phosphorus, while numerous uncontrolled nonpoint sources are in the area. The combined

[11]Nutrient sensitive waters are defined as waters subject to excessive plant growth and requiring limitations on nutrient inputs.

FIGURE 18.3 Potential Cost Savings with Trading across Point and Nonpoint Sources

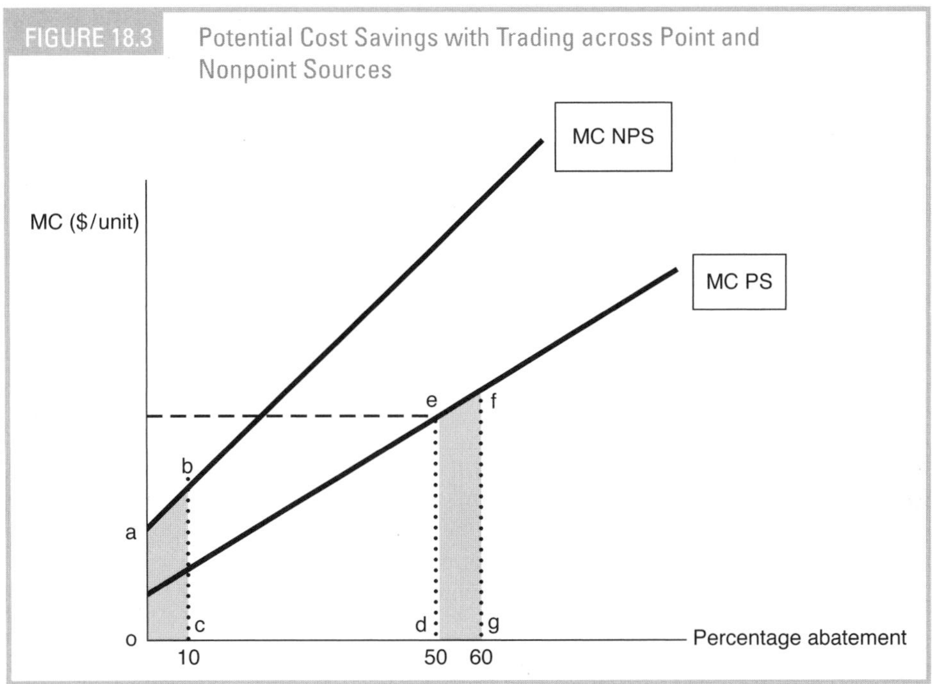

phosphorus load on the reservoir from point and nonpoint sources was projected to exceed its assimilative capacity.

The traditional way to rescue the projected phosphorus load would be to impose even more stringent controls on the point sources. The study found, however, that by following a balanced program controlling both point and nonpoint sources, the desired phosphorus target could be achieved at a cost of approximately $1 million a year less than would be spent if only point sources were controlled more stringently. The more general point to be carried away from this study is that as point sources are controlled to higher and higher degrees, rising marginal control costs will begin to make controlling nonpoint sources increasingly attractive. As the list of thirteen point–nonpoint trades in Table 18.3 demonstrates, we have apparently already reached that point.

Trades can sometimes achieve greater effluent reductions in addition to cost savings). Kibler and Kasturi (2007) describe one case for which reductions have actually been much greater than anticipated. When the Southern Minnesota Sugar Beet Industry needed to offset 6500 pounds of total phosphorus per year, they actually achieved 15,767 pounds per year reductions by trading. Does your state have a water pollutant trading program?

Atmospheric Deposition of Pollution

An additional complexity comes in the form of the nonpoint source pollution from the atmosphere that ends up in water bodies. Airborne pollutants, such as sulfur dioxide, mercury, and nitrogen, eventually find their way to rivers and lakes via atmospheric deposition. *Wet deposition* refers to pollutants that travel to the ground with rainfall. *Dry deposition* occurs when pollutants become too heavy and fall to the ground even in the absence of precipitation.

Debate 18.1 highlighted some of the issues surrounding one approach to dealing with air-borne deposition—fish consumption advisories due to mercury levels found in many fish. A quite different complication for water pollution control stems from a lack of coordination with air quality regulations. Simply put, they may or may not take into consideration the impacts of the air quality regulation on the soil (or in the water). The external benefits from air quality improvements are likely to be quite large. What does this suggest about the optimal level of air quality and the fact that air and water quality are controlled by separate offices within EPA?

The European Experience

Economic incentives have been important in water pollution control in Europe, where effluent charges play a prominent role in a number of countries. These charge systems take a number of forms. One common approach is illustrated by the former Republic of Czechoslovakia, which used charges to achieve predetermined ambient standards. Others, such as the former West Germany, used charges mainly to encourage firms to control more than their legal requirements. A third group, illustrated by Hungary and the former East Germany, shows how charge systems have been combined with effluent standards.

The former Republic of Czechoslovakia had used effluent charges to maintain water quality at predetermined levels for several decades. A basic charge is placed on BOD and suspended solids and complemented by a surcharge ranging from10 to 100 percent, depending upon the contribution of the individual discharge to ambient pollutant concentrations. The basic rates can be adjusted to reflect the quality of the receiving water. This system is conceptually very close to the ambient emissions charge system known to be cost-effective.

The charge system in the former West Germany was announced in 1976 and implemented in 1981. The level of charge is related to the degree of compliance with the standards. Firms failing to meet their required standards pay a charge on all actual emissions. If, according to the issued permit, federal emissions standards (which are separately defined for each industrial sector) are met, the charge is lowered to 50 percent of the base rate and is applied to the level of discharge implied by the minimum standard. If the firm can prove the discharge to be lower than 75 percent of minimum standards, one-half of the base rate is applied to the (lower) actual discharge level. The charge is waived for 3 years prior to the installation of new pollution control equipment promising further reductions of at least 20 percent. Revenues from the charges can be used by the administering authorities for administrative costs and financial assistance to public and private pollution abatement activities.

The approach used in Hungary and the former East Germany combines effluent charges with effluent standards. The charge is levied on discharges in excess of fixed effluent limits. In the Hungarian system, the level of the charge is based on the condition of the receiving waters, among other factors. Initially the Hungarian charges had little effect, but when the charge levels were raised, a flurry of wastewater treatment activity resulted.

Though these European approaches differ from one another and are not all cost-effective, their existence suggests that a variety of effluent charge systems are possible and practical. The German Council of Experts on Environmental Questions estimated the German effluent charge policy to be about one-third cheaper for the polluters as a group than an otherwise comparable uniform treatment policy. Furthermore, it encouraged firms to go beyond the uniform standards when it was cost-justified.

In a very different approach, Bystrom (1998) examines reducing nonpoint source nitrogen pollution by constructing wetlands in Sweden, where reducing nitrogen loads to the Baltic Sea is an important policy goal. Although it is well known that wetlands can help reduce nitrogen concentrations through the uptake of biomass, how cost-effective is this approach when it is compared to alternative, more traditional methods of control?

To answer this question, Bystrom estimates nonpoint source abatement costs for constructed wetlands and compares them to the costs of reducing nitrogen by means of land-use changes, such as the planting of fuel woods. This study finds that marginal abatement costs for wetlands are lower than transitioning to different crops, but still higher than the marginal costs of simply reducing the use of nitrogen fertilizer.

More recently, charges have been used in the Netherlands and in France for heavy metals and other discharges with revenues going toward water infrastructure (Olmstead, 2010).

Ireland was the first country to tax the use of plastic bags. Plastics pollution is a growing source of pollution, much of which ends up in the ocean. Example 18.2 examines the effect of the Irish bag levy.

Developing Country Experience

The move from command-and-control regulations to economic incentives for water pollution control has not seen as rapid a transition in developing countries. Several attempts to use discharge fees and marketable permits have failed. This may be due to lack of regulatory capacity—for example, lack of technical, political, and financial means to set up and monitor a fee or permit program effectively. Noncompliance and lack of infrastructure have hampered many programs. Example 18.3 explores Colombia's experience with a discharge fee program—one case deemed successful.

For developing countries, water pollution control is further complicated by poverty, lack of enforcement, and lack of technology. Deaths from waterborne diseases are much more frequent in developing countries. Of the 1.6 million deaths in 2003 attributed to water and sanitation, 90 percent were children under 5 and most were from developing countries. In 2004, 2331 deaths from cholera occurred in Africa. No deaths from cholera were recorded in the Americas. According to the World Health Organization, improved water supply reduces diarrhea morbidity by 6–25 percent, and improved sanitation reduces diarrhea morbidity by 32 percent.

EXAMPLE 18.2

The Irish Bag Levy

Rapid economic growth in Ireland in the 1990s was marked by a significant increase in the amount of solid waste per capita. The lack of adequate landfill sites resulted in escalating costs of waste disposal, which in turn led to more illegal dumping and littering. It was feared that tourism, one of Ireland's largest industries, would be negatively affected as a consequence of the degradation of the environment. The food industry, which based a significant amount of its marketing strategies on a healthy, wholesome reputation, also suffered as a result of the public perception of its role in the increased litter.

The most visible element of litter was plastic bags, so in 2002 the government introduced the Plastic Bag Environmental Levy on all plastic shopping bags (the" PlasTax"), with a few exceptions that were sanctioned for health and safety reasons. Retailers were charged a fee of 15 cents per plastic bag, which they were obliged, by the government, to pass on to the consumer. This levy was designed to alter consumer behavior by creating financial incentives for consumers to choose more environmentally friendly alternatives to plastic, such as "bags-for-life." (Bags-for-life are heavy-duty, reusable cloth or woven bags, which were made available in all supermarkets, at an average cost of €1.27.)

Expectations that this levy would bring about a 50 percent reduction in the number of plastic bags used were exceeded when the estimated actual reduction turned out to be 95 percent! In a single year, Irish consumers reduced their consumption of plastic bags from 1.26 billion to 120,000, while concurrently raising approximately €10 million in revenue for the government. Placed in the Environmental Fund, this revenue finances environmental initiatives such as recycling, waste management, and, most importantly, antilitter campaigns.

This levy has been viewed as a major success by the government and environmental groups alike. It has also been enthusiastically embraced by Irish consumers, thanks to an intensive environmental-awareness campaign that was launched in conjunction with the levy. Irish retailers, although skeptical in the beginning, have also recognized the huge benefits of this levy. Estimates suggest that their costs were offset by the savings from no longer providing disposable bags to customers free of charge, as well as the profit margin earned on the sale of "bags-for-life," whose sales have increased by 600–700 percent since the introduction of the levy. The amount of plastic being sent to Irish landfills has been dramatically reduced, bringing about a clear visual improvement. The success of this case has promoted the diffusion of this idea. For example, in 2008 China banned super thin plastic bags and imposed a fee on other plastic bags.

Source: Dungan, L. What were the effects of the plastic bag environmental levy on the litter problem in Ireland? Retrieved from http://www.colby.edu/~thtieten/litter.htm/

A study on the costs and benefits of meeting the United Nations Millennium Development Goal of halving the proportion of people without sustainable access to improved water supply and sanitation determined it would "definitely bring economic benefits, ranging from US$3 to US$34 per US dollar invested, depending on the region. Additional improvement of drinking water quality, such as

EXAMPLE 18.3

Economic Incentives for Water Pollution Control: The Case of Colombia

In 1997, Colombia experimented with a new nationwide program of pollution discharge fees. Polluters would be charged per unit of pollution emitted. Colombia has 33 regional environmental authorities (CARs) some of whom had discharge fees in place for 30 years. This was the first nationwide program.

This new program mandated that CARs would first collect and map out data on all discharging facilities that generated biological oxygen demand (BOD) and total suspended solids (TSS). They were then to set 5-year reduction goals for aggregate discharge in each basin and charge a fee per unit of BOD and TSS. The ministry set a minimum fee, but CARs could adjust this fee upward every 6 months if reduction targets were not being met.

The program ran into several problems, including uneven levels of implementation across CARs, incomplete coverage of dischargers, and widespread noncompliance by municipal sewage authorities. Between the start of the program in 1997 and 2003, municipal sewage authorities were assessed over 30 percent of all discharge fees, but only paid 40 percent of what they were charged. Given that some CARs were raising fees based on meeting reduction targets, noncompliance by one group of dischargers was responsible for large rate hikes for others.

Was the Colombia program thus unsuccessful? Surprisingly, evidence actually suggests it was successful! In a number of basins, discharges dropped significantly between 1997 and 2003. BOD discharge from point sources in the program dropped by 27 percent and TSS discharges fell by 45 percent.

One suggested reason for the apparent success of the program is that previously lacking enforcement had to be improved simply to set up a discharge program. Collecting information on discharge amounts and locations is also a necessary component for successful implementation. Increased transparency over command-and-control programs contributed to the program's success.

The author of this study suggests that one of the most important components of a successful program is adequate infrastructure.

Source: Blackman, A. (Spring 2006). Economic incentives to control water pollution in developing countries: How well has Colombia's wastewater discharge fee program worked and why? *Resources*, 20–23.

point-of-use disinfection, in addition to access to improved water and sanitation would lead to benefits ranging from US$5 to US$60 per US dollar invested" (Hutton & Haller, 2004).

China has implemented a different approach to enforcement than the type of sanction commonly used in the United States and Canada. China imposes a graduated pollution levy where the per-unit fine rises with the level of noncompliance (Wang & Wheeler, 2005). China also relies on self-reporting. Wang and Wheeler examine data from 3000 Chinese factories and estimate a model that incorporates the joint determination of levy and emissions. They show that progressive penalties, combined with self-reporting, is a significant deterrent. Regional variation in local enforcement, however, is a factor and inhibits universal compliance.

Oil Spills from Tankers

One of the chief characteristics of the current approach to oil spills is that it depends heavily on the ability of the legal system to internalize the costs of a spill through liability law. In principle, the approach is straightforward. Consider how liability for spills might affect the incentives for a tanker fleet. Forcing the owner of a vessel to pay for the costs of cleaning up the spill, including compensation for natural resource damages, creates a powerful incentive to exercise care. But is the outcome likely to be efficient in practice?

One problem with legal remedies is their high administrative cost; assigning the appropriate penalties is no trivial matter. Even if the court were able to act expeditiously, the doctrines it imposes are not necessarily efficient since the financial liability for cleaning up spills is limited by statute. This point is demonstrated in Figure 18.4, which depicts the incentives of a vessel owner to take precautions. The owner will minimize costs by choosing the level of precaution that equates the marginal cost of additional precaution, with the resulting reduction in the marginal expected penalty. The marginal reduction in expected penalty is a function of two factors: the likelihood of a spill and the magnitude of financial obligation it would trigger. This function slopes downward because larger amounts of precaution are presumed to yield smaller marginal reductions in both the likelihood and magnitude of resulting accidents.

The vessel owner's cost-minimizing choice with unlimited liability is shown as Q^*. As long as the imposed penalty equaled the actual damage and the probability of having to pay the damage once an accident occurred was 1.0, this outcome would normally be efficient. The external costs would be internalized. The owner's private costs would be minimized by taking all possible cost-justified precaution measures to reduce both the likelihood and the seriousness of any resulting spill; taking precautions would simply be cheaper than paying for the cleanup.

FIGURE 18.4 Oil Spill Liability

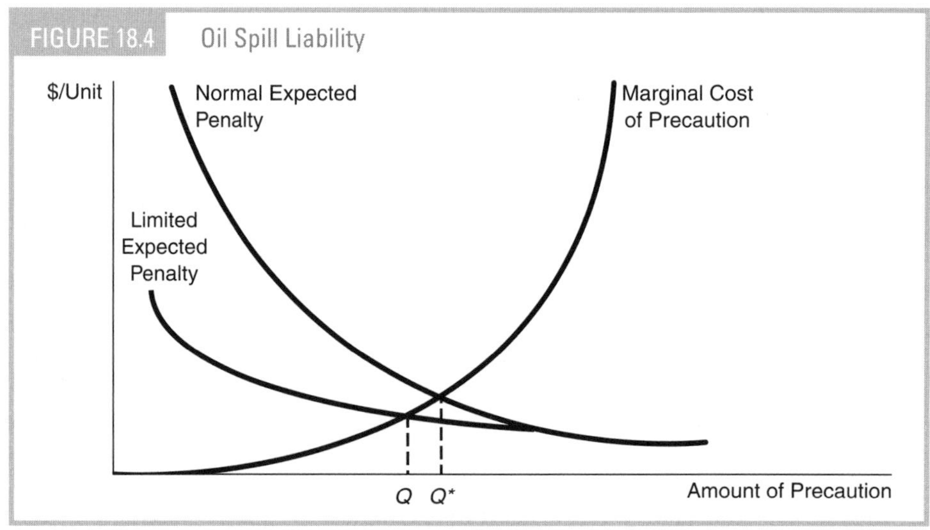

Limited liability, however, produces a different outcome. With limited liability, the expected penalty function rotates inward for levels of precaution lower than that level that would produce an accident resulting in damages exactly equal to the limit.[12] Lower levels of precaution imply damages that exceed the limit, but the vessel owner would not have to pay anything above the limit. (The only benefit to the vessel owner faced with limited liability of increasing precaution at lower levels of precaution is the reduction in the likelihood of a spill; in this range, increasing precaution does not reduce the magnitude of the financial payment should a spill occur.) The deviation in the magnitude of the limited expected penalty function from the normal expected penalty function is greatest at lower levels of precaution; it declines to zero at that precaution level where the expected magnitude of an accident is equal to the liability limit.

What is the effect of limited liability on the vessel owner's choice of precaution levels? As long as the liability limit is binding (which appears to routinely be the case with recent spills), the owner will choose too little precaution. (The owner's choice is shown as Q in Figure 18.3.) Both the number and magnitude of resulting spills would be inefficiently large.[13]

Garza-Gil et al. (2006) estimate the economic losses from the *Prestige* oil spill off the Spanish city of Galicia. Ultimately 63,000 tons were spilled (Table 18.1) and the tanker sank. This spill was considered one of the worst tanker spills due not only to the size of the spill but also to the "black tides" caused by the spill in valuable tourist regions of Northern Spain and Southern France. Garza-Gil et al. consider short-term (immediately following the spill) damages to the fishing industry and the tourism sector and find losses of almost 200 million euros. Including cleanup and restoration costs brings the total to 762 million euros. They were not able to include lost recreation opportunities or passive use-value losses. The current international liability framework does not allow for the inclusion of these values. (Recall the importance of these for the *Exxon Valdez* damage estimates discussed in Chapter 4.) What effect would omitting these values be expected to have on the incentives for risk-aversion by tanker owners?

An Overall Assessment

Although the benefit estimates from water pollution control are subject to much uncertainty, they do exist. While being careful not to place too much reliance on them, we can see what information can be gleaned from the studies in existence.

One early study concluded that the net benefits from water pollution control policy were positive but were likely to become negative as costs escalate in the future. Relying on benefits estimates derived from contingent valuation, Carson and Mitchell (1993) estimate that aggregate benefits from water pollution control

---

[12] To avoid confusion, note that the marginal expected penalty for additional precaution when the damage would exceed the liability limit is not zero. While further precaution does not lower the ultimate penalty in this range, it does lower the likelihood of an accident and, hence, the expected penalty.

[13] Suppose, at the efficient level of precaution, the magnitude of a resulting spill was less than the liability limit. How would this be depicted graphically? Would you expect the vessel owner's choice to be efficient?

in 1990 exceeded aggregate costs by $6.4 billion. They also found, however, that projected aggregate costs would exceed projected aggregate benefits because of the high marginal costs and the low marginal benefits associated with bringing the remaining bodies of water up to swimmable quality.

Griffiths and Wheeler (2005) summarize the costs and benefits of the most economically significant[14] water quality rules that are subject to benefit-cost analysis. For the five rules that relate to surface water, they find that two of them do not pass a benefit-cost analysis and for the other three, the range of benefits estimates bounds the costs. They point out that policies do not necessarily have to pass a benefit-cost test to be adopted; benefit-cost calculations are simply one source of information for the decision-making process.

Using cost-effective policies rather than the current approach, it would be possible to reduce costs substantially, without affecting the benefits. Cost-effectiveness would require the development of better strategies for point source control and for achieving a better balance between point and nonpoint source control. The resulting reduction in costs probably would allow net benefits to remain positive even with the more stringent control levels envisioned for the future. Even positive net benefits would not necessarily make the policy efficient, however, because the level of control might still be too high or too low (meaning the present value of net benefits would not have been maximized). Unfortunately, the evidence is not rich enough to prove whether the overall level of control maximizes the net benefit.

In addition to promoting current cost-effectiveness, economic incentive approaches would stimulate and facilitate change better than a system of rigid, technology-based standards. Russell (1981) assessed the importance of the facilitating role by simulating the effects on the allocation of pollution-control responsibility in response to regional economic growth, changing technology, and changing product mix. Focusing on the steel, paper, and petroleum-refining industries in the 11-county Delaware Estuary Region, his study estimated the change in permit use for three water pollutants (BOD, total suspended solids, and ammonia) that would have resulted if a marketable permit system were in place over the 1940–1978 period. The calculations assume that the plants existing in 1940 would have been allocated permits to legitimize their emissions at that time, that new sources would have had to purchase permits, and that plant shutdowns or contractions would free up permits for others to purchase.

This study found that for almost every decade and pollutant, a substantial number of permits would have been made available by plant closing, capacity contractions, product-mix changes, and/or by the availability of new technologies. In the absence of a marketable permit program, a control authority would not only have to keep abreast of all technological developments so emissions standards could be adjusted accordingly, but it would also have to ensure an overall balance between effluent increases and decreases so as to preserve water quality. This tough assignment is handled completely by the market in a tradable permit

---

[14]Defined as rules with an economic impact of more than $100 million.

system, thereby facilitating the evolution of the economy by responding flexibly and predictably to change.

Tradable effluent permits encourage, as well as facilitate, this evolution. Since permits have value, in order to minimize costs, firms must continually be looking for new opportunities to control emissions at lower cost. This search eventually results in the adoption of new technologies and in the initiation of changes in the product mix that result in lower amounts of emissions. The pressure on sources to continually search for better ways to control pollution is a distinct advantage that economic incentive systems have over bureaucratically defined standards.

Summary

Historically, policies for controlling water pollution have been concerned with conventional pollutants discharged into surface waters. More recently, concerns have shifted toward toxic pollutants, which apparently are more prevalent than previously believed; toward groundwater, which traditionally was thought to be an invulnerable pristine resource; and toward the oceans, which were mistakenly considered immune from most pollution problems because of their vast size.

Early attempts at controlling water pollution followed a path similar to that of air pollution control. Legislation prior to the 1970s had little impact on the problem. Frustration then led to the enactment of a tough federal law that was so ambitious and unrealistic that little progress resulted.

There the similarity ends. Whereas in air pollution a wave of recent reforms have improved the process by making it more cost-effective, little parallel exists for control of water pollution. Policy toward cleaning up rivers and lakes was based upon the subsidization of municipal waste-treatment facilities and national effluent standards imposed on industrial sources.

The former approach has been hampered by delays, by problems in allocating funds, and by the fact that about half of the constructed plants are not performing satisfactorily. The latter approach has given rise to delays and to the need to define the standards in a series of court suits. In addition, effluent standards have assigned the control responsibility among point sources in a way that excessively raises cost. Nonpoint pollution sources have, until recently, been virtually ignored. Technological progress is inhibited, rather than stimulated, by the current approach.

This lack of progress could have been avoided. It did not result from a lack of toughness. Rather, it has resulted from a reliance on direct regulation, rather than on emissions charges or tradable effluent permits, which are more flexible and cost-effective in both the dynamic and static sense. Recognizing this deficiency, watershed-based now trading programs are now gaining attention.

The court system has assumed most of the responsibility for controlling oil spills. Those responsible for the spills are assessed the financial liability for cleaning up the site and compensating for any resulting damages to natural resources. While in principle this approach can be efficient, in practice it has been hampered by liability limitations and the huge administrative burden an oil spill trial entails.

Discussion Questions

1. "The only permanent solution to water pollution control will occur when all production by-products are routinely recycled. The zero-discharge goal recognizes this reality and forces all dischargers to work steadily toward this solution. Less stringent policies are at best temporary palliatives." Discuss.
2. "In exercising its responsibility to protect the nation's drinking water, the government needs to intervene only in the case of public-water supplies. Private-water supplies will be adequately protected without any government intervention." Discuss.

Self-Test Exercises

1. Consider the situation posed in Problem 1(a) in Chapter 14.
   a. Compute the allocation that would result if 10 tradable effluent permits were given to the second source and 9 were given to the first source. What would be the market permit price? How many permits would each source end up with after trading? What would the net permit expenditure be for each source after trading?
   b. Suppose a new source entered the area with a constant marginal cost of control equal to $1,600 per unit of emission reduced. Assume further that it would add 10 units in the absence of any control. What would be the resulting allocation of control responsibility if the cap of only 19 total units of effluent allowed were retained? How much would each firm clean up? What would happen to the permit price? What trades would take place?
2. Suppose you have three production facilities that are polluting a river. Each emits 10 units of pollution. Their marginal cost functions for reducing emissions are, respectively, $MC_1 = \$3, MC_2 = \$4$, and $MC_3 = \$5$.
   a. If the objective is to cut emissions in half (to 15) cost-effectively, how much reduction should be assigned to each firm?
   b. What would be the total variable cost of controlling these emissions?
   c. What would be the total variable cost that would result from forcing each facility to control one-half of its emissions? Is this different from the cost associated with the cost-effective allocation? Why or why not?

Further Reading

Brouwer, R., & Pearce, E. (Eds.). (2005). *Cost benefit analysis and water resources management.* Cheltenham, UK: Edward Elgar. A collection of benefit/cost analyses case studies for water pollution control projects, flood control, and water allocation. Most of the cases occurred in Europe.

Fisher-Vanden, K., & Olmstead, S. (Winter 2013). Moving pollution trading from air to water: Potential problems and prognosis. *Journal of Economic Perspectives*, *27*(1),147–172. An analysis of water quality trading programs to date and the challenges that remain to implementing water quality trading.

Ohmstead, S. M. (Winter 2010). The economics of water quality trading. *Review of Environmental Economics and Policy*, *4*(1), 44–62. A thorough review of the literature on the economics of water quality.

Selman, M., Greenhalgh, S., Branosky, E., Jones, C., & Guiling, J. (March 2009). Water quality trading programs: An international overview. *WRI Issue Brief*, *1*. WRI (World Resources Institute). An overview and analysis of 57 water quality trading programs worldwide.

Additional References and Historically Significant References are available on this book's Companion Website: http://www.routledgetextbooks.com/textbooks/9780133479690

19 Toxic Substances and Environmental Justice

The fact that a problem will certainly take a long time to solve, and that it will demand the attention of many minds for several generations, is no justification for postponing the study. . . . Our difficulties of the moment must always be dealt with somehow, but our permanent difficulties are difficulties of every moment.

—T. S. Eliot, *Christianity and Culture* (1949)

Introduction

It is one of the ironies of history that the place that focused public attention in the United States on toxic substances is called the Love Canal. *Love* is not a word any impartial observer would choose to describe the relationships among the parties to that incident.

The Love Canal typifies in many ways the dilemma posed by toxic substances. Until 1953, Hooker Electrochemical (subsequently Hooker Chemical, a subsidiary of Occidental Petroleum Corporation) dumped waste chemicals into an old abandoned waterway known as the Love Canal, near Niagara Falls, New York. (Hooker was acquired by Occidental Petroleum in 1968.) At the time it seemed a reasonable solution, since the chemicals were buried in what was then considered to be impermeable clay.

In 1953, Hooker deeded the Love Canal property for $1 to the Niagara Falls Board of Education, which then built an elementary school on the site. The deed specifically excused Hooker from any damages that might be caused by the chemicals. Residential development of the area around the school soon followed.

The site became the center of controversy when, in 1978, residents complained of chemicals leaking to the surface. News reports emanating from the area included stories of spontaneous fires and vapors in basements. Medical reports suggested that the residents had experienced abnormally high rates of miscarriage, birth defects, and liver disease.

Similar contamination experiences befell Europe and Asia. In 1976, an accident at an F. Hoffmann-La Roche & Co. plant in Sevesco spewed dioxin over the Italian countryside. Subsequently, explosions in a Union Carbide plant in Bhopal, India, spread deadly gases over nearby residential neighborhoods with significant loss of life, and water used to quell a warehouse fire at a Sandoz warehouse near Basel, Switzerland, carried an estimated 30 tons of toxic chemicals into the Rhine River, a source of drinking water for several towns in Germany. In 2010, an explosion and fire at the BP/*Deepwater Horizon* drilling rig off Louisiana's coast in the Gulf of Mexico killed 11 people and ruptured an underwater pipe that caused a massive oil spill.

In previous chapters, we touched on a few of the policy instruments used to combat toxic substance problems. Emissions standards govern the types and amounts of substances that can be injected into the air. Effluent standards regulate what can be discharged directly into water sources, and pretreatment standards control the flow of toxics into wastewater treatment plants. Maximum concentration levels have been established for many substances in drinking water.

This impressive array of policies is not sufficient to resolve the Love Canal problem or others having similar characteristics. When violations of the standards for drinking water are detected, for example, the water is already contaminated. Specifying maximum contaminant levels helps to identify when a problem exists, but it does nothing to prevent or contain the problem. The various standards for air and water emissions that do protect against *point* sources do little to prevent contamination by *nonpoint* sources. Furthermore, most waterborne toxic pollutants are stock pollutants, not fund pollutants; they cannot be absorbed by the receiving waters. Therefore, temporally constant controls on emissions (a traditional method used for fund pollutants) are inappropriate for these toxic substances since they would allow a steady rise in the concentration over time. Finally controlling accidental discharges may require a rather different set of policies. Some additional form of control is necessary.

In this chapter, we describe and evaluate the main policies that deal specifically with the creation, use, transportation, and disposal of toxic substances and how those policies affect environmental justice. Many dimensions will be considered: what are appropriate ways to dispose of toxic substances? How can the government ensure that all waste is appropriately disposed of in a way that does not disproportionately disadvantage some socioeconomic groups? How do we prevent surreptitious dumping? Who should clean up old sites and how should the cleanup be financed? Should victims be compensated for damages caused by toxic substances under the control of someone else? If so, by whom? What are the appropriate roles for the legislature and the judiciary in creating the proper set of incentives?

Nature of Toxic Substance Pollution

A main objective of the current legal system for controlling toxic substances is to protect human health, although protecting other forms of life is a secondary objective. The potential health danger depends upon the toxicity of a substance to humans and their exposure to the substance. *Toxicity* occurs when a living organism experiences detrimental effects following exposure to a substance. In normal concentrations, most chemicals are not toxic. Others, such as pesticides, are toxic by design. Yet, in excess concentrations, even a benign substance such as table salt can be toxic.

While a degree of risk is involved when using any chemical substance, there are benefits as well. The task for public policy is to define an acceptable risk by balancing the costs and benefits of controlling the use of chemical substances.

Health Effects

Two main health concerns associated with toxic substances are risk of cancer and effects on reproduction.

Cancer. While many suspect the mortality rate for cancer may be related to increased exposure to carcinogens, proving or disproving this link is very difficult due to the latency of the disease. *Latency* refers to the state of being concealed during the period between exposure to the carcinogen and the detection of cancer. Latency periods for cancer run from 15 to 40 years, and have been known to run as long as 75 years.

In the United States, part of the increase in cancer has been convincingly linked to smoking, particularly among women. As the proportion of women who smoke has increased, the incidence of lung cancer has increased as well. Smoking does not account for all of the increase in cancer, however.

Although it is not entirely clear what other agents may be responsible, one suggested cause is the rise in the manufacture and use of synthetic chemicals since World War II. A number of these chemicals have been shown in the laboratory to be carcinogenic. That evidence is not necessarily sufficient to implicate them in the rise of cancer, however, because it does not take exposure into account. The laboratory can reveal, through animal tests, the relationship between dosage and resulting effects. To track down the significance of any chemical in causing cancer in the general population would require an estimate of how many people were exposed to specific doses. Currently, our data are not extensive enough to allow these kinds of calculations to be done with any confidence.

Reproductive Effects. Tracing the influence of environmental effects on human reproduction is still a new science. A growing body of scientific evidence, however, suggests that exposure to smoking, alcohol, and chemicals known as endocrine disruptors may contribute to infertility, may affect the viability of the fetus and the health of the infant after birth, and may cause genetic defects that can be passed on for generations.

Problems exist for both men and women. In men, exposure to toxic substances has resulted in lower sperm counts, malformed sperm, and genetic damage. In women, exposure can also result in sterility or birth defects in their children.

Policy Issues

Many aspects of the toxic substance problem make it difficult to resolve. Three important aspects that add to this difficulty are the number of substances involved, latency, and uncertainty.

Number of Substances. Of the tens of millions of known chemical compounds, approximately 100,000 are actively used in commerce. Many exhibit little or no toxicity, and even a very toxic substance represents little risk as long as it is isolated. The trick is to identify problem substances and to design appropriate policies as responses. The massive number of substances involved makes that a difficult assignment.

Latency. The period of latency exhibited by many of these relationships compounds the problem. Two kinds of toxicity are exhibited: acute and chronic. *Acute toxicity* is present when a short-term exposure to the substance produces a detrimental effect on the exposed organisms. *Chronic toxicity* is present when the detrimental effect arises from exposure of a continued or prolonged nature.

The process of screening chemicals as potentially serious causes of chronic illness is even more complicated than that of screening for acute illness. The traditional technique for determining acute toxicity is the lethal-dose determination, a relatively quick test performed on animals that calculates the dose that results in the death of 50 percent of the animal population. This test is less well suited for screening substances that exhibit chronic toxicity.

The appropriate tests for discovering chronic toxicity typically have involved subjecting animal populations to sustained low-level doses of the substance over an extended period of time. These tests are very expensive and time consuming. If the EPA were to perform these tests, given its limited resources, it could only test a few of the estimated 700 new chemicals introduced each year. If the industries were to do the tests, the expense could preclude the introduction of many potentially valuable new chemicals that have limited, specialized markets.

Uncertainty. Another dilemma inhibiting policy makers is the uncertainty surrounding the scientific evidence on which regulation is based. Effects uncovered by laboratory studies on animals are not perfectly correlated with effects on humans. Large doses administered over a 3-year period may not produce the same effects as an equivalent amount spread over a 20-year period. Some of the effects are *synergistic*—that is, their effects are intensified or diminished by the presence of other variable factors. (Asbestos workers are 30 times more likely than their nonsmoking fellow workers to get lung cancer if they smoke, for example.) Once cancer is detected, in most cases it does not bear the imprint of a particular source. Policy makers have to act in the face of limited information (see Example 19.1).

From an economic point of view, how the policy process reacts to this dilemma should depend on how well the market handles toxic substance problems. To the extent that the market generates the correct information and provides the

EXAMPLE 19.1

The Arduous Path to Managing Risk: Bisphenol A

One example of a potentially toxic substance that is working its way through the government regulatory bureaucracy is Bisphenol A (BPA). The food industry uses more than 6 billion pounds of BPA every year to make the resins that line food cans and the polycarbonate plastics used to make baby bottles and many other products. The Centers for Disease Control and Prevention (CDC) says that 95 percent of us carry measurable amounts of BPA in our blood.

In April 2008, the National Toxicology Program (NTP) at the National Institutes of Health (NIH) expressed some concern that exposure to BPA during pregnancy and childhood could impact the developing breast and prostate, hasten puberty, and affect behavior in American children. Not long after those concerns were expressed, the Canadian government moved to ban polycarbonate infant bottles containing BPA, the most popular type of bottle on the market.

Despite the absence of any such ruling from the US government, after the Canadian move the US market reacted. Major BPA manufacturers, including Playtex (which makes bottles and cups) and Nalgene, which makes portable water bottles, announced a shift to BPA-free products. Major retailers, including Walmart and Toys "R" Us, announced they would quickly phase out BPA-containing baby bottles.

In January 2010, the US Food and Drug Administration (FDA), which had previously found BPA to be safe, announced, "On the basis of results from recent studies using novel approaches to test for subtle effects, both the National Toxicology Program at the National Institutes of Health and FDA have some concern about the potential effects of BPA on the brain, behavior, and prostate gland in fetuses, infants, and young children. In cooperation with the National Toxicology Program, FDA's National Center for Toxicological Research is carrying out in-depth studies to answer key questions and clarify uncertainties about the risks of BPA."

Interestingly, while the federal government continued to study the problem, some states moved ahead with regulation. In April 2010, Maryland became the fifth state to ban the use of BPA in children's products, including baby bottles and sippy cups. In July 2012, the *Food and Drug Administration* followed suit and ruled that baby bottles and children's drinking cups could no longer contain BPA.

How this risk was handled in the United States is especially noteworthy in that both the market and the states reacted well before federal regulation was in place, but the federal government did ultimately follow their lead.

Sources: The National Institutes of Health Website. Retrieved May 23, 2013, from http://www.niehs.nih.gov/health/topics/agents/sya-bpa/; Food and Drug Administration Website. Retrieved May 23, 2013, from http://www.fda.gov/NewsEvents/PublicHealthFocus/ucm064437.htm; Environmental Working Group Website. Retrieved May 23, 2013, from http://www.ewg.org/bpa/

appropriate incentives, policy may not be needed. On the other hand, when the government can best generate information or create the appropriate incentive, intervention may be called for. As the following sections demonstrate, the nature and the form of the most appropriate policy response may depend crucially on how the toxic source and the affected party or parties are related.

Market Allocations and Toxic Substances

Toxic substance contamination can arise in a variety of settings. In order to define the efficient policy response, we must examine what responses would be forthcoming in the normal operation of the market. Let's look at three possible relationships between the source of the contamination and the victim: employer–employee, producer–consumer, and producer–third party. The first two involve normal contractual relations among the parties, while the latter involves noncontracting parties, whose connection is defined solely by the contamination.

Occupational Hazards

Many occupations involve risk, including, for some people, exposure to toxic substances. Do employers and employees have sufficient incentives to act in concert toward achieving safety in the workplace?

The caricature of the market used by the most ardent proponents of regulation suggests not. In this view, the employer's desire to maximize profits precludes spending enough money on safety. Sick workers can simply be replaced. Therefore, the workers are powerless to do anything about it; if they complain, they are fired and replaced with others who are less vocal.

The most ardent opponents of regulation respond that this caricature overlooks or purposefully ignores significant market pressures, such as employee incentives and the feedback effects of those incentives on employers. When the full story that includes these pressures is considered, regulation may be unnecessary or even counterproductive.

According to this market incentives worldview, employees will only accept work in a potentially hazardous environment if appropriately compensated for taking that risk. Riskier occupations should call forth higher wages. The increase in wages should be sufficient to compensate them for the increased risk; otherwise they will work elsewhere. These higher wages represent a real cost of the hazardous situation to the employer. They also produce an incentive to create a safer work environment, since greater safety would result in a lower risk premium and, hence, lower wages. One cost could be balanced against the other. What was spent on safety could be recovered in lower wages (see Figure 19.1).

The first type of cost, the marginal increase in wages, is drawn to reflect the fact that the lower the level of precaution, the higher the wage bill. Two such curves are drawn to reflect high-exposure and low-exposure situations. The high-exposure case assumes larger numbers of workers are exposed than in the low-exposure case. The low-exposure cost curve rises more slowly because the situation is less dangerous at the margin.

The second type of curve, the marginal cost of providing precaution, reflects an increasing marginal cost. The two different curves depict different production situations. A firm with a few expensive precautionary options will face a steeply sloped marginal cost curve, while a firm with many cheaper options will face a lower marginal cost at every comparable degree of precaution chosen.

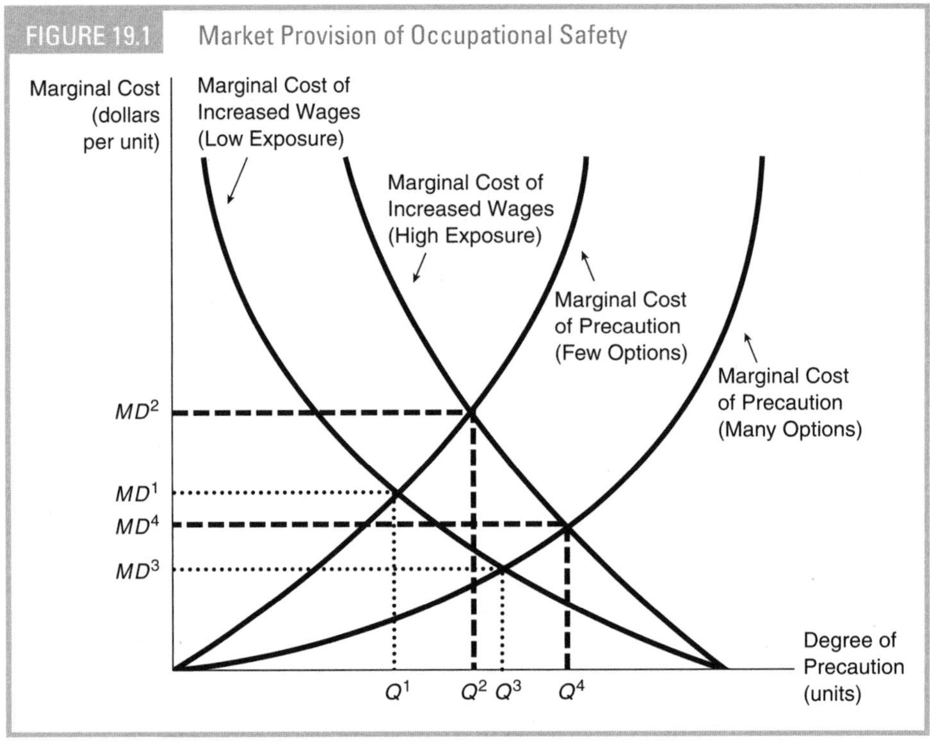

The graph depicts four possible outcomes—one for each possible combination of these four marginal cost curves. Note that very different choices will be made, depending on the circumstances. Also note that the level of risk chosen (as indicated by the marginal damage, labeled *MD*) and the degree of precaution are not perfectly correlated. The highest marginal risk is MD^2, but the associated level of precaution (Q^2) is not the largest. The reason, of course, is that the cost of taking precautions matters, and sometimes it is cheaper to accept the risk and compensate for it than it is to prevent it.

Because the marginal increased wages curve accurately reflects marginal damages (since the higher wages are demanded by workers to compensate them for damages), these market equilibria are also efficient. Thus, the efficient resolution of the occupational hazards problem varies not only from substance to substance, but also from plant to plant. As long as this stylized view of the world is correct, the market will tailor the appropriate degree of precaution to the situation.

Proponents of this view point out that this allocation would also allow more choices for workers than would, for example, a system requiring all workplaces to be equally safe. With varying occupational risk, those occupations with more risk (such as working to clean up toxic spills) would attract people who were less averse to risk. These workers would receive higher-than-average wages (to compensate them for the increased risk), but paying these higher wages would be cheaper to the firm (and hence, consumers) than requiring every workplace to meet the same risk standard. The risk-averse workers would be free to choose less risky occupations.

Do wages actually reflect risk? Existing empirical studies make clear that wages in risky occupations in countries like the United States do contain a risk premium (Viscusi & Aldy, 2003). Two conclusions about these risk premiums seem clear from these studies: (1) the willingness to pay for apparently similar risk reductions varies significantly across individuals, and (2) the revealed willingness to pay for risk reduction is substantial.

In those cases where wages accurately reflect risk is there any appropriate role for the government in controlling contamination in the workplace? Perhaps. The efficient solution may not always be considered the most ethical solution, a point that has been addressed in the courts. For example, if the employee is a pregnant woman and the occupational hazard involves potential damage to the fetus, does the expectant mother have the right to risk the unborn child, or is some added protection for the fetus needed? Furthermore, if the lowest-cost solution is to ban pregnant, or even fertile, women from a workplace that poses a risk to a fetus, is that an acceptable solution, or is it unfair discrimination against women? As Example 19.2 suggests, these are not idle concerns.

Ethical concerns are not the only challenges for market solutions. Wages may not reflect the actual risk. The ability of the worker to respond to a hazardous situation depends on his or her knowledge of the seriousness of the danger. With toxic substances, that knowledge is likely to be incomplete in general, but completely inadequate in settings such as developing countries. Consequently, the marginal increased wages function may be artificially rotated toward the origin. In this case, the employer would choose too little precaution and the market will not provide sufficient pressure to rectify this worker hazard. By having access to the health records of all employees, the employer could potentially be in the best position to assess the degree of risk posed, but the employer also has an incentive to suppress that information since publicizing the risk would mean demands for higher compensatory wages and possible lawsuits.

Information on the dangers posed by exposure to a particular toxic substance is a public good to employees; each employee has an incentive to be a free rider on the discoveries of others. Individual employees do not have an incentive to bear the cost of doing the necessary research to uncover the degree of risk. Thus, it seems neither employers nor employees can be expected to produce the efficient amount of information on the magnitude of risk.[1]

As a result, the government may play a substantial role in setting the boundaries on ethical responses, in stimulating research on the nature of hazards, and in providing for the dissemination of information to affected parties. It does not necessarily follow, however, that the government should be responsible for determining the level

---

[1]Unions would be expected to produce more efficient information flows since they represent many workers and can take advantage of economies of scale in the collection, interpretation, and dissemination of risk information. Available evidence suggests that the preponderance of wage premiums for risk has been derived from data involving unionized workers.

EXAMPLE 19.2

Susceptible Populations in the Hazardous Workplace

Some employees are especially susceptible to occupational hazards. Pregnant women and women in the childbearing years are particularly vulnerable. When an employer attempts to manage a work situation that poses a hazardous threat, either the susceptible population can be separated from the hazard or the hazard can be controlled to a sufficient level that its risk is acceptable to even the most susceptible employees.

The economic aspects of this choice are easily deduced from Figure 19.1. Suppose that the firm has few control options and is on the uppermost of the two marginal cost of precaution curves. By removing the susceptible population, it could face the low-exposure curve. Removal of the susceptible population results in lower marginal risk to the workers, lower costs to the firm, and less precaution taken. But is it fair to those who are removed from their jobs?

This issue came to a head in 1978 when American Cyanamid decided to respond to an occupational risk by banning all fertile women from jobs in the section manufacturing lead chromate pigment at Willow Island, West Virginia. After reviewing the decision, the Occupational Safety and Health Administration (OSHA) cited the company under the general duty clause of the Occupational Safety and Health Act, which requires an employer to provide a workplace free of hazards, and fined it $10,000. That was not the end of the story. In early 1980, the Oil, Chemical, and Atomic Workers Union sued the company under the 1964 Civil Rights Act on the grounds that the company had discriminated unfairly against women. In March 1991, the Supreme Court ruled that banning fertile women from any workplace posing a risk to a fetus was not an acceptable way to control risk. The workplace must be made safe for all.

Source: *International Union v. Johnson Controls,* 499 U.S. 187 (1991).

of safety in the workplace once this information is available and the ethical boundaries are determined. For situations that are sufficiently dangerous that no rational worker would voluntarily choose to work there, the role of the government would be to set and enforce a safety threshold.

This analysis suggesting that the market will not provide an efficient level of information on occupational risk is consistent with the enactment of "right-to-know" laws in several states. These laws require businesses to disclose to their employees and to the public any potential health hazards associated with toxic substances used on the job. Generally employers are required to (1) label toxic substance containers, (2) inventory all toxic substances used in the workplace, and (3) provide adequate training on the handling of these substances to all affected employees. Significantly, proponents of these laws suggest that the targets are not the large chemical companies, which generally have excellent disclosure programs, but the smaller, largely nonunion plants.

Product Safety

Exposure to a hazardous or potentially hazardous substance can also occur as a result of using a product, as when eating food containing chemical additives. Does the market efficiently supply safe products?

One view holds that the market pressures on both parties (consumers and producers) are sufficient to yield an efficient level of safety. Safer products are generally more expensive to produce and carry a higher price tag. If consumers feel that the additional safety justifies the cost, they will purchase the safer product. Otherwise they won't. Producers supplying excessively risky products will find their market drying up, because consumers will switch to competing brands that are safer, despite their higher price. Similarly, producers selling excessively safe products (meaning they eliminate, at great cost, risks consumers are perfectly willing to take in return for a lower purchase price) find their markets drying up as well. Consumers will choose the cheaper, riskier product.

This theory also suggests that the market will not (and should not) yield a uniform level of safety for all products. Different consumers will have different degrees of risk aversion. While some consumers might purchase riskier, but cheaper, products, others might prefer safer, but more expensive, products.[2]

Under this worldview it would be common to find products with various safety levels supplied simultaneously, reflecting and satisfying different consumer preferences for risk. Forcing all similar products to conform to a single level of risk would not be efficient. Uniform product safety is no more efficient than uniform occupational safety.

If this view of the market were completely accurate, government intervention to protect consumers would not be necessary to ensure the efficient level of risk. By the force of their collective buying habits, consumers would protect themselves.

The problem with the market's ability to provide such self-regulation is, once again, the availability of information on product safety. The consumer generally acquires his or her information about a product either from personal experience or from labels and warnings. With toxic substances the latency period may be so long as to preclude any effective market reaction arising from personal experience. Even when some damage results, it is difficult for the consumer to associate it with a particular source. While an examination of the relationships between purchasing patterns of a large number of consumers and their subsequent health might well reveal some suggestive correlations, it would be difficult for any individual consumer to deduce this correlation. Furthermore, it may be that the risk is so large that no knowledgeable consumer would accept that risk so that banning the product is the appropriate remedy. (Note that banning was the choice of several states in managing the risk from BPA, as described in Example 19.1.)

In situations where adequate information is available on the risks, consumers should have a substantial role in choosing the acceptable level of risk through their

---

[2]A classic example is provided by the manner in which Americans choose their automobiles. It is quite clear that some larger cars are safer and more expensive than smaller, cheaper ones, at least to their owners. Some consumers are willing to pay for this additional level of safety, and others are not.

purchases, but varying levels of access to information can make this problematic. (Recall Debate 18.1 on fish consumption advisories.)

Third Parties

The final case involves *third parties*, victims who have no contractual relationship to the source. Oil spills are one example. Another occurs when groundwater is contaminated by a neighboring wastewater treatment facility, by surreptitious dumping of toxic wastes, or by a neighbor's improper application of a pesticide. In all of these examples the victims are third parties. Since in third-party situations the affected party cannot bring any direct market pressure to bear on the source, the case for additional government intervention is stronger.

This does not necessarily imply, however, that executive or legislative remedies are appropriate. The most appropriate response may come from simply requiring better information on the risk or from using the judicial system to impose liability.

Liability law provides one judicial avenue for internalizing the external costs in third-party situations. If the court finds (1) that damage occurred; (2) that it was caused by a toxic substance; and (3) that a particular source was responsible for the presence of the substance, the source can be forced to compensate the victim for the damages caused. Unlike regulations that are uniformly (and, hence, inefficiently) applied, a court decision can be tailored to the exact circumstances involved in the suit. Furthermore, the impact of any particular liability assignment can go well beyond the parties to that case. A decision for one plaintiff can remind other sources that they should take the efficient level of precaution now to avoid paying damages later.

In principle, liability law can force potential sources of toxic discharges, including nonpoint sources, to choose efficient levels of precaution. Unlike regulation, liability law can provide compensation to the victims. Bringing suit to recover damages, however, is a costly process so these administrative costs must be balanced against the potential gains in efficiency when choosing the appropriate remedy for any particular situation.

The Incidence of Hazardous Waste Siting Decisions

Another element of managing risks involves dealing with the fairness of third-party situations that arise when hazardous waste facilities are being sited. Are market siting decisions likely to be both efficient and fair?

History

In 1979, Robert Bullard, then a sociologist at Texas Southern University, completed a report describing a futile attempt by an affluent African American neighborhood in Houston, Texas, to block the location of a hazardous waste site within their community. His analysis suggested that race, not just income status, was a probable factor in this local land use decision.

Environmental justice, as revealed though the siting of hazardous waste plants, became a national issue in 1982 when some 500 demonstrators protested against the location of a proposed PCB landfill in a predominantly low-income community in North Carolina. On returning from the protests, Walter Fauntroy, the District of Columbia congressional delegate, asked the General Accounting Office (GAO) to study the characteristics of hazardous waste sites in the EPA's Region 4 (Georgia, Florida, Mississippi, Alabama, Kentucky, Tennessee, North Carolina, and South Carolina). The 1983 study found that three out of four commercial hazardous waste facilities were in predominantly African American communities, and the fourth was in a low-income community.

In 1987, the United Church of Christ Commission for Racial Justice examined the issue of hazardous waste siting for the nation as a whole. According to their statistical analysis of communities with commercial hazardous waste facilities, they determined that:

- "Race proved to be the most significant among the variables tested in association with the location of commercial hazardous waste facilities. This represented a consistent national pattern."

In 1994, the Center for Policy Alternatives issued "Toxic Wastes and Race Revisited: An Update of the 1987 Report." That study found that commercial toxic waste facilities were even more likely to be located in minority communities at that time than in 1980, despite growing national attention to the issue.

Not all studies have reached this conclusion, but in a detailed review of the literature, Hamilton (2003) finds that for most US studies, low-income and minority residents do indeed face higher risks from hazardous waste facilities. Less detailed information exists on the exposure of these populations to hazardous waste risks in other industrialized countries.

Environmental Justice Research and the Emerging Role of GIS

The application of geographic information systems (GIS) technology has allowed studies of the distributional inequities with respect to either pollution or hazardous waste site location to become more sophisticated. GIS technology also allows analyses to be conducted at the facility level, the city level, or another geographical area. Most regional offices of the EPA, for example, now use demographic data from the US Census Bureau, combined with GIS mapping. This technique allows for the overlay of census data onto concentric rings around a hazardous waste facility or a Superfund site, for example, in order to discover who lives in close proximity to the site. The distribution of risks can also be mapped with assumptions about the radius of the externalities around a facility and data from epidemiological studies (Hamilton, 2006).

What have these most recent studies found? The results from these studies are quite varied, but they demonstrate that using only one measure of equity, such as low income, could prove misleading. Hamilton and Viscusi (1999), for example, consider multiple measures of equity, including racial distribution, mean household income, and potential cancer risks, and their work demonstrates how sensitive the results are to the specific measure that is used.

Other studies have utilized the EPA's Toxic Release Inventory (TRI) data. This data set contains self-reported information on toxic releases from all plants that are required to report. Using an air pollution index by zip code, Brooks and Sethi (1997) find that demographic groups most likely to face the threat of exposure to toxic air emissions include minorities, renters, people with incomes below the poverty line, and individuals with fewer years of schooling. Similar results were found by Sadd et al. (1999) for metropolitan Los Angeles. Using both GIS and census tract data, they find that census tracts with an emitting facility in the data set had higher percentages of minorities, including Latino residents, lower incomes (both per capita and household), higher percentages of industrial land, lower property values, and higher percentages of persons employed in manufacturing. Similar results were found for Hillsborough County in Florida (Chakraborty, 2001). Studies have also found significant negative effects of pollution on house values and incomes in New England states (Example 19.3).

What explains these findings? What do these findings imply for policy?

EXAMPLE 19.3

Do New Polluting Facilities Affect Housing Values and Incomes? Evidence in New England

Combining census data for New England for 1980 and 1990 with Toxics Release Inventory (TRI) data for manufacturing firms that began operations during that period, Hanna (2007) explores the effect of polluting facilities on the surrounding neighborhoods. The study looks specifically at how prices, wages, pollution, and incomes vary among census tracts in the New England states.

TRI data have only been collected since 1987, so Hanna uses data on new plants in order to measure how pollution changed over the 1980s. Hanna created an index of pollution exposure calculated as a weighted sum of the distance between the census tract and the pollution source times the TRI-reported releases for that pollution source. Some 167 New England sites were in the TRI data. Ten percent of the new plant emissions were of dichloromethane, an airborne contaminant classified as a probable human carcinogen. Significant negative effects of pollution on house values and incomes were found. Their estimates suggest that a house located 1 mile closer to a polluting manufacturing plant reduces its value by 1.9 percent.

Source: Hanna, B. G. (2007). House values, incomes, and industrial pollution. *Journal of Environmental Economics and Management*, *54*, 100–112.

The Economics of Site Location

One point of departure is to attempt to understand the dynamics of site location and how both income and race might play a role. Our analysis begins by recognizing that hazardous waste facilities are generally unpopular neighbors. Even if the treatment of hazardous waste makes sense for society as a whole, all potential recipient communities must face the NIMBY (Not in My Backyard) opposition.

Understanding the economics of site location requires consideration of the incentives facing both the owners of the proposed facility and the incentives of the recipient community. Since the owners want to maximize profits, they will look for a site that will be able to process the wastes at a low cost. Being located near the sources of the waste would be attractive as a means of holding down transport costs. Lower land costs would also be attractive since these facilities are frequently land-intensive. Finally, the site should pose as few liability risks as possible in order to limit future payouts.

The recipient community has its own agenda in order to ensure that it reaps benefits that outweigh costs. They would want to ensure, insofar as possible, that the site was safe for both employees and the inhabitants of the surrounding community. They would also want adequate compensation for assuming the risk. This compensation could take many forms (for example, employment, enhanced tax revenues, or new public services).

What does efficiency suggest about the characteristics of recipient communities? Low-income communities become attractive as disposal sites not only because land prices are relatively low in those communities, but also because those communities will typically require less compensation in order to accept the risk. Targeting low-income communities would be the expected, not the exceptional, outcome. Furthermore, once hazardous waste facilities are located in a community, the composition of that community is likely to become even more low income due to migration and the negative effects on surrounding property values. Assuming that the willingness to pay for risk-avoidance is higher for higher-income families, more lower-income families may be attracted by the unusually low land prices (or rents), while higher-income families may depart for less risky neighborhoods. Even if the community were not low income at the time of the siting, it is likely to become more so over time.

While even an efficient siting process might target a disproportionate share of these facilities in low-income communities, it is much more difficult to develop a clear economic rationale for why race is a more important predictor than income. Explaining that finding requires greater attention to market failures.

Efficient location requires both full information and adequate enforcement of agreements. In the absence of full information, recipient communities can fail to fully understand the risk and therefore are likely to undervalue it. One hypothesis to explain the importance of race is that minority communities have a less adequate flow of information than comparably situated white communities. This would imply they are more likely to be subject to flawed agreements that are biased against them. Another hypothesis is that they lack the power to enforce community will, perhaps because of underrepresentation on governing boards. This hypothesis implies that even potentially efficient agreements may be inefficiently implemented (Bullard, 1990). Taken as a whole, this evidence on the prominence of race as an independent predictor variable (over and above income) suggests not only that the current siting process may be discriminatory, but also that it is not efficient. Until such time as recipient communities can be guaranteed both full information and the capability to enforce the community's will, the hazardous waste siting process will remain seriously flawed.

One lingering issue of debate has to do with the direction of causality. In other words, these population groups could face higher exposures because a hazardous facility chose their community to locate in or were attracted by low land prices. On the other hand attracted by lower land and/or housing prices, people could have moved in after the hazardous waste site located in that community. This chicken-and-egg question has been explored in a few studies.[3] Example 19.4 illustrates one such study in Los Angeles.

EXAMPLE 19.4

Which Came First—The Toxic Facility or the Minority Neighborhood?

Pastor et al. (2001) explore "which came first" in Los Angeles County. Using data from 1970 to 1990, they explore whether toxic storage and disposal facilities (TSDFs) moved into a minority neighborhood or whether the TSDF was there first. Using geo-coded site locations and GIS, they were able to identify affected census tracts. By mapping the facility location and creating circular buffers of one-quarter mile and 1-mile, they were able to determine the potentially affected residents. Their data set contains 83 TSDFs, 39 of which are high capacity and handle most of the waste. Some 55 census tracts were within one-quarter mile of these facilities and 245 tracts were within 1 mile.

They find that areas receiving TSDFs during this time period were indeed low-income, minority areas with a disproportionate number of renters. After the hazards were in place, however, increases in minority residents were not disproportionate to the rest of the "move-ins." In other words, prior to any siting decision, neighborhoods with below-average incomes and above-average percentages of Latinos and African Americans were more likely to receive a TSDF. After the siting decision, little evidence suggests disproportionate in-migration along racial or ethnic lines.

The authors acknowledge two limitations of this study. One is that any analysis at the neighborhood level does not capture individual exposure rates, which may vary within the neighborhood. A second limitation arises from the fact that the perceived risks of living near a site are not certain. Some evidence suggests that people are more worried about hazards to which they have been exposed involuntarily. Perhaps perceived risk drives perceived fairness.

Source: Pastor, Jr., M., Sadd, J., & Hipp, J. (2001). Which Came First? Toxic Facilities, Minority Move-in and Environmental Justice. *Journal of Urban Affairs, 23,* 1–21.

---

[3]Boyce (2007) reviews some of the debate on the *direction* of environmental protection.

The Policy Response

Environmental Justice and Hazardous Waste Sites. In recognition of the problems associated with locating hazardous waste sites, the Office of Environmental Equity was officially established within the US Environmental Protection Agency on November 6, 1992. Its mandate is to deal with environmental impacts affecting people of color and low-income communities. Although the issue that precipitated the creation of this office was largely focused on the siting of hazardous waste facilities, the concerns of this office go well beyond that. Initial efforts are focused on gathering more information about the problem and strengthening enforcement inspections and compliance monitoring in impacted communities.

In 1994, President Clinton issued Executive Order 12898, "Federal Action to Address Environmental Justice in Minority Populations and Low-Income Populations." The goal of this order was to make sure that minority groups and low-income populations are not subjected to an unequal or disproportionately high level of environmental risks.

How effective has the order been? In 2004, the EPA issued an evaluation report of this Executive Order and did not award a good grade. In fact, the report suggests that Executive Order 12898 has not been fully implemented and that the EPA has "not consistently integrated environmental justice into its day-to-day operations." The report also states that the "EPA has not . . . identified populations addressed in the Executive Order, and has neither defined nor developed criteria for determining the disproportionately impacted."[4]

In a delayed response to this criticism in October 2012, the EPA issued a new screening tool, EJSCREEN, for use internally by agency managers and staff. EJSCREEN is designed to provide nationally consistent data and methods for screening areas of potential EJ concern that may warrant further consideration, analysis or outreach. It employs 12 environmental indicators plus race and income.

Simultaneous exposures to various types of risk make discerning the causal relationships even more complex. Those with lower incomes may live close to a plant with high emissions, but lower incomes are also associated with a poorer diet and less access to health care, both of which can also be associated with increased levels of illness (Hamilton, 2006).

Environmental Justice in Canada and Europe. The number of empirical studies outside the United States is rather limited, but some case studies have been conducted, particularly in Canada and Europe. These case studies are useful in helping to discern what kinds of strategies can be effective in the quest to achieve environmental justice in the siting of hazardous waste facilities.

Public participation has been cited as an important factor in the successful siting of hazardous waste facilities in the Canadian provinces of Alberta and Manitoba. ("Successful" in this case means not only that the facility was able to find a home, but also that no environmental justice concerns have arisen after the fact in the host communities.) The siting process in these provinces is not only voluntary, but it

[4]Report of the Office of the Inspector General, March 1, 2004.

also provides multiple stages at which the community can exercise veto power over the project.

Interestingly, the resulting locations are not always in low-income neighborhoods. In fact, one such location, the town of Swan Hills, has an average household income significantly higher than the average in the province and one of the lowest levels of unemployment (Rabe, 1994).

Why would any community accept such a facility? Potential jobs at the facilities were apparently one large factor as is the property tax revenue that might accrue.

One corollary of the jobs hypothesis might be that we would expect the presence of local high unemployment to increase the likelihood a community would accept a hazardous waste facility. That seems to be the case. In a survey of successful sitings in France, Hungary, Italy, the Netherlands, and Spain, for example, Dente et al. (1998) found that areas with higher unemployment are, as expected, more likely to accept facilities. They also find, however, that communities are more likely to accept waste if it is seen as "local" since, in that case, the residents of the host community will also be reaping the benefits from employment in the plants generating the waste.

The Role of Risk Perception. The NIMBY attitude has been explored in both the economics and cognitive psychology literatures. Delving into the psychology of risk perception, Messer et al. (2006) summarize the results of a study that evaluated the benefits of hazardous waste cleanup under the Comprehensive Environmental Response, Compensation, and Liability Act (CERCLA), more commonly known as Superfund. Although this legislation was passed in 1980, legal complexities in the act have delayed the cleanup of many Superfund sites. Messer et al. (2006) wanted to know if the length of delay affected the ultimate recovery of property values after the cleanup.

The authors examined four Superfund sites: Operating Industries, a landfill in Los Angeles; Montclair, West Orange, and Glen Ridge Townships in New Jersey, formerly the site of US Radium Corporation; Industri-plex and Water Wells G&H in Woburn, Massachusetts; and Eagle Mine in Colorado. Cleanup was significantly delayed and/or hampered at all of these sites.

They found that the designation of the site as a Superfund site, the cleanup itself, and the associated news items all negatively affected the property values. Media announcements were found to affect public perceptions of risk so profoundly that a "shunning" of the property may result. Current owners may not be willing to stay in their homes if their perceived costs of remaining are greater than the value of their homes and potential buyers are likely to be few and far between. In this study, property values continued to fall over time as cleanup was delayed. If cleanup was delayed for 20 years, for example, they found that the benefits of cleanup (measured by the recovery of property values) would be negligible in present value terms, since it would take another 5–10 years for property values to recover (Messer et al., 2006).

Compensation as a Policy Instrument. One policy device for attempting to achieve environmental justice is paying compensation or host fees to communities accepting hazardous waste facilities. In principle, this would serve to make sure that benefits, not merely the costs, accrue to the local community. Additionally, paying the compensation would internalize the cost of the environmental risk as that cost was passed on to those whose waste was being treated.

While compensation frequently is an effective device for finding common ground, as Debate 19.1 suggests, that is not always the case!

Does Offering Compensation for Accepting an Environmental Risk Always Increase the Willingness to Accept the Risk?

DEBATE 19.1

One week before a referendum in Switzerland on the siting of a nuclear-waste repository, a survey was conducted in the community where the repository was to be located. Researchers found that an offer of compensation to accept the facility *reduced* willingness to accept it! Specifically, Frey and Oberholzer-Gee (1997) and Frey et al. (1996) found that when asked whether they would accept a nuclear-waste repository without compensation, 50.8 percent of the respondents said "yes." This rate dropped to 24.6 percent when compensation was offered! The researchers suggest that acceptance rates drop with compensation because offering the compensation crowds out a feeling of civic duty. If respondents feel that accepting a facility is part of his or her civic duty, he or she will be less likely to feel this sense of responsibility once a payment is introduced. In this context, the authors believe that the compensation was viewed as a morally unacceptable bribe and, hence, should be rejected.

An alternative explanation might suggest that compensation could play a signaling role. Perhaps the risks are perceived as being small until such time as compensation is offered. At that moment, introducing compensation into the mix might be taken by the community as a signal that the risks are much higher than previously thought—indeed, so high that compensation must be paid!

How common is this outcome? In a very different setting (Japan), Lesbirel (1998) examined the siting of energy plants. In this context, the author found that compensation did, as expected, actually facilitate the siting of these plants. He interprets his findings as consistent with the belief that in Japan, institutional structures facilitate participatory negotiations on risk-management strategies that result in productive bargaining between the plants and host communities. This process effectively removes the moral stigma and eliminates the signaling role of compensation. Whether this characterization of the Japanese process continues to be valid following the Fukushima nuclear accident remains to be seen.

What is the moral of the story? This evidence suggests that compensation does not automatically increase the likelihood of a community accepting a hazardous facility, but it might. The context matters.

Sources: Frey, B. S., & Oberholzer-Gee, F. (1997). The cost of price incentives: An empirical analysis of motivation crowding out. *American Economic Review, 87*(4), 746–755; Frey, B. S, Felix Oberholzer-Gee, F., & Eichenberger, R. (1996). The old lady visits your backyard: A tale of morals and markets. *Journal of Political Economy, 104*(6), 1297–1313; Hayden, L. S. (1998). *NIMBY Politics in Japan: Energy siting and the management of environmental conflict*. New York: Cornell University Press.

Creating Incentives through Common Law

The common-law system is an extremely complicated approach to controlling risks. When a victim seeks recourse through the court system, a number of legal grounds can be used to pursue a claim. Not all of these may be available to every plaintiff (the person initiating the suit), since the appropriate doctrine depends partially on the legal tradition in the jurisdiction where the suit is filed. Two of the more common legal grounds are negligence and strict liability.

Negligence. Negligence is probably the most common legal theory used by plaintiffs to pursue claims. This body of law suggests that the defendant (the party allegedly responsible for the contamination) owes a duty to the plaintiff (the affected party) to exercise due care. If that duty has been breached, the defendant is found negligent and is forced to compensate the victim for damages caused. If the defendant is found to have exercised due care and to have performed that duty to the plaintiff, no liability is assessed. Under negligence law, the victim bears the liability unless it can be proved that the defendant was negligent.

Interestingly, the test conventionally applied by the courts in deciding whether the defendant has exercised due care, the Learned Hand formula, is fundamentally an economic construct. Named after the judge (yes, Learned Hand!) who initially formulated it, this test suggests that the defendant is guilty of negligence if the marginal loss caused by the contamination, multiplied by the probability of contamination, exceeds the marginal cost of preventing the contamination. This is simply a version of the expected net benefit formula developed in Chapter 3. The maximization of expected net benefits is efficient as long as society is risk-neutral. Therefore, the common-law approach embodied in negligence law in principle is compatible with efficiency in this case.

Sometimes the plaintiff can prove negligence on the part of the defendant by showing that the defendant violated a statute. In many states, any related statutory violation is taken as sufficient proof of negligence.

Strict Liability. Strict liability can be used by plaintiffs in some states and in some circumstances. Under this doctrine, the plaintiff does not have to prove negligence. As long as the defendant's activity causes damage, the defendant is declared liable even if the activity is completely legal and complies with all relevant laws.

Strict liability is usually applied in circumstances where the activity in question is inherently hazardous. Since the disposal of toxic substances is frequently considered such an activity, states are increasingly allowing toxic substance suits to be brought under this doctrine. In contrast to negligence, this doctrine transfers liability for damages to the source whether or not the source has exercised much care. One major consequence of that is that the responsible party has an incentive to begin immediately both the cleanup and the process of compensating victims. This was the case with the BP/*Deepwater Horizon* oil spill in the Gulf of Mexico in 2010.

Strict liability can also be compatible with efficiency because it sets a precedent that makes those who might be responsible for damages recognize that the damages will be internalized.[5] The decision maker dealing with toxic wastes must balance the costs of taking precautions with the likelihood of incurring the costs of lawsuits. In cases where the precautionary expenditures are particularly high and the damages low, only limited precaution is likely to be taken. However, for truly dangerous substances, strict liability can make it privately advantageous to take extraordinary precautions and avoid large damages.

Statutory Law

These liability remedies have been accompanied by a host of legislative remedies. The statutes have evolved over time in response to particular toxic substance problems. Each time a new problem surfaced and people were able to get legislators aroused, a new law was passed to deal with it. The result is a collage of laws on the books, each with its unique focus. We cover only a few of the main ones here.

Toxic Substances Control Act. This act requires the EPA to inventory the approximately 100,000 chemical substances in commerce; to require premanufacture notice to the EPA of all new chemical substances; and to enforce record keeping, testing, and reporting requirements so that the EPA can assess and regulate the relative risks of chemicals. At least 90 days before manufacturing or importing a new chemical, a firm must submit test results or other information to the EPA, showing that the chemical will not present "an unreasonable risk" to human health or the environment.

On the basis of the information in the premanufacture notification, the EPA may limit the manufacture, use, or disposal of the substance. The act is significant in that it represents one of the few instances where the burden of proof is on the manufacturer to prove that the product should be marketed, rather than forcing the EPA to show why it should not be marketed.

Comprehensive Environmental Response, Compensation, and Liability Act. Known popularly as the "Superfund Act," the Comprehensive Environmental Response, Compensation, and Liability Act of 1980 created a fund to be used for the cleanup of existing toxic waste sites. The initial revenue was derived mainly from taxes on chemical industries, but the agency also recovers money, using liability law, from potentially responsible parties (PRPs). It offers compensation for the loss or destruction of natural resources controlled by the state or federal government, but it does not provide any compensation for injured individuals.

---

[5]One well-known case where strict liability will not be efficient is when the victims can influence the likelihood of contamination and the magnitude of the damage caused. With full compensation, the victim's incentive to take precautions is undermined. In most toxic-substance cases, the role of the victim is minimal, so this potential source of inefficiency is not important.

To guide the EPA in determining which sites warrant further investigation, the *National Priorities List* (NPL) was created to establish national targeting priorities among the known releases or threatened releases of hazardous substances, pollutants, or contaminants throughout the United States and its territories.

This act, as amended, authorized federal and state governments to respond quickly to incidents such as the one that occurred in Times Beach, Missouri. Times Beach, a town of 2800 residents located about 30 miles southwest of St. Louis, had been contaminated by dioxin. Dioxin is a waste by-product created during the production of certain chemicals. One such chemical is Agent Orange, the defoliant used during the Vietnam War. The contamination occurred when a state oil hauler bought about 55 pounds of dioxin in 1971 from a now-defunct manufacturer, mixed it with oil, and under contract with the local government, spread it on unpaved roads as a dust-control measure. On December 23, 1982, after soil tests revealed dangerous levels of dioxin, the Centers for Disease Control recommended total evacuation of the town.

By February 22, 1983, the federal government had authorized a transfer of some $33 million from the Superfund to cover the cost of buying out all businesses and residents and relocating them. For its part, the State of Missouri agreed to pay 10 percent of the $33 million cost into the Superfund, and fund representatives were free to attempt to recover damages from the responsible parties. By June 1983, all but 40 families had been relocated. Federal and state agencies then burned more than 265,000 tons of contaminated soil. With the passage of time, the hazard has diminished. In 1999, the State of Missouri opened Route 66 State Park on the site, and the site has now been removed from the Superfund list.

The existence of the Superfund allows the governments involved to move rapidly. They are not forced to wait until the outcome of court suits against those responsible to raise the money or to face the uncertainty associated with whether the suits would ultimately be successful.

The Toxic Release Inventory

The Toxic Release Inventory (TRI) was enacted by the US Congress in January 1986 as a part of the Environmental Protection and Community Right to Know Act (EPCRA). EPCRA was enacted partially in response to two incidents. In 1984, methyl isocyanate killed thousands of people in Bhopal, India. A chemical release at a sister plant in West Virginia happened soon after. The public's (workers' and community members') demand for information about toxic chemicals was the impetus for EPCRA. Together with the Pollution Prevention Act (PPA) of 1990, it mandates the collection of data on toxic chemicals that are treated on-site, recycled, and combusted for energy recovery. The TRI is a publically available database designed to provide information to the public on releases of toxic substances into the environment. Most of the substances involved are not themselves subject to release standards.

TRI states that firms that *use* 10,000 or more pounds of a listed chemical in a given calendar year or firms that *import, process, or manufacture* 25,000 or more pounds of a listed chemical must file a report on each of the chemicals in existence within the plant if they also have 10 or more full-time employees. Approximately 650 chemicals are covered in the TRI. Most recently the TRI has been expanded to include lower reporting thresholds for certain persistent bioaccumulative toxic (PBT) chemicals. PBT chemicals are stock pollutants and can accumulate in body tissue. PBT chemicals include mercury, pesticides, and dioxins.

Reporting of emissions or use of listed chemicals is accomplished annually. (For the data, see http://www.epa.gov/tri/tridata/index.htm.) The reports include such information as the name of the company, the name of the parent company if it exists, the toxic released and frequency of release, and the medium in which the chemical is released. Data by state are also available and all data are available to the public. Firms must also separately report emissions to their state and local authorities as well as to fire and emergency officials.

Several other countries now use similar reporting mechanisms, known as Pollutant Release and Transfer Registers (PRTR). All have slight variations on the TRI. In Japan, the PRTR includes data on diffuse sources (e.g., automobiles). The Canadian PRTR, called the National Pollutant Release Inventory (NPRI), also collects data on the number of employees at each facility. The Mexican PRTR is voluntary and so data are limited. Australia, the Czech Republic, Norway, and the United Kingdom also all have PRTRs with on-site release data.

Has TRI reduced toxic emissions into the environment? EPA's annual reports reveal that substantial reductions have occurred. Although careful examination of the filings (e.g., Natan & Miller, 1998) found that some of these reductions merely reflect a change in definition, other reductions have been found to be genuine. Apparently, the reported magnitude of the reductions is overstated, but real reductions have occurred. Among the chemicals that are reported to TRI about 180 are known or suspected carcinogens. In 2011, the EPA reported that the air releases of these carcinogens decreased by 50% between 2003 and 2011.

Proposition 65

Proposition 65, the *Safe Drinking Water and Toxic Enforcement Act of 1986*, was established in the State of California by popular vote in November 1986, following the inception of the Toxic Release Inventory by the EPA. Proposition 65 is intended to protect California citizens and the state's drinking water sources from toxic chemicals. Proposition 65 requires companies producing, using, or transporting one or more of the listed chemicals to notify those who are potentially impacted. Chemicals are listed as carcinogenic or as causing reproductive harm. When their use or potential exposure levels exceed "safe harbor numbers" established by a group of approved scientists, the impacted people must be notified. The "safe harbor" threshold is uniquely determined for each chemical and depends upon its intrinsic potency or the potency of a released mixture. Proposition 65 also requires the governor of California to publish, at least annually, a list of chemicals known to the state to cause cancer or reproductive toxicity.

The program involves three forms of notification: (1) warning labels must be placed on all products that will cause adverse health effects when used for a prolonged period of time; (2) a company whose toxic emissions to air, ground, or water exceed levels deemed safe for prolonged exposure must provide public notification; and (3) workers must be warned of the potential danger if toxic chemicals defined by Proposition 65 are used in manufacturing a product or are created as a by-product of manufacturing.

Only companies with ten or more full-time workers are required to notify endangered people of exposure. Nonprofit organizations like hospitals, recycling plants, and government organizations, which account for over 65 percent of California's pollution, are not required to comply with Proposition 65.

Under the proposition, private citizens, other industry members, and environmental groups can sue companies that fail to notify people of exposure appropriately. Plaintiffs who make a successful legal claim can keep a substantial portion of the settlement; this encourages private enforcement of the law and reduces government monitoring. Industry members also have a strong incentive to monitor each other, so that one company does not cheat and look greener than its rivals.

Did this program change behavior? At least in controlling exposure to lead, it clearly did (see Example 19.5).

International Agreements

One of the issues erupting during the 1990s concerned the efficiency and morality of exporting hazardous waste to areas that are willing to accept it in return for suitably large compensation. A number of areas, particularly poor countries, appear ready to accept hazardous waste under the "right conditions." The right conditions usually involve alleviating safety concerns and providing adequate compensation (in employment opportunities, money, and public services) so as to make acceptance of the wastes desirable from the receiving community's point of view. Generally, the compensation required is less than the costs of dealing in other ways with the hazardous waste, so the exporting nations find these agreements attractive as well.

A strong backlash against these arrangements arose when opponents argued that communities receiving hazardous waste were poorly informed about the risks they faced and were not equipped to handle the volumes of material that could be expected to cross international boundaries safely. In extreme cases, the communities were completely uninformed as sites were secretly located by individuals with no public participation in the process at all.

The Basel Convention on the Control of Transboundary Movements of Hazardous Wastes and Their Disposal was developed in 1989 to provide a satisfactory response to these concerns. Under this convention, the 24 nations that belong to the Organisation for Economic Co-operation and Development (OECD) were required to obtain written permission from the government of any developing country before exporting toxic waste there for disposal or recycling. This was

EXAMPLE 19.5

Regulating through Mandatory Disclosure: The Case of Lead

Rechtschaffen (1999) describes a particularly interesting case study involving how Proposition 65 produced a rather major reduction in the amount of lead exposure by promoting new technologies, production-process changes, and pollution-prevention measures. He even goes so far as to suggest that Proposition 65 was apparently even more effective than federal law in addressing certain lead hazards from drinking water, consumer products, and other sources.

Rechtschaffen identifies several characteristics about Proposition 65 that explain its relative success. We mention two here.

First, despite periodic calls for such an integrated strategy, no coordinated federal approach to controlling lead hazards had emerged. Rather, lead exposures were regulated by an array of agencies acting under a multitude of regulatory authorities. In contrast, the Proposition 65 warning requirement applies without limitation to *any* exposure to a listed chemical unless the exposure falls under the safe harbor standard regardless of its source. Thus, the coverage of circumstances leading to lead exposure is very high and the standards requiring disclosure are universally applied.

Second, unlike federal law, Proposition 65 is self-executing. Once a chemical is listed by the state as causing cancer or reproductive harm, Proposition 65 applies. This contrasts with federal statutes, where private activity causing lead exposures is permitted until and unless the government sets a restrictive standard. Whereas under the federal approach, fighting the establishment of a restrictive standard made economic sense (by delaying the date when the provisions would apply), under Proposition 65 exactly the opposite incentives prevail. In the latter case, since the provisions took effect soon after enactment, the only refuge from the statute rested on the existence of a safe harbor standard that could insulate small exposures from the statute's warning requirements. For Proposition 65, at least some subset of firms had an incentive to make sure the safe harbor standard was in place; delay in implementing the standard was costly, not beneficial.

Source: Rechtschaffen, C. (1999). How to reduce lead exposure with one simple statute: The experience with Proposition 65. *Environmental Law Reporter,29.* 10581–10591.

followed, in 1994, by an additional agreement on the part of most, but not all, industrialized nations to completely prohibit the export of toxic wastes from any OECD country to any non-OECD country.

With the huge growth in sales of electronic devices and the valuable materials in the post-consumer *e-waste* resulting from these sales, enforcement of laws on exporting toxic materials in e-waste is getting more difficult (recall the e-waste discussion in Chapter 8).

Some used electronic goods exported to developing countries become electronic waste (e-waste) that is usually disassembled in those developing countries. The concern is the recovery process can be dangerous to the health of the disassemblers, particularly if it is done without the proper safeguards. E-waste often contains of toxic substances such as lead, mercury, cadmium, and flame retardants.

How much e-waste is being exported? This simple answer is we don't know.

According to the USEPA good data on e-waste exports do not exist. While the Basel Action Network, a Seattle-based nongovernmental organization announced in 2002 that as much as 80% of waste is exported, a recent survey by the US International Trade Commission (ITC) involving 5200 businesses found that US exports were only 7 percent of used electronic equipment sales. There are good reasons to be skeptical of both numbers.

Whatever the correct numbers are, it is clear that some exports clearly are injuring people in developing countries. Kinnaman and YoKoo (2011) report on studies that have found the following:

- Ambient dioxin and furan concentrations in the air around an e-waste dismantling site in China are the highest in the world. As a result, blood lead levels in children within proximity to this Chinese dismantling site significantly exceed the Chinese mean.
- Concentrations of lead, dioxins, and furans in e-waste dismantling sites in India also exceed World Health Organization guidelines.

A bill titled the Responsible Electronics Recycling Act, which would have banned US exports of electronic waste, was introduced in Congress in 2011, but not enacted.

Summary

The potential for contamination of the environmental asset by toxic substances is one of the most complex environmental problems. The number of potential substances that could prove toxic is in millions. Some 100,000 of these are in active use.

The market provides a considerable amount of pressure toward resolving toxic substance problems as they affect employees and consumers. With reliable information at their disposal, all parties have an incentive to reduce hazards to acceptable levels. This pressure is absent, however, in cases involving third parties. Here, the problem frequently takes the form of an external cost imposed on innocent bystanders.

The efficient role of government can range from ensuring the provision of sufficient information (so that participants in the market can make informed choices) to setting exposure limits on hazardous substances. Unfortunately, the scientific basis for decision making is weak. Only limited information on the effects of these substances is available, and the cost of acquiring complete information is prohibitive. Therefore, priorities must be established and tests developed to screen substances so that efforts can be concentrated on those substances that seem most dangerous.

In contrast to air and water pollution, the toxic substance problem is one in which the courts may play a particularly important role. Although screening tests will probably never be foolproof, and therefore some substances may slip through, they do provide a reasonable means for setting priorities. Liability law not only creates a market pressure for more and better information on potential damages associated with chemical substances, but also it provides some incentives to manufacturers of substances, the generators of waste, the transporters of waste, and those who dispose of it to exercise precaution. Judicial remedies also allow the level of precaution to vary with the occupational circumstances and provide a means of compensating victims.

Judicial remedies, however, are insufficient. They are expensive and ill-suited for dealing with problems affecting large numbers of people. The burden of proof under the current American system is difficult to surmount, although in Japan some radical new approaches have been developed to deal with this problem.

Is the burden posed by environmental risks and the policies used to reduce them fair? Apparently not. The siting of hazardous waste facilities seems to have resulted in a distribution of risks that disproportionately burdens low-income populations, and minority communities. This outcome suggests that current siting policies are neither efficient nor fair. The responsibility for this policy failure seems to lie mainly with the failure to ensure informed consent of residents in recipient communities and very uneven enforcement of existing legal protections.

The theologian Reinhold Niebuhr once said, "Democracy is finding proximate solutions to insoluble problems." That seems an apt description of the institutional response to the toxic substance problem. Our political institutions have created a staggering array of legislative and judicial responses to this problem that are neither efficient nor complete. They do, however, represent a positive first step in what must be an evolutionary process.

Discussion Questions

1. Did the courts resolve the dilemma posed in Example 19.2 correctly in your opinion? Why or why not?
2. Over the last several decades in product liability law, there has been a movement in the court system from caveat emptor ("buyer beware") to caveat venditor ("seller beware"). The liability for using and consuming risky products has been shifted from buyers to sellers. Does this shift represent a movement toward or away from an efficient allocation of risk? Why?
3. Would the export of hazardous waste to developing countries be efficient? Sometimes? Always? Never? Would it be moral? Sometimes? Always? Never? Make clear the specific reasons for your judgments.

4. How should the public sector handle a toxic gas, such as radon, that occurs naturally and seeps into some houses through the basement or the water supply? Is this a case of an externality? Does the homeowner have the appropriate incentives to take an efficient level of precaution?

Self-Test Exercises

1. Two legal doctrines used to control contamination from toxic substances are negligence and strict liability. Imagine a situation in which a toxic substance risk can be reduced only by some combination of precautionary measures taken by both the user of the toxic substance and the potential victim. Assuming that these two doctrines are employed so as to produce an efficient level of precaution by the user, do they both provide efficient precautionary incentives for the victims? Why or why not?
2. Firms whose economic activity might pose an environmental risk are sometimes required to post performance bonds before the activity is allowed to commence. The amount of the required bond would be equal to the present value of anticipated damages. Any restoration of the site resulting from a hazardous waste leak could be funded directly and immediately from the accumulated funds. Any unused proceeds would be redeemable at specified dates if the environmental costs turned out to be lower than anticipated.

   What is the difference in practice between an approach relying on performance bonds and one imposing strict liability for cleanup costs on any firm for a toxic substance spill?
3. Is informing the consumer about any toxic substances used in the manufacture of a product sufficient to produce an efficient level of toxic substance use for that product? Why or why not?

Further Reading

Jenkins, R. R., Klemicky, H., Kopitsz, E., & Alex Marten, A. (2012). Policy monitor–U.S. Emergency response and removal: Superfund's overlooked cleanup program. *Review of Environmental Economics and Policy*, *6*(2), 278–297.

Describes and evaluates a key component of the nation's response capability regulations to respond to actual and threatened hazardous releases, including deliberate releases by terrorists: the Superfund Emergency Response and Removal (ERR) Program.

Mendelsohn, R., & Olmstead, S. (2009). The economic valuation of environmental amenities and disamenities: Methods and applications. *Annual Review of Environment and Resources, 34*, 325–347. Reviews the evolution of our ability to estimate the economic value of environmental amenities and disamenities over the last four decades.

Sigman, H., & Stafford, S. (2011). Management of hazardous waste and contaminated land. *Annual Review of Resource Economics, 3*. A review of the hazardous-waste management from an economic perspective.

Additional References and Historically Significant References are available on this book's Companion Website: http://www.routledgetextbooks.com/textbooks/9780133479690

20 The Quest for Sustainable Development

The challenge of finding sustainable development paths ought to provide the impetus—indeed the imperative—for a renewed search for multilateral solutions and a restructured international economic system of co-operation. These challenges cut across the divides of national sovereignty, of limited strategies for economic gain, and of separated disciplines of science.

—Gro Harlem Brundtland, Prime Minister of Norway,
Our Common Future (1987)

Introduction

Delegations from 178 countries met in Rio de Janeiro during the first 2 weeks of June 1992 to begin the process of charting a sustainable development course for the future global economy. Billed by its organizers as the largest summit ever held, the United Nations Conference on Environment and Development (known popularly as the Earth Summit) sought to lay the groundwork for solving global environmental problems. The central focus for this meeting was sustainable development.

What is sustainable development? According to the Brundtland Report, which is widely credited with raising the concept to its current level of importance, "Sustainable development is development that meets the needs of the present without compromising the ability of future generations to meet their own needs" (World Commission on Environment and Development, 1987). But that is far from the only possible definition. Part of the widespread appeal of the concept, according to critics, is due to its vagueness. Being all things to all people can build a large following, but it also has a substantial disadvantage; close inspection may reveal the concept to be vacuous. As the emperor discovered about his new clothes, things are not always what they seem.

In this chapter, we take a hard look at the concept of sustainable development and whether or not it is useful as a guide to the future. What are the basic principles of sustainable development? What does sustainable development imply about changes in the way our system operates? How could the transition to sustainable development be managed? Will the global economic system automatically produce sustainable development or will policy changes be needed? What policy changes?

Sustainability of Development

Suppose we were to map out possible future trends in the long-term welfare of the average citizen. Using a timescale measured in centuries on the horizontal axis (see Figure 20.1), four basic culture trends emerge, labeled *A*, *B*, *C*, and *D*, with t^0 representing the present. *D* portrays continued exponential growth in which the future becomes a simple repetition of the past. Although this scenario is generally considered to be infeasible, it is worth thinking about its implications if it were feasible. In this scenario not only would current welfare levels be sustainable, but also growth in welfare would be sustainable. Our concern for intergenerational justice would lead us to favor current generations, since they would be the poorest. Worrying about future generations would be unnecessary if unlimited growth were possible.

The second scenario (*C*) envisions slowly diminished growth culminating in a steady state where growth diminishes to zero. The welfare of each future generation is at least as well-off as all previous generations. Current welfare levels are sustainable, although current levels of welfare growth would not be. Since the level of welfare of each generation is sustainable, artificial constraints on the process would be unnecessary. To constrain growth would injure all subsequent generations.

The third scenario (*B*) is similar in that it envisions initial growth followed by a steady state, but with an important difference—those generations between t^1 and t^2 are worse off than the generation preceding them. Neither growth nor welfare levels are sustainable at current levels, and the sustainability criterion would call for policy to transform the economy so that earlier generations do not benefit themselves at the expense of future generations.

FIGURE 20.1 Possible Alternative Futures

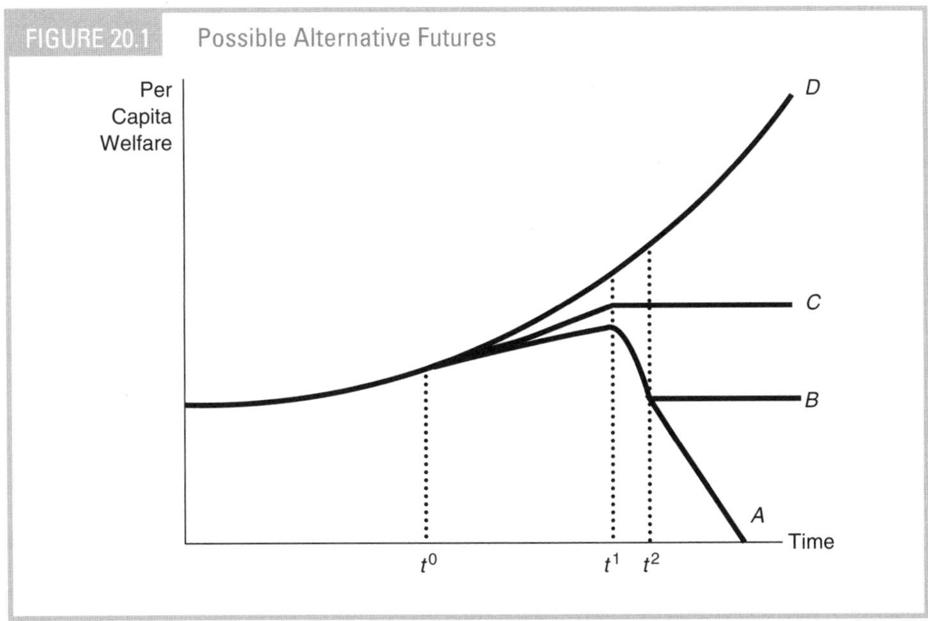

The final scenario (*A*) denies the existence of sustainable per capita welfare levels, suggesting that the only possible sustainable level is zero. All consumption by the current generation serves simply to hasten the end of civilization.

These scenarios suggest three important dimensions of the sustainability issue: (1) the existence of a positive sustainable level of welfare; (2) the magnitude of the ultimate sustainable level of welfare vis-à-vis current welfare levels; and (3) the sensitivity of the future level of welfare to actions by previous generations. The first dimension is important because if positive sustainable levels of welfare are possible, scenario *A*, which in some ways is the most philosophically difficult, is ruled out. The second is important because if the ultimately sustainable welfare level is higher than the current level, radical surgery to cut current living standards is not necessary. The final dimension raises the issue of whether the ultimate sustainable level of welfare can be increased or reduced by the actions of current generations. If so, the sustainability criterion would suggest taking these impacts into account, lest future generations be unnecessarily impoverished by involuntary wealth transfers to previous generations.

The first dimension is relatively easy to dispense with. The existence of positive sustainable welfare levels is guaranteed by the existence of renewable resources, particularly solar energy, as well as by nature's ability to assimilate a certain amount of waste.[1] Therefore, we can rule out scenario *A*.

Scenarios *B* and *C* require actions to assure the maintenance of a sustainable level of welfare. They differ in terms of how radical the actions must be. Although no one knows exactly what level of economic activity can ultimately be sustained, the ecological footprint measurements discussed later in this chapter suggest that current welfare levels are not sustainable. If that controversial assessment is valid, more stringent measures are called for. If scenario *C* is more likely, then the actions could be less drastic, but still necessary.

Current generations can affect the sustainable welfare levels of future generations both positively and negatively. We could use our resources to accumulate a capital stock, providing future generations with shelter, productivity, and transportation, but machines and buildings do not last forever. Even capital that physically stands the test of time may become economically obsolete by being ill suited to the needs of subsequent generations.

Our most lasting contribution to future generations would probably come from what economists call human capital—investments in people. Though the people who receive education and training are mortal, the ideas they bring forth are not: knowledge endures.[2]

Current actions could also reduce future welfare levels, however. Fossil fuel combustion could modify the climate to the detriment of future agriculture. Current chlorofluorocarbon emissions can, by depleting the atmosphere's ozone, raise the incidence of skin cancer. The storage of radioactive wastes could increase the

---

[1]One study estimates that humans are currently using approximately 19–25 percent of the renewable energy available from photosynthesis. On land the estimate is more likely 40 percent (Vitousek et al., 1986).

[2]While it is true that ideas can last forever, the value of those ideas may decline with time as they are supplanted by new ideas. The person who conceived of horseshoes made an enormous contribution to society at the time, but the value of that insight to society has diminished along with our reliance on horses for transportation.

likelihood of genetic damage in the future. The reduction of genetic diversity in the stock of plants and animals could well reduce future medical discoveries.

Suppose that higher levels of sustainable welfare are feasible. Would our market system automatically choose a growth path that produces sustainable welfare levels, or could it choose one that enriches current generations at the expense of future generations?

Market Allocations

Market imperfections, including intertemporal externalities, open-access resources, and market power create incentives that can interfere in important ways with the quest for sustainable development.

Allowing open access to resources can, and commonly does, promote unsustainable allocations. When resources are allocated by open-access, even the existence of renewable resources cannot assure sustainability. Diminished stocks are left for the future. In the extreme, it is even possible that some harvested species would become extinct.

Intertemporal externalities also undermine the ability of the market to produce sustainable outcomes. Emissions of greenhouse gases impose a cost on future generations that is external to current generations. Current actions to reduce the gases will impose costs on this generation, but the bulk of the benefits would not be felt until significantly later. Economic theory clearly forecasts that too many greenhouse gas emissions would be forthcoming for the sustainability criterion to be satisfied.

While market imperfections normally do exacerbate the problem of unsustainability, the more general conclusion that they always promote unsustainability, however, is not correct. Markets can sometimes provide a safety valve to ensure sustainability even when the supply of a renewable resource is threatened. Fish farming is one example where declining supplies of a renewable resource trigger the availability of an alternative renewable substitute. Even when the government intervenes detrimentally in a way that benefits current generations at the expense of future generations, as it did in the 1970s with natural gas, the market can limit the damage by making substitutes available. While government regulation made the transition significantly less smooth than it might have been, it did not prevent the transition altogether.

The flexibility and responsiveness of markets to scarcity can be an important component of the transition to sustainability, but the notion that markets would, if left to their own devices, automatically provide for the future is naïve, despite their apparent success in providing for generations in the past.

Efficiency and Sustainability

Suppose future governments were able to eliminate all market imperfections, restoring efficiency to the global economic system. In this idealized world, intertemporal and contemporaneous externalities would be reduced to efficient levels. Access to common resources would be restricted to efficient levels and excess harvesting capacity would be eliminated. Competition would be restored to previously cartelized natural resource markets. Would this package of policies be sufficient to achieve sustainability, or is something more required?

One way to examine this question is to examine a number of different models that capture the essence of intertemporal resource allocation. For each model the question becomes, "Will efficient markets automatically produce sustainable development?" The conclusion to be drawn from these models is very clear; restoring efficiency is *not* always sufficient to produce sustainability.

Take the allocation of depletable resources over time. Imagine a simple economy where the only activity is the extraction and consumption of a single depletable resource. Even when the population is constant and demand curves are temporally stable, the efficient quantity profiles show declining consumption over time. In this hypothetical world, later generations would be unambiguously worse off unless current generations transferred some of the net benefits into the future. Even an efficient market allocation would not be sustainable in the absence of transfers.

The existence of an abundant renewable backstop resource would not solve the problem. Even in this more congenial set of circumstances, the quantity profile of the depletable resource would still involve declining consumption until the backstop was reached. In the absence of compensating transfers, even efficient markets would use depletable resources to support a higher current standard of living than could ultimately be permanently supported.

In a historically important article, Dasgupta and Heal (1979) found a similar result for a slightly more realistic model. They assume an economy in which a single consumption good is produced by combining capital with a depletable resource. The finite supply of the depletable resource can either be used to produce capital or it can be used in combination with capital to produce the consumption good. The more capital produced, the higher is the marginal product of the remaining depletable resource in making the consumption good.

They prove that a sustainable constant consumption level exists in this model. The rising capital stock (implying a rising marginal product for the depletable resource) would compensate for the declining availability of the depletable resource. They also prove, however, that the use of any positive discount rate would necessarily result in declining consumption levels, a violation of the sustainability criterion. Discounting, of course, is an inherent component of dynamically efficient allocations.

In this model, sustainable development is possible, but it is not the choice made by markets, even efficient markets. Why not? What would it take to ensure sustainable allocations? Hartwick (1977) shows that the achievement of a constant per capita consumption path (which would satisfy our definition of sustainability) results when all scarcity rent is invested in capital. None of it should be consumed by current generations.

Would this be the normal outcome? No, it would not. With a positive discount rate, some of the scarcity rent is consumed, violating the Hartwick rule. The point is profound. Restoring efficiency will typically represent a move toward sustainability, but it will not, by itself, *always* be sufficient. Additional policies must be implemented to guarantee sustainable outcomes.

Not all economic models reach this discouraging conclusion. Specifically, a class of models with endogenous technical progress allows the possibility that efficient markets will produce sustainable outcomes. Endogenous technical progress means that the economic incentives inherent in the growth process produce a rate of technological progress that benefits future generations (remember that technological process shifts out the production possibilities). If the resulting rate is large enough to offset the declines to future generations caused by previous generations, efficient markets can produce sustainable outcomes.

Can we count on the fact that the endogenous rate to technological progress will be sufficiently high to generate a sustainable outcome? It is not guaranteed.

In Chapter 5, we pointed out that maintaining a nondeclining value of the capital stock (both physical and natural) provided an observable means of checking on the sustainability of current activity. If the value of the capital stock is declining, the activity is unsustainable. Can we automatically conclude that a nondeclining value of the capital stock implies the sustainability of current consumption levels? According to work by Asheim (1994) and elaborated on by Pezzey (1994), we cannot. Rising net wealth can coincide with unsustainability when the capital stock is being valued at the wrong (i.e., unsustainable) prices. When nonrenewable resources are being used up too rapidly, prices are driven down. Using these (artificially depressed) prices can create the false impression that the value of the depletion is less than the value of the additional investment and, therefore, that the value of the capital stock is rising. In fact, at the correct prices, the value of the capital stock may be falling.

Another study by Howarth and Norgaard (1990) reaches a similar conclusion from a different perspective. They derive competitive resource allocations across generations, assuming that each generation is assigned a specific share of the available depletable resources. This share is then varied and a new allocation calculated for each to reveal the effect of this intertemporal assignment of property rights to resources among generations. For our purposes, two of their conclusions are relevant: (1) the resulting allocations are sensitive to the initial allocation of the resource rights across generations; and (2) assigning all of the rights to the first generation would not produce a sustainable outcome. This study provides yet another perspective underlying the conclusion that efficient allocations of depletable resources do not necessarily produce sustainable outcomes.

How about with renewable resources? At least renewable resource flows could, in principle, endure forever. Are efficient market allocations of renewable resources compatible with sustainable development? John Pezzey (1992) has examined the sustainability of an allocation of a single renewable resource (such as corn) over time. Sustained growth of welfare can occur in this model, but only if two conditions hold: (1) the resource growth rate exceeds the sum of the discount rate and the population growth rate; (2) and the initial food supply is sufficient for the existing population. The first condition is sometimes difficult to meet, particularly with rapid population growth and slow-growing biological resources. Sustainable development of renewable resources is much harder in the presence of rapid population growth rates because the pressure to exceed sustainable harvest rates becomes harder to resist.

The second condition raises a more general and a more difficult concern. It implies the distinct possibility that if the starting conditions are sufficiently far from a sustainable path, sustainable outcomes may not be achievable without outside intervention. The simplest way to see this point is to note that a poor country that is reduced to eating all the seed corn to survive sacrifices its future in order to survive in the present. The double message that can be derived from these results is that (1) it is important to ensure, by acting quickly, that conditions do not deteriorate to the extent that survival strategies preclude investment; and (2) foreign aid is likely to be an essential part of sustainability policies for the poorest nations.

We must be careful to distinguish between what has been said and what has not been said. Restoring efficiency may well result in an improvement in sustainability, but efficiency may not be either necessary or sufficient for sustainability. Three different cases can emerge. In the first case, the private inefficient outcome is sustainable and the efficient outcome is also sustainable. In this case, restoring efficiency will raise well-being, but it is not necessary for sustainability. This case might prevail when resources are extraordinarily abundant relative to their use. In the second case, the private inefficient equilibrium is unsustainable, but the efficient outcome is sustainable. In this case, restoring efficiency not only increases current well-being, but it is also sufficient to ensure sustainability. In the final case, neither the private inefficient outcome nor the efficient outcome is sustainable. In this case, restoring efficiency will not be enough to produce a sustainable outcome. Some sacrifice by current generations would be necessary to ensure adequate protection for the well-being of future generations.

While efficient markets cannot always achieve sustainable development paths, this does not mean that unsustainability would be the norm. Indeed, the historical record suggests that the incompatibility of the efficiency criterion and the sustainability criterion has been the exception, not the rule. Capital accumulation and technological progress have expanded the ways in which resources could be used and have increased subsequent welfare levels in spite of a declining resource base. Nonetheless, the two criteria are certainly not inevitably compatible. As resource bases diminish and global externalities increase, the conflict between these criteria will become more important.

Trade and the Environment

One of the traditional paths to development involves opening up the economy to trade. Freer international markets provide lower prices for consumer goods (due to the availability of and competition from imported products) and the opportunity for domestic producers to serve foreign markets. The law of comparative advantage suggests that trade can benefit both parties. One might suspect (correctly) that as one moves from theory to practice, the story would become a bit more complicated.

The Role of Property Rights. From our previous studies in this book, it should be clear that trade can certainly inflict detrimental (and inefficient) effects on the environment when some nations (presumably those in the less developed South) have poorly defined property rights or have not internalized their externalities (such as pollution). In this kind of situation, the tragedy of the commons can become greatly intensified by freer trade. Poorly defined property rights in the exporting nations encourage the importing nations (by artificially lowering prices) to greatly expand their consumption of the underpriced resources. In this scenario, trade intensifies environmental problems by increasing the pressure on open-access resources and hastening their degradation.

Pollution Havens and the Race to the Bottom. The failure to control externalities such as pollution provides another possible route, known as the "pollution havens" hypothesis, for trade to induce or to intensify environmental degradation. According to this hypothesis, producers affected by stricter environmental regulations in one country will either move their dirtiest production facilities to countries with less stringent environmental regulations (presumed to be lower-income countries) or face a loss of market share due to the cheaper goods produced in the pollution havens.

Pollution levels in the pollution havens can change for three different reasons: (1) the composition effect, (2) the technique effect, or (3) the scale effect. According to the *composition effect*, emissions change as the mix of dirty and clean industries changes; as the ratio of dirty to clean industries increases, emissions increase, even if total output remains the same. (Note that this is the expected outcome from the pollution havens hypothesis.) The *technique effect* involves the ratio of emissions per unit output in each industry. Emissions could increase in pollution havens via this effect if each firm in the pollution haven became dirtier as a result of openness to trade. And finally the *scale effect* looks at the role of output level on emissions; even if the composition and technique effects were zero, emissions could increase in pollution havens simply because output levels increased.

In addition to suggesting a channel for degradation, the pollution havens hypothesis, if correct, could provide a justification for developing countries to accept lower environmental standards. In this view, lower environmental standards protect against job loss. In other words, it suggests a "race to the bottom" feedback mechanism where competitive incentives among nations force developing countries to keep environmental standards weak in order to attract jobs, and jobs move to those locations in search of the lower costs resulting from lower standards.

What is the evidence on the empirical validity of the pollution havens hypothesis and its race to the bottom implication? Earlier surveys of the empirical work, such as Dean (1992), found absolutely no support for the effect of environmental regulation on either trade or capital flows. Jaffe et al. (1995) reach the same conclusion in their survey of the effect of environmental regulations on US competitiveness. More recent studies reviewed by Copeland and Taylor (2004), however, have begun to find that environmental regulation can influence trade flows and plant location, all other things being equal, though the effects are still small.

Has there been a discernible exodus of dirty industries to developing countries? Apparently not. Studies that attempt to isolate composition, technique, and scale effects generally find that the composition effect (the most important effect for confirming the pollution havens hypothesis) is small relative to scale effects. Furthermore, in practice, technique effects normally result in less, not more, pollution (Hettige, Mani, & Wheeler, 2000). Though trade can increase pollution through the scale effect, these findings are quite different from what we would expect from a race to the bottom.

Actually, these results should not be surprising. Because pollution control costs comprise a relatively small part of the costs of production, it would be surprising if lowering environmental standards could become a major determinant of either firm location decisions or the direction of trade unless the costs of meeting those standards became a significant component of production cost.

The Porter "Induced Innovation" Hypothesis. The story does not end there. Michael Porter (1991), a Harvard Business School professor, has argued that more environmental protection can, under the right circumstances, promote jobs, not destroy them. Now known as the "Porter induced innovation hypothesis," this view suggests that firms in nations with the most stringent regulations experience a competitive advantage rather than a competitive disadvantage. Under this nontraditional view, strict environmental regulations force firms to innovate, and innovative firms ultimately tend to be more competitive. This advantage is particularly pronounced for firms producing pollution control equipment (which can then be exported to firms in countries subsequently raising their environmental standards), but it might also be present for firms that find, in retrospect, that meeting environmental regulations actually lowered their production costs. Some specific instances of regulation-induced lower production costs have been recorded in the literature (Barbera & McConnell, 1990), but few studies have found the Porter hypothesis to be universally true.

While it seems clear that innovation induced by environmental regulation could simultaneously increase productivity (lower costs) and lower emissions, it is less clear why this would necessarily always or even normally be the case. And if it were universally true, it is not clear why all firms would fail to adopt these techniques even in the absence of regulations.

The Porter hypothesis is valuable because it reminds us that a particularly ingrained piece of conventional wisdom ("environmental regulation reduces firm competitiveness") can be wrong. It would be a mistake, however, to use it as confirmation of the much stronger proposition that environmental regulation is universally good for competitiveness.

The Environmental Kuznets Curve (EKC). Although its proponents have come to recognize the potential problems for the environment posed by free trade, particularly in the face of externalities or poor property right regimes in the exporting countries, they tend to suggest that these problems will be self-correcting. Specifically, they argue that as freer trade increases incomes, the higher incomes will promote more environmental protection.

The specific functional relationship underlying this view comes from some earlier work by Simon Kuznets, a now deceased Harvard professor, and so has become known as the Environmental Kuznets Curve. According to this relationship, environmental degradation increases with higher per capita incomes up to some income level (the turning point). After the turning point, however, higher incomes result in reductions in environmental degradation. Some apparent confirmation of this view came from early studies that plotted variables such as SO_2 concentrations against per capita incomes using countries as the units of observation (data points).

The notion that increasing income from trade involves a self-correcting mechanism would have quite a different meaning if part of that correction involved exporting the pollution-intensive industries to other countries. This would change the meaning of the Kuznets curve considerably since it would involve a transfer of pollution, not a reduction of pollution. This conjecture is especially important in a finite world because it implies that developing countries would never experience the Kuznets turning point. Since they would have nowhere to go, the pollution-intensive industries could not be transferred again.

How is the EKC relationship affected by trade? Cole (2004) examines this question and finds that explicit consideration of trade effects in estimating the EKC relationship does not eliminate the turning point for most pollutants, but it does affect the timing. In particular, controlling for the transfer of pollution-intensive industries makes the actual turning point occur later than without considering these effects.

How about the general proposition that pollution problems are self-correcting with development? In general, that proposition has little empirical support (Neumayer, 2001; Pasten & Figueroa, 2012). The early studies used different nations as data points, but the interpretation suggested that an individual country would eventually increase environmental protection as its income increased. Subsequent studies that looked at how environmental protection varied over time as income increased within an individual country frequently did not find the expected relationship (Deacon & Norman, 2006; Vincent, 1997). Other studies found that it seemed to apply to some pollutants (such as SO_2) but not to others (such as CO_2) (List & Gallet, 1999; World Bank, 1992). And finally, as Example 20.1 illustrates, some case studies in countries that have experienced considerably freer trade regimes have generally experienced intensified, not reduced, environmental degradation.

What are we to make of this evidence? Apparently, environmental regulations are not yet a major determinant of either firm location decisions or the direction of trade. This implies that reasonable environmental regulations should not be held hostage to threats that polluters will leave the area and take their jobs with them; with few exceptions, firms that are going to move will move anyway, while firms that are not going to move will tend to stay whatever the regulatory environment.

When deterioration is caused by inadequate local property right regimes or inadequate internalization of externalities, it may not be necessary or desirable to prevent trade, but rather to correct these sources of market failure. These inefficiencies associated with trade could be solved with adequate property regimes and appropriate pollution control mechanisms. On the other hand, if establishing appropriate property regimes or pollution control mechanisms is not politically feasible, other means of protecting the resources must be found, including possibly restricting detrimental trade. However, caution must be used in imposing these trade restrictions, since they are a second-best policy instrument in this case and can even be counterproductive.[3]

[3]Barbier and Schulz (1997) note a case in which a trade restriction designed to protect against deforestation from excessive export logging sufficiently lowered the value of the forest that the land was deforested to facilitate its conversion to agriculture.

EXAMPLE 20.1

Has NAFTA Improved the Environment in Mexico?

The North American Free Trade Agreement (NAFTA) took effect in 1994. By lowering tariff barriers and promoting the freer flow of goods and capital, NAFTA integrated the United States, Canada, and Mexico into a single, giant market. The agreement has apparently been successful in promoting trade and investment. Has it also been successful in promoting environmental protection in Mexico?

According to a study by Kevin Gallagher (2004), it has not, although not necessarily due to the forces identified by the pollution havens hypothesis. Some effects clearly resulted in less pollution and others more, although on balance, air quality has deteriorated.

The pollution havens hypothesis might lead us to expect a relocation of heavily polluting firms from the United States to Mexico, but that apparently did not happen. None of the numerous statistical tests performed by the author supported that hypothesis.

In terms of positive effects on air quality from trade, Gallagher found significant shifts in Mexican industry away from pollution-intensive sectors; the post-trade Mexican industrial mix was less polluting than the pretrade industrial mix (the opposite of what would be expected from the pollution havens hypothesis). He even found that some Mexican industries (specifically steel and cement) were cleaner than their counterparts in the United States, a fact he attributes to their success in securing new investment for more modern plants with cleaner technologies.

The largest trade-related source of air quality degradation was the scale effect. Although the post-trade industrial mix generally shifted away from the most polluting sectors (meaning fewer average emissions per unit output), the promotion of exports increased output levels considerably. Increased output meant more emissions (in this case, almost a doubling).

One expectation emanating from the Environmental Kuznets Curve is that the increased incomes from trade would result in more environmental regulation, which, in turn, would curb emissions. That expectation was not met either. Gallagher found that both real government spending on environmental policy and the number of Mexican plant-level environmental compliance inspections fell by 45 percent after NAFTA, despite the fact that income levels reached the turning point expected by the pretrade studies.

Source: Gallagher. K. P. (2004). *Free trade and the environment: Mexico, NAFTA and beyond.* Palo Alto, CA: Stanford University Press.

While the foregoing argument suggests that the starkest claims against the environmental effects of free trade do not bear up under close scrutiny, it would be equally wrong to suggest that opening borders to freer trade inevitably results in a gain in efficiency and/or sustainability. The truth, it seems, depends on the circumstances, so pure ideology does not get us very far. The context matters.

Since new trade institutions are now emerging, new issues with enormous implications for the environment are emerging with them. Of particular interest are the environmental consequences of international trade rules under the General Agreement on Tariffs and Trade (GATT) and the World Trade Organization (WTO).

Trade Rules under GATT and the WTO

The General Agreement on Tariffs and Trade (GATT), the international agreement that laid the groundwork for the World Trade Organization (WTO), was first signed in 1947. That agreement provided an international forum for encouraging free trade between member states by regulating and reducing tariffs on traded goods and by providing a common mechanism for resolving trade disputes. Having now replaced the GATT forum, the WTO is the sole global international organization dealing with the rules of trade between nations.

As an organization devoted to freer trade, the WTO adjudicates disputes among trading nations through the lens of its effect on trade. Domestic restrictions on trade of any kind (including environmental restrictions) are suspect unless they pass muster. To decide whether they pass muster or not, the WTO has evolved a set of rules to define the border between acceptable actions and unacceptable actions.

These rules examine, for example, such things as "differential treatment." A disputed environmental action that discriminates against goods from another country (rather than holding imports and domestically produced goods to the same standard) is deemed differential treatment and is unacceptable. Disputed actions that are not the lowest-cost (and least injurious to trade) action that could have been taken to address the particular environmental problem are also unacceptable.

One of the most controversial rules involves a distinction between "product" concerns and "process" concerns (see Debate 20.1). At the risk of oversimplification, regulations that address product concerns (such as mandating the highest acceptable residual pesticide levels in foods) are acceptable, but regulations addressing the process by which the product was made or harvested (such as banning steel from a particular country because it is manufactured in coal-burning plants) are not acceptable. In the latter case, the steel from coal-burning plants is considered by the WTO to be indistinguishable from steel made by other processes, so the product is considered to be homogeneous and treating it as different is unacceptable.

The inability of any country to address process concerns in its imports clearly limits its ability to internalize externalities. In light of this interpretation, one way to internalize externalities in other countries would be to use means other than trade (international agreements to limit carbon emissions, for example). Another, as Debate 20.1 points out, is to use ecolabeling as a means of putting at least some market pressure on the disputed practices. How far that labeling can go without triggering a negative WTO ruling remains to be seen.

DEBATE 20.1 Should an Importing Country Be Able to Use Trade Restrictions to Influence Harmful Fishing Practices in an Exporting Nation?

Yellowfin tuna in the Eastern Tropical Pacific often travel in the company of dolphins. Recognizing that this connection could be exploited to more readily locate tuna, tuna fishermen used it to increase their catch with deadly effects for dolphins. Having located dolphins, tuna vessels would use giant purse seines to encircle and trap the tuna, capturing (and frequently killing) dolphins at the same time.

In response to public outrage at this technique, the United States enacted the Marine Mammal Protection Act (MMPA). This act prohibited the importation of fish caught with commercial fishing technology that results in the incidental kill or serious injury of ocean mammals in excess of US standards.

In 1991, a GATT panel ruled on an action brought by Mexico asserting that US law violated GATT rules because it treated physically identical goods (tuna) differently. According to this ruling, countries could regulate products that were harmful (as long as they treated domestic and imported products the same), but not the processes by which the products were harvested or produced in foreign countries. Using domestic regulations to selectively ban products as a means of securing change in the production or harvesting decisions of other countries was ruled a violation of the international trade rules.

The United States responded by mandating an ecolabeling program. Under this law, tuna caught in ways that killed dolphins could be imported, but those imports were not allowed to use the "dolphin-safe" label. Tuna caught with purse seines could only use the "dolphin-safe" label if special on-board observers witnessed no dolphin deaths. Disputes over some of the technical aspects of how this program is implemented are continuing.

Source: The official history of the case can be found at http://www.wto.org/english/tratop_e/dispu_e/cases_e/ds381_e.htm#top. (Last accessed on May 26, 2013.)

The Natural Resource Curse

One especially intriguing possible barrier to development might plague resource-abundant nations. Common sense suggests that those countries blessed with abundant resource endowments would be more likely to prosper. In fact, the evidence suggests the opposite—resource-abundant countries are less likely to experience rapid development (see Example 20.2).

The Growth–Development Relationship

Has economic growth historically served as a vehicle for development? Has growth really made the average person better off? Would the lowest-income members of the United States and the world fare better with economic growth or without it?

EXAMPLE 20.2

The "Natural Resource Curse" Hypothesis

Perhaps, surprisingly, robust evidence suggests that countries endowed with an abundance of natural resources are likely to develop less rapidly than countries with a more modest natural resource base. And it is not merely because resource-rich countries are subject to volatile commodity prices.

Why might a large resource endowment exert a drag on growth? Several possibilities have been suggested. Most share the characteristic that resource-rich sectors are thought to "crowd out" investment in other sectors that might be more likely to support development:

- One popular explanation, known as the "Dutch Disease," is usually triggered by a significant increase in revenues from raw material exports. The resulting boom draws both labor and capital out of traditional manufacturing and causes it to decline.
- Another explanation focuses on how the increase in domestic prices that typically accompanies the resource boom impedes the international competitiveness of manufactured exports and therefore export-led development.
- A third explanation suggests that the large rents to be gained from the resource sectors in resource-abundant countries would cause entrepreneurial talent and innovation to be siphoned away from other sectors. Thus, resource-rich countries could be expected to have lower rates of innovation, which, in turn, results in lower rates of development.
- Finally, countries endowed with natural resources can give rise to domestic institutions in which autocratic or corrupt political elites finance themselves through physical control of the natural resources.

While countries with large resource endowments may not have the significant opportunities for development that might have been expected, it is encouraging to note that lots of countries without large resource endowments have not been precluded from achieving significant levels of development.

Sources: Sachs, J. D., & Warner, A. M. (2001). The curse of natural resources. *European Economic Review, 45*(4–6), 827–838; Auty, R .M. *Sustaining development in mineral economies: The resource curse thesis.* London: Routledge, Inc.; Kromenberg, T. (2004). The curse of natural resources in the transition economies. *Economics of Transition, 12*(3), 399–426; Frankel, J. A. (April 2012). The natural resource curse: A survey of diagnoses and some prescriptions. *Harvard Kennedy School Faculty Research Working Paper Series RWP12-014.*

These turn out to be difficult questions to answer in a way that satisfies everyone, but we must start somewhere. One appropriate point of departure is clarifying what we mean by *development*. Some of the disenchantment with development can be traced to the way that development is measured. It is not so much that all growth is bad, but that increases in conventional indicators of development are not always good. Some of the enthusiasm for zero economic growth stems from the fact that economic development, as currently measured, can be shown to have several undesirable characteristics.

Conventional Measures

A true measure of development would increase whenever we, as a nation or as a world, were better off and decrease whenever we were worse off. Such a measure is called a *welfare measure* and no conventional existing measure is designed to be a welfare measure.

In contrast the conventional measures of national accounting we currently use are *output measures*, which attempt to indicate how many goods and services have been produced, not how well off we are. Measuring output sounds fairly simple, but it is not. The measure of economic development with which most are familiar is based upon the GDP (gross domestic product). This number represents the sum of the outputs of goods and services produced by the economy in any year. Prices are used to weight the importance of these goods and services in GDP. Conceptually, this is accomplished by adding up the value added by each sector of the production process until the product is sold.

Why weight by prices? Some means of comparing the value of extremely dissimilar commodities is needed. Prices provide a readily available system of weights that takes into account the value of those commodities to consumers. From early chapters we know that prices should reflect both the marginal benefit to the consumer and the marginal cost to the producer.

GDP is not a measure of welfare and was never meant to be one. Therefore increases in this indicator (growth) may not represent increases in development or well-being. One limitation of this indicator as a measure of welfare is that it includes the value of new machines that are replacing worn-out ones, rather than increasing the size of the capital stock. To compensate for the fact that some investment merely replaces old machines and does not add to the size of capital stock, a new concept known as net domestic product (NDP) was introduced. NDP is defined as the gross domestic product minus depreciation.

NDP and GDP share the deficiency that they are both influenced by inflation. If the flow of all goods and services were to remain the same while prices doubled, both NDP and GDP would also double. Since neither welfare nor output would have increased, an accurate indicator should reflect that fact.

To resolve this problem, national income accountants present data on *constant-dollar* GDP and *constant-dollar* NDP. These numbers are derived by "cleansing" the actual GDP and NDP data to take out the effects of price rises. Conceptually, this is accomplished by defining a market basket of goods that stays the same over time. Each year, this same basket is repriced. If the cost of the goods in the basket went up 10 percent, then because the quantities are held constant, we know that prices went up by 10 percent. This information is used to remove the effects of prices on the indicators; remaining increases should be due to an increased production of goods and services.

This correction does not solve all problems. For one thing, not all components of GDP contribute equally to welfare. Probably the closest, though still deficient, we could use in the existing system of accounts would be consumption, the amount of goods and services consumed by households. It leaves out government expenditures, investments, exports, and imports.

The final correction that could easily be made to the existing accounts would involve dividing real consumption by the population to get *real consumption per capita*. This correction allows us to differentiate between rises in output needed to maintain the standard of living for an increasing population and rises indicating more goods and services consumed by the average member of that population.

Real consumption per capita is about as close as we can get to a welfare-oriented output measure using conventional accounting data. Yet it is a far cry from being an ideal welfare indicator.

In particular, changes in real consumption per capita fail to distinguish between economic growth resulting from a true increase in income, and economic growth resulting from a depreciation in what economists have come to call "natural capital," the stock of environmentally provided assets, such as the soil, the atmosphere, the forests, wildlife, and water.

The traditional definition of income was articulated by Sir John Hicks (1939):

> *The purpose of income calculations in practical affairs is to give people an indication of the amount they can consume without impoverishing themselves. Following out this idea, it would seem that we ought to define a man's income as the maximum value which he can consume during a week, and still expect to be as well off at the end of the week as he was at the beginning. (p. 172)*

While human-created capital (such as buildings and bridges) is treated in a manner consistent with this definition, natural capital is not. As human-created capital wears out, the accounts set aside an amount called depreciation to compensate for the decline in value as the equipment wears out. No increase in economic activity is recorded as an increase in income until depreciation has been subtracted from gross returns. That portion of the gains that merely serves to replace worn-out capital is not appropriately considered income.

No such adjustment is made for natural capital in the standard national income accounting system. Depreciation of the stock of natural capital is by default incorrectly counted as income. Development strategies that "cash in" on the endowment of natural resources are in these accounts indistinguishable from development strategies that do not depreciate the natural capital stock; the returns from both are treated as income.

Consider an analogy. Many high-quality private educational institutions in the United States have large financial endowments. When considering their budgets for the year, these institutions take the revenue from tuition and other fees and add in some proportion of the interest and capital gains earned from the endowment. Except in extraordinary circumstances, standard financial practice, however, does not allow the institution to attack the principal. Drawing down the endowment and treating this increase in cash flow as income is not allowed.

Yet that is precisely what the traditional national accounts allow us to do in terms of natural resources. We can deplete our soils, cut down our forests, and douse ocean coves with oil, and the resulting economic activity is treated as income, not as a decline in the endowment of natural capital.

Because the Hicksian definition is violated for natural capital, policymakers can be misled. By relying upon misleading information, policymakers are more likely to undertake unsustainable development strategies. Adjusting the national income accounts to apply the Hicksian definition uniformly to human-made and natural capital could, in resource-dependent countries, make quite a difference.

Motivated by a recognition of these serious flaws in the current system of accounts, a number of other industrial countries have now proposed (or in a few cases have already set up) systems of adjusted accounts, including Norway, France, Canada, Japan, the Netherlands, and Germany. Significant differences of opinion on such issues as whether the changes should be incorporated into a complementary system of accounts or into a complete revision of the standard accounts remain to be resolved.

Alternative Measures

Are we fulfilling the sustainability criterion or not? Although that turns out to be a difficult question to answer, a number of indicators have now been designed to allow us to make some headway. These indicators differ in both their construction and the insights that can be derived from them.

Ecological Footprint. One example of an indicator, the Ecological Footprint, differs considerably from the others in that it is based upon a physical measure rather than an economic measure. The Ecological Footprint indicator attempts to measure the amount of renewable and nonrenewable ecologically productive land area that is required either to support the resource demands or to absorb the wastes of a given population or specific activities.[4] The footprint is expressed in "global acres." Each unit corresponds to one acre of biologically productive space with "world average productivity." Every year has its own set of equivalence factors since land-use productivities change over time. By comparing this "footprint" to the amount of ecologically available land, deficits or surpluses can be uncovered.

This indicator calculates national consumption by adding imports to, and subtracting exports from, domestic production. This balance is computed for 72 categories, such as cereals, timber, fishmeal, coal, and cotton. The footprint (in terms of acres) for each category of resource uses is calculated by dividing the total amount consumed in each category by its ecological productivity (or yield per unit area). In the case of carbon dioxide (CO_2) emissions, the footprint is calculated by dividing the emissions by the average assimilative capacity of forests to find the number of acres necessary to absorb the pollutants.

According to this indicator, the industrialized nations have the most unsustainable consumption levels (meaning that their consumption requires more ecologically productive land than is domestically available). This analysis also

[4]The details about this indicator can also be found on the Global Footprint Network Website at http://www.footprintnetwork.org/en/index.php/gfn/page/footprint_basics_overview/. Anyone can have his or her own ecological footprint calculated by answering a few questions at http://www.myfootprint.org/.

suggests that current global consumption levels cannot be sustained indefinitely by the current amount of ecologically productive land—we are in a deficit situation.

The Genuine Progress Indicator. One alternative indicator that has been developed is the Genuine Progress Indicator (GPI). While GDP is a measure of current production, the GPI is designed to measure the economic welfare generated by economic activity, essentially counting the depreciation of community capital as an economic cost. GPI starts with Personal Consumption Expenditures (a major component of GDP), but adjusts that data using 24 different components, including income distribution, environmental costs, and negative activities like crime and pollution, among others. GPI also adds positive components that are not included in the GDP, including the benefits of volunteering and household labor. Following an extensive analysis of the GPI both over time and across counties Kubiszewski et al. (2013) find a significant variation among these countries, but some major trends over the 1950–2003 period:

- "Global GPI/capita peaked in 1978, about the same time that global Ecological Footprint exceeded global biocapacity."
- "Life Satisfaction in almost all countries has also not improved significantly since 1975."
- "Globally, GPI/capita does not increase beyond a GDP/capita of around $7000/capita."

The Human Development Index. One reason for dissatisfaction with all of these measures of well-being is their focus on an average citizen. To the extent that the most serious problems of deprivation are not experienced by the average member of society, this focus may leave a highly misleading impression about well-being. To rectify this problem, in 1990, the United Nations Development Program (UNDP) constructed an alternative measure, the Human Development Index (HDI). This index has three major components: longevity, knowledge, and income.

Though highly controversial, because both the measures to be included in this index and the weights assigned to each component are rather arbitrary, the UNDP (2013) has drawn some interesting conclusions:

- The rise of the South is radically reshaping the world of the twenty-first century, with developing nations driving economic growth, lifting hundreds of millions of people from poverty, and propelling billions more into a new global middle class.
- More than 40 developing countries have made greater human development gains in recent decades than would have been predicted.
- These achievements are largely attributable to sustained investment in education, health care and social programs, as well as to an open engagement with an increasingly interconnected world.

Gross National Happiness. Bhutan is a small Asian country situated at the eastern end of the Himalayas. It shares borders with India and the People's Republic of China. In November 2008, the country adopted the Gross National Happiness index as an alternative to more conventional measures to guide its development strategy. This single number, Gross National Happiness index, which is based upon an extensive survey of the citizens of Bhutan, is based upon nine core *dimensions* that are regarded as components of happiness and well-being in Bhutan. The nine dimensions are as follows:

1. *Psychological Well-being*
2. *Time Use*
3. *Community Vitality*
4. *Culture*
5. *Health*
6. *Education*
7. *Environmental Diversity*
8. *Living Standard*
9. *Governance*

Gross national happiness is deemed to have risen over time if sufficient achievements in these nine dimensions have been obtained. Since it is very new, how well this index serves its intended purpose remains to be seen. Some early results from 2012 indicate that overall fewer women are happy than men (forty-nine percent of men are happy, while only one-third of women are). For the portion of the population that is in the lowest happiness group the biggest barriers to happiness stem from a lack of education, low living standards, and an unsatisfying use of time (including longer working hours).

How important is money to happiness? It seems like a simple question, but that simplicity can be deceptive (see Example 20.3).

Summary

Sustainable development refers to a process for providing for the needs of the present generation (particularly those in poverty) without compromising the ability of future generations to meet their own needs.

Market imperfections frequently make sustainable development less likely. Intergenerational externalities such as climate modification impose excessive costs on future generations. Free access to biological common property resources can lead to excessive exploitation and even extinction of the species.

Even efficient markets do not necessarily guarantee development that can be sustained. Restoring efficiency is desirable and helpful but can be insufficient as a means for producing sustainable welfare levels. While in principle dynamically

EXAMPLE 20.3

Happiness Economics: Does Money Buy Happiness?

In recent years, economists and psychologists have become interested in what has become known as the economics of happiness. What is that makes people happy and what role does income play?

A psychologist and an economist (Kahneman & Deaton, 2010) analyzed the responses of more than 450,000 US residents surveyed in 2008 and 2009 to several questions about their subjective well-being. Their results suggest a rather complex answer to this question, suggesting that it depends on how well-being is measured.

The authors defined two rather different subjective measures of well-being.

- One measure, labeled "Emotional Well-Being," refers to the emotional quality of an individual's everyday experience—the frequency and intensity of experiences of joy, fascination, anxiety, sadness, anger, and affection that make one's life pleasant or unpleasant. In this study emotional well-being is captured by two variables. The first, which deals with aspects of positive well-being, sums three binary (1 or 0) variables measuring self-reported happiness, enjoyment, and frequent smiling and laughter. The second, capturing a "blue effect," takes the average of two binary variables, measuring stress and worry. All questions asked the respondent to respond relative to his/her experience the previous day.
- The second measure, which the authors label "Life Evaluation," has the respondent rate his or her current life on a ladder scale in which 0 is "the worst possible life for you" and 10 is "the best possible life for you." Unlike the previous measure that focuses on a snapshot of feelings at a specific point in time, this question is a more overarching measure of well-being.

Before getting to the statistical results of how income affects these measures of well-being, consider some comparative observations revealed by these data. The authors found that most people were quite happy and satisfied with their lives. These results indicate that the US population ranks high on the Life Evaluation Index (ninth after the Scandinavian countries, Canada, The Netherlands, Switzerland, and New Zealand), and also does well in terms of happiness (5th), smiling (33rd), and enjoyment (10th), but much less well on worry (89th from least worried), sadness (69th from least sad), and anger (75th). Americans report very high levels of stress (5th among 151 countries).

In terms of income, the present study finds that "a lack of money brings both emotional misery and low life evaluation. . . . Beyond $75,000 in the contemporary United States, however, higher income is neither the road to experienced happiness nor the road to the relief of unhappiness or stress, although higher income continues to improve individuals' life evaluations" (p. 16491).

Sources: Bruni, L., & Porta, P. L. (2005). *Economics and happiness: Framing the analysis.* Oxford/New York: Oxford University Press. Kahneman, D., & Deaton, A. (2010). High income improves evaluation of life but not emotional well-being. *Proceedings of the National Academy of Sciences, 107*(38), 16489–16493.

efficient allocations can produce extraction profiles for depletable resources that are compatible with the interests of future generations, in practice this is not necessarily the case. When trade is used as part of the development strategy, it must be used carefully. The effects of trade on the environment are neither universally benign nor universally detrimental. Context matters.

We have examined a series of indicators that attempt to shed light on the degree to which current national practices are sustainable. Though all of these indicators are both incomplete and flawed, they all convey some important insights.

The Ecological Footprint provides helpful reminders that scale does matter and that the earth on which we all depend is ultimately limited in its ability to fulfill our unlimited wants. Though the Ecological Footprint finding that we have already exceeded the earth's carrying capacity is controversial, it does usefully lay to rest the naïve view that our ability to consume is limitless and emphasize that we had better start thinking about how to stay within those limits. The Ecological Footprint is also helpful in pointing out that affluence is fully as big a challenge to sustainability as poverty.

The Human Development Index reminds us that the relationship between income growth and the well-being of the poorest citizens of the world is far from a sure thing, in contrast to what some would have us believe. While income growth can provide a means for empowerment for the poor, it can only do so when accompanied by appropriate policy measures, such as ensuring universal health care and education and limiting the perverse effects of corruption. The index also identifies a number of low-income countries that have made great strides in ensuring that the fruits of development do reach the poor.

New sustainable forms of development are possible, but they will not inevitably be adopted. Economic incentive policies can facilitate the transition from unsustainable to sustainable activities. The search for solutions must recognize that market forces are extremely powerful. Attempts that ignore those forces are probably doomed to failure. Nonetheless, it is possible to harness those forces and channel them in directions that enhance the possibilities of sustainable outcomes. To take these steps will require thinking and acting in somewhat unconventional ways. Whether the world community is equal to the task remains to be seen.

Discussion Questions

1. Consider a possible mechanism for controlling population. According to an idea first put forth by Kenneth Boulding (1964) each individual would be given the right to produce one (and only one!) child. Because this scheme over a generation allows each member of the current population to replace himself or herself, births would necessarily equal deaths and population stability would be achieved.

   This scheme would award each person a certificate, entitling the holder to have one child. Couples could pool their certificates to have two. Every time a child was born, a certificate would be surrendered. Failure to produce a certificate would cause the child to be put up for adoption. Certificates would be fully transferable.

Is this a good idea? What are its advantages and disadvantages? Would it be appropriate to implement this policy now in the United States? For those who believe that it would, what are the crucial reasons? For those who believe it is not appropriate, are there any circumstances in any countries where it might be appropriate? Why or why not?

2. "Every molecule of a nonrenewable resource used today precludes its use by future generations. Therefore, the only morally defensible policy for any generation is to use only renewable resources." Discuss.
3. "Future generations can cast neither votes in current elections nor dollars in current market decisions. Therefore, it should not come as a surprise to anyone that the interests in future generations are ignored in a market economy." Discuss.
4. "Trade simply represents economic imperialism where one country exploits another. The environment is the inevitable victim." Discuss.

Self-Test Exercises

1. Because export taxes on are frequently seen as falling on foreign consumers, they tend to be favored as revenue sources by many countries. What assumptions are necessary for export taxes to be born entirely by foreign consumers? How likely is it that this set of assumptions characterizes the current world market for food commodities such as coffee or oranges?
2. If a natural disaster, such as the 2010 drought in Russia, hits food production, use supply and demand analysis to figure out how this affects consumers and producers. Does everyone lose or are some groups better off? Why?
3. Suppose the United States imposes a tariff on imported sugar. What are the consequences of this on consumers, domestic and foreign producers, and land use?

Further Reading

Copeland, B. R., & Taylor, M. S. (March 2004). Trade, growth, and the environment, *Journal of Economic Literature*, *42*, 7–71. An excellent survey of the lessons to be derived from the theory and empirical work focusing on the relationship between trade and the environment.

Deacon, R. T., & Norman, C. S. (2006). Does the environmental Kuznets curve describe how individual countries behave? *Land Economics*, *82*(2), 291–315. Examining time series data within countries, the authors find weak evidence of the existence of a Kuznets curve for SO_2 in wealthier countries, but no evidence for a Kuznets curve for other pollutants and for poorer countries.

De Soysa, I., & Neumayer, E. (2005). False prophet or genuine savior? Assessing the effects of economic openness on sustainable development, 1980–1999. *International Organization*,

59(3), 731–772. Estimates the effects of a dependence on trade, and foreign direct investment on sustainability as measured by the genuine saving rate. They find openness enhances sustainability.

Fischer, C. (2010). Does trade help or hinder the conservation of natural resources? *Review of Environmental Economics and Policy*, *4*(1), 103–121. This article reviews and takes stock of the lessons from the recent economics literature on the links between trade and the conservation of natural resources.

Frankel, J. A. (April 2012). The natural resource curse: A survey of diagnoses and some prescriptions. *Harvard Kennedy School Faculty Research Working Paper Series RWP12-014*. This paper reviews the literature on the Natural Resource Curse, focusing on six channels of causation that have been proposed.

Kubiszewski, I., Costanza, R., Franco, C., Lawn, P., Talberth, J., Jackson, T, & Aylmer, C. (2013). Beyond GDP: Measuring and achieving global genuine progress. *Ecological Economics*, *93*, 57–68. A synthesis of estimates of GPI over the 1950–2003 time period for 17 countries for which GPI has been estimated and analysis of the results.

Layard, R. (2005). *Happiness: Lessons from a new science.* New York: Penguin Press. Using integrated insights from psychology, economics, neuroscience, and sociology, a distinguished British economist explores the sources of human happiness.

Pasten, R., & Figueroa, E. B. (2012). The environmental Kuznets curve: A survey of the theoretical literature.*International Review of Environmental and Resource Economics*, *6*(3), 195–224. This paper reviews and summarizes most of the literature on the Environmental Kuznets Curve,

Additional References and Historically Significant References are available on this book's Companion Website: http://www.routledgetextbooks.com/textbooks/9780133479690

21 Visions of the Future Revisited

"Distinguishing the signal from the noise requires both scientific knowledge and self-knowledge: the serenity to accept the things we cannot predict, the courage to predict the things we can, and the wisdom to know the difference."

—Nate Silver, *The Signal and the Noise: Why So Many Predictions Fail—But Some Don't*

Introduction

We have now come full circle. Having begun our study with two lofty visions of the future, we proceeded to dissect the details of the various components of these visions—the management of depletable and renewable resources, pollution, and the development process itself. During these inquiries we gained a number of useful insights about individual environmental and natural resource problems. Now it is time to step back and coalesce those insights into a systematic assessment of the two visions.

Addressing the Issues

In Chapter 1, we posed a number of questions to serve as our focus for the overarching issue of growth in a finite environment. Those questions addressed three major issues: (1) How is the problem correctly conceptualized? (2) Can our economic and political institutions respond in a timely and democratic fashion to the challenges presented? (3) Can the needs of the present generation be met without compromising the ability of future generations to meet their own needs? Can short-term and long-term goals be harmonized? The next three segments of this section summarize and interpret the evidence.

Conceptualizing the Problem

At the beginning of this book, we suggested that if the problem is characterized as an exponential growth in demand coupled with a finite supply of resources, the resources must eventually be exhausted. If those resources are essential, society will collapse when the resources are exhausted.

We have seen that this is an excessively harsh and somewhat misleading characterization. The growth in the demand for resources is not insensitive to their scarcity. Prices matter.

Price is not the only factor that retards demand growth. Declines in population growth also play a significant role. Since the developed nations appropriate a disproportionate share of the world's resources, the dramatic declines in population growth in those countries has had a disproportionate effect on slowing the demand for resources. On the other hand, the rapidly rising consumption levels in high-growth, densely populated countries like China and India are having the opposite effect.

Characterizing the resource base as finite—the second aspect of the model—is also excessively harsh: (1) this characterization ignores the existence of a substantial renewable resource base and (2) it focuses attention on the wrong issue.

In a very real sense, a significant portion of the resource base is not finite. Plentiful supplies of renewable resources including, significantly, energy are available. The normal market reaction to increasing scarcity of individual depletable resources, such as oil, is to switch to renewable resources. That is clearly happening. The most dramatic examples can be found in the transition to wind, solar, and hydrogen fuel cells.

In addition, labeling the resource base as finite is also misleading because it suggests that our concern should be with "running out." In fact, for most resources we shall never run out. Millions of years of finite resources are left at current consumption rates. For most of these resources the rising cost (including environmental cost) of extracting and using those resources is the chief threat to future standards of living, not the potential for their exhaustion. The limits on our uses of these resources are not determined by their scarcity in the crust of the earth, but rather by the environmental consequences of their use. The implications of climate change, including rising sea level, heat extremes, droughts, and storm surges, are potentially so severe as to force a major reevaluation of our carbon-based energy choices. Similarly, the loss of biodiversity, which would be intensified by climate change, could irreversibly alter our ecosystems and reduce their resilience to future shocks.

Resource scarcity can be countered without violating sustainability by finding new sources of conventional materials, as well as discovering new uses for unconventional materials, including what was previously considered waste. We can also stretch the useful life of these reserves by reducing the amount of materials needed to produce the products. Striking examples include the diminishing size of a typical computer system needed to process a given amount of information and the substantially diminished amount of energy needed to heat a well-designed home.

For energy sources the issue is whether the transition to low-carbon fuels can proceed with sufficient speed and effectiveness so as to maintain economic well-being while preventing serious climate change damages.

Paradoxically, some of the most obvious cases of binding limits involve renewable resources, rather than depletable resources. Demand pressure, whether driven by population growth or rising incomes, is a key contributor to this phenomenon.

Expanding demand forces the cultivation of marginal lands and the deforestation of large, biologically rich tracts. The erosion of overworked soils diminishes their fertility and, ultimately, their productivity. Demand pressure can also contribute to the overexploitation of biological resources such as fisheries, even to the point of extinction. Trade can intensify these processes, especially when property regimes do not adequately protect the resources. For many resources the problem is not their finiteness, but the way in which they have been managed. It is important to recognize that "renewable" and "sustainable" are not synonyms.

Correct conceptualization of the resource scarcity problem suggests that both extremely pessimistic and extremely optimistic views are wrong. Impenetrable proximate physical limits on resource availability are typically less of a problem than the adverse atmospheric and biological consequences of their use. Transitions to renewable resources, recycled resources, carbon-free fuels, and less costly depletable resources have already begun. Whether the pace of the transition is sufficient remains to be seen.

Institutional Responses

One of the keys to understanding how society will cope with increasing resource scarcity and environmental damage lies in understanding how social institutions will react. Are market systems, with their emphasis on decentralized decision making, and democratic political systems, with their commitment to public participation and majority rule, equal to the challenge?

Our examination of the record seems to suggest that while our economic and political systems are far from infallible and have some rather glaring deficiencies, no fatal flaws are apparent.

On the positive side, markets have responded swiftly and automatically to deal with those resources experiencing higher prices. Demand has been reduced and substitution encouraged. Markets for recycling are growing and consumer habits are changing. Green buildings are proliferating. Renewable energy sources are being developed. No one has had to oversee these responses to make sure they occur. As long as property rights are well defined, the market system provides incentives for consumers and producers to respond to scarcity in a variety of useful ways (see Example 21.1).

As compelling as the evidence is for this point of view, it does not support the stronger conclusion that, left to itself, the market would automatically choose a dynamically efficient or a sustainable path for the future. Market imperfections frequently make sustainable development less likely. Treating resources such as the fish we eat, the air we breathe, and the water we drink as free-access resources can undermine their sustainable use. Left to its own devices a market will overexploit free-access resources, substantially lowering the net benefits received by future generations. In the absence of sufficient compensating increases in net benefits elsewhere in the economy, such exploitation could result in a violation of the sustainability criterion.

Externalities are also a barrier in the transition to sustainability. When many of the costs of using unsustainable resources are born by someone other than those

EXAMPLE 21.1

Private Incentives for Sustainable Development: Can Adopting Sustainable Practices Be Profitable?

Motivated by what it perceived to be great inefficiencies associated with its industry, the Interface Corporation, a carpet manufacturer, totally transformed the nature of its business. How it managed this transformation is instructive.

First, the company recognized that unworn carpet, usually under furniture, did not need to be replaced. In response, the company switched from selling traditional wall-to-wall carpet to selling a carpet tile system. Whereas in traditional practice, wear in any part of the carpet meant that the entire carpet had to be replaced; with carpet tiles only those specific tiles showing wear are replaced. As an added benefit, the reduction in carpet replacement simultaneously reduces the amount of potentially harmful glue fumes being released into the indoor air.

Next, Interface totally changed its relationship with its customers. Rather than selling carpet, Interface leased it. In effect, it became a seller of carpet services rather than a seller of carpets. Carpet tiles can be easily replaced overnight by Interface employees, eliminating the loss of productivity that could occur from halting company activities during the day. The cost to consumers is substantially lower not only because less carpet is replaced but also because leasing allows tax advantages. Leased carpet is treated by the tax code as an expense, not an asset, and, hence, lowers taxes.

The environment also benefited. In traditional industry practice, most used carpet was transported to a landfill. Much of the rest was remanufactured into much-lower-valued uses. Seeing that as a waste of resources, Interface created an entirely new product that, when recycled at the end of its useful life, could be remanufactured back into carpet. Not only was this production process less wasteful in terms of its drain on energy and raw materials, the product was also reportedly highly stain-resistant, four times as durable as regular carpet material, and easily cleaned with water.

These moves toward more sustainable manufacturing did not result from government mandates. Rather, an innovative company found that it could benefit itself and the environment at the same time.

Source: Hawken, P., Lovins, A., & Lovins, L. H. (1999). *Natural capitalism: creating the next industrial revolution.* Boston, MA: Little, Brown and Company.

making the resource choices, private and social costs will not align and the market process will be biased. Only when the externalities are internalized can sustainable resources compete on a level playing field.

Even efficient markets do not necessarily produce sustainable development. Restoring efficiency is frequently a desirable, but often insufficient means for producing sustainable welfare levels. While in principle dynamically efficient allocations can produce extraction profiles for depletable resources that are compatible with the interests of future generations, as we have seen in practice this is not necessarily the case. The market does have some capacity for self-correction. The decline of overexploited fish populations, for example, led to the rise of private aquaculture. In this case the artificial scarcity created by imperfectly defined property rights gave rise to incentives for the development of a private property substitute.

This capacity of the market for self-healing, while comforting, is not always adequate. In some cases, cheaper, more effective solutions (such as preventing the deterioration of the original natural resource base) are available. Preventive medicine is frequently superior to corrective surgery. In other cases, such as when our air is polluted, no adequate private substitutes are available. To provide an adequate response, it is sometimes necessary to complement market decisions with political ones.

The case for government intervention is especially compelling in controlling pollution. Uncontrolled markets not only produce too much pollution, but also they tend to underprice commodities (such as coal) that contribute to pollution either when produced or consumed. Firms that unilaterally attempt to control their pollution run the risk of pricing themselves out of the market. Government intervention is needed to ensure that firms that neglect environmental damage in their operating decisions do not thereby gain a competitive edge.

Significant progress has been made in reducing the amount of pollution, particularly conventional air pollution. Regulatory innovations, such as the sulfur allowance program and the Swedish NO_x charge, represent major steps toward the development of a flexible but powerful framework for controlling air pollutants. By making it less costly to achieve environmental goals, these reforms can limit the potential for a backlash against the policy. They have brought perceived costs more in line with perceived benefits.

It would be a great mistake, however, to assume that government intervention has been uniformly benign. The acid-rain problem, for example, was almost certainly made worse by an initial policy structure that focused on local rather than regional pollution problems, and using MTBE as a gasoline additive to reduce air pollution. While the former encouraged the export of pollution via tall stacks, the latter created new water pollution problems.

One aspect of the policy process that does not seem to have been handled well is the speed with which improvement has been sought. Public opinion polls have unambiguously shown that the general public supports environmental protection even when it raises costs and lowers employment. Historically, as shown by the early regulation of automobile pollution, policy-makers reacted to this resolve by writing very tough legislation designed to force rapid technological development.

Common sense suggests that tough legislation with early deadlines can achieve environmental goals more rapidly than weaker legislation with less tight deadlines. In this case common sense is frequently wrong. Writing excessively tough legislation with unreasonably early deadlines can have the opposite effect. Such regulations are virtually impossible to enforce. Recognizing this situation, polluters repeatedly exploited this weakness by seeking (and receiving) delays in compliance. In this particular regulatory regime it was frequently better, from the polluter's point of view, to spend resources to change the regulations than to comply with them. This would not have been the case with less stringent regulations, since the firms would have had no legally supportable grounds for delay.

Another flagrant example of counterproductive government intervention is to be found in treatment of both energy and water. By imposing price ceilings on natural gas and oil, the government removed much of the normal resiliency of the economic system. With price controls, the incentives for expanding the supply are reduced and the time profile of consumption is tilted toward the present. A similar story can be told about water. By holding water prices below the marginal cost of supply, water authorities have subsidized excess use.

Resources that in a normal market would have been conserved for future generations are, with price controls, consumed by the current generation. When price controls are placed on normal market transactions, the smooth transition to renewable resources that characterizes the normal market allocation is eliminated; shortages can arise.

In summary, the record compiled by our economic and political institutions has been mixed. It seems clear that simple prescriptions such as "leave it to the market" or "more government intervention" simply do not bear up under a close scrutiny of the record. The relationship between the economic and political sectors has to be one of selective engagement, complemented in some areas by selective disengagement. Each problem has to be treated on a case-by-case basis. As we have seen in our examination of a variety of environmental and natural resource problems, the efficiency and sustainability criteria allow such distinctions to be drawn, and those distinctions can serve as a basis for policy reform.

Sustainable Development

Historically, increases in inputs and technological progress have been important sources of economic growth in the industrialized nations. In the future, some factors of production, such as labor, will not increase as rapidly as they have in the past. The effect of this decline on growth depends on the interplay among the law of diminishing marginal productivity, substitution possibilities, and technological progress. The law of diminishing marginal productivity suggests slower growth rates, while technological progress and the availability of substitutes counteract this drag. One view foresees limits to technological progress imposed by the second law of thermodynamics, implying that the growth process must culminate in a steady or stationary state where growth ultimately, but inevitably, diminishes to zero.

The economy is currently being transformed. It is not business as usual. The increasing corporate focus on sustainability is playing a role. As citizens become better informed, they are beginning to use their power as consumers, employees, shareholders, and voters to let companies know that they support business behavior that is compatible with sustainable outcomes.

Recognizing that conventional measures of economic growth shed little light on the question, some crude attempts have been made to estimate whether or not growth in the industrialized countries has historically made the citizens of those countries better off. Results of these studies suggest that because growth has ultimately generated more leisure, longer life expectancy, and more goods and services, it has been beneficial. Yet other measures, such as the ecological footprint, convey a more cautionary story. They remind us that our inability to measure precisely the earth's carrying capacity for supporting human activity in no way diminishes the existence and importance of those limits.

Our examination of the evidence suggests that the notion that all of the world's people are automatically benefited by economic growth is naïve. Economic growth has demonstrably benefited some citizens, but that outcome is certainly not inevitable for all people in all settings. Expanding pollution and diminishing access to crucial resources such as water or land can offset or even more than offset the gains for at least some subset of the population. New sustainable forms of development are possible and desirable, but they will not automatically be adopted in either the high-income or the low-income nations.

The economic incentives approach to environmental and natural resource regulation has become a significant component of environmental and natural resource policy. Instead of mandating prescribed actions, such as requiring the installation of a particular piece of pollution control equipment, this approach achieves environmental objectives by changing the economic incentives of those doing the polluting. Incentives can be changed by fees or charges, transferable entitlements, disclosure strategies, or even liability law. By changing the incentives an individual agent faces, that agent can use his or her typically superior information to select the best means of meeting his or her assigned responsibility. When it is in the interest of individuals to change to new forms of development, the transformation can be amazingly rapid.

Public policy and sustainable development must proceed in a mutually supportive relationship. In some cases that relationship takes the form of public–private partnerships that involve explicit agreements between government and the private sector regarding the provision of public services or infrastructure (see Example 21.2). In other cases, it involves government regulatory action to ensure that the market is sending the right signals to all participants so that the sustainable outcome is compatible with other business objectives. Economic-incentive approaches are a means of establishing that kind of compatibility. The experience with the various versions of this approach used in the United States, Europe, and Asia suggests that allowing business great flexibility within a regulatory framework that harmonizes private and social costs in general is both feasible and effective.

How about global environmental problems? Economic-incentives approaches could be helpful here as well. Carbon pricing facilitates cost sharing among participants while ensuring cost-effective responses to the need for additional control. By separating the question of what control is undertaken from the question of who ultimately pays for it, the government significantly widens the control possibilities and lowers compliance costs. Conferring property rights for biological populations on local communities provides an incentive for those communities to protect the populations. Strategies for reducing debt can diminish the pressure on natural resources that might otherwise be "cashed in" to pay off the debt.

EXAMPLE 21.2

Public–Private Partnerships: The Kalundborg Experience

Located on an island 75 miles off the coast of Copenhagen, the city of Kalundborg has achieved a remarkable symbiosis among the various industries that provide the employment base for the city. The four main industries, along with small businesses and the municipal government, began developing cooperative relationships in the 1970s designed to lower disposal costs, attain less expensive input materials, and receive income from their waste products.

A coal-fired power plant (Asnaes) transports its residual steam to a refinery (Statoil). In exchange, Statoil gives Asnaes refinery gas that Asnaes burns to generate electricity. Asnaes sells excess steam to a local fish farm, to a heating system for the city, and to a pharmaceuticals and enzyme producer (Novo Nordisk). Continuing the cycle, the fish farm and Novo Nordisk send their sludge to farms to be used as fertilizer. Produced fly ash is sold to a cement plant and gypsum produced by its desulfurization process is sold to a wallboard manufacturer. Statoil, the refinery, sells the sulfur removed from its natural gas to a sulfuric acid manufacturer, Kemira.

This entire process resulted not from centralized planning, but simply because it was in the individual best interests of the public and private entities involved. Although the motives were purely financial, this synergetic situation has clear environmental benefits. It is therefore likely to be economically, as well as environmentally, sustainable.

Sources: Desroches, P. Eco-industrial parks: The case for private planning, *Report # RS 00-1.* Political Economy Research Center, Bozeman, MT 59718; http://www.symbiosis.dk/en

Europe and parts of Asia have more experience with effluent or emissions charges. This approach places a per-unit fee on each unit of pollution discharged. Faced with the responsibility for paying for the damage caused by their pollution, firms recognize it as a controllable cost of doing business. This recognition triggers a search for possible ways to reduce the damage, including changing inputs, changing the production process, transforming the residuals to less-harmful substances, and recycling by-products. The experience in the Netherlands and Japan, countries where the fees are higher than in most other countries, suggests that the effects can be dramatic.

Fees and auctioned allowances also raise revenue. Successful development, particularly sustainable development, requires a symbiotic partnership between the public and private sectors. To function as an equal partner, the public sector must be adequately funded. If it fails to raise adequate revenue, the public sector becomes a drag on the transformation process, but if it raises revenue in ways that distort incentives that, too, can act as a drag. Effluent or emissions charges an auctioned allowances offer the realistic opportunity to raise revenue for the public sector, while reducing the drag from more distortionary taxes. Whereas other types of taxation discourage growth by penalizing legitimate development incentives (such as taxing wages), emissions or effluent charges provide both incentives and revenue to support sustainable development. Some work from the United States suggests that the drag on development avoided by substituting carbon pricing for more traditional revenue-raising mechanisms, such as capital gains, income, and sales taxes, could be significant.

Incentives for forward-looking public action are as important as those for private action. The current national income accounting system provides a perverse economic signal. Though national income accounts were never intended to function as a device for measuring the welfare of a nation, in practice that is how they are used. National income per capita is a common metric for evaluating how well-off a nation's people are. Yet the current construction of those accounts produces information that can be highly misleading.

Rather than recognizing oil spills for what they are, namely a source of decline in the value of the endowment of natural resources in the area, under current accounting procedures cleanup expenditures increase measured national income; spills actually boost GDP! But the reason, of course, is that no account is taken of the consequent depreciation of the natural environment. The current system of accounts make no distinction between growth that is occurring because a country is drawing down or degrading its natural resource endowment with a consequent irreversible decline in its value, and sustainable development, where the value of the natural endowment remains intact. Only when suitable corrections are made to these accounts will governments be judged by the appropriate standards.

The power of economic incentives is certainly not inevitably channeled toward the achievement of sustainable growth. They can be misapplied as well as appropriately applied. Remember that tax subsidies to promote cattle ranching on the fragile soil in the Brazilian rain forest not only stimulated an unsustainable activity but it also imposed irreparable damage on an ecologically significant area. Incentive approaches must be used with care.

A Concluding Comment

Our society is evolving. The emerging complementary relationship among the economic system, the court system, and the legislative and executive branches of government is promising. We are, however, not yet out of the woods. Significantly, we the public must learn that part of the responsibility is ours. The government cannot solve all problems without our significant participation.

Not all behavior can be regulated. It costs too much to catch every offender. Our law enforcement system works because most people obey the law, whether anyone is watching or not. A high degree of voluntary compliance is essential for the system to work smoothly.

The best resolution of the toxic substance problem, for example, is undoubtedly for all makers of potentially toxic substances to be genuinely concerned about the safety of their products and to bite the bullet whenever their research raises questions. The ultimate responsibility for developing an acceptable level of risk must rest on the integrity of those who make, use, transport, and dispose of the substances. The government can assist by penalizing and controlling those few who fail to exhibit this integrity, but regulation can never completely substitute for integrity. We cannot and should not depend purely upon altruism to solve these problems, but we should not underestimate its importance either.

We also need to recognize that markets serve our preferences as consumers. Making sure our purchases and investments reflect environmental values will help markets move in the right direction. Fuel-efficient automobiles will enter the market much faster if many consumers demand them. Sustainably harvested fisheries will proliferate once consumers shun fish from those fisheries that are managed unsustainably. It is easy to see large corporations as villains, but it is tougher to notice the villains in our mirrors.

The notion that we are at the end of an era may well be true. But we are also at the beginning of a new one. What the future holds is not the decline of civilization, but its transformation. The road may be strewn with obstacles and our social institutions may deal with those obstacles with less grace and less finesse than we might have hoped, but we are unquestionably making progress.

Discussion Questions

1. Are you optimistic or pessimistic about the future? Why?
2. In thinking about the appropriate balance between the market and the government in achieving sustainability, do you think the government needs to take a stronger role or would you favor reducing government influence over the market? Why?

Further Reading

Hawken, P. (2010).*The ecology of commerce revised edition: A declaration of sustainability.* New York: Harper Collins. A classic in the field, this book makes the case for why business success and sustainable environmental practices need not—and, for the sake of our planet, must not—be mutually exclusive any longer.

Answers to Self-Test Exercises

Chapter 1

1. A shortage would promote higher prices, thereby lowering demand until it equaled the new smaller supply. Since this acts to reduce rather than intensify the shortage, it is a negative feedback loop.

   If consumers anticipate these higher prices, however, thereby buying and hoarding extra amounts before the prices rise, this is an example of a positive feedback loop because it intensifies the shortage.

Chapter 2

1. a. This is a public good, so add the 100 demand curves vertically. This yields $P = 1{,}000 - 100q$. This demand curve would intersect the marginal-cost curve when $P = 500$, which occurs when $q = 5$ miles.

   b. The economic surplus is represented by a right triangle, where the height of the triangle is \$500 (\$1,000, the point where the demand curve crosses the vertical axis, minus \$500, the marginal cost) and the base is 5 miles. The area of a right triangle is $1/2 \times$ base $\times$ height $= 1/2 \times \$500 \times 5 = \$1{,}250$.

2. a. Set $MC = P$, so $80 - 1q = 1q$. Solving for q finds that $q = 40$ and $P = 40$.

   b. Consumer surplus = \$800. Producer surplus = \$800. Consumer surplus plus producer surplus = \$1,600 = economic surplus.

   c. The marginal revenue curve has twice the slope of the demand curve, so $MR = 80 - 2q$. Setting $MR = MC$, yields $q = 80/3$ and $P = 160/3$. Using Figure 2.8, producer surplus is the area under the price line (FE) and over the marginal-cost line (DH). This can be computed as the sum of a rectangle (formed by FED and a horizontal line drawn from D to the vertical axis) and a triangle (formed by DH and the point created by the intersection of the horizontal line drawn from D with the vertical axis).

   The area of any rectangle is base $\times$ height. The base $= 80/3$ and the

$$\text{Height} = P - MC = \frac{160}{3} - \frac{80}{3} = \frac{80}{3}.$$

Therefore, the area of the rectangle is 6,400/9. The area of the right triangle is

$$\frac{1}{2} \times \frac{80}{3} \times \frac{80}{3} = \frac{3{,}200}{9}.$$

$$\begin{aligned}\text{Producer surplus} &= \frac{3{,}200}{9} + \frac{6{,}400}{9}\\ &= \frac{9{,}600}{9}.\end{aligned}$$

$$\begin{aligned}\text{Consumer surplus} &= \frac{1}{2} \times \frac{80}{3} \times \frac{80}{3}\\ &= \frac{\$3{,}200}{9}.\end{aligned}$$

d. 1. $\frac{\$9{,}600}{9} > \$800$

2. $\frac{\$3{,}200}{9} < \$800$

3. $\frac{\$12{,}800}{9} < \$1{,}600$

3. The policy would not be consistent with efficiency. As the firm considers measures to reduce the magnitude of any spill, it would compare the marginal costs of those measures with the expected marginal reduction in its liability from reducing the magnitude of the spill. Yet the expected marginal reduction in liability from a smaller spill would be zero. Firms would pay $\$X$ regardless of the size of the spill. Since the amount paid cannot be reduced by controlling the size of the spill, the incentive to take precautions that reduce the size of the spill will be inefficiently low.

4. If "better" means efficient, this common belief is not necessarily true. Damage awards are efficient when they equal the damage caused. Ensuring that the award reflects the actual damage will appropriately internalize the external cost. Larger damage awards are more efficient only to the extent that they more closely approximate the actual damage. Whenever they promote an excessive level of precaution that cannot be justified by the damages, awards that exceed actual cost are inefficient. Bigger is not always better.

5. a. Descriptive. It is possible to estimate this linkage empirically.

   b. Normative. A descriptive analysis could estimate the impacts of expenditures on endangered species, but moving from that analysis to a conclusion that expenditures would be wasted requires injecting values into the analysis.

c. Normative. A descriptive analysis could compare the effects of privatized and nonprivatized fisheries, but moving from these results to a conclusion that the fisheries must be privatized to survive normally requires an injection of values. If the data revealed that all privatized fisheries survived and none of the others did, the move to "must" would have a very strong descriptive underpinning.

d. Descriptive. This linkage could be estimated empirically directly from the data.

e. Normative. This statement could be descriptive if it was stated as "birth control programs actually contribute to a rise in population" since this is an empirical relationship that could be investigated.

However, as stated, it allows a much wider scope of aspects to enter the debate and weighing the importance of those aspects will normally require value judgments.

6. a. A pod of whales is a common-pool resource to whale hunters. It is characterized by nonexclusivity and divisibility.

   b. A pod of whales is a public good to whale watchers since it is characterized by both nondivisibility and nonexclusivity.

   c. The benefits from reductions of greenhouse gas emissions are public goods because they are both nondivisible and nonexclusive.

   d. For residents, a town water supply is a common-pool resource because it is both divisible and nonexclusive to town residents. It is not a common-pool resource for nonresidents since they can be excluded.

   e. Bottled water is neither; it is both divisible and exclusive. In fact it is a private good.

Chapter 3

1. With risk neutrality, the policy should be pursued because the expected net benefits (0.85 × \$4,000,000 + 0.10 × \$1,000,000 + 0.05 × −\$10,000,000 = \$3,000,000) are positive. Related Discussion Question: Looking at these numbers, do you think risk neutrality is how you would actually think about this situation? Or would you be more risk averse and weigh the third outcome more heavily than its expected likelihood?

2. a. Cost-effectiveness in this case (according to the second equimarginal principle) requires that that target be met (10 fish removed) and the marginal costs of each method be equal. We know that $q_1 + q_2 + q_3 = 10$ and that $MC_1 = MC_2 = MC_3$. The key is to reduce this to one equation with one unknown. Since $MC_1 = MC_2$ we know that \$10q_1 will equal \$5q_2, or $q_1 = .5q_2$. Similarly, $MC_2 = MC_3$, so $\$5q_2 = \$2.5q_3$ or $q_3 = 2q_2$. Substituting these values into the first equation yields $.5q_2 + 1q_2 + 2q_2 = 10$. So $q_2 = 10/3.5 = 2.86$ (to two decimal places.) That means $q_1 = 1.43$ and $q_3 = 5.72$. (The fact that this adds to 10.01 rather than 10.00 is due to rounding.)

   b. All three of these methods have a marginal cost that increases with the amount removed. Thus the cost of removing the first fish for each is cheaper than removing the second fish with that method, and so on. Consider the marginal cost of removing the last fish if all fish are removed by method three. In that case the marginal cost would be \$2.5 × 10 or \$25. Notice that the cost-effective allocation, the cost of removing the last fish when the marginal costs are equal (using q_1 for the calculation) is \$10 × \$1.43 = \$14.30. In the case of increasing marginal costs using a combination is much cheaper.

c. In this case you would only use method three because the marginal cost of removing each fish would be \$2.5. This is lower than the *MC* for method 1 (\$10) and lower than the *MC* for method 2 (\$5). Note that the marginal costs only have to be equal for the methods that are actually used. The marginal costs for unused methods will be higher.

3. Since the benefit cost test requires that the present value of benefits be greater than the present value of the costs, we can find the maximum allowable current cost by calculating the present value of the benefits. This can be calculated as \$500,000,000,000/$(1 + r)^{50}$ where r is either 0.10 or 0.02. Whereas with a 10 percent discount rate the present value is approximately \$4.3 billion, with a 2 percent discount rate it is approximately \$185.8 billion. Clearly the size of the discount rate matters a lot in determining efficient current expenditures to resolve a long-range problem.

Chapter 4

1. In order to maximize net benefits, Coast Guard oil-spill prevention enforcement activity should be increased until the marginal benefit of the last unit equals the marginal cost of providing that unit. Efficiency requires that the level of the activity be chosen so as to equate marginal benefit with marginal cost. When marginal benefits exceed marginal cost (as in this example), the activity should be expanded.

2. a. According to the figures given, the per-life cost of the standard for unvented space heaters lies well under the implied value of life estimates given in the chapter, while per-life cost implied by the proposed standard for formaldehyde lies well over those estimates. In benefit–cost terms, the allocation of resources to fixing unvented space heaters should be increased, while the formaldehyde standard should be relaxed somewhat to bring the costs back into line with the benefits.

   b. Efficiency requires that the marginal benefit of a life saved in government programs (as determined by the implied value of a human life in that context) should be equal to the marginal cost of saving that life. Marginal costs should be equal only if the marginal benefits are equal and, as we saw in the chapter, risk valuations (and hence the implied value of human life) depend on the risk context, so it is unlikely they are equal across all government programs.

3. a. The total willingness to pay for this risk reduction is \$200 million (\$50 per person × 4 million exposed people.) The expected number of lives saved would be 40 (1/100,000 risk of premature death × 4,000,000 exposed population). The implied value of a statistical life would be \$5,000,000 (\$200,000,000 total willingness to pay/40 lives saved).

b. The program is expected to save 160 lives ((6/100,000 − 2/100,000) × 4,000,000). According to the value of a statistical life in (a), the program will have more benefits than costs as long as it costs no more than $800,000,000 ($5,000,000 value per life × 160 lives saved).

Chapter 5

1. a. Ten units would be allocated to each period.
   b. $P = \$8 - 0.4q = \$8 - \$4 = \$4$
   c. User cost $= P - MC = \$4 - \$2 = \$2$
2. Because in this example the static allocations to the two periods (those that ignore the effects on the other period) are feasible within the 20 units available, the marginal user cost would be zero. With a marginal cost of $4.00, the net benefits in each period would independently be maximized by allocating 10 units to each period. In this example no intertemporal scarcity is present, so price would equal a $4.00 marginal cost.
3. Refer to Figure 5.2. In the second version of the model, the lower marginal extraction cost in the second period would raise the marginal net benefit curve in that period (since marginal net benefit is the difference between the unchanged demand curve and the lower *MC* curve). This would be reflected in Figure 5.2 as a parallel leftward shift out of the curve labeled "Present Value of Marginal Net Benefits in Period 2." This shift would immediately have two consequences: it would move the intersection to the left (implying relatively more would be extracted in the second period), and the intersection would take place at a higher vertical distance from the horizontal axis (implying that the marginal user cost would have risen).
4. a. The higher discount rate would lower the present value of the net benefit function in the second period. This would be reflected as a rotation of that function downward to the right. The new function would necessarily cross the PVMNB1 function at a point further to the right and lower than before the discount rate change. The fact that the intersection is further to the right implies that more is being allocated to period 1 and less to period 2. The fact that the intersection is lower implies that the present value of the marginal user cost has declined.
   b. Since a higher discount rate lowers the present value of allocations made to the second period, allocating relatively more of the resources to the first period will increase the present value derived from them. The present value of the marginal user cost is lower since the marginal opportunity cost of using the resources earlier has gone down.
5. a. Increasing the second period demand is reflected in the two-period model by a shift (not a rotation) in the PVMNB2 curve upward and to the left. After the shift, this new function will necessarily intersect the PVMNB1 curve closer to the left-hand axis and higher up on the Y-axis. This implies an increase in the relative amount allocated to the second period (thereby reducing the amount allocated to the first period) and a higher present value of the marginal user cost.

b. When demand is increasing in the future (hence making the marginal resources relatively more valuable), it makes sense to save more for the future. This is accomplished by a rise in the marginal user cost, which results in higher prices. The higher prices provide the incentive to save more for the future. More is consumed in the second period despite the higher prices because the demand curve has shifted out.

Chapter 6

1. From the hint, $MNB_1/MNB_2 = (1 + k)/(1 + r)$. Notice that when $k = 0$, this reduces to $MNB_2 = MNB_1(1 + r)$, the case we have already considered. When $k = r$, then $MNB_1 = MNB_2$; the effect of stock growth exactly offsets the effect of discounting, and both periods extract the same amount. If $r > k$, then $MNB_2 > MNB_1$. If $r < k$, then $MNB_2 < MNB_1$.
2. a. With a demand curve shifting out over time, the marginal net benefits from a given future allocation increase over time. This raises the marginal user cost (since it is the opportunity cost of using the resource now) and, hence, the total marginal cost. Thus, the initial user cost would be higher.

   b. Less of the resource would be consumed in the present; more would be saved for the future.
3. a. This turns out to have the same effect as the environmental cost pictured in Figures 6.6a and 6.6b. The tax serves to raise the total marginal cost and, hence, the price. This tends to lower the amount consumed in all periods compared to a competitive allocation.

   b. The tax also serves to reduce the cumulative amount extracted because it raises the marginal cost of each unit extracted. Some resources that would have been extracted without the tax would not be extracted with the tax; their after-tax cost to the producer exceeds the cost of the substitute. The price would be higher with the tax in all periods prior to the without-tax switch point. After that time the price would be equal to the price of the substitute with or without the tax.
4. The cumulative amount ultimately taken out of the ground is determined by the point at which the marginal extraction cost equals the maximum price consumers will pay for the depletable resource. In this model the maximum price is the price of the substitute. Neither the monopoly nor the discount rate affects either the marginal extraction cost or the price of the substitute, so they will have no effect on the cumulative amount ultimately extracted. The subsidy, however, has the effect of lowering the net price (price minus subsidy) of the substitute. The intersection of marginal extraction cost and the net price will, therefore, occur when a smaller cumulative amount has been extracted than would be the case in the absence of the subsidy.
5. They would not produce the same switch point. The switch would be faster under the subsidy. While they would result in the same cumulative amount of the depletable resource being extracted, the speed with which it would be

extracted would be faster with the subsidy. By raising the after-tax price the tax would reduce demand (and hence the speed with which the depletable resource would be used up), while the subsidy would, by lowering the marginal user cost, increase demand (and hence increase the rate at which the depletable resource was extracted).

Chapter 7

1. During a recession, the demand curve shifts inward, causing downward pressure on prices. If price is supported, then the quantity supplied must be reduced. Since the burden of holding the price up falls on the cartel, while the competitive fringe can keep on producing, the demand reduction causes production to fall most heavily in OPEC nations. This causes the cartel market share to fall. To protect their individual market shares, members start cutting prices. In growing markets, cartel market shares can be protected without cutting prices.

2. a. Producer surplus $= \frac{\$3{,}200}{9}$, $P = MC = \frac{\$80}{3}$.

   Consumer surplus $= \frac{\$9{,}600}{9}$, $q = \frac{80}{3}$.

   b. This is the mirror image of the monopoly allocation. The net benefits are identical in the two allocations, but they are distributed among producers and consumers rather differently. With this form of price control, the consumer surplus is larger and the producer surplus is smaller than the corresponding concepts when the allocation is governed by a monopoly. Essentially, the rectangle discussed in the answer to part (b) of the second problem in Chapter 2 goes to consumers with price ceilings and to producers in a monopoly.

3. The paper company. The high-cost energy is appropriately assigned to the five paper machines because that is the energy cost that would be eliminated if the machines were shut down. The company would not shut down all energy sources in proportion; it would shut down the most expensive sources. In making a shutdown decision, therefore, it is essential that the machines in question cover the cost of the energy that would be saved if the machines were shut down; otherwise, the company is losing money.

4. Peaking plants run only a small percentage of the time, so the capital expenditures remain unused most of the time. Operating costs are incurred only when they are needed. It makes sense, therefore, for utilities to design peaking plants so as to keep capital costs as low as possible, even if it means incurring higher operating cost. Base-load plants, on the other hand, run almost continuously, so the capital costs are prorated over a very large number of kilowatt-hours and therefore are less of a burden.

5. No. This could internalize some of the externalities associated with oil, but it would not internalize the climate change externalities of other fuels such as coal and indeed might exacerbate them as consumers switched from oil to coal.

6. a. *False.* While cartel members with small stocks of the depletable resource would be generally supportive, cartel members holding large reserves would be afraid that the high early price increases would force an earlier switch to renewables, leaving them with unsold stocks.

   b. *False.* By holding prices lower than they would otherwise be, placing a price control on a depletable resource would increase the speed with which the resource is extracted over time, but it would lower the cumulative amount ultimately extracted.

   c. *False.* By lowering the marginal user costs, a price control influences the extraction path of a depletable resource well before the time that the market price actually reaches the level of the price control.

   d. *Uncertain.* While internalizing the externality, as proposed here, is generally a move toward efficiency, the details do matter. For example, the level of compensation could be too high or too low. Remember that for efficiency the payments should exactly equal the damages caused. Excessive compensation can be inefficient because, by raising the expected cost of future operations above the efficient levels, it could preclude some efficient oil drilling. On the other hand, inadequate compensation, by ultimately understating the future expected cost, could promote excessive oil drilling.

7. The existence of a renewable energy credit market would lower the compliance costs associated with meeting a renewable portfolio standard by providing more flexibility to compliance units. For example, without such a market utilities would have to assure that they supplied the requisite amount of renewable power within their market area regardless of whether that market area was suitable for that renewable power or not. With a renewable energy credit market, producers can create the renewable power in those areas that are most suitable (e.g., have the requisite wind flow, water flow, or solar flux) and sell any excess to jurisdictions that could only generate their own renewable power at a much higher cost. Substituting this more efficiently produced (and hence lower-cost) power for the more inefficiently produced (and hence higher-cost) power, allows the standard to be met at a lower cost.

8. Incorporating national security concerns, but ignoring climate change impact means that domestic production is determined by the intersection of S_{d1} with P_{w2} and total consumption is determined by the intersection of P_{w2} with domestic demand. Note that this results in a lower price level (P_{w2} rather than P_{w3}), more domestic production (since domestic producers are ignoring the climate-change impact), and more domestic consumption (due to the lower price).

Chapter 8

1. a. Assume that only virgin ores are used. In this case, $P = MC_1$, so $10 - 0.5q_1 = 0.5q_1$ or $q_1 = 10$. This implies $MC_1 = 5$. The marginal cost of producing any units using recycled products is clearly higher than 5, so none will be used. Therefore, 10 units would be produced, and all of them would be produced using virgin ores.

   b. With the higher demand curve, the price will be high enough to stimulate the producer to make some of the product with recycled materials. The key to solving this problem is recognizing that the producer will equate the marginal costs of products made with recycled materials and those made with virgin ores. Using this fact, we can set $0.5q_1 = 5 + 0.1q_2$ or $q_1 = 10 + 0.2q_2$. Substituting this into the demand function yields

$$P = 20 - 0.5(10 + 0.2q_2 + q_2) \text{ or}$$
$$P = 15 - 0.6q_2.$$

Solving for $P = MC$ yields

$$15 - 0.6q_2 = 5 + 0.1q_2 \text{ or } q_2 = \frac{100}{7}$$

and

$$q_1 = 10 + 0.2\left(\frac{100}{7}\right) = \frac{90}{7}.$$

The solution can be verified by showing

$$P = MC_1 = MC_2 = \frac{45}{7}.$$

2. a. They will not have the same effect. Because the royalty is a per-ton fee, it raises the marginal cost of extraction to the firm, but the bonus bid, which does not affect the marginal cost of extraction, does not. If the mineral has an increasing marginal cost of extraction, less will be extracted with a royalty system than with a bonus bid system because the marginal cost of extraction (including the royalty payment) will hit the backstop price at a smaller cumulative amount extracted.

   b. The bonus bid is consistent with efficiency because it does not distort the allocation over time. The allocation that maximized firm profits before the bonus bid will still maximize it after the bonus bid. While the government shares the profits, it does so without distorting incentives. By raising the marginal cost of extraction, royalty schemes distort incentives.

   c. With a bonus bid scheme, the firm bears the risk. The government gets a fixed payment. The firm can either win big or lose big, depending on how valuable the deposit turns out to be. With the royalty scheme, the risk is shared. If the mine turns out to be very valuable, profits and government fees both go up. If the deposit turns out not to be very valuable, the firm gains little but so does the government.

3. Rising societal disposal cost is certainly one of the factors that should stimulate higher recycling rates, but it is by no means the only one. And as long as it is not the only factor, recycling rates will not automatically increase in response. First, this higher social cost must be reflected in increasing marginal disposal costs facing individuals in order to provide the incentive to recycle; rising social costs do not automatically result in rising individual marginal costs. Second, markets must exist for the recycled materials. Collecting them does no good if they can't be put to good use.

4. a. The sticker system would tend to be more efficient. Because the property tax approach to financing is not related to the amount of trash disposed of, the marginal cost of disposing of an additional bag under this system is zero. This is considerably lower than the cost to the town of disposing of the waste. The marginal cost to the consumer does not reflect the marginal cost to the town. In contrast, the sticker system imposes a marginal cost per bag that could, if the sticker price were calculated correctly, exactly equal the marginal cost to the town.

   b. Since the cost of the sticker does not have to be paid for illegally disposed trash, requiring stickers could promote illegal dumping. (People do, of course, have to pay any imposed fines if they get caught.) If illegal disposers tend not to get caught so illegal disposal is rampant, it could raise the costs to the town above $30.00 to recover and process the dispersed trash and would undermine the efficiency of the sticker system. A property tax financing system provides no incentives for illegal disposal since the cost is paid however a household chooses to manage its trash.

Imposing a deposit-refund on some large components of the trash would help to reduce illegal disposal because illegal disposal would now cost something—the consumer loses the deposit. However, a deposit refund system would raise no revenue for the town to cover its disposal costs since the deposit is returned to the consumer once the object is transported to the collection site.

Chapter 9

1. Since the amount of capacity needed would depend on the maximum flow during the year, the extra cost of expanding capacity during this high-flow period should be reflected in higher prices charged to users during these periods.

2. Assuming the rate was correct, the flat rate would be more efficient because it would confront the user with a positive marginal cost of further consumption. The marginal cost of further consumption with a flat fee is zero.

3. a. For the case in which the ground water comes from a private well that taps a private aquifer, with perfect information the owner would have an incentive to extract the water at an efficient rate. The private owner would face all costs, both present and future, and be able to balance them accordingly. The *social*

present value of marginal net benefit curves for both periods would be identical to the *private* present value of marginal net benefit curves for both periods. Note, however, the very important "full information" caveat. If the owner doesn't know what is there, he or she can't very well allocate it efficiently, regardless of how good the incentives are.

b. For the case in which the ground water is obtained from your private well that is drilled into an aquifer that is shared with many other users who have also drilled private wells, an efficient allocation would not be expected. Perverse incentives would arise both within any particular time period and over time. Because this is a divisible resource, within a time period, each user would know that any unit not extracted by him or her could well be extracted by a neighbor. The incentive is to take more than the efficient amount to avoid losing it. Over time, the users would act as if the marginal user cost is zero since the trade-off between the present and the future that characterizes the situation in part (a) is lost. Whereas in a private well whatever I don't use now I can simply use later, that is not true in a shared aquifer. Water not used by me now may well be used by someone else and be gone forever. This particular institutional arrangement encourages the overuse of water and thereby serves to intensify any problems of scarcity.

4. The key to using the tiered system for this purpose is to distinguish water needs by monthly volume. Specifically, the first block could contain a basic amount of water that fulfills essential purposes, while the second block contains all other water above that amount. The first block would be priced at a low level, while the second block price would reflect all of the scarcity rent generated by the marginal user cost as well as the marginal cost of extraction and distribution. Since the positive marginal user cost means that the marginal revenue for that block would be above the marginal extraction plus distribution cost, the utility could still cover its expenses despite the low cost of the first units. Meanwhile, because most households would consume at least some more water than allowed in the first block, the price they would face for the additional water would be the efficient (marginal cost) price in the second block. The fact that the price for the additional water would be the efficient price would preserve incentives to conserve an efficient amount.

Chapter 10

1. The congestion charge would raise the cost of transportation for commuters, while the increased number of lanes would reduce it (considering travel time). According to the bid rent function analysis, the congestion charge would make the residential bid rent function steeper and encourage more density in the urban area and less expansion into the suburban areas served by those expressways. Conversely, the new lanes would make the bid rent function less steep and encourage more people to move into the suburbs.
2. Land confers a bundle of entitlements to the owner. Conservation easements allow the transfer of only the specific entitlements of interest (typically the

development rights). For land conservation organizations, buying only the entitlements of interest is considerably cheaper than buying the land itself. Therefore, conservation groups could stretch a given budget over many more pieces of land with conservation easements than by buying the land outright. Donors may value some specific entitlements more than any market price they could get for them (and hence want to retain them, an option afforded by conservation easements), but for other entitlements the market price (or the value of the tax deduction) may be higher, making sale or donation the best option. An owner of a forest, for example, may wish to continue to harvest wood from that land, while being willing to donate the developments rights when he or she has little or no interest in selling the forest to a developer anyway.

3. The simplest difference is that relative to an income tax, property tax funding would make land and the improvements on that land more expensive to own. This, in turn, would raise the cost of all land-intensive activities such as forestry or farming relative to activities requiring much less land. It might also cause all firms engaging in land-intensive activities to consider if they could get away with using less land. It might cause some residents, for example, to downsize to smaller units.
4. Many answers, of course, are possible for this question, but here are a few possibilities.
   a. In this age group we could expect to have a smaller household size (as any children are grown and gone), thereby lowering the need for housing space. We might expect some of these households to downsize to smaller dwelling units.
   b. We might expect some movement back into urban areas as the need for space declines and difficulties with mobility arise.
   c. Access to schools could become less important and access to medical facilities more important.
   d. In the face of diminishing human energy to do landscaping and maintenance, condominiums could become relatively more attractive, since all their landscaping and maintenance is handled by the association in return for a monthly fee. Since most condominium units are smaller than owners' previous housing, this is also a way to downsize.
   e. As health problems commonly rise with age, assisted living facilities should become more common and some retirees will move to be closer to their children.
   f. As older households are likely to be less constrained by either work or parenting schedules, they are freer to move to locales offering especially high-quality, age-appropriate leisure-time activities.
   g. Since household net worth is probably higher after a lifetime of earning, this wealth might well also promote more seasonal second-home sales.

Notice that many of these hypotheses are testable by examining the appropriate data. Are condos becoming a greater percent of the residential housing stock? Are older households moving back into urban areas? Has second-home buying become more prevalent? Sounds like a good research project.

5. Because the ethanol subsidy raises the profitability of growing corn as a fuel, it should (1) increase the amount of domestic land allocated to agriculture (since more per acre is now earned), (2) increase the amount of domestic agricultural land allocated to fuel corn (since the net benefits per acre of that specific land use have increased), and (3) lower the amount of domestic land allocated to producing food crops as farmers, in response to these net benefit per acre changes, allocate more land to fuel and less to food crops (most obviously, but not only, corn).
6. Working at home reduces the amount of commuting and hence the cost of commuting. One implication is a lower incentive to locate close to work. If workplaces are densely located, working at home should make more remote locations relatively more attractive. Hence, according to this effect, the density of development might be expected to decline.

Chapter 11

1. The plot being turned into a housing development would have the shortest rotation period (youngest age) because the cost of delaying the harvest would be greatest in this case. It would include an additional cost—the cost of delaying the construction of the housing development—that would have to be factored in, causing net benefits to be maximized at an earlier harvest age.
2. The cost trend is the result of two offsetting trends. Harvesting cost is a function of the volume of wood, so it increases as the volume of wood increases. Since these costs are discounted, however, costs further in the future are discounted more. When the tree growth gets small enough, the discounting effect dominates the growth effect and the present values of the costs decline.
3. A relative increase in the demand for forest-base biomass fuels would increase the value of wood used for this purpose. To the extent that this added supply of fuel holds household energy costs lower than they would otherwise have been, consumers benefit, but they might lose if they use wood for other purposes (as its price would be likely to rise). The producers of this fuel will benefit, but producers of more traditional fuels would lose. Producers of products from wood other than fuels (say paper mills using the wood for pulp) would lose as their costs would rise. To the extent that this domestic biomass fuel substitutes for imported fuel, the state can expect an income increase as the funds formerly sent abroad are now spent locally where they have a higher multiplier effect.
4. The market would be expected to reach an efficient balance if the owner was actively engaged in selling both recreation and harvested wood. In this case the forest owner compares the marginal net benefits (reflected in their respective revenue streams) of various combinations of harvesting and recreation and chooses the combination that yields the highest net benefit. If, however, as is common, the private owner sells only harvested wood, recreational uses would be undervalued.
5. Certification is especially effective when the benefits being protected by the certification process are directly received by the purchaser. It is less effective when

conveying benefits that do not directly affect the purchaser. Both certification systems convey a considerable amount of information that is about externalities. For forests, for example, it can convey whether the wood is sustainably harvested, but sustainably harvested wood is apparently indistinguishable from unsustainably harvested wood in terms of its ability to be used to build a house, construct furniture, etc. The real benefits are indirect and psychological—knowing that the harvesting process is not degrading the environment. Organic-produce certification produces many of those same indirect psychological benefits, but in addition this form of certification conveys some information (the absence of pesticide residues, for example) that directly can affect the consumer. For this reason, organic-produce certification is probably a bit more likely to produce a more efficient outcome, all other things being equal.

6. A rise in the price of timber would make it more likely that harvested forests would be replanted and would make land conversion to another use less likely. Both of these reinforce components of sustainable forestry. On the other hand, it would also make the rewards from illegal harvesting higher, which is incompatible with sustainable forestry. Hence the answer depends upon the likelihood of illegal activity.

Chapter 12

1. a. The maximum sustainable yield is obtained when the marginal benefit of an additional reduction in the population size is zero: $20P - 400 = 0$ or $P =$ 20,000 tons. The maximum sustainable yield can then be calculated using the g equation: $g = 4(20) - 0.1(20)^2 = 40$ tons.
   b. The efficient sustained yield can be found by setting marginal cost equal to marginal benefit: $20P - 400 - 2(160 - P)$; therefore, $P = 32.7$, which is a larger population than the one that would produce the maximum sustainable yield.
2. a. No, despite the fact that this approach yields the efficient sustainable yield, this is not an efficient solution. Net benefits would not be maximized because costs would be too high. Everyone would have an incentive to capture as large a share of the quota for him- or herself as quickly as possible. This would lead to excessively large boats and would not guarantee that the fishermen who could catch the fish most cheaply would do the harvesting. The net benefits would be smaller than possible.
   b. Yes, this would be efficient. This quota system creates exclusive property rights and, therefore, eliminates the need to catch as much as possible and as soon as possible. Each fisherman can proceed on the most individually appropriate schedule because his or her share of the catch is guaranteed. Since the need to rush harvesting is eliminated, the need for excessively large boats is also eliminated. Fishermen with high harvesting costs would find it in their interest to sell their quotas to fishermen with low harvesting costs in order to maximize their return from their quota. These transfers guarantee that the fish are caught by those with the lowest harvesting costs, so net benefits are maximized.

3. The increase in the license fee is represented as a parallel upward shift of the total cost line, whereas the per-unit tax on effort is represented as a leftward rotation of the total cost curve around the zero effort point. The latter increases the marginal cost of fishing effort, while the former has no effect on the marginal cost.

   In the private-property fishery, the license fee will have no effect on effort (unless it is so high as to make fishing unprofitable, in which case the effort will drop to zero), while the tax on effort will unambiguously reduce effort.

   In the free-access fishery, both will reduce effort by exactly the same amount. (Remember, in the free-access fishery the equilibrium occurs where total cost equals total benefit. Since these two policy instruments raise the same revenue, both affect total cost by the same amount.)

4. When trying to reduce the degree of inefficiency from an open-access fishery, a regulation that increases the marginal cost of fishing effort by banning certain types of gear would be less efficient than a tax on effort. Although they both rotate the total cost of effort upward, the tax imposes a transfer cost, which is compatible with efficiency because it does not waste net benefits, and the gear restriction is incompatible with efficiency because in this case the net benefits are simply lost, not merely transferred.

5. a. In answering this question remember that the benefits are defined as price times the quantity of fish harvested. A fall in the price of fish would be reflected as a movement inward of that benefit curve.

      In the typical economic model of an efficient fishery, a fall in the price of fish would generally result in a smaller sustainable harvest. The efficient level of effort is determined where $MB = MC$. A fall in the price of fish lowers MB but leaves MC unchanged. The only way to reestablish $MB = MC$ is by increasing MB by lowering effort, which, because the efficient point is to the left of the maximum sustained yield, would lower the sustainable harvest.

   b. If the fishery allows free access, the effect is a bit more complex. Remember that for a free-access fishery the equilibrium level of effort occurs where $TB = TC$. In this case, because the TB curve has shifted downward, the effort level is reduced. That effect is the same as in (a). However, in this case, because the free-access equilibrium is normally to the right of the maximum sustained yield effort level, lowering the effort level means a higher sustained harvest. In essence, in this case, taking the pressure off the fish population allows that population to experience more sustained growth, which means that more fish can be caught with less effort.

6. a. This change is such that the after curve has a flatter slope but a higher intercept with the Y-axis. For the static efficient level of effort, where $MB = MC$, the MC would have fallen. Reestablishing $MB = MC$ would be accomplished by expanding effort (thereby, lowering MB—remember MB is the tangent to [or slope of] the TB curve) until it once again equaled MC. Increasing effort on this side of the maximum sustained yield point would necessarily *increase* the size of the sustained harvest.

b. In a free-access fishery, since the total cost is lower after the change, effort would expand. However, since this level of effort is to the right of the maximum sustained yield point, this increased effort would result in a smaller sustained yield.

Chapter 13

1. a. Carbon reduction credits are generally created in developing countries that do not have a cap on their emissions. Since their purpose is to be used as one means of complying with emissions limits imposed by a cap, they have no value in the country of origin. Making them transferable across national boundaries allows them to be sold to the highest bidder. This transferability provides incentives for the credit supplier to create the credits and to sell them to the highest bidders. The buyers who acquire the credits are likely to have the most to gain from their acquisition. Efficiency is enhanced because both the buyer and seller gain from the transaction and so net benefits are increased.

   b. Conservation banking allows landowners to fulfill their conservation obligations on one site by acquiring the requisite conservation entitlements from a much larger project on another site. If these entitlements were not transferable from one site to another, the original owner would have to fulfill the obligation on her own land. Because that approach would likely be smaller in scale, typically would involve less suitable, fragmented habitat, and would be more expensive, transferability allows the obligation to be met with lower cost and at a better (less fragmented) scale, while making more appropriate habitat available to the endangered species.

2. With a rise in demand in the recreational fishery its members are likely to want to increase their catch shares. In the absence of inter-sector transferability this is like to occur only if an administrative process changes the historical catch shares to allocate more to the recreational fishery and less to the commercial fishery. Any such change is likely to be opposed by the commercial fishery members since each share transferred represents a monetary loss for them. With inter-sector transferability, however, the recreational fishery members would have to buy the additional shares. They would do this by offering a higher price for catch shares, resulting in a shift in some shares from the commercial to a recreational fishery. Transferability reduces conflict because the transactions are voluntary and in this case the sellers gain, not lose.

Chapter 14

1. a. In a cost-effective allocation of emissions reduction, the marginal control costs should be equal. So $\$200q_1 = \$100q_2$. Furthermore, the total reduction is 21 units, so $q_1 + q_2 = 21$. Solving the first of these equations for q_1 yields $q_1 - 0.5q_2$. Substituting this into the second yields $0.5q_2 + q_2 = 21$. Solving this for q_2 results in $q_2 = 14$ and $q_1 = 7$.

b. From the text we know that in a cost-effective allocation with a single receptor

$$MC_1 = MC_2.$$

Therefore,

$$\frac{\$200q_1}{2} = \frac{\$100q_2}{1}.$$

Furthermore,

$$a_1(20 - q_1) + a_2(20 - q_2) = 27 \text{ or}$$
$$2(20 - q_1) + (20 - q_2) = 27.$$

From the first equation it is clear that in a cost-effective allocation, $q_1 = q_2$. It remains to derive the total amount of control using the second equation: $2(20 - q_1) + (20 - q_1) = 27$, so $q_1 = 11$ and $q_2 = 11$.

2. a. From the text we know $T = MC_1 = MC_2$. From Problem 1(a) we know $MC_1 = MC_2 = \$1{,}400$. Therefore, $T = \$1{,}400$.

   b. Revenue $= T(20 - q_1) + T(20 - q_2) = \$1{,}400(13) \times \$1{,}400(6) = \$26{,}600$.

3. a. The control authority would auction off 16 allowances (30, which is the current level of emissions, minus 14, which is the required reduction).

   b. The market-clearing price would be \$4.00. Since demand would equal supply and marginal abatement costs would be equal for all firms, a \$4.00 marginal abatement cost produces the required 14 units of reduction.

   c. With a \$4.00 price, Firm 1 would reduce emissions by 7 units so it would need to buy 3 allowances. Firm 2 would reduce emissions by 4 units and hence would need to buy 6 allowances, and firm 3 would reduce 3 units of emissions and therefore it would need to buy 7 allowances. Note that this produces the required 14 units of reduction and accounts for the 16 allowances that were made available by the control authority.

   d. We know that that the cost-effective allocation is achieved when the $MC_1 = MC_2 = MC_3 = \$4.00$. This allocation will be achieved with an emissions charge if the firms set their MCs equal to \$4.00. Hence the required tax rate is \$4.00.

Chapter 15

1. a. There would be 12 permits issued, each worth 1 ppm. The price of the permit will be that price that will clear the market; that is,

$$MC_1 = MC_2 = P.$$

We know that in equilibrium,

$$\frac{0.3q_1}{1.5} = \frac{0.5q_2}{1.0}, \text{ or } q_1 = 2.5q_2.$$

Further,

$$a_1(20 - q_1) + a_2(20 - q_2) = 12 \text{ or}$$
$$1.5(20 - 2.5q_1) + 1.0(20 - q_2) = 12.$$

Solving this equation yields $q_2 = 9$ and $q_1 = 20$. So,

$$P = \frac{0.3\,(20)}{1.5} = \frac{0.5(8)}{1.0} = \$4 \text{ per ppm.}$$

b. Permits auctioned off include:

First source $= P(20 - q_1)a_1 = \$4(20 - 20)1.5 = \$0$,

Second source $= P(20 - q_2)a_2 = \$4(20 - 8)1.0 = \$48$.

The six permits are worth $24, so the first source would sell all its permits for a gain of $24. The second source would keep its initial allocation of six permits and would buy six more at a cost of $24. The cost to the second source exactly balances the gain to the first.

2. Imposing the same tax rate on every unit of emissions would normally be expected to yield a cost-effective allocation of pollution-control responsibility if the environmental target were specified in terms of aggregate emissions. In that case, cost-effectiveness requires the marginal cost of emissions reduction to be equalized across emitters, and that can be achieved with a uniform tax rate. A uniform tax rate would not, however, be compatible with a cost-effective allocation of each control responsibility if the environmental target were an ambient standard. In this case, you want the marginal costs of concentration reduction (not emissions reduction) to be equalized across emitters. Since the location of emissions matters in this case (not merely the amount of emissions), a uniform tax rate will not be cost-effective.

3. Allowing the allowances to be traded after the allocation occurs is the process that achieves cost-effectiveness, so this allocation (and any others that allocated the correct number of total allowances) would be compatible with cost-effectiveness. Any cost-ineffectiveness remaining after the initial allocation would be removed by the trading. However, if firms have advanced knowledge that more permits will be allocated to those with higher emissions, this creates a cost-ineffective incentive to emit more during this interim period in order to qualify for additional allowances once the system begins. Since these additional emissions make the goal harder and more expensive to meet, costs are raised above the minimum.

Chapter 16

1. The emissions charge equalizes marginal cost, a required condition for cost-effectiveness. The subsidies induce utilities to choose options with a higher marginal cost. By equalizing their after-subsidy marginal costs, utilities will

minimize their outlays. This will not minimize total costs of control, since a greater reliance on carbon-capture technologies will result than would be cost-effective.

2. High revenues in this context arise from a combination of high charges and large amounts of uncontrolled emissions. This circumstance arises when the marginal cost of control function rises steeply at relatively low levels of control. Since the charge is equal to the marginal cost of control, high marginal control costs imply a high charge rate. Furthermore, if the function rises steeply at relatively low levels of control, then there are large amounts of emissions to which this high rate of charge is applied. Multiplying a high charge times a large amount of uncontrolled emissions yields high revenues.

3. a. *Uncertain.* Although in most circumstances being discussed this would be true (since a tax would internalize the external costs associated with the damages caused by greenhouse gases), it does depend on the level of the tax. It is possible to set a tax rate so high as to force the benefits from its imposition to be lower than the costs.

   b. *True.* Regional systems control only emitters in their jurisdictions, so unless all possible regions have control systems in place some emitters will remain uncontrolled. Leakage results from the flow of business from controlled entities to uncontrolled entities (because they can produce at lower cost and, hence, charge lower prices.) This flow of business from controlled to uncontrolled emitters results in an increase in emissions that at least partially offsets the reductions achieved within the region. A truly global system that included all emitters in the same emissions trading system or facing the same greenhouse gas emissions tax would exempt no one and hence eliminate the problem of leakage.

4. a. Since $P_A = MC_A$ and $P_B = MC_B$ at the level of reduction where each domestic cap is met, the price would be \$10 in Country A and \$40 in Country B. Each country would be reducing 40 tons.

   b. In the linked case $P = MC_A = MC_B$ because allowance can flow from one market to the other until the prices are equalized. Because Country A can abate at a fixed marginal cost of \$10, that will be the *MC* and the price for both markets. (Can you see why?) Achieving the desired 60 tons overall reduction implies that Country B will abate 10 tons ($MC_B = \$1 \times 10 = \$10$) and Country A will abate 50 ($MC_A = \$10$) tons. Thus country A would use 20 tons of its 50 ton abatement to satisfy its cap and export the remaining 30 tons of allowances to Country B. Country B would apply its 10 ton reduction to its cap and import 30 tons of abatement allowances from Country A.

5. Although the cooperative outcome would be collectively preferred, it is not the most likely outcome due to the free-rider effect. Although collectively nations would be better off if everyone cooperated, individual nations can well be better off if they choose not to join the agreement. This paradox about the divergene between individual and collective incentives can arise because nonjoiners can still obtain any of the benefits of the agreement and avoid the abatement cost obligations that accrue to those who join.

Chapter 17

1. Taxes do have two advantages in achieving aggregate emissions reductions. First, by lowering the cost per mile traveled fuel economy standards can encourage more miles traveled. Gasoline taxes *increase* the cost per mile traveled. Second, fuel economy standards apply only to new vehicles while gasoline taxes apply to the whole fleet of vehicles. Since new vehicles are only a small proportion of the fleet, taxes will likely produce a quicker result.

   Obviously, however, this advantage accrues to taxes only if implementing them is politically feasible and the tax rates are high enough to produce the desired change.

2. a. Labeling has the virtue that it seems to be politically feasible, and it can encourage a more fuel-efficient new vehicle fleet. However, it only affects new cars and it has no affect on how many miles the cars are driven. Furthermore, as we have noted in earlier chapters, labeling works best when it affects attributes that directly affect consumers. Saving energy certainly directly affects consumers, but some of the benefits of this approach, particularly those relating to national security and climate change, are externalities and therefore probably not likely to be completely internalized by prospective purchasers. These disadvantages would compromise its effectiveness.

   b. Older fuel-inefficient vehicles do typically disproportionately contribute to the problem, and therefore they are a useful target of opportunity, but they are still only part of the problem. By itself, this strategy does not internalize the large number of other externalities associated with the purchase of new automobiles or reducing emissions from the fleet of automobiles that are not old enough to be affected by this program. Furthermore, many of these older automobiles are owned by lower-income households. Depending on how these vehicles are retired (not compensating owners, for example), taking away their transportation could impose a considerable burden on the poor (particularly the rural poor who have no mass transit option).

   c. Pay-as-you-drive insurance *could* probably be a useful complement because, unlike the others, it forces on internalizing some of the externalities associated with miles driven. Thus it addresses a component that would not otherwise be addressed.

3. a. From a social point of view, efficiency would require that the marginal premium per mile driven include all costs that are specifically related to miles driven. These would include potential accident damage, contributions to climate change (greenhouse gas emissions), and national security damages (stemming from import dependence).

   b. A private company would be concerned about recovering the costs related to the claims it will have to pay out—accident damages, not the others. Internalizing the other damages would require the participation of the government.

Chapter 18

1. a. The price would be $1,400. In the final allocation, the first source would control 7 units and would hold 13 permits, whereas the second source would control 14 units and hold 6 permits. The first source would have to purchase 4 permits—the 13 it needs to minimize cost minus the 9 it was initially given—at a total cost of $5,600. The second source would sell 4 permits, thereby moving from the 10 held initially to the 6 it needs to minimize costs, so it would gain $5,600 from the sale.

   b. We know that in the final equilibrium, the marginal control cost will be equal. Since for the third source the marginal control cost is constant at $1,600, this will determine the final marginal control cost. The final permit price will be $1,600. The control allocation can be found for the first and second sources by choosing the level of control that yields a marginal control cost equal to $1,600. Thus $\$1{,}600 = \$200q_1$, so $q_1 = 8$ and $\$1{,}600 = \$100q_2$, so $q_2 = 16$.

   The third source will have to clean up sufficient additional emissions to meet the target. Uncontrolled emissions were stated to be equal to 50. The first two sources would clean up 24 units, leaving 26 units uncontrolled. Since the target emissions level is stated as 19 units, the third source would have to clean up the remaining 7 units ($q_3 = 7$). The third source would have to purchase three permits since it received no initial allocation. Two would be purchased from the second source, and one would be purchased from the first.

2. a. With these *constant* marginal cost functions, cost-effectiveness is achieved by securing as much reduction as possible from the facility or facilities with the lowest marginal cost. In this case, that means securing the first 10 units of reduction from the first facility and the next 5 from the second facility.

   b. The total variable cost in this case is simply the sum of the marginal costs for each unit of reduction. Therefore, the cost from reducing at the first facility would be $30 (10 units × $3) and the cost of the reductions at the second unit would be $20 (5 units × $4), so the total variable cost would be $50.

   c. The total variable cost if all 3 facilities were forced to reduce 5 units would be $15 (5 units × $3) + $20 (5 units × $4) + $25 (5 units × $5) = $60. The extra $10 over the cost-effective allocation results from the fact that this allocation of responsibility substitutes 5 units at $5 for the 5 units at $3. The extra $20 per unit reduced accounts for the additional $10.

Chapter 19

1. No. A potential toxic substance injurer facing an efficient negligent standard will minimize its cost by taking the efficient level of precaution and meeting that standard; he or she will therefore typically not be found negligent. Knowing that the best private solution for the potential injurer is to avoid being negligent, potential victims have an incentive to take whatever precaution they can do to minimize their damages.

With strict liability, however, the potential injurer is responsible for *all* damages regardless of his or her behavior. Since victims are compensated for all damages, their incentive to lower those damages is inefficiently low.

Victim precautionary incentives are higher (and more efficient) under an efficient negligence standard.

2. One main difference in practice between an approach relying on performance bonds and one imposing strict liability for cleanup costs on any firm for a toxic substance spill is that the former requires money to be deposited in an escrow account before the operation commences. For the firm, the performance bond ties up capital for the period the bond is in effect, a cost it does not incur with strict liability. For the government, a performance bond assures the availability of funds to clean up the toxic substance immediately should the need arise. This availability can make a significant difference if the firm responsible for the spill turns out to not have sufficient funds to be able to fund the cleanup (this is known as the "judgment proof firm" problem). In that case imposing strict liability would have little effect since the firm would be unable to fulfill its legal obligations.
3. Informing the consumer about any toxic substances used in the manufacture of a product is likely to represent a move toward efficiency for those risks actually borne by consumers. However, risks borne by the workers making the product or the workers recycling or disposing of the product after its useful life are externalities to the consumer, and informing the consumer is not likely to internalize those risks sufficiently to produce an efficient outcome.

Chapter 20

1. Export taxes will only be completely passed forward to the consumer if the demand is perfectly inelastic. In that case the consumer will simply pay the higher price (including the tax). If it is less than perfectly elastic, however, demand for that product will be reduced and the domestic producer will bear some of the burden in the form of lower sales.

   In world food markets it is unlikely that demand will be perfectly inelastic. Not only can consumers choose to consume less as the price rises, but they can switch to other suppliers or even to different food products.
2. A natural disaster, such as the 2010 drought in Russia, would shift the supply curve to the left and raise prices. Consumers would be unambiguously worse off as their net benefits would be reduced. Suppliers who lost their entire crop would be unambiguously worse off, but the effects on other suppliers can actually be positive. All of those suppliers (foreign suppliers, for example) whose crops were completely unaffected would be better off as the higher prices for their crops would raise their producer surplus. For suppliers that lost some, but not all, of their crops, it would depend on how the magnitude of the losses from the destroyed crops compared to the magnitude of the gain from selling the remainder at a higher price.

3. The U.S. tariff on imported sugar would raise the domestic cost of sugar to domestic consumers, would cause a relative increase in their consumption of domestically raised sugar and, it follows from that, a reduction in the amount of sugar imported from abroad. The increased profitability of the domestic sugar industry would allow it to compete for more land and other local resources. (To follow up on a specific example of this phenomenon, examine the controversies surrounding the effects of the Florida Sugar industry on the Everglades.)

Glossary

Absorptive Capacity—The ability of the environment to absorb pollutants without incurring damage.

Acid Rain—The atmospheric deposition of acidic substances.

Acute Toxicity—The degree of harm caused to living organisms as a result of short-term exposure to a substance.

Adjusted Net Savings—An indicator that attempts to measure whether an economy is acting sustainably when judged by the weak sustainability criterion. (Formerly called genuine savings.)

Aerobic—Water containing sufficient dissolved oxygen concentrations to sustain organisms requiring oxygen.

Age Structure Effect—Changes in the age distribution induced by the rate of population growth.

Agglomeration Bonus—A voluntary incentive mechanism that is designed to protect endangered species and biodiversity by reuniting fragmented habitat across private land in a manner that minimizes landowner resistance.

Alternative Fuels—Unconventional fuels such as ethanol and methanol.

Ambient Allowance System—A type of transferable permit system in which allowances are defined in terms of the right to affect the concentration at a receptor site by a given amount. This design can achieve a cost-effective allocation of control responsibility when the objective is to achieve a prespecified concentration objective at a specific number of receptor locations.

Ambient Standards—Legal ceilings placed on the concentration level of specific pollutants in the air, soil, or water.

Anaerobic—Water containing insufficient dissolved oxygen concentrations to sustain life.

Anthropocentric—Human-centered.

Aquaculture—The controlled raising and harvesting of fish. (Called "mariculture" when, as is the case with some salmon fisheries, the facilities are in the ocean.) Aquaculture can provide the opportunity to create a private-property regime for affected fisheries.

Asset—An entity that has value and forms part of the wealth of the owner.

Assigned Amount Obligations—The level of greenhouse gas emissions that ratifying nations are authorized under the Kyoto Protocol.

Asymmetric Information—A source of market failure that can arise when all of the economic agents involved in a transaction do not have the same level of information.

Automobile Certification Program—The testing of automobiles at the factory for conformity to federal emissions standards.

Average-Cost Pricing—When prices charged for resource use are based on average costs. (Sometimes used by regulatory agencies to ensure that regulated firms make zero economic profits, but it is not normally efficient.)

Base-Load Plants—Electric generators that produce virtually all the time. (They generally have high fixed costs, but low variable costs.)

Benefit-Cost Analysis—An analysis of the quantified gains (benefits) and losses (costs) of an action.

Benefits Transfer—Transferring benefits estimates developed in one context to another context as a substitute for developing entirely new estimates.

Best Available Technology Economically Achievable—A more stringent effluent standard than best practicable control technology, which has been defined by the EPA as "the very best control and treatment measures that have been or are capable of being achieved."

Bid Rent Function—This function relates the maximum price per unit of land as a function of distance from the urban center that would be offered for a type of land use such as residential or agricultural.

Biochemical Oxygen Demand—The measure of the oxygen demand placed on a stream by any particular volume of effluent.

Block Pricing—A form of pricing in which the charge per unit consumption is held fixed until a threshold is reached where a new per-unit charge is imposed for all consumption beyond the threshold. For increasing block pricing, the per-unit charge after the threshold is higher.

Bycatch—Untargeted fish that are unintentionally caught as part of the harvest of targeted species.

Cap-and-Trade System—A form of emissions trading where the government specifies a cap on emissions and allocates allowances to emission sources, either by gifting or auctioning, based upon this cap. These allowances are freely transferable among sources. Distinguished from the credit form of emission trading.

Carbon Tax—A policy that would control climate modification by placing a per-unit emissions tax on carbon-emitting sources.

Carrying Capacity—The level of population a given habitat can sustain indefinitely.

Cartel—A collusive agreement among producers to restrict production and raise prices. In this case the group tends to act like a monopolist and to share the gains from collusive behavior.

Chapter 11—A provision in the North American Free Trade Agreement that protects investors from government regulations that decrease the value of their investments.

Choke Price—The maximum price anyone would be willing to pay for a unit of the resource. At prices higher than the choke price, the demand for that resource would be zero.

Chronic Toxicity—The degree of harm caused to living organisms as a result of continued or prolonged exposure to a substance.

Clean Development Mechanism—An emissions trading mechanism set up under the Kyoto Protocol that allows industrialized countries to invest in greenhouse gas reducing strategies in developing countries and to use the resulting certified reductions to meet their assigned amount obligations.

Closed System—No inputs enter the system, and no outputs leave the system.

Coase Theorem—A remarkable proposition, named after Nobel Laureate Ronald Coase, that suggests that in the absence of transaction costs, an efficient allocation will result regardless of the property rule chosen by the court.

Cobweb Model—A theory in which long lags between planting decisions and harvest can influence farmer's production decisions in such a way as to intensify or dampen price fluctuations.

Command and Control—Controlling pollution via a system of government-mandated legal restrictions. Under this approach the government has the responsibility not only for setting the environmental targets, but also for allocating the source-specific responsibilities for meeting those targets.

Common-Pool Resource—A resource that is shared among several users.

Common-Property Regimes—A property rights system in which resources are managed collectively by a group.

Community Land Trust—An organization set up to acquire and hold land for the benefit of a community. Frequently used to provide affordable access to land for members of the community.

Comparative Advantage—In trade theory a comparative advantage prevails for products that have the lowest opportunity cost of production.

Compensating Variation—A method for evaluating the welfare effects of a price increase. It is the increase in income it would take to make the consumer as well off as he or she was before the price increase.

Competitive Equilibrium—The resource allocation at which supply and demand are equal when all agents are price takers.

Composite Asset—An asset made up of many interrelated parts.

Composition of Demand Effect—Shifts in demand brought about by changes in the relative cost of inputs. (For example, rising costs of ores coupled with stable prices for recycled inputs could make the products of firms relying more heavily on recycled inputs relatively less expensive and hence more attractive to consumers.)

Congestion Externalities—Higher costs imposed on others resulting from an attempt to use resources at a higher-than-optimal capacity.

Congestion Pricing—Charging higher tolls during peak hours to discourage vehicle traffic (and the resulting air pollution) and encourage public transit ridership.

Conjoint Analysis—A survey-based technique that derives willingness to pay by having respondents choose between alternate states of the world where each state of the world has a specified set of attributes and a price.

Conjunctive Use—The combined management of surface and groundwater to optimize their joint use and to minimize the adverse effects of excessive reliance on a single source.

Conservation Easements—Legal agreements between landowners and land trusts or government agencies that permanently limit uses of land in specifically defined ways in order to protect its conservation value.

Constant Dollar—Purging increases in output measures that are due to price increases.

Consumer Surplus—The value of a good or service to consumers above the price they have to pay for it. Calculated as the area under the demand curve that lies above the price.

Consumption—The amount of goods and services consumed by households.

Consumptive Use—In water law this refers to water that is removed from the source without any return.

Contingent Ranking—A valuation technique that asks respondents to rank alternative situations involving different levels of environmental amenity (or risk). These rankings can then be used to establish trade-offs between more of the environmental amenity (or risk) and less (or more) of other goods that can be expressed in monetary terms.

Contingent Valuation—A survey method used to ascertain willingness to pay for services or environmental amenities.

Conventional Pollutants—Relatively common substances found in most parts of the country, and presumed to be dangerous only in high concentrations.

Corporate Average Fuel Economy (CAFE) Standards—Minimum average miles-per-gallon standards imposed on each auto manufacturer for new vehicles sold in a specific vehicle class. Autos are in one class and SUVs and light trucks in another.

Criteria Pollutants—Conventional air pollutants with ambient standards set by the Environmental Protection Agency (includes sulfur oxides, particulate matter, carbon monoxide, ozone, nitrogen dioxide, and lead).

Current Reserves—Known resources that can profitably be extracted at current prices.

Damped Oscillation—In the absence of further supply shocks, the amplitude of price and quantity fluctuations decreases to the point of equilibrium.

Debt-Nature Swap—The purchase and cancellation of developing-country debt in exchange for environmentally related action on the part of the debtor nation.

Deep Ecology—The view that the environment has an intrinsic value, a value that is independent of human interests.

Degradable—Pollutants that are capable of being decomposed chemically or biologically.

Demand Curve—A function that relates the quantity of a commodity or service consumers wish to purchase to the price of that commodity.

Deposition—Pollution that transfers from the air to the earth's surface (land or water).

Development Impact Fees—One-time charges designed to cover the additional public service costs of new development.

Differentiated Regulation—Imposing more stringent regulations on one class of sources (such as new vehicles) than on others (such as used vehicles).

Discount Rate—The rate used to convert a stream of benefits and/or costs into its present value.

Dissolved Oxygen—Oxygen that naturally occurs in water and is usable by living organisms.

Divisible Consumption—One person's consumption of a good diminishes the amount available for others. (For example, if I use some timber to build my house, you receive no benefits from that timber.)

Double Dividend—A second welfare advantage that accrues to revenue-raising pollution control policy instruments (over and above the welfare gain due to pollution reduction) when the revenue is used to reduce distortionary taxes (thereby reducing the welfare losses associated with those taxes).

Downward Spiral Hypothesis—A positive feedback loop in which increasing population triggers a cycle of sustained, reinforced environmental degradation.

Dry Deposition—Occurs when air pollutants get heavy and fall to the earth's surface (land or water) as dry particles.

Dynamic Efficiency—The chief normative economic criterion for choosing among various allocations occurring at different points in time. An allocation satisfies the dynamic efficiency criterion if it maximizes the present value of net benefits that could be received from all possible ways of allocating those resources over time.

Dynamic Efficient Sustained Yield—The sustained yield that produces the highest present value of net benefits.

E-Waste—Waste involving used electronics such as TVs, tablets, or mobile phones.

Ecological Footprint—A sustainability indicator that attempts to measure the amount of ecologically productive land that is required to support the resource demands and absorb the wastes of a given population and their economic activities.

Economies of Scale—The percentage increase in output exceeds the percentage increase in all inputs. Equivalently, average cost falls as output expands.

Ecosystem Services—Services supplied by nature that directly benefit at least one person.

Ecotourism—A form of tourism that appeals to ecologically minded travelers. It can serve as a source of revenue to protect the local ecosystem.

Efficient Pricing—A system of prices that supports an efficient allocation of resources. Generally, efficient pricing is achieved when prices are equal to total marginal cost.

Emissions Allowance System—A type of transferable permit system in which the permits are defined in terms of the right to emit a stipulated amount of emissions. This design can be used to achieve a cost-effective allocation of control responsibility for uniformly mixed pollutants.

Emission Charge—A charge levied on emitters for each unit of a pollutant emitted into the air or water.

Emission Standard—A legal limit placed on the amount of a pollutant an individual source may emit.

Emissions Banking—Firms are allowed to store emissions reduction credits or allowances for subsequent use or sale.

Emissions Reduction Credit (ERC)—Part of a transferable permits system. Any source reducing emissions beyond required levels can receive a credit for excess reductions. These can be banked for future use or sold to other sources.

Emissions Trading—An economic incentive-based alternative to the command-and-control approach to pollution control. Under emissions trading, a regulatory agency specifies an allowable level of pollution that will be tolerated and allocates emission authorizations among sources of pollution. Total emissions authorized by these allowances cannot exceed the allowable level. Pollution sources are free to buy, sell, or otherwise trade allowances.

Enforceability—Property rights should be secure from involuntary seizure or encroachment from others.

Entropy—Amount of energy not available for work.

Environmental Kuznets Curve—An empirical relationship that shows environmental degradation first increasing, then decreasing, as per capita income increases.

Environmental Sustainability—This definition of sustainability is fulfilled if the physical stocks of designated resources do not decline.

Equivalent Variation—A method for evaluating the welfare effects of a price increase. It is the reduction in income that would leave a consumer indifferent between accepting the income reduction or accepting the price increase.

Estate Tax—A tax paid on the fair market value of a property after the owner's death.

Eutrophic—A body of water containing an excess of nutrients.

Exclusivity—All benefits and costs accrued as a result of owning and using the resources should accrue to the owner, and only the owner, either directly or indirectly by sale to others.

Extended Producer Responsibility—The belief that manufacturers of products should have the responsibility to take the packaging and the products back at the end of their useful lives in order to promote efficient packaging and recycling. (Also called the "take-back" principle.)

Expected Present Value of Net Benefits—The sum over possible outcomes of the present value of net benefits for a policy, where each outcome is weighted by its probability of occurrence.

Expected Value—In situations where the value of a resource depends on which of several outcomes might prevail, the expected value of a resource is the sum over all outcomes of the likelihood of each outcome multiplied by the value that would prevail in that outcome.

External Diseconomy—The affected party is damaged by an externality. (For example, my well is polluted by chemicals from a factory next door.)

External Economy—The affected party is benefited by an externality. (For example, my neighbor decides not to develop a wetland that serves as a recharge area for my water supply.)

Externality—The welfare of some agent, either a firm or household, depends on the activities of some other agent. The externality can take the form of either an external economy or external diseconomy.

Feebates—A system that combines taxes on purchases of new high-emitting vehicles with subsidies for new purchases of low-emitting vehicles. The revenue from the taxes is supposed to serve as the primary source of funding for the subsidies.

Feedback Loop—A closed path that connects an action to its effect on the surrounding conditions that, in turn, can influence further action.

First Law of Thermodynamics—Neither energy nor matter can be created or destroyed.

Fixed Cost—Production costs that do not vary with output.

Fleet Average Standard—Used in the Corporate Average Fuel Economy Standards, this standard is imposed on the sales weighted average of vehicles sold rather than forcing every vehicle to meet it.

Free-Rider Effect—When a good exhibits both the consumptive indivisibility and nonexcludability properties, consumers may enjoy the benefits of goods purchased by others without paying anything themselves. (For example, countries that decide not to take any steps to control global warming can "free ride" on the steps taken by others.)

Full-Cost Pricing—In water management this pricing system seeks to recover not only all of the costs of providing water and sewer services but also the cost of replacing older water systems.

Fund Pollutants—Pollutants for which the environment has some absorptive capacity; if the rate of emission exceeds this capacity, then fund pollutants accumulate.

Gaia Hypothesis—An example of a negative feedback loop suggesting that, within limits, the world is a living organism with a complex feedback system that seeks an optimal physical and chemical environment.

Genetically Modified Organisms—A term that designates crops that carry new traits that have been inserted through advanced genetic engineering methods involving the manipulation of DNA.

Genuine Progress Indicator—A sustainability indicator that attempts to establish the trend of well-being over time by taking into account the effects of development on resource depletion, pollution damage, and distribution of income.

Global Environmental Facility—An international organization, loosely connected to the World Bank, that provides loans and grants to developing countries to facilitate projects that contribute to solving such global problems as protecting the oceans, preserving biodiversity, protecting the ozone layer, and controlling climate modification. The fund uses the "marginal external cost" rule to allocate funds.

Government Failure—An inefficiency produced by some government action.

Greenhouse Gases—Global pollutants that contribute to climate modification by absorbing the long-wave (infrared) radiation, thereby trapping heat that would otherwise radiate into space. (Includes carbon dioxide, methane, and chlorofluorocarbons, among others.)

Groundwater—Subsurface water that occurs beneath a water table in soils, rocks, or fully saturated geological formations.

Groundwater Contamination—Pollution that leaches into a water-saturated region.

Hartwick Rule—The weak sustainability criterion can be fulfilled if all scarcity rent from depletable resources is invested in capital.

Health Threshold—A standard to be defined with a margin of safety sufficiently high that no adverse health effects would be suffered by any member of the population as long as the pollutant concentration is no higher than standard level.

Hedonic Property Values—The values of environmental amenities (or risks) that are determined from differences in the values of property exposed to different levels of the amenities (or risks).

Hedonic Wage Studies—A valuation technique that allows the value of an environmental amenity (or risk) to be determined from differences in the values of wages paid to workers exposed to different levels of the amenity (or risk).

High-Grading—Discarding low-value fish such as juveniles in favor of high-value fish in order to increase the income derived from a harvest quota.

Host Fees—Fees collected from disposers that are used to compensate a community hosting a regional landfill. Designed to increase the willingness of communities to host these facilities.

Human Development Index—A socioeconomic indicator constructed by the United Nations Development Program that is based upon longevity, knowledge, and income.

Hypothetical Bias—Ill-considered responses that may arise in surveys based on contrived rather than actual situations or choices.

Impact Analysis—An analysis that attempts to make explicit, to the extent possible, the consequences of proposed actions. May mix quantitative with qualitative information and monetized with nonmonetized information.

Income Elasticity—Measures the percentage change in demand for commodities or services in response to a 1 percent change in income.

Individual Transferable Quotas (ITQs)—A means of protecting a fishery and the income derived from it by limiting the number of fish caught. Individual fishermen are allocated quotas that entitle them to portions of the authorized total allowable catch. These quotas can be transferred to other fishermen or used to legalize their harvest.

Indivisible Consumption—One person's consumption of a good does not diminish the amount available for others. (For example, the benefits I receive from controlling greenhouse gases do not diminish the benefits you receive.)

Information Bias—Arises when contingent valuation survey respondents are forced to value attributes with which they have little or no experience.

Intangible Benefits—Benefits that cannot be easily assigned a monetary value.

Interactive Resources—The size of the resource stock is determined jointly by biological considerations and actions taken by humans.

Isoquant—A curve showing possible combinations of two inputs that produce the same output level.

Joint Implementation—A project-based emission trading mechanism set up under the Kyoto Protocol in which an investor from one industrialized country can get emission reduction credits for certified greenhouse gas reductions resulting from investments in a project in another industrialized country.

Junior Claims—Used in water management, this class of rights for specified amounts of water is subordinate to senior claims. In times of water scarcity, these rights become valid once the senior claims have been fulfilled.

Kyoto Protocol—An international agreement to control greenhouse gases that went into effect in February 2005.

Land Trust—An organization specifically established to hold conservation easements and to ensure that the use of land conforms to the terms of the easements.

Latency—The period between exposure to a toxic substance and the detection of harm caused by that substance.

Law of Comparative Advantage—A country or region should specialize in the production of those commodities for which it has a comparative advantage.

Law of Diminishing Marginal Productivity—In the presence of a fixed factor, successively larger additions of variable factors will eventually lead to a decline in the marginal productivity of the variable factors.

Law of Diminishing Returns—The relationship between inputs and outputs when some inputs are increased and others are fixed, eventually leading to the decreased productivity of the variable inputs.

Lead Phaseout Program—A transferable permit program designed to lower the costs of phasing out lead in gasoline as well as to eliminate lead earlier than otherwise would have been possible. It allocated transferable rights to use lead in refining gasoline to refiners. The number of rights declined over time until at the end of the program they expired.

Leapfrogging—Refers to a situation where new development takes place not at the edge of current development, but further out, skipping over tracts of land that are closer in.

Liability Rules—Rules that award monetary compensation from an injurer to an injured party after damage has occurred. Valuation must be accomplished by the courts.

Low-Emission Vehicles—A class of vehicles that can satisfy much more stringent emissions standards than currently imposed on conventional vehicles.

Marginal Cost of Exploration—The marginal cost of finding additional units of the resource.

Marginal-Cost Pricing—Basing the prices charged for resource use upon marginal costs. (This pricing scheme is generally consistent with efficiency.)

Marginal External Cost Rule—Used by the Global Environmental Facility to disperse funds. According to this rule, the facility will fund additional expenses associated with investments that contribute to the global environment (produce positive global net benefits), but cannot be justified domestically (since the domestic marginal costs exceed domestic marginal benefits). Countries are expected to pick up that portion of the expenses that can be justified domestically (where the domestic marginal benefits exceed domestic marginal costs).

Marginal Extraction Cost—The cost of mining an additional unit of resource.

Marginal Opportunity Cost—The additional cost of providing the last unit of a good as measured by what is given up.

Marginal User Cost—Present value of forgone future opportunity costs at the margin.

Marginal Willingness to Pay—The amount of money an individual is willing to pay for the last unit of a good or service.

Marine Reserve—A specific geographic area that prohibits harvesting of fish and enjoys a high level of protection from other threats such as pollution.

Market Economy—An economic system in which resource allocation decisions are guided by prices that result from the voluntary production and purchasing decisions by private consumers and producers.

Market Failure—An inefficient allocation produced by a market economy.

Maximum Sustainable Yield—The maximum harvest that could be sustained forever.

Minimum Viable Population—The level of population below which regeneration is negative, leading ultimately to extinction.

Model—Formal or informal framework for analysis that highlights some areas of the problem in order to better understand complex relationships.

Monopoly—A situation in which the seller side of the market is dominated by a single producer.

Montreal Protocol—An international agreement to control ozone-depleting gases.

Multilateral Fund—A fund set up by the parties to the Montreal Protocol to help developing countries meet the phaseout requirements for ozone-depleting gases.

Myopia—Nearsightedness; excessive concern for the present.

Natural Capital—The endowment of environmental and natural resources.

Natural Equilibrium—Stock levels of biological populations that persist in the absence of outside influences.

Natural Resource Curse Hypothesis—Suggests that countries with abundant natural resources are likely to grow more slowly than their lesser endowed counterparts.

Negative Feedback Loop—A closed path of action and reaction that is self-limiting rather than self-reinforcing.

Negligence—A doctrine in tort law suggesting that the party responsible for a tortious act owes a duty to the affected party to exercise due care. Failure to fulfill that duty can lead to a requirement for the injurer to pay compensation to the victim.

Net Benefit—The excess of benefits over costs resulting from some allocation.

New Scrap—Waste composed of the residual materials generated during production. (Also called preconsumer scrap.)

New Source Review Process—All large new or expanding sources are subject to preconstruction review and permitting. These firms are typically subjected to more stringent requirements. The specific requirements depend on whether the source is attempting to locate in an attainment or a nonattainment area.

Nonattainment Region—A region in which the pollution concentrations exceed the ambient standards, so more stringent environmental regulations are in effect.

Noncompliance Penalty—A charge used to reduce the profitability of noncompliance with pollution control requirements. It is designed to eliminate all the economic advantage gained from noncompliance.

Nonconsumptive Use—In water law this refers to a use that does not involve diverting the water from the source or that does not diminish its availability. (Swimming for example.)

Nonexcludability—No individual or group can be excluded from enjoying the benefits a resource may confer, whether they contribute to its provision or not.

Nonpoint Sources—Diffuse sources such as runoff from agricultural or developed land.

Nonrenewable Resource—Resources that cannot be reproduced during a human timescale, so their supply is finite and limited.

Nonuniformly Mixed Pollutants—For these pollutants, the damage they cause is a function not only of the amount of emissions but also the location of the emissions sources. (Examples include particulates and lead.)

Nonuse (Passive-Use) Values—Resource values that arise from motivations other than personal use.

Normative Economics—The branch of economics that is concerned with evaluating the desirability of alternative resource allocations. It is concerned with "what ought to be."

Nutrient Sensitive Waters—Water bodies that have excessive levels of nutrients causing algal blooms, low oxygen levels, and increased fish kills.

Occupational Hazards—Risks undertaken during the course of a job.

Old Scrap—Waste recovered from products used by consumers. (Also called postconsumer scrap.)

Open-Access Resources—Common-pool resources with unrestricted access.

Open System—A system that imports and exports matter or energy.

Opportunity Cost—The net benefit forgone because the resource providing the service can no longer be used in its next-most-beneficial use.

Optimal—Best or most favorable option.

Optimization Procedure—A systematic method for finding the optimal means of accomplishing an objective.

Option Value—The value people place on having the option to use a resource in the future.

Output Measure—A measure currently used in national income accounting to indicate how many goods and services have been produced.

Overallocation—More than the optimal level of a resource is dedicated to a given use or time period.

Overshoot and Collapse—A forecast that involves exceeding the natural carrying capacity of the environment, with the consequence that society collapses.

Oxygen Sag—A point of low dissolved oxygen concentration generally located around effluent injection points.

Ozone-Depleting Gases—Global pollutants that destroy the stratospheric ozone layer. (Includes chlorofluorocarbons and halons, among others.)

Pareto Optimality—An allocation such that no reallocation of resources could benefit any person without lowering the net benefits for at least one other person. (Named after economist Vilfredo Pareto.)

Pay-as-You-Drive (PAYD) Insurance—A system in which an individual's annual premium for automobile insurance is calculated by multiplying a rating factor times the number of miles driven. It is designed to reduce inefficiency by internalizing those costs of accidents that are related to the amount of driving.

Peak Periods—Times of especially high resource demand. (For example, the demand for electricity during the hottest part of the summer when air-conditioning is in heavy use.)

Peaking Units—Those electricity-producing facilities used only during peak periods. (They generally have low fixed costs, but high variable costs.)

Peak-Load Pricing—Charging resource users during the peak period the higher cost of supplying resources during that period. The surcharge during the peak period is designed to cover the cost of expansion since the need to expand is triggered by increased demands during the peak period.

Pecuniary Externalities—External effects that are transmitted through higher prices. (For example, the value of my land increases because surrounding employers expand their operations, thereby creating a scarcity of housing in the immediate area.) Unlike most externalities, pecuniary externalities do not generally result in inefficient allocations.

Performance Bond—An amount of money required to be placed into a trust fund by those initiating risky projects to cover the costs of any anticipated damages.

Persistent Pollutants—Inorganic synthetic pollutants with complex molecular structures that are not effectively broken down in water.

Planning Horizon—The time period over which the benefits and costs are considered in time-related decisions. For a specific investment such as a power plant, for example, the planning horizon might correspond to the useful life of the project. For forestry, it could either correspond to the age of the stand of trees when harvested (the finite planning horizon) or extend forever (the infinite planning horizon). In addition to considering the age at which to harvest the stock (the focus of the finite planning horizon model), the infinite horizon model must also take into account a perpetual sequence of forestry decisions (such as restocking, harvesting, preservation, and so on).

Point Sources—Sources of pollution that discharge effluent through a readily identifiable emission point such as an outfall or discharge pipe. (Most industrial and municipal sources are point sources.)

Pollution Havens Hypothesis—Stricter environmental regulations in one country either encourage domestic production facilities to locate in countries with less stringent regulations or encourage increased imports from those countries.

Porter Induced Innovation Hypothesis—Firms facing stringent environmental regulations derive a competitive advantage because they are forced to innovate. Innovation typically increases productivity.

Positive Economics—The branch of economics that is concerned with describing alternative resource allocations without forming a judgment as to their desirability. Concerned with "what is."

Positive Feedback Loop—A closed path of action and reaction that is self-reinforcing rather than self-limiting.

Potential Reserves—The amount of resource reserves potentially available at different price levels.

Present Value—The current discounted value of a stream of benefits and/or costs over time.

Present Value Criterion—Resources should be allocated to those uses that maximize the present value of the net benefits received from all possible uses of those resources.

Price Controls—The establishment of maximum or minimum prices by the government.

Primary Effects—The direct, measurable effects of an action.

Primary Standard—An ambient air pollution standard designed to protect human health.

Prior Appropriation Doctrine—Entitlements for water are allocated to the agent who diverts and first puts water to a beneficial use.

Private Marginal Cost—The cost of producing an additional unit of the resource that is borne by the producer.

Producer Surplus—The value of a good or service to producers above the cost to them of producing it. Calculated as the area below the price line that is above marginal cost.

Product Charges—A charge imposed on a product that is associated with emissions (such as a gasoline tax). This indirect form of controlling emissions is used when placing the charge directly on emissions proves difficult.

Property Rights—A bundle of entitlements defining the owner's rights, privileges, and limitations for use of the resource.

Property Rules—Legal rules that govern the initial allocation of entitlements. Valuation of the entitlements is left to the market.

Property Tax—A tax on the value of land and the improvements on it.

Proposition 65—A California law that requires companies producing, using, or transporting one or more of the specified substances in amounts over the "safe harbor" threshold to notify those who are potentially impacted.

Prototype Carbon Fund—An intermediary set up to encourage developing-country reductions in greenhouse gases. It acts as a kind of mutual fund by picking promising investment opportunities under the clean development mechanism for donor countries and transferring the resulting emission reduction credits to the donors for use in meeting their assigned amount obligations.

Public Good—A resource characterized by nonexclusivity and indivisibility.

Real Consumption Per Capita—Constant-dollar consumption divided by population.

Real-Resource Costs—As opposed to transfer costs, these are costs borne by both private parties and society as a whole because they involve the loss of net benefits, not merely their transfer.

Receiving Areas—Those areas under a transferable development rights system where rights acquired from owners in the sending area can be used.

Recycling Surcharge—Imposed at the time of commodity purchase, this charge attempts to recover from the consumer the cost of recycling and/or disposal of the commodity after its useful life.

Regional Pollutants—Pollutants that can cause damage some distance from the emission source. (Examples include the precursors for acid rain and tropospheric ozone.)

Regressive Distribution—Net benefits from a policy received by various income groups represent a larger portion of the income of the rich than of the poor.

Renewable Energy Credit—An official record granted to producers of qualified renewable energy that can be sold separately from the power to allow the recovery of the extra costs associated with renewable power. It can be used to prove compliance with a renewable portfolio standard.

Renewable Portfolio Standards—These standards specify enforceable targets and deadlines for producing specific proportions of electricity from renewable resources.

Renewable Resources—Resources that can be naturally regenerated over time on a human time scale.

Rent Seeking—The use of resources in lobbying and other activities directed at securing increased profits through protective regulation or legislation.

***Res Nullius* Regime**—A property rights system in which no one owns or exercises control over resources. Resources covered by this regime can usually be exploited on a first-come, first-served basis.

Resource Endowment—The natural occurrence of resources in the earth's crust and atmosphere.

Resource Taxonomy—A classification system used to characterize the nature of natural resource stocks in terms of the certainty of the stock estimates and the economic likelihood of their recovery.

Return Flow—A term used in water management that refers to the unconsumed portion from an upstream user's water allocation that will eventually return to the watercourse (and, hence, be available to a downstream user).

Riparian Rights—Allocates the right to use water to the owner of the land adjacent to the water, as long as no adverse effects are imposed on other rights holders.

Risk-Free Cost of Capital—Rate of return earned on an investment when the risk of earning more or less than expected returns is zero.

Risk-Neutrality—An agent who has no preference between options that produce the same expected value.

Risk Premium—Additional rate of return required to compensate the owners of the capital when the expected and actual returns may differ. It represents compensation for a willingness to undertake some risk.

Scale Effects—How the size of an operation affects average costs.

Scarcity Rent—Producer's surplus that persists in long-run equilibrium due to fixed supply or increasing costs.

Second Law of Thermodynamics—Entropy, the energy not available for work, increases.

Secondary Effects—Indirect consequences of an action; beyond primary effects.

Secondary Standard—An ambient standard designed to protect those aspects of human welfare other than health.

Sending Areas—Areas where the owners of land can sell rights in a transferable development rights system.

Senior Claims—Used in water management, this class of claims entitles the holder to a priority for specified amounts of water. These rights have a higher priority in times of low water availability than junior claims.

Social Marginal Cost—The cost of producing an additional unit of the resource that is borne by society at large. Generally includes private marginal costs plus external marginal costs.

Socialist Economy—A centrally planned economy where the means of production are controlled by the government.

Sprawl—An inefficient land use pattern where the uses are excessively dispersed.

Stable Equilibrium—A level of stock that will be restored following temporary shocks.

Starting-Point Bias—Arises when a contingent valuation survey respondent is asked to check off his or her answer from a predetermined range of possibilities and the answers depend on the range specified by the survey instrument.

Static Efficiency—The chief normative economic criterion for choosing among various allocations when time is not an important consideration. An allocation satisfies the static efficiency criterion if it maximizes the net benefits from all possible uses of the resource.

Static Efficient Sustained Yield—The sustained catch level in a fishery that produces the largest annual recurring net benefit.

Stationary Source—An immobile pollution source. (Industrial sources, for example, as opposed to automobiles.)

Statistically Significant—Observed differences are unlikely to result from pure chance.

Stock Pollutants—Pollutants that accumulate in the environment because the environment has little or no absorptive capacity for them.

Strategic Bias—A respondent provides a biased answer to a contingent valuation survey in order to influence a particular outcome.

Strategic Petroleum Reserve—A petroleum stockpile established by an importing nation to minimize the damage that could be done by an embargo imposed by a foreign supplier. It would serve as an alternative source of supply for a short period.

Stratosphere—The atmosphere that lies above the troposphere. It extends to about 31 miles above the earth's surface.

Strict Liability—A tort law doctrine requiring that the party responsible for pollution contamination compensate victims for damage caused. Differs from negligence in that the victim does not have to prove negligence by the injurer.

Strong Sustainability—This definition of sustainability is fulfilled if the value of the natural capital stock does not decline.

Suboptimal Allocation—An allocation that could be rearranged so that one or more people could be made better off while no one was made worse off. (Also called an inefficient allocation.)

Subsidies—Payments or tax breaks from the government that make the cost to the buyer lower than the marginal cost of production.

Substitution—Replacing one resource with another. May occur, for example, when the original resource is no longer cost-effective or is diminishing in quantity or quality.

Sulfur Allowance Auction—Run by the Chicago Board of Trade, this annual auction requires utilities to place a proportion of these allowances up for sale each year. The proceeds are returned to the utilities. (This is called a "zero revenue auction" since the government derives no revenue from it.) It ensures the continual availability of permits and provides good public information on prices.

Sulfur Allowance Program—A transferable permit program targeted at electric utilities that was designed to reduce sulfur emissions from 1980 levels by 10 million tons. Involves an auction and an emissions cap.

Surface Water—The freshwater in rivers, lakes, and reservoirs that collects and flows on the earth's surface.

Sustainability Criterion—A criterion for judging the fairness of allocations of resources among generations. Generally requires that resource use by any generation should not exceed a level that would prevent future generations from achieving a level of well-being at least as great.

Sustainable Forestry—Forestry practices that are consistent with one of the definitions of sustainability, though most commonly this term refers to compatibility with the environmental sustainability criterion.

Sustainable Yield—Harvest levels that can be maintained indefinitely; achieved by setting the annual harvest equal to the annual net growth of the population.

Synergistic—The dose-response relationship is dependent upon several interrelated factors.

"Take-Back" Principle—The belief that manufacturers of products should have the responsibility to take the packaging and the products back at the end of their useful lives in order to promote efficient packaging and recycling. (Also called extended producer responsibility.)

Tangible Benefits—Benefits that can reasonably be assigned a monetary value.

Technological Progress—An innovation in process or technique that allows more output or services to be derived from a given set of inputs.

Thermal Pollution—Pollution caused by the injection of heat into a watercourse.

Third Parties—Victims who have no contractual relationship to a pollution source. (They are neither consumers of the product produced by the source nor employed by the source.)

Total Cost—The sum of fixed and variable costs.

Toxic Release Inventory—A system for reporting toxic emissions releases from individual facilities in the United States. By making the data public, it was designed to warn communities of the risks they face and to encourage reductions prior to regulation.

Toxicity—The degree of harm caused to living organisms as a result of exposure to the substance.

Transactions Costs—Costs incurred in attempting to complete transactions. (For example, in buying a home, these might include payments to the broker for arranging the sale, to the bank for one-time special fees, and to the government for the required forms. The value of the time expended in negotiating would also be a transactions cost.)

Transfer Coefficient—A coefficient used in simulating pollutant flows. It relates the degree to which pollution concentrations at a specific receptor site are increased by a one-unit increase in emissions from a specific source.

Transfer Cost—A cost to a private party that is not a cost to society as a whole, because it involves a transfer of net benefits from one private party to another.

Transferability—Property rights can be exchanged among owners on a voluntary basis.

Troposphere—The atmosphere that is closest to the earth. Its depth ranges from about 10 miles over the equator to about 5 miles over the poles.

Two-Part Charge—As used in water management, this type of charge combines volume pricing with a monthly fee that doesn't vary with the amount used. The monthly fee is designed to help cover fixed costs.

Underallocation—Less-than-optimal levels of a resource are dedicated to a given use or time period.

Uniform Emission Charge—A charge on effluent that applies the same per-unit rate to all sources regardless of their size or location.

Uniform Treatment—A strategy to reduce effluent levels by a specified percentage at each emissions level.

Uniformly Mixed Pollutants—For these pollutants, the damage done to the environment depends on the amount of emissions that enters the atmosphere. The location of emissions is not a matter of policy concern. (Examples include ozone-depleting gases and greenhouse gases.)

User Cost—Opportunity cost created by scarcity. It represents the value of an opportunity forgone when the resource can no longer be used in its next-best use. (For example, for a unit of a depletable resource used now, the user cost is the net benefits that would have been received by saving it and using it during the next time period.)

Usufruct Right—Holders of this right may use a resource (normally subject to restrictions), but do not have full ownership rights.

Variable Cost—Production costs that vary with output.

Volume Pricing—Making the cost of the service a function of the volume used. Used in both trash disposal and water distribution.

Weak Sustainability—Resource use by previous generations should not exceed a level that would prevent future generations from achieving a level of well-being at least as great. This definition of sustainability is fulfilled if the total capital stock (natural capital plus physical capital) does not decline.

Welfare Measure—A measure of development that increases or decreases in relation to how well-off society is.

Wet Deposition—Occurs when air pollutants fall to land or water during rain or snow events.

Zero Discharge—No emissions of the targeted pollutant are allowed.

Zero Emission Vehicle—Automobiles that directly emit no air pollutants. (Examples include vehicles powered by solar energy and fuel cells. Electric automobiles are also normally included despite the fact that producing the electricity typically results in pollution.)

Zoned Effluent Charge—A charge on effluent that applies different per-unit rates to sources depending on their location. Generally sources closer to, and upstream from, locations with more serious pollution problems face higher rates.

Name Index

Subject Index